Timeline of Psychology

Prehistory	The use of trepanning to control behavior and health
Circa 1,600 B.C.E.	Egyptian medical papyrus that includes instructions for treating head wounds
Circa 400 B.C.E.	Hippocrates suggests the brain is the source of mental illness
Circa 335 B.C.E.	Aristotle suggests that mental activity is located in the heart
1487	The Malleus Maleficarum applies a "guilty until proven innocent" procedure to identify witches. Subsequently, many mentally ill are burned at the stake.
1492-1541	Philippus Theophrastus Bombastus von Hohenheim (Paracelsus) writes on a wide variety of psychological topics
1547	Bethlehem Hospital in London is converted into an asylum
1693	Witch trials in Salem Massachusetts are common.
1773	First American mental health hospital opens in Virginia
1793	Phillipe Pinel frees the asylum patients from LaBicetre in Paris
1812	Benjamin Rush publishes the first American textbook on psychiatry
1865	Gregor Mendel publishes his work on genetics
1873	John Stuart Mill establishes associatively based rules of experimental methodology
1879	Wilhelm Wundt establishes the first psychology laboratory at the University of Leipzig
1892	American Psychological Association is established
1893	Sigmund Freud and Josef Breuer establish the beginning of psychoanalysis with the publication of *On the Psychical Mechanisms of Hysterical Phenomena*
1898	Ivan Pavlov discovers classical conditioning
1898	Edward Thorndike publishes his doctoral dissertation on instrumental learning
1900	Ramon y Cajal proposes the synaptic gap
1905	The Binet-Simon test is established and becomes the basis for later intelligence tests in the United States
1907	Alzheimer's disease is discovered by Alois Alzheimer
1913	John Watson develops behavioral theory
1921	Henry Dale and Otto Loewi discover chemical transmission across nerve cells
1924	Law enforcement uses the first lie detector test
1929	The EEG is developed sufficiently to become a useful tool
1935	The first frontal lobotomy is performed
1936	The first EEG laboratory begins service at Massachusetts General Hospital
1938	B. F. Skinner publishes *The Behavior of Organisms*
1943	The hallucinogenic properties of LSD are discovered
1949	Egas Moniz shares the Nobel Prize for the development of the frontal lobotomy
1951	Chlorpromazine (Thorazine) was first tested. It became the primary treatment for schizophrenia and led to a widespread period of deinstitutionalization over the coming decade
1952	The DSM is first published
1953	Nathaniel Kleitman and Eugene Aserinsky discover REM sleep
1954	James Olds and Peter Milner discover the reward center of the brain
1958	Joseph Wolpe develops systematic desensitization therapy
1963	The Community Mental Health Act facilitates the deinstitutionalization of psychiatric patients in the United States
1963	The antianxiety drug, Valium, is first sold in the United States
1970	Masters and Johnson develop the process of sex therapy
1972	The CT scan is first introduced as a diagnostic tool
1973	Karl von Frisch, Konrad Lorenz and Nikolaas Tinbergen share the Nobel Prize for their discovery of imprinting in ducklings
1975	Endorphins are discovered in the human brain
1981	The MRI scan is first introduced as a diagnostic tool
1981	Ritalin is used to treat ADHD
1981	Roger Sperry shares the Nobel prize in Medicine for his work on cerebral specialization through his work on split-brain patients
1995	The APA searches for empirically supported mental health treatments
2000	The human genome is mapped completely
2002	Daniel Kahneman, a psychologist, shares the Nobel prize in economics for work related to human decision making
Circa 2012	You take a General Psychology course

Psychology

The Scientific Approach

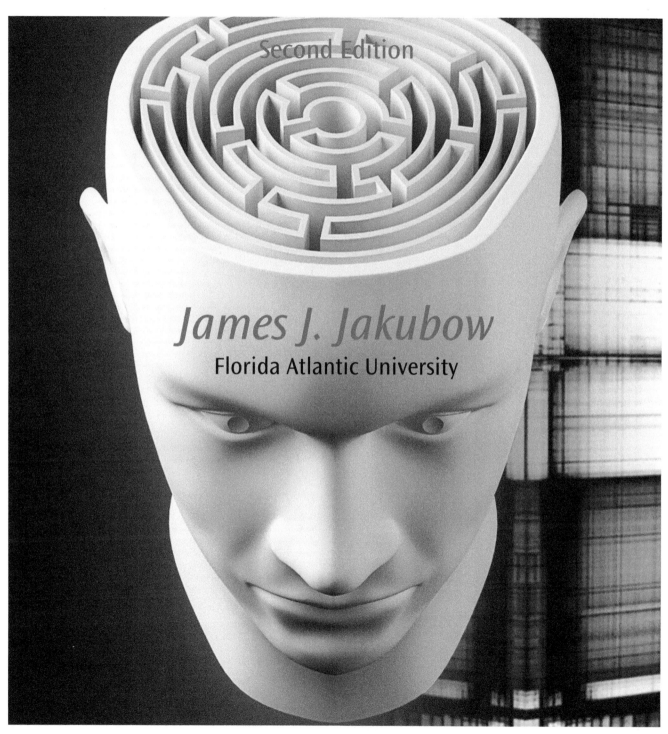

Second Edition

James J. Jakubow

Florida Atlantic University

Kendall Hunt
publishing company

Cover images © Shutterstock, Inc.

www.kendallhunt.com
Send all inquiries to:
4050 Westmark Drive
Dubuque, IA 52004-1840

Contents

Chapter 7 ■ Learning   301

UNIT THREE: COMBINING THE BASIC FUNCTIONS OF PSYCHOLOGY

UNIT ONE

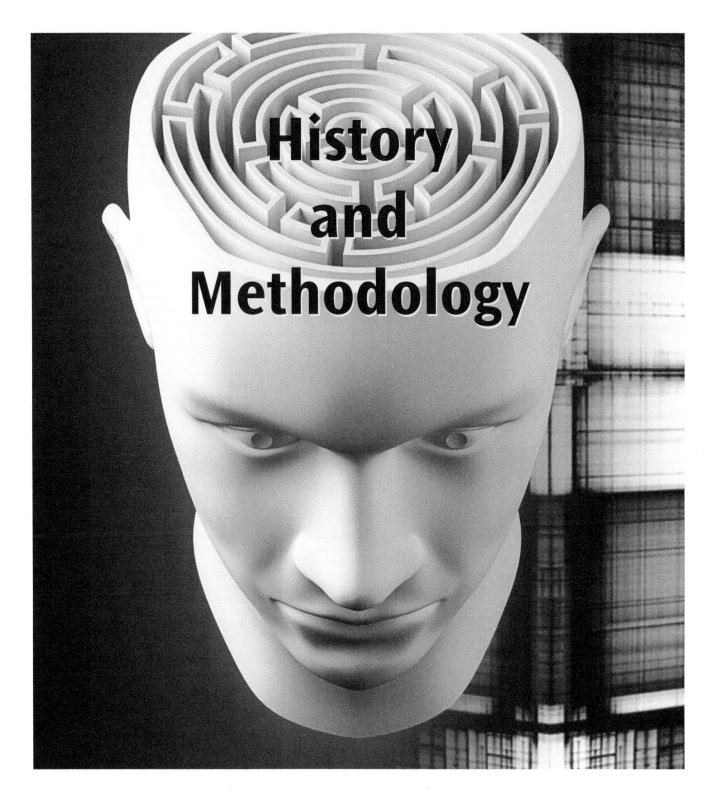

History
and
Methodology

1 Introduction to Psychology

BIOLOGY AND PHILOSOPHY

Wouldn't it be nice if people came with an instruction manual? If they did, you could always have the best experiences with everyone you meet. You could avoid arguments and increase your happiness. So much unpleasant personal and social strife would disappear from your life. Understanding people perfectly means that you might always get what you want and so would everyone else.

Unfortunately, the instruction manual for humans has yet to be completely written. Psychologists have been busy writing a small proportion of it for a little more than a century. The process of writing that manual has uncovered an entirely new understanding of human beings. Research has given us a new appreciation for the development of intellectual functioning from childhood through adulthood. People who were thought to be uneducable can now learn to live independent and productive lives. Diseases and injury that were once believed to produce permanent damage can now be treated or overcome through psychological interventions. This is the effect of writing that instruction manual, to predict and manage behavior for the betterment of humanity.

Writing that manual has not been easy. The human brain is one of the most complex organs in the known universe. Its complexity is staggering, involving billions of neurons and trillions of microscopic interconnections. The challenges to understanding the brain have been immense. The attempts to understand it, however, have definitely been worth the effort. All of our experiences, thoughts, opinions, and memories are housed in a three-pound ball of neural tissue residing inside our skull. Whether we learn to build skyscrapers 1,600 feet into the air, discover new species of animals at the bottom of the ocean, or develop a green economy, our ability to do so will primarily come from our ability to organize ourselves in a manner that maximizes our intellectual capacity.

Psychological research over the past century has showed us that people have an untapped intellectual capacity greater than most people are aware. Almost anyone can memorize thousands of names or telephone numbers or pages of textbooks, or become proficient in highly advanced fields of study. The ability of savants to perceive and reproduce music, art, and mathematics with ease tells us that we all have potential that has yet to be discovered.

The field of psychology looks quite a bit different today than it did a century ago. What we believe we can do, as well as our constraints, are different today than they were when psychology was in its infancy. Where the future of psychological research will take us is not clear; however, to understand our full potential and our chances for improvement we must take the journey. Like any journey, we will start at the beginning. The roots of psychology can be documented back to the Neolithic period following the last Ice Age. This is where we will begin.

The full potential of the human brain has yet to be determined.

© Orla, 2011. Used under license from Shutterstock, Inc.

Prescientific Psychology: The Time Before 1600 CE

Approximately 10,000 BCE, the glaciers of the northern hemisphere were retreating and the people who lived between the Tigris and Euphrates rivers began to develop agriculture. It is from this time, at various locations around the globe, that archaeologists have found the first attempts to perform medical or psychological treatments on the head. The practiced treatment evident in the archaeological record is **trepanning**. Trepanning is a surgical technique in which a hole is cut into the skull of a patient. Archeologists have often assumed that trepanning was done as a way to let evil spirits out the head. There are no written records to prove that analysis; however, it seems to fit well with later writings regarding biology and evil spirits. Moreover, there is evidence from the postcolonial period that the Mesoamericans practiced trepanation for just these reasons.

Ancient doctors may have conducted trepanning for other reasons as well. For example, there is some evidence doctors used trepanning to treat headaches. Moreover, there may have been knowledge that a blow to the head followed by a loss of consciousness could be treated by trepanning. In this case, it would have alleviated pressure on the brain due to swelling or intracranial bleeding. How well the technique worked in the Neolithic age is uncertain. Certainly, many

Trepanning or trepanation: The act of boring a hole out of the skull. Typically it is believed that doing so allows for evil spirits to exit the mind of the patient.

of the skulls found that were trepanned showed signs of bone regrowth indicating that the patient survived. In contrast, however, many of those skulls exist in a form with the hole still open, indicating that the patient did not live long enough for all the removed bone to completely grow back.

Ancient Philosophers

Ancient philosophers contributed to the development of psychology. With respect to Western culture, the ancient Greeks had a significant influence on the development of psychological thought. Although individuals such as Aristotle, Socrates, and Democritus covered areas we categorize today as psychology, almost all of their ideas are currently irrelevant save for the general impression that they gave to the field. The loss of relevance of their work largely stems from their use of a purely philosophical approach as opposed to a scientific method. Unfortunately, the logic of scientific methodology would not be developed for another 1900 years.

After the ancient Greeks, religious philosophers developed most of the philosophical works regarding human nature in Western society. This approach also failed to produce any significant improvement in the understanding of human nature for the same reasons that constrained Greek philosophy. The common problem experienced by the religious philosophers was that each one had a different set of assumptions about the nature of humankind. Because each philosopher applied different assumptions, they all reached different conclusions. Consequently, there was much discussion about human nature but little widespread agreement as to which ideas were correct.

One of the worst applications of religious philosophy occurred during the end of the medieval times in Europe. The medieval period was a time filled with superstitious thinking. For instance, during the 15th century, there came to be a widespread concern that witches and evil spirits could control human behavior. Stories of witches, sorcerers and magical creatures thrived during this time. Eventually, in 1487 the Malleus Maleficarum (Latin: The Witches Hammer) was written by Heinrich Kramer—an Alsatian clergyman—and James Sprenger—a Swiss monk. Kramer and Sprenger attempted to make people aware of the hazards of witches and the evil spirits they conjure. The following quote from the Malleus Maleficarum indicates both the superstitious time during which they lived as well as the extent of logic they applied to the stories they heard (Pachter, 1951/2007).

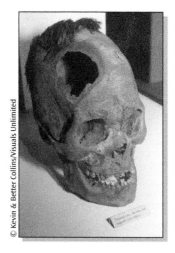

This skull is from the Peruvian Paracas culture that dates as far back as two thousand years ago.

Witches were believed to collect souls for Satan in exchange for special favors.

... there are as many different unclean spirits as there are different desires in men. For it is manifest that some of them, which the common people call Fauns, and we call Trolls, which abound in Norway, are such buffoons and jokers that they haunt certain places and roads and, without being able to do any hurt to those who pass by, are content with mocking and deluding them, and try to weary them rather than hurt them. And some of them only visit men with harmless nightmares. But others are so furious and truculent that they are not content to afflict with an atrocious dilation the bodies of those whom they inflate, but even come rushing from on high and hasten to strike them with the most savage blows. (p. 106)

Beyond discussing the qualities and temperaments of magical creatures, Kramer and Sprenger attempted to describe (a) the conditions that allow witchcraft to occur, (b) the treatments against witchcraft and (c) the judicial proceedings against witches. Today, we would argue that the logic behind the Malleus Maleficarum is convoluted and promotes guilty verdicts for anyone

Malleus Maleficarum: Latin for "Witches Hammer." It became the most respected text on the characteristics of witches and evil spirits in the late medieval period. The text describes how to try a witch for heresy.

© inginsh, 2011. Used under license from Shutterstock, Inc.

A Norwegian troll.

accused of witchcraft. During its time, however, it was used to great effect against people who appeared to be mentally ill. If you consider that an individual who is delusional and hallucinating reports experiences of seeing devils in the forest, then many people of this time might take their story at face value. Because that period offered no useful treatments for psychiatric disorders of this type, no intervention stopped the delusions or hallucinations. Consequently, it appeared the individual had a special bond with evil spirits and should therefore be put to death—at least according to Kramer and Sprenger. This book and its proceedings would be applied at least until the early 18th century—another 200 years. Fortunately, these 200 years also saw a change in the application of logic to both human behavior and the physical world. One of the people who brought about this change is Philippus Theophrastus Bombastus von Hohenheim (1492–1541). He is generally remembered by his Latin name, **Paracelsus**.

Paracelsus and the Alchemists

Paracelsus was a person with one foot in medieval superstition and one foot in the coming scientific revolution. He was greatly involved with medieval alchemy—a superstitious attempt at chemistry—and he spent his life trying to improve its effectiveness. Although alchemy generally attempted to transmute metals into gold, it more broadly attempted to change any element into medicinally valuable substances. Therefore, alchemists often were familiar with medical applications of plants and minerals. Generally, however, they believed in the magical properties of these plants and minerals and assigned their medical treatments accordingly.

The medical treatments applied by alchemists were published over hundreds of years in texts full of secret codes. People described as experts in the field authored them and no one questioned their authority or the value of their treatments. The treatments were applied because they were assumed correct due to the authority of the author. If a treatment did not work, it was assumed to be the doctor's fault or the patient's "refusal" to participate in the treatment. It certainly could not be the fault of the expert author.

Paracelsus also followed the authoritative literature of the time. He did begin, however, to apply his own thinking to medical practice and found that his approaches were often more effective than the ones contained in these authoritative texts. Paracelsus began to apply a trial and error approach that evaluated every self-made concoction for a particular disease. He was able to develop one

Paracelsus:
A medical doctor and alchemist who began to study the effects of drugs through trial and error. He also wrote extensively on human psychology during the late medieval period.

Alchemy:
Although usually associated with superstitious attempts to turn base metals into gold, alchemy also attempted to understand the basic medical properties of plants and minerals. It is a prescientific form of chemistry.

of the first useful treatments for the new venereal disease of syphilis that New World explorers were bringing back to Europe in the early 16th century. This highly toxic treatment required the afflicted individual to take a bath in a mixture of dilute mercury and sulfur! To his credit, he became known as one of the most popular European doctors in the late medieval period.

Although Paracelsus is known for developing medical treatments, he began applying his efforts at human psychology. Paracelsus wrote books regarding the nature of human behavior, dreams, placebo effects, trances, personality, and other topics. Given the influence of religious philosophers at this time, any mention of psychology generally referred to how the human soul operated. You might say that medieval psychology attempted to understand the "operating characteristics" of the human mind/soul. For Paracelsus, however, the soul was not an ethereal part of the body. Rather, it was just another physical entity of the body and was understandable by the same physical laws that governed alchemy and medicine.

Part of the reason that Paracelsus believed that the soul was part of the body was the fact that he could control how a person thought. That is, if he could control the soul (read this as *thought*), then it must be a physical entity and not an ethereal body. Along these lines, he found that if his patients believed he could cure them, then they were more likely to improve. In the cases that Paracelsus believed the problem was more psychological (mind/soul) than physical, he applied a process of social influence to affect the patient. In this way, he convinced the patients that they could be cured if they performed some simple meditations. For example, one treatment that he applied was to make small wax figurines that he told his patients represented their sicknesses. After the patient was told to focus on the wax figurine as a symbol of their sickness, they would melt it to symbolically destroy the problem. As silly as it seems in today's modern world, this placebo approach worked for patients who had complete belief that their doctor controlled the metaphysical properties of the universe. Paracelsus also applied this approach to make people have particular dreams as seen in this quote from (Pachter, 1951/2007).

> "If this person believes in what I say, he will be sure that it will come true, and see it before his imagination. If he goes to bed with this idea strongly entrenched in his mind, he will experience exactly what I told him." (p. 232)

Paracelsus lived in a scientifically transitional period. For hundreds of years the application of superstitions, philosophy, and astrology dominated the study of human behavior. Moreover, any investigation into psychological characteristics always involved what we refer to today as higher order thinking. There were no basic experiments on human behavior in the same way that alchemists manipulated substances in a trial and error fashion. In fact, there were no trial and error experiments on human psychology at all. By the time of Paracelsus' death in 1541, there would be another three centuries before the development of scientific psychology. To get there from 1541 required a great many developments. One of them would be the discovery of electricity in the nervous system. That finding would not occur for at least another century after Paracelsus' death.

Stories of witchcraft and alchemy produce many of the horror genre references we use in modern times.

The scientific basis of placebo effects will be discussed later in this chapter.

The Seventeenth Century and the Development of the Scientific Method

As the scientific method began to develop, its application was generally toward astronomy and the developing field of physics. Early scientific research revolved around the measurement of the basic physical laws we are aware of today (e.g., motion, light, heat, etc.). In the grand scheme of things, the next

Rene Descartes was honored for his achievements by having his likeness placed on this French stamp.

Sir Isaac Newton is celebrated on a Polish stamp.

You may take batteries for granted today, however, at this time they were technology of the highest magnitude.

closest step toward the development of scientific psychology would be the application of scientific reasoning to biology. Anatomical studies constituted the majority of early biological research. Researchers at this time could not understand the brain very well given their primary research tool, visual inspection. Moreover, the anatomical studies conducted could not last more than a few days due to the body's decomposition.

Anatomical research provided clues to the workings of human biology, especially the work that tracked the pathways of nerves through the body. Another approach that proved useful was the study of the nervous system through the overt behavior of the living subject. Rene Descartes produced some of the earliest respected works that combined both of these topics. He published his theory in the *Treatise of Man* (1662/2003). In this book, he proposed that the nervous system was similar to a hydraulic plumbing system. According to Descartes's approach, the mind, which is located in the head, causes the ventricles of the brain to squeeze and thereby push pressurized fluid through the nerves so they can operate the muscles. Descartes's particular approach required that the body be separate from the mind and that the nerves be hollow tubes capable of passing pressurized fluid.

Descartes's contemporaries found two primary flaws in his theory. The first was that he conceived the mind as a nonphysical entity. If the mind is nonphysical, then no one can be expected to actually locate or study its physical properties because, by definition, it has none. The second problem was related to his proposal that nerves are hollow tubes. One of the earliest and most well respected microscopy scientists, Antonie van Leeuwenhoek, could not verify experimentally that the nerves were hollow tubes filled with fluid.

Apart from Leeuwenhoek's microscopic work, other theoreticians suggested alternatives to Descartes's hydraulic-nerves theory. One of the primary theoretical challenges came from Sir Isaac Newton. Newton proposed mechanisms in the nervous system that were based upon his knowledge of physics. Specifically, he suggested that nerves transmitted vibrations from the muscle to the brain (sensation) or from the brain to the muscle (voluntary control of movement). The concept of vibration followed the same waveform analysis that Newton applied in physics. This approach also rejected Descartes's mind/body distinction because sensation and voluntary control operated through the same physical mechanisms. Although in development for decades, Newton first published his vibration theory of the nervous system in a small section of the second edition of the *Principia Mathematica* (1713).

The Eighteenth Century and Biological Electricity

The following century would capture the development of early batteries—more specifically, Leyden jars. One of the uses of these Leyden jars was to electrocute the legs of a doctor's paralyzed patients. The reasoning for this stemmed from the idea that nonworking nerves were clogged and could not distribute signals throughout. Because electrocuting someone caused them to jerk, it seemed likely that the electricity was unclogging the nerves. Electricity might produce faster signals in the nerves and faster signals might blast through the clogged nerves, which would effect a cure for the paralysis. Forerunners of this technique in the late 18th century included Christian Gottlieb Kratzenstein, who found that electrocuting the legs of paralyzed patients sometimes caused them to report tingling sensations in their legs or feet. This tingling—understood today as part of the peripheral nervous system not directly related to a spinal injury—allowed for another route of information into the patient's brain. Kratzenstein incorrectly believed that he could effectively treat paralysis in this matter. Consequently, he also applied electricity to dead birds to see if he could resuscitate them back to life. These experiments, of course, failed.

Luigi Galvani conducted further work on the nervous system's electrical signals. After his laboratory assistant accidentally touched an electrified panel to the leg of a dead frog, they found that the leg jerked. The movement of the leg is similar to the rapid movements one gets when shocking a living person. This suggested to Galvani that the nerves might not be hollow tubes filled with fluid, but tubes that conducted electricity. Galvani referred to this effect as animal electricity. He then passed this information to his nephew, Giovanni Aldini.

Aldini, who would later develop a reputation for being a quack doctor, assessed whether electricity would make the faces of beheaded criminals grimace. Aldini would take the head of a freshly decapitated criminal and place the paddles of the Leyden jar near its mouth and ears. Such tests showed that, in fact, the head would make grimacing faces due to the electrical stimulation. Aldini also used electric shocks to treat medical disorders. In fact, Aldini had his gout patients place their feet into a bucket with electric eels so that they could be shocked for the expected medical benefits. Moreover, while Kratzenstein attempted to resuscitate dead birds, Aldini attempted to resuscitate executed criminals. He did so by taking the bodies of people hung to their deaths and exposing them to the electric shocks from his Leyden jars. These experiments with humans failed just as Kratzenstein's attempts with birds failed.

One of the few beneficial uses of Aldini's electric shock treatments was in treating melancholy, a mild form of depression. His results indicated that an electric shock to the head of a person with melancholy produced an improved mood in the patient. Technologically, Aldini had poor measures of electrical current and no measure of mood assessment other than his own opinion. Regardless, his attempts constitute the first instances of electroconvulsive therapy, a technique that is still in use today. Aldini's positive outcomes prompted him to electrocute himself. He reported that the shocks to his own head produced a "sleepiness for days." By today's standards, we would view Aldini's self-experimentation as harmful. He, however, believed he was doing himself more good than harm.

The Nineteenth Century and Research Directly Leading to the Development of Psychology

Neuroanatomy

During the first half of the 19th century, French and German physiologists conducted most of the work that directly led to the development of psychology. For instance, aided by Galvani's concept of animal electricity, Ernst Muller developed the Doctrine of Specific Nerve Energies. This doctrine grew from the observation that the brain appeared to be made of a unitary substance. Today, we would recognize that substance as neural tissue. Muller reasoned that if the brain was built with the same material throughout, then signals from the eyes and ears and skin should all produce the same sensations. Because that clearly is not the case, he proposed that each area of the brain functioned to produce different sensations, or specific nerve energies. Broadly, what this implied was that the brain was compartmentalized into control sections for different sensory or motor functions. The Doctrine of Specific Nerve Energies led to experiments that sought to find evidence of brain compartmentalization.

One way to study this inferred compartmentalization is to choose an area of the brain, destroy it, and then determine which behavioral deficits develop once the subject recovers from surgery. This type of work is referred to as ablation experiments. The Frenchman Pierre Flourens, circa 1825, developed ablation experiments. Flourens used this ablation technique on rabbits and pigeons to

Kratzenstein and Aldini performed their experiments in the late 18th century. Because of the bizarre nature of their work and its widespread use throughout Europe, it is believed that many citizens outside of medicine were also aware of it. One of those citizens was likely Mary Shelly, the author of the novel *Frankenstein*.

Animal electricity: A term used in the 17th and 18th centuries that referred to the vague understanding that nerves conduct electricity through animals. Frequently, it is contrasted with atmospheric electricity, the type of electricity early researchers observed in lightning.

Gout: A form of arthritis caused by increased levels of uric acid in the blood that result in the deposit of painful crystals in your joints.

A statue of Darwin outside the Natural History Museum in London.

(a)　　　　　　　　　　　　　　(b)

Drugs and surgical tools were important for 19th century biologists.

map the outer surfaces of their brains by systematically destroying small sections and determining the overall structure of deficits that developed once they had recovered.

By the 1870's, a new technique developed that contrasted with Flourens' ablation procedure. Rather than ablating sections of brain, the German biologists, Eduard Hitzig and Gustav Fritsch, stimulated the outer surface of the brain with a mild electric current. This allowed for the determination of brain function by exciting its activity rather than eliminating its activity. Using dog subjects primarily, Fritz and Hitzig would stimulate the brain with a mild electrical current. The effect they sought was reflexive motor activity. These electrical stimulation experiments were conceptually similar to those of Flourens in that Fritz and Hitzig believed that a single area of brain could have its function determined by stimulating it or ablating it. The ablation and stimulation techniques are still applied in biological research today. They are currently used with such high precision that individual neurons can be ablated or stimulated while causing minimal damage to the surrounding tissue.

Ablation:
A surgical technique in which a portion of the brain is destroyed so that the researcher can assess that section's function by determining the behavioral deficit that results afterward.

During the late 19th century, it may have appeared that the conclusions from this research applied only to rabbits, birds, and dogs, so the information would have had limited value. That possibility disappeared once Charles Darwin published *On the Origin of the Species* in 1859. Darwin's work proposed underlying neuroanatomical similarities in various creatures due to their common ancestry. Darwin's theory proved highly valuable to 19th-century biologists. It tied together the neuroanatomical divisions of the brain across a wide range of animal species, including humans. Because human beings were not experimented upon in the same way animals were, it would take many years to assess the behavioral deficits from stroke and head injury victims before anatomical maps comparing human and nonhuman brain structures would reveal their similarities. Those similarities, in addition to many other biochemical similarities, means that animals are often useful subjects for testing biological phenomena when ethical regulations prohibit the use of humans.

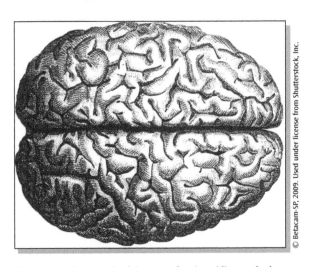

The brain begins its history of scientific study by first being ablated.

Sensation and Perception

Weber and Fechner

In the first few decades of the 1800's, Ernst Weber and Gustav Fechner conducted the first experiments on what we know today as Sensation and Perception. Weber, a physician, and Fechner, a physicist, became interested in how the physical attributes of stimuli outside our bodies (e.g., light, sound and weight, etc.)

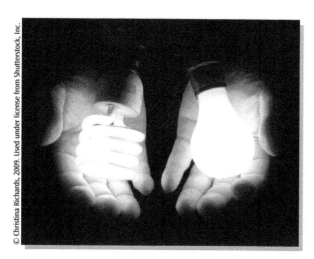

Modern three-way light bulbs allow you to see the effects of psychophysics in your own home.

Psychophysics:
The field of psychology that examines how physical energy outside your body is received and converted into a mental perception.

Somatosensory:
The sense of touch.

Linear input-output:
When any changing input into a natural system results in a correspondingly equal change in output. Frequently seen in physical systems such as adding 1 pound weights to a scale and seeing that the meter spins 10 degrees for each pound added.

convert into perceptions. Their primary discovery was that the perception of stimuli does not linearly follow energy intensity. Everyone is aware of this effect with common household three-way light bulbs. If the bulb you are using operates at 50, 100 and 150 Watts, there is a linear increase in light intensity across the three settings. Therefore, if our perceptions of light were linearly related to the actual amount of light outside our eyes, we would then perceive a linear increase in light intensity. This, of course, is not what actually happens. People perceive the increase in light from the 50 W to the 100 W setting as far greater than the increase in light from the 100 W to 150 W setting. This helps show that a constant increase in illumination is perceived as smaller increases in light intensity. In 1821, Weber published the first book on this newly developed field he named **psychophysics**.

Weber's work is best known for his investigations of the visual and **somatosensory** systems, specifically the ability to distinguish between differently weighted items. The field of psychophysics immediately became important to the slowly developing field of psychology. Psychophysics clearly shows that humans and animals do not function as the **linear input-output** systems seen in the physical sciences (e.g., force, motion, chemical reactions, etc.). When it came to living beings, the input-output relationships were curvilinear. This distinction was an important one in the development of psychology. It contrasted strongly with the linear relationships seen in the physical sciences and indicated that nervous systems did not operate by the same rules.

Helmholtz

The actions of that new curvilinear system were analyzed by one of the 19th century's greatest all around scientists, Herman von Helmholtz. Helmholtz received training in medicine and physics. He would spend most of his life conducting experiments on both biology and physics. Throughout his career, he made significant discoveries in both physics and biology. In fact, Helmholtz's influence was so great that college textbooks on general physics, general psychology, biological psychology, and medical ophthalmology still refer to his work.

Helmholtz conducted much work on the visual system. He developed the first ophthalmoscope, which is the device the doctor uses to look at the back of your eye during an eye exam. Helmholtz also conducted experiments circa 1850 that lent great support to Thomas Young's 1802 theory on color vision. That theory is the Young-Helmholtz theory of color vision. It is largely accepted as fact today and will be discussed in the later sensation and perception chapter.

Due to his work on the medical aspects of vision, Helmholtz was named as one of the three founding members of the field of ophthalmology.

For more information on Thomas Young, please see the chapter on Sensation and Perception.

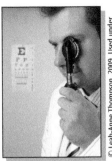

The prototype for this ophthalmoscope was created by Helmholtz.

Subtraction method:
A process in which simple *response* durations are subtracted from (*response + decision*) durations to determine the duration of the *decision*.

Helmholtz's accurate estimation of the speed of neural signals was one of his most relevant discoveries for psychology. In the mid-1800's, most biologists believed that nerves sent signals at the speed of light. Helmholtz assessed this by marking two points on an individual's body and clocking their reaction times from each area. If stimulation occurred on your shoulder and on your foot, Helmholtz could estimate the speed of your reaction to each stimulus and determine the difference between your reactions for the stimulus closer to your brain versus the one further away. The difference between those two points would allow for an estimate of the speed of neural transmission. This type of procedure was termed the subtraction method.

Helmholtz's speed estimates of 50 meters/sec (164 feet/sec) remain accurate to this day. Research over the next century revealed a few additional variables in the determination of neural speed. All things being equal, the fastest neural signals travel at 120 meters/sec or 394 feet/sec. That is 1.3 football fields in one second! This also means that a six foot man determining the comfort of a new pair of shoes requires 0.015 seconds for the signal to go from his foot to his brain—a tad more than 1/100th of a second. Once researchers discovered the speed of neural transmission, they could use it to estimate all sorts of mental processes. For instance, a Dutch eye doctor would soon use it to determine the length of time it takes to make a simple decision.

Reaction Time Experiments

Donders

Franciscus Donders began to investigate human reaction times during the 1860's at Utrecht University in Holland. Donders, a physiology professor, may be best remembered as a co-founder of the field of ophthalmology, along with Hermann von Helmholtz. Stemming from Helmholtz's work in neural speed, Donders used a variation of Helmholtz's subtraction method to determine the duration of a simple decision.

Donders proposed that reaction times to stimuli require only the observation of the stimulus and a reaction to it. If one were to add an extra stimulus in the experiment, one which required a decision to respond or not, then the difference between (a) simply responding to a stimulus or (b) responding to two stimuli if only the correct one were present, would allow for the measurement of the decision itself. The time difference in responding in a two-stimulus procedure versus a one-stimulus procedure gives an estimate of how long it takes to make the decision to respond. This subtraction process, in a more carefully designed form, has become a primary measurement tool in psychology.

Donders' work opened up a wide range of possibilities for those interested in studying human cognitive processes. His technique gave an objective, easily measured datum to the developing field of psychology. Despite his methodological advances, his work was not enough to cause the development of psychology departments in academic institutions. Another person would make that final step; this time, a physician turned scientist.

Psychology Begins

Wundt

Wilhelm Wundt was born in 1832; he was the son of a minister. Numerous times his father's ministry failed to develop large congregations. Consequently, the Wundt family had to move repeatedly to smaller towns. Wundt's upbringing was generally considered strict, even for the period in which he lived. In his memoirs, he reported that his grandfather would keep him in dark closets for long periods as punishments for misbehavior. This, however, did not stop young Wilhelm from having poor grades in school and a reputation for daydreaming. Furthermore, he had to repeat the first year of high school due to his poor performance.

© Semen Lixodeev, 2009. Used under license from Shutterstock, Inc.

The "personal equation" of astronomy affects the development of psychology's reaction time experiments.

It was not until he went to the University of Heidelberg that he began to show any academic promise.

Wundt developed an interest in science and began to conduct experiments on himself. One such experiment involved determining the effects of a restricted salt diet. As his academic training took him down the pathway of medicine, he found himself covering long night shifts at a hospital. On one such evening, while he was very sleepy, he almost poisoned a patient by feeding him a spoonful of iodine rather than the prescribed medicine that was nearby. This caused Wundt such personal grief that he decided he should not continue to train as a physician, but rather become an academic physiologist. In the years to come when he began to study psychology, he would look back to that near accidental poisoning and try to understand it by analyzing his consciousness. This pivotal event helped develop consciousness into its own field of study.

After medical school, Wundt moved to the University of Heidelberg and became the laboratory assistant of Hermann von Helmholtz. While there, Wundt attempted to determine the duration of a thought with a so-called Thought Meter. Wundt's attempts estimated thought-durations at approximately 0.125 s. Most psychologists today would argue that his estimate was much too long.

Reportedly, Wundt and Helmholtz argued frequently over psychological theories and who was responsible for discovering which find. In one such instance, the writings of astronomer Adolf Hirsch encouraged Wundt to improve upon the reaction time measures used at observatories to set clocks to astronomical events. Astronomers refer to reaction time variability as the "personal equation." Wundt and Helmholtz argued forcefully over which of them was responsible for developing the experiments that helped solve those problems.

In 1871, Helmholtz moved to the University of Heidelberg to pursue his interests in physics. Wundt expected to be promoted into Helmholtz's position but was passed over and given a low paying teaching position. Angry over this perceived slight, he took a position at the University of Zurich in 1874 and moved again to the Philosophy department at the University of Leipzig in 1875. It is at this point that Wundt established his own psychological laboratory.

In his research, he was interested in how thoughts work. In his laboratory, he abandoned the purely philosophical approach used since the time of the ancient Greeks. He turned his attention to the use of scientific principles and focused on objective measures of behavior such as reaction times and psychophysical measurements. His approach, therefore, was to focus on measurable aspects of behavior that could be used to understand internal events, such as thoughts.

Many science historians identify this laboratory as the first psychological laboratory. Clearly, Wundt, Helmholtz, and others were working on the concepts of psychology for many decades. What characterizes Wundt's Leipzig laboratory as unique, is his mixture of philosophy, biology and the overall set of questions he addressed. Moreover, when one reviews the opening of psychology departments across Europe, North America, and Japan, either Wundt or one of Wundt's students trained most of the faculty contained therein. Clearly, the spread of psychological laboratories leads directly back to Wilhelm Wundt.

The Twentieth Century and the Formation of Modern Psychology

The discovery of DNA has affected all fields of study that have a biological approach.

Across the twentieth century, the field of psychology developed ever more rapidly. As the physical sciences developed computer systems and miniaturized electronic equipment, psychologists made use of these advances in their own research. For example, before the inception of inexpensive desktop computing systems, most psychological laboratories made use of electromechanical relay equipment to control their experiments. Developments in biology, such as the mapping of the human cortex during brain surgeries and the discovery of DNA, resulted in further developments in therapies for mental illness and brain injuries. Psychology has not only developed due to borrowed advances in electronics. In contrast, social events have influenced the development of psychology as well.

The passage of two world wars, the development of national ethical standards for research and a civil rights movement influenced the first 75 years of research of the 20th century. Each time, both the social and biological control of behavior has been investigated to all our benefit. These world events influenced which areas psychologists focused upon, and therefore, which aspects of human behavior we better understood. The rate at which psychological information advances has increased ever more rapidly over the past one and a quarter centuries. The 21st century offers such rapid changes in development that the next fifty years of research may change psychology as much as it has changed since 1879, when Wundt opened the first psychological laboratory. The methodologies applied by psychologists are the topics for the next section. Follow it carefully and you will understand how psychologists conduct their work.

DEFINING PSYCHOLOGY

Psychology as the Study of Thoughts and Feelings

Therapists try to analyze your thoughts by using what you say as a way to infer what you are thinking.

When I tell people that I am a psychologist, they generally say something to the effect of "Well, don't psychoanalyze me," and then they redirect me to their spouse who—they say—is in need of some therapy. This generally reflects the perception that people believe psychology is all about clinical work—finding out why people do strange things. Of course, that is partly true. Each year, most newly awarded Ph.D.'s are in the clinical arena. This, however, is not the full story. Psychologists work in a wide range of areas that reflect basic scientific research in brain-behavior relationships as well as the helping professions. What is common to all these areas, that is central to psychology, is that each area studies the behavior of its subjects as opposed to thoughts and feelings specifically.

To be certain, the history of psychology reflects psychologists concern over the internal mental events of people. What has always been true, however, is that the scientific investigations of thoughts and feelings have always been designed to measure behavior specifically. You might wonder how that may be the case. It certainly is not the impression one gets from the popular media. Certainly, most of the descriptions given in the media refer to thoughts, wants and emotions. Drug addicts "crave" their drug, angry spouses "want" their spouse to change and clinical professionals frequently analyze your thoughts and feelings. With everyone concerned about thoughts, could there be anything wrong?

Emphatically, there is a problem with concentrating on thoughts, feelings, and emotions only. The problem is that thoughts, feelings, and emotions cannot be **directly measured**. To consider this strange idea—an idea you have probably never heard of before—consider the following examples.

Imagine experiments in which only thoughts, feelings, or emotions are measured. We might have a situation in which we want to measure the feelings of a husband toward and his wife during an unpleasant divorce. How could we do so?

<aside>
Directly measured:
A datum that is publicly observable. The overt behavior is not used to infer the existence of an unseen mental event.
</aside>

In this hypothetical example, we might hook our male subject up to a brain-recording device that measures his feelings when his wife is present. What is being measured in this experiment? You may believe that it is his feelings. What kind of data do you think our machine will give us? If we have attached some form of electrode to the man's head then we should receive the electrical output associated with his emotions. A very important question we need to ask ourselves now is, "Is the measure of electrical activity the same as a measure of feelings?" If the answer to that question is no, then you need to look elsewhere for his emotions. What you have measured is the electrical activity from his brain. That electrical activity very well may be associated with his feelings. Electrical activity, however, is not a measure of feelings itself. In fact, in this instance the electrical activity measured is a conglomeration of all the electrical activity occurring in his brain during the time that he saw his wife. We can be certain, then, that our measure of electrical activity is contaminated with other measures.

Let's suppose we take another approach. Let's say, this time, we measured changes in the chemicals from the man's blood. If we measure chemical changes that correlate directly to the time that his wife is present or absent, then can we say we have measured the man's feelings? Again, we are in the same situation as before. The blood chemicals may change systematically with the presence and absence of the man's wife, however, blood chemicals are not feelings. Moreover, there are no tests available today that can associate specific blood chemicals to specific feelings.

This same problem exists when studying dreaming. Dreaming is a very popular topic in psychology. To study dreams, one must get a verbal report from the dreamer because dream researchers do not have direct access to the dreamer's experience. No one can hook you up to a computer and watch your dreams while you are having them. The analysis of dreams must start with verbal reports from the dreamer. If the dreamer does not remember their dreams then there are no dream reports to analyze. If the dreamer remembers the dream incorrectly, then no one will know that the story she tells is inaccurate. Can you really be sure that you remember your dreams correctly? Can you be certain that your experimental subject is recalling their dreams accurately? The answer to both questions is no.

This same measurement problem will be present for every physiological quality we take from the man. So then, you may be wondering, "How do we ever measure this man's feelings?" The answer is, we don't. Each time we attempt to measure directly thoughts or feelings we run into the same problem. We have to accept that we cannot directly measure thoughts and feelings in psychology.

FREUDIAN SLIP

Despite Freud's questionable status in psychology today, most people are aware of him sufficiently that this joke makes sense.

That, however, has not stopped researchers from trying to understand thoughts and feelings. The way in which psychologists have studied internal events has always required researchers to associate an overt behavior with the mental events they hope to understand. This accuracy of the inference of a mental event has been debated in psychology since the time of Wundt. I am not trying to answer this problem now; however, any psychology student should be aware that (a) internal mental events are never directly accessible and (b) internal events are always inferred from their behavioral correlates. Moreover, there is no technological or philosophical way around this problem. It simply has to be accepted. Consequently, all psychological research is inherently behavioral.

Psychology as the Study of Behavior

Behavior:
Any measure of movement from a living organism. This includes throwing a ball, walking, writing, or talking about one's feelings and dreams.

So what constitutes a behavior? Its most basic characteristic is muscular activity. Commonly, behavior is referred to as "overt behavior" or "overt responding." Simple examples of behavior are walking, talking, describing your dreams, discussing your feelings, answering questions on an exam, and driving a car. It does not include sitting still, remaining motionless, not talking, or playing dead. The absence of behavior in those examples is not behavior itself. Counting non-behavior is like trying to count the amount of nothings that fill up a hole.

For example, assume a man in therapy has the problem of making insulting comments to others. He enters therapy in the hopes of eliminating this bad habit. When the therapist tries to reduce the incidences of these behaviors, she will focus on increasing appropriate measurable behaviors in particular social contexts (e.g., saying "You look nice today"). She will not attempt to count the absence of the inappropriate behavior. Why is that the case? This is so because the absence of behavior cannot be counted. Only behavior that occurs—and can be measured objectively—can be counted. Therefore, if you estimate the progress of our patient in therapy by showing his "lack of inappropriate behavior," then you place yourself in a position in which you need to count events that never happened! It should be obvious to you that this is not possible. To measure how much progress is occurring, you should (a) count the lessening number of inappropriate comments he makes and (b) count his instances of appropriate behavior. This will give you a clear operational definition of the behavior you wish to measure. Any operational definition is a clearly defined, objective definition of a behavior that is publicly observable and can be directly measured. If the patient is progressing in therapy, then you will know it objectively because of the manner in which you objectively measure the behavior in question.

Operational definition:
A clearly defined, objective definition of a behavior that is publicly observable and can be directly measured.

© Jelena, 2009. Used under license from Shutterstock, Inc.

Applying the Behavioral Rule Throughout Psychology

Ultimately, no matter what we attempt to study in psychology we need to (a) identify specifically the behavior we want to measure and (b) count only its occurrences. If you are still not convinced of this fact then try to imagine the alternative, the field of psychology in which behavior is not measured.

Suppose we were to evaluate someone's thoughts without the benefit of a behavioral measure. For instance, our subject thinks of something and then we evaluate it. Because we are not evaluating a measure of behavior, how will we assess our subject's thoughts? We could watch and wait for him to move but that would not matter in this example because any overt action on the part of the subject cannot be used in this example. We need to assess his behavior without behavior. We could stick his head in a brain scan machine but that would give us a picture of his brain and the areas that were working. Unfortunately, it would not let us know which words were being thought of or the grammatical arrangement they were placed in. We would sit, wait and never learn anything because it is impossible to measure mental events directly.

Now consider all the interesting ideas you want to study in psychology. Are you interested in your thoughts, feelings, dreams or those things in others? Do you believe that by understanding how thoughts function that you can understand people better? Well, it is true that most psychologists believe that as well. Not having direct measures of internal mental events is bothersome; however, it has not stopped psychologists from using the behavioral correlates of subject-reported-thoughts as the basis for research.

HISTORICAL ROOTS OF BEHAVIORISM

The History of Behavioral Psychology

The roots of behavioral thinking go back as far as ancient Greece, specifically to Aristotle. The more recent developments in the 19th century derive from the biological research conducted during the brain mapping experiments previously discussed. Researchers such as Muller, Fritz, Hitzig and Flourens, all examined the behavior of their experimental animals. It is true they wondered what their subjects' experiences were; however, they had no technological developments to overcome their animal's lack of language. As psychology developed toward the end of the 19th century, experiments with human subjects were commonplace. Consequently, many researchers accepted their subjects' verbal descriptions of thoughts and feelings as accurate descriptions of what effect the experiment had on them. As we will see in future chapters, this led researchers to work with some very inaccurate information.

As time passed, greater reliance was placed on subject's descriptions of experiences. This led to a nearly complete focus on what people said in experiments as the datum of interest. So much so, that subject descriptions were sometimes understood in a deductive manner. This means that if one behavior was observed from the subject that another event—an unknown mental event—must be associated with its occurrence. If that behavior changed then it was presumed that the mental event changed as well. Moreover, it is now known that the researchers unknowingly modified their subject's memories of their experiences and that the subjects, even under the best conditions, did not always remember everything accurately. The reliance on these unmeasured mental events became so prevalent that there began a backlash in the early 20th century. That backlash was the development of the behavioral school of psychology.

During the first decade of the 20th century, American psychology was full of unscientific concepts. It was then that John Watson, a psychology professor at Johns Hopkins University in Baltimore, formalized the behavioral school of psychology. The concept of behavioral psychology essentially suggests that researchers must focus on the behavior of their subjects because mental events are inaccessible. Therefore, by definition, psychology is a science of behavior. This approach later linked closely with animal research because those subjects exhibited no language. Its application, however, would eventually spread throughout most fields of psychology.

© Dhoxax, 2009. Used under license from Shutterstock, Inc.

Aristotle seems to be personally responsible for all of Western civilization.

Science of behavior: If all psychological measures are inherently behavioral then psychology is a science of behavior. Any measure taken from a person, whether it is a brain scan or other biological measure, must ultimately relate back to the overt actions of a person.

At that time, psychologists outside of animal research clung to their attempts to measure mental events. Moreover, they made dubious claims that they could accurately measure thoughts and feelings. This approach was most prevalent in the study of clinical psychology. Early 20th century theories of human clinical psychology were largely derived from the belief that what people stated in therapy—and what they did not state—all described a rich internal mental life that controlled the person's overt behavior. The legacy of that work is still with us today (Lee, 1998). From the end of the 19th century until today, some researchers have argued that they can measure mental events directly or, at least measure them indirectly but accurately. Regardless of how this argument resolves itself, I hope it is clear to the reader that any work conducted in psychology must always involve measures of behavior. Whether a researcher claims those measures are reflections of internal mental states or not is irrelevant.

Major Figures in Behavior

The father of behaviorism is John Watson. He obtained that title because he constructed the first formalized description of a behavioral science in his seminal article, "Psychology as the Behaviorist Views it" (Watson, 1913). The period in which Watson wrote that article saw the popularity of mentalistic concepts arise from the work being completed in clinical psychology. Watson believed that the focus on mentalism in American psychology would stop the field from developing into an experimental science. He therefore aggressively fought against mentalistic approaches by identifying their failures to commit to a scientific methodology. His efforts paid off in that behavioral theory became the predominant approach in American psychology by the 1950's.

After Watson, the next person who further developed the behavioral approach was B. F. Skinner. Skinner started his academic training at Harvard University researching animal behavior using Watson's behavioral approach. Through a series of experimental insights, Skinner advanced the equipment used to study laboratory animals. He also developed the behavioral approach beyond Watson by relying on the much larger database of the late 1930's compared with the one Watson accessed in the early 1920's. This allowed Skinner to extend behavioral thinking to applications with humans in ways that Watson could not.

Speaking Behavioralese

We use everyday language when we casually speak to our friends. Everyday language, casual speaking, is filled with mentalistic terminology. Some of the most common greetings we give each other include references to internal thoughts and feelings. Greetings such as "How are you?" and "How do you feel today?" The phrase "Penny for your thoughts" even implies that thoughts are individual items that can be bartered for cash. We use the concepts of thoughts and feelings without *realizing* that we use them. In fact, they are so embedded in our language that I, the author, cannot even discuss them without using them myself, such as my use of the term *realizing* in the previous sentence.

A quick check of a thesaurus will show anyone the many terms that exist in English for internal mental events (search the terms *thoughts* and *feelings*). It is not necessary to use these terms when discussing the scientific description of behavior, however. The careful use of language in describing behavioral operations is possible; however, it may be difficult. It certainly takes practice. Let's try now to apply scientific terminology to the study of psychological events with all the mental events extracted out.

Throughout the history of behavioral psychology, the application of scientific phraseology has been worked rigorously. One of the most basic components

John loves Susan.

© Tomasz Trojanowski, 2009. Used under license from Shutterstock, Inc.

of scientific language use is the reliance on the *stimulus input-response output* process observed in all living organisms. Recognizing this input-output process is very important. To call humans biological input-output machines does not take away from the overall behavioral complexity they exhibit. It also does not mean that exposing them to random stimuli results in them randomly twitching reflexively all day long either. Rather, it is recognition that stimulus events elicit behavior. Moreover, those events may control different people in different ways based upon each of their individual learning histories.

> Internal mental events: Will, obstinacy, caprice, impulse, desire, eagerness, indifference, satiety, sanity, insanity, idea, reasoning, belief, curiosity, etc.

To address a specific example, let's analyze the comment, "John loves Susan." Comments about love are very common; we hear them all the time. People speak of loving their friends, their life, or even ice cream. We immediately distinguish between the types of love and their meaning in each case. If John states that he loves Susan, he may also say other things that we feel are related such as "floating on air when he meets her" or "getting butterflies in his stomach when she is around." We do not really believe that John can levitate when he sees Susan or that literal butterflies are in his stomach. Rather, we have learned in our culture that these comments are descriptions of feelings that John would express in any number of ways. Each way centers on John's physical experiences and their relation to Susan's presence. More importantly, we cannot directly access John's feelings regarding Susan, which is an issue we dealt with in a previous section. What we can measure is what he says about her and about himself when she is present or absent. John's attitude may change greatly when Susan is around. If she is present and he becomes the friendliest person we know, then we attribute that to Susan's presence and her influence on him.

The casual descriptions of behavior that involve mentalistic terminology generally refer to the thoughts and feelings of the speaker. To avoid the mentalistic terminology, one must view a person as a complex input-output machine. It has been clear for many decades that specific stimulus inputs into a nervous system contribute to specific outputs. Because behavior may be viewed as this input-output system, it becomes obvious that one should associate behaviors with particular stimulus inputs. This results in descriptions such as "The presence of Susan made it more likely that John showed up." In this example, John's behavior is directly connected to Susan's presence. The interrelationship of John to Susan is expressed in that statement. It says nothing about John's thoughts, feelings or motivations. The phrase is a clean description of the overt, publicly observable behavior that John exhibited. No assumptions about John's thoughts were made.

Is she angry (mental state) with her husband or is she displaying anger?

When defining exactly what "love" means in regards to John and Susan, we must first define specific target behaviors that will define our definition. If we were just to discuss the concept of love, anyone who listened to us may have a different definition of what needed to be covered. With multiple definitions of love, we certainly would wind up with confusion regarding our concepts. Alternatively, if we define a few specific target behaviors, then we will alleviate any misunderstanding that may occur to those who read our work. For example, we could define John's "love" for Susan by measuring the duration of time he speaks to her each day. The measurement of speaking-duration may not seem like an accurate measure of love. Remember, however, that we cannot access John's feelings directly. What we can measure is what those presumed emotions cause John to do. Stated more cleanly, John states that he loves Susan and correspondingly we measure that he speaks to her for approximately four hours each day. Moreover, when he is questioned about this, he states that he would rather speak with Susan than do anything else. John may do other things as well such as going to the drugstore for her when she is sick, picking her flowers in the park as a gift, or even getting her car washed. For the sake of recording, each of those responses may be measured in different ways. Each of those ways will produce a slightly different view of John's "love."

> The verbal descriptions of the patients constitute the behavioral measures the therapist analyzes.

Observing and Recording Behavior

Suppose that as time goes by, John and Susan fall out of love for each other. Because they want to stay together, they go to couples therapy. The therapist will then talk to John and Susan separately and together to listen to what is bothering them about their mate. Because the therapist does not live with his patients or socialize with them outside of therapy, the only way for her to learn about their problems is to ask questions. The verbal descriptions the patients give allow the therapist to evaluate their progress. If their stories do not make sense, it may require some clarification. If the clarification does not come then the patient may be intentionally giving false information. When John and Susan discuss each other to the therapist, the therapist will try to reconcile each story with what the other has said to make a logical picture of what is happening in the relationship. If questioning them does not work out, then the therapist may have to step up her evaluation technique.

> **Reactivity:**
> The changed behavior of a person during times in which they believe they are being watched.

If this occurs, the therapist will need to observe and record John and Susan's behavior with respect to each other. If the therapist follows John and Susan around, her presence in their environment may influence how they behave. For example, John may behave less angry toward Susan when the therapist is present and Susan, who may feel she is misunderstood, may react more strongly to John so that she can express to the observing therapist what her needs are. When the presence of an observer influences the observed subjects, the process is called **reactivity**.

The therapist may need to remain out of John and Susan's environment. So how can she measure their behavior if she is not present? One possibility is that the therapist places discrete video cameras in John and Susan's house. Initially, the presence of the cameras may influence John and Susan's behavior. Over time, however, it would be expected that their normal pattern of behavior will emerge. What the therapist is looking for is how John and Susan treat each and which behaviors precede an argument. By recording their behavior at home, the therapist can record the number of instances of specific target behaviors that immediately precede arguing. Because any number of comments from John may make Susan angry, the therapist may not be able to categorize them easily. The therapist can count, however, the number of times Susan begins to argue with John after he speaks. Susan's arguing as well, must be defined in concrete terms. The therapist may identify the raised volume of her voice or count the number of negative adjectives she uses to describe John.

> The therapist has to be flexible regarding which response to measure. She may have to evaluate them for a while before she realizes which measure will work best under these conditions.

BEHAVIORAL SCIENCE METHODS

Folk Psychology

You will probably hear a variety of answers when you ask people what they think the field of psychology entails. Most people will describe psychology as something that everyone makes attempts at doing, such as watching and describing the behavior of others. Some people will suggest that psychology is all about clinical work. For example, therapists working with people to solve their emotional problems. Many people believe they understand human behavior so well through observation and insight that they know unequivocal facts. They may associate their friend's thriftiness with their history of poverty. Others may associate their friend's big spending habits with histories of poverty. Other examples include seeing a "fear of rejection" in obese people. Those cases may be contrasted with other instances in which bulimics are viewed as showing a "fear of rejection." Many of those unjustified correlations grow out of cultural stereotypes and establish much of Folk Psychology.

Folk psychology is the understanding of human behavior through the traditional culturally specific understanding of people. It is often the comments your grandmother used to make regarding her life experiences. For example, one folk psychology comment I have personally heard on a number of occasions is that "Crazy people are the ones that go into psychology because they want to learn about themselves."

The comment makes many assumptions about why people find an interest in psychology. Those assumptions, however, have not been tested scientifically. Simply put, they are untested ideas that have been passed around for decades and generally result in some acceptance because they seem to make sense or because they are heard so often.

Frequently, folk psychology has a set of phrases—or proverbs—that are contradictory but can be used in a wide variety of situations. Some of the more common ones are "Look before your leap" and "He who hesitates is lost." Another is "Absence makes the heart grow fonder" and "Out of sight, out of mind." When one looks closely at these statements, they may apply accurately under a select set of conditions; however, those conditions may be linked by other changes in the social context. That simply does not make for good science. We cannot choose our explanations based upon untested assumptions of behavior. It would be equally as wrong to make a system of explanation for human behavior based upon cultural proverbs. When would we actually test our understanding for facts?

Illusory Correlations

When dealing with human behavior, it is common for different characteristics to be associated. For example, you may notice that small children like to play with toys but adults never do so. You may notice that it is harder to approach attractive people and strike up a conversation with them then it is with someone you believe is unattractive. The belief that some things are associated, or go together, is very common in psychology. In fact, these correlations between events are extremely important for understanding human behavior. They frequently allow us to assume the presence of one unseen characteristic if we first find its correlate.

We often find ourselves in trouble when we inappropriately correlate two conditions that really do not go together. If we make assumptions based upon race, gender or religion, we often find these correlations do not hold. Of course, that is not always the case. Sometimes the correlations will work, and sometimes they will not. Stating that a correlation exists does not guarantee that it will be

Bulimia:
An eating disorder usually characterized by binge eating followed by self-induced vomiting.

Folk psychology:
A form of commonsense psychology generally characterized by the use of cultural proverbs to understand human behavior (e.g., Birds of a feather flock together; The squeaky wheel gets the grease, etc.)

present in all cases. In fact, it probably won't. Psychology is very much a statistical science, which means that one is always assessing scientific truth based upon the statistical likelihood of a particular condition existing. Therefore, it is usually true that any known relationship among variables will exhibit exceptions. For example, it is well known that smoking is correlated with a variety of medical problems; however, there are smokers who never get sick. It is important to identify and measure statistically the correlation between any two characteristics. More importantly, it is necessary for psychologists to distinguish between the varieties of correlations that exist for any one person.

Because you are a living being with a nervous system, live in society and have frequent contact with other humans, you most certainly have established correlations among the various characteristics of people you meet. To do so is a normal pattern of behavior. What you are learning to do now, however, is distinguish among the various relevant components so that your decisions become more accurate. One of the best ways to do this is to walk-through some commonly known mistakes regarding correlations. These are referred to as Illusory Correlations. Illusory correlations generally are inaccurately made correlations. That is, people believe the identified characteristics are associated despite the fact that they are not. One common example of this is the adoption/conception illusory correlation.

The inaccurate assumptions are as follows; if a couple tries to conceive a child and has difficulty doing so then they may adopt. If they adopt, the woman will then become pregnant afterward because of the reduction in stress that she experiences as a result of no longer trying to conceive. Often, people "recognize" the presence of this illusory correlation in family members. Medically, this implies that emotional stress has a significant factor regarding egg fertilization. This, however, is not true. Anyone who believes this illusory correlation will likely believe that stress can influence fertilization. This may seem to make sense given the wide range of medical problems often associated with stress. In this particular instance, however, there does not appear to be an accurate connection.

Look at **Figure 1.1**, this figure shows the relationship between adoption and pregnancy in a simple 2 X 2 table. This table shows four possible outcomes in the relationship between getting pregnant and adoption. Both pregnancy and adoption conditions are dichotomous. That is, you are either pregnant or are not pregnant, and you either adopt or do not adopt. The assumption behind the illusory correlation is that when a couple adopts it increases the couple's chance of conception. If the couple does not adopt then their chance of conception remains low. Those two particular cells in the table reflect the main components of the illusory correlation. When one only focuses on these two cells, it may appear that couples are more likely to conceive if they have already adopted than if they have not. To be more scientific, however, one must also consider the alternative cells—these are the ones that are frequently ignored. How often do couples conceive if they do not adopt? How often do couples fail to conceive after adopting? Directly measuring all four cells and evaluating all the information together in a statistical test is the only way to make a balanced conclusion regarding the correlation between adoption and conception.

Does adoption help you conceive?		Conceive (2nd)	
		Yes	No
Adopt (1st)	Yes	Supports illusory correlation	Scenario ignored
	No	Scenario ignored	Supports illusory correlation

FIGURE 1.1 ■ The basic relationship between adoption and conception.

Low Probability Events

Psychologists rely on statistics to make logical decisions regarding behavior. The laws of behavior developed in psychology come from statistical estimates regarding the amount of control one variable will have on some behavior. You will see many lawful relationships of human behavior that are based upon statistical reasoning in this textbook. In almost all cases, however, one will find exceptions to the rule. For example, it may seem very unlikely that anyone will win the lottery twice. There are, however, a growing set of instances is in which people are winning the lottery multiple times. How can this happen? Well, statistics provides the answer.

Few people win the lottery, however, even fewer win it twice.

One basic statistical rule implies that the larger the population one draws from, the greater the total number of instances will exist in the low probability ranges. Stated differently, the larger the population you draw from the more often you will see unlikely events. **Table 1.1** shows how the unlikely 2 percent of a distribution increases its number of events as the size of the population increases.

In contrast to the greater number of low probability events in large populations, new students to psychology must learn that the occurrence of unlikely events does not violate the general laws they come from. For example, when addressing the relationship between smoking and cancer, many people will indicate they have heard of someone who smoked heavily for decades but never developed cancer. That very well may be true. The reality, however, is that there is a strong correlation between tobacco use and various forms of cancer. If people let a single exception diminish the overwhelming evidence that predicts cancer, then they are performing themselves a disservice.

Descriptive Methods

The beginning of many scientific research programs often begins with the descriptive methodology. The descriptive methodology is a process for acquiring information through the simple observation and description of what is

TABLE 1.1 ■ The Total Number of Events Observed as a Function of Population Size.

Probability multiplied by population size	Total number of observed events
0.001×100	The event will be seen once each time the population turns over ten times
$0.001 \times 1,000$	The event will be seen once in the population
$0.001 \times 10,000$	The event will occur 10 times in the population
$0.001 \times 100,000$	The event will occur 100 times in the population
$0.001 \times 1,000,000$	The event will occur 1,000 times in the population
$0.001 \times 10,000,000$	The event will occur 10,000 times in the population
$0.001 \times 100,000,000$	The event will occur 100,000 times in the population
$0.001 \times 1,000,000,000$	The event will occur 1,000,000 times in the population

Having a microphone and camera pointed you will almost certainly modify how you answer questions.

observed. Stated very simply, one only needs to describe what they observed without further analyzing it. The descriptive methodology is very useful once a new research program begins. The lack of knowledge in some new research areas negates the usefulness of completing complex experiments. It is much more useful to simply watch and observe your subjects and take that information for further analysis.

Psychologists frequently refer to three general forms of descriptive methodology. They are case studies, naturalistic observation, and polls. Case studies have a long history in psychology. They became popular around the turn of the 20th century when early clinical psychologists, who had very little information regarding mental illnesses, studied interesting cases. With little background data or theory to support their ideas, these early clinicians attempted to understand their patients by describing their symptoms. This data was then analyzed theoretically in an attempt to understand their patients and, more broadly, psychology.

Many clinical constructs were developed during the early 20th century using case studies. There was no more popular version than what was contributed by Sigmund Freud. Freud's analysis of his patients resulted in a very large and complex theoretical model that became known as Freudian psychoanalysis. Psychoanalysis became very popular in the early 20th century. Little experimental support for its concepts was found in the following decades, however. As research failed to support Freud's theories, Freudian psychoanalysis fell out of favor with psychologists. Today, few graduate psychology programs in psychoanalysis exist. In contrast, the popular media is the place where Freudian ideas are presented frequently. This is usually seen when media therapists give advice regarding a person's *ego, complex and defense mechanisms*. Little evidence exists that support the existence of these concepts; however, the public and the popular media distribute these ideas habitually.

Case studies need not result in bad science, however. Oftentimes, even in medical scenarios, unique patients with peculiar symptoms must be analyzed specifically and intensely because there are no other patients with similar problems. One such current issue is related to brain damage and memory. In the vast majority of cases, individuals who receive a blow to the head, and receive brain damage, find themselves with memory problems. In very few cases, however, individuals receiving blows to the head have recovered from their injuries only to find enhanced memories and increased intelligence. If psychologists did not follow these individuals to determine how the injury has influenced their memory capacity, then we would all lose an opportunity to learn something about how the brain works. This is certainly an incredibly interesting finding from the field of neuropsychology and it holds potentially valuable information about human psychology.

The second form of descriptive methodology is naturalistic observation. Naturalistic observation is a process in which one observes the behavior of their subject in its natural environment. The researcher does not attempt to disturb their subject, only to observe it. One of the most common uses of naturalistic observation is in ethology; the scientific study of natural behavioral patterns in the wild. Ethological research is presented frequently on nature science programs such as the *Animal Planet* channel. Naturalistic observation is applied also in a variety of social psychological research venues. In many cases, psychologists have studied the social behavior of humans in their natural habitat. Those natural habitats have been elevators, parking

Case studies:
The focused study of a single individual who typically has a special characteristic rarely found among others.

Naturalistic observation:
Observing subjects in their natural habitats without disturbing them.

Polls:
A form of survey in which people are asked to give their opinion. Polls may be used for any form of questioning; however, they are most commonly seen during political elections.

© Ed Phillips, 2009. Used under license from Shutterstock, Inc.

Filling out a paper survey may make you feel more relaxed than during an interview, but your answers may not be completely honest if you think you may be identified as having made them.

lots, shopping malls and even churches. The purpose of using naturalistic observation is generally to collect data on your subjects before you are ready to create a new, more formalized theory regarding their behavior.

The third general form of descriptive methodology is polling. Generally, polling comes in the form of political polling. Frequently during the times of presidential elections, telephone surveys are conducted to assess which candidate is most popular. Polling is very much a descriptive methodology; however, it is much more statistical in nature than either naturalistic observations or case studies. Neither of those forms is typically analyzed with the use of statistical tests.

Correlational Method

The second of the big three research methodologies is correlation. Unlike the descriptive methods, in which one observes their subjects, the correlational method seeks to collect two forms of data from each subject. These data will be any two characteristics. One common example is the measurement of both height and weight. Two psychological measurements may be depression and duration of marriage. The two characteristics, however, can be physical and psychological (e.g., height, intelligence). The term correlation specifically refers to the co-relation of two variables. This correlation is then measured for strength. This strength is statistical strength; how likely it is that one variable will change in value when the other one changes in value.

A basic understanding of how correlations work begins with how the two forms of data are plotted on a graph. **Figure 1.2** shows various correlation plots. The leftmost figure shows a positive correlation between the variables. A positive correlation is the name given when both variables increase at the same time. If there is a positive correlation between height and weight, then knowing someone's height will allow us to predict with greater accuracy their weight. In addition, knowing their weight will allow us to predict reasonably well their

Height and weight are correlated.

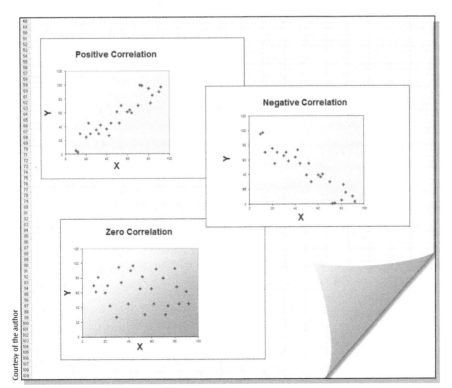

FIGURE 1.2 ■ A positive, zero and negative correlation.

weight. It is not being suggested, however, that knowledge of height will give us an exact estimate for weight. It is suggesting, however, that we will be more accurate at estimating weight if we first know a person's height.

The second figure shows no correlation between the variables. Notice that there is no trend across the figure in the data. In fact, the data appear to be scattered randomly around the graph. At each level of variable X the level of variable Y may be low or high. Because there is no consistency in one measure with respect to the other, we cannot predict any better than just knowing the mean of variable X and the mean of variable Y. Some unrelated variables producing zero correlations are hair length with body height, IQ with shoe size or adult finger length with the total number of years spent in school.

The final figure shows a negative correlation. A negative correlation is named such because as one variable increases the other decreases. This gives the graph of a negative correlation its characteristic downward slope from left to right. The name negative does not imply anything bad about the correlation. It simply refers to the direction in which the function travels. An example of a negative correlation might be the number of friends a person has and the likelihood that they experience a major depressive episode. Generally, more friends mean you will be better protected from the harmful influences of extreme stress.

Correlations may be positive, zero, or negative. As was mentioned above, the measurement of correlations is related to specific mathematical procedures. Those procedures restrict the value of the correlation to a range from -1.0 to +1.0. These values mean something very specific and the consumer of correlational data must understand how to read the sign and value of the correlation. Any correlation that has a positive value indicates that it is a positive correlation. Any correlation that has a negative value indicates that it is a negative correlation. Correlations that are near zero give an impression of randomly scattered data points. Sometimes zero correlation graphs are referred to as "buckshot graphs" because they resemble the scattering of buckshot that was fired at a target.

The numerical value of a correlation conveys how strong the correlational relationship is. This number must be understood as an absolute value. The higher the absolute value of the number is, the stronger the correlation. Whether the correlation is a negative or a positive value is irrelevant. The strength of the relationship is conveyed in the absolute value of the number. Therefore, a correlation of -.95 is greater than a correlation of +.29. A correlation of +.57 is stronger than a correlation of +.12. There is no clearly defined cut off between a weak correlation and a strong correlation. One only needs to compare the difference between two correlations to determine which is stronger and by how much.

Correlation vs. Causation

Correlations play a very useful role in scientific research. All relationships between variables may be viewed in terms of correlations. There are, however, limitations to the value of correlational information. Most importantly, researchers must always remember that correlations do not mean causation. That phrase, which is a central tenet in the behavioral sciences, suggests that any correlation observed does not guarantee that a cause and effect relationship exists between them. Does your height control your weight? Does your weight control your height? Does self-esteem control depression or can depression affect self-esteem? Determining whether one variable only affects the other or they both interact cannot be done by knowledge of a significant correlation between them.

To understand clearly how correlation does not logically lead to a cause and effect relationship, I will walk you through a simple but powerful example. Each year in Florida when the orange crop is high, there is also is a high yield of grapefruits. Year after year, this positive correlation exists. When more oranges are grown then more grapefruits are grown. When fewer oranges are grown then

Correlation does not mean causation: This statement is central to all fields of science and warns behavioral researchers to be aware of inappropriately making cause and effect connections between variables that are only correlated.

fewer grapefruits are grown. Now that we have a correlation to work with, we can evaluate whether a cause and effect relationship exists.

In what manner, through the processes of nature, will cause the growth of oranges to influence the growth of grapefruits? Is it possible that spores are released from the orange trees that fertilize the trees on grapefruit farms? Could it be that the grapefruits release healthy nutrients into the air that are carried into the orange groves? Actually, with little knowledge of farming, most people can eliminate those two suggestions immediately. What then may cause this positive correlation to exist? The most likely answer is that the weather has influenced the growth of both oranges and grapefruits during the same growing season. Although orange yield and grapefruit yield are correlated, there is no cause and effect relationship between them. The point being made is that correlations are induced sometimes through a third variable that the researcher has overlooked.

What would happen if a correlation were more difficult to understand than in the grapefruit example? What if there was a positive correlation between level of poverty and likelihood of committing a crime? Would researchers be safe in suggesting that poverty causes crime? Just how can poverty cause crime? Does having less money than others force you into a reflexive set of movements that result in a robbery? Obviously, the answer is no. Is it possible that committing crimes causes poverty? Could the more money you steal result in greater poverty? Again, this seems unlikely. In fact, a cause and effect relationship does not seem very well supported for this issue. Poverty and crime must be linked through a third variable. Which variable (or variables) link poverty and crime are not given to you in your initial correlation. This is when further research needs to be conducted. It is up to the researcher to use logic, theory and experimentation to determine which variables they are.

Might these grapefruits one day fertilize an orange grove?

Confounds

In a correlational study, two variables are associated with one another. The correlational methodology does not allow cause-and-effect relationships to be identified between the two variables. Moreover, the possibility that an unknown third variable is present cannot be ruled out. Another potential source of confusion in the correlational approach is the presence of confounds. A confound is present when one variable is changed but in reality two variables change as a result.

For example, when correlating height and weight in a population of teenagers, we know that taller individuals tend to weigh more. One of the potential confounds in this experiment is that taller individuals may eat more [height/eating]. It might be easiest to understand this as height and eating being positively correlated. This confound would not be an experimental problem if ingesting food had no influence on your height—but it does. The amount of protein one ingests during the developing years will influence their adult height. Therefore, [height/eating] will be confounded with weight. This occurs because the experimenter is attempting to correlate height and weight but each time they measure a taller or shorter person they are measuring someone who also eats more or less than his group members. Researchers typically expect confounds to exist in any correlational study, especially those collected from outside the well-controlled laboratory. The presence of confounds always decreases the strength of your experimental conclusions.

In the following section on experimental methodology, however, all confounds must be eliminated. It is of great interest to the experimenter to eliminate any potential confound from their experiment so that their data reflect the relationship between what the experimenter manipulates and its outcome on behavior.

Confound:
The condition during which the experimenter changes one variable but unknowingly changes two.

Laboratory science affords the greatest control over your subject matter.

Random assignment:
The process by which subjects in an experiment are assigned to groups through random decision processes. Random assignment is used so that no extraneous processes influence the experiment.

Data are almost always collected as some sort of numerical representation.

Population characteristics:
The specific characteristics of the subjects needed for an experiment. Population characteristics frequently involve the identification of basic demographic information.

Experimental Method

Both the previously discussed descriptive and correlational methodologies give researchers tools to understand human behavior. Those tools, however, have a number of known flaws that restrict their use to particular research designs. To overcome these limitations, researchers need better techniques. One of those techniques is the experimental method.

Unlike the descriptive method in which the subjects were observed only, and the correlational method in which cause and effect relationships are frequently unknown, the experimental method controls as many variables as possible so that researchers maximize the likelihood of identifying a cause and effect relationship. Therefore, this is the strongest and most preferred technique of the three.

In the correlational method, two variables are measured. The researcher, however, controls neither variable. For example, when a researcher measures height and weight, she neither makes you taller nor reduces your mass. Simply put, the variables are measured in the state they exist in regardless of their relationship to each other. The experimental method takes this technique one-step further by holding one variable constant and systematically manipulating the other variable. The benefit of using the experimental methodology is that it makes it more likely that a researcher will identify a cause and effect relationship than in the descriptive or correlational methodologies.

The experimental method involves the **random assignment** of subjects to groups. Consider how groups were created in the previously described correlational method. The subjects in those experiments each held two variables that were measured by the researcher. The reason the subjects had each of two characteristics in the state they were in (e.g., depression and marriage status) may have been due to any number of previous events. In short, there is no control over which variables, or the strength of the variables, that the subjects exhibit. As a result, the conclusions of a correlational study are always open to alternative interpretations because unknown factors may be influencing subject characteristics. In contrast, experimental methodology sidesteps this problem by randomly selecting subjects for the experiment and using random assignment to place them into groups.

Before an experiment begins, the researcher has to decide which population of subjects to use in the experiment. The researcher may choose subjects with any set of characteristics that are appropriate for the experiment. For example, some subjects may need to be female and bilingual. Some subjects may need to be over 6 ft. tall and have had previous treatment for depression. These characteristics are referred to as the **population characteristics**. Population characteristics must be chosen very carefully because the subjects used in the experiment will influence greatly the results of the experimental manipulation. When one discusses which type of subjects were used the term subject population is frequently used. Subject population is referring to the population characteristics of the subjects.

Once the subject population has been identified, the subjects need to be selected for the experiment. Because researchers cannot force people to partici-pate in their research, advertisements are generally posted which are used to draw people into the experiment. Once subjects volunteer for the experiment, they are assigned through random processes into any one condition of the experiment. Why would researchers use random processes to assign subjects to experimental conditions? The answer is to avoid allowing any biases to influence which conditions the subjects are exposed to during the experiment. This is a concern because the researcher may unknowingly exhibit bias in establishing groups that may lend support for the expected outcomes. Here is an example of how bias may influence the arrangement of subjects in four groups.

Assume a researcher is studying procrastination. Once the researcher hangs a sign up for volunteers it may be true that the least procrastinating subjects may sign up for the experiment first. All of the worst procrastinators sign up for the experiment later. If the researcher worked to fill the control group first and then later the experimental groups, there would exist a bias in the procrastination characteristics across the groups. This certainly would influence the outcome of the experiment and would be completely inappropriate.

> **Subject population:** The name of the group of subjects chosen for an experiment that have the required population characteristics.

Independent and Dependent Variables

In any experiment, the researcher needs to determine which variable they will manipulate and which variable they will measure. The name of the variable that the researcher manipulates is the independent variable. The name of the variable that the researcher measures for outcomes is the dependent variable. The independent variable is so named because it is *independent* of the opera-tions in the experiment. It is supposed to imply that its levels of operation are separate from the rest of the experiment. The dependent variable implies that it is dependent upon the manipulations the researcher makes. More specifi-cally, the value of the dependent variable is *dependent* upon the value of the independent variable.

> **Independent variable:** The variable that the experimenter manipulates or controls.

Suppose a researcher wanted to study the effects of therapy on depres-sion level. Consequently, the number of therapy sessions a patient receives is compared to the patient's level of depression. To begin the experiment, the researcher needs volunteers that would be randomly assigned into various groups. Let us assume the researcher has decided to run three separate therapy-length conditions. The first condition is one-month long, the second condition is two months long and the third condition is four months long. The researcher knows that the effects of therapy must be measured against an untreated control group and therefore adds one more group. This final group is the control group. The control group does not receive therapy at all but rather spends an equivalent amount of time talking to a therapist about non-psychiatric issues.

> **Dependent variable:** The variable that the experimenter measures. The dependent variable and data are the same thing.

As each group finishes its period of therapy, the therapist begins assessing the subjects' levels of depression. The measure of depression is the dependent variable. Hypothetical data for this experiment are shown in **Figure 1.3**. This figure shows that the highest level of depression is in the untreated control group. Successive durations of therapy result in lowered levels of depression. Although no statistical test is used on these data, the visual display is intended to show that longer periods of therapy are associated with less depression. The group with four months of therapy shows the lowest level of depression in the graph.

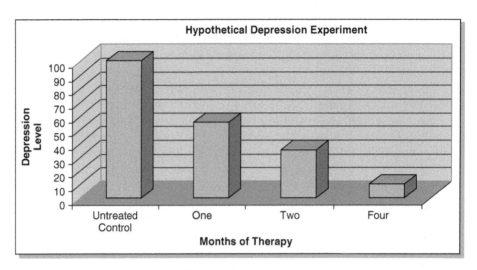

FIGURE 1.3 ■ Hypothetical therapy data.

Group Designs

There are varieties of ways to conduct experiments in the behavioral sciences. Some of the most common experimental procedures are group designs. The simplest group designs establish two separate conditions in which one group is exposed to the independent variable and the other group is exposed to a control variable. The control variable should be as similar to the independent variable as possible; however, it should not contain the relevant variable components. For example, if smoking were the independent variable in an experiment on nicotine addiction, the relevant variable in smoking is the nicotine exposure. All of the other components such as the inhalation of warm smoke, carbon dioxide, tar and ash all need to be present in both the control group's and experimental group's smoke. The only difference between them should be the presence of nicotine. If only one difference exists between the control group and the experimental group then any difference measured (read that as dependent variable) between the groups may be attributed logically to that one variable.

Group design experiments begin with selecting the subjects for the experiment. Subjects are selected based upon the hypothesis the researcher is addressing. If the researcher is studying teaching procedures in fifth grade students, then it would only make sense that fifth graders be used as subjects. Once the researchers have chosen the particular population they will work with, they need to acquire volunteers for the experiment. Suppose for example, the

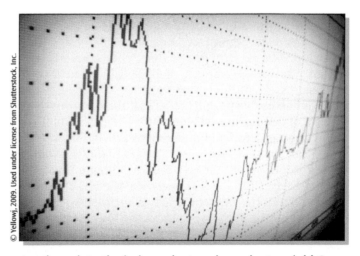

Are these data the independent or dependent variable?

researcher goes to a local grammar school and acquires permission to seek volunteers from the current class of fifth graders. The students would likely be sent home with permission slips for their parents to sign if the parent and child both agree to participate in the experiment.

Students may not participate if they do not wish to or if their parents are against their participation. To be certain, which students volunteer for an experiment is to some degree modifying the subpopulation of subjects who give data in the experiment. For example, if the only students who participate in the experiment are from families in which the parents are extremely involved in their child's education, then that particular difference may modify the outcome of the experiment in the broader group of fifth grade students—the population selected for study.

Once the researcher has collected enough volunteers to conduct the experiment, the subjects will be randomly assigned into two groups. The two groups created are the control and experimental groups. The experimental group will be exposed to the independent variable manipulation and the control group will not be exposed to it. Let's suppose that the researcher is testing the role of flow charts to help children understand biological concepts. Therefore, in addition to their regular textbook reading on the circulatory system, the researcher will also allow students in the experimental group to see a series of flow charts as well.

Therefore, the control group will be exposed to a textbook reading on the circulatory system and the experimental group will be exposed to a textbook reading plus flow charts. Subsequently, both groups will be given a multiple-choice exam on the material they learned. The average performance in the control group versus the experimental group will then be compared (see **Figure 1.4**).

Although this experiment has been designed properly, it may be improved upon. A simple improvement would be to add more experimental-groups. For example, our current experimental group is exposed to a circulatory system flow chart. Other experimental groups may be exposed to increasingly complex figures describing the same information. If the level of complication in the flow chart is systematically changed, then we may get an idea of how much complexity adds to learning and at what point it detracts from it. By increasing the number of groups and having each group exposed to a higher level of complexity, our potential to understand the relationship between flow charts and learning in fifth graders is improved.

Controls for Living Organisms

Expectations

When establishing control groups for human subjects, special procedures must be used. These control procedures are not seen in the physical sciences because they are control procedures for expectation effects. Expectations are related simply to what the subjects believe will happen in the experiment. The belief that one or another manipulation will occur may cause the subjects to change their behavior without knowing it. A classic example of this expectation effect comes from an experiment by Rosenthal & Fode (1963). These researchers established a two-group study to assess student's expectations of laboratory animals. Both groups of subjects were told that they had to train a lab rat to press a bar. One group was told that they were using dumb rats. The

Pregnant women should not participate in experiments on smoking.

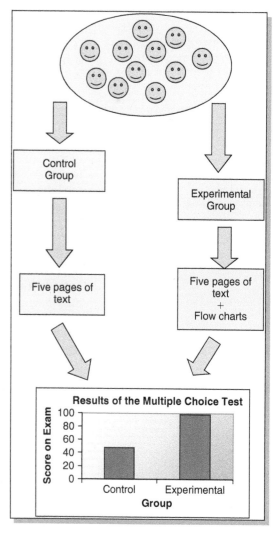

FIGURE 1.4 ■ The hypothetical fifth grader study.

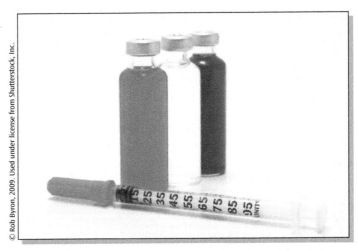

© Rob Byron, 2009. Used under license from Shutterstock, Inc.

If three people were given drug out of each of these different vials then they would all expect to see different reactions in each other.

Expectation Effects: The influence of a subject's expectations for what may happen in the experiment.

Placebo: An inert substance given to the control group in a drug experiment. The use of a placebo controls for the subject expectations that come with taking a pill in an experiment.

If that seems farfetched, just remember how human subjects unconsciously influence the behavior of a rat to learn or not learn to press a bar.

other group was told they were using smart rats. The researchers distributed rats from the same population to both groups of subjects so that there was no true difference in intelligence between the groups of rats. It was the researcher's intention to determine whether the human subjects belief that they had smart or dumb rats would influence whether or not the rats learned the task.

The researchers found that the human expectations of rat intelligence had a strong influence on whether or not the rat learned the task. It is believed that because some subjects expected their rats to do well, they may have treated them in a matter that was more supportive of learning than those who believed they had dumb rats. This expectation, therefore, clearly influenced the outcome of the experiment. Such differences may be found in more subtle ways in all experiments involving human subjects. The subjects' expectation of what the researcher is examining will influence their behavior and therefore modify the outcome of the experiment. Psychological researchers are well aware of this fact and put great effort into controlling its influence in their experiments.

One condition in which expectation effects are controlled always is in drug research. For ethical reasons subjects must be told the type of medication they may be taking in a drug study. If the researcher explains that some of the side effects of a stimulant drug may be an upset stomach or headache, the subjects may begin to experience the symptoms of an upset stomach or headache despite having been given a **placebo**. A placebo is an inert substance used to control for the act of taking a medication during the experiment. If a pill is being given to an experimental group in a study, the control group will be given an inert pill that looks the same but will not contain the active drug ingredient. The purpose of the placebo is to control the same expectation effects that were described previously. All subjects are told of the side effects that may occur with the particular medication. Some subjects may then begin to experience those side effects because of expectations. It is important to know how many people experience those effects because of expectations and compare that with the number of people that experience the side effects that were given the drug. The difference between those two groups is the measurement of the true side effects.

To maximize further the control of expectations that may occur in an experiment, a researcher may apply a double-blind procedure. A double-blind procedure in part controls for the researcher's expectations rather than the subject's expectations. For example, if a researcher is motivated to believe his drug will control a psychological problem, he may influence the behavior of the subjects in the various groups nonconsciously so that the conclusions of the experiment support their ideas. To control for the researcher's beliefs, one must separate the researcher from the subjects so that they are not influenced. The researcher, however, may have important work to do for the experiment such as distributing the pills into different cups for distribution to the subjects. Once the researcher has done so, he may leave them in a room, have his assistant come collect them and then distribute them to the subjects. In this manner, the assistant who is interacting with the subjects does not know which substance—drug or placebo—is given to the subject. This helps ensure that the assistant will not bias her interactions with the subjects.

Double and Triple Blind non-Drug Experiments

This same form of experimental logic may be applied to nondrug experiments as well. In research involving the social behavior of people, a researcher may wish to remove their expectations from the experiment so that there is no contamination of the data. To do so, a researcher may produce a script. A script is typically a set of directions that each subject receives upon entering the experiment. If it is possible to have the directions written down so that the subject can read them independently then that works best. In some cases, however, a researcher must interact with the subjects directly. Under those conditions, the researcher is best to treat everyone the same. To do so, the researcher—who is aware of the various experimental conditions— writes a variety of scripts and passes them to her research assistants. Each assistant, however, is unaware of the differences in the scripts and therefore does not know which condition any subject is exposed to. Now, the subjects each receive the proper instructions, the assistant does not bias their subjects and the researcher does not influence the outcome of the data.

Experiments are confusing enough. Why have unknown variables influence your subjects if you do not have to.

The further use of a triple blind control procedure may also be applied. In this case, the researcher would produce a set of directions that would be sent to an assistant and then that assistant would further assign a secondary assistant to actually implement the directions. Of course, the control offered by the triple-blind procedure will be enhanced by eliminating as much of the interaction between assistants as possible. Often times in experimental research, assistants who are not fully informed of the experiments purpose are used as those intermediary assistants. Therefore, the use of someone who does not fully understand the experiment is quite useful as a laboratory worker. Although an experimental assistant must have some training, it often times is useful to control just how much they know before they begin to interact with the subjects.

THE OVERALL RULES OF SCIENCE

Two Goals of Science: Prediction and Control

The two goals of science are **prediction** and **control**. All scientists wish to be able to predict future events as well as control them. Prediction is a function that may not involve any control; however, any control will come with prediction. Therefore, scientists consider control a more valued measure of the knowledge of your field.

Scientists show that they have great understanding of their subject matter if they can accurately predict future events. Knowing with some degree of statistical certainty that an individual will become depressed after a series of failures is far more powerful than just associating failures with depression. Predicting accurately

Prediction:
The ability to predict accurately future behavior.

Control:
The ability to control behavior. Regardless of how well you can predict behavior, the ability to control it is valued more than prediction.

Control is best if you can make your subjects act as obediently as a robot.

when and to what degree a depression will occur will support the idea that the researcher's theory is accurate. If one's theory allows for the accurate prediction of future events, then the next increase in knowledge comes from controlling the events of the environment. If one can control the environment to either induce or eliminate a depressive episode—and predict those outcomes accurately—then the theoretical explanation is given even greater value.

Each time one moves from prediction to control, it indicates that your level of understanding of the subject matter has improved. It is possible that prediction is well established but that it is difficult to control the subject matter. That is, one may be able to predict events accurately, but have little control over the relevant factors in question. Such a scenario would occur if we assumed in a hypothetical example that genetics were the only controlling factor in depressive episodes. Under these circumstances, we may be able to predict depressive episodes by determining whether our subject has the depression-genes; however, we would have no ability to control them because gene manipulation in humans is currently underdeveloped as a safe and effective clinical technique.

Such events occur frequently at the outer envelope of scientific understanding. It is often very frustrating to be able to predict events well but be unable to control them. Examples of such occur in clinical therapy when you can predict that your patient will act in an undesirable manner but you are unable to stop it. It occurs when you know you will get stuck in a traffic jam but are unable to take an alternate route. It occurs when you can detect a tornado with Doppler radar but you can do nothing to eliminate its arrival.

The Cyclic Nature of Scientific Research

When researchers collect data, it feeds into a broader understanding of what they are doing. That broader understanding is analyzed through the three steps of science. Those steps are the hypothesis, experimentation and theory steps (see **Figure 1.5**). The hypothesis step is when the researcher decides how to ask a relevant question in his field of study. For instance, a researcher studying depression may have noticed by chance that many of his subjects have been exposed to very stressful life situations within the previous five years. This casual observation may lead the researcher to ask a specific question regarding the stress-depression connection. The question, formally a hypothesis, might take the form of "All people who are diagnosed with depression have a significant stressful life event within the previous five years." This hypothesis will be easy enough to address in the next step, the process of experimentation.

In the process of experimentation, the researcher attempts to address scientifically the presented hypothesis. If the hypothesis is about the timing of stressful life events and the onset of depression, then the researcher can set up a study in which he questions people who are being treated for depression to determine if they have been exposed to significant stress over the previous five years. Whether the researcher finds evidence that supports his hypothesis or not, the conclusion of his experiment will be fed into the third step of the process, the theory step.

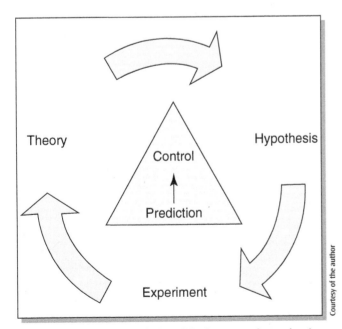

FIGURE 1.5 ▨ The relationship between hypothesis, experimentation and theory.

The theory step requires the researcher to take his data and feed them back into his original theory about depression. Let's assume that his theory stated that depression is caused by stress. If the data he collects do not support his theory, then he would revise his theory. Afterward, he would derive a new hypothesis from the revised theory and again enter the experimentation phase. The process would repeat itself indefinitely until the experimental evidence supports each hypothesis derived from the theory.

STATISTICS

Basic Probability

In the history of the behavioral sciences, many lawful relationships have been discovered. One of the primary roles of this textbook is to describe those many relationships to you, the student. Despite there being lawful relationships amongst psychological variables, many things in the behavioral sciences appear to be somewhat random. For example, the best way to predict whether one will identify a particular set of conditions (e.g., randomly selecting someone with a particular disease) is to estimate its statistical likelihood. That likelihood will be based on probabilistic processes. In other words, the assumption of randomness in social relationships is always made. Moreover, it is consistently supported by the data psychologists collect.

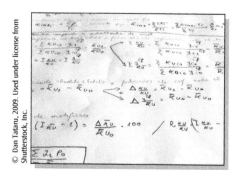

There is no avoiding mathematics in science.

The probability of obtaining subjects with particular social characteristics, personal histories, physical traits, etc. can be estimated statistically. Therefore, behavioral scientists can accurately predict the likelihood of obtaining subjects with particular characteristics based upon the number of subjects chosen and the way in which the subjects are selected. Consequently, the concept of randomness is one of the most fundamental ideas applied when addressing the acquisition of behavioral characteristics in populations.

Randomness is often described as the changing of events with no reason. This, however, makes no sense with respect to our understanding of the physical universe in which we live. Theoretically, all things seem to be produced by the actions of other things. When scientists refer to randomness, they are generally accepting that some process is occurring that they do not understand. Consequently, the broad outcomes of randomness may be predictable despite our lack of knowledge of the random mechanisms themselves. This does not automatically mean that scientists believe things happen for no reason. Rather, randomness refers to the fact that scientists can predict a general pattern of events despite the inability to control that pattern.

Understanding statistics may help you predict your chances of meeting someone special.

ANALYZING CORRELATIONS

I previously described how correlations are used in research. In this section, I will discuss how they are calculated. More specifically, I will give you a set of basic rules to follow so that you can calculate easily a correlation value using the spreadsheet software *Excel*. The steps will be easy to follow. You will only need to collect some simple data to correlate together, place those data into an Excel spreadsheet and calculate your correlation by using a function command. For simplicity, you can analyze

Continued

the heights and weights of a few of your friends, analyze the number of hours they spend exercising per week with their resting heart rate or the total amount they spend on gasoline per week with the number of miles they drive per week. Feel free to correlate any other two things if you wish.

Correlations may be calculated easily. You will need to determine which data you would like to correlate together. You may use any of the above three or something of you own choosing, however, I should point out that the height and weight data are easily obtained from anybody without much effort. It should be the easiest way to get you through this demonstration.

For simplicity, I will refer to your data as height and weight data although you can change that to anything that you are actually measuring. To start, you will need to set aside a piece of paper with two columns on it. One column will be entitled height and the other weight. Collect the height in inches and the weight in pounds. If you collect the height in feet and inches you will have to convert that score (e.g., 5'4") into inches before you work with the data in the spreadsheet. As you collect the data, place your subject's height and weight next to each other in your columns and fill up your data sheet. When you set this up, assume you will be collecting data from approximately twenty people. I am not going to assume you are choosing your subjects by random assignment so you should choose people that you believe have a wide range of heights or weights. That is, find some short and tall people or look for thin and heavy people. Don't be overly fussy. Make this as easy as you can.

You will need to add your data to an Excel spreadsheet once you have it collected. Almost everyone has access to Excel, whether you are a PC or Macintosh computer user. For those that do not, all the public computers on campus have Excel installed on them. If you are using a publicly available Florida Atlantic University campus computer, then just click on the *Start* icon on the lower left hand area of the screen; select *All Programs*; locate *Microsoft Office* then *Excel*. Once you open it, you will be given a new spreadsheet to work with.

	A	B	C	D	E
1	Height	Weight			
2	66	125			
3	61	120			
4	62	130			
5	70	165			
6	75	200		0.885139	
7	72	140			
8	68	145			
9	74	185			
10	60	110			
11	65	117			
12					
13					

Courtesy of the author

Enter your data in columnar form just in the way I requested you collect your data on the piece of paper. It does not matter which column or row you start with inside the spreadsheet. If you wish, start at columns A and B for row 1. Do not make two rows with your data. Be sure to make two columns. Enter the data person by person, so that each person's height and weight are next to each other in the spreadsheet. You can then calculate your correlation coefficient once your data are input.

To calculate the correlation coefficient, use the function CORREL. In any empty cell, type "=**correl(**" and then click and drag over the height column, press the comma command and then click and drag over the weight column. Once you do, type in a final ")" and your correlation coefficient will be automatically calculated and appear in the cell you just entered the function command into.

If you look at figure XX, you will see a zoomed in shot of my ten sample data. I labeled the columns height and weight, placed in the ten sample data points I created and placed the CORREL function into cell D6. Note that I clicked on cell D6 so that the actual function I typed in would appear in the function line near the top of the screen. It reads "=CORREL(A2:A11,B2:B11)." Notice that when I clicked and dragged for the height and weight columns respectively, Excel automatically placed A2:A11 and B2:B11 into the function for me. I only had to add the comma between two those sets of data so that the program understood which set of data to use for the first or second variable. Finally, the results of the hypothetical height and weight data show a correlation coefficient of 0.885139 which would more likely be presented as r = 0.88. That is all it takes to calculate a correlation coefficient. Most people would like to see their data graphed as well. Graphing these data in Excel is also easy provided we make a simple graph.

The essential way in which to set up a random process is to guarantee that each opportunity to measure something is both equal and independent of all other opportunities. For example, if flipping a coin results in a 50/50 chance of obtaining heads, then each flip of a coin should always result in a 50/50 chance of obtaining heads and each flip of the coin should have no influence on any future flip of the coin. The idea that each flip of the coin does not influence any other flip of the coin is referred to as the assumption of independence. The independence of events is very critical to obtain when randomly distributing your subjects to various groups in an experiment. The assumption that each flip of a coin results in a 50/50 chance of obtaining heads is the assumption of equality. The abstract mathematical procedures used to develop these statistical rules are expressed in the biological and social data collected by researchers.

For example, assume you have one hundred people. Of those, fifty are male and fifty are female. It would not be a surprise to find in an equal and independent selection process that a sample of thirty of those individuals results in approximately fifteen males and fifteen females. No one would automatically expect that there would be exactly fifteen males and fifteen females, but rather that the collection of subjects would be very close to that which would be theoretically expected. The fact that you collect thirteen males and seventeen females on one attempt and sixteen males and fourteen females on your second attempt would be attributed to randomness. So then, you may ask; is it possible that only one male and twenty-nine females are chosen? The answer is that it's possible, although it is very unlikely. In fact, the more you deviate from the expected theoretical outcome under these circumstances (e.g., one-half male subjects and one-half female subjects) the lower the probability of observing that outcome will occur. It is not impossible, just unlikely.

Equal:
Refers to the equal probability of each coin toss. As a coin is flipped in the air there should always be a 50 percent chance that heads will appear.

Independent:
Refers to the unrelated relationship of each coin toss. If coin tosses are independent then each toss has no influence on any future coin toss.

Central Limit Theorem

Whenever subjects are selected for experiments, behavioral scientists rely on statistical procedures. These procedures suggest that the greater the number of subjects collected, the more likely the researcher will calculate the true mean of

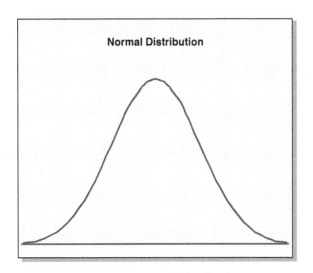

Normal Distribution

FIGURE 1.6 ▇ The normal distribution.

the population. That is, if the researcher is measuring the heights of her subjects, the larger the sample size she uses the more likely she will measure the actual mean height that exists in the larger population. When selecting larger and larger groups of subjects the conclusions have greater and greater accuracy. This process is known as the Central Limit Theorem.

The central limit theorem is a mathematical theory that describes the relationship between sample size and the accuracy of the group mean. How this occurs may be understood easily by extending the sample size all the way to the size of the population itself. In the above example with one hundred males and females, the sample size drawn from the population was thirty individuals. What would happen to the accuracy of our mean height measurement if we drew a sample of one hundred people from this population of one hundred people? Our sample would measure exactly what the population characteristics were, of course. As we select a sample less than the size of the population, however, we begin to introduce error into our measurement.

The size of the error increases as the sample size gets smaller and smaller relative to the original population size. Therefore, if we have a sample of five individuals from a population of 1000, we would expect our estimate of the original population to be quite filled with error. If, however, we drew a sample of one hundred people using the processes of equality and independence in each selection, then our estimate of the original population would gain a considerable amount of accuracy. There is no exact cutoff in which we go from being inaccurate to accurate; however, collecting larger sample sizes results in greater accuracy.

The Normal Distribution

The normal distribution, also known as the bell curve, is a specific mathematical description of data with a bell shaped form (see **Figure 1.6**). Many forms of behavioral and biological data are expressed in bell shaped curves. Mathematicians have proven that this form of distribution would be expected if random factors were controlling the distribution of characteristics throughout the population. This occurs because a single probability for the occurrence of some characteristic measured over time results in bell shaped curves.

Consider these examples first discovered in the late 19th century by Sir Francis Galton. Both the height and weight of people fall on normal distributions. This characteristic is expected due to the underlying random, or unknown, variables in operation that establish one's height and weight. Scientists believe this indicates that random processes are present in many forms of biological data. Measuring these processes through random events indicates that random processes control those events.

Law of Large Numbers

Law of large numbers: Indicates that as a population grows in size the total number of low probability events will increase despite keeping probability constant.

One of the interesting facts we can gather from the normal distribution is the Law of Large Numbers. The law of large numbers refers to the fact that as populations grow in size they become more likely to produce low probability events. This is not related to an increased chance of low probability events but is related to the total number of events that do occur. To understand how this works, consider an example in which there are only one hundred people. Of these one hundred people, only one lucky person has won the lottery.

Winning the lottery is a low probability event itself. It is even less likely that our subject will win the lottery a second time. Although these facts hold true, it is also true that the size of the population will in part determine how many people will win the lottery twice. In a very small population, the likelihood of finding someone who wins the lottery is extremely small. In a very large population, however, the likelihood of finding someone who wins the lottery twice may be higher. How can that happen?

When the New Jersey Lottery was introduced in the early 1970's it became very popular. As the number of players increased, the number of people that won multiple times also increased. This occurred despite the fact that the chance of winning remained the same as it had always been. As the number of people who played the lottery increased given the overall size of the New Jersey population at that time, it became likely that a few people would win the lottery twice. And they did, in fact. This frequently astounded many people and resulted in much media attention. The likelihood of winning the lottery twice is very low, however, in a very large population, the total number of low probability events increases because there is a larger population of small probability events.

An application of the law of large numbers helps explain why such varieties of strange things are seen in large crowded cities. When one travels to a crowded city such as Manhattan, it is not surprising to see the full range of people present in society; from the richest to the poorest, the drug addicts and the "green volunteers." Any sector of society that may be hidden in a suburb or rural area is accessed easily in a big city. In fact, large crowded cities are known frequently as being places where you come across the unpleasant sides of urban life. Simply put, the law of large numbers indicates that with a large population crowded into a small space, it will be much easier to see the full range of people in the society. Stated differently, people generally see a wider range of the population in a large crowded city and less populated areas seem more homogeneous. Given that you are more likely to see the "odd" things in a city, cities develop a reputation for containing oddities. The combination of the law of large numbers and expectations determines the basis of your experience when you are there.

COMPARING THE BEHAVIORAL AND PHYSICAL SCIENCES

Lawful Results and Free Will

When reviewing the history of science, it rapidly becomes clear that the physical sciences developed before the behavioral sciences. The physical sciences were in part led by astronomy circa 1600 CE. Immediately afterward, however, it quickly turned into physics, the *study of the entire natural or physical world* (Nolan, 1993). It then takes almost another three centuries before psychology develops. Why should psychology take so much more time to develop than the physical sciences? We need to look at what was involved in the development of both areas of study before we can understand this difference.

One of the characteristics that seems to have made the physical sciences easier to study is that inanimate objects generally behave more lawfully than do people. In fact, much of this regularity comes from the absence of a "memory" in nonliving things as opposed to living ones. By memory, I mean that studying physical things does not necessarily result in changed properties of that thing. For example, when—or if (Wikipedia "Galileo Galilei," 3/30/09, Physics section para. 1)—Galileo dropped balls from the Tower of Pisa, each instance of ball dropping did not cause the balls to become lighter or heavier. Rather, every trial at measuring the duration with which the balls fell to the ground resulted in a consistent measure, or at least with the capacity of Galileo to measure it. This is certainly not true with living organisms.

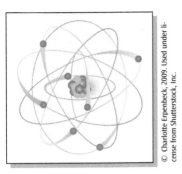

The monistic view of science suggests that the universe is filled with only matter and energy.

Einstein's universe is lawful, so was Einstein's behavior.

The physical and behavioral sciences have different characteristics due to the difference in subject matter.

Creatures with nervous systems have true memories. Consequently, each event that they are exposed to changes them. Therefore, living beings make poor subject matter when you are searching for consistency. This also makes human behavior seem very varied and unrelated to the environment. In other words, living things, especially humans, appear to have free will. In contrast to the study of inanimate objects in physics, people do not appear to be controlled by their environment.

The complications with people have been evident since the earliest philosophical writings about human behavior. They have always been described as free thinkers. It is frequently stated that they can exert their will over their own body or express behavior that is unrelated to their environment. An example of such a thing is when I write, "There is a giant green spider hanging from the ceiling." There is no giant green spider in the room as I write these statements, however. Neither do I believe that there is a giant green spider hanging over the head of the student who reads this text. If there are no giant green spiders present when we make that statement then we must be able to function independent of environmental stimulation, correct? People have used that type of argument in an attempt to prove that humans have free will. If they do, they should be able to exhibit behavior that changes frequently, cannot be constrained logically and is unrelated to the lawful operations of science.

Since the time that scientific psychology has started, it has become clear that three basic factors control human beings. They are biology, personal learning histories and present environmental conditions. There seems to be very little indication that humans exhibit free will. If they did, then psychological experimentation would frequently result in negative findings. All the subjects of an experiment would behave differently given that they all exhibit free will. In contrast, human and animal behavior may be predicted accurately through a mixture of genetics, personal history and current conditions. Humans appear to be as understandable as the rest of the physical world.

Comparing the Rate at Which the Physical and Behavioral Sciences Develop

Frequently, the public perception of psychological advances is that they come much more slowly than in the physical sciences. Historically, physical science experiments are completed more rapidly for a variety of reasons. One of those was previously stated above; the subject material generally does not contain "memory." Another reason is that physical science research can take place twenty-four hours per day in laboratories around the world. Psychological research is rarely studied so aggressively.

Suppose you are examining a way to make smokeless gunpowder. You can change the recipe for gunpowder in a systematic manner and determine which way produces the least amount of smoke. Because you can do this work under controlled conditions, your conclusions are likely to be accurate. Moreover, your research can progress day and night because gunpowder works the same regardless of the time of day.

In contrast, if you try to find the fastest way to teach a fifth grader then you can only use the child during the day when they are awake and motivated to learn. You will need to obtain permission from the parents and school system and the results from your study of a single child may not necessarily apply to all fifth-graders. If you try to use the same subject more than once, then you will find yourself with a subject that is changing noticeably across the experiments. Teaching a child repeatedly will improve his or her ability to learn so that they will become more educable across the experiment. This is certainly detrimental to your research program because each time you test your child you will reach a different set of conclusions.

If you cannot produce consistent results then it is not clear whether your subject is changing or the new experiments you are conducting are working differently. In contrast, we expect physical science experiments to produce the same results each time the experiment is conducted. Generally, physical science experiments deal with material that produces less variability and can be studied 24 hours per day. In contrast, behavioral science experiments use living subjects that constantly change their qualities because of the experimental treatments.

A changing subject matter complicates experimentation drastically. This effect has made a very large impression on experimental psychologists. These comments, however, may lead a new student of psychology to believe that studying human behavior is a hopeless endeavor. That, however, is incorrect. A range of other methodologies and statistical procedures help control for these issues with living subjects. Despite the valuable influence those control procedures have on facilitating valid research conclusions, they still tend to take long periods to complete. Consequently, you will see in this text that studying human behavior often takes lengthy periods. One clear example is the forty year experiments conducted on personality and intelligence. If you want to study how personality and intelligence change over the lifespan, you cannot expect to complete your work in one afternoon!

Four vs. Forty Forces

Another difference between the physical and behavioral sciences is related to the number of fundamental factors in each field. Physicists suggest that there are four fundamental forces in nature. They are the strong force, weak force, electromagnetic force and gravity. In contrast, psychologists do not refer to any fundamental psychological forces. There are some factors, however, that are present in all psychological conditions. Some of the most obvious are sensation, learning, and memory. Although they are not identified as fundamental forces of psychology, they are common factors in all behavior. Each chapter of this text will contain at least three lawful relationships relevant to the understanding of human behavior. A new student to psychology should realize that they are all important and ignoring anyone of them will result in a gap in your knowledge.

What Is an Exact Science?

Often times the physical sciences are described as exact sciences. In contrast, many new psychology students have heard that psychology is not even a science. What constitutes an exact science and why would someone believe that psychology is not a science? An exact science is something that does not truly exist. No field of science is exact. This would indicate that any measure taken is perfectly accurate. Comments like this would only be applied if someone did not understand the role of decimal places in mathematical measurement. It is impossible in any field of science to measure anything accurately to an infinite number of decimal points, unless when you are counting whole items such as books or apples. The concept of an exact science seems to come from the popular notion that the physical sciences can measure things accurately to many decimal places. In contrast, very few things, and probably nothing that is discussed in the science media, are known to be measured on the order of decimal places in psychology.

It is true that the meaning of many psychological measurements are not relevant when it comes to even a single decimal place. For instance, IQ measurements are never given in decimal places. Moreover, the differences in a few points of measured IQ are always suspect at being truly relevant. Therefore, if you and your friend have IQs of 115 and 118 most psychologists will consider you equal in intelligence. The three-point difference is likely within the range of

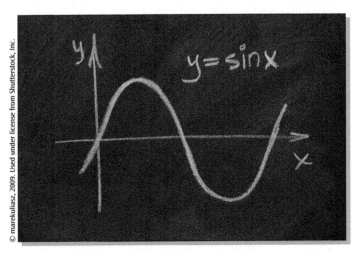

How many decimal places could you show in a table when you calculate this sin(x) wave?

typical variability between measurements. Intelligence, which is not a single unified function of your brain, does not exist in a form that current measurement devices can realistically depend upon decimal places for information.

There are instances, however, in which decimal places are relevant. Some measures of learning, memory and reaction time may be measured very accurately. In those cases, decimal places must be taken very seriously. As was discussed earlier, however, given the greater variability in behavioral data, one should expect less relevance in the decimal places of psychological measurements. If humans functioned like memory-less inanimate objects, then it would not be a surprise that some measurement could be relevant to its eighth decimal place.

Are the Behavioral Sciences Integrated?

The previous discussion of the four fundamental forces indicates that physics is highly integrated. One may wonder then whether the behavioral sciences are also integrated. They are. They are not integrated in the same manner as the physical sciences, however. Essentially, the physical sciences are integrated through the four fundamental forces of physics. Once you view the methodologies of physics, however, one sees there are many different laboratory procedures used to study those forces.

In the behavioral sciences, the integration is reversed. The behavioral sciences are integrated through methodology but not in fundamental phenomena. Core methodological components include the use of statistics and the control procedure. Control procedures do not exist in the same form in the physical sciences as they do in the behavioral sciences. Certainly, inanimate objects do not exhibit expectations. With less variability and less need for control conditions, the physical sciences are more likely to apply mathematical modeling to their data. Mathematical modeling is also applied in the behavioral sciences; however, the way in which behavioral science data is collected is generally less conducive to mathematical analyses.

Given the integration of the behavioral sciences through methodology, most psychologists deal with the same methodological procedures and statistical analyses as do all other behavioral scientists. The specific field one works in, however, may deal with very different forms of data. For example, researchers studying memory deficits in Alzheimer's disease will use the same methodological approach in their research as do others studying marital therapy. The database for Alzheimer's disease and marital therapy are completely

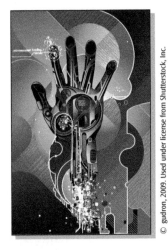

The integration in the physical sciences and the behavioral sciences is different. That, however, does not mean that they cannot work together toward common goals. When both fields are brought together, you will find developments such as bionic limbs and the future of cybernetic organisms.

different, however. Understanding one of those databases gives very little understanding to the other, however, the underlying link between them is the use of statistics, control procedures and methodology.

WHAT DO PSYCHOLOGISTS DO?

To state it as simply as possible, psychologists study why people and animals act they way they do. Psychologists comprise a field that may be understood as applied biology. Although traditional biologists focus on the genetic and cellular properties of their subjects, psychologists focus on the environmental components that control behavior. How can we predict the behavior of humans and animals and how do we control that behavior? The application of anything genetic, physiological or environmental that can help us answer those questions is what will be used in our work. The type of work one does in psychology is very much influenced by the level of college education one obtains. Today, the least amount of training you need to work in psychology is a bachelor's degree.

Therapy is probably the most popular field of interest for psychology students.

Bachelor's Degree

People who obtain a bachelors degree in psychology have a wide range of opportunities to apply their knowledge of human behavior. Many individuals with a bachelor's degree take positions in social service agencies. These positions range from various forms of counselors in state-run social service programs such as foster care or adoption agencies, or in nonprofit organizations devoted to supporting social service programs. With a bachelor's degree, you may also find work in a variety of institutions as a staff counselor treating drug addicted individuals, the mentally ill, mentally retarded or autistic. Typically, these positions include daily interaction with the residents of the facilities, operating their behavior management programs and managing their behavior through the controlled use of language. A bachelor's degree is also the least amount of training needed before being involved in any large-animal training programs such as those with dolphins.

Some psychologists do classified government work.

Master's Degree

If you stay in school for further training, you may receive a master's degree. People who obtain a master's degree in psychology have a wider range of opportunities than those with a bachelor's degree. Individuals with bachelors or masters degrees may also hold positions in the criminal justice system and the federal government. Agencies such as the FBI, CIA and Homeland Security frequently search for employees with an understanding of human behavior. Many individuals with a master's degree choose to work in counseling psychology. Master's level counselors may be licensed in a number of areas of specialty such as Marriage and Family counseling, Addictions or Mental Health. Although master's level counselors do work in private practice, it is more likely they work in social service agencies, within hospitals and in education.

Ph.D. and Psy.D.

One may obtain a Ph.D. or Psy.D. after the master's degree. Frequently, the terminal degree in psychology opens one up to the widest range of employment possibilities. Typically, a person holding the Ph.D. or Psy.D. (clinically oriented Ph.D. without a

Forensic psychology relates to criminal activity. Psychologists who profile criminals have become a popular television characters.

For psychologists, basic research in the laboratory generally takes places at academic institutions.

Psychology students are frequently interested in animal training. Jobs working with large sea mammals are typically very rare and often require a masters degree in animal behavior. People who do obedience training with house pets may not have even attended college.

dissertation) will work in hospitals or private practice. Clinical psychologists generally deal with problems that are more entrenched than those seen by master's level clinicians. They are more likely to work with individuals with biologically based psychological disorders such as schizophrenia and major depressive disorder. Doctors of psychology are able to hold positions within medical hospitals, psychiatric hospitals, counseling centers and academic positions such as professors. Those interested in conducting psychological research should pursue the Ph.D. and focus on training related to scientific research. **Table 1.2** is a list of some of the areas in which doctors of psychology work. Each of these areas, however, will have bachelors- and masters-level positions available appropriate for those levels of training.

TABLE 1.2 ▪ Fields of Psychology

Type of Psychologist	Type of Work
Clinical/Counseling	Conducts therapy with patients individually or in groups
Developmental	Studies, or applies the knowledge of studies, to people of a specific age range. Generally, developmental psychologists are trained to examine behavior as a function of development.
Educational	Works with educational settings to conduct research or apply new finding to classroom settings
Engineering	Often work with physical or computer engineers in the design of machines to be used by humans
Experimental	Typically conducts basic research in an academic institution
Forensic	Supports the criminal justice system by predicting the characteristics of types of criminals
Health	Applies the results of research to behavior change which supports healthful habits
Industrial/Organizational	I/O psychologists generally work within large corporations to determine how to make organizations work more effectively or efficiently.
Neuropsychology	A clinical field that generally treats people with brain damage as a result of head injuries, stroke, or disease
Quantitative	The application of mathematics to modeling human behavior through theoretical models
School	Essentially, a school's clinical specialist
Sports	Works with professional athletes to improve their skills

REFERENCES

Descartes, R. (1662/2003). *Treatise of man.* (T. S. Hall, Trans.) New York: Prometheus Books. (Original work published 1662).

Galileo Galilei, 3/30/09, Retrieved April 3, 2009, from Wikipedia: http://en .wikipedia.org/wiki/Galileo_Galilei

Kantowitz, B. H., Roediger III, H. L., & Elmes, D. G. (1994). Experimental psychology: *Understanding psychological research.* New York: West Publishing Company.

Lee, C. (1998). *Alternatives to cognition: A new look at explaining human social behavior.* Mahwah, New Jersey: Lawrence Erlbaum Associates.

Nolan, P. J. (1993). *Fundamentals of college physics.* Dubuque, IA: Wm. C. Brown Publishers.

Robinson, A. (2007). *The last man who knew everything: Thomas Young, the anonymous genius who proved Newton wrong and deciphered the Rosetta Stone, among other surprising feats.* New York: Plume.

Rosenthal, R., & Fode, K. L. (1963). The effect of experimenter bias on the performance of the albino rat. *Behavioral Science, 8,* 183–189.

Watson, J. B. (1913). Psychology as the behaviorist views it. *Psychological Review, 20,* 158–177.

KEY TERMS

ablation
animal electricity
aristotle
b. f. skinner
behavior
behavioral correlate
case studies
central limit theorem
charles darwin
christian gottlieb
kratzenstein
confound
control
correlation
correlation does not
  mean causation
correlational
  methodology
deductive
democritus
dependent variable
descriptive
  methodologies
directly measured
double blind procedure
equal and independent
ernst muller

ernst weber
expectation effects
experiment
experimental
  methodology
folk psychology
franciscus donders
giovanni aldini
group designs
gustav fechner
gustav fritsch
  & eduard hitzig
hermann von
  helmholtz
hypothesis
illusory correlation
independent variable
internal mental events
john watson
law of large numbers
linear input-output
luigi galvani
naturalistic observation
negative correlation
normal distribution
objective definition
operational definition

pearson product
  moment correlation
pierre flourens
placebo
polls
population
  characteristics
positive correlation
prediction
psychophysics
random assignment
reactivity
r-value
science of behavior
script
somatosensory
subject population
subtraction method
theory
trepanning
triple blind
  procedure
verbal descriptions
wilhelm wundt
young-helmholtz
  theory of color vision
zero correlation

Chapter 1: Introduction to Psychology

END OF CHAPTER QUIZ

1. Which technique discussed in this chapter was used by ancient peoples to release evil spirits from the mind?
   a. Mystical dances
   b. Drugs derived from local plants
   c. Trepanning
   d. Prayer

2. Who believed that the nervous system functioned like a hydraulics system?
   a. Descartes
   b. Leeuwenhoek
   c. Galvani
   d. Flourens

3. This person was one of the first people to attempt reanimating dead animals with electricity.
   a. Galvani
   b. Aldini
   c. Muller
   d. Kratzenstein

4. The compartmentalization of the rain was described through the _____ by Muller.
   a. Doctrine of specific nerve energies
   b. Theory of ablation
   c. Psychophysics
   d. Use of electricity

5. Darwin's first book describing evolutionary theory, *On the Origin of Species*, was first published in:
   a. 1839
   b. 1849
   c. 1859
   d. 1869

6. Ernst Weber was responsible for developing the field of:
   a. Psychophysics
   b. Biopsychology
   c. Psychosurgery
   d. Psychology

7. Mental chronometry is still used today to study:
   a. Reaction times
   b. Visual processing
   c. Cognitive thought processes
   d. Psychophysics

8. Which of the following had the LEAST effect on the development of psychology in the 20th century? (HINT: Which one was NOT discussed in the chapter):
   a. World War I
   b. World War II
   c. Discovery of DNA in the 1950's
   d. The self-potential movement of the 1970's

9. Which of the following people developed the school of Behaviorism?
   a. Fritz
   b. Flourens
   c. Wundt
   d. Watson

10. Who is credited with developing the field of psychology and in what year is psychology said to have begun?
    a. Wundt, 1879
    b. Fechner, 1859
    c. Pavlov, 1898
    d. Muller, 1849

11. A(n) ____ is a standardized definition that allows something to be identified in a publicly observable form.
    a. Case study
    b. Population
    c. Naturalistic observation
    d. Operational definition

12. This term refers to the times that other scientists repeat your experiments to see if they can get the same results.
    a. Case study
    b. Replication
    c. Experimental condition
    d. Operational definition

13. If you wish to study the opinions of the 10,000 female students at FAU, you can most efficiently do so by:
    a. Measuring the entire population
    b. Conducting case studies
    c. Generating a theory
    d. Taking a random sample

14. Which of the following groups is exposed to the independent variable?
    a. Control group
    b. Experimental group
    c. Placebo group
    d. Population

15. Which of the following constitute a population?
    a. People who do not like traffic jams
    b. Asian Americans
    c. People who exercise three or more times per week
    d. People who buy themselves massages on their birthdays
    e. All of the above

16. Which type of graph in your textbook shows correlational data?
    a. Bar graphs
    b. Line graphs
    c. Scatterplots
    d. Polar coordinate graphs

17. Why does it appear that humans have free will?
    a. Because of the potential for human imagination
    b. Humans are the only intelligent creatures on earth
    c. Because humans are intelligent enough to have determined that they have free will
    d. Because human behavior often appears unrelated to the environment and is therefore poorly predicted

18. Which of the following relates to the "most frequently occurring score"?
    a. Mean
    b. Median
    c. Mode
    d. Standard deviation

19. Which of the following relates to the "average distance between scores"?
    a. Mean
    b. Median
    c. Sum of squares
    d. Standard deviation

20. How are the behavioral sciences integrated?
    a. Through databases
    b. Through theories
    c. Through underlying physical causes
    d. Through methodologies

21. Which of the following is an exact science?
    a. Physics
    b. Chemistry

    c. Biology
    d. Psychology
    e. None of the above

22. An integrated set of principles that organize and predict events.
    a. Hypothesis
    b. Theory
    c. Experiment
    d. Statistical analysis

23. A specific question that can be asked in a controlled setting is called a(n):
    a. Experiment
    b. Data analysis
    c. Hypothesis
    d. Theory

24. Naturalistic observations are part of which general research design?
    a. Surveys
    b. Correlation
    c. Experimentation
    d. Description

25. An illusory correlation results from:
    a. Poorly conducted random sampling techniques
    b. Ignoring relevant data that suggest contrary conclusions
    c. Improperly conducted statistical tests
    d. Two correlations embedded in the same data

26. Which type of correlation is the following: "The more years you spend in school the higher your IQ."
    a. Negative correlation
    b. Illusory correlation
    c. Positive correlation
    d. Buckshot correlation

27. To control for expectations, a psychologist working with people needs to use:
    a. Random control procedures
    b. Double blind procedures
    c. Placebo-control or nontreatment-control groups
    d. All of the above

28. A scientist manipulates a(n) ___ variable and measures a(n) ___ variable.
    a. Dependent, independent
    b. Independent, dependent
    c. Control, independent
    d. Independent, control

29. Which of the following degrees is needed at a minimum to be able to conduct form therapy with a patient with personal stress problems?
    a. Bachelor's degree
    b. Master's degree
    c. Ph.D.
    d. Psy.D.

30. Which of the following describes mathematically the relationships between sample size and statistical accuracy?
    a. Normal distribution
    b. Central limit theorem
    c. Pearson's product moment correlation
    d. Probability theory

31. A zero correlation reflects:
    a. No relationship between x and y
    b. A small relationship between x and y
    c. A small or big relationship between x and y
    d. A big relationship between x and y
    e. The relationship between x and y depends on the sign (+/-)

32. Why does a significant correlation not guarantee that there is a cause-and-effect relationship?
    a. That question is false. All significant correlations reflect a cause-and-effect relationship
    b. Because x might not influence y
    c. Because y may not influence x
    d. Because z may influence x and y
    e. B, C and D are correct

33. Why would you use the experimental methodology over the correlational methodology? Because the experimental methodology allows one to:
    a. Correlate two variables together
    b. Write up a case history
    c. Describe the subjects thoughts about the experiment
    d. Control the most number of variables related to the experimental question

34. What is the value of random assignment?
    a. It avoids spreading bias across groups
    b. It is more fair
    c. It helps with establishing correlations
    d. It causes bias

35. Population characteristics are:
    a. The demographic characteristics of the group you expect to apply your data to
    b. The demographic characteristics of your subjects

    c. The characteristics of the broader population in your society
    d. The demographic characteristics of the group from where you are taking your subjects

36. Subject population refers to:
    a. The subjects you are using
    b. The subjects you are not using
    c. The subjects rejected from the experiment
    d. The set of subjects for the next experiment

37. Which of the following answers has the independent variable identified in CAPITALS?
    a. You shock a subject and measure his SCREAMS OF PAIN
    b. You test different spices in dog food to assess DOG PREFERENCES
    c. You give DRUGS to different groups to see which dose makes them fall asleep
    d. You use depression level as a way to estimate the SIZE OF THE PERSON'S SOCIAL CIRCLE

38. Which of the following answers has the dependent variable identified in CAPITALS?
    a. You SHOCK a subject and measure his screams of pain
    b. You test different SPICES in dog food to assess dog preferences
    c. You give drugs to different groups to see which dose makes them FALL ASLEEP
    d. You use DEPRESSION LEVEL as a way to estimate the size of the person's social circle

39. What is a placebo?
    a. An inert substance
    b. An inert substance used to produce drug effects
    c. An inert substance used to control for the act of taking a drug
    d. An active drug used to compare effects with the tested drug in question

40. Why would an experimenter use a double-blind procedure? To control for:
    a. Drug effects
    b. Possible experimenter bias
    c. Placebo effects
    d. Side effects

41. Why would an experimenter use a triple-blind procedure? To control for:
    a. Drug effects
    b. Possible experimenter bias
    c. Placebo effects
    d. Side effects

42. This term refers to the predefined manner in which research subjects are treated.
  a. Script
  b. Libretto
  c. Draft
  d. Play

43. What are the two primary goals of science?
  a. Theory development and prediction
  b. Prediction and analysis
  c. Control and theory development
  d. Prediction and control

44. In the big scheme of things, which of the following is more important?
  a. Prediction
  b. Control
  c. Theory
  d. Data

45. A question that may be formed in such a way that an experiment will either support or refute it.
  a. Experiment
  b. Theory
  c. Hypothesis
  d. Correlation

46. The process of controlling the environment so that you can manipulate a variable and accurately measure its effects on another variable.
  a. Experiment
  b. Theory
  c. Hypothesis
  d. Correlation

47. This thing may be either mathematical or verbal (language description) in nature. It is a scientist's best estimate of what is happening between varieties of factors that have been experimented upon.
  a. Experiment
  b. Theory
  c. Hypothesis
  d. Correlation

48. The need for "equal and independent" to be addressed in an experiment is related to which of the following issues?
  a. Theory
  b. Control
  c. Randomization
  d. Placebo effects

49. As the n-size of your sample grows, it becomes more likely that your measurements of that group are accurate.
  a. Central limit theorem
  b. Normal distribution
  c. Law of large numbers
  d. Experimental research

50. Regardless of the number of subjects or data points you have, you can accurately estimate how many fall within certain limits if that set of data is:
  a. Normally distributed
  b. Equal and independent
  c. From the law of large numbers
  d. Centrally distributed

UNIT TWO

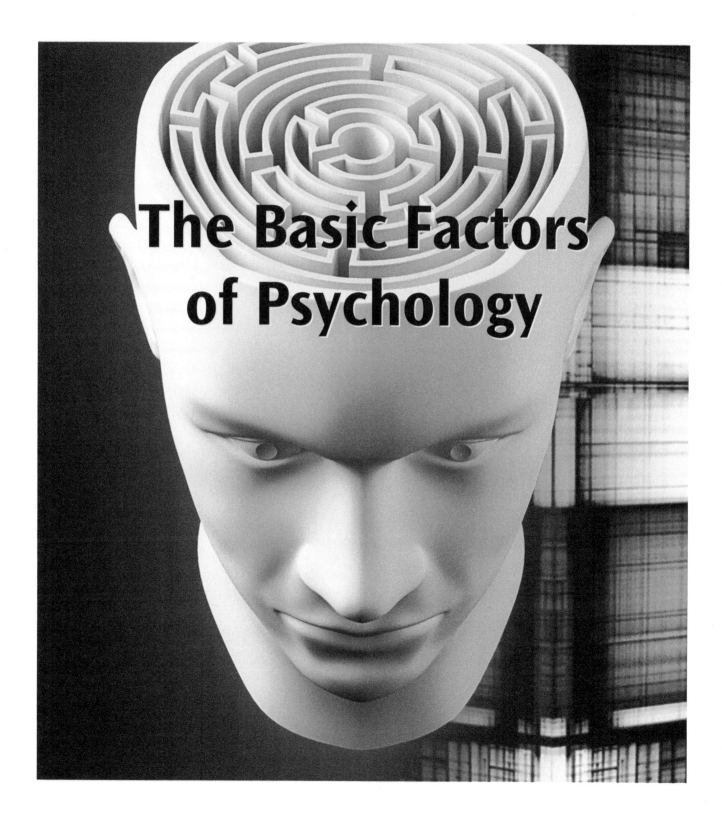

The Basic Factors
of Psychology

2 Neuroscience and Behavior

Egas Moniz and the Frontal Lobotomy

Egas Moniz, a medical researcher from Portugal, earned the Nobel Prize in Physiology or Medicine in 1949 for his work on the prefrontal leukotomy. In years to come, this procedure would be known as the fontal lobotomy.

The lobotomy was a technique first developed in animals during the end of the 19th century. Researchers studying brain function observed that lobotomies reduced aggression in the animals receiving them. In a more technically refined manner, Moniz learned to destroy sections of the outer surface of the human frontal cortex to influence the symptoms of schizophrenia, a disorder characterized by delusions and hallucinations. The outcomes initially seemed to improve the symptoms in some patients; however, it had no effects on others. Unfortunately, the surgical procedure also caused the deaths of some patients.

Moniz's procedure produced a permanent reduction in emotional outbursts and resulted in a much more controllable person. He evaluated treatment outcomes over time and found that the frontal lobotomy dampened the emotional behavior of the patients but did not eliminate their hallucinations. Moreover, their emotional flatness was so pervasive that it led the family members of treated patients to make comments to the effect that the "soul" of their relative was missing.

Doctors in the 1930's described the emotional flattening of patients with schizophrenia as a success. During this time, however, there were few treatments for that disorder. Some of the available techniques included heavy doses of sedatives, forcibly placing the patient in a bath of cold water until they calmed down, or using straight jackets and shackles. None of these techniques had permanent positive effects on the patient's recovery either. These techniques were the medical community's desperate attempt to affect some good in the patient. Instead, society went from caring for a person with schizophrenia to caring for a person with schizophrenia who now had brain damage.

By today's standards, the frontal lobotomy is entirely unacceptable. The permanent damage to neural tissue and the poor reduction in schizophrenic symptoms, make it a treatment that does more harm than good. This is truer today with the current set of available drug treatments as an alternative.

Moniz's work was valued during the time he conducted his initial studies. In contrast, however, his work serves as a reminder that some medical treatments that initially appear useful are not without their drawbacks.

References
http://nobelprize.org/nobel_prizes/medicine/laureates/1949/

CHAPTER OUTLINE

NEURAL BASES OF BEHAVIOR

> Neural cells must be quite small for ten-trillion to make up your nervous system.

The neural cell is the building block of the nervous system. It has a characteristic structure that is found throughout the brain, spinal cord, limbs and trunk of the body. When you understand the structure and function of this basic cell type, you will understand how the estimated ten-trillion neural cells in your body (one-hundred billion in your brain) work together to produce useful behavior. The neural cell has three primary anatomical components that will become our focus for understanding the neural basis of psychology. These components are the soma, dendrite and axon. These three components will control the one-way direction of information flow through the brain and the location of genetic material—which will control your brain's ability to adapt to new memories. We will begin by discussing the soma and its genetic material. Afterward, we will discuss the dendrite and axon because they control the transportation of information throughout the nervous system. This will then allow us to connect their functions to issues of intercellular communication.

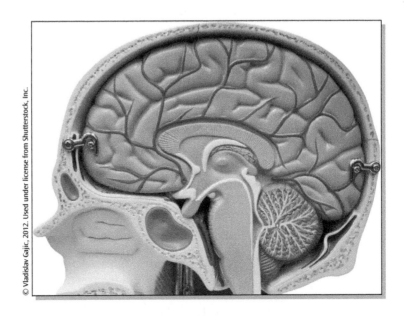

Electricity in the Cell

Batteries

Introduction to the Problem

By the time a student has graduated from high school, they have learned in biology class that electrical signals travel through the nerves of our bodies. For anyone who has watched a science program produce animations of this electricity, it is generally shown as a pulse of bright light traveling through a nerve. That presentation has both accurate and inaccurate components. It is true that the electricity in our nerves travels as a localized packet but that is where the animations give a decidedly skewed view of biological electricity. The animations of a brightly lit pulse through a nerve give one the perception that biological electricity is similar in form to the electricity that comes from a wall outlet. That, however, is not true. The electricity that runs our electronic equipment has different chemical characteristics from the biological electricity in your body. To understand the differences we must begin to look at both forms of electricity. For example, the electricity from a wall outlet is the movement of free electrons through metal wires. This type of electricity is similar to the type of electricity you obtain from a standard household battery. Because that is something that you are likely familiar with, the following discussion will describe the properties and functions of household electricity so that we can use it as a context for understanding biological electricity.

The Design of a Battery

Electrostatic Pressure

Electrochemistry is predicated upon the difference in electrical charge across a barrier. The common household battery is a simple example of this. A battery has a positive end, denoted by the "+" sign and a negative end denoted by the "–" sign. If you were able to see the inside of a battery—and I do not recommend

© valdis forms, 2012. Used under license from Shutterstock, Inc.

Electrostatic pressure: Electrostatic pressure is the force of diffusion generated by housing ions of a similar type within one area.

Diffusion: Diffusion is the distribution of atoms from areas of high concentration to areas of lower concentration.

Voltage: Voltage is an electrical measurement.

Voltage, amperes and ohms are the three basic measures of electricity.

A digital multimeter used to measure the voltage, amperes and ohms of electricity

© Bragin Alexey, 2012. Used under license from Shutterstock, Inc.

you cut one open—you would see a barrier that splits the internal environment in half. The material at the negative pole has a negative charge. A negative charge indicates that the material on that side of the battery has "extra" electrons that it will readily release. The material at the positive pole has a positive charge. A positive charge indicates that the material has "too few" electrons relative to the negative side and will readily accept any free ones.

The difference in the two sides of the battery create electrostatic pressure—measured in volts—which partially accounts for the movement of the electrons from the negative pole to the positive pole. Electrostatic pressure is based on the chemical principle that substances of the same charge repel each other and that substances of opposite charges attract each other. Because the negative end of the battery is filled with negatively charged ions, the force created by housing all those like ions together pushes the electrons out through a wire to reach the positive end of the battery. Sometimes electrostatic pressure is described analogously to liquid under pressure. Imagine, one container filled with water that is under high pressure and another container with no water in it at all. If one connected the two containers together with a pipe and opened a valve between them, then the water in the high-pressure container would squirt through the pipe and run to the empty container until the amount of water in each container was equal. This is analogous to what happens with electrostatic pressure and the electrons that travel along a wire from the negative pole to the positive pole.

Diffusion

If a wire were connected from the negative pole to the positive pole of a battery, then the force of the extra electrons at the negative pole relative to the attractive force at the positive end—electrostatic pressure—will cause the electrons to run through the wire and reach the positive pole. Upon arriving at the positive pole, they will be accepted by the positively charged environment. Of course, using the battery will eventually "drain" it of power because once the electrons travel to the positive side there will be a decreasing difference in diffusion between the two poles. Eventually there will be an equal concentration of electrons at both poles. That will be the condition when the battery is "dead." It will no longer operate any equipment because there is no longer any force pushing the electrons from the negative pole to the positive pole. Diffusion is another chemical property that will drive the electricity through your nervous system.

Voltage

The measure of the potential of a battery to do work is known as voltage. The voltage is not actually a physical thing so much as it is the difference in attractive (positive) and repulsive (negative) forces across the barrier of the battery. The greater the difference between these forces the greater the voltage of the battery. This voltage difference is exactly what is being measured when you describe the properties of electrochemical signals in your neurons. Voltage is used to measure the difference between the charged particles inside your neurons and the charged particles that are outside of your neurons. This difference will contribute significantly to the function of your nervous system.

Measuring Electricity from a Battery

The device to measure electricity from a battery is called a voltometer. A voltometer will measure the voltage, amperes and ohms from the electrical system that it is powering. Most common household batteries operate at 1.5 V. It works by applying a lead from the voltometer to each of the positive and negative ends of the battery. When a battery is attached to an electronic appliance, it sends electrons from the negative pole of the battery through the electronic device and returns to the positive end of the battery. The flow of electrons powers the electronic device. For example, attaching a battery to a light bulb will cause the light bulb to operate because the electrons will leave the negative end of the battery, travel through the light bulb—illuminating its filament—and then exiting the positive lead of the light bulb and returning to the positive end of the battery. This same basic process operates with any electronic device such as your cellular phone, computer or portable radio.

Biological Electricity

Introduction to the Problem

It is necessary to understand the basics of electricity before attempting to understand the electricity in your nerves. When we take what we know about electricity and batteries and apply it to the nervous system, however, only some of the information transfers well. For example in the previous section, we discussed how electrons move along wires to power devices such as cellular phones. With respect to the electricity in your nervous system, electrons are not traveling in the same manner. Instead of electrons moving through your neurons in the same manner as they flow through wires, **biological electricity** is based on the movement of sodium (Na+) and potassium (K+) across cell membranes. The differences caused by the movement of these ions produces voltage changes that travel along the neuron. This voltage difference travels as a punctate unit that constitutes the electrical activity of the nervous system. The next section will describe the design of a cell membrane, the barrier that separates the sodium and potassium. This section will begin to show you why biological electricity is different than the movement of electrons that power electronic equipment.

The Design of a Cell Membrane

I previously mentioned how a battery's internal barrier separates it's positive and negative poles. Within your neural cells, there is an analogously arranged barrier. This barrier is called the **cell membrane**. The cell membrane is the outer surface of each neural cell. The barrier establishes the inside from the outside of the cell. The cell membrane is made from two layers of fat; a **lipid bilayer**. This lipid bilayer keeps charged ions of different types separated from one another. Sodium (Na+) is outside of the cell and is positively charged. Inside the cell, potassium (K+) and large anions—negatively charged particles—are present. To produce an electrical signal in the neuron, a passageway must open up allowing charged particles to cross the cell membrane so that there is a change in the voltage across it.

Diffusion and Electrostatic Pressure

An **action potential** is the formal name for the electrical signal that travels along a neuron. When scientists speak about electrical activity in the nervous system, they are referring to this packet of electricity that travels through the neurons as a punctuate grouping of charged particles. To understand how to produce an action potential, one should begin at the point at which they are produced. There are two places to choose; the tip of a dendrite and the axon hillock. Let us start at the tip of the dendrite.

The beginning of an action potential at the dendrite requires that an exchange of charged particles cross the cell membrane at that location. When the cell is stimulated—a topic we have not yet discussed—a process exchanging charged particles across the cell membrane will begin. The

Biological electricity: Biological electricity is the name given to the electricity within your nervous system.

Cell membrane: The outer surface of a neuron that is made from two layers of fat (lipid bilayer).

Lipid bilayer: A molecular double–layer of fat molecules is called a lipid bilayer. It is used to create the vesicles within axons as well as the cell membrane of neurons.

Action potential: An action potential is the formal name for the packet of electrical activity that travels through a neuron. The action potential is always a +40 mV in strength.

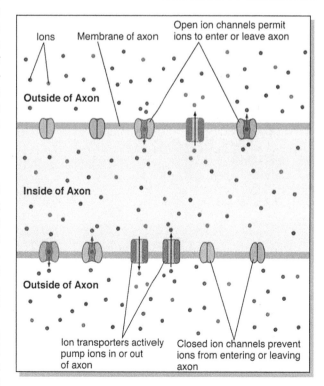

FIGURE 2.1 Ion channels and ion transporters

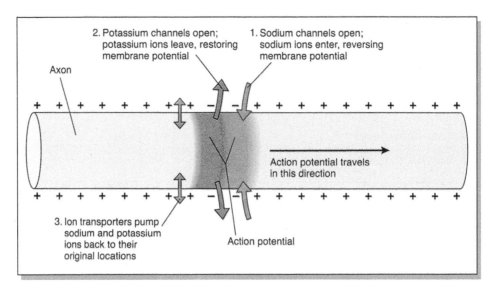

FIGURE 2.2 ■ The movement of sodium and potassium ions to produce an action potential

Sodium, chlorine, calcium and potassium are the most common charged particles in the nervous system that influence action potentials.

Resting potential: The name refers to the level of voltage in a cell at rest. The voltage is equal to −70 mV.

particles will travel through pores in the cell membrane. There will be channels for the charged particles such as sodium (Na+), chlorine (Cl−), calcium (Ca^{2+}) and potassium (K+).

The way in which an electrochemical signal is produced at the neuron begins with the different ions that are inside and outside of the cell. Outside the cell, the charged particle of relevance is sodium (Na+). Inside the cell, the primary charged particle of relevance is potassium (K+). The overall voltage difference between the charges outside the cell relative to inside the cell is −70 mV. This value is referred to as the cell's resting potential. It is given that name because −70 mV is the voltage present in all neural cells when there are no action potentials.

When the cells are stimulated, they open channels that allow the sodium to rush into the cell. Sodium rushes into the cell for two reasons. First, there is a higher concentration of sodium outside the cell than inside the cell. Second, sodium is positively charged and the inside of the cell is comparatively negatively charged (opposite charges attract). When the sodium enters the cell, it changes the initial voltage difference from −70 mV to +40 mV. Once the positively charged sodium ions begin to rush into the cell, the overall voltage difference between the inside and outside of the cell becomes +40 mV. This is because the positively charged sodium ions have just entered the cell.

This change in voltage potential has a disruptive effect on the cell membrane itself. It causes more sodium channels to open just next to the area that has turned +40 mV. Consequently, the +40 mV "electrical signal/voltage difference" moves in the direction of the newly opened ion channels. Ultimately, the electrical signal (action potential) travels through the dendrite until it reaches the soma. When it reaches the soma, there are not enough ion channels in the cell membrane to keep the action potential moving and so the exchange of charged particles stops and the action potential dies out. The changed concentration of charged particles, however, is dumped into the soma where they can integrate with other charged particles arriving through other dendrites that have sent signals into the soma. The sum result may be an increase in concentration of charged particles that may produce a new signal in the neuron.

When the integration of charged particles occurs in the soma, there are some general rules that establish whether a new signal will be produced. Those rules are that a +10 mV charge must occur within a 10 ms period. If those conditions are met, then the cell will produce a new action potential. If a new signal develops, it will appear at the axon hillock—the very beginning of the axon just next to the soma.

Dendrites

The primary role of the **dendrites** is to bring information into the neuron. Of course, that information is brief pulses of biological electricity. Because the dendrites bring information into a cell, they must be connected to other cells. The specific arrangement of the dendrites of any cell can vary for each neuron. Anatomists have shown that the branches of the dendrites appear similar to the roots of a plant. They extend from the cell body of the neuron, branch out and divide as they stretch out. Ultimately, the number of connections that the dendrites make to other cells may be in the order of ten thousand. To understand fully how signals are passed from one cell to another and how the electricity travels through the cell itself will require a discussion of the dendrites, axons and neurotransmission. For now, however, our discussion of the dendrites will center on where they generate action potentials, where they send those signals and what ultimately happens to the signals themselves.

It is likely that you have previously heard of receptors in the body. Generally, the discussion of receptors takes place within a context of the discussion of drugs. Drugs do affect receptors; however, other naturally occurring drug substances within your body also affect receptors. The names of these naturally occurring substances are called neurotransmitters. Neurotransmitters are released from the end of an axon, the very end of a neuron, and cross a gap to reach the dendrite of the next neuron. When the neurotransmitters reach the dendrite, they have the ability to land on a random scattering of receptors. Receptors on the dendrite are essentially large protein molecules that are sticking out of the cell membrane. Just like any large protein molecule, they will have a particular shape that will bond with other substances that have a complementary shape. The neurotransmitters that are released from the neurons naturally have a complementary shape to the dendritic receptors. When neurotransmitters land on these receptors, a chemical bond takes place that causes an opening to occur in the cell membrane. That

> **Dendrite:** The portion of a neuron that generates an action potential due to the activity of neurotransmitters affecting its receptors is called the dendrite. This section of the neuron sends the action potentials toward the soma.

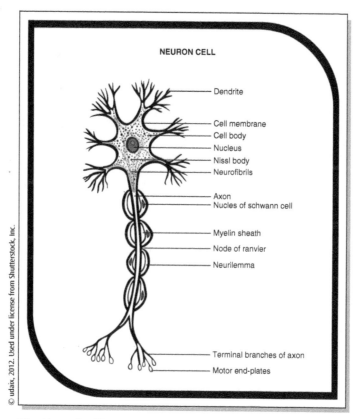

© udaix, 2012. Used under license from Shutterstock, Inc.

The Neural cell

opening is referred to as an ion channel. These are the same type of ion channels discussed in the section on biological electricity. There are many different types of channels on dendrites. One of the most common is the sodium channel. As we talk about ion channels throughout this section, we will focus on sodium channels. The reason we will do so is because sodium channels are one of the most common types to initiate electrical signals in dendrites.

Ion Channels

Ion channels are designed in such a way that they only allow certain types of ions through them. For example, sodium-potassium channels are one of the most common. With sodium-potassium channels, only sodium and potassium can pass through the membrane. In fact it is designed in such a way that sodium can only pass from the inside of the cell to the outside of the cell and potassium can only pass from the outside of the cell to the inside. Other channels only allow chlorine or calcium to pass through them. Each of these channels has a role in establishing electrical activity in the neuron itself, and therefore plays a part in the overall functioning of the cell.

In general, ion channels are controlled by the neurotransmitters designed to influence them. For instance, once the neurotransmitters land on the receptors, the receptor-neurotransmitter combination will cause a mechanical twisting of the receptor itself that will stimulate the ion channel and allow ions to pass through the cell membrane. Receptors embedded in the surface of the dendrite typically have control over the ion channels in their general vicinity. As the receptor-neurotransmitter combination twists, it will eventually cause the neurotransmitter to snap off the receptor and return to the axon from which it came. When that happens, the ion channel that was open will close. Therefore, no more charged particles will be able to cross the cell membrane in that area. Consequently, the control over ion channels in any particular location on the dendrite is dependent upon the presence of a neurotransmitter landing on the appropriate receptor on the dendritic surface.

EPSPs and IPSPs

When neurotransmitters contact their receptors, the effect can be to increase or decrease the likelihood of the dendrite producing an action potential. The reason that neurotransmitters may increase or decrease this chance is based upon the type of charged particle that crosses the cell membrane. The most common charged particles that cross cell membranes are sodium, potassium, calcium and chlorine. Sodium ($Na+$), potassium ($K+$) and calcium (Ca^{2+}) are all positively charged ions. As we saw earlier, when positively charged ions enter the cell, an overall change in voltage toward the positive direction occurs. Changing the voltage a minimum of +10 mV will result in the production of a new action potential. Both sodium and calcium can enter the cell and increase the chance of an action potential. Potassium, however, primarily resides within the cell when the cell is at rest. Therefore, the movement of potassium is to leave the cell which makes the inside of the cell more negatively charged. Chlorine, a negatively charged ion primarily exists outside of the cell and will have the same influence as potassium leaving the cell. In both cases, the cell will develop a more negative voltage. The loss of potassium or the introduction of chlorine will result in more difficulty producing an action potential in the cell. To state that in other terms, they will make the cell more inhibitory. This is the same as stating that the cell will have a more difficult time firing.

The production of a positive voltage change in a cell is referred to as an **excitatory postsynaptic potential** (EPSP). The reduction of a negative voltage change in a cell is referred to as an **inhibitory postsynaptic potential** (IPSP). The production of EPSPs and IPSPs are very important in understanding the nervous system. Some neurotransmitters naturally produce EPSPs and others naturally

Ion channel: The channel pathway that ions take to cross a cell membrane is called an ion channel.

Excitatory postsynaptic potential (EPSP): The EPSP is the proper name for an action potential derived at the dendrite.

Inhibitory postsynaptic potential (IPSP): The IPSP is not an action potential but rather a negative voltage applied to a neuron making it more difficult for an EPSP to occur.

produce IPSPs. Drugs may modify the function of cells by increasing or decreasing the likelihood of the production of EPSPs and IPSPs. We will further discuss the role of drugs and postsynaptic potentials in a later section on psychopharmacology.

Soma and Signal Integration

As action potentials are generated at the beginning of the dendrite, they will follow the full length of the dendrite and eventually reach the soma. The soma serves many functions as far as cellular communication is concerned. Currently, our discussion centers upon the use of the soma as the place where action potentials from the dendritic branches meet and integrate. The soma is also the location of the genetic material inside of the neuron. The soma contains literally thousands of substances of which we will only discuss a few.

The soma is the location of EPSP and IPSP integration from all dendritic branches. Previously, we discussed how neurotransmitters cause different types of ion channels to open up and generate either EPSPs or IPSPs. This process is occurring at each dendritic branch. As each action potential is generated in a dendrite, it will travel to the soma where it will be integrated with other action potentials from other dendritic branches. The integration of positive and negative ions occurs at the end of the dendrite where the action potential is generated and it also takes place in the soma. This integration determines whether the cell produces a new signal. The rule for determining a new signal will require that a +10 mV signal is generated in the soma within a 10 ms duration.

Axons

The process of signal integration determines whether a new action potential is going to be generated by the neuron. If no new action potential is produced, then that signal will terminate. That is, from wherever this signal was originally generated, its pathway influencing the nervous system has ended. Alternatively, a new action potential may be generated. This will reflect the ongoing life of whichever signal originally started the whole trail of signals through the nervous system.

Once the process of signal integration initiates a new action potential, that new signal will begin in the axon hillock. The axon hillock is the initial portion of the axon just off the soma. The new action potential will travel the full length of the axon at one speed and, of course, as a +40 mV signal. If the axon branches into different directions then the full +40 mV signal strength will carry on in all directions until it reaches the very end of each branch. The end of an axon is called the axon terminal or terminal button. The passage of the action potential through the axon follows the same ionic-exchange process described for the dendrite. In the axon, however, there are additional components that modify the speed of the action potential through the axon. Those factors are the diameter of the axon and myelination.

Affecting the Speed of the Action Potential

Axon Diameter and Glia

The diameter of an axon is positively correlated with the speed that an action potential can travel. The thinnest diameter axons produce the slowest action potentials and the largest diameter axons produce the fastest action potentials. This effect has no influence on the voltage of the action potential itself. All action potentials are always +40 mV.

Soma: The soma is another name for the cell body. The soma houses the genetic material of a neural cell.

Signal integration: Signal integration refers to the integration of voltages of the various EPSPs and IPSPs that reach the soma within a neural cell.

Axon hillock: The axon hillock is where new action potentials are formed within the cell after signal integration.

Axon: The axon is the section of the neuron that produces an action potential, houses neurotransmitters and is responsible for sending signals away to other neurons.

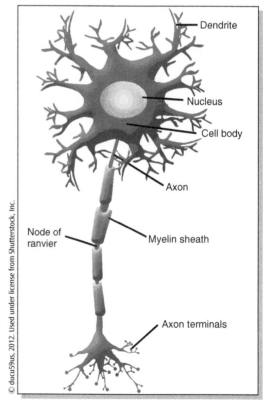

The major portions of a multipolar cell

Myelin: Myelin is the alternative name for glia. Myelin is the fatty insulating cover around an axon.

Glia: The alternative name for myelin is glia. It is the fatty insulating cover around an axon.

Oligrodendrocyte cell: Oligrodendrocyte cells are the glial cells in the central nervous system.

Salutatory conduction: Salutatory conduction refers to the process by which action potentials can only transfer ions across the axonal membrane at the nodes of Ranvier. It increases the speed at which the action potential can pass down the axon.

Nodes of Ranvier (ROW vee ay): The nodes of Ranvier are tiny gaps in between each successive myelin cell along an axon. These nodes produce salutatory conduction that speeds the rate at which the action potential travels.

Terminal button: The terminal button is another name for the axon terminal. It is the very end of an axon where the neurotransmitters are housed in the vesicles.

Vesicles: Vesicles are the fatty bubbles present in the axon terminal (terminal button) that houses the neurotransmitters.

Another factor that influences action potential speed is whether the axon is myelinated. Myelin, which comes from a type of cell called glial cells (glia), is a fatty substance that insulates axons. Myelin is one of the few structures one can see in the brain with the naked eye because it produces a whitish hue. In the central nervous system, myelin comes from cells called oligrodendrocyte cells. These cells wrap themselves around the axon and insulate it from spreading its electrical activity to any of its adjoining cells. This keeps the electrical activity from producing an "electrical short" (allowing the action potentials to jump from one axon to another).

Myelin speeds the rate of action potentials through a process called salutatory conduction. Salutatory conduction means "jumping conduction." In salutatory conduction, the action potential does not open and close ionic channels along the membrane of the entire cell as it once did in the dendrite. Rather, ionic exchanges must take place within small gaps between each succeeding piece of myelin. Because the myelin insulates the axon, the only place for ion channels to open is in the tiny gaps in between each oligrodendrocyte cell. These tiny gaps are called the nodes of Ranvier. The nodes of Ranvier allow just enough of the charged particles through to maintain the action potential from gap to gap. Because the action potential does not have to wait the full length of time for sodium and potassium channels to open and reset themselves, the overall flow of ions through the axon is conducted more quickly. Therefore, myelinated axons send signals more quickly.

Terminal Button and Vesicles

As an action potential travels down the axon it will eventually reach the end of the line, the terminal button. This is where the action potential terminates because it has nowhere else to go. Once an action potential reaches the end of an axon, new biochemical processes must initiate so that this signal can be transferred to the next cell in the pathway. If it is transferred, it will be converted from an electrical signal to a chemical signal before reaching the next neural cell.

The terminal button is a unique place within a neuron. The very end of each axon widens at its tip. Within the very end of this section reside small bubbles called vesicles. Vesicles are fatty bubbles that are filled with a chemical signal called a neurotransmitter. The neurotransmitter that resides in these vesicles is generally specific to the cell itself; however, multiple forms of neurotransmitter may exist in the end of an axon. The vesicles are formed from the same material that creates the cell membrane; that is, the lipid bilayer. It is necessary to recognize that vesicles and cell membranes are made from the same material because part of the process of signaling from one cell to the next will involve the vesicles merging with the cell membrane. When it does, its contents will be sent out of the cell to reach the receptors on the next cell.

Once the action potential reaches the end of the axon terminal, the presence of the action potential causes calcium channels to open to allow calcium to enter the cell. This will initiate the movement of the vesicles toward the very end of the axon terminal.

Neurotransmission

In the process of neurotransmission, the vesicles are pushed against the inside wall of the end of the axon. In this location, they dock against protein molecules that pull the vesicles open and allow the neurotransmitters to dump out into the synaptic gap. The synaptic gap is the space in between the very end of an axon and the beginning of the next cell, the dendrite. It is essentially an alleyway between the two cells. Once the neurotransmitter is released into the synaptic gap, it continues on its journey until it reaches the dendrite. The dendrite, as we discussed earlier, is the location of the receptors. Once the neurotransmitters have influenced the receptors, they are returned in the direction of the axon from whence they came. This process is referred to as reuptake.

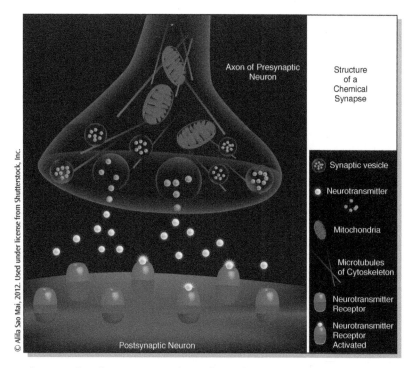

The transfer of neurotransmitters from the axon terminal (presynaptic) to the dendrite (postsynaptic)

Neurotransmission: Neurotransmission is the name given to the chemical signaling that occurs between two neural cells.

Reuptake: Reuptake is the process by which neurotransmitters return to the axon that released them.

Intercellular communication: Communication between two neurons is referred to as intercellular communication.

Reflex: A reflex is a biologically hardwired response to a particular stimulus.

Reuptake

The process of **reuptake** is the process of reabsorbing any neurotransmitter back into the axon. When the neurotransmitters reach the axon from whence they came, they are reabsorbed across the cell membrane and back into the axon itself. There, floating by themselves, they are reabsorbed by empty vesicles in need of neurotransmitters. Once the vesicles refill themselves, they will again be ready to release their contents into the synaptic gap. This, of course, will not occur until another action potential reaches the very end of this axon terminal.

INTERCELLULAR COMMUNICATION

One of the primary functions of the brain is to control behavior. The only way for the brain to send signals to the various areas for processing is to have an **intercellular communication** system. The intercellular communication system includes neuroanatomical connections between cells. It also contains a system of chemical signals and genetic processes. To understand how the brain sends signals from one location to another, we need to discuss the basic neuroanatomical layout of the intercellular communication system. Although all intercellular communication systems include neurotransmission, we are going to focus on the neuroanatomical components that send signals from one neural cell to another. The first system to be addressed is related to a simple reflexive response.

Receptor to Motor-Neuron Reflex Arc

One of the simplest forms of intercellular communication is represented in the basic **reflex**. The basic reflex involves three neurons: one from the sensory receptor, another in the spinal cord and one leading from the spinal cord back to the muscle near the location where the sensory receptor resides. In this

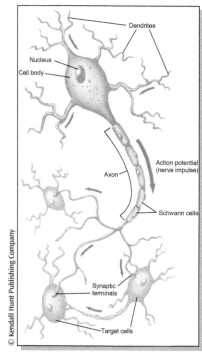

FIGURE 2.3 ■ A simplistic representation of the interconnection between neurons

system, sensory stimulation sends action potentials back to the spinal cord. At this location, the cell connects with an interneuron that sends a separate signal to the brain. This separate pathway is related to voluntary (e.g., brain controlled) adjustments of the reflex response. Finally, this interneuron connects with a motor neuron that returns a signal to a muscle that modifies the subjects response—usually withdraw from painful stimulation. For example, if a straight pin stuck your finger, then that painful sensory signal would lead back your spinal cord, send a signal to the brain and a separate signal to a motor neuron that would return to the location of the pinprick. This will enable the muscles in that area of the finger to contract and withdraw the sensory receptor from the location of the painful stimulus. Previously mentioned, however, a separate signal is sent to the brain. How does that separate signal modify how the subject may act?

The signal sent to the brain engages any relevant brain activity in the management of the hand withdraw reflex. The relevant areas will contain previous learning and memories as well as the entire conglomeration of current perception and thinking of the subject. For example, in cases during which you are burning your hand because you are carrying a hot pot, you can override the reflex by your motivation to not drop the pot. The motivational component, which is described very vaguely here, is derived from the activity in the brain. It involves all of the learning, memories, and current perception of the situation that determines to what degree the subject will hold the hot pot. If a person is motivated to not drop the pot because it will ruin their dinner, then they will instead burn their hands. Despite the presence of the actively processed hand withdraw reflex, the person may be able to hold on to their dinner. Without the separate signal sent to the brain, there would be no way for the subject to stop the hand-withdraw reflex from dominating their final motor output and the hot pot would be dropped.

More Complex Intercellular Connections

The **three-cell reflex** arrangement is one of the simplest intercellular systems the human nervous system contains that is relevant to observable human behavior. If, however, we considered the complete set of pathways modifying the

Three–cell reflex: The three–cell reflex is the simplest type of spinal reflex that exists. It involves one sensory neuron, an interneuron in the spinal cord and a motor neuron extending back to muscles near the location of stimulation.

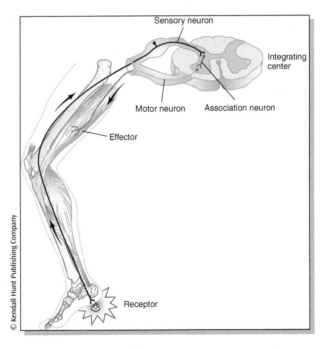

FIGURE 2.4 ■ A cross section of the anatomical connections of a reflex arc within the spinal cord.

hand-withdraw reflex—control from the brain—then we would need to identify many more circuits. This, of course, would be an enormous undertaking. The language and emotional motivation systems that influence whether the subject overrides the reflex would be extremely complex. In fact, current neuroanatomical research cannot meet this demand. It is simply too extensive given the small size of the neurons and the numerous pathways involved in the processing. This, however, does not mean that we cannot discuss the system in more general terms.

For what reason might someone hold onto the hot pot and override their hand-withdraw reflex? It might be that they are near the table and will not need to hold it for long. It might be that they are hungry and if they drop it then they will both lose their dinner and have a big mess to clean up. In addition, they might hold on to the pot because someone important to them is watching. Each of these reasons constitutes a separate overall pathway which will lead to the same result; holding onto the hot pot.

To discuss this issue, we will have to simplify what is an enormous degree of complexity. Let us suppose that our subject held onto the pot while his mother—who was standing within his visual field—was yelling "Don't drop that pot, darn it!" The hand-withdraw reflex of our subject would be expected to make him drop the pot. Because he did not, we can ask what environmental event modified the reflex. It appears—in our example—that it has something to do with his abrasive mother. To understand her influence in terms of his biology, we need to understand their history. The example stated that she was in his field of view and was yelling at him. These two sensory routes, vision and hearing, will ultimately lead to brain output that will connect with the spinal interneuron at the location where the pain receptor junctions with the motor neuron in the spinal cord. The visual stimulus of his mother will need to travel to the area in the back of the brain where vision is analyzed. Then components of that analysis will have to evoke memories of his mother in similar situations as well as the general character of their relationship. The auditory stimuli will perform the same activity except that it will take place along the sides of the brain where hearing is analyzed. Moreover, the specifics of his mother's movements, clothing and tone of voice will further modify his response. It may be that he loves her and holds onto the pot to make her happy. In other situations, different subjects might drop it because they hate her. There is—at this time in history—no realistic way to describe all the pathways in which his brain may analyze the influence of his mother's behavior.

Despite all this complexity, there really is quite a bit that is understood about the brain, however. For instance, we know that the general flow of information is relatively similar between all members of our species. That is, the locations and connections between the various hubs of analysis in our brains are relatively similar. There must be relevant differences, however, that allow each of us to express unique patterns of behavior given our genetic and environmental backgrounds.

Central nervous system (CNS): The portion of a nervous system comprised of the brain and spinal cord.

NEUROANATOMY

General Structures

Central Nervous System

Distinguishing the Two Branches of the Nervous System

The overall structure of the nervous system is comprised of two parts. The first part is the central nervous system (CNS) and the second part is the peripheral nervous system (PNS). It is necessary to be able to distinguish why one section

Peripheral nervous system (PNS): The PNS is any part of a nervous system that is not the brain or spinal cord. The PNS can be subdivided into the somatic nervous system (muscular control) and autonomic nervous system (internal organs and glands).

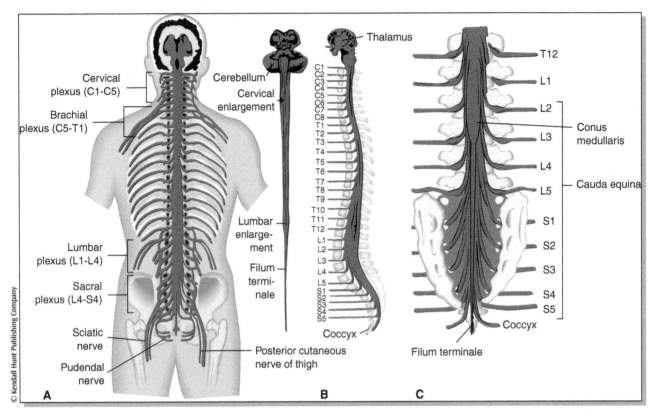

© Kendall Hunt Publishing Company

FIGURE 2.5 ■ *The two main branches of the nervous system are the CNS (brain and spinal cord) and the PNS (all other neurons).*

Blood–brain barrier: This system is created from three anatomical components. They are the endothelial cells, cerebrospinal fluid and skeletal structure covering the central nervous system (CNS).

Bone encasement: Bone encasement is one third of the blood–brain barrier system.

Cerebrospinal fluid (CSF): This substance is produced near the center of the brain and flows through channels to completely cover the outside of the brain and spinal cord. It serves to cushion the brain and to block outside substances from reaching the central nervous system. Therefore, it is part of the blood brain barrier.

of the nervous system is referred to as "central" and the other section is referred to as "peripheral." The description in the following sections will show how the blood brain barrier separates the central and peripheral nervous systems. In addition, we will discuss the difference in the ability of the cells of the peripheral nervous system to regenerate themselves relative to that of the central nervous system. This distinction, which is probably something you are already aware of, accounts for the reason why brain or spinal cord damage is often times permanent whereas damage to cells in the peripheral nervous system—such as your hand—can result in a substantial recovery.

Blood Brain Barrier

The **blood brain barrier** is a three-tiered system that protects the central nervous system over and beyond that which the peripheral nervous system is protected. This protection reveals the special status the central nervous system has in the entire nervous system. The first section of the blood brain barrier is **bone encasement**, the second part is the **cerebrospinal fluid** and the third part is made from **endothelial cells**, special cells that make the capillaries in the brain.

Bone encasement of the central nervous system is the most obvious anatomical component of the blood brain barrier. The sections of the nervous system that are encased in bone are your brain and spinal cord. Your brain is housed within your skull and your spinal cord—which runs about three-fourths of the way down your back—through the center of the vertebrae in an opening called the **spinal foramen**. This gives the central nervous system an advantage in safety beyond that of the peripheral nervous system. The encasement by bone protects your brain and spinal cord from any damage that you may incur from either falling or being hit.

The second section of the blood brain barrier involves the use of cerebrospinal fluid. Cerebrospinal fluid is a clear liquid similar to blood plasma that fills the tiny space that surrounds the entire central nervous system. For example, imagine a thin coating of fluid that surrounds the entire brain and spinal cord. That fluid is the cerebrospinal fluid. This fluid, of course, does not just sit alongside of the central nervous system itself; it is actually sandwiched within three layers of tissue that cover the entire central nervous system.

The three layers of tissue that surround the central nervous system are referred to as the **meninges**. Each layer of tissue has a separate name; the outermost layer is referred to as the **dura mater**, the second layer of tissue is called the **arachnoid membrane** and the third innermost layer of tissue is called the **pia mater**. The area between the arachnoid membrane and the pia mater is referred to as the **subarachnoid space**. The subarachnoid space forms a cavern system through which the cerebrospinal fluid can flow. It does so through the **arachnoid trabeculae** that extends from the arachnoid space to the pia mater. I refer to it as a cavern system because it looks like stalactites and stalagmites in a cave that have reached from floor to ceiling.

The cerebral spinal fluid that passes through this cavern system is generated in the brain. Four hollow sections in the lower areas of your brain (**ventricles** 1-4) are filled with cerebrospinal fluid. That fluid is generated in the ventricles. The fluid then flows out through a single canal system down through the back of the brain. Once near the lower back base of the skull, the cerebrospinal fluid follows paths that allow it to surround the brain and spinal cord.

Just like the bone encasement of the entire central nervous system, the cerebrospinal fluid helps to protect the central nervous system tissue from outside influences. The primary role of the cerebrospinal fluid is to wash away any material that crosses from the arterial system into an area near the central nervous system. That is, it functions as a flowing liquid barrier that washes away any external substances that may prove dangerous for the central nervous system.

The third section of the blood brain barrier involves something called endothelial cells. Endothelial cells are the cells that make up the capillaries within the brain. These cells are unique with respect to all cells which make up the capillaries in that they are more tightly compacted than the other capillary-creating cells throughout the body. Consequently, any large molecules flowing through the arterial system of the brain have a more difficult time crossing the capillary barrier and entering the central nervous system. The endothelial cells generally protect the central nervous system from large molecules. Smaller structures and those that are very soluble in fat, may still cross the endothelial cells.

Apart from the three components of the blood brain barrier, there is one additional way to classify central nervous system tissue separately from peripheral nervous system tissue. This final point is not related to the protection of the central nervous system from outside forces or chemicals; however, it is related to the activity of the central nervous system tissue and its ability to regenerate the cells that make it up.

Neural Cell Regeneration

As many people are already aware, neural cells in the central nervous system do not regenerate themselves very well. Many people are aware of this fact because they know that brain damage and spinal cord injury result in permanent deficits. This, of course, is in contrast to the damage that occurs in the peripheral nervous system. In the peripheral nervous system, one may damage cells and they will regenerate themselves so that a pathway is reestablished. This is often seen when someone loses a limb and then has it surgically reattached. If the cells of the peripheral nervous system did not regenerate, then the reattachment of a limb would not work. In recent years, there have been many instances described in the media in which a person had lost a limb and had it reattached. The reason that a limb can be re-attached is related to the regenerative capacity of the peripheral nervous system. Once the neural cells of the peripheral nervous system are aligned during the surgical reattachment procedure, a biochemical

Endothelial cells: The tightly packed cells creating the capillaries of the brain are called endothelial cells. They are part of the blood brain barrier because they stop large molecules from crossing from the blood supply into the central nervous system tissue.

Spinal foramen: The spinal foramen is the opening in the center of a vertebra that allows the spinal cord to be encased in bone as it runs down the back.

Meninges: A three layer covering that surrounds the complete central nervous system. It is comprised of the dura mater, arachnoid membrane and the pia mater. The pia mater is the layer closest to the brain tissue.

Dura mater: The dura mater is the outermost tissue level of the meninges.

Arachnoid membrane: The middle layer of the meninges.

Pia mater: The pia mater is the innermost tissue of the three layers of the meninges. It is the softest and most flexible tissue of the three and lies along the brain and spinal cord.

Subarachnoid space: The subarachnoid space is the location that cerebrospinal fluid flows through within the meninges.

Arachnoid trabeculae: Legs extending from the arachnoid membrane to the top of the pia mater.

Ventricles: Four hollow chambers in the brain are filled with cerebrospinal fluid (CSF)

Neurogenesis refers to the development of new neural cells. There is some evidence that new neural cells may develop in adulthood but more research is still needed before fully understanding this issue.

Plasticity: The ability of neurons to connect and disconnect from other neurons is called plasticity. Applications of plasticity and neurogenesis are at the forefront of neuroscientific research

process begins which cleans away any of the dead neural tissue and produces a signal which causes the cells to regenerate. Those cells grow toward each other and eventually reconnect. This, however, is in direct contrast to what happens in the central nervous system.

In the central nervous system, damaged cells are eliminated but there is not a proper biochemical process to regenerate cell growth and direct it along its previous pathway. Therefore, damage to the brain or spinal cord tends to be permanent. In recent decades there has been some evidence indicating that central nervous system tissue regenerates itself very modestly. That, however, is not sufficient to eliminate any serious damage that may occur during a spinal cord injury, stroke, or closed head injury. In effect, any central nervous system tissue damage that occurs in an adult is essentially permanent.

Biological researchers continue to work on this topic in an attempt to regenerate central nervous system tissue. Whereas strides have been made in recent years, we appear to be a long way from having a safe and effective treatment for central nervous system tissue damage. One of the approaches neuroscientists have taken is to attempt to enhance the role of **neurogenesis** in the central nervous system. Neurogenesis is the brain's natural capacity to produce new neural cells. This process takes place most frequently in the hippocampus—an area associated with memory formation—and in the olfactory system. If the process of neurogenesis is controlled, then damage to the central nervous system might be overcome by enhancing the growth of new cells in the damaged area. The process is not without a biological precedent. Frogs can have their eyes removed and turned upside down or placed in the opposite eye and the neurogenesis process will reconnect the visual pathway so that vision is reestablished. A similar process in humans would result in the end of permanent brain or spinal cord injury. Overall, this process of neurogenesis in conjunction with the brain's ability to rewire itself is referred to as brain **plasticity**; a term which refers to the brain's ability to rewire or repair itself. The process of brain plasticity is very important in modern neuroscience as a research and clinical issue. The more that is understood with respect to how the brain rewires or repairs itself, the more will be understood about how experience influences brain function.

Brain

An Overview of Brain Structure

The adult brain is a three-pound organ made entirely of neural cells and myelin. The outer surface of the brain is grayish in color, hence its nickname "gray matter." You will recall from the previous discussions of neural cells that axons are myelinated and dendrites and cell bodies are not. Because any myelinated axons have a whitish hue, you can surmise that the surface of the brain is comprised entirely of cell bodies and their dendritic interconnections. This is in sharp contrast to what lies below the surface of the brain. A cross section of the brain will show that much of the inside of this organ has a whitish hue. Hence, the inside of the brain is comprised primarily of myelinated axons. This indicates that this lower section of the brain reveals a system of interconnections between various areas of the surface of the brain. An overview of how the brain develops into this form is described in the next section.

An Overview of Brain Development

The central nervous system begins to appear at about 18-days after conception and the brain appears about six days later. The nervous system first develops as a hollow tube that will develop into the spinal cord and brain. Throughout the process of development, the brain will continue to grow along the same axis that contains the developing spinal cord.

As the brain grows larger, it involves the division and migration of cells from the tip of the spinal cord toward the outer surface of the developing brain. In this manner, the brain grows continually from the outside, not the inside. Once the cells migrate to the outside of the brain, they attach themselves to other cells that have already made the journey. As this process repeats over the coming months, the brain will develop to nearly its adult size. The brain will continue to develop after birth; however, its rate will be slow compared to its prenatal period.

Although this process of development may seem like neural cells produce a random selection of interconnections; that is far from the truth. For instance, the motor cortex shows a distribution of interconnections that reflect the surface of your body. For example, the distribution of cells across the motor cortex show a pattern which stretch—in reasonable order—from your head to your feet. This map of the body produces a structure that organizes brain circuitry well. This same structure also holds for the primary somatosensory cortex—an area which is one of the first places in which sensory information is processed by the brain. The manner in which these interconnections form is regulated by the location of the neural cells in the brain and the local biochemical signals they produce.

As the brain continues to grow, it will cease extending out along the axis of the spinal cord. Instead, it will fold back upon the end of the spinal cord from which it grew. In a general sense, the growth backward is similar to the way in which a mushroom cap folds over the stem that generated it. This mushroom cap analogy of the brain will help you remember where various areas of the brain reside. For example, when you discuss areas of the brain that control such things as higher-level reasoning in humans—as opposed to basic life sustaining functions—you will be able to deduce approximately where in the brain they exist. This is because the basic life sustaining areas of the brain tend to be clustered at the base of the mushroom stem and the higher-level reasoning skills tend to be spread throughout the outer surface of the mushroom cap. By 20 weeks after conception, the brain will be approximately 2 inches long and have the basic shape of an adult brain. Its three main sections (forebrain, midbrain and hindbrain) will involve distinctly different neural operations that will maintain the health and maintenance of the organism. When the brain is finally developed, it will weigh approximately three pounds and will involve, minimally, billions of neural cells.

In the following sections, the anatomical organization of the brain will be reviewed from the areas controlling basic life-sustaining functions (hindbrain) to the higher order functions (forebrain). When we reach the forebrain, we will look at the various subsections that give us the biological bases of personality, language and intelligence.

Hindbrain

The hindbrain is the section of the brain closest to the end of the spinal cord. The hindbrain is made of three sections; the medulla oblongata, cerebellum and pons. Each of the areas of the hindbrain is primarily related to the control of basic life sustaining activities and bodily management functions that are needed to keep a person alive.

The first structure, the medulla oblongata, is commonly referred to as the medulla. The medulla is the first section of brain just after the spinal cord ends. The primary role of the medulla is controlling activity of the cardiovascular system, respiration and muscle tone. Damage to the medulla will oftentimes result in death given that signals from the brain would not be able to control the heart or lungs.

The second section of the hindbrain is the cerebellum. The cerebellum gets its name from the Latin term for "little brain." It is referred to as the little brain because, by itself, it appears to be a miniature version of the entire human brain. The cerebellum primarily controls balance and coordination with respect to

Forebrain: The outermost third of the brain. It accounts for more brain tissue than the hindbrain or midbrain.

Midbrain: The midbrain is essentially the center section of the brain. It primarily processes hormonal activity and sensory integration.

Hindbrain: The hindbrain is the section of the brain closest to the spinal cord. It primarily controls functions related to basic life sustaining activities such as breathing and heart rate.

Medulla oblongata: The first section of the brain after the spinal cord. The medulla is generally associated with basic life sustaining functions (e.g., heart rate, breathing, blood pressure).

Cerebellum: The cerebellum is also known as the little brain because it looks like a brain itself. It has a primary role in the processing of balance and coordination.

Pons: The pons is an area of the hindbrain just above the medulla (first section of the brain beyond the spinal cord). The pons holds circuitry that controls sleep, breathing, hearing and balance.

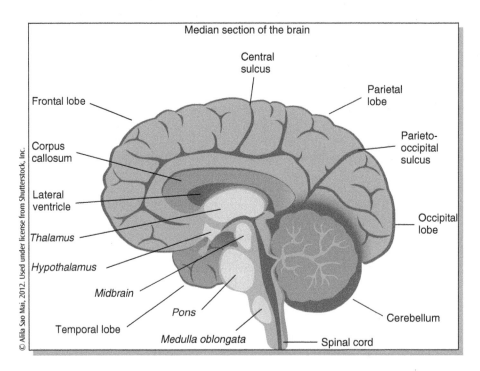

Median section of the brain

© Alila Sao Mai, 2012. Used under license from Shutterstock, Inc.

gross motor activity. Generally, animals with very good balance or motor coordination tend to have an especially large cerebellum. As we will see in later sections, the role of plasticity will cause a more highly developed cerebellum in human athletes. In contrast, most average folks have a smaller and less integrated cerebellum.

The third section of the hindbrain is the pons. The pons lies farther along the brainstem than the medulla. It can be easily identified because it has a bulbous appearance at the base of the brain. The pons contains an area referred to as the reticular formation that is very important to sleep and arousal (In this sense, arousal refers to general wakefulness). For example, if damage to the reticular formation were to occur, it could place a person into a permanent coma. The pons is also related to basic motor activity because it transfers information from the cerebellum (motor coordination) to the rest of the brain.

Midbrain

The midbrain contains a variety of areas that control sensation and sensory integration. The **reticular formation**, which extends from the hindbrain through the midbrain, is also responsible for the control of general arousal. Other than the reticular formation, the midbrain contains areas that help integrate visual and auditory information as well as distribute sensory information to the cortex. In general, the midbrain is involved in arousal, attention, muscular movement, and a variety of reflexes. One of the more interesting areas of the midbrain is related to the processing of pain information. In an area named the **periaqueductal gray area**, specific circuits control pain perception as well as the motor behaviors related to fighting and mating.

Forebrain

The forebrain is by far the largest section of the brain. It certainly occupies far more space than the hindbrain and midbrain put together. The forebrain is the primary neural real estate devoted to higher-order intellectual functioning. The primary controls come from the outer surface of the forebrain, an area referred to as the **cortex** (Cortex comes from the Latin work for "bark" such as the bark on a tree). In contrast, however, varieties of subcortical areas of the forebrain are important for overall functioning. Many of these subcortical areas are related to

Reticular formation: The reticular formation controls general arousal in the hindbrain.

Periaqueductal gray area: The periaqueductal gray area is a group of circuits in the midbrain that are involved in pain perception.

Cortex: The outer surface of the brain which is made from six layers of neurons.

motor activity, sensory processing, and the transfer of information from lower areas of the brain to the cerebral cortex. Of the many areas of the forebrain, we will focus on the four lobes of the brain's surface and four highly relevant subcortical areas.

Thalamus The thalamus gets its name from the Greek word meaning "inner chamber." The thalamus is located in the lower section of the forebrain just next to the basal ganglia (a group of areas related to motor behavior). In general, the thalamus is a subcortical region that receives sensory input from all locations of the body and then relays that information to a specific processing area of the brain's cortex. The one exception to this rule is related to the sense of smell, olfaction. Otherwise, all sensory input into your body from your skin, eyes, ears etc. are all relayed to the thalamus before being passed on to the location of primary analysis in the cortex. As such, the thalamus functions primarily as a central distributor of sensory information into the cerebral cortex. Consequently, the neurons coming from any particular area of the body will tend to cluster at specific locations on the thalamus. Damage to that one particular area, which may be a rather small area, will result in widespread sensory processing damage.

Thalamus: The thalamus is a centrally located area of the brain that helps to direct sensory input and motor output signals to their target locations.

Hypothalamus The hypothalamus is a structure that lies just below the thalamus. Its name, hypo-thalamus, identifies its location. The hypothalamus is a small structure; however, it has a great deal of importance. It influences the endocrine system (the hormonal system), and has a substantial influence over fighting, feeding, fleeing and mating (biologists often refer to these responses as the Four F's). The hypothalamus has a very complex interconnected structure. This might be expected given the breadth of responses it controls. In addition, the hypothalamus significantly influences the anterior pituitary gland, which is frequently called the master gland (the anterior pituitary gland resides next to the hypothalamus). The anterior pituitary gland has a substantial influence on many hormonal systems. In particular, it influences hormones related to the development and expression of reproductive organs and activities, respectively. As we will see later in this book, our hormonal activity at puberty, as well as hormonal activity related to emotional behavior, will often be influenced by the hypothalamus or glands that are influenced by the hypothalamus. As such, the hypothalamus is itself a very important structure and one that should catch the attention of any psychology student.

Hypothalamus: An area of the brain that is frequently associated with hormonal activity.

Endocrine gland: Any gland that releases hormones is called an endocrine gland. The endocrine system is another name for the hormonal system.

Limbic system The limbic system is not a compact location of the brain. Actually, it is a wide variety of circuits within the lower section of the forebrain all of which are related to emotional behavior. The limbic system has a variety of subcomponents, each of which has a particular job. Two of those components are well known in the field of psychology. They are the hippocampus and the amygdala.

The hippocampus is well known in the field of psychology because it is directly related to the memory system. In fact, most of the time that psychologists refer to the hippocampus they are referring to its memory function. It is highly integrated and has been associated with the formation, indexing and retrieval of memories. That is, the hippocampus does not actually store memories itself, but rather indexes the location in the brain where particular memories are accessed. Therefore, whenever a memory is retrieved, the hippocampus activates its indexing capacity and locates the places where the memories reside. Subsequently, it has a role in pulling memories from various locations into a single unit. For example, your memory of having watched a television program will require the hippocampus to locate the visual and audio components of that memory and

Limbic system: The section of the forebrain that processes emotions is the limbic system.

Hippocampus: The hippocampus is a section at the end of the limbic system involved in the formation and retrieval of memories.

Amygdala: A brain area that is generally associated with the processing of fear and aggression.

Post–traumatic stress disorder (PTSD): PTSD is a psychological disorder in which previous memories involving fear or aggression return as flashbacks to the patient.

Basal ganglia: An internal section of the brain involved in the processing of motor behavior. Destruction of cells in the basal ganglia is partly responsible for the symptoms of Parkinson's disease.

Fissures: The fissures are large grooves on the surface of the brain. They are contrasted with the small grooves of the brain called sulci.

Sulci: Sulci are the small fissures on the surface of the brain.

Frontal lobe: The most anterior lobe of the brain is the frontal lobe. It is most generally known for processing motor behavior as opposed to analyzing sensory input.

Parietal lobe: The parietal lobe is under the crown of your head. The parietal lobe has a primary function in analyzing the somatosenses (e.g., touch).

retrieve them in such a manner that they can be recombined into the event that was originally encoded. Damage to the hippocampus will most certainly create a variety of memory problems.

The hippocampus is well known to psychologists because it has a primary role in controlling memories with highly charged emotional components, in particular, fear and aggression. Fear and aggression are frequently correlated. Events that evoke fear are frequently the same events that evoke aggression. Moreover, the area of the brain that controls the expression of fear and aggression, the amygdala, is physically near the hippocampus. This relationship between memory formation and fear/aggression has been cited as a possible reason for the development of the psychiatric disorder called Post-Traumatic Stress Disorder (PTSD).

Basal ganglia The basal ganglia are a collection of subcortical nuclei in the forebrain. It has three main components, they are the globus pallidus (pale globe) the caudate nucleus (nucleus with a tail), and the putamen (the shell). Overall, the basal ganglia are involved in the control of movement. Oftentimes, psychologists refer to the basal ganglia when they discuss the deficits that result from Parkinson's disease. Parkinson's disease destroys dopamine containing neural cells throughout the basal ganglia. This cell loss accounts for some of the motor behavior impairments that are symptomatic of this disorder.

Four cortexes The outer surface of the brain is referred to as the cortex. Cortex means "bark" in Latin. The areas that lie across the surface of the brain are referred to as cortical areas. In contrast, however, areas that lie beneath the cortex are referred to as subcortical areas. That is, they are areas under the surface of the brain. The human cortex contains many convolutions. These convolutions are generally referred to as the wrinkles across the surface of the brain. These wrinkles produce a variety of bulges as well as grooves (in fact, one may think of them as mountains and valleys). The technical term for one of the mountains is gyrus. The valleys, however, have two names. The largest valleys are referred to as fissures and the smallest ones are referred to as sulci. The value of the brains convolutions is that it increases the overall surface area of the cortex. In fact, you can greatly increase the amount of brain material that fits inside the skull using a convoluted outer surface. To reason by analogy, if you lay down a 6 ft. X 6 ft. blanket and then simply wrinkle the blanket so that the overall surface on the floor is reduced, then you would get an idea of the value of convoluting the brain's surface. In fact, the convolutions of the brain approximately triple the total surface of the brain compared to if it had a smooth surface. The outer surface of the brain is approximately 2.5 ft.^{2} and the cortex is approximately 3 mm thick.

Across the surface of the brain, one can find a variety of functions that analyze sensory input and control motor output. For instance, some sections of the cortex only analyze sensory information and other areas control motor activity only. The type of motor activity may be general, such as controlling walking or the movements of your head and hands. In addition, they may also be specific, such as controlling your ability to speak—which requires specially integrated circuits that coordinate the movements of lung and tongue.

The cortex contains four lobes. Three of these lobes are devoted to sensory input and one is devoted to motor output. Starting from the anterior section of the brain—the part closest to the nose—and moving clockwise, the cortex contains the frontal, parietal, occipital and temporal lobes. The frontal lobe is the only lobe dedicated to controlling motor behavior. The remaining three lobes process sensory information. The type of sensory information that is analyzed in each lobe is specific to only one or two sensory systems. For example, the parietal lobe primarily analyzes touch, the occipital lobe primarily analyzes vision and the temporal lobe primarily analyzes hearing. Balance, smell and taste are analyzed in the temporal and parietal lobes, which gives us a few exceptions.

Within each lobe, there exists a primary and association cortex area. The primary cortex in each lobe is the area that first receives input from the sensory organs directing signals into the brain. In the case of the frontal lobe, the primary cortex is the last section that analyzes motor responses before they are sent out to the muscles. The association cortex areas of each lobe are generally identified as the places where memories reside. For example, any memory of a visual event should be held in the association cortex of the occipital lobe (the lobe analyzing vision). Any memory for auditory events should be stored in the association cortex of the temporal lobe (the lobe analyzing hearing). The association cortex for the frontal lobe holds memories for motor behavior. In other words, the motor patterns of how to reach out and pick something up or the memories needed to plan a new action are stored in this area.

Frontal Lobe The frontal lobe primarily controls motor behavior. It lies in front of the central sulcus and runs toward the front (anterior) of the brain. The back (posterior) section of the frontal lobe along the central sulcus is the location of the primary motor cortex. Because the frontal cortex controls motor behavior, its primary motor cortex is the final cortex location that analyzes motor responses before they are distributed to muscles throughout the body. The distribution of control of the muscles runs in an organized pattern across the primary motor cortex. Therefore, areas of the body that are near each other tend to be adjacently located along the primary motor cortex. It is known that the number of neural cells on a section of the primary motor cortex is associated with the number of motor neurons sent to that area of the body. This will either reflect the size of the body part or its relative importance with respect to motor control. For example, the lips are a relatively small area of the body but are highly perfused with motor neurons.

Parietal Lobe Moving behind the frontal lobe, the parietal lobe is found at the top back portion of the brain. It is primarily involved in the processing of

Occipital lobe: The posterior lobe of your brain is called the occipital lobe. Vision is analyzed in the occipital lobe.

Temporal lobe: The temporal lobe runs along the sides of the head near the temples.

Primary cortex area: Primary cortex areas are the first locations within the parietal, occipital and temporal lobes that sensory information is analyzed. Within the output system of the frontal lobe, the primary cortex area is the last place signals are analyzed before exiting the cortex.

Association cortex area: Any area secondary to the initial evaluation of sensory stimuli that is involved in the housing of memories.

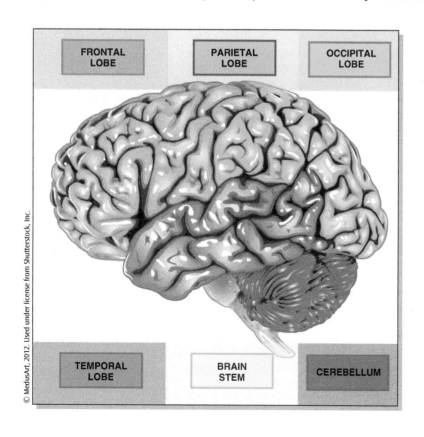

FRONTAL LOBE PARIETAL LOBE OCCIPITAL LOBE

TEMPORAL LOBE BRAIN STEM CEREBELLUM

© MedusArt, 2012. Used under license from Shutterstock, Inc.

somatosensory information (touch). The primary cortex for the parietal lobe resides along the posterior ridge of the central sulcus. In fact, the primary somatosensory cortex lies just across the central sulcus from the primary motor cortex. The primary motor and somatosensory cortexes are linked together across the central sulcus. The same distribution of body parts reflected in the primary motor cortex is reflected in the distribution of body parts in the primary somatosensory cortex. For instance, if you can locate an area on the primary motor cortex that controls the flexion of your leg, then you need only cross the central sulcus to locate the corresponding area of the primary somatosensory cortex that receives touch signals from that leg. It is known that the number of neural cells on a section of the primary somatosensory cortex is associated with the number of sensory neurons received from that area. This will either reflect the size of the body part or its relative importance with respect to sensory processing. For example, the hands are a relatively small body part but they send a proportionally large number of sensory neurons into the brain.

Occipital Lobe

The occipital lobe is located in the posterior section of the brain. Its primary function is the analysis of visual information. When visual information from the eye reaches the occipital lobe, it first enters the primary visual cortex. This area does most of the initial processing of vision before the more integrated components of vision are analyzed. Those more integrated components involve the processing of motion, advanced color analysis, shading and perceptual modifications based upon memory. The primary visual cortex is located in a strip that stretches laterally across the back of the brain in approximately the center of the occipital lobe. It is easy to locate because it runs along the calcarine fissure, a primary anatomical location of the brain.

Temporal Lobe

The temporal lobe lies along the lower sides of your brain. More specifically, it lies below the frontal lobe and in front of the occipital lobe. It has gotten its name because it resides along the temples of your skull. The temporal lobe is most closely associated with the processing of auditory information. This should be easy to remember because the sides of your head are where your ears are located. The primary auditory cortex for the temporal lobe exists in a strip along the side of the brain. It cannot be easily identified visually because the primary auditory cortex lies within the lateral fissure, which, of course, if covered by the folds of the fissure itself.

Specialized circuits

Language Center The ability to communicate through language is one of many unique aspects of human behavior. Language communication typically occurs verbally, however it can occur through any variety of means. For instance, language that is written, spoken, sung or used in various codes such as semaphore or Morse code, all involve the application of language. That the use of language is unique in humans requires us to specify the particular location in the brain that controls this response pattern.

Language is spread across the frontal and temporal lobes and therefore cross the lateral fissure. For approximately 90 percent of all humans, language is located in the left hemisphere. For the remaining 10 percent of all individuals, it is in the right hemisphere. The presence of language in the right hemisphere is a natural variation on brain anatomy and does not reflect the presence of any neurological deficit.

The presence of language in only one hemisphere reflects the general rule of lateralization. That is, some anatomical circuits tend to reside only on one side of the brain. The left hemisphere, which tends to hold the language center, is known to be the location where sequenced events are analyzed. Sequenced events are any series of events that need to be processed in sequential order so they can be decoded properly. It appears the capacity of the left hemisphere to analyze sequences is related to language use that always involves analyzing stimulus sequences (grammar). Consider if you took this sentence and randomly re-arranged the words. Do you think you might understand what I was trying to convey to you? How do you think you would understand a lecture if all the words from the instructor were made in random order?

Well over a century's worth of work has been applied to the study of the biology of language. In fact, medical doctors have been systematically evaluating speech impairments after stroke and head injury since the early 1800's. As people have acquired head injuries that have resulted in speech impairments, medical pathologists have been able to associate those symptoms with specific areas of brain tissue damage during autopsies on those same patients. Doctors in the mid-19th century uncovered two general areas related to language function.

The first area is referred to as Broca's area. It was named after Pierre Broca, the French physician who first discovered it along the frontal cortex bordering the lateral fissure. Damage that occurs to Broca's area results in deficits of speech production. The ability to produce sounds, however, is connected to the ability to comprehend sounds as well. Therefore, although Broca's aphasics seem to understand language fully, they actually lose some of the ability to process grammar and mix up the subject and object of sentences. For instance, if one heard the sentence "The dog chased the cat" they might understand that a cat chased a dog.

The second area, named Wernicke's area, was named after the 19th century German physician who discovered it along the posterior section of the temporal lobe bordering the lateral fissure. Wernicke's area is related to language comprehension. Wernicke's aphasics have difficulty understanding the meaning of speech and, in extreme cases, making any normal speech other than gibberish. Given the difficulty in speech comprehension, these patients may not be able to understand what is said to them or be able to communicate effectively back to the speaker.

Facial Recognition Center It appears that the ability to detect faces comes from a specialized circuit at the end of the visual analysis system in humans. This area is referred to as the fusiform face area. Visual processing begins in the occipital lobe, however, extensions of circuits lead to the temporal lobe at the base of the brain. This is the location of the fusiform face area. In rare cases in which the fusiform face area is damaged, an individual will develop a neurological disorder called prosopagnosia. The symptoms of prosopagnosia show that an individual cannot distinguish by memory one human face from another. Although the individual can distinguish among the various facial details such as the nose, lips and eyes, the ability to pull each of those separate stimuli into a cohesive whole is lost. In many cases, individuals with prosopagnosia will come to recognize others by the sound of their voice, the sound that they make when they walk, or their clothes. If, however, two people had similar physical features and were dressed the same, an individual with prosopagnosia might confuse them unless a non-visual cue could distinguish them. Such a cue might be their perfume or their characteristic physical gestures.

Broca's area:
An area of the language center that manages speech production.

Wernicke's area:
Wernicke's area is an area of the language center that manages language comprehension.

Fusiform face area:
The fusiform face area is an area of the brain that received its name because it is active while recognizing human faces.

Prosopagnosia:
Prosopagnosia is a neurological disorder in which the patient can no longer identify individuals by their face. Patients with prosopagnosia cannot detect or remember human faces.

© Andi Berger, 2009. Used under license from Shutterstock, Inc.

Phantom limb:
A phantom limb is the perception of the presence of a limb that had been amputated. Sometimes individuals born without limbs also have phantom limb sensations.

Phantom Limb Sensations Whether a person was born with a missing limb or lost it during their life, they may experience phantom limb sensations. A phantom limb sensation is one in which the afflicted person reports feeling the presence of the limb that is not there. Patients with these sensations htxave reported a wide variety of sensations such as pain, pressure, cold or warm temperatures, wetness and itching.

The neuroscientific explanation for phantom limb sensations is that the proximal nerve ending—the part remaining after amputation—develops a neuroma. A neuroma is a nodule at the end of the nerve. It is believed that this nodule sends signals back to the brain circuits that analyze sensory stimuli from that area of the body. Therefore, the pre-existing brain circuitry analyzes the sensations as coming from an existing limb. Despite the person's personal knowledge that their limb is gone, their brain continues to function in the matter for which it was designed originally.

This reflects a limitation of brain circuitry that you may not be aware exists. Regardless of the location of the original signal into the brain, a finger or a neuroma from a nerve that once led to a finger, the signals that reach the sensory analysis circuitry will always give one the perception that it is detecting the finger because that is what that circuit was designed to do. Moreover, you could go into the brain directly and stimulate the circuit for pain from the finger and it will give you the same result.

Mirror cells:
Mirror neurons refer to a series of circuits within the forebrain that allow one to duplicate the behavior of others. Learning by observation would be impossible without mirror neurons.

Mirror Neurons During the 1990's, research showed that an area of the premotor cortex (frontal lobe) in the brains of monkeys became active when they watched others performing grasping or holding tasks. The investigators referred to the cells in this area of the brain as mirror cells. Further research showed that these cells play a primary role with respect to the animal's ability to learn through observation.

Similar circuits reside within the human brain as well. Brain scans indicate that mirror cells become active when humans watch and imitate the behavior of other people. In neurological disorders in which individuals express difficulty copying the response patterns of others, such as in autism, there is reduced mirror neuron activity.

Blindsight A unique characteristic of our visual system became apparent as some individuals developed damage to the right parietal lobe of the brain. Damage to this area may produce a neurological disorder referred to as **blindsight**. Blindsight is a disorder in which a person has the ability to see, at least moderately, but is unaware of their ability to see. People afflicted with blindsight will state honestly that they are completely blind. In contrast, however, if you ask a blindsight patient to reach out and take an object with their hand, they will be able to do so despite the fact that their perception is that they simply guessed correctly.

The reason a person can see but not be aware that they can see results from humans having two visual systems, a mammalian visual system and an older reptilian visual system. The mammalian visual system is connected to our language center and when it is used, the things that we see are routed to the language center so that we can talk about them. Being able to discuss our experiences certainly constitutes a conscious awareness of them. The reptilian visual system does not have this connection to the language center, therefore, things that it conveys to the brain are not in their consciousness—which typically requires language.

Split Brains As described earlier, the left and right hemispheres of the brain have specialized functions despite the fact that they primarily exhibit similar functional properties. Because the left hemisphere is connected to language processing, it has been referred to as the "dominant" hemisphere, in relation to the non-language right hemisphere. Once, however, surgeons began to split the tissue connecting the left and right hemispheres as a treatment for severe—potentially deadly—seizure disorders, it was found that the right hemisphere is not submissive to its left partner. The story of surgically splitting the brain between its hemispheres begins in 1961.

Two neurosurgeons in Los Angeles, Philip Vogel and Joseph Bogen, suggested that some forms of severe epilepsy are instigated by the spread of electrical activity between the left and right hemispheres. Therefore, they concluded, if the brain was split by cutting the **corpus callosum**, they would be able to reduce the severity of the seizures. The corpus callosum is a wideband of axon fibers that run between the left and right hemispheres of the brain. It is responsible for integrating action potentials from the left and right hemispheres. By cutting the corpus callosum to minimize the spread of an epileptic attack, the neurosurgeons would also eliminate the cross-hemisphere signaling that is part of normal cognitive activity. Prior research on ablating the corpus callosum in animals indicated that little or no disruption of normal behavior should result from the surgery. This gave them the opportunity to apply it to the human patients with such severe epileptic activity that they might die if there was no application of a new safe and effective treatment.

The results of operations on humans indicate that few side effects are present. In fact, the patients seem relatively normal upon waking from surgery. Typically, patients who receive the **split-brain** operation live relatively normal lives. In fact, meeting one of these individuals is unlikely to result in you recognizing any odd behavior on their part. Therefore, cutting the corpus callosum does not initially appear to produce any serious side effects. It was not until further psychological testing conducted on these patients showed the cognitive deficits in their post-operative lives.

When the corpus callosum is severed in the split-brain operation, the optic chiasm remains intact because it is lies beneath the corpus callosum and is specific to vision, not the general distribution of signals from the left and right hemispheres. The optic chiasm helps the left and right eyes send visual

Blindsight: Blindsight is a disorder in which a person perceives her or himself blind and is unaware that they have a limited visual ability.

© Corel

This painting was made by arranging images of flowers. If a split–brain patient saw it with only their left brain, then they would only recognize the flowers. If only their right brain detected the image, then they would see the face, but not the flowers.

Corpus callosum: The area of neurons that connect the left and right hemispheres of the brain is called the corpus callosum. It is made from myelinated axons crossing between the two hemispheres.

Split brain: A split brain is one that has had the corpus callosum surgically severed thereby producing two independent brain hemispheres.

information to the opposite hemisphere. It lies beneath the corpus callosum and transfers visual information from the left and right side of each eye into the left and right hemispheres, respectively. More precisely, the left side of each eye sends information into the left hemisphere. The right side of each eye sends information into the right hemisphere. Only the sides of the eye closest to the nose need to cross over to the opposite hemisphere.

Early research began to show that any information in the left visual field of a split-brain patient would be sent to the right side of each eye. Consequently, if a patient were asked to stare at a "+" at the center of a computer screen, then words could be presented on the left and right sides of the screen that would be sent to the right and left sides of their hemispheres respectively. For example, suppose the words BULL and FROG appear on the left and right sides of the computer screen respectively. This will cause the word BULL, which is in the left visual field, to be sent for processing in the right hemisphere. In contrast, the word FROG, which is in the right visual field, would be sent to the left hemisphere for processing. Because language typically resides in the left hemisphere, the subject would recognize they had seen the word FROG but not that they had seen the word BULL. That is, there would be a conscious awareness of having seen FROG but no awareness in language of the word BULL. This, however, does not mean that the word BULL did not affect the subject. To assess the effect of the stimulus BULL, one needs to use another testing procedure.

To show that the word BULL had influenced the subject's behavior, one could ask the person to use their left hand to point to a series of words to determine which one they had seen. Keep in mind, however, that the patient in this case will indicate that they had not seen any other word other than FROG. When shown a series of words, or a series of pictures, a split-brain patient could use their left hand to accurately point to the word BULL. Why would a split-brain patient have to use their left hand? The reason is the right hemisphere controls the left side of the body. Therefore, any processing that occurs in the right hemisphere will be reflected by actions in the left side of the body. That is, the left hand could be used to point to the word that was processed by the right hemisphere. Even though the split-brain patient is not aware of having seen the word BULL they will use their left hand to accurately point to a picture of a BULL or the word BULL.

Spinal nerve:
Spinal nerves are any bundled set of nerves that exit the spinal cord at the junctions between vertebrae and variously extend into the trunk and limbs.

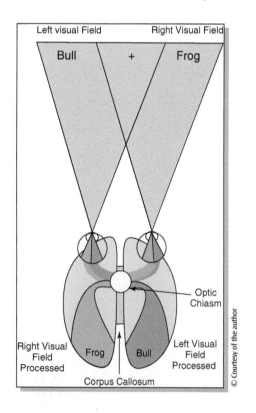

Peripheral Nervous System

The previous discussions were about various sections of the central nervous system. The CNS, however, is only one part of a two-part nervous system. The other section of the nervous system is the peripheral nervous system. The PNS primarily sends information from sensory receptors to the brain and from the brain to the muscle. It does not serve a primary role in thinking; however, it does make up the pathways for basic spinal reflexes that do influence behavior.

Spinal Nerves

The **spinal nerves** are nerve bundles that branch off the spinal cord and navigate the trunk and limbs of the body. They extend from both sides of thirty-one vertebrae along the spinal cord. The pathways of the spinal nerves branch similarly to the way in which I discussed the branching of neurons in the past. That is, the branches start as a thick stalk. As they travel through the body, they branch off and become smaller at each division. The spinal nerves establish the primary pathway for which sensory receptors in the skin send information into the brain. They are also the main pathway for motor signals from the brain to the muscles.

Autonomic and Somatic Nervous Systems

The peripheral nervous system has two main branches. They are the somatic and autonomic nervous systems. The somatic nervous system is involved in the relay of sensory information into the central nervous system as well as the control of muscular movements. The other branch of the peripheral nervous system is called the autonomic nervous system. The autonomic nervous system is designed to regulate smooth muscle activity as well as that of the heart and glands. Smooth muscle is found in the skin where it controls piloerection, in the blood vessels and in the eyes. It is also found in the gastrointestinal tract, bladder and other internal organs. The autonomic nervous system has two anatomically distinct sections: the sympathetic division and the parasympathetic division. The sympathetic division controls the activity of the body during periods of excitement. The parasympathetic division controls the activity of the body during periods of relaxation.

Sympathetic and Parasympathetic Nervous Systems

The sympathetic division of the autonomic nervous system controls preparatory responses for when someone is excited or under stress. For example, at a time

Somatic nervous system: The somatic nervous system is one subdivision of the peripheral nervous system. It controls motor behavior.

Autonomic nervous system: The portion of the nervous system that controls glandular activity and muscles that are not connected to the skeletal system. For example, it regulates the volume of blood in the digestive system, dilates pupils and affects hormonal releases.

Sympathetic nervous system: The sympathetic nervous system is one of two subsections of the autonomic nervous system. The sympathetic branch becomes active during the fight or flight syndrome (compare with the parasympathetic nervous system).

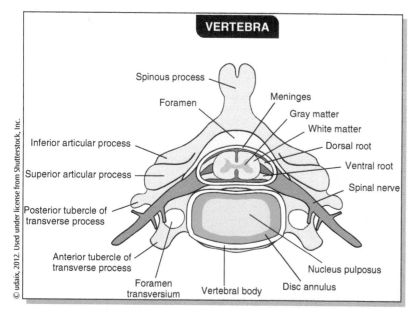

VERTEBRA

Spinous process
Foramen
Meninges
Gray matter
White matter
Inferior articular process
Dorsal root
Ventral root
Superior articular process
Spinal nerve
Posterior tubercle of transverse process
Anterior tubercle of transverse process
Nucleus pulposus
Foramen transversium
Vertebral body
Disc annulus

© udaix, 2012. Used under license from Shutterstock, Inc.

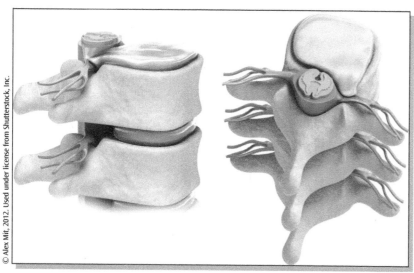

© Alex Mit, 2012. Used under license from Shutterstock, Inc.

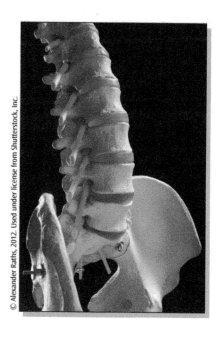

© Alexander Raths, 2012. Used under license from Shutterstock, Inc.

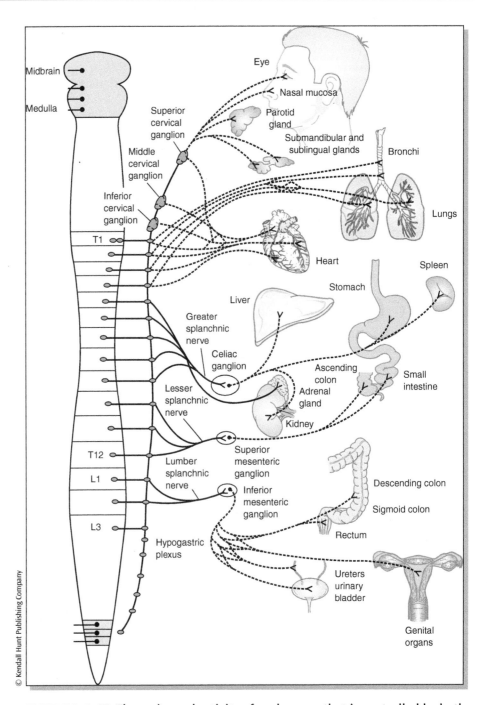

FIGURE 2.6 ▨ The reciprocal activity of each organ that is controlled by both the sympathetic and parasympathetic nervous systems.

when you are almost in an automobile accident, see a bear in the woods, or even run a great distance, your sympathetic nervous system becomes active. It supports the release of adrenaline (epinephrine) and increases the flow of blood to skeletal muscles. The sympathetic nervous system is attached to the spinal cord through approximately the center one-third of the spinal cord. The branches of the sympathetic nervous system attach themselves to the organs needed to control stress responses. For example, it is connected to the eyes for dilating the pupils, the lungs for breathing faster, the heart for beating faster and the pancreas for releasing more energy-producing glucose. One common effect of the sympathetic nervous system that everyone has experienced is the "butterflies" that one gets in their stomach while nervous. The reason for this is

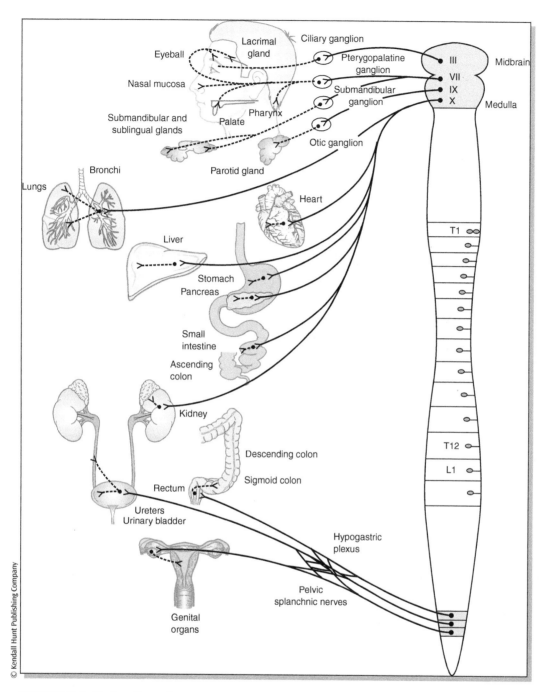

FIGURE 2.6 ■ (continued).

that as the blood is redirected to the extremities and adrenaline is released, the digestive system is slowed down and causes a feeling of sickness.

The **parasympathetic division** of the nervous system connects with the spinal cord in its upper and lower thirds. It controls the state of the internal organs appropriate for relaxation. During periods of relaxation, blood is moved away from the limbs and back to the internal organs where it can help in digestion and other internal operations. There is a reduced need for glucose and the body will make more effort to reserve its stores for when it is needed later. Both the sympathetic and parasympathetic nervous systems actively exert their influence on their branch of the autonomic nervous system. Therefore, the perceptual duality of excitement through relaxation that you experience is

Parasympathetic nervous system: The autonomic nervous system can be subdivided into two sections; the sympathetic nervous system and the parasympathetic nervous system. The parasympathetic nervous system controls the operation of your internal organs when you are at rest (compare with the sympathetic nervous system).

Gene: The gene is a single section along a DNA molecule.

Chromosome: A chromosome is a folded string of DNA visible to the naked eye.

Deoxyribonucleic acid (DNA): A very long double helix molecule created by stringing together a series of genes.

Functional unit of heredity: The functional unit of heredity is a name given to describe one of the primary functions of a gene. It obtained that name because genes cannot be changed without affecting their function.

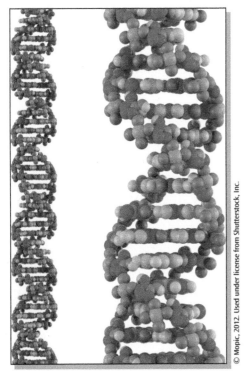

© Mopic, 2012. Used under license from Shutterstock, Inc.

actually the combined effect of two divisions of the autonomic nervous system actively competing with each other.

GENETICS

The previous discussions of the nervous system described its anatomical design. That design, however, must be encoded into the genes so that all members of a species begin life with a similar anatomical structure. The location and function of genetic material is the topic of the following section. The first issue we will discuss is the location of the genes in the body.

All the cells in your body contain your entire genetic code. In the nervous system specifically, the **genes** are located within the soma. This makes the soma a place of special importance for biopsychologists. The soma contains thousands of substances of which we will discuss only a few. One of the most pervasive is the cytoplasm, the fluid in which all the cell's contents float. The internal structure of the soma contains a nucleus. A nucleus is a sphere containing small pores that allow substances to move in and out of it. Within the nucleus resides the complete set of genes that include the basic blueprint for creating you.

If one were to look at the inside of a nucleus with a powerful microscope, then the complete set of **chromosomes** that are responsible for producing your physical and psychological characteristics could be seen. The chromosomes float around in the cytoplasm of the nucleus until they are biochemically signaled to initiate their activity. You have no doubt seen images of chromosomes before; they look like squiggly little X's that are lined up in images within the pages of biology textbooks. The X that you see is actually two copies of the same chromosome connected at the center by a structure known as the centromere. Each copy of the chromosome may not be identical to its partner; however, they are far more similar than dissimilar.

If you were to take that X-shaped chromosome and remove the centromere, you would then have two separate copies of it. By taking a close look at one of its copies, you would see that it looks like a long string folded very tightly. That the chromosome is folded so tightly, allows it to fit into a smaller space. Unraveling the entire chromosome shows that what once fit into the nucleus of the cell is now a lengthy string. It also moves us toward seeing the basic structure of the molecule itself.

The unraveled chromosome may only look like a gelatinous string to us now. In fact, that tiny string is visible by the naked eye (uncovering the chromosomes from a plant cell is a common laboratory experiment in General Biology class). If you were able to view that chromosomal string at a higher magnification, then you would be able to see the characteristic double helix structure of **deoxyribonucleic acid** (DNA).

The chromosome itself is made from DNA and DNA gets its name from its chemical structure. If you specify particular areas along the DNA strand, you will be able to identify specific genes. Genes are subsections along the entire chromosomal strand that have their locations identified by special codes at either end of the gene. They are referred to as the **functional unit of heredity** because the genes cannot be added to or subtracted from. If genes are changed at all, then they do not produce the same protein that they originally did. On a practical basis, they are not the same gene that you started with.

The primary role of genes is to produce proteins. This is a very important point. As a psychology student, you will need to understand how a gene that codes for a protein can come to control some relevant complex social behavior such as anxiety, risk-taking or memory. An answer to this question will take considerably more reading than just in this chapter. It will start to make sense once we connect the biological and environmental foundations of human behavior.

If you take the entire chromosome and stretch it out in front of you, then different sized sections along its length will constitute the genes for any of the proteins needed by your body. For example, a specific section of the chromosome may produce human growth hormone, another section may control your eye color and another may be for creating your fingernails. The specific location of each gene across your 46 chromosomes is placed in a consistent location across all human beings.

Once you have located the genes, you may wonder how they encode information or manage useful biological functions. The following section will describe just those issues. As you will come to understand, the gene itself is not the protein that performs a function somewhere inside your body. Rather, the genes are instructions that first need to be copied before they can have their instructions produce the needed protein. The needed protein is then sent to the required location to perform its job. The genetic copying and production processes are described in the next section.

Transcription and Translation

When the body is in need of some protein such as a neurotransmitter, hormone or substance to support new synaptic connections, the gene for that substance

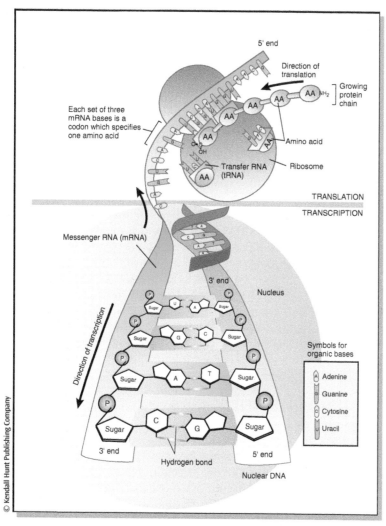

The general process of transcription and translation

Transcription: Transcription is the process by which a gene is decoded within the nucleus of the soma. For the gene to be converted into a useful protein, the process of translation must then take place.

Translation: Translation is the process by which a decoded gene is moved outside the nucleus and decoded by ribosomes into a protein. The translation process follows the transcription process.

Skeletal muscles: Skeletal muscles are those muscles attached to the skeletal system. They are the muscles that allow us to move around our bodies. The somatic branch of the peripheral nervous system controls skeletal muscles. They are also referred to as striated muscle because they have visual striations to their appearance.

Smooth muscles: Smooth muscles are those controlled by the autonomic branch of the peripheral nervous system. They are in various locations around the body such as the arteries, bladder, iris of the eye, intestines and uterus. Their anatomy contrasts with striated skeletal muscle.

Cardiac muscle: Cardiac muscle is another name for your heart.

will have to be copied in the first of a series of steps. Second, the gene's copy will be converted into the needed substance. Following its construction, the substance will be sent to the location that it is needed. The beginning of the process for copying a gene requires a section of the chromosome to be unraveled given the fact that the chromosome is folded so tightly. The unraveling and gene copying process is called transcription.

Once the section of the chromosome containing the gene is unraveled, the section of DNA containing the gene will be split apart. That is, the chromosomal double helix that constitutes the gene will be biochemically unzipped so that the two strands making the double helix are separated like the two strands of a zipper. The opened zipper of DNA will then begin to create a copy of itself that will become the set of instructions needed to produce the actual protein. This copied set of instructions is called messenger ribonucleic acid (mRNA). Once a copy of the gene has been created, the strands of the DNA will reattach its ends together and return to its tightly packed state until it is once again signaled to produce a protein. Remember that the chromosomes are housed within the nucleus, so the copied gene needs to exit the nucleus through a pore before protein production begins. The second primary step in making a protein is referred to as translation.

Translation begins outside of the nucleus. It is the process in which the copied gene—an instruction—is translated into the protein that the instructions dictate. Once outside the nucleus, the protein's blueprint are approached by a substance called a ribosome. The ribosome will take a primary role in getting the new protein formed. Once the translation process is complete, a new protein exists. It will then be sent to the proper location for use. Some of the proteins that are relevant to psychology are neurotransmitters (which stay within the cell), hormones (which are sent into the blood supply) and substances to create new cellular connections (which are sent to the axons or dendrites).

MUSCLES

Overall, I have described the nervous system as essentially an input-output system. Sensory input leads to brain processing which ultimately leads to motor output. The primary job of the brain may be conceptualized as a process to control movement. Moreover, many of its other functions such as sensory processing or planning, are simply other actions that lead to bodily movement as well. Therefore, it is worth trying to understand how and where these output signals are going. Of course, the output is going to the muscles. The main question is how does the brain control muscular activity? As we will see in the next sections, there are three basic forms of muscle in your body. The first is skeletal muscle that controls the actions needed to move us around in our environment. Secondly, there is smooth muscle that is related to the operation of internal organs and glands. Finally, there is cardiac muscle. Obviously, the use of cardiac muscle is important; however, in the field of psychology it has only a small influence on our psychological processes.

Muscular Activity as Output

Skeletal Muscle

Skeletal muscles have gotten that name because they are the muscles that move our skeletons. Most skeletal muscles are attached to each end of a bone they serve. There are few exceptions, such as your eye muscles. There are two primary forms of activity from muscles. They are the flexion and extension movements. The contraction of a flexor muscle produces flexion. Flexion refers to the drawing in of a limb. Extension is produced by contracting an extensor muscle. Extension is

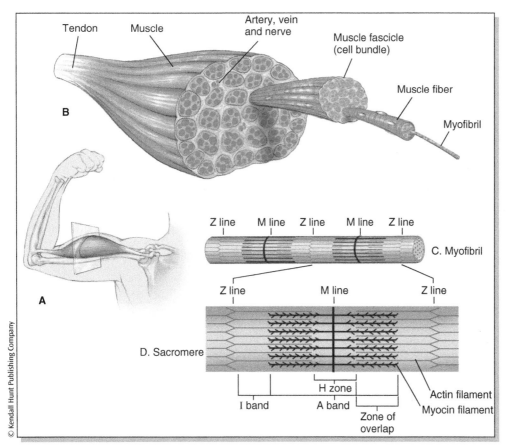

A cross section of striated muscle.

when a limb moves in an outward motion. Flexion and extension muscles tend to be on opposite sides of the bone they serve. One common example is the bicep and tricep muscles. Therefore, whether flexion or extension occurs, muscles are always contracting. They simply contract different muscles to produce an inward or outward movement of a limb.

Each skeletal muscle is comprised of two types of muscle fibers, the extrafusal muscle fibers and the intrafusal muscle fibers. Extrafusal muscle fibers are served by the output signals of the alpha motor neurons. The alpha motor neurons extend from spinal nerves to the muscle and exert the control emanating from the brain. Control of extrafusal muscle fibers gives muscles their motive force—their ability to move.

When muscles contract they make use of a neuromuscular junction. A neuromuscular junction is the location where an axon from the nervous system junctions with the muscle. Neuromuscular junctions universally use the neuro-transmitter acetylcholine. Its action at the synapse produces a depolarization and causes a contraction of the muscle itself.

The intrafusal muscle fibers are specialized sensory organs that provide feedback to the brain. Axons attached to the intrafusal muscle fibers send the brain feedback with respect to how much the muscle is stretched. Overall, the muscles are served by brain signals that contract a muscle and other feedback signals that let the brain know how much the muscle is being stretched or contracted. Other feedback cells send signals to the brain that determine the location and movement of your limbs in space. These feedback cells are part of the kinesthetic system. They are not processed well in an alcohol-intoxicated person and therefore serve as a valued field sobriety test for police suspecting someone driving while intoxicated.

Acetylcholine (ACh): The primary neuromuscular neurotransmitter is acetylcholine. It is also present in the brain.

Kinesthetic system: The kinesthetic system is made from sensory neurons in your muscles that allow you to determine where your body parts are without the addition of sight.

Smooth and Cardiac Muscle

The two remaining forms of muscle are smooth muscle and cardiac muscle. Neither smooth nor cardiac muscles are directly involved in moving our bodies. They do have important functions, however, that support normal living. Smooth muscles are involved in pupil constriction, eye lens adjustment and piloerection. They are typically affected by hormonal activity and generally reflect a person's emotional state (recall that the emotion-controlling limbic system influences the endocrine system). The influence of the hormonal system on the autonomic muscles is part of the basis for the traditional lie detector test, the polygraph.

The use of the original polygraph test was that if a guilty person were asked questions about a crime they committed it would make them worry and that would be evidenced in their autonomic responses. The polygraph does not work very well despite its continued use by law enforcement. In fact, biofeedback, a form of psychological therapy designed to help a person overcome anxiety problems, trains a person how to control their autonomic responses to help them feel better. If anyone can train their autonomic responses then the lie detector test can be manipulated to give inaccurate results.

Cardiac muscle is the final muscle type discussed. It is primarily related to pumping blood through our vascular system. Without cardiac muscle, the distribution of oxygen would not occur and cells throughout our body would die very quickly. Cardiac muscle is different from skeletal or smooth muscle because it produces its own pacemaker-like activity. That is, cardiac muscle produces its own signal for contraction without the need for brain activity. In fact, in hunting communities it is commonly known that by removing the heart from a recently

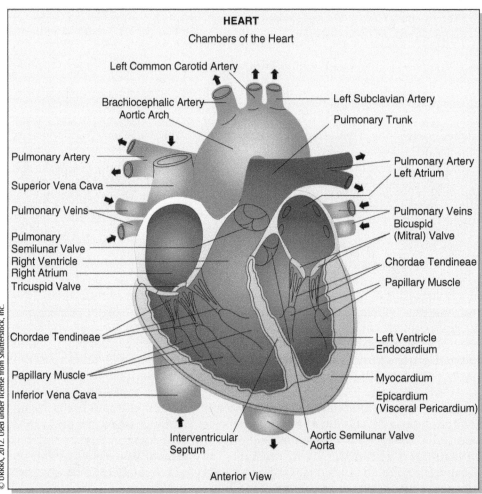

HEART

Chambers of the Heart

Left Common Carotid Artery

Brachiocephalic Artery
Aortic Arch

Left Subclavian Artery

Pulmonary Trunk

Pulmonary Artery

Pulmonary Artery
Left Atrium

Superior Vena Cava

Pulmonary Veins

Pulmonary Veins
Bicuspid
(Mitral) Valve

Pulmonary
Semilunar Valve

Right Ventricle

Right Atrium

Tricuspid Valve

Chordae Tendineae

Papillary Muscle

Chordae Tendineae

Left Ventricle
Endocardium

Papillary Muscle

Myocardium

Inferior Vena Cava

Epicardium
(Visceral Pericardium)

Interventricular
Septum

Aortic Semilunar Valve
Aorta

Anterior View

killed animal you will be able to see it beat on its own. This is often used for dramatic flair in many horror films.

Spinal Cord Reflexes

Although many behaviors are controlled by the brain, a number of basic reflexive responses are controlled by circuits that begin in the limbs, travel to the spinal cord and then return to the muscle near the location of the original stimulus. These circuits establish reflexes. There are two basic reflexive responses in humans. These responses are the monosynaptic stretch reflex, and the polysynaptic reflex. In the following section, we will look at each reflex system briefly to get an idea of some of the most basic forms of human behavior.

Monosynaptic Stretch Reflex

The monosynaptic stretch reflex is oftentimes considered to be one of the simplest reflex pathways in the nervous system. One of the most common examples of it is the patellar tendon reflex. The patellar tendon reflex requires one to sit on a table with the lower portions of the legs hanging lightly. Then, someone taps the patellar tendon just below the kneecap and your leg jerks forward. The tapping stimulus causes your quadriceps muscle on the top of your thigh to contract. This makes your leg jerk forward. Electrophysiological measures indicate that it takes approximately 15 ms between the tapping stimulus and the leg reflex response. That is much too short to involve any brain activity because signals would then have to run through the spinal cord, travel through brain circuits for processing and then return from the leg. Such an extensive circuit would require additional time.

> Monosynaptic stretch reflex: The monosynaptic stretch reflex is a basic spinal reflex that helps maintain one's balance based upon the stretching of calf muscles in the leg.

The basic role of the monosynaptic stretch reflex is to produce a rapid response to a simple stimulus. With respect to the patellar tendon reflex, its use is to maintain one's balance. While you are standing, the patellar tendon reflex maintains components of balance and posture. As you begin to lean to one side the muscles of the leg are stretched which elicit a reflexive contraction that regains your balance. Many people are not aware of this reflex. If, however, you carefully watch people standing still you will easily notice they lean from side to side. Oftentimes, the individual swaying is not even aware of it. Moreover, we oftentimes shift our weight so frequently and are so focused on other things (such as talking to someone) that we are not aware of how much we sway while we are standing. This leaning and righting is part of the patellar tendon reflex. If this reflex were not present, the only control for balance would come from our vestibular system, which resides in the inner ear. Control from such a distant location would require a great deal more processing time given the length of the neural pathway needed to be traveled. Therefore, we would more easily fall over.

Polysynaptic Reflexes

The monosynaptic reflex arc is the only known reflex that works through a single synaptic connection in the spinal cord. Obviously, that is how it got its name. In contrast, however, most basic reflexive responses require multiple synaptic connections. Two common examples are the finger withdrawal reflex to painful stimuli and the ejaculation of semen.

Polysynaptic reflexes control a wide variety of reflexive responses. A practical application of their function involves the counteracting agonist-antagonist muscle contractions that occur in pairs of opposing muscles. As mentioned previously, pairs of muscles often work together such as the bicep and tricep muscles. If a muscle contracts, then the opposing muscle needs to relax and stretch. The neuroanatomical basis for this activity comes from the arrangement of neural connections in the spinal cord where the afferent and efferent nerves

> Polysynaptic reflexes: Polysynaptic reflexes come from complex spinal circuitry that is often involved in flexion and extension motor behaviors.

of those two muscles junction. If the flexion and extension functions of opposing muscles did not work together, then both muscles might contract at the same time. This, of course, would cause the arm to become rigid. Although these are reflexive responses, they may be modified by brain activity. That is, any memory stored in the brain may exert its influence from it stored location, down into the spinal cord and modify the reflexive response at the location where the afferent and efferent neurons junction in the spinal cord.

Control of Movement by the Brain

There are varieties of basic reflexive responses. A rapidly stretched muscle will trigger the monosynaptic stretch reflex, standing will trigger a posture reflex and an object moving quickly toward your face will elicit a startle reflex. These basic reflexes do not modify themselves very well and they are not produced through learning but rather are there from the existing anatomical architecture present at birth. Most of our social behavior, however, develops through learned behavior.

Learned actions are stored in the frontal lobe. These memories are modified by the primary motor cortex before they are sent to the muscles they control. You can observe the presence of the brain systems combined with the spinal reflex systems at the same time. For example, a person can walk, talk, chew gum and make hand motions all at the same time. To be able to do so requires the initiation of learned behavior (hand gestures), specialized circuits (language) and reflexive responses (postural control).

Organization of the Motor Cortex

Somatotopic organization: Somatotopic organization refers to the organizational layout of the primary motor cortex and the primary somatosensory cortex. The arrangement of areas along these cortexes changes similarly with movements across the body.

The primary motor cortex lies at the posterior section of the frontal lobe. It is organized in a very systematic fashion that is referred to as somatotopic organization. Somatotopic organization refers to the distribution of body parts mapped across the motor cortex. For each body part mapped on the primary motor cortex, a cluster of neural cells control the movements of that body part. If one were to stimulate experimentally the motor cortex area of your arm, then your arm would make some movement.

On the primary motor cortex, many neurons need to be active to control most basic forms of behavior. For any specific behavior, the response will begin once a majority of the systems neurons becomes stimulated. Subsequently, the entire system will begin to operate. Neuroscientists have been able to use single cell recordings to predict whether an overt response will occur a few seconds after the motor neurons begin to come online. Measurements show their increasing activity before the overt response is evident. In short, by measuring the neural activity in the motor cortex one can predict the presence of a behavior about 2 seconds before it actually occurs!

Previous discussions of the brain's lobes indicated that the frontal lobe is devoted to motor behavior. The association area of the frontal cortex is where memories for motor responses are stored. Because the frontal lobe stores output information, the primary motor cortex is the final cortex area traversed before the signals are sent out to the muscles they control. In contrast, the other three lobes store sensory memories. In the three sensory lobes, sensory input first reaches the primary cortex and then moves on to the association cortex. Therefore, the primary cortexes of the sensory and motor lobes work in opposite order.

As signals are sent out of the primary motor cortex, they undergo a final modification from the primary somatosensory cortex. Remember, the primary somatosensory cortex lies just across the central sulcus from the primary motor cortex. In fact, the somatotopic organization of the motor cortex corresponds in a one to one relation to the organization of the primary somatosensory cortex.

That is, if you can find the location for sensory information from your lips then you need only cross the central sulcus to find the area that controls the motor output for the lips.

METHODOLOGICAL TECHNIQUES

In general, the field of biology has generated many ways in which to measure living and dead tissue of the brain. Some of the oldest techniques, such as ablation, are still used today. They are used, however, in a much more delicate manner than they were one hundred years ago. Moreover, they can clarify the function of much smaller areas of brain tissue as well. In fact, a single neural cell can be ablated so that its function with respect to the surrounding cells can be assessed. Understanding some of these older techniques also helps us understand the historical processes in the field of biological psychology. These are the techniques described in the following section.

Measuring Dead Tissue

Ablation

Ablation may be produced and studied in one of two ways. The first way is natural. Natural ablation is essentially brain damage that occurs to people because they are the unfortunate victims of accidents, strokes, head injuries and drowning. We may do everything in our power to avoid these problems but they are going to happen anyway. The second way ablation techniques are used is through laboratory experiments. In laboratory experiments, the subjects are typically nonhuman. In contrast to the work with humans mentioned above, laboratory ablations are completed as part of a scientific program of inquiry into the workings of the brain.

Ablation: The intentional destruction of neural tissue is called ablation.

Natural

Natural ablations have been studied throughout the entire history of biological psychology. Especially during the 1800's, medical doctors took close notice of those patients who had received blows to the head or other kinds of brain damage. Evaluating brain damage in the 19th century was difficult because there were no brain scan techniques available. Consequently, what most doctors did was to evaluate any deficits the patient developed because of the injury. Once the patient died—provided the doctor had permission from the family—an anatomical study of the patient's brain could be conducted to look for areas of damage. It was generally assumed that any area of dead tissue found was the area responsible for the deficits the patient revealed in life. It is through this drawn-out deductive process that many of the basic functions of the human brain were discovered. In particular, Broca's area and Wernicke's area, both of which are involved in language production and analysis, were discovered through these techniques.

Natural ablation: The destruction of neural tissue through natural processes such as a stroke or head injury is called a natural ablation.

Laboratory Experiments

The history of laboratory-controlled ablations goes back to the 19th century. During a time when physicians were analyzing the deficits produced from brain injuries in their human patients, medical researchers began to produce ablations in laboratory animals. This research was designed to evaluate the function of various areas of the cortex. Fritz and Hitzig performed some of the most famous work in this area. These two German scientists systematically ablated sections

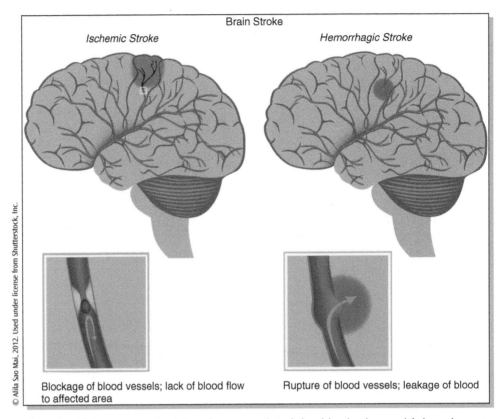

Since the 19th century, physicians have associated dead brain tissue with impairment after a stroke.

of the cortex of dogs to evaluate which areas controlled various forms of motor behavior. This type of experimental work produced the first mappings of the brain's cortex. Ultimately, however, this type of research was limited by the techniques available in the 19th century. Better techniques would become available in the 20th century. By the 1960's, individual neurons could be ablated and their role within a small grouping of cells could be assessed. Such techniques are far more specific than Fritz and Hitzig could have conducted. Today, the functions within a single cell can be assessed which is an entirely new level of analysis beyond simple ablation.

One might think that by now all the ablation experiments should have been completed. Given the widespread integration of the brain, ablations in any area influence multiple systems elsewhere. Therefore, depending upon what one is looking for, the same area of brain may need to be ablated multiple times (in different animals, obviously) to determine the influence of one area on a particular neuroanatomical pathway. Therefore, despite reaching the 21st century, biological scientists still rely on the use of ablation as an experimental technique in animals. Moreover, the unfortunate accidents of life still help neuroscientists map and understand the human brain as well.

Measuring the Living Brain

It took until the development of the electroencephalogram (EEG) before any measures of the living brain could be taken. The EEG existed as the only brain scan technique from the 1930's until the 1960's. After the 1960's, other techniques increased the functionality and accuracy of brain scans. Today we often take brain scans for granted. Many of the current techniques, however, have not been around for more than about three decades.

Brain Scan Techniques

Biomedical researchers have provided the scientific community with a variety of brain scan techniques. New techniques are being developed all the time and the following sections will cover some of the most recent inventions as well as some as the oldest ones. The following sections are divided into the static and functional measures sections. Static measures are those that give a snapshot image of the brain. That is, there is no measure of change over time and the image can be held much the same as any photograph.

Functional measures are taken across time. Because psychological variables tend to change over time, these techniques tend to be more valuable in scientific research. Consequently, they produce much more information then static images. Because functional measures are taken across time, they are generally held as files on a computer or on long strips of paper. Generally, to conduct research with functional measures, one needs specialized software to read and analyze the data.

Static Measures

Computed Tomography

The computed tomography (CT) scan has been applied to a variety of medical applications since its development during the early 1970's. Frequently referred to as a CAT scan, the CT scan is essentially a three-dimensional x-ray generated by taking multiple two-dimensional x-rays around a central point and then having computer software combine the information together to form a simulated three-dimensional image on a computer screen. The CT scan has found itself useful in the study of psychology during times in which a person may have either tumors or foreign objects embedded in the brain. Of course, these objects are generally going to be removed surgically and it pays to know exactly where they

Static measure (brain scan): A static measure is a snapshot image of the brain. The image does not show change over time.

Functional measures (brain scan): Functional measures are any measure taken over time.

Computed tomography (CT): The CT scan is a simulated three–dimensional image of the brain formed by taking x–rays in each of the three planes.

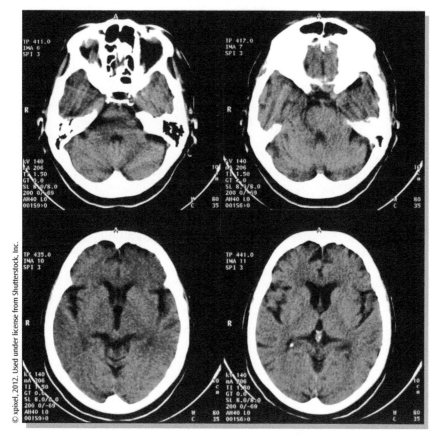

A computed tomography (CT) scan of the brain with ventricles

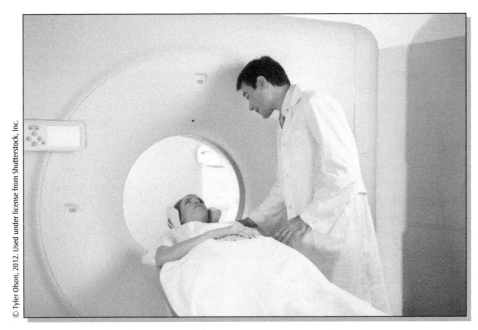

© Tyler Olson, 2012. Used under license from Shutterstock, Inc.

A patient entering the MRI machine

are before you go fishing around inside someone's skull. The CT scan gives surgeons the opportunity to locate the object prior to the surgery and to make predictions regarding which forms of damage may occur to the person's cognitive functioning based upon the surgical process of retrieving it.

Magnetic Resonance Imaging

The **magnetic resonance image** (MRI) scan has been applied to a wide variety of medical purposes. In fact, many readers of this text may recognize the application of MRI to the evaluation of soft tissue damage in a person's back, neck or knee. In psychology, however, the MRI scan has been used to locate dead tissue, tumors and foreign objects located in the brain. The MRI produces its image by using the magnetic properties of the soft tissue of the brain. By exposing the subject to a strong magnetic field and aligning the atomic spin of the atoms of the brain, one can then send a radio frequency through it and use the reflected signal as the basis for determining the internal structure of the brain. This technique tends to be more accurate than the CT scan; therefore, it is the preferred measure over computed tomography especially when one is looking for soft tissue damage.

Diffusion Tensor Imaging

Diffusion tensor imaging (DTI) is an outgrowth technology from magnetic resonance imaging. Whereas MRI scans show both gray and white matter of the brain, the DTI method focuses on the white matter specifically. It does this by creating images of the brain by tracing the pathway water takes as it diffuses in the brain. Water diffusion generally follows pathways such as myelinated axons. Therefore, by following the pathway of diffused water, one can trace the location of myelinated axons. This technique stands in contrast to the previous brain scan techniques discussed because they all focused on the gray matter of the brain. That is, gray and white matter would be scanned, however, the researchers focused on the activity of the gray matter as locations of signal processing. The DTI technique now gives us an idea of the interconnections between various areas of the brain. The images it has produced have been strikingly different than the other brain scan techniques we discussed because they focus on lengthy axonal connections between various areas of gray matter and not the gray matter itself.

Magnetic resonance imaging (MRI): A brain scan technique that passes a strong magnetic wave through the body of the subject is called an MRI. Through the additional use of a radio wave, the scanning machine can read how the radio frequency bounces back differently and uses that information to produce an image of the inside of the scanned object.

Diffusion tensor imaging: A form of brain scan technology that tracks the direction water flows along myelinated axons.

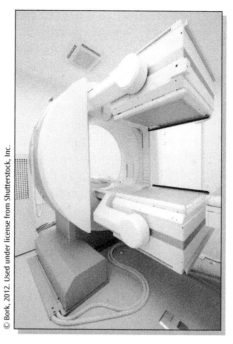

A mannequin wearing an EEG skull cap   *A PET scanner*

Functional Measures

Electroencephalograms

The **electroencephalogram** (EEG) is a brain scan technique that came into use during the 1930's. The technique allows one to read the electrical activity given off by the brain. To do so, small flat metal pads are pasted onto the scalp. These metal pads detect the electrical activity of the brain through the skull and scalp and send the information to a recording device. The placement of the recording pads gives a general indication of the overall amount of electrical activity in that vicinity of the brain. The use of the EEG has been metaphorically compared to hanging a microphone over a soccer stadium during the World Cup. That is, you may know when there is more or less activity during the game; however, you do not know what is specifically being said between the two fans in row H, seats 4 and 5.

Positron Emission Tomography

Positron emission tomography (PET) allows one to evaluate the brain by assessing where glucose (sugar) is being absorbed. To perform a PET scan, one must inject the subject with a radioactive form of glucose and then allow it to distribute around the body. As the brain is engaged in various cognitive tasks arranged by the researcher, the subject will need more glucose in the areas with increased activity. These areas, therefore, will be more highly radioactive because of the accumulation of glucose in those areas. The value of the PET scan allows researchers to evaluate which areas of the brain are active during which intellectual tasks. These measures allow researchers to distinguish between the areas of the brain that control language, mathematics, hearing, vision, etc.

Functional Magnetic Resonance Imaging

The **functional magnetic resonance imaging** (fMRI) scan is based upon the same technology of the MRI discussed above. The difference between the MRI and the fMRI is that the fMRI takes repeated measures over time. This way, changes in magnetic activity from the brain can be assessed across time. Which magnetic properties of the brain are changing over time? The changes are due to changes in

Electroencephalogram (EEG): The reading of electrical activity from the brain through small, flat metal pads (electrodes) glued to the scalp.

Positron emission tomography (PET): PET is a brain scan technique that uses radioactive glucose. As select areas of the brain become more active during intellectual tasks, the PET scanner reads where the radioactive glucose accumulates. Higher concentrations of radiation indicate that those areas of the brain are more active because they are in more need of glucose as an energy source.

Functional magnetic resonance imaging (fMRI): Functional magnetic resonance imaging is the same as magnetic resonance imaging (MRI) except that the image is taken multiple times per second so that a pattern of activity over time may be determined.

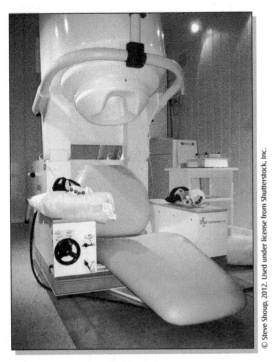

The magnetoencephalogram

Magnetoencephalography (MEG): A brain scan technique that measures the differences in magnetic properties of a subject's blood and brain and converts that to an image.

Microelectrode: An extremely thin electrode device that may be used to deliver electric current to the brain or to read the electric current in the brain.

blood flow through the brain. Just as with the PET scan described above, changes in intellectual activity change the local blood volume through the areas most active. These changes in blood flow are detected by the fMRIs as changes in magnetic activity. These measures are the primary basis of the fMRI.

MEG

Similar to the PET and fMRI measures, the **magnetoencephalogram** (MEG) is a brain scan technique that measures the magnetic properties of blood traveling through the brain. The magnetic fields measured by the MEG are extremely small and are detected by superconducting detectors called SQUIDS (superconducting quantum interference devices). The MEG is one of the newest brain scan technologies to become available. It has only been consistently used within the past decade.

Electrodes

All cells within the nervous system produce action potentials. Cells in the brain comprise circuits that control all of our behavior. Scientists wish to study the circuits to determine which pathways exist and how they function in relation to each other. One potential way to determine the activity of cells in the brain is to use a microelectrode.

Microelectrodes are thin metal wires that are inserted into the neural tissue and are attached to a connecting socket outside of the skull. Connecting sockets are held in place by dental plastic that is placed there during surgery. The careful use of stereotaxic equipment will allow a researcher to identify very specific locations of the brain in which the tip of the electrode needs to be inserted. Once it is there, the activity of the cells in that region are read and correlated with the environmental input to which the subject is exposed. Once the experiment is finished, however, the placement of the electrode in the brain has to be determined through autopsy to justify that the recordings had actually come from the proper area of the brain. Clearly, the use of electrodes in the brain is applied with animals and not humans.

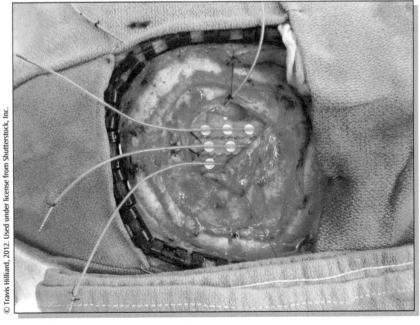

Electrodes placed on the surface of the brain during surgery.

In contrast to reading brain activity, one can stimulate the area instead. By using this same essential procedure, a microelectrode can be used to send a small electrical input into the brain to stimulate a particular area so that the scientist can evaluate what increase in behavior may occur as a result of the increased stimulation. In some cases, inhibitory cells are stimulated in this manner and therefore the scientist would expect to see a reduction in a particular pattern of behavior. Either way, the microelectrode can be inserted into neural tissue to either read or stimulate an area of the brain.

Microdialysis

The brain is full of chemicals. Substances such as neurotransmitters and hormones are released at different times based upon the functioning of the brain. To understand when a particular neurotransmitter—or other substance—is released into the brain requires a real-time measure of the function of that area. To do so, one uses microdialysis technology.

Microdialysis is a process by which the presence and concentration of chemicals in the brain can be measured. It works through a tiny probe that is inserted into brain tissue similar to that of an electrode. For example, if one wanted to study the release of the inhibitory neurotransmitter glycine in the brain during dreaming—a time during which the brain blocks motor activity to the body—then a microdialysis probe may be inserted into the area that is suspected of producing glycine. Once REM sleep occurs, the system will be able to measure the presence of glycine during that time.

The system functions by using a small probe with an input and outtake drainage system. One metal tube is for pumping fluid into the brain and the other tube is for receiving the material from the brain. As the first tube sends fluid down into the brain it mixes with any substances presently at the probe's tip and the second tube draws the material up for analysis.

> Microdialysis: A procedure using thin metal cannulae that are inserted into the brain of a research subject. The cannulae extract out chemicals from the local area to determine the concentration of various substances (e.g., neurotransmitters, hormones) during psychological or biological manipulations.

Controlling the Living Brain

The above sections have described how to take measurements from the living brain. Sometimes, however, rather than reading what the brain is doing you may want to control what the brain is doing. How then can one go about influencing the activity of the brain? There are a number of techniques and a few are listed below.

Physiological Methods

Electrodes

Our previous discussion of electrodes involved the reading of electrical activity from the brain. Electrodes, however, are essentially wires. Therefore, one may read electrical activity from the brain or one may send electrical activity into the brain. When one sends electrical activity into the brain through an electrode, the location of the tip of the electrode is the area stimulated. Stimulation in this matter is somewhat sloppy experimentally. Given the size of the electrode and the total area that is stimulated, many different circuits leading to different areas of the brain may become stimulated. This technique, however, has been used successfully in many research programs. For example, the implantation of an electrode into the reward center of the brain can serve to stimulate the subject in such a way so that their responses continue to occur. Although these techniques are used experimentally, they would most certainly be used with non-humans. The only time such techniques are used with humans is if there is a serious medical need to stimulate an area of the brain for the person's medical benefit. Therefore, experimental studies using electrodes to stimulate the brain are almost certainly coming from animal studies. The next brain stimulation technique is more likely to be used with humans, is safer and can be used for research purposes.

Transcranial Magnetic Stimulation

The previous brain scan measurements that we discussed relied heavily on the magnetic fields of the soft tissue and blood of the brain. With transcranial magnetic stimulation (TMS), a magnetic field is sent into the brain to stimulate an area and thereby induce its activity. Generally, TMS produces reflexive responses in the subjects being stimulated.

The TMS device is generally shaped like the numeral 8 and involves coiled wires that produce a magnetic field. The center of the 8 is placed over the skull near the brain section that is to be stimulated. Once the magnetic field is turned on, the magnetic waves cross the skull and into the brain. Whereas sometimes TMS can be used to induce a reflexive response, thereby identifying an area of brain tissue that controls a particular response, it has also been used successfully to stimulate an area and thereby reduce its activity. For instance, TMS has been used successfully to stimulate a section of the brain that helps humans detect motion. Once that area is stimulated, it becomes temporarily inhibited and the person loses the ability to recognize movement.

Psychopharmacology

Traditionally, one of the most common ways to influence the living brain is by administering drugs. Modern psychopharmacology has produced a wealth of agents to influence a wide variety of psychological disorders. Some of the most common agents are related to the control of anxiety disorders. Such substances, when ingested into the stomach, are absorbed by the blood supply and typically travel to all parts of the brain. The drug will only have a significant influence on psychological functioning if it's molecular shape fits receptors. Generally, drug effects are strongly associated with their molecular shape and their degree of fat solubility. Molecular shape influences whether the drug will affect a particular receptor and fat solubility will influence whether the drug crosses cell membranes sufficiently to reach receptors. New drug agents are always being produced and psychology students should stay abreast of these updates as they may have significant influence on your understanding of the brain.

> **Transcranial magnetic stimulation (TMS):** Transcranial magnetic stimulation is the application of a handheld device that emits a magnetic wave through the surface of the brain and elicits activity from the stimulated cortex areas.

> **Psychopharmacology:** Psychopharmacology is the study of how drugs influence behavior.

© jordache, 2012. Used under license from Shutterstock, Inc.

The application of medical pharmacology has been around for thousands of years

Genetic Methods

Gene Knockout Techniques

Gene knockout techniques are one of two types of targeted mutations discussed in this section on the genetic methods to control the living brain. Targeted mutations are mutated genes that are produced in the laboratory and inserted into laboratory animals. Those animals are typically mice. The mutated gene, which is typically referred to as a knockout gene, is designed in the laboratory to not produce a particular protein. Once it is inserted into the genetic structure of the mouse subject, the mouse will no longer produce the protein that it once did. Consequently, scientists can assess what affect that protein had exerted. Knockout genes work conceptually similar to the role of ablation as previously discussed. Ablation, just as with knockout genes, shows deficits that occur because of a removed function from the brain. The disruption caused by this technique, however, may also influence other areas and therefore any disruption seen may not be completely attributable to the knockout gene.

Gene knockout: The knockout process is a biotechnology used to eliminate the gene of a research animal as a way to determine its use.

Gene Replacement Techniques

Another form of targeted mutation involves the replacement of genes with other active genes. New genes inserted into the DNA code of a mouse may be used to increase the production of a particular protein or produce an entirely new protein. One unique use of gene replacement techniques in the laboratory is to cause a fluorescent dye to be produced by the body so that sections of the mouse brain become fluorescent and are easily identifiable during the data acquisition procedure of the experiment.

Gene replacement: Gene replacement is the removal of an existing gene and its replacement with a new copy. Gene replacement therapy is predicated upon the idea that medical science will be able to perform this treatment to eliminate any disorder resulting from the activity of a corrupted gene.

© iQoncept, 2012. Used under license from Shutterstock, Inc.

The application of genetic therapy provides much excitement but is still an experimental technique.

KEY TERMS

Ablation
Action potential
Amperes
Amygdala
Arachnoid membrane
Arachnoid trabeculae
Association cortex area
Autonomic nervous
  system
Axon
Axon hillock
Basal ganglia
Biological electricity
Blindsight
Blood brain barrier
Bone encasement
Broca's area
Calcium (Ca2+)
Cardiac muscle
Central nervous system
  (CNS)
Cerebellum
Cerebrospinal fluid
Chlorine (Cl-)
Chromosome
Computed tomography
  (CT)
Cortex
Dendrite
Deoxyribonucleic acid
  (DNA)
Diffusion
Diffusion tensor imaging
Dura mater
Electroencephalogram
  (EEG)
Electrostatic pressure
Endothelial cells
Excitatory postsynaptic
  potential (EPSP)
Fissures
Forebrain
Frontal lobe
Functional magnetic
  resonance imaging
  (fMRI)

Functional measures
  (brain scan)
Functional unit of
  heredity
Fusiform face area
Gene
Gene knockout
Gene
Hindbrain
Hippocampus
Hypothalamus
Inhibitory postsynaptic
potential (IPSP)
Intercellular
  communication
Ion channels
Limbic system
Lipid bilayer
Magnetic resonance
  image (MRI)
Magnetoencephalogram
  (MEG)
Medulla oblongata
Meninges
Microdialysis
Microelectrodes
Midbrain
Mirror neurons
Monosynaptic stretch
  reflex
Myelin
Natural ablation
Neural reflex arc
Neurogenesis
Neurotransmission
Nodes of Ranvier
  (ROW-vee-a)
Occipital lobe
Ohms
Oligrodendrocyte cell
One-hundred billion
Parietal lobe
Periaqueductal gray
  area
Peripheral nervous
  system (PNS)

Phantom limb
Pia mater
Plasticity
Polysynaptic reflexes
Pons
Positron emission
  tomography (PET)
Post-traumatic stress
  disorder
Potassium (K+)
Primary cortex area
Prosopagnosia
Psychopharmacology
Reflex
Reticular formation
Reuptake
Salutatory conduction
Signal integration
Skeletal muscles
Smooth muscles
Sodium (Na+)
Soma
Somatic nervous
  system
Somatotopic
  organization
Spinal foramen
Spinal nerves
Split brain
Static measure
  (brain scan)
Subarachnoid space
Sulci
Temporal lobe
Ten trillion
Terminal button
Thalamus
Three-cell reflex
Transcranial magnetic
  stimulation (TMS)
Transcription
Translation
Vesicles
Voltage
Wernicke's area

Chapter 2: Neuroscience and Behavior

END OF CHAPTER QUIZ

1. Which of the following brings information into a cell?
   a. Dendrite
   b. Axon
   c. Myelin
   d. Soma

2. Which of the following sends information away to other cells?
   a. Dendrite
   b. Axon
   c. Myelin
   d. Soma

3. The gap between cells.
   a. Interneuron
   b. Lesion
   c. Synapse
   d. Vesicle

4. Chemical messengers released from the presynaptic (axonic) terminal.
   a. Neurotransmitters
   b. Hormones
   c. Glial cells
   d. Vesicles

5. The venom of the black widow spider is to _____ as botulin is to _____.
   a. Paralysis; convulsions
   b. Convulsions; paralysis
   c. Depression; elation
   d. Elation; depression

6. There are naturally occurring morphine-like and THC-like substances in your brain.
   a. True
   b. False

7. The central nervous system is made up of the:
   a. Spinal cord, thalamus, and cortex
   b. Brainstem and cortex
   c. Brain and spinal cord
   d. Autonomia and somatia

8. The difference between the Autonomic and Skeletal nervous systems is the difference between:
   a. Leg and hormones
   b. Stomach and intestine
   c. Liver and lungs
   d. Heart and bicep

9. The peripheral nervous system is made up of:
   a. Everything that is not the central nervous system
   b. Spinal nerves
   c. Sensory neurons
   d. Motor neurons and cranial nerves

10. Which section of the nervous system activates the "fight or flight" reflex?
    a. Parasympathetic
    b. Sympathetic
    c. Somatic
    d. Enteric

11. Some reflexes will work without a connection to the brain.
    a. True
    b. False

12. Hormones are controlled through which system?
    a. Endocrine
    b. Neural
    c. Sensory
    d. Motor

13. In order to monitor the electrical activity in the brain, researchers would use a(n):
    a. MRI.
    b. PET scan.
    c. EEG.
    d. CT scan.

14. Which process uses radioactive glucose?
    a. CT scans
    b. MRI
    c. PET scans
    d. EEG

15. Which process is the formation of a 3-dimensional x-ray image?
    a. CT scans
    b. MRI
    c. PET scans
    d. EEG

16. Which process uses very strong magnets to realign the molecules in your soft tissue?
    a. CT scans
    b. MRI
    c. PET scans
    d. EEG

17. The limbic system controls:
    a. Hormonal activity
    b. Emotions
    c. Sensation
    d. Motor development

18. Hormones, sexual behavior, feeding, emotions, and memory are located very near the same area in the brain.
    a. True
    b. False

19. Split brain patients have which part of their brain destroyed?
    a. Corpus callosum
    b. Left hemisphere
    c. Reticular formation
    d. Frontal lobe

20. That a brain can LESS easily adjust to damage later in life than earlier in life indicates a reduction in:
    a. Synaptic connections.
    b. Aphasia.
    c. Plasticity.
    d. Neurotransmitters.

21. The main role of the dendrite is to:
    a. Send signals to other cells
    b. Bring electricity into a neuron
    c. Control genetic processes
    d. House the synaptic vesicles

22. The all-or-none law states that:
    a. All cells will fire at the same time
    b. Many cells will stay off at the same time
    c. All cells contain only one neurotransmitter
    d. Each action potential from a particular cell has the same strength and speed

23. What happens to vesicles when a cell fires?
    a. They dissolve
    b. They merge with the cell wall
    c. They are pushed into this synaptic gap
    d. They are destroyed by neurotransmitters

24. All nervous system activity has two basic components. What are they?
    a. Sensory input and motor output
    b. Sensory input and memory processing
    c. Sensory input and learning
    d. Memory processing and motor output
    e. Learning and memory and motor output

25. Most of the cells inside the brain are classified as:
    a. Sensory neurons
    b. Interneurons
    c. Motor neurons
    d. Pyramidal neurons
    e. Axonal fibers

26. Sensory input and motor output generally follow which type of pathway?
    a. Point-to-point connections
    b. Circuitous routes
    c. Flexible pathways
    d. Pathways which always passed through the thalamus
    e. There is no consistency in either of those pathways

27. Brain plasticity refers to:
    a. Fake connections
    b. Rigid connections
    c. Flexible connections
    d. The ability of the brain to modify itself

28. Which are the two main branches of the nervous system?
    a. The sympathetic nervous system and parasympathetic nervous system
    b. The central nervous system and the peripheral nervous system
    c. The central nervous system and the sympathetic nervous system
    d. The peripheral nervous system and the parasympathetic nervous system
    e. The sensory system and the motor system

29. Drugs can influence your behavior because they have similar molecular shapes to naturally occurring substances in your brain.
    a. True
    b. False

30. Which of the following is not a typical neurotransmitter system used to understand psychological processes?
    a. Glutamate
    b. GABA
    c. Acetylcholine
    d. Monoamines
    e. Steroids

31. Which of the following brain scan techniques is considered a static (snapshot) measure?
    a. CT
    b. EEG
    c. MEG
    d. PET
    e. fMRI

32. Which of the following brain scan techniques is considered a functional measure that uses radioactive glucose?
    a. CT
    b. MRI
    c. MEG
    d. PET
    e. fMRI

33. This brain scan technique is essentially a three dimensional x-ray.
    a. CT
    b. MRI
    c. EEG
    d. PET
    e. fMRI

34. This technique takes a static measure of your brain and uses strong magnetic waves.
    a. CT
    b. MRI
    c. EEG
    d. PET

35. This brain scan technique reads the electrical activity from the surface of your scalp.
    a. CT
    b. MRI
    c. EEG
    d. MEG
    e. fMRI

36. This is a functional measure of magnetic activity from your brain.
    a. MRI
    b. EEG
    c. MEG
    d. PET
    e. fMRI

37. Which of the following is the lowest brain area?
    a. Medulla
    b. Cerebellum
    c. Reticular formation
    d. Thalamus

38. The primary role of the limbic system is to control:
    a. Sensory input
    b. Motor output
    c. Balance
    d. Emotion
    e. Memory

39. If the reward system were damaged, a person would feel:
    a. Unmotivated to do anything
    b. Sad
    c. Happy
    d. Confused
    e. As though they had memory loss

40. Which of the following is not a lobe from your cortex?
    a. Parietal
    b. Occipital
    c. Cerebellar
    d. Temporal
    e. Frontal

41. Memories are located in one area of the brain called the hippocampus.
    a. True
    b. False

42. Ninety percent of all people have their language center located in the:
    a. Left hemisphere
    b. Right hemisphere
    c. Left parietal lobe
    d. Right parietal lobe
    e. Occipital lobe

43. Neurotransmitter pathways generally develop because:
    a. Neurons with similar neurotransmitters are more likely to connect than neurons with dissimilar neurotransmitters
    b. Certain neurotransmitters are isolated in certain areas of the brain
    c. Neurons with dissimilar neurotransmitters are unable to connect
    d. Certain brain areas can only work with certain neurotransmitters

44. Which set of characteristics below best shows the natural correlation with respect to neurotransmitter pathways?
    a. Brain area, neurotransmitter type
    b. Brain area, sensory/motor processing
    c. Neurotransmitter type, sensory motor processing
    d. Brain area, sensory/motor processing, neurotransmitter type

45. Which area of the brain connects the two hemispheres?
    a. Thalamus
    b. Medulla
    c. Cerebellum
    d. Corpus callosum
    e. Occipital lobe

46. A split-brain patient who sees something in their right field of vision can comment on it.
    a. True
    b. False

47. Which chemical signal may travel the furthest?
    a. Neurotranmitters
    b. Neuromodulators
    c. Hormones
    d. GABA

48. Which of the following systems does the endocrine system have no influence on?
    a. Feeding
    b. Emotions
    c. Sexuality
    d. Wakefulness
    e. The endocrine system affects all the above systems

49. Which of the following areas plays a role in the hormonal feedback system related to stress?
    a. Medulla
    b. Thalamus
    c. Hypothalamic-pituitary-adrenal axis
    d. Reticular formation
    e. All these areas influence the hormonal stress feedback system

50. There is an identifiable mind separate from your physical brain.
    a. True
    b. False

3 Nature and Nurture Working Together

Behavior Genetics and the Prison of Biology

In this chapter, we entertain the idea that genes can control your behavior. If that idea is correct, then what mechanism controls the process? Genes are collections of molecules. They cannot think on their own, they are not responsible for giving you ideas, and they are not the voice you hear inside your head. The function of genes is to code for proteins. Therefore, in the big picture some of your behavior starts with genes, moves on to proteins and then, somehow, winds up as a publicly observable behavior. Biologists and psychologists are a long way from completely explaining how this works; however, there are some clues in the system that indicate how it works.

When families are measured across generations, some general traits may be more prevalent in one family than in others. For example, depression, among other forms of mental illness, is seen in higher proportions in some families. This indicates that a gene may be controlling the incidence of depression. This is even more so the point when you see children reared in adoptive families that still suffer from the same mental health issues that were present in their biological family. This issue of genes also shows up in the study of personality.

Personality researchers have identified five general characteristics that appear to be central to everyone's personality. Moreover, the particular expression of those personality traits has a tendency to follow through families over generations. So how can these mental health and personality characteristics follow family lines?

One possible answer is to look at the type of characteristic that transfers across generations. The five personality characteristics all have strong emotional aspects to them, such as your capacity to deal with stress. Moreover, many of the mental health problems that transfer across generations have strong emotional components as well. Some of those are anxiety, depression, and bipolar affective disorder (previously known as manic-depression). If genes control the emotional characteristics of ones psychological make up, then those genes may be influencing the anatomical structure of the circuits controlling emotional responding. This explanation could bridge a gap between genes and behavior. This, however, is not the whole story.

If a person with a high tendency for anxiety never learns to effectively deal with anxiety provoking stimuli (e.g., snakes, heights, barking dogs, etc.) then you might develop a person with a significant anxiety problem. If, however, that person is raised in a culture that supports the idea that one should face their fears, then he or she might learn effective ways to deal with anxiety. Moreover, the people in their life might reinforce their attempts at "facing their fears" which would lend some social support to help treat their problem. This may ultimately lead to a person who is still more anxious compared to most others, albeit much less anxious than the person in the former scenario.

It is intriguing that environmental differences can produce two completely different people despite their similar genetic heritage. Since the time researchers have begun studying family

Continued

103

Behavior Genetics and the Prison of Biology   *Continued*

behavioral traits, much has been learned about the genetic and environmental causes of behavior. Currently, it appears clear that both genes and environment contribute to your overall psychological make up. Overall, however, there still seems to be much more to do before it can be stated confidently that we really understand the mechanism by which it works.

CHAPTER OUTLINE

Nature: Nature is the general term that refers to biological influences on psychology.

Nurture: Nurture is the general term that refers to environmental influences on psychology.

Nature versus nurture: This phrase was developed by Sir Francis Galton in the 1880's and refers to the possibility that either biological influences or environmental influences are the basis for human psychology. Currently, it is believed that both nature and nurture influence all psychological traits.

NATURE VS. NURTURE

Scientific and Social History

The concept of nature versus nurture has been a component of psychology since its inception. Nature refers to the control of human behavior by biological means. This generally refers to genetics, neuroanatomy and neurochemistry. Of course, any physical trait that can be identified will be a component of the nature factor. Nurture refers to the control of human behavior through the environment. This generally refers to prior learning and memory that modifies an individual's behavior. Common examples of control by nurture include the period of world history in which you live, your culture, language and current social events.

Many arguments have been made that attribute human behavior solely to either biological factors or environmental factors. These arguments have been made since the "nature versus nurture" phrase was coined by Sir Francis Galton in the 19th century. Currently, it appears that there is evidence for both nature and nurture in the control of human behavior. To develop a broader understanding of this concept, and to understand where it came from, I will discuss the history of nature and nurture in the following section. The beginning of the story will take place in ancient Sparta.

Eugenics in Ancient Western History

Eugenics is a word that means different things to different people. Long ago in various locations around the world, eugenics was a way to make sure that only the strong and healthy survived to use the resources of society. In modern times, eugenics has been connected to social bias and murder the likes of which have not been seen for centuries. At its heart, eugenics refers to the management of the gene pool by society. The way in which society does so is to evaluate each person's worthiness to live and only allow healthy individuals to survive. One should note, however, that eugenics programs focused upon the biological control (nature) of human behavior and did very little with the nurture component. There was little provision provided for the improvement of human behavior through eugenics programs. For example, if one was identified as lacking intellectually, then eugenics thinking would identify that person as permanently intellectually inferior. There would not be an attempt to improve their level of intelligence by actively educating the individual.

Statue of King Leonidas

Throughout history, the use of eugenics has been actively applied to various degrees around the world. In Western civilization, the application of eugenics was first documented to occur in ancient Sparta (circa 500 BCE). The ancient Spartans were known for maintaining a militaristic society. Their cultural values were geared toward preparing for war. Throughout their history, the men in society were trained consistently for military roles starting from a young age. One phrase from ancient Sparta, which gives us an indication of how militaristic they were, was "Come back with your shield or on it." This phrase was uttered by mothers to their sons going off to war. It meant that their son should either return carrying their shield or be draped over it in death. In such a militaristic society, one might expect the physical health of each individual to be of utmost importance. Compared by today's standards, the ancient Spartans did so to an extreme.

> **Eugenics:** Eugenics is the application of artificial selection to human beings.

Whenever a new child was born in ancient Sparta, village elders would evaluate the new child for strength and medical problems. If the child was identified as sickly, then it was taken from the family and murdered. In some instances, the child was left in the woods to be eaten by wild animals and in other instances; he or she was thrown into a chasm on Mount Taygetos. There was not, however, any attempt to allow the child to grow up with the expectation that special training might make him or her increase their overall potential. Spartan society accepted that the village elders were protecting everyone from wasting resources on the sickly. In this way, anyone with a birth defect would neither waste society's resources nor produce another sickly child.

Eugenics in Modern Western History

After Darwin published The Origin of Species in 1859, much debate centered on how human behavior could be controlled by heritable influences. Many biologists of the time accepted the idea that inheritance could influence medical or psychological health. Such things as birth defects or mental illness could be transferred across generations. Consequently, it was believed that if you identified a family that produced a child with an abnormality, then you could eliminate that disorder by stopping any of those family members from reproducing. Just as in ancient Sparta, the 19th century eugenicists did not consider that an environmental input such as a healthy diet, exercise, drugs or surgery could repair the identified medical or psychological problem. Eliminating the heritable trait responsible for the disorder sounded like a good

© Sami Kallioniemi, 2012. Used under license from Shutterstock, Inc.

An entrance to the Auschwitz concentration camp

idea to many scientists during Darwin's time. The question was; how could you go about doing it?

Darwin's cousin, Sir Francis Galton, was a wealthy scientist and contemporary of Darwin's. During this time, Galton coined both the phrases Nature vs. Nurture and eugenics. Eugenics, from the Greek *eugenes*, means "good birth." It was used by Galton to refer to the management of inherited traits throughout society. Of course, this implies that a eugenics program will only provide support to those individuals identified as healthy or otherwise physically acceptable. Despite coining the phrase Nature versus Nurture, Galton and the rest of the eugenicists tended to focus on the nature component of health and disease and almost entirely ignored the nurture component.

Eugenics was conceived of in two ways; **negative eugenics** and **positive eugenics**. The process of negative eugenics was the process of eliminating a sickly person from society by killing them. Positive eugenics, however, applied only sterilization to the sickly individual so that they could not reproduce. Positive eugenics did not suggest that society had the right to kill an individual but that it did have the right to protect its overall resources by not allowing more sickly individuals to be born. At the time, it would have been difficult to get most members of society to agree to the application of negative eugenics programs. Scholarly people, however, began to promote the application of positive eugenics programs. These programs became especially well funded in the United States.

Eventually, thirty-three states in the U.S. promoted positive eugenics programs through law by the time World War II ended. By the late 1960's, there had been approximately 60,000 sterilizations performed in the U.S. Many of the sterilizations were applied to people who were identified as feebleminded. The term feebleminded was commonly applied to individuals with low intelligence scores that did not completely fit the category of mental retardation. The interest in sterilizing feebleminded individuals was to stop them from producing any more feebleminded or retarded persons.

The measures used to establish whether someone required sterilization was based upon the known medical and psychological principles of the time. The psychological principles, which generally involved intelligence tests, were the primary tool. At this time, it was widely believed that intelligence was controlled by biological forces (nature) and therefore was a constant throughout your entire life. That is, no amount of special academic training could improve

Negative eugenics: This term refers to the application of artificial selection processes to human populations in which killing undesirable members of society is practiced.

Positive eugenics: This term refers to the application of artificial selection processes to human populations in which killing undesirable members of society is not practiced. In a positive eugenics program, such as in the United States during the early 20th century, undesirables were sterilized but not murdered.

your level of intelligence. Today, it is clear that the measures of behavioral viability and prognosis applied by the eugenicists were poor. Unmistakably, they went well beyond the limits of what psychologists could actually measure at the time. Ultimately, what was seen was that social bias drove much of the decisions regarding who was feebleminded. The historical record shows that most individuals identified for sterilization fit the character of social biases drawn from the 19th and early 20th centuries.

Laws forbidding interracial marriages were developed through eugenicist ideology. These laws were referred to as antimiscegenation laws. The idea that different races should not marry—and have children—came from the idea that different races have different inherent levels of intelligence. Therefore, by mixing races you would produce an overall decline in those groups with higher intelligence levels and degrade the overall gene pool.

The earliest eugenicist sterilization policy was passed into law by the Indiana legislature in 1907. It provided for the forced sterilization of criminals, the feebleminded and rapists. Although 1907 marks the beginning of the legal application of eugenicist policies in the U.S., one of the last antimiscegenation laws to be removed from legal statute was in Alabama in 2000.

By the time World War II ended, the concentration camps in Europe were uncovered. Their discovery placed much public attention on the American eugenics programs. The European application of negative eugenics, the killing of people identified as unfit for reproduction, placed a heavy political burden upon the Americans who continued to apply eugenic ideas. It may be argued that the awareness of concentration camps in Europe became the primary impetus to end the American eugenics programs.

Antimiscegenation laws: Antimiscegenation laws restricted interracial marriages in the United States. The idea was supported by the early 20th century eugenicists who suggested that mixing races would result in an overall decrease in intelligence levels throughout the gene pool.

Modern Conceptions of the Nature-Nurture Debate

Today, the argument over nature and nurture seems reasonably settled. Most psychologists will argue today that both biology and environment help determine psychological traits. In short, if there were no nervous system then you would get no behavior out of an individual. In addition, without any particular environmental input there would be nothing initiating brain activity.

Psychology students need to look beyond the old nature versus nurture debate and recognize that psychological traits involve both biological and environmental influences. The degree to which biology or environment influences any one particular trait may be weighted more heavily toward biology for some

Getting hungry is mostly biological, but what we choose to eat is mostly cultural.

© Ariwasabi, 2012. Used under license from Shutterstock, Inc.

behaviors or more heavily toward environment for others. Any discussion of biology versus environmental control of behavior must be understood within the context of a specific response system. For example, becoming hungry and eating may be a trait that is more heavily influenced by innate biological factors. In contrast, however, what you eat when you become hungry is largely determined by your culture and personal history. In terms of language, the fact that you speak is likely derived from innate biological structures that develop in your brain at a young age. Which language you learn to speak, however, is largely dependent upon your geographic location and parents.

I think it would be shortsighted to argue that we currently understand fully the degree to which biology or the environment manages our behavior. In contrast, however, we can develop statistical estimates that reveal their influence on our psychological response systems. What does seem constant, however, is that both biology and environment always influence the control of psychological traits.

> **Phylogeny:** Phylogeny refers to the influences that affect heritable traits over generations.

Phylogenetic Change: Evolution

The work of many 19th-century biologists led to a great deal of research on phylogeny. **Phylogeny** is the study of genetic change over generations. Part of that work was observed in the research conducted by Charles Darwin. Darwin's research, which primarily used the descriptive and correlational methods, developed a body of evidence indicating that animals change over long periods into a variety of species. How and why that process takes place was addressed by Darwin and is the topic of the next section.

Darwin's work highlighted the role of the functional nature of biological structure. That is, any characteristic an animal possesses must have some functional significance. For example, the claws and sharp teeth of the lion must allow it to catch and eat prey. Animals that live in snow-covered areas should have a lighter coloration to camouflage them from predators. Flying birds can travel great distances and migrate during the changes of the seasons. Darwin's work gave rise to the theory of functionalism, a theory that suggested living organism's characteristics must perform useful functions. Experimentally, to understand the purpose of a particular trait of an animal, we need to understand what function that trait serves. It is always necessary to understand traits within the contexts they were created. Otherwise, the trait may not make much sense.

Charles Darwin. The father of evolutionary theory.

© Nicku, 2012. Used under license from Shutterstock, Inc.

One good example of a functional analysis of an animal's trait comes from the analysis of moths and butterflies with large eyespots on their wings. Eyespots look similar to the eyes of large predators such as owls. Moths and butterflies generally require camouflage for protection; however, when the backs of their wings are folded they are colored similarly to the types of trees on which they reside. Once predatory birds approach the butterflies, the butterflies open their wings showing the eyespots which results in the predatory birds flying away. This effect, which is seen in nature, has also been reproduced in the laboratory giving the researchers the opportunity to manipulate the characteristics of the eyespots.

> **Evolution:** Evolution is the process by which creatures change their form and function because of natural selection pressures over long periods.

Natural Selection

Darwin produced the theory of **evolution** in an attempt to explain how animals develop their functional characteristics. One of the cornerstones of the theory of evolution is the concept of **natural selection**. Darwin realized that not all members of the species are the same and that these differences were inherited biological traits. Moreover, the traits present across the members of the species

> **Natural selection:** Natural selection is the process by which genetically controlled characteristics that increase the probability of survival and reproduction for a species appear more frequently in the gene pool over time.

were likely to influence the degree to which the subject could reproduce relative to other members of its group. If small differences in the rate of reproduction occur between members of a group over very long periods of time, then some traits will become more prevalent within a group and that change will be the basis by which genetic change occurs within the population. Therefore, natural selection is generally concerned with minor changes that occur over long periods. Those changes produce gradual modifications in the genetic makeup of the population.

Eyespots on the Buckeye Butterfly

Darwin and his colleagues knew nothing of the role of DNA in inheritance. In fact, during his time, a common term which referred to the biological entity which helped to transfer information between generations was germ plasm. In general, the germ plasm referred to whatever substance was transferred during sexual reproduction across generations. The development of the differences between members of the species is produced due to random mutations. Mutations may come about because of exposure to natural forms of radiation or may also come from biochemical mistakes made during the process of cell division. It is most likely that any mutation that occurs in the species will produce a deleterious effect. Over the long run, however, a very small number of mutations may actually produce a selective advantage for that individual. If that individual has the opportunity to reproduce, then that mutated gene will become more prevalent in the population gene pool and the survival characteristics of all members of the group will improve.

As mutations occur over time, geographic isolation from other members of the species will enhance those differences. For example, over geologic time tectonic forces may force some sections of land out into the ocean to become a new island. Over the course of millions of years, the surviving members of the species on the island become completely isolated from their original mainland group. This isolation results in a separate set of mutations from their ancestors on the mainland. Such is the case with the island of Madagascar off the southeastern shore of Africa. Over geologic time, Madagascar became separated from Africa and produced a wide range of unique creatures that have a genetic history with those on the African mainland but are now unique to the island itself.

One of the practical advantages to understanding the theory of evolution is that it helps a biological researcher understand why similarities exist across animal species. In fact, the area of comparative psychology often compares the anatomical structure of the brain across similar species that do not have the exact same brain areas. Therefore, the differences in the structures of the brain may be correlated with the changes in behavior between the two species. If both creatures have a similar genetic history, then one may be able identify through genetic analysis when the split occurred between them. Moreover, understanding the environments in which the split occurred will help to understand why the change in behavior occurred between species.

Artificial Selection

Wild foxes are generally very skittish around humans. Attempting to touch or pick up a wild fox will most likely result in being bitten. Dmitry Belyaev of the Russian Academy of Sciences Institute of Cytology and Genetics addressed the question of whether or not wild foxes could be domesticated. To address this issue, one-hundred female foxes and thirty male foxes were used in an experiment and allowed to produce offspring. Of those offspring, the tamest were allowed to move on to produce the second generation of foxes. The number of aggressive reactions they made when the experimenters attempted to feed, handle or touch them determined the tamest of these animals. The procedure of allowing only the tamest foxes to reproduce was applied over thirty generations.

vector set: ★ FARM ANIMALS ★

© Akaiser, 2012. Used under license from Shutterstock, Inc.

Farm animals have been bred for physical and behavioral characteristics for thousands of years

Artificial selection:
Artificial selection refers to the human controlled development of heritable properties. Artificial selection has been practiced on farms for millennia as farmers have attempted to breed larger animals for food sources. It has also been practiced in biology labs as ways to test genetic theories.

After 40 years, and approximately 45,000 births, the most recent set of foxes were much more human-friendly. That is, the previously wild foxes had become domesticated. They no longer exhibited fearful or aggressive behavior toward the human experimenters; rather, they acted much like a breed of house pets. This experimental approach established evidence that selective breeding could modify the behavior of foxes. Among other things, these data were used to help understand how domesticated dogs came from wild wolf populations.

Both biologists and psychologists have argued that similar, natural, processes have occurred in human kind over the course of millions of years to modify the universal patterns of human behavior. Rather than the artificial selection process used in the fox study, the processes of natural selection occurred over the course of eons and were influenced by the Earth's climate, tectonic plates, the availability of food and volcanic activity. All these factors and more modified the likelihood that humans would survive to a new generation.

Unique to humans is our ability to adapt to different environments. People may be found in the coldest climates on Earth as well as the hottest, the highest altitudes and the lowest altitudes. Our ability to produce tools to adapt to different environments as well as to modify our food selection techniques has enabled us to thrive on all the continents of the world.

By evaluating the common traits across human beings, one can put together a picture of our evolutionary history. Such common biological functions such as morning sickness or our tendency to enjoy fatty or sweet tasting foods are all related to the survival function of which foods we eat given the environment or biological state that we are in. Because sweets and fats had survival value and were in short supply in our long-ago evolutionary history, we developed a tendency to eat foods with those qualities. Currently, however, famine is very rare in industrialized societies but we retain our tendency to enjoy fatty and sweet foods. Therefore, much of the rise in obesity in industrialized societies reflects our evolutionary history and the fact that our biological history is, to some extent, not working to our advantage today with the current food supply.

If one extends evolutionary principles to human psychology, then there are ready answers to why there exist some universal behaviors in humans. Universal behaviors such as common facial expressions across all cultures, the relationship between the development of walking and stranger-anxiety, and why it is much less likely to see a biological father abuse or murder their children compared with stepfathers. These issues, and others like them, will be addressed through this and future chapters. For now, however, it is worth noting that common patterns of human behavior typically are understood through an application of evolutionary theory.

Selection by consequences: This term refers to the change in behavior that occurs over time because of the consequences obtained for behaving.

Ontogenetic Change: Selection by Consequences

The process of evolution shows how the results of genetic activity influence the evolution of the species (phylogeny). In particular, traits that make the species more adaptable to their environment will make them more likely to survive. In contrast, if developed traits make the species less adaptable to the environment then they will more likely become extinct. If one applies that same adaptability concept to the development of behavior across an individual lifespan then one is describing **selection by consequences**. Selection by consequences is a conceptually similar approach to behavior as evolution is to heritability. Simply put, if an exhibited behavior makes it more likely that a person will obtain a reward of some sort (e.g., food, social praise, etc.) then that same behavior will be more likely to occur in the future. In contrast, if an exhibited behavior makes it less likely that a person will obtain a reward then it will be less likely to occur in the future. Ultimately, this suggests that one's life is full of the responses that have garnered success in all previous environments. That, however, does not mean that those responses are the most successful ones for the current environment.

Selection by consequences is an **ontogenetic** effect. That is, the change occurs across the lifespan of the individual as opposed to a **phylogenetic** effect that occurs across multiple generations. In a simplistic way, phylogenetic change is related to genetic activity whereas ontogenetic change is often related to learning and memory. Therefore, a conceptual consistency exists between the phylogenetic process of natural selection and the ontogenetic selection by consequences process.

Successful people do successful things. We recognize successful people based upon the patterns of behavior that they exhibit. What one would expect from a successful person is patterns of behavior that support actions such as planning and organization, time management and listening skills. Of course, depending upon the particular environment one is in, a different set of behavioral patterns will be more likely to lead to success. This previous set should work well in the work environment as well as with family members. Those may not be the best patterns of behavior to exhibit if one were a member of a street gang or a standup comedian. Successful survival in the street gang may involve more engagement of action—not pontificating—and aggressive behavior. Standup comedians may rely more on an understanding of what makes things funny. Depending on what the primary reward is, the pattern of behavior will be different.

In the field of clinical psychology, it often helps to understand why someone may be exhibiting an odd pattern of behavior. The identified pattern is maladaptive as a result of it not supporting the acquisition of social rewards in the current environment. Often times, however, understanding the history of the individual will lead to understanding why that pattern of behavior exists now and how it used to produce social rewards. For example, an individual who appears withdrawn and keeps to himself may be viewed by many people as standoffish or as a loner. People may view that person and say, "Why doesn't he ever talk to us?" Because he does not interact much with other people he may not be invited to lunch or spoken to by his coworkers. If you asked this individual whether they wanted to interact with other people they might tell you yes. The question would remain then, why do they not interact with other people?

Oftentimes people who live in stressful environments (e.g., an emotionally abusing, degrading environment) learn to keep to themselves to avoid "rocking the boat" and making problems. People in these scenarios may learn to avoid interactions with other people despite the fact that they wish they had friends. Oftentimes they learn that is better to avoid interacting with others than it is to try to engage them in relationships. If this type of scenario lasts for a lengthy period, it may become a natural pattern of the individual. Therefore, once they go to work and find themselves in social situations, they simply will not interact very much with other people because of their own personal life history. The current maladaptive behavior, not interacting with other people, exists because of the rewarding consequences they earned during the time they lived in the emotionally abusing environment. It is times like these that a clinical psychologist may be able to intervene and train the individual in more appropriate ways of behaving.

Ontogeny (ontogenetic): Ontogeny refers to the influences that occur across an organism's life.

Phylogeny (phylogenetic): Phylogeny refers to the influences that affect heritable traits over generations.

Animals learn useful behavior by being rewarded for it and so do you.

© GoodMood Photo, 2012. Used under license from Shutterstock, Inc.

Much of evolutionary psychology is concerned with why people pursue certain mates.

Evolutionary biology:
Evolutionary biology is the study of biology with an evolutionary perspective.

Evolutionary psychology:
Evolutionary psychology is the study of psychology with an evolutionary perspective. It examines how traits common across all humans today may have developed because of evolutionary pressures.

Evolutionary Psychology

Humans across the world show a wide variety of similarities. We share a similar biology and—in particular—a similar architecture of brain circuitry. The field of behavioral genetics is primarily interested in determining to what degree genetics and environmental influence affect our behavior to create the similarities between us. Humans have 46 chromosomes, 23 contributed by each of our parents. The set of approximately 25,000 genes we have are turned on and off at different developmental periods. The signaling for these changes comes in part from environmental input into our nervous system.

Behavioral geneticists primarily focus on twin and adoption studies. They studies allow us to use naturally occurring differences between people to evaluate the relative roles of genetics and the environment. All psychological characteristics are known to have a biological aspect as well as an environmental component. One of the fields that behavioral geneticists tap for information is the field of molecular genetics. Researchers in molecular genetics study the molecular structure of genes and attempt to relate their structure to behavioral control by tracing their biochemical activities. There is a great deal of cooperation between psychologists and molecular geneticists in determining which specific genes influence human behavior.

The application of molecular genetics to the study of human behavior attempts to connect the biochemical activity of genes through to the ultimate behavioral outcomes. Molecular geneticists study the basic biochemical processes that turn genes on, off and overall translate them into proteins that are used somewhere within the body. How those genes came to be in the first place and what their function originally was designed for is less a question for molecular geneticists and more so a question for evolutionary biologists. When **evolutionary biology** is applied to the understanding of human behavior it is often referred to as **evolutionary psychology**. That is, the application of natural selection principles to the understanding of human behavioral characteristics.

Gender Differences in Human Mating Strategies

Researchers have long since recognized the differences in sexual responsiveness between males and females. These differences are not just in Western society but are consistent across all human cultures. In general, males are more easily aroused sexually relative to females and females are more selective regarding their choice of mates relative to males. Because these gender differences occur cross-culturally, psychologists have studied the difference from an evolutionary perspective. The evolutionary perspective of mate selection suggests that whichever gender invests more into the raising and care of the young, should be more selective about with whom they mate. The effect is seen throughout the animal kingdom. For animals in which the female takes primary responsibility for the raising of the young, the females are very selective about with whom they choose to mate. For animals that share the responsibility of raising the young, the females are less choosy. In cases such as the seahorse in which the male takes primary responsibility for carrying the developing eggs, the males are the choosy gender and the females compete to attract them. The same general function as described above exists in human mating strategies. Cross cultural research has shown that males are more likely to engage in recreational sex (e.g., sex with strangers, one-night stands) relative to females. In contrast, females tend to be very selective and find mates that show signs of willingness to make long term commitments.

© corepics, 2012. Used under license from Shutterstock, Inc.

Which approach males and females use reflect their long and short term interests.

The evolutionary perspective suggests that males and females have adopted these two strategies to obtain sex due to the parental investment required by each of their genders. For males, sex has little repercussions overall. That is, if sex results in a pregnancy, then it is not the male who becomes pregnant. Consequently, sex is a relatively brief activity for most males of which they suffer little biological consequence. In contrast, however, females can become pregnant. The addition of pregnancy after sex results in a comparatively large investment in effort that females must make. At the end of the pregnancy, the child is born and it will take well over a decade before he or she will be considered independent. Therefore, it would be more adaptive for females to search for mates who like them for her relatively permanent qualities (e.g., personality factors) rather than any other potentially temporary characteristic she exhibits such as physical beauty, social status or symbols of wealth.

In contemporary society, there is easy access to prophylaxis and online sexual-encounter services. If they wanted, could not females engage in as much sex as men wish they would? Well, technically the answer is both yes and no. Although these products and services are readily available, females—as a group—do not feel drawn to make use of them. The expectation from evolutionary theory is simply that females are not designed to regularly engage in short-term sexual activity but rather to look for long-term relationships. In contrast, males are regularly sensitive to any potential sexual signals from females and behave accordingly.

What Looks Good in a Mate?

Apart from the suggestions evolutionary psychology gives for mating strategies, it also suggests the traits that males and females look for in mates. If the evolutionary perspective suggests that male sexuality is driven by attempts to produce pregnancies, then the best choice for female partners would be those most likely to become pregnant. Across cultures, most men should tend to prefer women with youthful appearances. Research shows that youthfulness has been correlated with greater fertility (Buss, 2012). Females who are healthy have smooth skin and a youthful appearance and have characteristics associated with the ability to get pregnant. This suggests that across cultures men will tend to prefer women that are younger than they are and have characteristics indicative of good health. Once measured in cross-cultural research, We find that these predictions are supported in cross-cultural research (Buss, 2012).

Which of these two images do you think appeals more to men or women?

In contrast, mate selection for females should be different if you are going to hold a pregnancy for nine months and raise a child for years afterward. Consequently, females should be more interested in males who exhibit signs of strength and resources (e.g., money, social power). The strength and resources of the male should protect the mother and child during the lengthy period in which the mother is weakened by the pregnancy (e.g., tiredness, nausea and difficulty getting around) and unable to acquire resources while she raises the child. Resources take time to acquire so it would be expected that females should have a tendency to find attractive males that are older. Once measured in cross-cultural research, we find that these predictions are also supported in cross-cultural research (Buss, 2012).

Putting the Evolutionary Approach in Perspective

Critics of evolutionary psychology like to point out that regardless of the way in which humans behave now, you could always make suggestions about the long-ago evolutionary history that may have induced a particular pattern of behavior that exists today. That argument is difficult to argue against. It is essentially impossible to lose an argument when you are arguing in hindsight from an evolutionary perspective. If you are not there and did not record what was happening over millions of years then it's only mere speculation of what may have happened that led to the patterns of behavior that exist today. Artificial selection as well as natural selection processes may be observed today, especially in creatures with short generation spans, but that does not guarantee that an evolutionary explanation of human psychological traits is accurate. It may be, but it is difficult prove at the current time.

Problems with the evolutionary approach to behavior, whether it is human or nonhuman, always come from saying different strategies of behavior emerged across different creatures. For example, humans tend to mate with one person over the course of their life. Evolutionary psychologists often argue that this is a result of establishing in a monogamous relationship that the child actually belongs to the father; the issue of paternity being a primary concern with respect to humans. In contrast, however, bonobo chimps have a strategy in which females mate with many males. This, of course, muddles the issue of paternity but seems to work just fine in the bonobo population. How could such different strategies appear in two types of primates? It is not clear.

Attempts to understand human behavior through evolutionary methods always include some degree of speculation. This, however, does not mean that you cannot find evidence for different patterns of behavior. It may be that those explanations are simply not available yet. As more is known about molecular genetics, neuroanatomy, and the similarities and differences in brain structure across

The behavior of our ancient ancestors established portions of our contemporary behavior. Scenes like this were probably not too common.

primates, researchers will be in a better position to understand why different patterns of behavior occur based upon current biological and environmental conditions without referring to evolutionary history. Evolutionary history may be important, but it is probably much more important to focus on the here and now in understanding differences in behavior rather than become concerned with what happened millions of years ago.

DISTINGUISHING NATURE FROM NURTURE

When anthropologists look around the globe at human cultures, they find many similarities. Of course, they also find many differences as well. Those aspects of human behavior that are consistent across cultures are understood in terms of a shared biological heritage across all human beings. The unique components are frequently associated with the individual history of that society. The reasons explaining why there are common patterns of behavior as well unique aspects across societies are one of the primary issues of this chapter. To understand these issues one must delve into the shared biological heritage of all humans as well as address the components of environmental input modifying each culture. In the next section, we will address the issue of shared biological inheritance.

Genetic Influences on Behavior

Every one of us has strengths and weaknesses. When we review our strengths and weaknesses, can we automatically attribute them to the genes we obtained from our parents? Do we know we can attribute them to our upbringing, such as the way our parents took care of us until we were adults? The understanding of which aspects of human behavior are a result of biological functions as opposed to environmental influences was debated scientifically since the third quarter of the 19th century. Today, researchers known as behavioral geneticists evaluate the differences in our characteristics from the standpoint of biology and environment. To understand the research methodologies that behavioral geneticists use and the database from which they make their conclusions is the primary issue in the following section.

Behavioral geneticists: Researchers that attempt to study how genes can influence behavior are called behavioral geneticists.

Behavioral Genetics

The story of genetics is consistent across human kind. All humans have 46 chromosomes, 23 donated by your mother's eggs and 23 donated by your father's sperm. These chromosomes are composed of a chain of molecular deoxyribonucleic acid (DNA). Genes are the smallest segments of these grand DNA molecules. Genes are small sections of DNA that cannot be broken down or added to without changing their function (generally changing a gene leads to disastrous consequences). Because each gene has a specific function to perform, it has been called the functional unit of heredity. Biologists estimate that we have approximately 25,000 or so genes; however, the majority of these appear to be dormant. Between humans, there is an enormous amount of similarity. All people share approximately 99.9 percent of their DNA. Surprisingly, the action of that $1/10^{th}$ of 1 percent difference is where we generally focus all our social attention.

Small but important differences also exist between chimpanzees and humans. Despite the 1.2 percent difference between human and chimpanzee DNA, there is an enormous difference in human behavior relative to chimpanzees. Scientists are interested in determining how the differences in genetics and environment produce these large effects. As a model to understand such a complex issue, one might try looking at something simpler such as understanding the genetic and environmental factors controlling your weight.

Your weight may seem like a simple issue to grasp, however, your genes and environment determine it and they have not been easy to understand. Your weight may be influenced by your sensitivity to the smell of certain foods, your sensitivity to tastes and the ability of your stomach to distend—all primarily genetic issues. They may also be influenced by how good a cook your parents were as you were raised, your daily free time and your access to food through either money or more primary resources—all primarily environmental issues. To determine what is contributing to a person's overall weight we must look at many different factors. To tease apart the genetic and environmental factors controlling your weight—or anything else—behavioral geneticists have come up with some creative methodological procedures. These procedures have led to a considerable amount of knowledge since the 1980's.

© Kenneth Sponsler, 2012. Used under license from Shutterstock, Inc.

In the 1980s, the rate of twinning was estimable by race. Since then, those differences have largely been erased. This is evidence that twinning is affected by both biological and environmental factors.

Twin Studies

Identical and Fraternal Twins

The study of twins helps researchers determine whether differences in weight, personality or other traits are related to the environment or their genetic background. The way in which twin studies do this is by examining identical twins that were raised together or raised apart. In addition, fraternal twins that were either raised together or raised apart are similarly studied. In this manner, researchers can determine whether the effects of similar genes or similar environments modify human behavior.

Purposely conducting a twin study from scratch, however, would definitely violate ethical standards. That is, one would have to create a set of identical twins and then purposely separate them or allow them to be raised together so that you could assess the influence of the same or different environment in relation to their genetic background. This, of course, is ethically unacceptable. Separations at birth do occur naturally—generally through adoption—and behavioral geneticists use these events as a way to understand the basics of human nature.

Many studies have indicated that there are both influences from genetic background as well as environment. Studies of this type have essentially put an end to the nature versus nurture debate. Consistently, researchers find that both genes and environment influence human behavior. Issues of greater interest now are; (a) what type of influence can affect behavior and (b) how much that factor can influence behavior. The questions of how much and which type of control are of primary interest today.

Identical twins who develop from a single fertilized egg are the most genetically similar individuals on the planet, although it has been recently found that identical twins may have some genetic differences between them (Bruder, et al., 2008). Regardless, they are more similar than any two individuals on the planet. Fraternal twins develop from two separate fertilized eggs and are as genetically similar as general siblings except they shared a placental environment. Evaluating the shared womb environment is certainly something not seen in non-twin siblings given that two children would likely be born about one year apart.

Studies conducted around the world on thousands of pairs of identical twins have indicated that they are more alike in personality and intellectual characteristics then fraternal twins or general siblings. Even patterns of social behavior are also more similar. For example, identical twins with a divorced sibling have a 5.5 times greater likelihood of divorce themselves than if their twin was not divorced. If you compare fraternal twins, however, the difference only goes up 1.6 times if your twin is divorced. These effects, which also control for environmental influences, indicate that our genes will influence to some degree whether or not we will get divorced. This, however, is not the full story. Certainly, environmental influences affect whether or not we are unhappy in our marriages. The sensitivity to these effects have to be processed through our biology and in some way—in ways we do not understand—affects our likelihood for divorce.

Adoption Studies

Another research methodology that helps distinguish between genetic and environmental influences is adoption studies. Adoption studies allow for the comparison between parent and sibling between same or different environments. That is, a child

Twin studies: A twin study is the generic name given to the study of heritability in children born into the same family, especially twins, triplets etc.

Identical twins: A set of twins derived from a single fertilized egg spitting into two separate individuals. Identical twins are more similar genetically than any other two individuals.

Fraternal twins: Twins derived from the fertilization of two eggs by two separate sperm cells during the same gestation period.

© Susan Law Cain, 2012. Used under license from Shutterstock, Inc.

Fraternal twins are no more genetically similar than general siblings are because they are both conceived from different eggs and sperm. Developing inside their mother at the same time, however, produces a long-term environmental influence that can be measured in adulthood.

Adoption studies: An Adoption study is the name given to the study of heritability in adopted and non-adopted children.

raised by their own parents can be compared to that child's twin who was put up for adoption and raised by another couple. The twin raised by the adoptive couple does not share a genetic similarity with their caregiver but does share a genetic similarity with their biological parents. During the course of development, especially during adulthood, the personality characteristics of the child can be compared to the adoptive parents as well as to the original biological parents to determine whether or not traits from the biological family are evidenced in the adopted child or if the new caregivers alone developed the traits of the child.

Results of such experiments have indicated primarily that biology is the factor determining personality traits much more strongly than environment. That is, adopted children are more similar to their biological parents than to the adoptive parents. These effects are remarkable and very different to what most people tend to believe. In fact, it has been stated that two adopted children raised together in the same home are no more likely to share personality characteristics with each than with any randomly selected child from the same neighborhood (Myers, 2010). Similar types of effects can also be seen with macaque monkeys who live in zoos that are raised by their own parents or foster parents.

Overall, these statements indicate that biology primarily establishes the basic characteristics of personality far more greatly than environmental influence. This of course raises the question of why children who live in the same household may appear so different in personality than those children who live in different households. This question, is oftentimes been referred to as one of the most important puzzles in the history of psychology (Pinker, 2002).

So is it true then that adoptive parenting has no influence on the child? The answer to that question is a resounding no. Rather than basic personality characteristics, environmental influences tend to have greater influence on children's attitudes, values, social manners, religious faith and politics (Brodzinsky & Schechter, 1990). Moreover, the parents and adoptive homes are carefully screened by the adoptive agencies, which is something that does not happen for the natural biological parents. Therefore, often times the parents of adoptive homes are identified as well suited for parenting before obtaining their children. Many of the characteristics of adoptive parents as such are then often

Studying adopted children allows researchers to estimate how similar they are relative to their biological parents.

passed to the children that they raise. The adoptive parents who may be viewed as "self-giving" tend to pass those self-giving patterns onto their adoptive children. Evidence indicates that adoptees are often raised with fewer problems than are experienced by children who are raised by their own biological parents (Bohman & Sigvardsson, 1990). Altogether, this indicates that the environmental influences on adoptive children are beneficial. More importantly for our current purposes, they are environmental influences.

Temperament Studies

The term **temperament** refers to an individual's emotional excitability. Emotional excitability is often described in terms such as placid, quiet, easy-going, fidgety, reactive, cheerful, predictable and relaxed (Chess & Thomas, 1987). Studies on temperament indicate that temperament is a relatively permanent characteristic of personality. The temperaments of newborns are consistent with the same temperaments they express at nine months of age. Similar studies indicate that there is a consistency in temperament between the first year of life and adulthood. Further support for this concept of a biologically derived temperament that is permanent across the lifespan comes from the comparison of identical and fraternal twins.

Temperament: Temperament refers to one's overall level of emotional reactivity.

Heritability

Heritability is related to the likelihood that one can acquire a trait through genes. It is measured as the **proportion of variation** among individuals with and without the trait. The heritability of a trait may vary depending upon the range of differences in the population and the environment studied. It is estimated statistically that biology affects 50 percent of the variability among the personality characteristics of humans. The proportion of variation that is determined statistically is related to the amount of variability in the data as it changes across conditions. That is, as you change conditions from biological factors to environmental factors the type of personality characteristics change. Admittedly, this is a rather obtuse point and it is related to the way in which the statistical tests used to measure human behavior have been fashioned. For now, however, accept as best you can the idea that 50 percent of the "variability" between biological and environmental factors is influenced by biology.

Heritability: Heritability refers to the likelihood that a genetic trait will be inherited by offspring.

Proportion of variation: This term refers to the amount of variance accounted for in a statistical correlation.

If one-half of all personality characteristics are influenced by biology, then can we extend that prediction to account for one-half of all differences between

Biology and environment establish the conditions that create a child's personality. Neither child in this image is guaranteed a bright future, however, one of them is more likely to experience it.

different cultures? The answer is, not necessarily so. Determining the differences between individuals can be estimated with the proportion of variance that we discussed in the previous paragraph. Those influences, however, do not always refer to the average performance of a general group. For example, most Americans are both taller and heavier today than they were one-hundred years ago. These differences, however, cannot be linked to a recent rapid change in genetics that occurred over the past century. Rather, the explanation is better understood through changes in nutrition and diet habits (environmental differences). In contrast, however, the differences between individuals today should still be controlled by the same genetic factors that were present one-hundred years ago. If we were to return to a standard diet from circa 1910 then it would be expected that our children would become shorter and we would all become thinner. Consequently, both genetics and the environment have clear influences on our characteristics.

The previous section has indicated that both biology and environment influence our behavior. The question we can ask now is; how is our development affected by the interaction of our genes with environmental influences? One way to understand this issue is by looking at gene self-regulation. Genes are self-regulating which means that they can change their functions slightly based upon the environmental input that reaches them. One nice example of self-regulating genes comes from the African butterfly (*Bicyclus anynana*). This butterfly has a temperature-controlled genetic switch that makes the butterfly turn green and show eyespots in the summer and brown without eyespots in the fall. Therefore, the butterfly has genes that are sensitive to environmental input and modify their function accordingly. This type of self-regulating process seems to account for a number of patterns of human behavior. That is, depending upon the environmental input that a person experiences, genes may modify their patterns of behavior in ways that establish their personality characteristics. One of the places that we see evidence for this is in the environmental role in inducing schizophrenic symptoms from a person who has the genes for the disorder.

Overall, the understanding of gene-environment interaction leads most researchers to conclude that both factors influence the development of human personality as well as other characteristics. Therefore, asking whether biology or environment is more important really has no clear answer. Both biology and environment affect the development and expression of characteristics. Certainly, biology and environment always influence psychological characteristics. The real question is to what degree does biology or the environment influence anyone particular personality characteristic. The determination of the proportion of variance for genetic and environmental control over human response systems is the contemporary approach to nature and nurture.

Consider a situation in which a pair of identical twins has one slight difference between them; one child tends to be more adaptive to stressful situations. Throughout the course of their lives, the one who is more stress adaptive tends to persevere in stressful scenarios for longer periods and also tends to expose herself to recreational stress (e.g., roller coasters, skydiving, extreme camping). Throughout the course of their lives, they may experience separate careers, different levels of income, different peer groups and ultimately may become quite different than one may have considered given their similar genetic backgrounds.

What this example provides is a way to understand how a small difference between people may lead to big differences after a long period. Slight differences between individuals can be enhanced enormously over long periods. In fact, as we will see in the intelligence chapter, some theories of intelligence indicate that large differences may come about because of minor differences between individuals that are enhanced over the course of a lifetime.

One way in which these differences may develop comes from each individual selecting an environment that suits their biological characteristics. In the above example, a more stress resilient individual may tend to expose themselves to greater levels of stress than their stress-averse twin. Stress, which is a rather vague term, may appear in many different forms. Stress can come about because of economic instability or exposure to noise. A stress adaptive person who is also physically strong may have personality characteristics that fit well for a life in the military. An equally stress resilient person who is physically small would not. In fact, that person's small physical size may lead him to sources of stress that are unrelated to physical fighting but are still competitive (e.g., nonviolent games).

Therefore, it is necessary to understand that from the time of conception onward, a series of interactions between our genes and the environment make us what we are. Our personality characteristics and intelligence are developed in this manner. In no way should anyone consider nature versus nurture as a proper question today. One should always consider how genes and the environment interact to produce something different separately from either of those two sources of control. Moreover, we should be looking closely to see if genes or the environment weighs more heavily in any given human behavior.

A more complete understanding of genetics tells us that multiple genes often control single factors. One such factor is your weight. Although there are multiple genes that influence weight, some subset of them will be influenced by nutrition (e.g., how much carbohydrates or protein we eat). Therefore, our weight will in part be related to our preferences for the food for which we have access. Which genes control our tendency to exercise will also influence how many calories we burn. This in turn will affect our likelihood of obesity. Thinking of obesity as a single gene issue is an oversimplification. There are genes that influence what we find tasteful, genes that influence how quickly we recognize that our stomachs are full, genes that influence our tendency to exercise and other genes that influence our resilience against a low calorie diet. Taken together, all these influences affect whether or not we develop obesity and the subsequent problems associated with it such as diabetes. What may look like a simple issue—obesity—may actually be quite complex when you consider the genetic and environmental issues controlling it.

Environmental Influences on Behavior

Personal History

The terms nature and nurture refer to biology and environment respectively. Both of these factors become active at the moment of conception. That is, prior to birth, a prenatal infant is exposed to environmental influences in the womb that will last for a nine-month period. What kind of environmental influences can affect the prenatal infant? Recall that our definition of nurture refers to any stimulation from outside the organism. Therefore, the nurture of a prenatal infant refers to its nutrition, any toxins or drugs that the mother may be taking, the child's access to the mother's blood supply as well as the presence of a sibling (e.g., twin, triplet, etc.) that may also be in the uterus. All of these factors ultimately influence the early development of the child.

Nurture is most likely to be seen in instances of social behavior, however. Research has shown that the development of the brain and the total number of synaptic connections that it makes early in life are influenced by the amount of social activity that a laboratory rat receives (Renner & Rosenzweig, 1987). It appears that similar processes also occur in humans although it would be unethical to conduct a similar experiment intentionally. Rather, such data comes from the natural differences between people that live and die at an early age (Field et al., 2006).

Experiments with rats indicate that housing a rat by itself or separately in an environment with other rats produces a difference in the size of the brain and number of synaptic connections present. The rats that are housed together tend to have about a 10 percent increase in brain weight and an increase in approximately 20 percent in the number of synaptic connections compared to rats that are housed alone. The effect of environmental stimulation on brain development has led researchers to assess the possibility that massaging prenatal infants will improve their overall health. In fact, it turns out that massaging premature infants does help them develop faster and improve their medical status (Field, et al., 2006).

Similar types of processes occur if someone is blind since birth as a result of cataracts. If a child is born with cataracts and the cataracts are removed then the child's occipital lobe may develop normally and the child may develop normal visual functioning. In contrast, however, if the cataracts are not removed the brain tissue that would have analyzed visual information is then redirected to be used by the surrounding areas of the brain (such as hearing) and the ability to develop accurate vision later once the cataracts are removed is then reduced (Gregory, 1978). You may recall that the brain's ability to rewire itself is referred to as plasticity.

Plasticity occurs every day in adults. Any time you learn a new skill, such as playing a musical instrument, the brain must wire itself in a manner that supports that new behavior (Karni, et al., 1998). Therefore, as you learn you also rewire your brain. Because you are learning new things every day, especially those of you who are consistently studying in college, you are rewiring your brain on a daily basis. To a greater or lesser degree, everyone's brain is rewiring itself all the time because we are always being exposed to new events during the course of the day. Those of us that actively train some particular skill may actively modify those areas of the brain more rapidly. This process is normal and is expected to occur in the brains of all living organisms.

Understanding the environmental influences on human development raises many questions about early development in the child's life. How much control is exerted by parents and how much control is exerted by peers? Much research has indicated that many of the patterns of social behavior that children exhibit

Although poverty is correlated with various types of social problems, it also serves as a motivating factor to succeed. It also encourages others to help. Neither wealth nor poverty guarantees your future successes or failures.

are primarily derived by peer influences rather than parental influences. When children reject food items at the home dinner table they may be more likely to eat them in front of their peers who are eating the same items. Children who have parents that speak with an accent almost always learn to speak with respect to the accent of their peers. Children and teenagers who learn to smoke almost always do so because of peer influence.

Knowing that the behavior of a child or teenager is developed in part by parental biology, parental influence and peer influence requires care in attributing any particular behavior of the subject to either parent or peer. Ultimately, it seems most likely that any pattern of behavior will be both parentally and peer influenced. Overall, any pattern of behavior that develops in a child is likely a result of the individual history of that person with respect to their biology and social influences by both their parents and peers.

Cultural Influences on Behavior

Nature and nurture are the primary themes in this chapter. When we discuss learned influences on behavior, we clearly are discussing the role of the environment. The capacity to learn the principal beliefs, values and philosophy of a culture provides us with the opportunity to modify the behavior of children to exhibit the most adaptive behavioral patterns for the current conditions of the world.

There is some evidence that non-human primates exhibit the rudimentary components of culture. Evidence supporting this idea comes from the presence of "local customs" of tool use, grooming and courtship that occur across different troops of primates. Some of those components of non-human culture are learned behaviors acquired by watching the adult members of the species. The fact that learned behavior is passed from one generation to the next is the basis for what we would call culture.

Culture is commonly defined as the common behaviors, ideas, and attitudes shared by a group of people and taught to each succeeding generation. Culture provides us with numerous advantages. The knowledge acquired by any one individual can be transferred to others in the same generation or across multiple generations. We do so primarily by our oral traditions and by writing. It may be argued that the greatest amount of cultural information in any society is based within its accumulated books and media. Cultural learning modifies which behaviors will help us survive and reproduce. Keep in mind, the fastest way to adapt to a rapidly changing world is through learning, not through natural selection.

Learning a language has an enormous influence on our overall ability to survive and reproduce. The entire history of human knowledge written into books, the internet and any other media device comprises all of the cultural learning of humankind acquired over thousands of years. The entire set of human knowledge is given to each succeeding generation who may append it. Each generation will modify that information in a manner that will support their ability to survive and reproduce. For example, archaeologists believe that archery was developed during the Upper Paleolithic period (Late Stone Age) about 12,000 to 42,000 BCE. From then until now, archery has essentially stayed the same. The strength of the bow was directly related to the force acquired from the bow's arms. The first major advancement in archery after thousands of years came in 1966 with the invention of the compound bow. The compound bow uses a series of pulleys to reduce the tension the archer applies once the string is

Culture: Culture is the general view of the world from a whole society.

© lev dolgachov, 2012. Used under license from Shutterstock, Inc.

Regardless of your cultural training, the pattern of behavior you learn generally works for the society you live in. It is typically when you move to another country that you begin to see the irrational patterns in yours and others behavior. Can you predict a problem with mixing a young woman in provocative clothes with alcohol?

pulled completely back making it easier to aim the arrow. This advance makes the compound bow more accurate and has since become the more commonly used bow in our contemporary age.

Despite the differences across cultures, there are a number of behavioral similarities observed in the individuals across all cultures. For example, adults respond to a baby's cooing, crying and babbling similarly. Baby talk is a common human trait that typically initiates a child-adult interaction. Of course, whether you are learning Chinese or English, the particular sounds that the parent makes to the child at this time will be different. This, however, does not negate the fact that responding to the child's noises draws the parent into a verbal interaction with the infant. This consequently exposes the child to sounds from the adult language that the baby will copy.

Sometimes different cultural patterns seem to reflect differences in races. For example, lower rates of cardiovascular disease in Japan relative to the United States seem to reflect a difference in mean biological traits between the two countries. If, however, one does not recognize the different dieting pattern between the countries, then one may associate the difference with a racial genetic trait between Japanese Asians and North American Caucasians. Similar types of effects may also be seen within single countries. One such effect is the mean differences in blood pressure between black and white Americans. Generally, medical doctors have recognized that black men in the United States have higher blood pressure on average than Caucasian men. This difference, if accepted on face value, may seem to reflect differences in race. Further research, however, has shown that the difference is related to mean dieting patterns between the two groups, of which a higher mean salt content is present in the diet of black Americans. Overall, this indicates that differences between groups need to be evaluated carefully so that the proper factors contributing to the differences are understood properly. This issue, of course, goes back to the chapter 1 discussion of correlation. Remember, correlation does not mean causation regardless of the factors being evaluated.

FINDING NATURE AND NURTURE IN GENDER DEVELOPMENT

A common illustration of nature and nurture (phylogeny and ontogeny) working together is the development of gender. From the time of a person's conception, people ask whether "it's going to be a boy or girl." After finding out, they begin referring to the child with the appropriate gender related pronoun. It is common for people to speak to the child in a gender related manner and even purchase him or her clothing of particular colors that match their physical gender. Even though all male and female infants may be essentially helpless cooing, crying babies in need of complete help from other people, adults will classify them in male or female categories and treat them accordingly.

Physical gender, as determined by your chromosomes, is certainly a biological issue. How we behave as males and females, however, is largely derived by social learning. That social learning will be part of our culture and our specific life history. There is integration between biology and environment as well. For example, chromosomal activity influences physical development and may modify the physical characteristics that influence our gender-related treatment from others. One common example of such an effect is androgen insensitivity syndrome (AIS) (Diamond & Watson, 2004). Males with AIS have the male XY chromosomal pattern but have all the outward physical characteristics of a female. Researchers have seized on the available opportunities in gender related research to evaluate how phylogeny and ontogeny influence development.

Perceived and Real Gender Differences

Notwithstanding the differences often portrayed between males and females, we are actually much more alike than we are different. One reason for that comes from our genes. Of our 46 chromosomes, 45 of them are unisex. Only one chromosome accounts for our gender. Moreover, in evolutionary history, males and females living together have suffered through the same hardships and have met the same successes. Given the similar history over millions of years, one would expect males and females to be quite similar.

It is a common social phenomenon that people concentrate on the differences between them and ignore the obvious similarities. Despite all the discussion of differences between males and females, any psychology student should recognize that we are far more similar than we are different. Some of the differences that people tend to focus on are related to aggression, social power and social connectedness. We will discuss these three in the next few paragraphs.

Social psychologists generally recognize that men do exhibit more physical aggression than do women. These differences in aggression exist cross culturally as well. Cross-cultural studies show that males tend to exhibit more physical aggression than women do. One social statistic that identifies this result is in violent crime rates. In the United States, there is a 9 to 1 difference in favor of males for exhibiting violent crime. In addition, involvement in hunting, fighting and military service is primarily male activities.

Cross culturally, most people tend to perceive males as being more dominant, forceful and independent. In contrast, women tend to be viewed as more deferential, nurturing and socially connected. When groups form, the power generally goes to the males whether you are discussing courtroom juries or company leadership. As leaders, men tend to be more directive and autocratic whereas women tend to be more democratic. Female bosses are more likely to listen to subordinates opinions than male bosses are. Males generally tend to offer opinions of what they would like to see happen, whereas women are more likely to support others ideas. The differences in the way males and females behave socially tends to support the inequities of social power. For example, male patterns of behavior are more dominant than female patterns. Expressing or demanding opinions tends to result in more people doing as you say as opposed to listening to others' ideas and offering support. When we see these cross-cultural differences, we have to ask if they are genetically controlled or if there is common social training across cultures that produce these effects.

Another difference between males and females is related to the amount of social interaction each seeks out. Generally, males tend to be less involved in social groups whereas females tend to get involved with more people in their lives. The reason for the existence of these differences is not clear, however, they do begin early in life. Typically, males play in large groups with a focus on a particular activity, such as a soccer game. These games generally involve little verbal interaction between the group members. In contrast, females tend to play in smaller groups and usually with a single friend. Female play tends to be less competitive relative to male play and involves activity that is more social. In both play and non-play settings, females tend to be more open and responsive to feedback than males.

© stefanolunardi, 2012. Used under license from Shutterstock, Inc.

Personally, I hate shoe shopping so much that I will set aside one hour, go to one store and force myself to buy something regardless of whether I like the shoes or not. My one pair of dress shoes contrasts strongly with my wife's twenty pairs. In eleven years, she has bought every pair of shoes our children have ever gotten— although I am sometimes standing in the background holding onto my credit card.

When males and females are compared with respect to their social networking there continues to be differences. For example, male and female subjects could accurately estimate 66 percent of the time which student e-mails were written by other males or females. With respect to computer use, females spend more time e-mailing friends and less time playing games (games tend to be the preferred male activity). Studies conducted in France indicate that women make 63 percent of the telephone calls. When women are speaking to other women on the telephone, they tend to stay connected for longer periods than males (Smoreda & Licoppe, 2000). Data such as these have lent some support to the idea that women speak more than males. Further research, however, has indicated that the total number of words spoken per day is very similar between males and females (Mehl et al., 2007).

The Chromosomal Characteristics of Gender

Children's gender is indistinguishable during the first seven weeks after conception. It is about this time that sex chromosomes become active and establish your biological gender. During sex, females always contribute an X chromosome and males contribute an X or Y chromosome. When the male contributes an X chromosome, the child will have two X chromosomes and will necessarily become female (XX). If the male contributes a Y chromosome then the child will be male (XY).

The Y chromosome includes a single gene that triggers a master switch to produce the principal male hormone, testosterone. Once the switch is on, the presence of testosterone will begin to produce external male genitalia. As you may know already, females also have testosterone. The difference between males and females in relation to this master switch is the total concentration of testosterone produced in the child. Greater concentrations lead to the development of a male. Lower concentrations of testosterone produce a female.

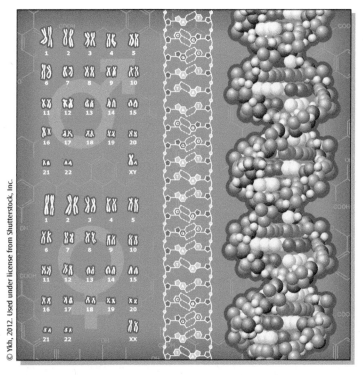

Researchers have been surprised to find that some gender-related characteristics are nearly unchangeable.

When problems in the development of testosterone develop, the external genitalia of the child may change. For example, when females have an excess of testosterone prenatally, their external genitalia may appear male. At birth and during the beginning of their life, they may act in a more traditional male manner. For example, they often play more aggressively than typical girls and prefer to play with guns rather than dolls. There is some research that indicates these females will be more likely lesbian, however, most will become heterosexual (Berenbaum & Bailey, 2003).

These data seem to suggest that prenatal hormones influence sexual orientation and gender related behavior. Experiments with rats and monkeys also indicate that typical patterns of male or female behavior mirror the same effects seen in humans. With respect to humans, however, females exposed to greater concentrations of prenatal testosterone are generally viewed socially as physically masculine. This may lead to masculine treatment of these individuals by society. This social effect may further drive the pattern of masculine behavior. This is an important point of which to make. Once a biological influence develops, it will be further modified by social interactions. If a female looks masculine, or if a male looks feminine, the degree and type of social interactions they experience may differ based upon their appearance. At a young age, this may modify the child's gender related behavior and ultimately develop different gender typed patterns of behavior as an adult.

The John Joan Case

Other evidence that biological influences modify gender comes from the John Joan case. The John Joan case involved a pair of male identical twins of which one lost his penis during a botched circumcision. The doctor involved suggested to the parents that gender was a socially derived function and that their son could have his testicles removed, plastic surgery to produce a vagina, and be successfully raised as a girl. As Joan grew up, she tended to play in rough-and-tumble ways. She preferred more male activities relative to female activities despite the fact that she was being raised as a girl and was administered female hormones.

Although the John Joan case illustrated the failure of involuntary sex reassignment, about 1:10,000 American males happily undergo the transition like the transsexual in the above image.

By the time Joan had reached puberty, she was not sexually interested in boys. It was approximately at this time that Joan's parents explained to her about her early life sex change. Shortly thereafter, Joan rejected her female identity and began to live her life as a male. He first had plastic surgery to develop the outward appearance of a male and stopped taking female hormones. By adulthood, he lived his life as a male, met a woman and was married. He was stepfather to his wife's previous children until his death in 2004 (Diamond, 1997).

One of the lessons of the John Joan case is that gender development and sexual orientation are influenced by biological factors. This case and others like it have largely eliminated the idea that gender is derived by environmental factors alone. Today, most researchers accept that gender and sexual orientation are influenced by both biological (genetic, chromosomal) and environmental factors (culture, life history).

Gender Related Behavior

Gender role: A characteristic pattern of behavior that is associated with a gender is called a gender role.

Males and females have **gender roles** in every society on earth. Gender roles are expectations about the way men and women should behave in their society. Gender roles are not determined by biological factors alone; rather they are primarily influenced by culture (learning, ontogeny). Sociological studies across the 20th century have shown that there have been enormous changes in the gender role patterns of females across the world. For example, in 1900 New Zealand was the only democracy to allow women to vote. By 2000, Kuwait was the only one that did not grant that right. Only one in thirty American law students were female in 1960 but by 2000 that number had risen to about fifty percent. Only 29 percent of Americans agreed that it was "all right for a girl to telephone a boy to ask for date" in 1950 but by the end of the 20th century that number had risen to 70 percent (Myers, 2007).

Gender identity: Gender identity is a person's perception of their identified sex role.

Other than gender roles, society provides for us a **gender identity**. Gender identity is defined as the sense of being male or female in your society. To a varying degree, all people become **gender typed**. Gender type refers to the degree to which someone expresses his or her gender role in society. For example, a strongly gender typed female would exhibit all of the traditional feminine traits in her society and very few of the masculine traits.

Gender-typing: The development of a traditional gender role is called gender typing.

Social learning theory: This term refers to the theoretical approach that all social behavior develops through learning.

Most of our understanding of gender roles, gender identity and gender typing come from **social learning theory**. Social learning theory suggests that we learn social behavior by observing and imitating others. When we observe others obtain rewards and punishments for their behavior, we then copy or avoid their patterns accordingly. For example, when a small boy sees that his father always holds the television remote control and asks his wife to bring him a beer (and she does) then he will learn to act accordingly as an adult. Societies are filled with gender typed patterns of behavior that come through social learning. In Western society, one of the most common instances is the use of blue for boys and pink for girls. Deviating from this pattern often raises the ire of its recipient (try giving an eight-year-old boy a pink toy and you will see what I mean). As children grow up learning their social rules, they tend to form into gender typed groups because the patterns they exhibit are more easily expressed around others with the same behavior.

This discussion of gender related behavior highlights the roles of genetics and the environment in producing a final psychological make up. Gender is first determined by genetics in our XX or XY chromosomal patterns. These chromosomes are activated during development and provide us with the physical characteristics associated with masculinity or femininity. The activation of these chromosomes plays out through the release of hormones. For males, testosterone is the primary hormone initiating the physical traits of masculinity. Estrogen is the corresponding hormone for females.

© shivanetua, 2012. Used under license from Shutterstock, Inc.

Across the globe, military operations are almost entirely male activities.

Although sex hormones have a significant role in developing our physical bodies, they also have a significant influence over our behavior. Common patterns of male or female behavior may be enhanced or suppressed by changing hormone levels. This is especially true in the developing child. Higher or lower concentrations of sex hormones enhance or reduce gender typed behavior. If, with androgen insensitivity syndrome, a developing male will not have sufficient receptors for his testosterone then he will fail to develop his masculine physical traits. Moreover, his psychological traits will be more similar to females.

Our bodies will direct others in society to see us as male or female. This will consequently influence how we are treated. The male or female pattern of treatment established by culture will be applied throughout all of our interactions with others. Consequently, we see that the final behavioral product of gender typed behavior is related to our **genes, hormones and learning** experiences. The combination of these three factors is the driving force behind current thinking about psychological traits. The idea is formally expressed in what is now known as the **biopsychosocial model of psychology**. This approach has been applied successfully in numerous areas of psychology and is the topic of discussion in the following section.

> **Genes, hormones and learning:** Genes, hormones and learning are the three primary factors establishing one's psychological traits.

> **Biopsychosocial model of psychology:** The biopsychosocial model of psychology suggests that all human behavior is a combination of biology, personal history and cultural influences.

THE BIOPSYCHOSOCIAL APPROACH TO PSYCHOLOGY

History

The history of medicine is filled with logic and superstition, progress and misconduct. The end of the 18th century was about the last time physicians referred to evil spirits as being involved in the illnesses they examined. Because, by then, the medical model was developed. The medical model in biology and medicine assumed that all illness was attributable to the physical operations of the body. This was accounted for through the chemical actions of oxygen, nutrients and minerals as well as the presence of germs that would not be discovered for decades hence. The medical model has reigned supreme in the field of medicine since that time. As the field of psychology developed in the late 19th century, the medical model was adapted for psychological operations. Some of the early research in psychology was focused upon the physical operation of the brain and how it controls behavior and other psychological characteristics.

Two of the factors researchers most heavily focused upon were heredity and neuroanatomy. Unfortunately, for researchers of that time, little work could be conducted in either field due to their lack of technical sophistication. For instance, work on heredity did not involve work on genes because DNA was not discovered until the early 1950's. Work on heredity in the 19th century generally involved experiments with plants, such as those conducted on pea plants by Gregor Mendel. Research on neuroanatomy was little more than basic anatomical studies of the nervous system. German and French researchers conducted some of the first brain mapping studies on the cortexes of dogs and birds. Laboratory techniques in biology, however, could not discern the specific pathways of neural cells in the brain and researchers were left to infer the existence of neural circuits based upon their systematic lesioning of brain surfaces. Separate from the study of brain circuits on heredity, biological researchers were becoming more interested in the internal chemical signaling systems of the body; the study of hormones.

By the 20th century, more was known about endocrinology—the hormonal system. During the first four decades of the 20th century, most information regarding the endocrine system was unrelated to behavior. It was not until a series of experiments on the neural and hormonal control of sexual behavior of rats that more work was conducted on **behavioral endocrinology**. Behavioral endocrinology is the scientific study of behavior controlled by the hormonal system. Beach's text, *Hormones and Behavior* (Beach, 1948) was the first textbook devoted to the new field of behavioral endocrinology. This new field opened up the possibility that the social events of animals or humans may influence hormonal activity that may in turn affect our biological systems.

Behavioral endocrinology: Behavioral endocrinology refers to the study of how hormones influence behavior.

One of the contributions the behavioral sciences gave to medicine and psychiatry was social research. Researchers in anthropology, sociology and psychology contributed a wealth of data in the early 20th century with respect to how environmental conditions influence biological functioning. Early cultural studies by anthropologists showed that a patient's trust in the village medicine man greatly influenced their prognosis. Similar effects were also seen in Western society; however, Western doctors ignored the issue largely as a placebo

Genetic studies started with plants and animals before moving onto humans

effect unrelated to true biological functioning. As decades passed, more research was collected on the topic until the 1970's in which it was clear that environmental conditions (psychological functioning) had a substantial influence on whether surgeries or drugs cure medical problems. This information ran counter to the traditional medical model of medicine. The traditional medical model suggested all biological activity was caused by biochemistry or physiological systems. The suggestion that one's experience, thoughts or feelings may have a significant influence on medical health went against established medical thinking.

Engel (1977) wrote the first theoretical article suggesting the medical model was no longer viable for medicine. That same year an article describing the biological, psychological and social factors involved in drinking and alcoholism was published by Ewing (1977). Since this time, both physicians and behavioral scientists have integrated the biological, psychological and social factors involved in disease—whether it is medical or psychiatric.

Biological Influences

There are numerous biological influences on behavior. One of the most commonly identified is your genes. Genetics establishes the biochemical basis of heredity and the transfer of characteristics from one generation to the next. Although it may have been debated in the 19th century whether human behavior was influenced by heredity, it is now known that it does. In contrast, the environment also influences human behavior; therefore, no psychological theory completely based upon genetic arguments is likely to be supported by scientific investigations.

The endocrine system has a substantial role in our development especially with respect to the creation of secondary sexual characteristics and puberty. Research throughout the 20th century has concluded that hormones also modify personality characteristics. Personality differences between genders are often associated with genetics; however, hormone concentrations in the blood stream also influence personality and intellectual functioning. For example, a male who takes high doses of estrogen, a female hormone, will become less aggressive and more interested in social connectedness. When the hormone regimen is stopped, the man will return to a more typical male pattern of behavior. The reverse is also true when females take high doses of testosterone, the primary male hormone. Hormones also influence intellectual functioning and have a role in maintaining the high verbal skills of females and spatial abilities of males. When males take female hormones then their verbal skills increase. When females take male hormones their spatial reasoning capacity increases. When the hormone regimen is stopped, each gender returns to its normal baseline level (Einstein, 2007; Nyborg, 1983).

Although the majority of genes between males and females are similar, the single sex chromosome will initiate a sequence of events to cause the neuroanatomy of males and females to develop separately. The hypothalamic nucleus, an area associated with male sexual behavior, is approximately 2.5 times larger in males that it is in females. In addition, the corpus callosum is larger in women than it is in men. It is interesting that the corpus callosum is larger in women because two other areas, the anterior commissure and the massa intermedia, are both larger in females and additionally perform the role of connecting the left and right hemispheres (Carter, 2010).

The prenatal environment of an infant clearly influences its development. In the case of identical twins, differences in the diameter of the umbilical cord between the twins influence each child's access to oxygen and nutrients. Consequently, changes in the diameter of the umbilical cord will influence the child's birth weight. In a set of twins, one sibling is likely to have a slightly larger diameter umbilical cord. The difference in birth weight is associated with differences in

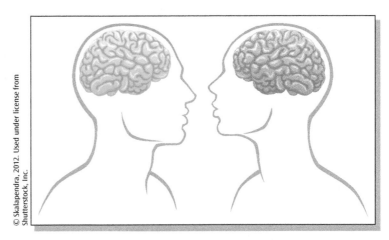

Research has shown neuroanatomical differences between the brains of males and females.

intelligence and personality that can be measured statistically in adulthood. Although these effects cannot be seen within a single pair of twins, the difference can be measured in large groups. This simply indicates that the effect is small. For our purposes presently, a small effect is still an effect. Of primary concern is that the prenatal environment influences the infant's access to oxygen and nutrients through the umbilical cord and these effects can be measured well into adulthood.

Psychological Influences

Engel (1977) addressed the need for the biopsychosocial model of medicine. He did not specifically define the term "psychological" in his article, however. References to psychological effects throughout the literature on biopsychosocial theory imply they are the personal events in the life of the subject. It is implied they are events the subject has greater control over. For instance, the psychological effects of parent-child relationships allow you to modify your behavior to change the outcomes of the relationship. In contrast, however, the following section on Social Influences refers to scenarios of time and culture that one cannot control (a natural disaster). The implication is that psychological influences are specific to the individual and involve events they can directly influence. Effects of social influence will happen to the individual but they also happen to all (or most) individuals. Moreover, everyone has little control over these social influences.

The psychological influences on medical and mental health should encompass any emotional or cognitive event the subject experiences. In short, the subject's thoughts, feelings and behavioral reactions to events are relevant factors in understanding what is managing their development and behavior. The experience of stress also fits into this category. During the early 20th century, stress was understood as a psychological variable with no physical component. Throughout the 20th century, however, the definition of stress has become increasingly biological. That is, whereas stress may stem from certain social events (loss of a job, a death in the family) it's processing and ultimate effects are biological. The work of Hans Selye (1936) has contributed much to the understanding of how psychological events have physical consequences. The period from the 1930's through to the 1970's saw rapid growth in the understanding of how stress causes physical damage to the organism. It is not clear how far this effect travels into the psychological realm, however. Medical research shows no evidence that a positive attitude will influence the medical prognosis of cancer patients even slightly (Chu et al., 2009; Lilienfeld et al., 2010).

© marco cappalunga, 2012. Used under license from Shutterstock, Inc.

I have only ever heard medical and psychological researchers state the positive benefits of exercising a moderate amount on a regular basis.

The recognition that psychological events can influence medical health helped develop the field of **psychoneuroimmunology**. Ader and Cohen developed the term psychoneuroimmunology in 1977. They developed it after using Pavlovian conditioning to associate a taste cue with an immunosuppressive drug to produce a conditioned immunosuppressive response in rats. Since that time, the field of psychoneuroimmunology has rigorously examined the connection between psychological events and biological stress reactions. The data are consistent in showing that psychological effects can influence medical health status, however, we are nowhere near the point at which we can "think ourselves" healthy. An effect that robust remains out of the reach of psychoneuroimmunological treatments.

> **Psychoneuroimmunology:** This term refers to the overall influence of learning, neural biology and the immune system.

Social Influences

Social influences may be the category of life events we cannot fully control. The most common example of **social influence** is our culture. Cultures are general patterns of behavior observed within people of a specific geographic location. Culture reflects the history of that group and often retains customs and rituals that are no longer relevant but simply exist due to tradition. Some customs cause individuals to accept certain roles in society based upon their demographic characteristics such as race, ethnicity, age or gender. Therefore, cultural values may place you as a top ranking leader or the lowest ranking follower. Which role you receive will be dependent upon your demographic characteristics and not upon your motivation or skill set. The inability to pursue your desired training or career path, marry the person you love or parent the children you create will cause stress that may play out in psychological or biological illnesses.

> **Social influences:** This term generically refers to the cultural influences on the psychological makeup of an individual.

Regardless of cultural traditions and biases, historical events contemporary with your life will also influence your development and psychological characteristics. In a time of great wealth your psychology may be influenced equally but in opposite direction to a time of great economic poverty. In countries at war, the civilian population will frequently suffer increases in both psychological and

© steve estvanik, 2012. Used under license from Shutterstock, Inc.

The influences of a civil war on your personality might be permanent.

medical illnesses (posttraumatic stress disorder, premature births) induced by the exposure to the military operations. Such outcomes also occur in areas hit hard by natural disasters. Two common examples are Hurricane Katrina in 2005 and the 2011 Tohoku earthquake and tsunami that knocked out the Fukushima Daiichi nuclear power plant in northern Japan.

KEY TERMS

adoption studies
antimiscegenation laws
artificial selection
behavioral
  endocrinology
behavioral geneticists
biopsychosocial model
  of psychology
culture
eugenics
evolution
evolutionary biology
evolutionary
  psychology

fraternal twins
gender identity
gender roles
gender typed
genes, hormones,
  and learning
heritability
identical twins
natural selection
nature
nature versus nurture
negative eugenics
nurture
ontogeny

phylogeny
positive eugenics
proportion of variation
psychoneuro-
  immunology
selection by
  consequences
social influences
social learning theory
temperament
  studies
twin studies

Chapter 3: Nature and Nurture Working Together

END OF CHAPTER QUIZ

1. Which of the following describes your total gene make up?
   a. DNA
   b. Genome
   c. Chromosome
   d. Protein

2. Heritability means:
   a. The likelihood of inheriting a genetic trait
   b. The guarantee of inheriting a genetic trait
   c. The likelihood of developing a mental disorder
   d. The guarantee of developing a mental disorder

3. In the field of Behavior Genetics, the term "interaction" means:
   a. How genes and environment interact
   b. How statistical processes interact
   c. How people interact
   d. How people with different genes interact with each other behaviorally

4. Where will you find Y-chromosomes?
   a. In males only
   b. In females only
   c. In both males and females
   d. Only during genetic disorders

5. Which of the following statements is TRUE?
   a. Chromosomes are made with hydroxyl chains
   b. The nucleus is smaller than the chromosomes
   c. Strings of genes make up the chromosomes
   d. Chromosomes are shaped like circles

6. How many chromosomes does the MOTHER contribute during conception?
   a. 12
   b. 23
   c. 34
   d. 46

7. A fertilized egg is called a:
   a. Nucleus
   b. Nucleotide
   c. Zygote
   d. Guanine

8. The Russian fox-breeding experiment bred foxes to be:
   a. Aggressive like guard dogs
   b. Beefy (more muscle mass)
   c. Friendly to humans
   d. Good trackers/pointers

9. Which of the following statements would an evolutionary psychologist agree with?
   a. Attractive women get married faster than unattractive women
   b. Women become like their own mothers after 10-years of marriage
   c. Men like to "hunt" women
   d. Men are more likely to be attracted to women who look young and healthy

10. Behavioral characteristics CAN be bred into animals.
    a. True
    b. False

11. Evolutionary psychologists PRESUME behavioral characteristics can be bred into humans.
    a. True
    b. False

12. Fraternal twins have the same DNA.
    a. True
    b. False

13. Which of the following terms refers to the process by which biological characteristics that support survival and reproduction become more prevalent in the gene pool?
    a. Mutations
    b. Evolutionary homeostasis
    c. Natural selection
    d. Genome

14. What is the most common tool of behavior geneticists?
    a. Laboratory experimentation
    b. Brain slicing
    c. DNA blood tests
    d. Twin studies

15. Temperament studies indicate that:
    a. Temperament is consistent across the lifespan
    b. Temperament is inconsistent across the lifespan
    c. Fraternal twins are more alike than identical twins
    d. Identical twins are as similar as two strangers

16. Which of the following appears to have a strong genetic influence?
    a. Temperament
    b. Intelligence
    c. Personality
    d. A, B & C all seem to have a genetic component

17. Behavior geneticists theorize that biology controls about ___ of the variation between individuals with respect to personality characteristics.
    a. 10-20%
    b. 20-30%
    c. 30-40%
    d. 40-50%

18. Which set of siblings has the most similar set of personalities?
    a. Fraternal twins
    b. Fraternal twins from separate placentas
    c. Identical twins from the same placenta
    d. Identical twins separated at birth

19. Teaching a person a new skill will result in which of the following?
    a. Great time and effort
    b. New patterns of electrical activity in the brain of the subject
    c. A change in personality
    d. Hormonal influences

20. Social Learning Theory and Gender Schema Theory both try to characterize
    a. The development of gender-typed behavior
    b. The development of hormonal responses throughout puberty
    c. Mate selection
    d. A single major factor controlling sexual preferences

21. Which of the following locations is best identified as the location of genetic material?
    a. Dendrite
    b. Axon
    c. Nucleus
    d. Terminal button
    e. Synapse

22. The primary job of genes is to:
    a. Code for proteins
    b. Establish behavioral patterns
    c. Establish medical health
    d. Establish personality characteristics
    e. Control development

23. Which of the following is the largest set?
    a. The basic elements of DNA
    b. Genes
    c. Chromosomes
    d. Genome

24. Which of the following will the environment of an unborn child not be able to influence?
    a. Learn its father's voice
    b. Favor particular music
    c. Learn to favor particular tastes
    d. Learn to favor particular colors
    e. Influence its intelligence relative to its twin

25. Differences in intelligence between twins may be determined by the different placental blood connections the twins received. These differences can be determined with great accuracy in a SINGLE PAIR of adult twins.
    a. True
    b. False

26. The main difference between natural selection and artificial selection is:
    a. Natural selection is controlled naturally by humans
    b. Artificial selection is controlled naturally
    c. There is no difference between natural and artificial selection
    d. Natural selection occurs without human intervention and artificial selection occurs due to human intervention

27. What happened to the behavior of the foxes in the Russian Fox Breeding experiment?
    a. They became more aggressive
    b. They became better hunters
    c. They refused to bite children
    d. The acted like domesticated dogs
    e. They became afraid of humans

28. Psychologists apply the natural selection concept to the development of human behavioral traits.
    a. True
    b. False

29. Psychologists believe that genetics can influence which friends you choose and whether you commit a crime.
    a. True
    b. False

30. Which of the following groups do behavior geneticists not typically study?
    a. Twins raised together
    b. Triplets raised apart
    c. Adopted siblings
    d. Aunts and nephews
    e. Biological siblings raised apart

31. Which of the following measures do behavior geneticists not typically measure?
    a. Intelligence
    b. Personality
    c. Language spoken
    d. Temperament
    e. Athleticism

32. Heritability refers to:
    a. The likelihood of inheriting a family trait
    b. Personality
    c. Chromosomes
    d. Emotional regulation

33. Which of the following characteristics are unlikely to be inherited?
    a. Intelligence
    b. Personality
    c. Adult food preferences
    d. Temperament
    e. Athleticism

34. Which of the following characteristics do both genes and environment not influence?
    a. Height
    b. Weight
    c. Personality
    d. Intelligence
    e. All of the above are affected by genes and environment

35. About how much of your personality is likely a result of your upbringing (e.g., parents, neighborhood, financial status, etc.)?
    a. 0%
    b. 25%
    c. 50%
    d. 75%
    e. 100%

36. Which of the following represents a time during which your brain is changing minimally?
    a. When you learn a new phone number
    b. When you read your textbook
    c. When you drive or walk home
    d. When you are exercising
    e. When you are relaxing quietly and not thinking about anything

37. The name given to the general behavior pattern you learn from a particular geographic location.
    a. Personality
    b. Traits
    c. Culture
    d. Character

38. Cultural patterns are based upon:
    a. Naturally occurring social pressures over time
    b. Human controlled social pressures
    c. Religious organizations
    d. Government regulations
    e. Naturally occurring laws

39. Which of the following do not control the development of gender identity?
    a. Sexual attraction
    b. Genes
    c. Hormones
    d. Learning

40. Gender identity begins with:
    a. Puberty
    b. Hormones
    c. Inherited chromosomal pattern
    d. Social learning

41. Which of the following is correlated with greater environmental stimulation?
    a. More exercise
    b. More CNS regeneration
    c. Fewer illnesses
    d. More brain synapses

42. Which of the following is correlated with greater environmental stimulation?
    a. Fewer illnesses
    b. Higher brain weight
    c. More exercise
    d. More CNS regeneration

43. Which of the following add to the number of neural connections made during the early years of life?
    a. Environmental stimulation
    b. Good nutrition
    c. Physical exercise
    d. An education
    e. All of the above

44. What is the benefit of massaging a premature child?
   a. Weight gain and neurological development are faster
   b. They can reach for things more easily
   c. It promotes physical activity
   d. They become less susceptible to viruses

45. At birth the brain has ___ brain connections which are ___ by puberty.
   a. Extra; eliminated
   b. Too few; developed
   c. Extra; developed
   d. Too few; reduced further

46. Differences in culture reflect:
   a. Genetic diversity
   b. Hard wired programming
   c. The effects of environment
   d. The role of biology

47. Which of the following areas are children least suited to learn relative to adults?
   a. A second language
   b. Algebra
   c. Cultural values
   d. Musical skills

48. Which of the following areas are children best suited to learn relative to adults?
   a. A second language
   b. A world view
   c. Cultural values
   d. Musical skills
   e. Children are better suited to learn all of the above

49. Research on the genetic traits of families suggests that:
   a. Children will most likely develop a personality based upon their genetic background
   b. Children will most likely develop a personality based upon their environmental background
   c. Something other than genes or environment is producing the personalities of children
   d. Children will most likely develop a personality based upon a combination of their genetic and environmental backgrounds

50. In which of the following cases might parenting affect a child's personality?
   a. In extreme cases such as abuse
   b. In food preferences
   c. In intelligence scores
   d. In career choice

Answers: 1. b; 2. a; 3. a; 4. a; 5. c; 6. b; 7. c; 8. c; 9. d; 10. a; 11. a; 12. b; 13. a; 14. d; 15. a; 16. d; 17. d; 18. a; 19. b; 20. a; 21. c; 22. a; 23. d; 24. e; 25. b; 26. d; 27. d; 28. a; 29. a; 30. d; 31. c; 32. a; 33. c; 34. e; 35. c; 36. e; 37. c; 38. a; 39. a; 40. c; 41. d; 42. b; 43. e; 44. a; 45. a; 46. c; 47. b; 48. e; 49. d; 50. a

4 Psychology Over the Lifespan

The Role of Time in Development

When one considers the many changes that occur over the lifespan, it quickly becomes clear that there is much to disentangle. Time, learning and memory all change. Our ability to learn or remember may increase or decrease at different points, but our perception of time is that it only moves forward. We cannot move time backward and we cannot speed it up or slow it down. Therefore, time is a variable we do not control. This poses quite a problem for anyone studying development because you are working with an uncontrolled variable. If you cannot make one year pass in five minutes or let your subject age while you run time backwards, then you do not have control over time.

This then leads to an interesting question. What are you controlling in a developmental psychology experiment? In almost all cases, researchers control the same experimental variables that most memory, learning and social psychologists control. Typically, these are related to problem solving, intelligence, academic skills, moral development and social behavior, just to name a few. So where in this mix is the time-dependent "developmental process?"

Development is predicated upon the passage of time and without controlling time itself, researchers have to consider other variables that are confounded with time as possible independent variables. Psychologists frequently refer to a "genetic unfolding" of development. This implies that a natural timing of genetic changes is responsible for the dependent variable changes observed in intelligence, memory, social behavior, etc.

Answers like that are highly doubtful. Back in the Nature-Nurture chapter, it was described how genes themselves are unlikely causes for particular forms of behavior. Do you recall the many references to how a gene is an unlikely explanation for robbing a convenience store? Do you think that "unfolding genes" will account for a robber's weapon of choice? Probably not.

Ultimately, it is not clear what is happening in developmental psychology over time. That does not mean, however, that developmental psychologists have not made some educated guesses. Those guesses are that changes associated with time are part biological and part social. When you want specific answers in an experiment, however, that answer is not satisfactory.

Outside of biology and the environment, there are no other categories of control over living organisms. Psychologists have to refine their theorizing to variables that are likely related to the specific experiment. For example, cognitive changes through age's three to seven are likely the result of genetic and physiological changes as well as social development. It is likely that the changes that occur through puberty are hormonally related. Social changes may modify the thinking patterns of middle age adults. Whether one concentrates on genetic, hormonal, physiological or environmental factors as the driving forces behind the behavior of your subject, is determined by the specific developmental questions you ask with respect to the time of the subject's life.

Until someone develops a time machine that can slow down, speed up, or run time backwards, psychologists will continue to have to make educated guesses about which variables confounded with time are responsible for the changes they see in their subjects.

CHAPTER OUTLINE

Some of his classmates called him "Spielbug." Girls thought he was nerdy and unattractive. His father, Arnold, a pioneer in the use of computers in engineering, was hardly ever around and, to make matters worse, frequently uprooted his family, moving from Ohio to New Jersey, to Arizona, and finally to Northern California. Steven Spielberg was a perpetual new kid on the block. He was also, by all accounts, an unusual child, both in his appearance (he had a large head and protruding ears) and in his fearful and awkward behavior (McBride, 1999). Spielberg himself has said that he "felt like an alien" throughout his childhood. He desperately wanted to be accepted, but didn't fit in. So, at age 12, he began making films, "little 8mm things. I did it to find something that, for me, could be permanent" (quoted in R. Sullivan, 1999, p. 66). Spielberg continued to make movies as a teenager, often casting his three sisters in roles. He discovered that making movies was one way to win his peers' acceptance, as well as some small measure of power—for he sometimes induced his worst enemies to appear in his films.

When he was 16, Spielberg's parents divorced, and Spielberg blamed his father's constant traveling for the breakup. His unhappiness only deepened when his father remarried, taking for his second wife a woman Spielberg couldn't stand. At the same time that he withdrew from his father, Spielberg continued to have a close relationship with his mother, Leah, a concert pianist and artist. The split with his father lasted some 15 years.

In many ways, Spielberg's films, like the rest of his life, are shaped by his childhood. Spielberg himself has said about *E.T., The Extra–Terrestrial*, "The whole movie is really about divorce . . . . Henry's [the main character's] ambition to find a father by bringing E.T. into his life to fill some black hole—that was my struggle to find somebody to replace the dad who I felt had abandoned

Kosslyn, Stephen M.; Rosenberg, Robin S., *Fundamentals of Psychology in Context*, 3rd Edition, © 2007, pp. 528–585. Reprinted by permission of Pearson Education, Inc., Upper Saddle River, NJ.

me" (R. Sullivan, 1999, p. 68). Many of Spielberg's other films feature children who are separated from their parents (such as the girl in *Poltergeist* and the boy in *Close Encounters of the Third Kind*). And *Back to the Future* might represent his longings to change the past, if only he could. Only when he turned 40 did he turn to adult contexts. As he matured, Spielberg's identification with oppressed people in general (not just oppressed children) led him to make movies such as *The Color Purple, Schindler's List*, and *Amistad*.

Steven Spielberg married and had a child, but eventually divorced his first wife, actress Amy Irving. His own experiences made him extremely sensitive to the effect of the divorce on his son, Max, and he made every attempt to ensure that Max did not feel abandoned. When he married again, he became deeply involved with his family (which includes seven children, some of them adopted). There was a happy development in the previous generation's father—son relationship as well: Arnold became a well-loved grandfather and a regular presence in the Spielberg household.

Spielberg's journey is one version of the universal story of human development: A skinny kid beset by fears and with few friends becomes one of the most powerful figures in the global entertainment industry; from a fragmented family life develops a man's resolve to make the best possible life for his own family; across generations, a father and a son come to like each other, now as a grandfather and a father, after 15 years of estrangement. *Developmental psychologists* study exactly these sorts of events in our lives—the fascinating and varied process of human development over the life span. In this chapter, we begin by considering prenatal development and the newborn, and we see that even here genes and environment are intimately intertwined. We next turn to infancy and childhood and observe the interplay between maturation and experience in shaping a child's physical, mental, emotional, and social development. Then we consider adolescence, a crucial time in development, bridging childhood and adulthood. And finally, we discuss adulthood and aging, gaining insights that help us understand how Arnold Spielberg could develop from a less-than-optimal father into a terrific grandfather.

IN THE BEGINNING: FROM CONCEPTION TO BIRTH

Steven Spielberg has been celebrated as one of the most successful moviemakers of all time. He just seemed to have a natural bent for making movies (he never attended film school). Where did his talent come from? In this section, we begin at the beginning and think about the foundations of our skills and abilities.

Prenatal Development: Nature and Nurture From the Start

For each of us, life began with the meeting of two cells, a sperm and an egg (or ovum, which in Latin means "egg"). These specialized cells are sex cells, or *gametes*. The sperm penetrates the egg, and the genetic material of the sperm melds with that of the ovum. The ovum is not a passive partner in this dance of life; the sperm is drawn to the egg by chemical reactions on the surface of the

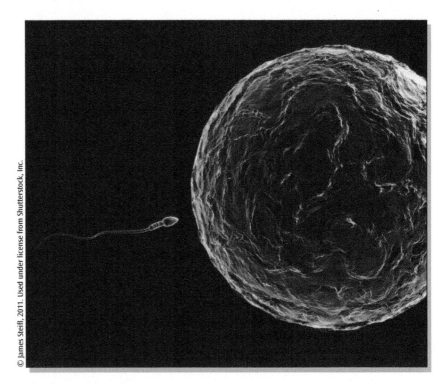

© James Steifl, 2011. Used under license from Shutterstock, Inc.

At the moment of conception, a sperm penetrates an ovum. The egg, however, is not a passive recipient; by changing its surface properties, it actively regulates the behavior of the sperm.

egg. And when a sperm has been accepted within the egg, other reactions prevent additional sperm from penetrating. The ovum is a supercell, the largest in the human body. Even so, it is barely the size of a pinprick, and sperm are much smaller (about 1/500 of an inch). But despite their small sizes, within the ovum and sperm reside all the machinery necessary to create a new life. And, even at this earliest stage of development, *genes* (*nature*) and the *environment* (*nurture*) are intimately intertwined.

From Zygote to Birth: Getting a Start in Life

The genetic heritage of every normal human being is 23 pairs of chromosomes, one member of each pair coming from an egg and the other from a sperm. A *chromosome* is a strand of DNA (*deoxyribonucleic acid*) in the nucleus of the cell. A molecule of DNA is shaped like a twisted ladder—the famous double helix—in which the "rungs" are formed by the bonds between pairs of chemicals. Each *gene* on the chromosome is a series of particular rungs (see Chapter 3). All cells in the human body except the gametes (eggs and sperm) contain all 23 pairs of chromosomes; each gamete contains only a single member of each chromosome pair. In an egg, one of these 23 is a chromosome known as X; in a sperm, the corresponding chromosome is either an X chromosome or a shorter one called a Y chromosome.

In the Beginning

Maturation: The developmental process that produces genetically programmed changes with increasing age.

Much of early development is determined by maturation, the process that produces genetically programmed changes with increasing age. But from the very start, genes and the environment interact. Although the genes in both the sperm and the egg have a major impact on the characteristics of the person who will eventually develop, the environment plays a crucial role in whether the sperm ever reaches the egg. Sperm actually "surf" on subtle muscle contractions in the uterus; these waves usually move in the correct direction in fertile women, but they either move in the wrong direction or are weak in infertile women (Kunz et al., 1997; Lyons & Levi, 1994). In addition, the fluid in the uterus must be the right consistency and must have the right chemical composition for the sperm to complete their journey (Mori et al., 1998; Shibahara et al., 1995; Singh, 1995).

The fertilization of the egg by the sperm creates a cell called a zygote, in which the chromosomes from the egg and from the sperm pair up so that the zygote contains the full complement of 23 pairs. If the sperm contributes an X chromosome, the off-spring will be female (XX); if Y, male (XY). The Y chromosome contains a gene (the SRY *gene*, for "sex-determining region of the Y chromosome") that produces a chemical substance that ultimately causes the zygote to develop into a male; if this substance is not present, genes on the X chromosome will produce other substances that cause the baby to be female (Goodfellow & Lovell-Badge, 1993; Hawkins, 1994).

> **Zygote:** A fertilized ovum (egg).

Dance of the Chromosomes

The two members of each pair of chromosomes (other than the XY pair in males) are similar—but they are not identical. For example, the gene for the shape of your earlobes is on the same spot on both chromosomes, but because of its particular chemical composition, the gene on one chromosome may code for an attached earlobe and the gene on the other for an unattached earlobe. The gametes are formed from specialized cells that, while themselves containing the full 23 pairs, in the course of division produce cells with half that number, with only one member of each pair. So, because the members of each pair are not identical, the genetic contents of the resulting gametes are not all the same. And there's another wrinkle, which further contributes to our wonderful human variety: In the course of cell division, the chromosomal decks of cards are shuffled so that pieces of the chromosomes in each pair in the parent cell are exchanged, as shown in **Figure 4.1**, to form new combinations of genes. Each zygote thus consists of a unique combination of genes. In fact, in theory, each human couple can produce some 70 trillion genetically different children! The chance of your getting the particular combination of genes you received is roughly the same as the probability that a meteor will hit a particular 5-foot-by-5-foot square patch of land on the surface of the Earth!

Division and Differentiation

Once formed, the zygote begins to divide. The production of certain hormones causes genes to turn on and off in a specific sequence, guiding the zygote's development (Brown, 1999). Soon a cluster of cells has developed. After 3 days, about 60–70 cells have formed and organized themselves into a hollow sphere called a *blastocyst*. This sphere proceeds through an orderly progression, first forming into a tube, then developing features that in early stages look much like those of relatively primitive animals, then more complex ones.

Human development in the womb is divided into trimesters, three equal periods of 3 months each. The first trimester is divided into three stages: The developing baby starts off as a zygote, becomes an embryo when the major axis of the body is present (about 2 weeks after conception), and then becomes a fetus when all major body structures are present (about 8 weeks after conception; thereafter, the developing baby is called a fetus until he or she is

> **Embryo:** A developing baby from the point where the major axis of the body is present until all major structures are present, spanning from about 2 weeks to 8 weeks after conception.

> **Fetus:** A developing baby during the final phase of development in the womb, from about 8 weeks after conception until birth.

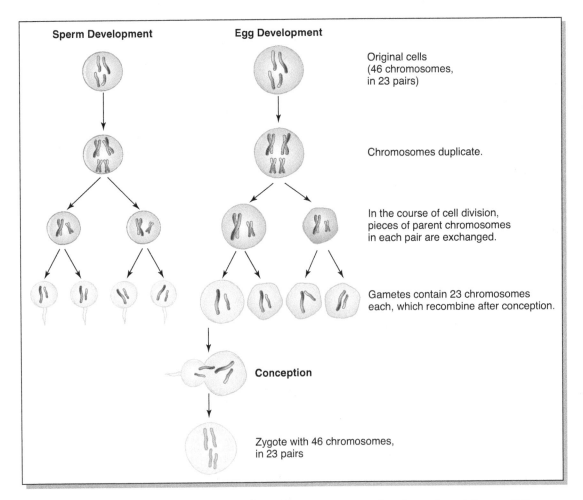

Sperm Development   Egg Development

Original cells
(46 chromosomes,
in 23 pairs)

Chromosomes duplicate.

In the course of cell division,
pieces of parent chromosomes
in each pair are exchanged.

Gametes contain 23 chromosomes
each, which recombine after conception.

Conception

Zygote with 46 chromosomes,
in 23 pairs

FIGURE 4.1 ■ The chromosomes in eggs and sperm are not simply copies of those of the parent, but rather unique combinations of the material in the two chromosomes in each pair of the parent's chromosomes. The sperm and egg combine to form the basis of a unique individual (or individuals, in the case of identical twins).

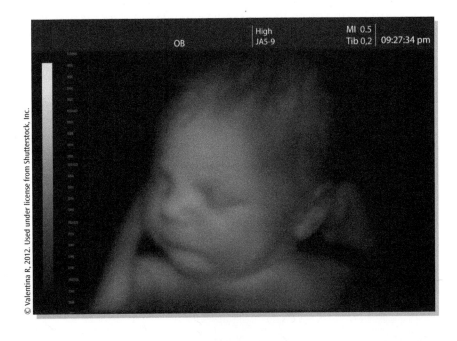

born). At the end of the second trimester, the great bulk of the neurons each individual possesses are in place (Nowakowski, 1987; Rakic, 1975; Rodier, 1980), but they are not completely fixed; researchers have found that new neurons can be produced even in adult brains (Gould et al., 1999).

The path from zygote to birth is not always smooth. Perhaps surprisingly, about half of all fertilized eggs contain some kind of abnormality in their chromosomes. Most of these eggs are spontaneously aborted (in fact, about 30% of zygotes don't even make it to the embryo phase), and more male embryos than female embryos are aborted (Vatten & Skjaeaerven, 2004)—but even so, about 1 in 250 babies is born with an abnormality that is obvious (for example, he or she may not respond appropriately to light or loud noises), and probably more have abnormalities that are not obvious (such as subtle defects in particular brain areas, which will become evident only later in life; Plomin et al., 1997; Sadler, 1995).

Learning and Behavior in the Womb

A popular—and misleading—image shows the fetus floating peacefully asleep in the womb. But in truth, the fetus is active nearly from the start, at first with automatic movements, such as the heart beating, and then with large-scale coordinated behaviors. As the fetus develops, the heart rate slows down (but becomes more variable), the fetus moves less often but more vigorously when it does stir, and the heart rate and movement patterns become coordinated. Some researchers have even reported sex differences in behavior in the womb, with male fetuses more active than females (Almli et al., 2001; DiPietro et al., 1996;). After 20–25 weeks of gestation, the fetus is sensitive to both sound and light (Nilsson & Hamberger, 1990; Pujol et al., 1990). How do we know this? Because if a fetus is examined, as is sometimes medically necessary, by a special light-emitting instrument called a *fetoscope*, it will actually move its hands to shield its eyes. As the fetus develops, its movements become increasingly coordinated, and by 28 weeks, it responds to external stimulation. A bit later, its heart rate can change if the mother is startled (Kisilevsky & Low, 1998; DiPietro et al., 1996), and sometime between 25 and 34 weeks, a fetus can detect human speech (Cheour-Luhtanen et al., 1996; Zimmer et al., 1993). In fact, researchers have found that fetuses older than 33 weeks even pay attention to music (Kisilevsky et al., 2004).

In addition, there is evidence that fetuses can learn. In a classic study (DeCasper & Fifer, 1980), pregnant women read the story *The Cat in the Hat* aloud twice each day during the 6 weeks before their babies were born. A few hours after birth, the babies were tested. The researchers put earphones on the babies' little heads and a special pacifier-like device in their mouths. Sucking faster or slower on this device allowed the infants to hear either their mother's voice or another woman's voice reading the story. The infants sucked at the speed that produced their own mother's voice. Perhaps even more impressive, the researchers also gave the infants the opportunity to choose between hearing their mother read *The Cat in the Hat* or another story—and the infants preferred the story their mother had read aloud before they were born!

Moreover, characteristics of the fetus predict those of the child after birth. For example, fetuses that had more variable heart rates later developed into more linguistically able toddlers and demonstrated more sophisticated forms of symbolic play (Bornstein et al., 2002).

Teratogens: Negative Environment Events

A teratogen is an external agent, such as a chemical, virus, or type of radiation, that can cause damage to the zygote, embryo, or fetus. Because of events at

teratogen: Any external agent, such as a chemical, virus, or type of radiation, that can cause damage to the zygote, embryo, or fetus.

different stages in the course of development, different organs are vulnerable to teratogens at different times.

Maternal Illness

Unfortunately, the central nervous system is vulnerable at virtually every phase of prenatal development. For example, the development of the brain can be disrupted if the mother catches a virus, such as chicken pox or rubella (3-day German measles); more than half the babies born to mothers who contract rubella will be mentally retarded if the developing child is in the embryonic period at the onset of the disease. In addition, a mother who is HIV-positive can pass the virus on to the baby during gestation or birth (but only about one third of these babies contract the virus). The HIV virus causes brain damage, leading to problems in concentration, attention, memory, movement control, and the ability to reason (Clifford, 2000; Grant et al., 1999).

Alcohol and Drugs

Another potential teratogen is alcohol, which can damage a woman's eggs before fertilization (Kaufman, 1997) as well as affect the developing baby throughout pregnancy, starting with the embryo phase. If the mother drinks enough alcohol during pregnancy, the baby may be born with *fetal alcohol syndrome*; part of this syndrome is mental retardation (Streissguth et al., 1989, 1999). If a mother consumes any alcohol during pregnancy, research suggests that she should take antioxidants, such as vitamins C and E, which may reduce the damage to the fetus (Cohen-Kerem & Koren, 2003). In addition, using heroin or cocaine during pregnancy can cause a host of problems: physical defects (Singer et al., 2002b), irritability, and sleep and attentional problems in the newborn (Fox, 1994; J. M. Miller et al., 1995; Vogel, 1997). Although prenatal exposure to cocaine may have only subtle effects in infancy (such as slowed language development; Lester et al., 1998), such exposure may have long-lasting consequences—some of which may become more marked in subsequent years (Chapman, 2000; Lester, 2000; Singer et al., 2002a). In addition, the problem is not restricted to mothers. Certain drugs (both prescription and illegal, such as cocaine) can affect the father's sperm and thereby affect the growing fetus and child (Yazigi et al., 1991).

Caffeine and Smoking

Major diseases and strong drugs are not the only threats to healthy prenatal development. Excessive amounts of caffeine (three cups of coffee a day, according to one study) can lead to miscarriage or low birth weight, irritability, and other symptoms (Eskenazi, 1993; Eskenazi et al., 1999). Smoking during pregnancy affects both mother and fetus; it is correlated with higher rates of miscarriage, lower birth weights, smaller head size, stillbirth, and infant mortality, and it can cause attentional difficulties in the infant (Cornelius & Day, 2000; Floyd et al., 1993; Fried & Makin, 1987; Fried & Watkinson, 2000). Smoking may even damage the fetus's genes (de la Chica et al., 2005). A mother's smoking also significantly increases the chance that her baby will die from *sudden infant death syndrome* (SIDS; Pollack, 2001). Smoking during pregnancy alters the way the infant's autonomic nervous system operates, which may contribute to SIDS (Browne et al., 2000).

Diet and Pollution

A mother's poor diet can lead her infant to have fewer brain cells than normal (Morgane et al., 1993) and can increase the risk that the child will develop a host of psychological disorders—including antisocial personality disorder (Neugebauer et al., 1999) and schizophrenia (Susser et al., 1996). In addition, the lack of even a single important vitamin or mineral can have significant effects. For example, insufficient folic acid (a type of vitamin B) can disrupt the early development of the neural tube that gives rise to the brain and spinal cord (Nevid et al., 1998), and thereby cause birth defects. Most important, if the mother does not have enough folic acid, the infant can be born without the top of the skull or with *spina bifida*, which occurs when the spine does not close properly. Spina bifida requires immediate surgery and can lead to problems in bladder and bowel control (and can even prove fatal). Folic acid is also essential for producing the iron-containing protein needed to form red blood cells. (However, there can be too much of a good thing: Folic acid supplements are associated with a higher incidence of fraternal twins [Källén, 2004].)

Furthermore, if the mother eats fish with high levels of methylmercury, this can cause the infant to be born deaf or to have visual problems; it may also impair auditory processing (Murata et al., 1999). Moreover, other environmental pollutants as well as ionizing radiation can have effects ranging from birth defects and cancer to behavioral difficulties (such as in paying attention). And, in other animals at least, these effects can be passed on to the third generation, to the offspring of the offspring (Friedler, 1996).

Maternal Stressors

The fetus is exquisitely sensitive to the mother's stress level. For example, when a pregnant woman takes a mildly stressful cognitive test (the Stroop color-word test, in which a person must ignore the colors named by words when naming the colors of the ink used to print them), the fetus stops moving, and its heart rate becomes more variable (DiPietro et al., 2003). Given this sensitivity, we should not be surprised that stressors in the mother's life can endanger the developing fetus. When the stress is severe enough, infants may subsequently experience attentional difficulties, be unusually anxious, and exhibit unusual social behavior (Weinstock, 1997). In fact, fetuses with mothers of lower socioeconomic status, who are often more stressed than those of higher socioeconomic status, move less often and less vigorously and show other differences from fetuses whose mothers are better-off (Pressman et al., 1998). There are several biological reasons for these effects: When the mother is stressed, more of her blood flows to parts of the body affected by the fight-or-flight response (such as the limbs and heart), and less flows to the uterus. She produces hormones such as cortisol, which slows down the operation of genes that guide prenatal development of the brain, suppressing brain growth (Brown, 1999). There is evidence that the babies born to stressed mothers have smaller heads than those born to unstressed mothers, which may be related to the poorer behavioral functioning scores observed for such babies (Lou et al., 1994). That said, you shouldn't despair about the fact that life often presents stress: There's evidence that *mild* stress may actually be good for the developing fetus (DiPietro, 2004).

Figure 4.2 illustrates the times during gestation when particular organs are especially vulnerable.

© Andrey Arkusha, 2011. Used under license from Shutterstock, Inc.

Social support can be advantageous for a pregnant mother. Reductions in stress during pregnancy are associated with better health for the developing child.

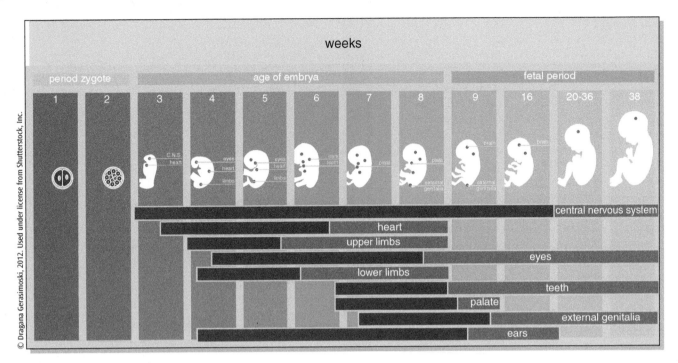

FIGURE 4.2 ■ Prenatal development by week. The darker and lighter lines indicate more or less vulnerability to teratogens, respectively.

Positive Environmental Events: The Earliest Head Start

The previous paragraphs might seem to suggest that our species would be better off if maturation alone controlled development. But environmental effects are not all bad, and some prenatal experiences help the fetus. For example, researchers found that mothers who ate chocolate every day during pregnancy later rated their 6-month-old babies as having more positive temperaments than did mothers who did not eat chocolate so regularly (Räikkönen et al., 2004). However, this may say more about the effects of the candy on the mother than on her infant! Other findings show more conclusively that the prenatal environment can play a positive role in development. Consider the following study by Lafuente and colleagues (1997).

Uuderstanding Research

Stimulating the Unborn

Question

Can playing music to an unborn child enhance development during infancy?

Alternatives

(1) Playing music to a fetus enhances development during infancy. (2) Playing music to a fetus impairs development during infancy. (3) Playing music to a fetus does not affect development during infancy.

Logic

If playing music to a fetus enhances subsequent development, then infants who heard music should later score higher on standard measures of cognitive and motor function than infants who did not hear music.

Method

Each of 172 pregnant women was randomly assigned to an experimental or a control group. The participants in the experimental group were given a waistband with a tape recorder and small speakers, which they used to play tapes of violin music for a total of about 70 hours (on average), starting at about 28 weeks after conception and continuing until the birth of the baby. The researchers then tracked the development of the babies during their first 6 months of life. The pregnant women in the control group did not play music to their fetuses.

Results

The infants of mothers in the experimental group were more advanced than those of mothers in the control group; for example, they had better motor control and better vocal abilities of the sort that precede language.

Inferences

Playing music to a fetus (and perhaps providing other forms of stimulation) can enhance subsequent development. Steven Spielberg's mother played the piano frequently while she was pregnant. Could these prenatal concerts have had longterm positive effects on him? (Note that this study differs in its design and conclusion from those on the Mozart effect, in which music is played for brief periods to adults, who are then tested on aspects of IQ.)

Think Critically!

The mothers presumably heard the music along with their fetuses. Is it possible that the positive effects of the music on the infant arose because the mother was affected by the music? Perhaps it made her more relaxed, and thus less prone to the effects of stressors. Or perhaps the music made the mother more tolerant of the discomforts of late pregnancy, and thus more responsive to the infant—and that is what was responsible for the infant's advanced development. Can you think of a way to rule out these explanations for the effects of the music? Can you think of ways to test them directly?

The Newborn: A Work in Progress

The human brain is not fully developed at birth, perhaps because the baby's head would not fit through the birth canal if he or she had a full-size adult brain. Much human brain development continues after birth (Johnson, 2001), and thus the newborn's abilities to think, feel, and behave differ from those of older children and adults. For example, newborns cannot be classically conditioned to associate a tone with an air puff that causes them to blink (Naito & Lipsitt, 1969; Sommer & Ling, 1970); in the rat, researchers have shown that this ability emerges only after key parts of the cerebellum have matured during infancy (Freeman & Nicholson, 2001; Rush et al., 2001).

Nevertheless, although the typical infant may seem thoroughly incompetent—capable of eating, sleeping, cooing, crying, drooling, and not much else—such an assessment is off the mark. A baby is not a blank slate, waiting for learning or maturity to descend. On the contrary, babies come equipped with a surprising range of abilities and capacities.

Sensory Capacities

Even at the earliest phases of development, babies have the beginnings of sophisticated sensory capabilities. They are born sensitive to the range of frequencies of women's voices (Hauser, 1996) and have a relatively sensitive sense

Human children develop much slower than most other animals. This kitten can run at 6 weeks of age but the child may not even roll over until about 6 months of age.

of smell. Even babies who are fed by bottle prefer the odor of a woman who is breast-feeding another infant to that of a woman who is not breast-feeding (Porter et al., 1992).

Newborns also prefer to look at normal faces rather than faces with scrambled features, but this preference turns out to be part of a more general one for visual patterns that have more elements in the upper half than in the lower half (Cassia et al., 2004; Turati, 2004). Only with time do infants come to process faces like adults do (de Haan et al., 2002). Moreover, 2-day-old infants prefer to look at attractive faces (as judged by adults) than at unattractive faces (Slater et al., 2000).

In addition, 2-day-old infants can learn to pair information coming from different senses, such as vision and hearing. For example, Slater and colleagues (1997) showed such infants two visual stimuli, which differed in both color and orientation; at the same time as they presented one of the stimuli, they also presented a distinctive sound. They then switched the pairings and found that the infants paid more attention to the new combinations. These results showed that even 2-day-old infants can put visual and auditory stimuli together; if they couldn't, they wouldn't have noticed the changed pairings.

Reflexes

Infants also come equipped with a wide range of reflexes, the most important of which are summarized in **Table 4.1**. A *reflex* is an automatic response to an event, an action that does not require thought. Some of the reflexes shown by infants, such as sucking, have obvious survival value, and some, such as the *Moro reflex* (in which the startled baby throws its arms wide, as if to grab hold of someone), may have had survival value for our ancestors. Other reflexes, such as the *Babinski reflex* (in which the baby's big toe flexes while the other toes fan out when the sole of his or her foot is stroked), are less obviously useful.

Some reflexes evolve with time. For example, 5- to 6-month-olds blink when they see a picture of a looming object, which appears to be moving toward them. At this age, the infants blink when the image reaches a certain size. In contrast, 6- to 7-month-old infants blink in preparation for the object's actually hitting them—which requires them to take into account not just the size of the image, but also the speed with which that size changes (Kayed & van der Meer, 2000).

TABLE 4.1 ■ Reflexes Present at Birth.

	Stimulus	Response	Periods
Withdrawal Reflex	Poking foot	Leg flexion	About ten days
Stepping Reflex	Child dangled over table	Stepping movements	About two months
Sucking Reflex	Placing a finger in the mouth	Sucking response	About three months
Rooting Reflex	Stroking the cheek	Child turns head toward stimulation and begins sucking reflex	About four months
Palmar grasp Reflex	Pressing the child's palm	Grasping the object	About four months
Moro Reflex	Sudden loud noise	Rapidly extends and flexes arms and legs, begins crying	About five months
Swimming Reflex	Being face-down in water	Kicks and strokes the water	About six months
Tonic neck Reflex	Turn head to one side	One arm straightens, the other arm and leg bends	About seven months
Plantar Reflex	Pressing on the ball of the child's foot	Toes curl under	About twelve months
Babinski Reflex	Stroking the sole of the foot	The big toe flexes while the others fan out	About twelve months
Eye blink Reflex	Bright light	Eyes shut	Present for life

Curiously, many of the reflexes that babies have at birth disappear after a while. Some of these reflexes appear to be simpler versions of later behaviors, such as walking or swimming. Should we try to preserve these reflexes? It has been shown, for example, that the stepping reflex can be retained longer if the baby's leg muscles are exercised and become stronger (the reflex appears to disappear in part because the baby gains weight and the legs can no longer support the body; Thelen, 1983, 1995). However, infants who walk earlier do not walk *better* than infants who walk later.

Temperament: Instant Personality

A friend describing the birth of his second son expressed amazement as he realized, when handed the child immediately after birth, that the infant was *already different* from his first son, calmer and steadier. Our friend should not have been surprised. From their earliest hours, babies show the makings of individual personalities. They demonstrate differences in *temperament*, in their innate inclinations to engage in a certain style of behavior. Some babies may be inclined toward "approach," others toward "withdrawal" (Thomas & Chess, 1996). Infants who tend to show an approach response generally react positively to new situations or stimuli, such as a new food, toy, person, or place. Infants who are inclined to show a withdrawal response typically react negatively to new situations or stimuli, by crying, fussing, or otherwise indicating their discomfort (Chess & Thomas, 1987). Some babies are considered "easy" in that they do not cry often and are not demanding, whereas others are "difficult" in that they are fussy and demanding.

Biological Factors

That such differences are present virtually from birth suggests, at least in part, the operation of biological factors. Some of these differences may reflect events that occurred in the womb. For example, newborns who had lower levels of iron display more negative emotion and are less alert and easily soothed (Wachs et al., 2005). In addition, babies who had a fast heart rate in the womb are more likely to become inhibited, fearful children (Kagan et al., 1988). Indeed, heart rate differences between inhibited, fearful babies and uninhibited, relaxed babies have been found at 2 weeks of age (Snidman et al., 1995). Further, at 14 and 21 months of age, inhibited babies often have narrow facial structures, whereas uninhibited babies often have broader faces. These differences may reflect the fact that facial growth at these ages can be affected by high amounts of cortisol in the blood (Kagan et al., 1998). Babies who had greater EEG activation in the right frontal lobe at 9 months of age tended to be inhibited at 14 months (Calkins et al., 1996); this is interesting because greater EEG activation in the right frontal lobe in adults has been identified with a relatively less happy mood. The influence of biological factors on temperament is also evident in the fact that at 24 months of age, identical twins have more similar temperaments than do fraternal twins (DiLalla et al., 1994). Indeed, this study of twins showed that the tendency to be inhibited has a high heritability (that is, its variability among people in general is largely accounted for by genetic differences).

For temperament, like other characteristics, the story of development over the life span reveals themes of both stability and change. Even in the first week of life, temperament varies in different settings (Wachs et al., 2004). Moreover, as you saw in Chapter 11, not all inhibited infants became shy children and adults. In fact, only children who are extremely inhibited or uninhibited are likely to stay that way; the majority of children, who fall in the middle ranges, can change dramatically (Kerr et al., 1994; Robinson et al., 1992; also Kagan et al., 1998; Schwartz et al., 1996). Nevertheless, for those infants who exhibit marked inhibited or uninhibited behavior, early temperament is likely to provide an enduring core characteristic of later personality.

Nurturing Experiences

Some of the stability of temperament may arise not from innate predispositions, but from early nurturing experiences. Probably the most compelling evidence of this comes from research with nonhuman animals. Meaney and his colleagues (Anisman et al., 1998; Liu et al., 1997; Meaney et al., 1991; Zaharia et al., 1996) have shown that simply handling rat pups during the first 10 days after birth has enormous effects on the way the animals later respond to stressful events. As adults, these animals don't become as nervous as other rats (as reflected by fewer feces, less "freezing" responses, and more exploration) when put in a large open field, and they have lower cortisol responses (and thus are less vulnerable to the negative effects of prolonged exposure to cortisol. They are also less prone to learned helplessness (Costela et al., 1995). The effects of handling occur naturally when the mother rat licks her pups and engages in nursing with an arched back (so the pups are directly under her); off-spring of mothers that behaved this way later had lower amounts of the type of RNA that produces cortisol (Liu et al., 1997) and changes in the sensitivity of the hypothalamic-pituitary-adrenal axis (Weaver et al., 2004). There is good reason to believe that similar effects extend to humans: Touching infants not only can enhance growth and development, but also can reduce the EEG activation in the right frontal lobe that is associated with depression (even in 1-month-old infants!) and can boost immune function (Field, 1998; Field et al., 1986; Jones et al., 1998). Moreover, parents who perceive their infants as having a particular sort of temperament appear to influence the development of such a temperament (Pauli-Pott et al., 2003).

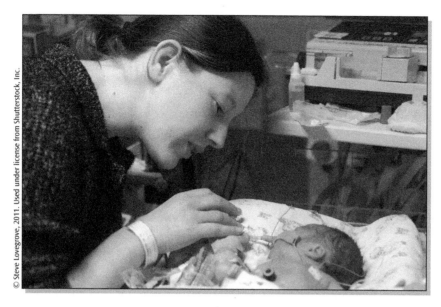

Social interactions with premature infants have been positively correlated with faster development and a sooner discharge from the hospital.

INFANCY AND CHILDHOOD: TAKING OFF

Steven Spielberg has repeatedly noted that his ability to make movies that appeal to children and to "the child inside adults" stems from the fact that he's never grown up himself. But although he may retain many childlike characteristics, the filmmaker has indeed matured. That is, his motor, perceptual, cognitive, and even social abilities have long outstripped those of even a preadolescent child. In this section, we see how this development occurs.

Physical and Motor Development: Getting Control

If we continued to grow throughout childhood at the same rate as during infancy, we would all be giants. A newborn can look forward to being 50% longer on his or her first birthday and 75% longer on his or her second. But growth does not continue at this rate; rather, it usually occurs in a series of small spurts. Similarly, control over various parts of the body does not occur simultaneously and smoothly, but in phases. Good motor control (that is, control of the muscles) is a necessary first step for normal interaction with the world. Developmental psychologists have spent many years studying the precise ways in which babies' movements change as they grow. Two of the early pioneers, Arnold Gesell (Gesell & Thompson, 1938) and Myrtle McGraw (1943), described a series of milestones that all babies, from all races and cultures, pass in an orderly progression. In general, control progresses from the head down the trunk to the arms, and finally to the legs; at the same time, control extends out from the center of the body to the periphery (hands, fingers, toes). By the age of 2, the child has good control over all the limbs. However, fine motor control—of the sort needed to play piano or type on a keyboard—develops more slowly. And some of us do this better than others; Spielberg, for example, was notoriously clumsy and uncoordinated throughout his childhood.

In spite of the dramatic improvements with age, even young infants have remarkable control of their movements. For example, when reaching for a ball in order to toss it into a tub on the floor, 10-month-old infants reach more quickly than if they are going to drop the ball down a tube—which shows that they are planning the pair of movements in tandem (Claxton et al., 2003).

The early theorists believed that the consistent and universal order of motor development implies that this development is entirely maturational. However, later studies of motor control showed that this view cannot be correct (Thelen & Ulrich, 1991). For example, consider the unanticipated consequences of having infants sleep on their backs, in an effort to reduce the chances of SIDS (this is advocated by the "Back to Sleep" movement, which has helped to reduce SIDS in the United States by about 30% since 1994; Association of SIDS and Infant Mortality Programs, 2002). Ratliff-Schaub and colleagues (2001) found that premature infants who slept on their backs had more difficulty holding their heads up and lowering them with control than did infants who slept on their bellies. Moreover, other back-sleeping babies were slow to roll from their backs to bellies, to sit up, to creep, crawl, and to pull themselves to a standing position (B. E. Davis et al., 1998). However, the children walked at the same age, regardless of how they slept. In fact, since babies have begun sleeping on their backs, some never learn to crawl. "It was an occasional phenomenon before, and now about a third of babies skip the step of crawling and go right to walking," says Dr. Karen Dewling (quoted by Seith, 2000). Thus, developing some aspects of motor control involves more than maturation; it also involves learning about the body and the world (Adolph, 2000; Thelen, 1995).

Developing motor control is important not simply because it allows the child to get around, but also because it helps the child develop capacities as varied as distance perception, visual search, and even using gestures to communicate. As Campos and colleagues (2000) put it, "travel broadens the mind." **Figure 4.3** presents average age ranges for major motor developments (but keep in mind that various factors, such as the opportunities to use specific muscles, affect these ages).

Perceptual and Cognitive Development: Extended Horizons

A parent probably would not tell as elaborate a story to a 3-year-old as to a 10-year-old. The reason is obvious: The younger child not only has a shorter attention span and understands fewer concepts about objects and events,

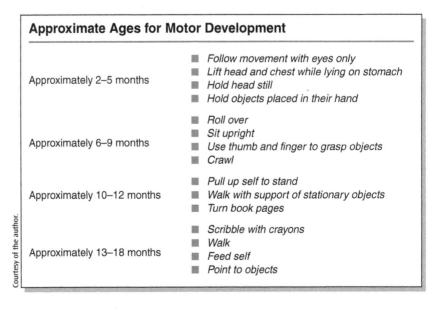

Approximate Ages for Motor Development

Approximately 2–5 months	■ *Follow movement with eyes only* ■ *Lift head and chest while lying on stomach* ■ *Hold head still* ■ *Hold objects placed in their hand*
Approximately 6–9 months	■ *Roll over* ■ *Sit upright* ■ *Use thumb and finger to grasp objects* ■ *Crawl*
Approximately 10–12 months	■ *Pull up self to stand* ■ *Walk with support of stationary objects* ■ *Turn book pages*
Approximately 13–18 months	■ *Scribble with crayons* ■ *Walk* ■ *Feed self* ■ *Point to objects*

Courtesy of the author.

FIGURE 4.3 ■ The ages shown in the table are approximate and are influenced by many factors.

but also can grasp only simple concepts about relations between objects and events (such as that one object can physically cause another to move). Where do these concepts come from? In part from perception, the organization and identification of information received through the senses; in part from cognition, or mental processes; and in part from the social environment.

Perceptual Development: Opening Windows on the World

Along with the rest of the body, the sensory organs develop with age. For example, young infants view the world blurrily, as if through thick gauze; with age, their visual acuity increases, in part because of developments in the eye, particularly in the lens and the retina (Banks & Bennett, 1988).

Infant Visual Perception

How do we know that infants can't see well? You obviously can't ask them, so how might you determine what babies are capable of seeing? Psychologists working in this area have developed a number of clever techniques. For example, to determine depth perception, infants are placed on a level sheet of glass that at first lies directly on a floor, but then extends over a part of the floor that has been stepped down. In this *visual cliff* experiment, researchers have found that even 6-month-old infants don't want to crawl out on the glass over the "deep end"—even when coaxed by their mothers—thus demonstrating that they can perceive depth before they can talk (Gibson & Walk, 1960).

But the visual cliff task is of no use with babies who are not yet able to crawl, so it is possible that even younger babies can see depth. How can we tell? In one study, researchers measured infants' heart rates when they were placed on the shallow or deep end of the visual cliff and found that 2-month-old babies had slower heart rates on the deep side (Campos et al., 1970); slower heart rates indicate that someone is paying closer attention, which suggests that the infants could in fact tell the difference between the two depths.

Other techniques for examining infants' visual perception measure the amount of time they spend looking at stimuli. For example, the *habituation technique* (also sometimes called the *looking time technique*), illustrated in **Figure 4.4**, is based on the fact that all animals—including humans of all ages—*habituate* to

Will this child have sufficient depth perception to avoid crawling off the ottoman and falling to the floor?

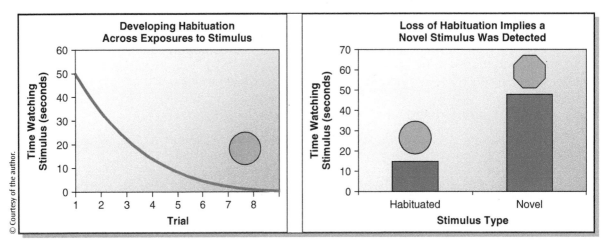

FIGURE 4.4 ▨ Hypothetical data showing a test to determine whether an infant can distinguish a red ball from a red octagon.

a stimulus: If a baby looks at a particular shape long enough, he or she will no longer find it interesting—and thus will prefer to look at something new. This technique can be used to discover what babies can see, hear, or feel as "different." If you simply added a copy of the habituated stimulus, it would be no more interesting than the original—the infant has to perceive it as different to find it interesting. By varying how two stimuli differ (in shape, distance, color, pattern of movement, and so on) and noting the circumstances in which babies prefer a new stimulus after habituating to a previous one, it is possible to discover what differences they can detect. Habituation techniques have shown that babies can detect depth between 2 and 3 months of age. In fact, 8-week-old babies can see depth as represented by sets of points flowing on a screen, the way we do when we see a spaceship whizzing through a cloud of meteors in a movie—and these infants can even see shapes that are depicted three-dimensionally by sets of flowing points (Arterberry & Yonas, 2000).

Newborns aren't very attentive companions, but they will notice if you make direct eye contact with them; in fact, even infants 2–5 days old prefer to look at faces that look directly at them rather than faces in which the eyes are averted (Farroni et al., 2002). Thus, looking time can be used not simply to assess habituation, but as a more general reflection of what an infant notices. Such techniques have shown that newborn infants only notice isolated portions of objects; within about 2 or 3 months, they can perceive overall shapes (Spelke et al., 1993) and even organize line fragments into three-dimensional forms (Bhatt & Bertin, 2001). By about 6 months of age, they can organize sets of isolated squares into horizontal or vertical stripes (Quinn et al., 2002), can visually "chunk" groups of objects into units (Feigenson & Halberda, 2004), and can mentally fill in when their view of a moving object is briefly obstructed (Johnson et al., 2003). As they grow older, babies need less stimulus information to recognize patterns. It is tempting to speculate that their enjoyment of playing "peek-a-boo" may reflect this developing ability, in that they can use top-down processing (see Chapter 4) and their knowledge about objects to infer a whole from a part.

Understanding Pictures

Steven Spielberg is counting on the fact that you will relate emotionally to his images in a film in the same way you would relate to the events and characters if you met them in reality. Nonetheless, when watching a movie, you are in no doubt that you are seeing an image, not the thing itself. Apparently, however, 9-month-old infants aren't quite sure about which properties of objects are captured by pictures. DeLoache and her colleagues (1998) showed infants high-quality color photographs and observed the babies' reactions. The babies reached for and touched the pictures as if they were seeing the actual objects, and sometimes actually tried to pick them off the page! It wasn't as if the babies thought that the pictures *were* objects; they weren't surprised or upset when they couldn't pluck them off the page. Rather, they apparently *did not know* what pictures were and so were exploring their properties in the way that seemed most sensible. But 10 months later, at 19 months of age, the babies pointed toward the objects in the pictures and no longer tried to manipulate them. Babies apparently have to learn what pictures are, and this learning takes time. This finding transcends culture and experience: Babies from the Ivory Coast of Africa and babies from the United States acted the same way in this experimental situation—even though the children in this study from this part of Africa had never before seen pictures in books.

Infant Auditory Perception

Compared with visual perception, auditory perception appears to be more fully developed at an earlier age. For example, researchers played consonant or dissonant versions of two sequences of tones to 4-month-olds. When the sequence was consonant, the infants looked longer at the audio speakers than when it was dissonant. Not only did they look away when the stimulus was dissonant, but they were more physically active. The researchers suggested that infants are innately tuned to find consonance more pleasing than dissonance (Zentner & Kagan, 1998). Apparently, to appreciate dissonant music, you must learn to overcome preferences that may be innate. But infant audition is unlike that of adults in a crucial way: When listening to sequences of tones that "do not conform to the rules of musical composition" (Saffran & Griepentrog, 2001, p. 74), even 8-month-old infants initially focus on absolute pitches, not relations among pitches (Saffran, 2003). Adults, in contrast, focus on relations among pitches. Thus, part of auditory development is a shift away from attending to absolute pitch to attending to relative pitch, which is more useful for music and for speech (because individual voices differ in absolute pitch).

Perceptual development continues beyond the first year of life. When, for instance, toddlers (2- and 3-year-olds) are shown an array of objects and asked whether it includes a specific object, they look haphazardly from place to place (Vurpillot, 1968). But 6- to 9-year-olds will search the array systematically, left to right, then top to bottom, as if they were reading a page. In general, by about age 11, children have perceptual abilities that are similar to (although often slower than) those of adults (Lobaugh et al., 1998; Piaget, 1969; Semenov et al., 2000), but some aspects of perceptual processing (used in organizing complex patterns) probably continue to develop until late adolescence (Sireteanu, 2000).

Long-Term Memory Development: Living Beyond the Here and Now

We adults have both explicit and implicit long-term memories. Is the same true of infants?

Infant Explicit Memory

Many studies have documented that even 3-month-old infants can store information explicitly (Rovee-Collier, 1997). How could researchers find this out? The key idea is that recognition taps explicit memory, whereas priming taps implicit memory (priming occurs when performing a task "greases the wheels," making the same or a related task easier to perform in the future). In one study conducted to assess recognition, researchers attached one end of a ribbon to an infant's foot and the other to a mobile that hung over the crib. The mobile was decorated with plus marks of a particular size. The infants soon learned that

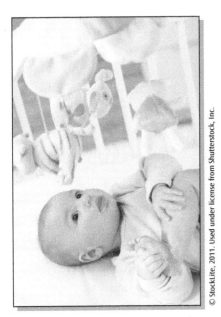

Kicking pulls a string that moves the mobile. Infants learn to kick their legs to make the mobile move. Such simple apparatuses allow researchers to assess the development and loss of memories in infants.

© StockLife, 2011. Used under license from Shutterstock, Inc.

kicking would move the mobile, which they found reinforcing—and hence they kicked at a higher rate. The researchers waited a day and then showed the infants either the identical mobile from the previous trial or one with plus marks that were either larger or smaller than on the original. The infants kicked at a higher rate only when the plus marks were the initial size. This is evidence that they recalled the original mobile explicitly (Gerhardstein et al., 2000).

Infant Implicit Memory

What about implicit memory? To test whether even 3-month-old infants have such memory, the same researchers used the kicking test but now waited 2 weeks before retesting, which is a time period longer than that for which infants can recall that kicking moves the mobile (typically only up to 6–8 days after learning). They had each infant watch while the investigator held the ribbon attached to the mobile and moved it at about the same rate that the infant had moved it before. This priming event was sufficient to reactivate the memory, leading the infants to recall the relationship between kicking and moving the mobile. However, the explicit memory was not activated: Now infants increased their kicking when they saw mobiles that had all sizes of plus marks, not just when the plus marks were the original size (Gerhardstein et al., 2000). Additional studies have shown that only 7.5 seconds of priming are necessary to reactivate the memory (Sweeny & Rovee-Collier, 2001). Moreover, the priming stimulus doesn't have to be part of the to-be-remembered event; even at 6 months of age, a "forgotten" memory can be reactivated by showing the infant another event that was associated with the to-be-remembered event (Barr et al., 2001, 2002). In fact, other researchers have shown that the brain responds differently when 6-month-old infants see a novel face than when they see one that's been primed (by having been shown previously; Webb & Nelson, 2001).

Memory Development

You might be tempted to think that memory is like height and weight: You get more of it as you age. Not exactly. For example, in one study, researchers found that although adults recognize location better than children do, older children actually recognize color better than adults do (Gulya et al., 2002). Such findings are additional evidence that "memory" is not a single entity, but is instead comprised of multiple systems—and these systems develop at different rates.

Language-based types of memory take on increasing importance as a child gets older. For example, in one study, Simcock and Hayne (2002) asked young children to learn to operate a machine that apparently shrank the sizes of toys. Six months or a year later, the researchers tested the children's memory for this event. They found that in recalling various aspects of the event, the children used only words that they knew at the time when they initially experienced it; that is, no words learned in the intervening period were used. This finding suggested to the researchers that the "children's verbal reports of the event were frozen in time, reflecting their verbal skill at the time of encoding, rather than at the time of test" (p. 229). We noted that adults have remarkably poor memory for events that occurred during early childhood—perhaps this is one explanation.

Brain Development and Memory

For the most part, long-term memory does improve from early childhood to adulthood. Why? Some improvement is probably due to the development of the brain (Bauer, 2002). For example, development of the hippocampus might explain why 6- to 12-month-olds show poorer recognition of an object when the context (the color of the background) is changed, whereas 18- to 24-month-olds were not affected by a context difference (Robinson & Pascalis, 2004). Changes in brain function underlie many aspects of memory development, as shown in part by the finding that an adult's brain is activated in more areas than is a 4-year-old's brain when a previously studied item is seen—and the adult's brain is activated more quickly after the item is presented (Marshall et al., 2002). In fact, even 14-year-olds differ from adults in their patterns of brain activation during memory tasks (Hepworth et al., 2001). But not all improvement in memory with age is due to brain development—events at other levels of analysis are also important. For example, adults—in particular, mothers—systematically help young children learn to label and organize to-be-remembered material (Labrell et al., 2002; Low & Durkin, 2001).

Stages of Cognitive Development: Piaget's Theory

Thinking is more than perceiving and remembering; it also involves reasoning. It's obvious that babies don't have the mental capacity of adults; they can't even understand most problems, let alone solve them. The gradual transition from infant to adult mental capacity is known as *cognitive development*. The great Swiss psychologist Jean Piaget (1896–1980) developed a far-reaching and comprehensive theory of cognitive development. Interest in Piaget's theory helped generate other lines of research that have focused on how the gradual improvement in information processing, the maturation of the brain, and the social environment contribute to cognitive development.

Piaget was originally trained in biology, but early in his career, he worked in Paris with Alfred Binet's collaborator, Theodore Simon, helping to standardize Binet's newly developed intelligence tests for children. Piaget was curious about the types of reasoning mistakes children are likely to make. This new interest connected with his long-term fascination with biology and the nature of the mind, leading him to a general investigation of the reasoning processes of children at various ages. Piaget believed that babies begin with very simple, innate schemas, mental structures that organize perceptual input and connect it to the appropriate responses. For the youngest infant, such schemas trigger grasping and sucking at the nipple when the infant is hungry and in the presence of a bottle or breast. According to Piaget, the process of assimilation allows the infant to use existing schemas to take in new stimuli and respond accordingly.

Schema: In Piaget's theory, a mental structure that organizes perceptual input and connects it to the appropriate responses.

Assimilation: In Piaget's theory, the process that allows the use of existing schemas to take in new sets of stimuli and respond accordingly.

For this child to play doctor with the stuffed bear requires approximately two years of normal development or else he will not be able to do it.

© FotoShock, 2012. Used under license from Shutterstock, Inc.

Accommodation: In Piaget's theory, the process that results in schemas' changing as necessary to cope with a broader range of situations.

For example, the schema for sucking a breast can also be used for sucking a bottle or a thumb. In contrast, the process of accommodation results in schemas' changing as necessary to cope with a broader range of situations. As the child develops, the schemas develop in two ways: First, they become more fully *articulated*; for example, more precise motions are used to locate the nipple and suck. Second, they become *differentiated*; an original schema for sucking may give rise to two separate schemas, one for bottles and one for thumbs, which in turn may give rise to schemas for drinking with a straw, drinking from a cup, and eating solid food.

These two processes—assimilation and accommodation—together are the engine that powers cognitive development. Piaget's theory of development hinges on what results when assimilation and accommodation work in tandem, which he claimed produces a system of rules—in Piaget's terms, a "logic"—that guides the child's thought. Depending on the available schemas, different kinds of logical operations are possible. Thus, according to Piaget, the child's thinking changes systematically over time as new schemas develop.

Piaget described four major stages, or periods, of cognitive development, as shown in **Table 4.2**; each period is governed by a different type of logic and includes many substages, with key characteristics. The periods overlap slightly, and they may occur at different ages for different children; thus, the ages given in the table are only approximate.

Sensorimotor Period

The infant's experience begins in the *sensorimotor period*, which extends from birth to approximately 2 years of age. According to Piaget's theory, infants initially conceive of the world solely in terms of their perceptions and actions. In this period, infants lack the ability to form mental representations that can be used to think about an object in its absence. In the early stages of the sensorimotor period, the infant does not yet have object permanence, the understanding that objects (including people) continue to exist even when they cannot be immediately perceived. For example, a rattle dropped by an infant over the side of the high chair is quickly forgotten—and more than forgotten: Out of sight means not just out of mind but out of existence! Piaget claimed that by the end of the sensorimotor period, by about age 2, the toddler understands that objects

Object permanence: The understanding that objects (including people) continue to exist even when they cannot be immediately perceived.

TABLE 4.2   Piagetian Developmental Stages.

Category	Approximate Age Range	Behavioral Qualities
Sensorimotor stage	0–2 years	Behavior is directly related to what is currently affecting the child. The child shows little capacity to plan future behavior.
Preoperational stage	2–7 years	The development of a symbolic manipulation process speeds the development of language, pretend play and simple mathematics. The child begins to recognize that others have thoughts and feelings different than their own.
Concrete operational stage	7–11 years	Basic reversible logical rules may be followed. The child can systematically organize objects into concrete categories.
Formal operational stage	11 years through adulthood	Abstract thought begins to develop and is applied to concrete objects (e.g., rocket ships) and intangible concepts (e.g., love, justice).

exist even when they are no longer perceived. In addition, Piaget claimed that a second major achievement of the sensorimotor period—at around 9 months of age—is the ability to imitate.

Preoperational Period

Once out of the sensorimotor period, the toddler enters the *preoperational period*, from roughly age 2 until age 7. Armed with the ability to form mental representations, children in the preoperational period are able to think about objects and events that are not immediately present. As a result, they can imitate actions that occurred in the past. This newfound capacity for mental representation allows the child to engage in fantasy play. Whereas the infant might play with a bar of soap in the bath by squeezing it and watching it pop up, the preoperational child, performing the same actions, might think of the soap as a submerged submarine that is breaking the surface.

A cook asks two boys who have just ordered a large pizza, "How many slices do you want me to cut your pizza into, 8 or 12?" One boy immediately answers, "Please cut it into 12 pieces, because I'm very hungry!" This is a joke for older children and grown-ups, but not for preoperational children, whose thoughts are limited in part because they do not yet have a "logic" for manipulating, or *operating* on, mental representations. Therefore, they often reason on the basis of appearances. One of Piaget's important discoveries is that these children do not understand **conservation**, the principle that properties such as amount or mass remain the same even when the appearance of the material or object changes, provided that nothing is added or removed. Many studies have documented that preoperational children do not conserve, and so they do not realize that cutting a pizza into 12 pieces instead of 8 does not increase the total amount of pizza. A classic example, illustrated in **Figure 4.5**, is that preoperational children do not understand that pouring liquid from a short wide glass into a tall thin glass does not alter the amount of liquid. Similarly, they typically think that flattening a ball of clay decreases the amount of clay and that spreading the objects in a row farther apart changes the number of objects in the row.

Both sensorimotor and preoperational children show **egocentrism**, which does not mean "selfishness" in the ordinary sense of the word, but instead the inability to take another's point of view. For example, children in this period will hold a picture they've drawn up to the telephone, to "show" it to a grandparent. They mistakenly assume that others see the same things they do.

> **Conservation:** The Piagetian principle that certain properties, such as amount or mass, remain the same even when the appearance of the material or object changes, provided that nothing is added or removed.

> **Egocentrism:** In Piaget's theory, the inability to take another person's point of view.

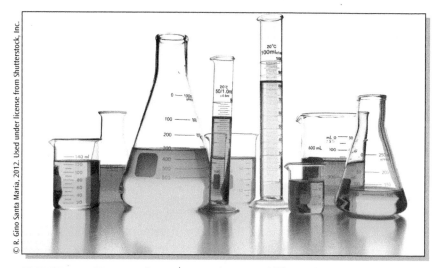

FIGURE 4.5 ■ Tests for conservation use differently sized and shaped containers to manipulate the height of the same volume of liquid.

Concrete operation: In Piaget's theory, a (reversible) manipulation of the mental representation of an object that corresponds to an actual physical manipulation.

Concrete Operations Period

By the end of the preoperational period, at about age 7, children develop the ability to take another person's perspective. This ability is linked to the fact that they can now perform concrete operations, manipulating mental representations in much the same way as they can manipulate the corresponding objects. At this point, children are able to begin to classify objects and their properties, to grasp concepts such as length, width, volume, and time, and to understand various mental operations such as those involved in simple arithmetic. This *period of concrete operations* is Piaget's third period of cognitive development, which takes place roughly between the ages of 7 and 11. Concrete operations allow the child to reason logically, partly because this mode of conceptualizing is *reversible*; that is, it can be used to make or undo a transformation. For example, having seen the liquid being poured into a tall thin glass, the child can mentally reverse the process and imagine the liquid being poured back into the original container. Seeing that no liquid has been added or subtracted in the process, the child realizes that the amount in both glasses must be the same.

Formal Operations Period

By definition, concrete operations cannot be used for reasoning about abstract concepts; children in the period of concrete operations cannot figure out, for example, that whenever 1 is added to an even number, the result will always be an odd number. To be able to reason abstractly, Piaget said, requires that the child be capable of formal operations, reversible mental acts that can be performed even with abstract concepts. This ability emerges roughly at the age of 11 or 12, at the onset of what Piaget termed the *period of formal operations*. Rather than simply understanding the logic of "what is," as occurs with concrete operations, the emerging adolescent is now able to imagine the possibilities of "what could be." Formal operations allow children to engage in abstract thinking, to think about "what-would-happen-if" situations, to formulate and test theories, and to think systematically about the possible outcomes of an act by being able to list alternatives in advance and consider each in turn. For example, formal operations would permit a child to think about how best to spend his or her money and to weigh the benefits and drawbacks of each possible budget decision.

Formal operation: In Piaget's theory, a mental act that can be performed (and reversed) even with an abstract concept.

The Child's Concepts: Beyond Piaget

Do children follow the stages Piaget described? When researchers use techniques different from Piaget's in order to see what children do or do not understand, they often come up with results that differ from his. Although Piaget employed very clever tasks (such as those used to assess conservation), those tasks typically assessed only easily observable aspects of behavior. When more subtle measurements are taken, evidence sometimes emerges that children can show competence well before they have reached the appropriate Piagetian stage.

Earlier Competencies

The capacities of infants often far exceed those claimed by Piaget. For example, Andrew Meltzoff and his colleagues (notably, Meltzoff & Moore, 1977) have found that 2- to 3-week-old infants can show true imitation, and others have found that even 2-day-old infants can imitate happy and sad facial expressions (Field et al., 1982). And there's evidence that 9-month-old infants can add and subtract (McCrink & Wynn, 2004). Moreover, given what's been learned about infant memory, you won't be surprised that other researchers have shown that babies as young as 3 months old can have object permanence—they know that previously seen objects continue to exist after they are removed from sight. This refutes Piaget's idea that object permanence does not establish itself until the child is a

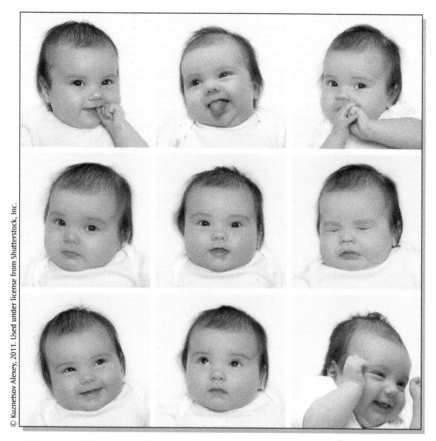

Infants can learn to imitate the facial expressions of adults at nearly two weeks of age.

toddler (Baillargeon, 1993, 2004; Spelke et al., 1992). Moreover, when appropriately tested, children as young as 3 years show that they understand the conservation of amount or mass (Gelman, 1972).

Piaget's theory seems to underestimate the sophistication of young children's conceptions of the world. Infants demonstrate an understanding of some physical laws even before they have developed the kinds of perceptual-motor schemas that Piaget claimed are the foundations of such knowledge. For example, even 4-month-old infants are aware of temporal intervals, showing surprise when a predictable sequence of flashing lights is interrupted (Colombo & Richman, 2002). Moreover, from experiments using looking-time methods, researchers have concluded that even young infants realize that objects need to be physically supported to remain stable (**Figure 4.6**), that objects can't move *through* other objects, and that objects don't flit from place to place but shift along connected paths (Spelke, 1991; Spelke et al., 1992).

In contrast to Piaget's idea that formal operations are necessary to formulate and test theories, more recent research findings have suggested that in many ways the young child relates to the world as a young scientist. Faced with a bewildering set of phenomena, children try to organize stimuli and events into categories and develop theories of how those categories interact (Carey, 1985, 1988, 1995b; Keil & Silberstein, 1996; Spelke et al., 1992; Wellman, 1990). Even 1-year-old babies begin to organize categories (Waxman, 1992), and preschoolers develop sophisticated ways to determine whether an object belongs in a particular category. For example, they begin to understand that animals beget animals of the same type and that the internal biology—not the external appearance—defines the type (Keil, 1989a, 1989b).

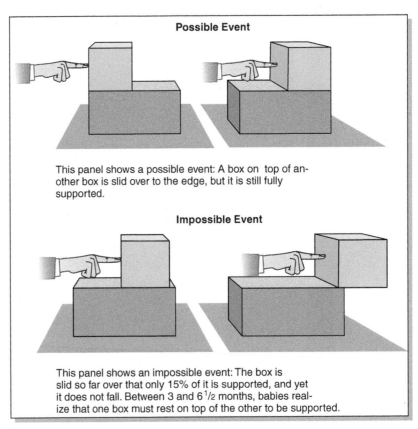

FIGURE 4.6 ▓ Early Perception of Possible Events.

Theory of Mind

In addition, current thinking suggests that children develop a theory of mind, a theory of other people's mental states—their beliefs, desires, and feelings. This theory allows them to predict what other people can understand and how they will react in a given situation (Flavell, 1999; Frye et al., 1998; S. Johnson, 2000; Lillard, 1999; Wellman, 1990). One way to assess theory of mind is to tell children a story and see whether they draw the proper inferences about the protagonist's mental state. In one story used for this purpose, a boy hides his candy in a drawer, but after he leaves the room, his mother moves the candy to a cupboard. Children are then told that the boy returns and is asked where he thinks his candy is hidden. By age 4 (which is before the age at which Piaget believed that children rise above their egocentric outlook), children believe that the boy thinks the candy is still where he put it originally, but children under 4 often believe that the boy thinks that the candy is in the cupboard. In order to get this right, the child must understand that belief does not necessarily reflect reality.

How does a theory of mind work? It is possible that children learn to "put themselves in another person's place," seeing things through another's eyes (J. R. Harris, 1995). It is also possible that children build a theory of the situations that give rise to other people's feelings (for example, seeing a child scream after being stung by a bee leads to the theory that bee stings hurt; Wellman, 1990); this approach has been called the *theory theory* (see Gopnik, 1996).

How does a theory of mind develop? The underlying process partly relies on the mother: Mothers who talk about their children's mental states more often have children who are more adept at using a theory of mind; in addition, children who have high verbal abilities also tend to develop a sophisticated theory of mind (Meins et al., 2002).

In addition, the particular theory of mind a child develops depends in part on the surrounding culture. In many African tribes, calamities such as AIDS or

A theory of mind is the name for the ability to infer accurately what another person may be experiencing.

fires are believed to have supernatural causes (Lillard, 1999). Even within a culture, different subgroups can develop different types of theories. Lillard and colleagues (1998, as cited in Lillard, 1999) asked children to explain the behavior of a character in a story and found that children growing up in cities tended to use psychological explanations—for example, referring to the character's likes and dislikes—even at 7 years of age. In contrast, children growing up in the country rarely (only 20% of the time, compared with 60% for urban children) used such explanations; instead, rural children usually relied on aspects of the situation to explain behavior. It is not clear why this difference exists. Although researchers agree that culture plays a role in the development of a theory of mind, culture cannot explain the evidence that children as young as 6 months begin to develop a theory of mind. For example, after being habituated by watching someone reach for the same toy repeatedly, infants of this age looked longer when a person reached for a new toy than when the person used a new movement to reach for the familiar toy (Woodward, 1998). Apparently the infant inferred that the person had the goal of reaching for the familiar toy and was surprised when the goal changed—but not when the motion changed. Such effects were not found when the infants saw inanimate objects (which were similar in size and shape to a human arm) touch or pick up the toy (Baldwin [2000], S. Johnson [2000], and Shimizu & Johnson [2004] report similar findings).

In short, the finding that many abilities are evident much earlier than Piaget predicted challenges his idea that all of a given child's thought reflects a single underlying logic, a logic that changes with increasing age and development. Moreover, later research has shown that many children do not enter the period of formal operations until high school, and some never enter it at all (Hooper et al., 1984; Lunzer, 1978). Nevertheless, Piaget has been proven correct in his observation that there are qualitative shifts in children's performance of specific tasks as they age. He must also be credited with discovering many counterintuitive phenomena, such as failure to conserve and egocentrism, that all subsequent theories of cognitive development must be able to explain.

Information Processing and Neural Development

Efforts to explain the findings sparked by Piaget's theory have looked at specific changes in the way children process information and at how their brains mature. The brain develops dramatically from birth to about 3 years of age, and it continues to show substantial growth until the child is about 12 years old (Tsekhmistrenko et al., 2004). But what is this enhanced brain able to do? The *information-processing approach* is based on the idea that perception and cognition rely on a host of distinct processes in the brain, not all of which necessarily develop at the same rate.

Researchers have thus studied very specific aspects of cognitive development and have found that some mental processes do indeed develop more quickly than others. For example, even very young children are adept at using sensory memory (the very brief memory of perceptual stimulation) and at accessing information they have successfully stored in long-term memory (the relatively permanent store of information). However, anyone who has spent time with children knows that young children often perform more poorly than older children in many tasks. There are many reasons for this: Young children are not able to focus attention effectively; they are not able to formulate and follow plans effectively (Scholnick, 1995); and they do not have as much stored information that can be used in organizing and remembering input (Chi, 1978). Moreover, young children are simply slower at mental processing than older children and adults (Kail, 1988, 1991). Finally, a particularly important reason why young children may perform more poorly than older children is that their *working memory*—their ability to use information held in an active state—does not stack up well against that of older children or adults.

Development of Working Memory

Working memory capacity increases with age throughout childhood (Case, 1977, 1978). As working memory capacity increases, a child becomes able to perform tasks that were previously beyond reach.

The finding that working memory increases with age explains many of the phenomena documented by Piaget, such as the out-of-sight/out-of-mind behavior that he interpreted as showing a lack of object permanence (Baird et al., 2002). In this case, a *quantitative* change in capacity (the increase in its size) can lead to a *qualitative* change in performance (the transition to a new stage; Case, 1992b; Pascual-Leone, 1970). By analogy, if you have a relatively small amount of RAM memory in your computer, then you will be able to run only relatively simple programs (such as basic text editing or e-mail), but not more complicated ones (such as a complex word-processing program or large slide-show presentation). If you increase the amount of memory, you will be able not only to run more complex programs, but also to run multiple programs at the same time. A quantitative change in the amount of memory underlies qualitative changes in performance.

Working Memory and Strategies

Increases in working memory capacity can also affect other factors that change with age—such as the number and types of strategies a child can use. Robert Siegler's (1996) *wave model* rests on the idea that cognitive development is like a series of waves, where the waves are sets of strategies. Each wave crests at a different age, and more sophisticated strategies become possible with increasing age—but older strategies are not abandoned altogether, they are just used less often. For example, when shown a square grid that contains blocks in some of its cells and asked to report the number of blocks, children can use one of three strategies: they count clusters of blocks and add them up; they count the number of empty cells and subtract them from the total number of cells; or they guess, based on an overall impression. Younger children have difficulty using the subtraction strategy, in part, because they don't accurately calculate the total number of cells (Luwel et al., 2001). As children become older, they have more strategies to select among (Chen & Seigler, 2000; Jansen & van der Maas, 2002; Lautrey & Caroff, 1996; Siegler, 1989, 1996; Siegler & Svetina, 2002). Some strategies are automatic, and once learned will continue to be used in familiar settings; other strategies require conscious thought, and it is these that are most affected by the growth of working memory (Crowley et al.; 1997, Crowley & Siegler, 1999).

Working Memory and Brain Development

What accounts for the child's improvements in working memory with age? The initial immaturity of the brain may be key. The brain undergoes rapid growth spurts (Epstein, 1980) around the ages that Piaget identified as marking transitions to new periods. Some of the increase in brain weight with age may be due to *myelinization* (the laying down of myelin, a fatty substance that serves as an insulator, on the axons), which increases the speed and efficiency of neural transmission, and some may be due to larger numbers of synapses and long-distance connections (Case, 1992c; Thatcher, 1994; Thompson et al., 2000). These changes would not only increase the speed of information processing (Demetriou et al., 2002), but also would allow more information to be activated at the same time— which, in turn, would increase working memory capacity. In fact, as more white matter matures in two different parts of the frontal lobes between the ages of 8 and 18, working memory improves (Nagy, Westerberg & Klingberg, 2004).

Vygotsky's Sociocultural Theory: Outside/Inside

Appreciating the importance of events at different levels of analysis leads us to look beyond any single source to explain psychological events. Thus, it isn't surprising that at least some aspects of cognitive development reflect social interactions. Russian psychologist Lev S. Vygotsky (1896–1934) emphasized the role of social interaction during development (Vygotsky, 1978, 1934/1986). Whereas Piaget believed that the child constructs representations of the world in the course of experiencing it first-hand, Vygotsky believed that the child constructs representations of the world by first absorbing his or her culture; the culture, as represented in the child's mind, then serves to guide behavior (Beilin, 1996; Kitchener, 1996). According to Vygotsky, adults promote cognitive

A good memory is an invaluable tool during your life.

development by guiding and explicitly instructing children, and cultural creations, particularly language, play a crucial role in development (Cole & Wertsch, 1996; Karpov & Haywood, 1998).

One of Vygotsky's key ideas is that once children learn language, they begin to use "private speech" to direct themselves (Berk, 1994a; Smolucha, 1992; Vygotsky, 1962, 1988). **Private speech** (also sometimes called *inner speech*) is language used by the child in planning or in prompting himself or herself to behave in specific ways. Children initially begin to use language in this way by actually speaking aloud to themselves, but eventually private speech becomes internalized and silent. As Vygotsky predicted, researchers have found that young children use private speech more when trying to solve a difficult task (such as folding paper in a particular way or arranging events into a story) (Berk, 1992a, 1994b; Duncan & Pratt, 1997) than when working on an easy task. They also use private speech more after they have made an error (Berk, 1992a, 1994b). Preschoolers (aged 3 to 5) also use private speech more frequently when they have to decide what to do in a free play situation than when they are put in a highly structured play situation (Krafft & Berk, 1998).

It might be tempting to think that culture is one influence on cognitive development, and the brain another. But this would be an error. The two factors interact: Culture affects the brain, and vice versa. For example, culture determines which language or languages you learn, which in turn affects how your brain processes sounds. By the same token, aspects of the brain affect culture; for example, we don't have customs that require more working memory capacity than the brain provides.

> **Private speech:** The language used by a child in planning or in prompting himself or herself to behave in specific ways; also called *inner speech*.

Social and Emotional Development: The Child in the World

The psychological development of a child includes more than the improvement in mental processing and the acquisition of knowledge and beliefs. Equally impressive development occurs in the child's social interactions, such as the ability to form relationships.

> **Attachment:** An emotional bond that leads a person to want to be with someone else and to miss him or her when separated.

Attachment: More Than Dependency

In our closest relationships, we develop deep attachments to other people. **Attachment** is an emotional bond that leads us to want to be with someone and to miss him or her when we are separated. The tendency to form such an emotional bond begins during infancy, when normal infants become attached to their primary caregivers.

Origins of Attachment

What is the origin of the infant's attachment? Decades ago, a prominent theory—sometimes called the "cupboard theory" because it centered on food—held that infants become attached because their caregivers feed them and thus become associated with positive feelings (Sears et al., 1957). However, classic experiments by Harry Harlow and his collaborators disproved this and similar theories (for example, Harlow, 1958). These researchers found that baby monkeys became much more attached to a model "mother" that had a pleasing texture and a more realistic face than to another "mother" that lacked these characteristics, even though the latter was the only one from which they received food. The impulse to seek comfort from something soft is an innate rather than a learned characteristic of mammals.

British psychoanalyst John Bowlby (1969) developed a theory of attachment that has become widely accepted among developmental psychologists. According to Bowlby, children go through phases during the

A baby monkey raised without parental care generally exhibits poor social behavior in adulthood.

development of attachment. Just as in Piaget's stages, the order of the phases is thought to be determined biologically, but the precise ages of the transitions depend on experience. A major shift, usually occurring between 6 months and 2 years, is characterized by separation anxiety, which is fear of being away from the primary caregiver. This shift may arise on the heels of a transition in cognitive development—specifically, infants can now think about and remember objects (including the primary caregiver) for relatively long periods when the objects are no longer present.

Types of Attachment

Not all babies become attached to their caregivers in the same way. Ainsworth and her colleagues (1978) developed a way to assess attachment using a scenario they called the *Strange Situation*. The setup involves a staged sequence of events designed to discover how a child reacts when left with a stranger or alone in an unfamiliar situation. If the child has developed secure attachment, he or she should show separation anxiety, becoming upset when the mother leaves, and should not be soothed equally well by a stranger as by the mother. Studies using the Strange Situation revealed four types of attachment:

- *Secure attachment* (about 60–70% of American babies) is evident if babies venture away from the mother, are upset when she leaves and not well comforted by a stranger, but calm down quickly when the mother returns.
- *Avoidant attachment* (about 15–20% of American babies) is evident if babies don't seem to care very much whether the mother is present or absent and are equally comfortable with her and a stranger; when she returns, they do not immediately gravitate to her.
- *Resistant attachment* (about 10–15% of American babies) is evident if babies do not use the mother as a base of operations but rather stay close to her and become angry when she leaves; some of these babies may go so far as to hit the mother when she returns, and they do not calm down easily thereafter.
- *Disorganized/disoriented attachment* (5–10% of American babies) is evident if the babies become depressed and have periods of unresponsiveness along with spurts of sudden emotion at the end of the procedure.

Data indicate that the type of attachment established between parent and child is partly due to cultural factors.

However, these differences have proven to be matters of degree, not sharply defined categories (Fraley & Spieker, 2003). Various factors influence the kind of attachment an infant will show. For example, if the mother was a heavy user of cocaine or other illicit drugs while pregnant, her infant is more likely at age 18 months to have disorganized/disoriented attachment (Swanson et al., 2000). In addition, mothers who are more sensitive to their babies' moods and behaviors had more securely attached infants (Tarabulsy et al., 2005). Moreover, the children of poor Black mothers are less securely attached than those of White mothers, which may reflect the adverse effects of poverty on a mother's ability to remain highly sensitive to her child (Bakermans-Kranenburg et al. 2004).

The type of early attachment can have long-lasting effects. Infants with secure attachment who were later studied at age 11 were found to have closer friendships and better social skills than children who had not been securely attached as infants (Shulman et al., 1994). In fact, the type of attachment determines how some genes operate: At least in monkeys, certain genes that underlie aggression and excessive drinking of alcohol are only activated (and thus only have their effects) when the monkey had an insecure early attachment—not when it experienced secure attachment (Suomi, 2003). Furthermore, secure attachment can lead a child to be more comfortable with exploring, which leads to better learning and can lead to more intimate love relationships later in life (Sroufe & Fleeson, 1986; Weiss, 1986).

Is Daycare Bad for Children?

Obviously, a child will not have an opportunity to become attached to a parent who is never around. This was a major concern of Steven Spielberg, whose own father was often absent. However, according to Scarr (1998), "Exclusive maternal care of infants and young children is a cultural myth of an idealized 1950s, not a reality anywhere in the world, either now or in earlier times" (p. 95). Since 1940, less than half of all persons in the United States have lived in a "traditional" family with a full-time working father and a mother who works only in the home, and the percentage has been declining since 1950. In the United States today, over half of the mothers of babies younger than 1 year work outside the home (Behrman, 1996). Most of these children are in some form of daycare.

Is daycare bad for children? This question has been the subject of a long and sometimes intense debate; parents have felt trapped between guilt about

Daycare can be an enjoyable experience for both the children and staff.

not staying at home with their children and the necessity of supporting their families. To begin, it's worth noting that high-quality daycare (with small adult-child ratios and appropriately trained staff) enriches a child's learning experiences and improves his or her cognitive abilities (Duncan, 2003; Loeb et al., 2004). In addition, children who were securely attached to their primary caregiver before entering daycare had lower cortisol levels while they were getting used to daycare than did children who were not securely attached; this finding suggests that daycare is less stressful for securely attached children (Ahnert et al., 2004).

But—looking at the other side of the coin—what are the effects of daycare on how well children are attached to their primary caregiver? Research examining the strength of attachment of children raised at home versus those raised partly in daycare centers has found that children who entered daycare relatively early in life were as strongly attached to their mothers as those who entered relatively late (Scarr, 1998; see also NICHD Early Child Care Research Network, 1997; Roggman et al., 1994). Moreover, children were more securely attached to mothers who were strongly committed to their jobs, returned to work relatively early, and had relatively little anxiety about sending their children to daycare (Harrison & Ungerer, 2002). However, other research has shown that slightly more of the home-raised children show secure attachment in the Strange Situation (Scarr, 1998). Moreover, there is evidence that children who spend more time in "nonmaternal care" during their first 4½ years behave more aggressively and defiantly than children who spend more time with their mothers (Belsky, 2001, 2002; NICHD Early Child Care Research Network, 2003). But these behaviors are fluid and change as the children grow older (Barry, 2002).

Self-Concept and Identity: The Growing Self

A critical aspect of social development is the emerging sense of who you are and how you stand relative to other people. Psychologists use the term **self-concept** to refer to the beliefs, desires, values, and attributes that define a person to himself or herself. A key part of Steven Spielberg's self-concept as a child was his many fears, both large and small (McBride, 1999).

For young children, the self-concept is necessarily grounded in the level of cognitive development. Thus, preschoolers think of themselves in very concrete

Self-concept: The beliefs, desires, values, and attributes that define a person to himself or herself.

Knowledge of your appearance is a portion of your self-concept.

terms, in terms of behaviors and physical appearance (Keller et al., 1978). At what age do children begin to conceive of themselves as having specific characteristics? To find out, a dab of red paint was placed on babies' noses without their knowledge, and the babies then looked in a mirror. Some babies of about 15 months of age will notice the smudge and rub it off. By age 2, virtually all children have this response (Amsterdam, 1972; Lewis & Brooks-Gunn, 1979). However, this test may in fact assess understanding of temporary changes in appearance, not self-concept (Asendorpf et al., 1996). Other researchers have argued that the roots of the self-concept are present in children much younger than toddlers. Bahrick and her collaborators (1996) found that even 3-month-olds prefer to look at the face of another child of the same age rather than at their own face, which suggests that they are already familiar with the appearance of their face. Even newborns distinguish between touching themselves and being touched by someone else, a distinction that may mark the beginning of a self-concept (Rochat & Hespos, 1997).

By 3 years of age, children begin to appreciate that they have distinct psychological characteristics, such as being happy in certain situations and not in others (Eder, 1989). Children of about 8 to 11 begin to describe themselves in terms of personality traits, perhaps as "energetic" or "musical." The oldest children in this age range also describe themselves in terms of social relations (Rosenberg, 1979), such as the relationships they have with their siblings and friends. This ability to self-label depends on reasoning abilities that develop during what Piaget described as the period of formal operations.

Culture clearly affects a person's self-concept. In the collectivist cultures of Japan, China, and other Asian countries, children's self-concepts typically revolve around their relations to the group (Markus & Kitayama, 1991). In contrast, in the individualist cultures of most Western countries, children's self-concepts typically revolve around defining themselves as distinct entities that must negotiate with, and navigate through, the group.

Gender Identity and Gender Roles

A central part of your self-concept is your identity as a member of one gender, which in turn leads you to adopt certain roles.

Gender Identity: Not Just Being Raised with Pink or Blue

Gender identity: A person's belief that he or she is male or is female.

Gender identity is the belief that you are male or female. Part of your gender identity arises from how you are raised (Tenenbaum & Leaper, 2002), and part of it comes from the social context in which you grow up (Horowitz & Newcomb, 2001). Given the pervasive influence of events at all three levels of analysis, you might expect that biological factors also play a role—and they do. The role of such factors is vividly illustrated in the following case history (Colapinto, 2000): At 8 months of age, a boy's penis was accidentally sliced off as a split foreskin was being surgically repaired. The family and surgeons decided that it would be best to raise the boy as a girl, and so his testicles were removed and a vagina was surgically formed. The boy, previously known as "John," was now called "Joan," and her past as a boy was never discussed. Joan was treated in every way like a girl, and her friends and classmates had no reason to suspect that she was in any way extraordinary. When Joan was 9 years old, psychologist John Money (1975) wrote a famous paper in which he reported that Joan had a female gender identity, in sharp contrast to her identical twin brother, who had a strong male gender identity. This report, and others like it, led researchers to believe that gender identity was essentially neutral at birth and was formed by culture and upbringing.

However, Diamond and Sigmundson (1997) revisited John/Joan some 20 years later and recounted a very different story. They found that as a young child, she sometimes ripped off her dresses and tried to urinate standing up. At

14, she refused to have any more vaginal surgery or to live as a girl. She was not attracted to boys and considered suicide. Even though she had been treated as a girl and even received female hormones that caused breasts to develop, she was deeply unhappy and confused. Her father finally broke down and told her about the accident. Instead of being upset on learning that she had been born a boy, she was greatly relieved. She renounced her female identity, underwent surgery to remove her breasts and reconstruct a penis, and was determined to establish a relationship with a woman. Joan became John once again. He eventually married and adopted his wife's children from a previous marriage. However, the early trauma cast a long shadow: John committed suicide in 2004, when he was just 38 years old.

What was going on here? John's brain had been exposed to high levels of androgens in the womb, which led his brain to develop in male-typical ways. These male predispositions were not something that could be arbitrarily changed simply by treating him as a female. Indeed, certain disorders result in exposure of a genetically female fetus to high levels of male hormones in the womb, and studies of such children have shown that this exposure can affect gender identity. These girls later preferred to play with boys' toys and to participate in boys' games (Berenbaum, 1999; Berenbaum & Hines, 1992). Boys can also be affected by the hormonal environment; boys who experience a relatively low amount of male sex hormones in the womb engage in less rough-and-tumble play than do boys who are exposed to the usual amount (Hines & Kaufman, 1994).

The Development of Gender Roles

Gender roles are the culturally determined appropriate behaviors of males versus females. It is one thing to identify yourself as male or female, but something else entirely to understand what behaviors are appropriate for your gender (Martin & Ruble, 2004). Gender roles vary in different cultures, social classes, and time periods; for example, a proper woman in Victorian England (or, perhaps, 19th-century America) would probably be very surprised to learn that a woman

Gender roles: The culturally determined appropriate behaviors of males versus females.

© AISPIX, 2011. Used under license from Shutterstock, Inc.

Most developmental psychologists would guess that this girl wants to treat the bear as a baby that needs loving attention. The boy probably wants to kick or throw it into the air. These are two characteristic types of play seen in girls and boys.

can be a senator or the president of a major corporation today. Conceptions about gender roles develop early. Indeed, by age 2, children have apparently learned about gender role differences (Caldera & Sciaraffa, 1998; Witt, 1997). Some preschool boys apparently believe that if they play with cross-gender toys (say, dishes instead of tools), their fathers will think that was "bad" (Raag & Rackliff, 1998).

Freud argued that children identify with the same-sex parent, and that this is the main way in which gender roles develop (see Chapter 11). But Eleanor Maccoby believes that identification with the same-sex parent may be the *result* of gender role development, not the cause. Her account rests on events at all three levels. At the level of the group, in Maccoby's view, peer-group interactions are key to learning gender roles. It is in the peer group, she argues, that boys first learn about how to gain and maintain status in the hierarchy and that girls develop their styles of interaction (Maccoby, 1990, 1991). Maccoby and Jacklin (1987) found that 4-year-old children spent triple the amount of time playing with same-sex peers as with opposite-sex peers, and this proportion shot up to 11 times more when the children were 6 years old. According to Maccoby (1990, p. 514), "Gender segregation . . . is found in all the cultural settings in which children are in social groups large enough to permit choice."

Why does gender segregation occur? Maccoby (1988) suggests that part of the answer may lie in biological, particularly hormonal, differences. Boys play more aggressively than do girls, and their orientation toward competition and dominance may be aversive to many girls. However, shifting to the level of the person, Maccoby (1990) also notes that girls may not like playing with boys because they believe that boys are too difficult to influence; the polite manner in which girls tend to make suggestions apparently doesn't carry much weight with boys. Girls find this response (or lack of response) frustrating and retreat to the company of other girls.

Moral Development: The Right Stuff

A key aspect of social development is the emergence of more complex ideas of morality, which center on the ability to tell right from wrong. As children grow older, their developing cognitive abilities allow them to draw more subtle infer-ences. The young child may feel that a girl who knocks over a lamp and breaks it is equally to blame if she smashed it intentionally, bumped it by accident while horsing around, or fell against it accidentally when the dog jumped on her. An older child is able to make clear distinctions among the three cases, seeing decreasing blame for each in turn. Piaget was a pioneer in the study of moral as well as cognitive development. His studies often involved telling children stories in which he varied the intentions of the characters and the results of their actions, and then asking the children to evaluate the characters' morality. Lawrence Kohlberg extended Piaget's approach and developed an influential theory of moral development.

Kohlberg's Theory

Moral dilemma: A situation in which there are moral pros and cons for each of a set of possible actions.

Kohlberg presented boys and men with **moral dilemmas**, situations in which there are moral pros and cons for each of a set of possible actions. He asked par-ticipants to decide what the character should do and to explain why. This is the famous dilemma that confronted Heinz (Puka, 1994).

> In Europe, a woman was near death from a special kind of cancer. There was one drug that the doctors thought might save her. It was a form of radium that a druggist in the same town had recently discov-ered. The drug was expensive to make, but the druggist was charging 5 times what it cost him to make the drug. He paid $400 for the radium, and charged $2,000 for a small dose of the drug. The sick woman's

husband, Heinz, went to everyone he knew to borrow the money, but he could only get together about $1,000, half of what it cost. He told the druggist that his wife was dying, and asked him to sell it cheaper or let him pay later. But the druggist said, "No, I discovered the drug and I'm going to make money from it, so I won't let you have it unless you give me $2,000 now." So Heinz got desperate and broke into the man's store to steal the drug for his wife.

Should Heinz have done that? Why?

Kohlberg was not so much interested in what the participants decided as in the way that they reached their decisions. What kinds of factors did they consider? Which conflicts did they identify (such as the conflict between the value of human life and the value of private property), and how did they try to resolve these conflicts? Kohlberg interviewed boys and men at length, and from their responses he identified three general levels of moral development (Kohlberg, 1969; Rest, 1979), which are ordered as follows:

- The *preconventional level* rests on the idea that good behaviors are rewarded and bad ones are punished. Correct action is what an authority figure says it is. A preconventional response to the Heinz dilemma might be, "If you let your wife die, you will get in trouble" (this and the following examples are adapted from Kohlberg, 1969, and Rest, 1979).
- The *conventional level* rests on the role of rules that maintain social order and allow people to get along. For example, a child reasoning at this level wants to be viewed as a "good person" by friends and family and tries to follow the Golden Rule ("Do unto others as you would have them do unto you"). Morality is still closely tied to individual relationships ("If he lets his wife die, people would think he was some kind of heartless lizard").
- The *postconventional level* (also called the *principled level*) rests on the development of abstract principles that govern the decision to accept or reject specific rules. In the most advanced stage at this level, principles are adopted that are believed to apply to everyone. ("Human life is the highest principle, and everything else must be secondary. People have a duty to help one another to live").

Evaluating Kohlberg's Theory

Some researchers have questioned the generality of Kohlberg's levels. For example, some have found that the levels don't apply well to people in non-Western cultures. Okonkwo (1997) studied Igbo students in Africa with Kohlberg's methods and found that in some cases the responses did not fit into any level. Although the responses clearly relied on moral reasoning, the reasoning sometimes involved factors such as family interdependence and the supreme authority of a divine being. Perhaps the strongest objection to Kohlberg's theory came from Carol Gilligan (1982), who argued that because the theory was based on studies of boys and men, it applies only to males. She believed that females tend to focus on an *ethic of care*, a concern and responsibility for the well-being of others. In contrast, Kohlberg's higher levels of moral development focus on abstract rights and justice, which Gilligan saw as a male-oriented perspective.

However, later studies have shown that differences in how males and females reason about moral issues do not reflect fundamental differences in the way their minds work. Although there is evidence that males and females do emphasize different principles in their moral reasoning (Wark & Krebs, 1996), this difference seems more a reflection of their daily activities (and the assumptions and general orientations that result from such activities) than an enduring gender difference. For example, if people are presented with dilemmas that feature concerns about raising children, men and women reason in the same ways (Clopton & Sorell, 1993). In addition, males and females score comparably on

© Gina Sanders, 2011. Used under license from Shutterstock, Inc.

The moral choices males and females make may be more closely tied to their daily concerns as opposed to inherent strategy differences.

Kohlberg's tests, and both sexes reveal concerns with both caring and justice (Jadack et al., 1995; Walker, 1995). Furthermore, it is not clear that Kohlberg's levels are like traits, which characterize a person in all situations. Rather, people may use different types of moral reasoning, depending on the details of the dilemma (Trevethan & Walker, 1989).

In addition, we must distinguish between *moral reasoning* and *moral behavior*: The fact that someone reasons in a particular way doesn't guarantee that he or she will act on this reasoning. Moral behavior may be governed not simply by reasoning, but also by various aspects of your character, such as your *conscience*—which leads you to appreciate what is morally correct and feel obligated to follow this path. A conscience may develop far earlier than sophisticated moral reasoning. For example, Grazyna Kochanska and her colleagues (1994) have found that conscience typically develops at about age 3. In fact, how well an infant imitated his or her mother at ages 14 and 22 months predicted the degree to which he or she would feel guilty after transgressing at ages 33 and 45 months (Forman et al., 2004). However, having a conscience at an early age is not just about imitating adults; it has a lot to do with temperament and how a child interacts with his or her mother more generally (Kochanska, 1997). Fearful children, who are shy and anxious, learn moral standards best if their mothers gently discipline them and encourage them to do right instead of threatening them about the consequences of doing wrong. Fearless children, who are outgoing and who actively explore their surroundings, learn moral standards best when their mothers provide direct feedback, such as taking a toy away or making angry comments. But such direction has the greatest impact if these fearless children have a close, emotionally secure relationship with their mothers (Fowles & Kochanska, 2000). Fearful children may develop a conscience earlier than fearless children, in part from feeling anxious and guilty at the mere thought of doing something wrong (Kochanska et al., 2002).

And conscience is not the only aspect of character that can direct moral behavior. Another is the capacity to feel *empathy*, the ability to put yourself in another person's situation and feel what they feel. Indeed, Martin Hoffman (2000) shows that by early adolescence most children have sophisticated abilities to feel and act on empathy in a wide range of moral situations. For example, the children appreciate the unfairness of another person's not receiving a just reward for his or her efforts.

In short, many factors affect how people behave in moral situations, and some of these factors develop much earlier than does the ability to reason logically about morality. Our behavior is not just a result of how we reason, but also of who we are.

ADOLESCENCE: BETWEEN TWO WORLDS

Steven Spielberg's adolescence was different from that of many of his peers in many ways; nonetheless, the challenges he faced in those years—forming friendships, testing limits, coming to terms with a new and unfamiliar body—are essentially universal. Because his family had moved so often, none of his friends from early childhood were still with him in high school; most of his classmates, in addition, were firmly established in cliques. Spielberg craved their acceptance and used his newfound love of moviemaking and storytelling as a way of gaining it. Nevertheless, his obsession with movies and his lack of interest in the usual teenage pursuits of dating and sports continued to set him apart.

Not surprisingly, Spielberg's adolescence was not an easy time for him or, sometimes, for those around him. On one occasion, he and some friends spent 3 hours throwing rocks through plate-glass windows at a shopping mall, causing about $30,000 worth of damage (McBride, 1999, p. 88). He later said that *Poltergeist* was "all about the terrible things I did to my younger sisters" (McBride, 1999, p. 89). He fought his father's wishes for him to study math and science, declaring that someday he was going to be a famous movie director and didn't need to know those kinds of things (McBride, 1999). Extreme behavior, yes. Adolescent behavior, yes.

Physical Development: In Puberty's Wake

Adolescence begins with **puberty**, the time when hormones cause the sex organs to mature and secondary sexual characteristics, such as breasts for women and a beard for men, to appear. These changes typically begin between ages 8–14 for girls and between ages 9–15 for boys. **Adolescence** is the period between the appearance of these sexual characteristics and, roughly, the end of the teenage years. Although girls usually experience their first period (*menarche*) about 2 years after the onset of puberty, typically between 12 and 13 years of age today (Chumlea et al., 2003), various factors influence when this occurs. In fact, in the mid-19th century, girls had their first period at about 17 years of age. In recent years, the age of puberty has declined—for both girls and boys—throughout the developed and developing world, including the United States (Finlay et al., 2002; Herman-Giddens et al., 2001), Europe (de Muinck Keizer-Schrama & Mul, 2001), China (Huen et al., 1997), and Brazil (Kac et al., 2000). This may reflect a *secular trend* in society: As children receive better health care and consistently better nutrition and lead less physically strenuous lives, puberty occurs earlier. For example, in rural Brazil, girls whose fathers were unemployed and those from low-income families had their first periods later than girls from more prosperous backgrounds (Tavares et al., 2000). Another study documented that American boys of various ethnic backgrounds are taller and heavier today than in previous generations, and these boys also develop public hair and mature genitalia at a younger age than was previously considered the norm (Herman-Giddens et al.,

Puberty: The time when hormones cause the sex organs to mature and secondary sexual characteristics, such as breasts for women and a beard for men, to appear.

Adolescence: The period between the onset of puberty and, roughly, the end of the teenage years.

2001). Could better nutrition explain this trend? Studies have shown that overweight girls tend to experience their first periods before those who are not overweight (Kaplowitz et al., 2001), which suggests a link between diet and the age of onset of puberty. However, Black American girls tend to be overweight less often than White American girls, but are younger when they have their first periods (Herman-Giddens et al., 1997). Thus, diet alone cannot explain the secular trend. In addition, for at least some girls who have a certain gene, stress (especially caused by having an absent father) apparently triggers early puberty (Comings, et al., 2002). Many theories have been proposed to explain the trend, ranging from the effects of additives in food (such as hormones added to animal feed and then passed on to human consumers; Teilmann et al., 2002) to various chemical pollutants in the environment (such as polybrominated biphenyls, or PBBs; Blanck et al., 2000)— but the reason or reasons underlying it are still not understood. **Figure 4.7** summarizes pubertal events in girls and boys.

Physical development during adolescence also, of course, includes growth. During infancy and childhood, the body grows from the trunk outward; the upper arms grow before the lower arms, which in turn grow before the hands. At puberty, the trend is reversed: Rapid growth of the hands, feet, and legs is followed by growth of the torso (Wheeler, 1991). Do you remember when you stopped needing larger shoes but still needed larger coats? That's why. The uneven growth during adolescence can lead to an awkward, gawky look, which doesn't do wonders for a teen's sense of self-confidence.

Once the sex hormones start operating in earnest, the shoulders of young boys grow large relative to their hips, and vice versa for girls. At age 11, girls typically are taller and heavier than boys because their major growth spurt starts about 2 years before that of boys. By age 14, however, boys' heights and weights have taken off, whereas girls have stopped growing or have begun to grow more

Early on girls grow faster than boys, however, boys tend to grow for a longer duration and eventually become taller.

© Sandra Gligorijevic, 2011. Used under license from Shutterstock, Inc.

Major Pubertal Events in Boys and Girls		
Years	**Boys**	**Girls**
8–10		■ *The development of breast buds*
10–12		■ *Public hair begins to grow* ■ *Vagina, labia, ovaries and uterus grow rapidly* ■ *Breasts continue to enlarge* ■ *Growth spurt in height*
12–13	■ *Testes grow larger* ■ *Pubic hair begins to grow*	■ *Menarche occurs* ■ *Underarm hair develops*
13–16	■ *Penis enlarges* ■ *Voice deepens* ■ *First ejaculation of semen* ■ *Body and facial hair may appear* ■ *More rapid increase in height*	■ *Breast become rounder* ■ *Ova mature* ■ *Conception is possible about one-year after menarche* ■ *Voice deepens*
16–18	■ *More facial and body hair grows* ■ *Voice deepens further*	

Courtesy of the author.

FIGURE 4.7 ■ Hormones, exercise, and nutrition may all affect the onset of pubertal events.

slowly. American girls typically stop growing at around age 13 (some may continue to grow until about age 16), but American boys usually continue to grow until about their 16th birthdays (and some may continue growing until they are almost 18 years old; Malina & Bouchard, 1991; Tanner, 1990).

Cognitive Development: Getting It All Together

The adolescent's ability to reason can become dramatically more powerful, but nevertheless be plagued with biases and distortions.

More Reasoned Reasoning?

The major cognitive development of adolescence, achieved by some but not all adolescents, is the ability to reason abstractly. Piaget's period of formal operations covers the cognitive achievements of these adolescents. According to Piaget, formal operational thinking allows a person not only to think abstractly, but also to think systematically about abstract concepts and possible scenarios. In one of his experiments, now regarded as a classic, Piaget gave a child a set of weights, string that could be attached to the weights, and a bar to which the string could be attached, allowing the weight to swing like a pendulum. The child was asked to vary both the weight and the length of the string in order to discover what factors would make the weight swing most quickly. Adolescents in the formal operational period are not only able to figure out the possibly relevant factors (size of weight, length of string, how high the weight is raised before being dropped, force with which it is pushed), but also to understand that to discover the role of each variable, they must alter only one thing at a time. These adolescents have grasped the very essence of scientific experimentation: holding everything else constant while systematically varying one factor at a time. In short, all the cognitive machinery necessary to think scientifically can be present by about 11 or 12 years of age. But not all adolescents develop these abilities this early, and some never do.

Most adolescents in Western societies are able to grasp the rules that underlie algebra and geometry. The ability to think systematically about abstractions also allows them to think about concepts such as justice and politics, as well as about relationships and the causes of human behavior. In fact, there's evidence that the adolescent brain is better prepared to learn algebra than is the adult brain! Researchers found that adolescents and adults used parts of the frontal and parietal lobes when they first learned rules of algebra and used those rules to solve equations—but after practice, adolescents' parietal lobes stopped being activated, whereas those brain areas in adults continued to be activated (Luna, 2004; Qin et al., 2004).

How does the ability to think abstractly and logically emerge? It is tempting to conclude that it is a result of the development of working memory, which does not function at adult levels until about 19 years of age (Luna et al., 2004). Moreover, one might speculate that this ability emerges at this time because it depends on the final stages of brain maturation (and the brain does, in fact, continue to develop well into adolescence—Sowell et al., 1999). However, assuming that events at any one level alone could account for such a sweeping change would be rash indeed. Cole (1990) has found that, in many traditional African societies, even the adults cannot use the kinds of abilities described by Piaget's idea of formal operations, but there is no indication that their brains have failed to develop fully. Culture must play a role, perhaps shaping the developing child's thought, as Vygotsky theorized.

But thinking is more than using logic or knowing how to grapple with abstractions. As discussed in Chapter 8, emotion guides much of our reasoning, and such processing relies on the ventromedial (lower-center) frontal lobes.

Evidence suggests that this brain area is not fully mature during adolescence, and thus emotions do not guide teenagers' thinking effectively (Hooper et al., 2004). It is tempting to speculate that this maturational lag may sometimes explain a lack of "common sense" during this stage of life.

Adolescents have sometimes been portrayed as being prone to distortions in their thinking. For example, at least some adolescents may use self-serving distortions, such as deciding that there's no need to ask because their parents really won't mind if they borrow the family car late at night (Barriga et al., 2000; Gerrard et al., 2000). In particular, they have been seen as unable to make well-reasoned judgments about themselves. This assumption contains a grain of truth, but bear in mind that adults aren't so good at making judgments about themselves either. When researchers asked adults and adolescents to assess the probability of various misfortunes happening either to them or to someone else, both age groups made remarkably similar estimates (Quadrel et al., 1993). It is sobering to note that both groups tended to *underestimate* the amount of risk they would face in various circumstances (such as having a car accident or being mugged). Both groups exhibited signs that they thought they were, to some extent, invulnerable. Both adults and adolescents sometimes use heuristics and shortcuts that can produce faulty reasoning (Jacobs & Klaczynski, 2002; see Chapter 8).

Adolescent Egocentrism: It's All in Your Point of View

The enhanced cognitive abilities of adolescents allow them to take other points of view easily—in particular, to see themselves as they imagine others see them. Theorists have claimed that these improved abilities can lead to two kinds of distortions in adolescents' conceptions of how others view them (Greene et al., 2002).

First, the *imaginary audience* is a belief sometimes held by adolescents, in which they view themselves as actors and everyone else as an audience (Elkind, 1967; Elkind & Bowen, 1979). This view can lead teenagers to be extremely self-conscious and easily embarrassed; a pimple feels like a beacon, not unlike Rudolph's nose. Although many adolescents do not succumb to such cognitive distortions (Vartanian, 2001), those who do—perhaps because they believe others may be watching them—are less likely to engage in risky behaviors (Galanaki, 2001). However, some researchers argue that often there is nothing "imaginary" about the audience (echoing the old joke that even paranoids sometimes have enemies), and that adolescents have realistic concerns about others' opinions (Bell & Bromnick, 2003).

Second, some teenagers have a *personal fable*, which is a story in which they are the star and, as the star, have extraordinary abilities and privileges. Teenagers may have unprotected sex and drive recklessly because they believe that they are immune to the possible consequences (Lapsley, 1990; Lapsley et al., 1988). These tendencies, and other social behaviors, are clearly influenced by peers. However, adolescents are influenced primarily by their families with regard to basic values and goals (Brown et al., 1986a, 1986b).

Who do you think is the imaginary audience?

Social and Emotional Development: New Rules, New Roles

A bridge between childhood and adulthood, adolescence is a time of transition. The adolescent must forge a new identity, which emerges as he or she negotiates a new place in the world (Marcia, 1993). This negotiation involves not only coming to grips with changing roles in the larger society, which requires obeying new sets of rules, but also learning to live with cognitive and biological changes that affect interactions with others in many ways.

"Storm and Stress": Raging Hormones?

The picture of adolescents as moody and troubled is nothing new. In the 18th century, German authors developed an entire genre of stories (the best known is Johann Wolfgang von Goethe's *The Sorrows of Young Werther*) about passionate, troubled young people so immersed in anguish and heartache that they committed impetuous acts of self-destruction. This body of literature came to be called *Sturm und Drang*, which translates roughly as "storm and stress." G. Stanley Hall (1904) popularized this term among psychologists when he wrote his now-classic two-volume work on adolescence.

The notion that adolescents experience a period of "storm and stress" has waxed and waned in popularity (Arnett, 1999). Anna Freud (1958) not only believed that adolescent "angst" (anguish) was inevitable but also that "normal" behavior during adolescence was in itself evidence of deep *abnormalities* in the individual. A strong reaction to this view soon followed, and only a few years ago, many psychologists were dismissing the idea as another popular misconception. However, additional studies have shown that there is in fact a tendency for normal adolescents to have three sorts of problems (Arnett, 1999):

(1) Adolescents tend to have conflicts with their parents (Laursen et al., 1998). The *frequency* of the conflicts is greatest in early adolescence, whereas the *intensity* of the conflicts is greatest in midadolescence (Laursen et al., 1998). Adolescent—parent conflicts occur most often between mothers and their daughters who are just entering adolescence (Collins, 1990). These conflicts can be even worse if the parents are not getting along or become divorced. Steven Spielberg claims that *E.T.* is really about the trauma he suffered during the divorce of his parents (McBride, 1999, p. 72); he broke down sobbing at the end of its first screening (p. 333).

(2) Adolescents experience extreme mood swings (Buchanan et al., 1992; Larson & Richards, 1994; Petersen et al., 1993), and by the middle of the teen years, about one third of adolescents are seriously depressed (Petersen et al., 1993)—and such depression is associated with increased levels of delinquency (Beyers & Loeber, 2003). Adolescents also often report feeling lonely and nervous.

(3) Adolescents may be prone to taking risks. Anticipating Anna Freud's view, Hall (1904) went so far as to say that "a period of semicriminality is normal for all healthy [adolescent] boys" (Vol. 1, p. 404). Steven Spielberg's rock-throwing episode at the shopping mall is a perfect example of what Hall had in mind. Adolescents are relatively likely to commit crimes, drive recklessly, and have high-risk sex (Arnett, 1992; Gottfredson & Hirschi, 1990; Johnston et al., 1994). Such behaviors are related to problems in regulating emotions (Cooper et al., 2003), and they tend to peak in late adolescence.

Many adolescents don't have these problems; rather, as Arnett (1999) documents, such problems are simply "more likely to occur during adolescence than at other ages." (p. 317). But why do they occur at all? Many people assume that they are an unavoidable result of the hormonal changes that accompany puberty. The notion that the emotional turmoil of adolescence is rooted in biology was neatly captured by Greek philosopher Aristotle's remark that adolescents "are heated by Nature as drunken men by wine."

In fact, the hormonal changes that go along with puberty do make the adolescent prone to emotional swings (Brooks-Gunn et al., 1994; Buchanan et al., 1992). But hormones only predispose, they do not cause; environmental events trigger the emotional reactions (Dodge & Pettit, 2003). Moreover, the biological effects can be indirect. For example, hormonal changes can lead adolescents to want to stay up late at night and sleep late in the morning (Carskadon et al., 1993). If they are forced to wake up early to go to school, their general mood will no doubt be affected.

In sum, adolescents are more likely than people of other ages to experience "storm and stress," which arises in part from the workings of hormones. However, this is only a tendency, and the degree to which an adolescent will experience such turmoil depends on personal and cultural circumstances.

Evolving Peer Relationships

The adolescent's relationship with his or her parents casts a long shadow. Both young men and women who have a more positive relationship with their mothers later have more positive intimate relationships with others (Robinson, 2000). Parental and peer relationships have a major impact on self-esteem (Wilkinson, 2004). However, many kinds of life experiences affect whether a young man or woman will develop intimate relationships. For example, perhaps counterintuitively, military service can enhance the ability to form intimate relationships (for example, by helping someone learn to trust and rely on others; Dar & Kimhi, 2001). Most adolescents develop pre-dominantly same-gender networks of friends, and women's friendships tend to be stronger than men's (Roy et al., 2000). The one exception to this generalization is gay young men—who tend to have more female than male friends; moreover, gay young men tend to be less emotionally attached to their love interests than are heterosexual young men (Diamond & Dube, 2002). In addition, as portrayed in countless Hollywood "nerd films," some adolescents can be rejected by their peers. For example, girls can effectively use indirect aggression (for example, by spreading false rumors) to exclude other girls from their circle (Owens et al., 2000). Hurt pride or lowered self-esteem is not always the only result of such rejection. Many gay or bi-sexual students report being victimized at school, which apparently contributes to their being at risk for suicide and substance abuse and for their engaging in high-risk behaviors (Bontempo & D'Augelli, 2002).

Teenage Pregnancy

In general, American teenage girls engage in amounts of sexual activity comparable to those of girls in other industrialized societies, but American teens do not use contraception as effectively. In 2001, 33.4% of births in the United States were to unmarried mothers. However, American teens are having fewer children; in 2001, they had 25.3 births per 10,000, compared to 27.4 in 2000—an 8% decline (Wetzstein, 2002).

Which teenagers are likely to become pregnant? Those at greatest risk are poor and do not have clear career plans—and their father is likely to be absent (Ellis et al., 2003). Maynard (1996) reports that a third of the teenagers who become pregnant drop out of school even before they become pregnant. Further, over half of teenage mothers were living in poverty when they had their children. For many of these young women, particularly Black Americans, having a baby is part of "coming of age" and is in many ways equivalent to a career choice (Burton, 1990; Merrick, 1995). Unfortunately, the adult children of teen mothers are likely to leave school early, be unemployed, and be in trouble with the law for violent offences—and they themselves tend to become parents at an early age (Jaffee et al., 2001).

However, the specific consequences of having a child depend on the mother's subsequent behavior and social group: If teenage mothers do not drop out of school, they are about as likely to graduate as girls who did not give birth, and Black Americans appear to suffer the fewest economic consequences of having given birth as a teenager. Apparently, Black American teenage mothers tend to live at home, continue school, and benefit from the assistance of other members of their families (Burton, 1990, 1996; Rosenheim & Testa, 1992).

ADULTHOOD AND AGING: THE CONTINUOUSLY CHANGING SELF

Steven Spielberg was an unhappy teenager and—in some aspects of life—a spectacularly successful young adult. But being successful in his chosen career did not mean that he was successful in all aspects of life. His first marriage ended; his relationship with his father was strained; and he was concerned that he himself would not measure up as a father (several of his movies deal with difficult relationships between fathers and sons). When he had children of his own, he realized that he needed to be an adult for them; he, and his relationships, had to change, and they did.

Famous filmmaker or not, the grown-up Steven Spielberg is in a very different phase of life than his children are; he is also in a very different phase of life than his father is. This is the human condition, and we now turn to an exploration of the stages of adult development.

Becoming an Adult

When do you become an adult? In some cultures in Africa and elsewhere, for example, there are distinct *rites of passage*, sometimes marked with circumcision, that have a 13-year-old becoming an adult overnight; in other African cultures, a boy can become a man at any age, depending on when his father dies. In Western countries, most people aged 18–25 do not think of themselves as adults, and thus this period has been dubbed *emerging adulthood* (Arnett, 2000). Most people in Western societies follow a progression as they mature into adults, which consists of leaving their parents' home, getting a job (often after having attended college), finding a spouse, and perhaps starting their own family. However, this pattern is by no means universal; the transition from adolescent to adult need not be this patterned or direct. In fact, after an initial period of independence, some people may become more dependent on their parents—moving back in with them for extended periods and not entering into marriage or other usual adult activities (Cohen et al., 2003).

The period of emerging adulthood typically is marked by substantial positive changes in the perceptions of relationships between an individual and his or her parents; in contrast, this period is not marked by large shifts in the individual's attitudes toward religion (Lefkowitz, 2005). In addition, old conflicts with siblings tend to dampen down during this period, and people develop warmer feelings toward their brothers and sisters (Scharf et al., 2005). Moreover, people in this age range who think of themselves as adults tend to have a firmer grip on their self-identity, to have a clearer idea of the characteristics of their desired romantic partners, to be less depressed, and to engage in fewer risky behaviors than do people who do not view themselves as adults (Nelson & Barry, 2005).

Many issues in young adulthood can persist into middle adulthood.

The Changing Body: What's Inevitable, What's Not

By your early 20s, it is unlikely that you will grow taller, and your weight has typically stabilized for many years to come. For the next several decades, changes in your body should be relatively minor. True, you may come to need bifocals, and your hair may begin to gray or to thin. But the basic bodily systems continue to function well. However, after age 50 or so, noticeable changes in the body begin to occur (Lemme, 1995).

Aging has two aspects: changes that are programmed into the genes and changes that arise from environmental events (Busse, 1969; Rowe & Kahn, 1998). Many changes that come with aging arise not from inevitable processes, but rather from lack of adequate nutrition (such as fragile bones that result from osteoporosis-related calcium deficiency), lack of exercise (resulting in obesity in some elderly people and frailty in others, or just plain sluggishness and poor health; Brach et al., 2004), or lack of meaningful activities (which can lead to feelings of helplessness or apathy; Avorn & Langer, 1982; Langer & Rodin, 1976; Rodin & Langer, 1977; Rowe & Kahn, 1998). By the same token, environmental events—such as taking calcium supplements or lifting weights—can help to counter or diminish such problems.

Learning to Live with Aging

A major challenge of aging is to accommodate to those changes that are inevitable and to forestall undesirable changes when you can. Many older people develop diseases or conditions that are uncomfortable or even painful, such as arthritis or collapsed vertebrae. However, in most cases, older people can cope with pain effectively, particularly if they adopt a "can-do" attitude (Melding, 1995; Rowe & Kahn, 1998). One of the inevitable age-related changes in women is *menopause*, the gradual ending of menstruation that typically occurs between the ages of 45 and 55; following menopause, eggs are no longer released and pregnancy is not possible (Wise et al., 1996). Hormonal changes that accompany menopause can lead to various bodily sensations (such as "hot flashes"); the knowledge that childbearing is no longer possible, along with the decline in youthful appearance, can adversely affect a woman's self-concept and self-esteem. On the other hand, for many women, the physical discomforts are slight, if present at all, and the idea of sexual intercourse without the threat of an unwanted pregnancy provides new pleasure. Some women feel "postmenopausal zest" and are reinvigorated by this change and the freedom it represents. For men, after about age 40, sperm production begins to fall off—but, unlike the cessation of egg production after menopause, men never fully lose the ability to produce sperm. Men do experience declining vigor (strength and energy) with age, which can affect sexual performance.

© Robert Kneschke, 2012. Used under license from Shutterstock, Inc.

Weight lifting can fight off osteoporosis.

Why Do We Age?

Why do all of us inevitably become less vigorous as we age? The combined effects of changes in the body have been likened to the effect of hitting a table with a hammer over and over (Birren, 1988). Eventually, the table will break, not because of the final blow, but because of the cumulative effects of all the blows. Some researchers believe that aging and death are programmed into the genes. An often cited piece of evidence for this idea was reported by Hayflick (1965), who found that human cells grown in the lab will divide on average only about 50 times, and then simply stop. However, all the findings that suggest programmed death can also be interpreted in other ways. For example, instead of accepting that the genes have been programmed for death, we might assume that errors accumulate over time, and finally, there are so many errors that the genes no longer function properly. If you photocopy a drawing or a page of text, and then copy the copy, and so on, you'll see how errors in reproduction multiply over repeated copying. In the case of the body, the damage may not be caused by the copying process itself, but rather by the repeated effects of bodily chemicals on each copy (Arking, 1991; Harman, 1956; Levine & Stadtman, 1992).

Perception and Cognition in Adulthood:
Taking the Good with the Bad

Cognitive abilities remain relatively stable through most of adulthood, but signs of a decline in some abilities begin to appear by age 50. The good news is that aging itself probably doesn't cause neurons to die (Long et al., 1999; Stern & Carstensen, 2000), but the bad news is that aging does impair communication among neurons, possibly by disrupting neurotransmitter functioning (S-C. Li et al., 2001) or by degrading the white matter of the brain, which provides the connections among neurons (Guttmann et al., 1998). These changes in the brain will eventually catch up with you and lead you to perform more slowly and be more prone to making errors. Indeed, by age 60, people perform most cognitive tasks more slowly than do younger people (Birren et al., 1962; Cerella, 1990; Salthouse, 1991b). The harder the task, the larger the difference in the time taken by young adults and elderly ones.

But how large is a "large" difference in time? Although even healthy elderly people require more time to carry out most tasks, the elderly are usually only a second or so slower than young people (Cerella et al., 1980), a difference that is often barely noticeable in daily life.

Shortly before death, however, many people exhibit *terminal decline* (Kleemeier, 1962). Their performance on a wide range of cognitive tasks takes a dramatic turn for the worse (Berg, 1996). This decline appears most dramatically in those who will die from cerebrovascular diseases, such as strokes and heart attacks, and it may be related to such disease states (Small & Bäckman, 2000). Thus, terminal decline is probably not an inevitable final chapter of the book of life (Bosworth & Siegler, 2002). More common is a gradual degradation in cognitive performance in the years leading up to death (Johansson et al., 2004; Small et al., 2003).

Perception: Through a Glass Darkly?

During early and middle adulthood, worsening vision can usually be corrected with eyeglasses. Later in life, however, more severe visual difficulties emerge. More than half of the 65 and older population has *cataracts*, a clouding of the lenses of the eyes; in older people, the pupil (the opening of the eye through which light enters) also becomes smaller. Surgery can remove cataracts and

Herbal treatments suggest they can help cognitive function. More research, however, must be completed before an accurate decision can be made.

result in greatly improved vision. But when such surgery has not been pre-scribed, moderate optical difficulties cause many older people to need greater contrast to see differences in light (Fozard, 1990). Contrasts between lit and unlit surfaces, such as shadows caused by steps, can define differences in depth, and if older people cannot perceive such definition, they are more likely to stumble over a step. Simply providing more light will not necessarily help older people to see well; because of the clouding of the lenses, more light causes more glare. Thus, the best level of illumination is a compromise between what produces the best contrast and the least glare. However, some declines in visual perception have nothing to do with the physical condition of the eyes, but rather reflect changes in how the brain functions. For instance, the elderly do not classify the identities of faces as well as younger people do—but they nevertheless classify facial expressions as well as younger people do (Kiffel et al., 2005).

Hearing is also affected by age. After age 50 or so, people have increased difficulty hearing high-frequency sounds (Botwinick, 1984; Lemme, 1995). Because consonants (such as *k*, *c*, *p*, and *t*) are produced with higher-frequency sounds than are vowels, older people often have trouble distinguishing between words that differ by a single consonant, such as *kill* and *pill*. Older people also have more difficulty shutting out background noise, a problem that may actually be worsened by hearing aids, which boost the loudness of both irrelevant back-ground sounds and relevant sounds.

Unlike vision and hearing, the sense of taste does not decline with age (Bartoshuk et al., 1986; Ivy et al., 1992). Even in 80-year-olds, the taste buds are replaced frequently. But what we think of as the sensation of taste comes in part from smell, and the sense of smell does decline after the middle 50s (Doty et al., 1984; Ivy et al., 1992; Schiffman, 1992). As a result, as people move beyond middle age, they may prefer spicier foods; they may also have difficulty noticing if food has gone bad (Lemme, 1995).

Memory: Difficulties in Digging It Out

Parts of the brain that produce the neurotransmitter acetylcholine become impaired with age (Albert & Moss, 1996; D. E. Smith et al., 1999); this neurotrans-mitter is crucial for the proper functioning of the hippocampus, which plays a key role in explicit memory. The less efficient processing in this part of the brain is probably one reason why older people often have trouble with some kinds of memory (Schacter, 1996); in fact, the hippocampus and related brain structures are smaller in older adults, and the sizes of these structures are correlated with recall ability (Rosen et al., 2003).

Even so, aging affects some aspects of memory more than others. *Semantic memory* (memory for facts, words, meanings, and other information that is not associated with a particular time and place) remains relatively intact into very old age (Light, 1991), and the storing of new *episodic memories* (memory for specific events) is often relatively effective. People in their 70s and 80s do fairly well if they are given a list of words and then asked to pick out these words from a longer list that also contains other words (Craik & McDowd, 1987). Moreover, the elderly have good implicit memory (Fleischman et al., 2004), and they can recall the gist of a description and its implications at least as well as younger people (Radvansky, 1999).

However, the elderly have difficulty when they must actively recall specific episodic memories: For example, they do poorly if they are given a list of common words to remember and later asked to recall them (Craik & McDowd, 1987). Tasks that require the *recall* of specific information appear to rely on the frontal lobes to dig the information out of memory, and processes accomplished there are not as efficient in the elderly as they are in younger people. Indeed, the frontal lobes—along with many other brain areas—become smaller in old age (Ivy et al., 1992; Raz et al., 1997; Resnick et al., 2003). In fact, even healthy people over age 67 or so have trouble with the same tasks that are difficult for patients with frontal lobe damage (such as sorting cards first by one rule, then switching to another rule; Schacter, 1996). Furthermore, just as patients with frontal lobe damage sometimes show *source amnesia* (forgetting the source of a learned fact), so do elderly people (Craik et al., 1990; Glisky et al., 1995; Schacter et al., 1991, 1997; Spencer & Raz, 1995). For example, Schacter and colleagues (1991) asked people to listen to novel facts (such as "Bob Hope's father was a fireman"), which were read aloud by either a man or a woman. When later asked to recall which voice read the facts, 70-year-olds were much less accurate than young people, even when they could recall the facts themselves (Schacter and his co-workers [1994] describe similar findings). Moreover, the elderly are also prone to creating false memories, which are fabricated on the basis of misleading information (Jacoby et al., 2005).

Frontal lobe impairment is probably also responsible for difficulties the elderly have with tasks involving working memory (De Beni & Palladino, 2004). Such deficits are especially evident when elderly people must hold information in mind while doing something else at the same time (Craik et al., 1995). If strategies are needed to perform a task (such as figuring out the most efficient way to move through a store to collect different items), the frontal lobe impairments of the elderly can affect their performance (Gabrieli, 1996; S-C. Li et al., 2001). As Salthouse (1985) suggests, slowed cognitive processes may also lead the elderly to use inefficient strategies, strategies composed of many steps, each relatively simple. Ironically, there is evidence that elderly people are actually more likely than younger people to use strategies that rely more on their frontal lobes, attempting to compensate for less efficient processing in other parts of the brain (Gutchess et al., 2005).

Intelligence and Specific Abilities: Different Strokes for Different Folks

It might seem likely that as you age, your accumulated life experience should add up to an increasingly important determinant of your intelligence. But this is not so. Researchers were surprised to discover that although overall level of intelligence is remarkably stable from age 11

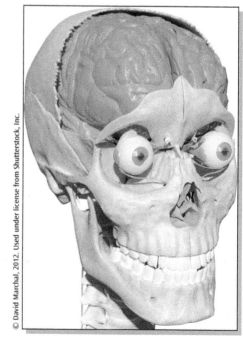

© David Marchal, 2012. Used under license from Shutterstock, Inc.

Cell loss in the frontal lobe may contribute to memory problems in old age.

to age 78 (Deary et al., 2004), genetic influences on general intelligence actually increase with age (Finkel et al., 1995; Plomin et al., 1994).

Changes in Fluid and Crystallized Intelligence

Investigators have asked whether aging affects all types of intelligence in the same way. In particular, they have examined the effects of age on *fluid intelligence*, which involves flexibility in reasoning and the ability to figure out novel solutions, and *crystallized intelligence*, which involves using knowledge as a basis of reasoning (see Chapter 9). It might seem that crystallized intelligence, which, by definition, relies on experience, would be less influenced by age than would fluid intelligence. How could we tell? These two types of intelligence have been assessed in **longitudinal studies**, which test the same group of people repeatedly, at different ages. These findings suggest that *both* types of intelligence are stable until somewhere between the mid-50s and the early 70s, when both decline (Hertzog & Schaie, 1988). However, the very strength of longitudinal studies—the continuing use of the same group—also leads to a weakness: The participants become familiar with the type of testing, and this familiarity can influence their performance on later assessments. As shown in **Figure 4.5**, **cross-sectional studies** involve testing different groups of people, with each group composed of individuals of a particular age. The key here is to ensure that the groups are equated on all possible measures other than age (such as sex, educational level, and health status). Such studies have led most researchers to believe that fluid intelligence begins to decline as early as the late 20s (Salthouse, 1991a), whereas crystallized intelligence may actually grow with age and decline only late in life (Baltes, 1987; McArdle et al., 2002; Li et al, 2004).

Longitudinal study: A study in which the same group of people is tested repeatedly, at different ages.

Cross-sectional study: A study in which different groups of people are tested, with each group composed of individuals of a particular age.

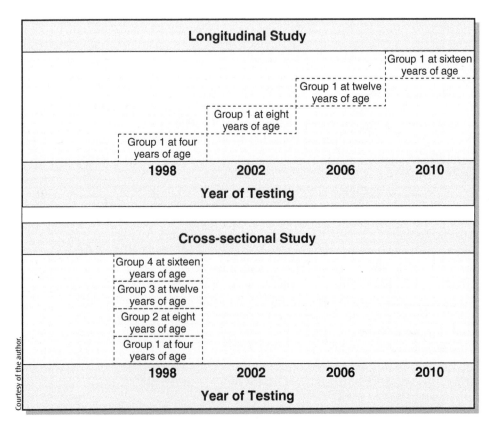

FIGURE 4.5 ■ Longitudinal studies test the same people over many years whereas the cross-sectional study tests people of different ages all at the same time.

The increase in crystallized intelligence in old age often gives the elderly an advantage in telling interesting life stories.

Changes in Specific Abilities

Crystallized intelligence, rooted in experience, may be thought of as underlying much of what we mean by "wisdom." The ability to draw on such intelligence may explain why researchers found that older adults were rated as telling more interesting, higher-quality, and more informative stories than younger adults (James et al., 1998). This should be cheering news for Steven Spielberg, who plans to keep telling stories as long as he can.

Moreover, in some respects, old people actually reason better than young people. For example, in one study, researchers asked young and old participants to indicate their preferences when given either two or three alternatives—for example, chocolate or vanilla ice cream versus chocolate, vanilla, or strawberry ice cream. Young people were inconsistent, perhaps choosing vanilla when only two choices were offered, but chocolate when strawberry was included. Old people were much more consistent and "logical" in their choices (Tentori et al., 2001).

General intelligence is distinct from special abilities, such as the ability to do arithmetic or to imagine objects rotating. Not all the special abilities of a given person are affected by aging to the same degree. For example, a longitudinal study by Schaie and colleagues (Schaie, 1983, 1989, 1990b; Schaie et al., 2004) examined the effects of aging on five measures of special abilities, including the ability to recognize and understand words and the ability to rotate shapes mentally. He found that by age 60 about three fourths of the participants maintained their level of performance from the previous 7 years on at least four of the five abilities tested, and by age 81 more than half the participants maintained this level of performance. For any given person, some aspects of intelligence were affected by aging more than others (Schaie & Willis, 1993; Schaie et al., 2004). The same is true for many types of skills, which age affects in different ways for different people (Stern & Carstensen, 2000).

Compensating for Declining Abilities

People can often compensate for declining abilities by using abilities that are still intact (Baltes, 1987; Baltes et al., 1984). Some typists can retain their speed as they age by looking farther ahead on the page, thus taking in more as they go

(Salthouse, 1984). Similarly, tennis players may compensate for reduced speed and vigor by developing better strategies (Lemme, 1995; Perlmutter, 1988). In fact, people with more education tend to function better than those with less education when their brains have been impaired by diseases, such as Alzheimer's disease. The *cerebral reserve hypothesis* states that education either strengthens the brain itself (for example, by building in backup circuits) or helps people develop multiple strategies; thus, when part of the brain is damaged, they can draw on these reserves and continue to function reasonably well (Cohen et al., 1996; Stern, 2002). In fact, simply having more leisure activities in old age may help build such cognitive reserves (Scarmeas et al., 2001).

The Less-Differentiated Brain

At least some of the cognitive changes in old age reflect changes in how the brain works. We've already noted some of these changes, especially in the functions of the hippocampus and frontal lobes. But a much more sweeping change must also be noted: As we age, the parts of our brains become less specialized. This *dedifferentiation*, as it is called, is evident in many neural systems (Li et al., 2004; Logan et al., 2002; Park et al., 2004)—and is supported by the finding that scores on different parts of intelligence tests are more highly correlated in the elderly than in younger people (Deary et al., 2004). In fact, even the specializations of the two cerebral hemispheres become less sharply defined with aging (Cabeza, 2002). Such a lack of specialization may give rise to slower or less efficient information processing.

Social and Emotional Development During Adulthood

The phrase "growing up" might seem to imply that psychological development is like height: After a certain age, you reach a plateau, and that's where you stay. Not so. At least in mentally healthy people, psychological development continues throughout the life span. In discussing Steven Spielberg's 15-year split with his father, an expert on father-son relationships, James Levine, commented: "In such a split, you don't recognize that under the anger is sadness. There's denial: pretending it's not important to heal the rift. But a split in the father—child relationship always has an effect" (quoted in Sullivan, 1999, p. 67). Still, as in Spielberg's case, relationships change and evolve over time.

Theories of Psychosocial Stages in Adulthood

Psychosocial development: The effects of maturation and learning on personality and relationship.

Some theorists, Freud included, believed that personality stops developing in childhood. But Erik Erikson (1921–1994) proposed three stages of adult **psychosocial development**, due to effects of maturation and learning on personality and relationships, in addition to five stages of psychosocial development through childhood and adolescence (see Table 12.3). The adult stages were defined by issues that adults are most likely to confront and need to resolve.

- The first stage, *intimacy versus isolation,* occurs in young adulthood. To navigate this stage of development successfully, the young adult must develop deep and intimate relations with others and avoid becoming socially isolated. Steven Spielberg had serious difficulty being intimate with people, which may be one reason why his first marriage dissolved (McBride, 1999).
- The second adult stage, characterized by *generativity versus self-absorption,* occurs during the middle adult years. The challenge here is for men and women to think about the future and decide what their contributions will be for their children or for society at large. People who are highly generative agree with the African proverb "The world was not left to us by

our parents. It was lent to us by our children" (which is inscribed on a wall in the UNICEF office in New York). People who fail at the task of this stage will be faced with a sense of meaninglessness in life. Steven Spielberg not only cares for his own children but also makes it a point to help young directors who are just starting out; such altruistic behavior is another type of generativity.

■ The third adult stage, characterized by *integrity versus despair,* occurs during old age. The task here is to be able to reflect back on life and feel that it was worthwhile, thereby avoiding feelings of despair and fear of death.

Many theorists have picked up where Erikson left off (Gould, 1978; Havinghurst, 1953; Vaillant, 1977). Some have focused on one aspect of Erikson's theory. For example, McAdams and his colleagues developed ways to assess generativity (McAdams & de St. Aubin, 1992), and they found that adults who are concerned about providing for future generations tend to be more satisfied with their lives (McAdams et al., 1993) and to view life optimistically—believing that even bad events will eventually have a happy outcome (McAdams et al., 2001).

Other theorists have extended Erikson's approach by proposing additional stages. For example, Levinson (Levinson, 1977, 1978, 1986, 1990; Levinson et al., 1978), basing his work on interviews with 40 men, developed an influential theory of developmental transitions in men's lives. Perhaps the most important and interesting aspect of Levinson's theory is the *midlife transition,* which occurs when a man begins to shift from thinking of his life as marked by the time passed since birth to thinking of his life as marked by the time left until death. This transition typically occurs somewhere between the ages of 40 and 45. This change in perspective can have profound consequences, often leading a man to question the path he has chosen. According to Levinson, many men have *midlife crises,* which can lead them to end marriages and begin others, change jobs, or make other major life changes. In Steven Spielberg's case, this crisis seems to have caused him to deal with conflicting emotions about being Jewish; one result was his movie *Schindler's List,* in which he confronted his fears and ambivalence about his Jewish identity (which were particularly severe because of his strong need for acceptance; McBride, 1999).

Despite stereotypes to the contrary, we can do many different things in our later years.

Continued Personality Development

We must distinguish between the changes in perspective represented by the psychosocial changes and changes in personality; evidence indicates that personality does not change substantially during adulthood (Costa et al., 2000; Johnson et al., 2005; Schaie et al., 2004). In fact, Costa and McCrae (1988) tested more than a thousand adults, both men and women, using standardized measures (not interviews) of the Big Five personality dimensions: openness to experience, conscientiousness, extraversion, agreeableness, and neuroticism (see Chapter 11). The participants ranged in age from 21 to 96 years. In addition to asking the participants to complete the measures, the researchers also asked 167 spouses to fill in the measures about the participants. Eighty-nine men and 78 women were tested twice, 6 years apart; thus, both cross-sectional and longitudinal data were collected. The results were clear: There were very few differences in any of the dimensions of personality over the years, and when such differences were found, they were very small. Moreover, Costa and McCrae found that personality was equally stable over time for men and women. They concluded that "aging itself has little effect on personality. This is true despite the fact that the normal course of aging includes disease, bereavement, divorce, unemployment, and many other significant events for substantial portions of the population" (p. 862). As a matter of fact, objective tests have shown that even when a person feels that his or her personality has changed (over the course of 6–9 years) during middle age, it really hasn't (Herbst et al., 2000).

Apparent changes in personality over time probably reflect not so much changes in the person as changes in the life challenges that he or she is confronting at the time: For many people, aging is accompanied by changes in marital status, parenting, and job-related factors. Such major life changes often become less frequent or severe as a person grows older, which could explain the finding that people become increasingly consistent in the degree to which they can be described by particular traits until around age 50, and thereafter are stable (Roberts & DelVecchio, 2000). Consistency, in this sense, refers to the relative ordering of people according to a trait—with increasing age, your ranking relative to other people will become more stable. This stability could reflect, in part, your settling into a niche in life, and thus restricting the range and variety of situations you encounter.

Mature Emotions

The poet Robert Browning wrote, "Grow old along with me! / The best is yet to be / The last of life, for which the first is made." He may have been more right than he realized. In one study, people of different ages were prompted to report their emotions at various times over the course of a week (Carstensen et al., 2000). The researchers found that as people enter old age, they tend to experience more extended periods of highly positive emotions and less enduring spells of negative emotions than do younger people. Moreover, positive emotions were evoked as regularly for the elderly as for the young. Negative emotions, on the other hand, arose increasingly less often until about age 60 (when they leveled off).

But the news is even better than this. Older people are, well, more "mature" in their emotional responses. With age, people become better able to regulate emotions (Gross et al., 1997). In fact, elderly Americans of European and Chinese ethnic backgrounds had smaller changes in heart rate when watching emotional films than did younger people (Tsai et al., 2000). But this doesn't mean that their emotions are blunted or diminished; even when heart rate changes were smaller, older participants had subjective responses comparable to those of younger participants.

Adult Relationships: Stable Changes

Perhaps as a result of their increased ability to grapple with emotions, older people tend to change their outlook on life. Laura Carstensen and her collaborators have developed the *socioemotional selectivity* theory, which rests on the idea that older people come to focus on the limited time they have left, which in turn changes their motivations (Carstensen & Charles, 1998; Lang & Carstensen, 2002). Consistent with this theory, these researchers find that as people age, they come increasingly to value emotionally fulfilling relationships. This leads older people to prefer the company of those with whom they are emotionally close. The same findings hold true both for White and Black Americans (Fung et al., 2001).

In general, as people age, they interact with fewer people, but these interactions tend to be more intimate (Carstensen, 1991, 1992)—older people don't miss the broader social networks that they had when they were young (Lansford et al., 1998). Relationships earlier in life tend to include more friends than relatives, but with age the mix reverses, with more time spent with relatives than with friends. This pattern is even more pronounced among Latinos than Americans of European descent (Levitt et al., 1993). In later life, a relationship long dormant can be picked up and reestablished with minimal effort (Carstensen, 1992); after young adulthood, temperament and personality variables are relatively stable, which makes it easy to "know" someone again even after a long lapse.

During young adulthood, people are concerned that their relationships with friends and relatives are equitable—that neither party gives more than he or she receives (Lemme, 1995; Walster et al., 1978). As people age, such concerns recede into the background. In successful marriages, the members of the couple think of themselves as a team, not separate people who are in constant negotiations (Keith & Schafer, 1991). Because they are in it for the long haul, people trust that the balance of favors and repayment will even out over time. Thus, older couples resolve their differences with less negative emotion than do younger couples (Carstensen et al., 1995).

Death and Dying

We began this chapter with the very earliest phase of development, and we close it with the last of life's experiences. The psychology of death has two faces: The effects on the person who is dying and the effects on friends and relatives.

Grief is the emotion of distress that follows the loss of a loved one, and bereavement is the experience of missing a loved one and longing for his or her company. People in the United States tend to go through the grieving process in three phases (Lemme, 1995; Lindemann, 1991):

Contrary to stereotypes, the elderly tend to experience more happiness than younger people.

(1) Until about 3 weeks after the death, the bereaved person is in a state of shock. He or she feels empty, disoriented, and, sometimes, in a state of denial and disbelief; these feelings eventually settle into a state of deep sorrow. (This shock may be buffered by having to make funeral arrangements, deal with lawyers, and so on, but it nevertheless exists during this period.)

(2) From 3 weeks to about a year following the death, the bereaved person experiences emotional upheavals, from anger to loneliness and guilt. During this time, people often review their relations with the deceased, wondering whether they should have done things differently, whether the death was inevitable. During this phase, people may think that they catch glimpses of the deceased in crowds or hear the person talking to them.

(3) By the beginning of the second year, grief lessens. The bereaved person may largely stop thinking of the deceased and, in the case of a spouse's death, be ready to become committed to a new intimate relationship. However, bereavement may continue indefinitely, particularly when a person is reminded of the deceased by special places or events, such as anniversaries or birthdays. Indeed, even years after an adult child has died, the parents tend to be more depressed and their health declines more rapidly, compared to parents who have not experienced such a loss. But such a tragedy may also bring the parents closer together, leading them to become more satisfied in their marriage (de Vries et al., 1997).

Grief: The emotion of distress that follows the loss of a loved one.

Bereavement: The experience of missing a loved one and longing for his or her company.

Wortman and Silver (1989) shook up this area of research by challenging key assumptions about the response to the death of a loved one. In particular, they challenged the idea that we must "work through" our loss, and that eventually we should expect to recover from the loss. That is, for many years, mental health clinicians urged the bereaved to "work through" their grief, which involves talking to others about their feelings and striving to finish the relationship with the dead (Lindstrom, 2002). But there is little evidence that such practices help

(Davis et al., 2000). In fact, many clinicians now recommend suppressing or avoiding negative thoughts and emotions (not discussing them freely), focusing on positive emotions, and maintaining an internal relationship with the deceased.

The effects of the death of a friend or loved one depend on many factors. You might think that the death of a mate would have more severe effects if the marriage was conflicted, given the "unfinished business" at the end. But this has not turned out to be true (Carr et al., 2000). You also might think that the death would be easier to bear if you had a lot of forewarning. Again, this is not necessarily so (Carr et al., 2001). When forewarned, some people begin grieving before the death, and the accompanying depression doesn't necessarily let up afterwards; however, if women don't become depressed when forewarned that their husbands will die, this leaves them particularly vulnerable to becoming depressed after the death (Carnelley et al., 1999). In addition, a woman's reaction to her husband's death will be different if she was dependent on him (more anxiety after his death) than if she was not (less anxiety; Carr et al., 2000). And a bereaved person's reaction depends in part on the age of the deceased. Most deaths in the United States and Canada tend to occur at a relatively old age; the average age of death in some Latin American countries is much younger. The grief for someone who has had a full life is different from the grief for someone who has been cut down in his or her prime.

Concern about our own deaths apparently does not increase with age: Death anxiety either stays the same over the course of life or actually decreases near the end (Lemme, 1995). Women report fearing death more often than men do (Lonetto & Templer, 1986). However, this finding could simply mean that women are more honest or self-aware, or that men—consciously or unconsciously—avoid confronting the topic. In addition, because women tend to live longer than men, they may have had more opportunity to witness and to become concerned about death. Cultural differences clearly influence the ways in which people view and react to death (Kalish & Reynolds, 1977; Platt & Persico, 1992). Researchers who studied the Maya people of Central America found that they did not try to fight death. Elderly people announce that their time has come and then retire to a mat or hammock and wait to die. They refuse food or water, ignore attempts by others to talk to them, and soon die. Their attitude toward death is fostered by their strong belief in an afterlife in paradise (Steele, 1992). In contrast, people of the Kaliai, a tribe in Papua New Guinea, almost never die of old age, instead meeting death in battle or as a result of an accident. Thus, they do not view death as a natural occurrence; they look for someone to blame for such deaths, usually a sorcerer (Counts & Counts, 1992).

Looking at Levels

Keeping the Aging Brain Sharp

In old age, particularly in the years just before death, many people do not function as well mentally as they did earlier in life, even if they are physically healthy (Small & Bäckman, 2000). Is this deterioration inevitable? As people age, the brain receives less blood, which means that it is sustained by fewer nutrients and less oxygen (Ivy et al., 1992). The blood supply to the brain decreases with age because the blood vessels themselves become smaller. Why does this happen? One reason may be that the brain cells are not working as hard, so they need less blood—which in turn leads the vessels to adjust (Ivy et al., 1992). This is like Catch-22: The neurons don't work as effectively because they receive fewer blood-borne nutrients and less oxygen, but the reason they don't receive as much is that they haven't been functioning as effectively as they did before.

But focusing on the brain alone is not enough. At the level of the person (at least in the United States), the elderly have absorbed societally transmitted negative conceptions about aging—and these stereotypes apparently can undermine the will to live. In one study, young and elderly people were shown positive or negative words concerning old age; the words were presented too briefly to be seen consciously—and hence functioned as unconscious "primes." The elderly participants were more likely to say that they would reject treatment for serious illness after being primed with negative words than they were after being primed with positive words; the negative words apparently activated stored negative concepts about aging. For the young participants, the type of words used as primes made no difference (Levy et al., 1999–2000).

As usual, we must also consider events at the level of the group. Social interactions clearly affect how well older people can cope with stress (Krause, 2004), which in turn affects the stress response; and older people experience cognitive degradation when they lose social support (Aartsen et al., 2004). But more than that, it is tempting to hypothesize that if you managed to engage your elderly parents, grandparents, or other family members in more challenging tasks, you could literally increase the blood supply to their brains and improve their thinking abilities. This result is plausible because "mental workouts" appear to enhance cognitive function in the elderly (Rowe & Kahn, 1998); in fact, training over the course of only 10 sessions can substantially improve memory, reasoning, and speed of processing in the elderly (Ball et al., 2002). Moreover, dendrites continue to grow normally even into old age (Coleman & Flood, 1986), and as neurons die, new connections may be formed to compensate for losses (Cotman, 1990). In one study, when elderly rats were moved from their standard cages into a rat playpen full of toys and other rats, they developed heavier brains with more extensive connections among neurons. Moreover, other researchers have found that mice that live in an enriched environment (complete with lots of attractive toys, other mice to play with, and opportunities to explore and exercise)

Research suggests that keeping your brain active by problem solving or doing puzzles protects you from cognitive decline.

retain more neurons as they age (Kempermann et al., 1998). Indeed, simply giving animals the chance to exercise enhances neuronal growth and improves survival rates (Cotman & Berchtold, 2002; van Praag et al., 1999). Very likely the same would be true for humans who were provided with more stimulating environments (Avorn & Langer, 1982; Langer & Rodin, 1976; Rodin & Langer, 1977; Rowe & Kahn, 1998). In fact, researchers have found that the brain generally becomes smaller with aging, but that people with more education have less severe size reductions (Coffey et al., 1999).

Thus, if your otherwise healthy parents or grandparents are understimulated by their surroundings (as occurs in some nursing homes as well as in many home environments), this could affect their brains. The changes in their brains could in turn lead them to avoid mental challenge and engagement, which in turn could lead to changes in self-concept and level of self-esteem. These changes then may lead them to become lethargic and to avoid social interaction. And not interacting with others could lead to even less effective neural functioning, and so on. Clearly, there is ample opportunity for events at all three levels to interact.

However, it is unlikely that all of the functions that are impaired with age can be helped simply by getting your grandparents to use their brains more, or even by changing their conceptions of what it means to be elderly. MRI scans of more than 3,600 apparently normal elderly people (aged 65 to 97) revealed that slightly over one third had brain lesions. These were often small and usually affected subcortical structures, but some of the lesions were probably large enough to perhaps affect a specific cognitive function (Bryan et al., 1997). Damage to the white matter can also disrupt cognition in the elderly (Koga et al., 2002). Thus, possible effects of changing beliefs and of social interactions must be considered within the context of changes in the brain. As always, events at the three levels interact.

KEY TERMS

accommodation
adolescence
assimilation
attachment
bereavement
concrete operation
conservation
cross-sectional study
egocentrism
embryo

fetus
formal operation
gender identity
gender roles
grief
longitudinal study
maturation
moral dilemma
object permanence
private speech

psychosocial
  development
puberty
self-concept
separation anxiety
schema
teratogen
theory of mind
zygote

Name: _____   Date: _____

Chapter 4: Psychology Over the Life Span

END OF CHAPTER QUIZ

1. The name of chemical or biological substances that may cause birth defects.
   a. Teratogen
   b. Menarche
   c. Drugs
   d. Virus

2. Which of the following is the name of a basic reflex present at birth.
   a. FAS reflex
   b. Mouthing reflex
   c. Climbing response
   d. Rooting reflex

3. The name given to the process by which a duckling follows the first object it sees after it hatches.
   a. Attachment
   b. Critical period
   c. Intimacy
   d. Imprinting

4. The Piagetian stage most closely associated with abstract thought and a period of myelination of the brain.
   a. Sensorimotor stage
   b. Preoperational stage
   c. Concrete operational stage
   d. Formal operational stage

5. The name given to the phenomenon during which a child acts as though all people have the same thoughts.
   a. Egocentrism
   b. Conservation
   c. Autism
   d. Cognition

6. A fertilized egg is called a:
   a. Blastula
   b. Germinosis
   c. Chimera
   d. Zygote

7. Fetal alcohol syndrome is a result of the presence of a _____ during prenatal development.
   a. Vitamin deficiency
   b. Rooting reflex
   c. Placental toxin
   d. Teratogen

8. Newborn infants show a preference for looking at human faces over all other visual stimuli.
   a. True
   b. False

9. Which of the following is the MOST common measure of infant cognitive abilities?
   a. Crying
   b. Rolling over
   c. Habituation to stimuli
   d. Latency to speak

10. The name given to "orderly biological growth processes."
    a. Maturation
    b. Schema
    c. Formal operations
    d. Cognition

11. As a child ENTERS Piaget's Preoperational Stage, which behaviors have already developed?
    a. Stranger anxiety, mathematics, walking
    b. Conservation, egocentrism, pretend play
    c. Walking, abstract symbol recognition
    d. Walking, stranger anxiety, passing tests for object permanence

12. Which Piagetian Stage of development starts at about age 6 or 7?
    a. Sensorimotor
    b. Preoperational
    c. Concrete Operational
    d. Formal Operational

13. Which aspects of the Concrete Operational Stage of Development are most important before formal schooling can begin?
    a. Understanding conservation, mathematical transformations
    b. Object permanence, pretend play
    c. Stranger anxiety, abstract logic
    d. Abstract logic, mathematical transformations

14. Harlow's monkey experiments identified a(n)_____ during the development of attachment in monkey social behavior.
    a. Critical period
    b. Increase in imprinting
    c. Cognitive enhancement with artificial mothers
    d. Decrease in stranger anxiety

15. Stranger anxiety and separation anxiety both develop at the time that _____ develops.
    a. Speaking
    b. Attachment sensitivity
    c. Walking
    d. Concrete thinking skills

16. Adolescence begins at which period?
    a. Formal Operations
    b. Menopause
    c. Puberty
    d. Menarche for both males and females

17. Kohlberg's stage of development in which the individual is concerned with concrete rewards and punishments.
    a. Preconventional
    b. Conventional
    c. Postconventional

18. Which of the following parenting styles do psychologists GENERALLY recognize as being the most effective in North America?
    a. Authoritative
    b. Permissive
    c. Authoritarian

19. The best parenting style is the one that conforms to the child's traits.
    a. True
    b. False

20. Menopause marks a period of depression in mid-life for women.
    a. True
    b. False

21. Developmental psychology may be said to include all areas of psychology just so long as there are measures taken over time.
    a. True
    b. False

22. Which of the following does not represent the typical chimera?
    a. Two sperm + one egg
    b. A fertilized egg fuses with an unfertilized egg
    c. Two fertilized eggs fuse together
    d. Two embryos fuse together
    e. Two eggs are fertilized by sperm from two different men

23. The germinal period lasts about:
    a. 2 weeks long
    b. 6 weeks long
    c. 16 weeks long
    d. 27 weeks long

24. The embryonic period lasts about:
    a. 2 weeks long
    b. 6 weeks long
    c. 16 weeks long
    d. 27 weeks long

25. The fetal period lasts about:
    a. 2 weeks long
    b. 6 weeks long
    c. 16 weeks long
    d. 27 weeks long

26. With which probability does a fertilized egg attach to the uterine wall?
    a. 25%
    b. 50%
    c. 75%
    d. 100%

27. This stage encompasses the organogenesis period.
    a. Germinal period
    b. Embryonic period
    c. Third trimester
    d. Fetal period

28. During which period does the brain develop at its fastest rate?
    a. First trimester
    b. Germinal period
    c. Embryonic period
    d. Fetal period

29. Which of the following is not a teratogen?
    a. Aspirin
    b. Nicotine
    c. X-ray radiation
    d. Caffeine
    e. All of the above are teratogens

30. Early childhood includes this adaptive capacity.
    a. Language learning at age 3-months
    b. An excess of neural connections
    c. The ability to walk by age 6-months
    d. Highly developed vision on the day of birth

31. Which of the following is the name for the basic "eating reflex" that is present at birth?
    a. Grasping
    b. Moro-startle
    c. Rooting
    d. Stepping
    e. Babinski

32. Which of the following do infants show no preference for on their day of birth?
    a. Human faces
    b. Their mother's voice

c. Flesh-tone colors
d. Their mother's smell
e. Tastes from the mother's diet

33. What does the general rule of thumb suggest that most children should be speaking by age three?
   a. One word sentences
   b. Two word sentences
   c. Three word sentences
   d. Three or more word sentences

34. Which of the following is the typical measure for assessing infant cognitive capacity?
   a. Learning
   b. Memory
   c. Sensory integration
   d. Grasping
   e. Habituation

35. If a child shows a declining response to the same stimulus then it is safe to suggest that the child is:
   a. Forgetting the stimulus
   b. Remembering the stimulus
   c. Excited by other stimuli
   d. No longer able to sense the stimulus

36. A daycare program might try to get this Piagetian age group to clap their hands and sing along with a song for the first time in their lives.
   a. Sensorimotor stage
   b. Preoperational stage
   c. Concrete operational stage
   d. Formal operational stage

37. A grammar school might try to get this Piagetian age group to do subtraction for the first time in their lives.
   a. Sensorimotor stage
   b. Preoperational stage
   c. Concrete operational stage
   d. Formal operational stage

38. An after school program might try to get this Piagetian age group to discuss the environmental impact of the U.S.-Soviet cold war.
   a. Sensorimotor stage
   b. Preoperational stage
   c. Concrete operational stage
   d. Formal operational stage

39. The development of walking, stranger anxiety and separation anxiety at about 1-year of age leads to the following:
   a. Children go with babysitters very easily at this time
   b. More often than not, 1-year olds walk up to people they do not know

c. Crying near any stranger or during any period in which the caregiver is out of sight
d. Aggressive behavior toward other children

40. Harlow's experiments with monkeys established that basic attachment is controlled by:
   a. Feeding
   b. Touch
   c. Socialization
   d. Harlow's original experiments did not answer the question clearly

41. When the monkey was not feeding, where did it spend most of its time?
   a. One the wire mesh mother
   b. On the terry cloth mother
   c. Playing with the other monkeys
   d. Cowering in a corner

42. Could the "emotional" problems of Harlow's monkeys be reversed through therapy?
   a. Yes, they could be reversed
   b. No, they could not be reversed at all
   c. It could neither be reversed or not reversed but instead the monkeys approached a Zen-like state in which their minds altered their perceptions, dude

43. The time during which Harlow's monkeys could learn proper social behavior is called a:
   a. Social attachment period
   b. Sensitive period
   c. Developmental period
   d. Critical period

44. The time during which humans can learn proper social behavior or language is called a:
   a. Social attachment period
   b. Sensitive period
   c. Developmental period
   d. Critical period

45. The beginning of adolescence is identified by:
   a. The onset of puberty
   b. The beginning middle school
   c. Bodily changes
   d. Increased height

46. Which of the following skills uniquely develops at the time of puberty?
   a. Language skills
   b. Strength
   c. Memory capacity
   d. Abstract reasoning

47. For most women, menopause is a:
   a. Period of freedom
   b. Sad period marked by the "empty nest syndrome"
   c. Period of loss
   d. Period marked by mood swings due to changing hormone levels

48. Your father always tells you the same story about when he grew up:
   a. Fluid intelligence
   b. Crystallized intelligence
   c. Memorial intelligence
   d. Contextual invariance

49. In which stage of Kohlberg's model do people become concerned with concrete rewards and punishments?
   a. Preconventional stage
   b. Conventional stage
   c. Post-conventional stage

50. Which of the following parenting styles would include the following statement; "Do it because I said so!"
   a. Authoritarian
   b. Permissive
   c. Authoritative
   d. Neglectful

5 Sensation and Perception

A Rose by Any Other Name

What are some of your favorite odors? Could they be the smell of cookies baking in the oven, a special perfume worn by someone close to you, or the smell of evening jasmine under a moonlit sky? Everyone may have a favorite odor; however, not everyone has considered exactly how your nose goes about detecting those odors. How do you go from the free-floating molecules that were shaken loose from a rose petal to the romantic experience they conjure up? These were the types of questions raised by Richard Axel and Linda B. Buck, the winners of the 2004 Nobel Prize for Physiology or Medicine.

Axel and Buck began their foray into olfaction when, in the late 1980s, they began to discuss how humans can detect nearly 10,000 separate odors given the chemical similarity of many of those substances. In fact, one of the striking problems regarding olfaction is how brain cells can sensitively distinguish the differences between so many odors.

As neuroscientists, Axel and Buck viewed odor detection from a cellular basis. From that standpoint, distinguishing between two odors means there must be some controlling biochemical or genetic process. One of the things Axel and Buck looked for first were the odor receptors in the nose, which were still undiscovered at that time. Soon afterward, they turned their attention to the isolation of the genes responsible for growing those receptors and distinguishing their physical properties. They found that there are about one thousand genes controlling as many receptor types for odors. These one thousand receptor types are replicated until 10 million total receptors are present in the nasal cavity.

It appears that any odor releases a set of molecules, which, in their entirety, sets the condition for an odor experience. This occurs by having the molecules breathed up the nasal cavity until they land upon the receptors of the olfactory epithelium. The mixture of active receptors then travel to a set of glomeruli—integrated sets of 2,000 receptor axons—before being relayed to the primary olfactory cortex in the brain.

Axel and Buck earned the Nobel Prize for their systematic dissemination of the genetic components of the olfactory process. In addition, they found that active genetic processes in the olfactory system control the acquisition and storage of odor information. Understanding this complex process makes it easier for neuroscientists to uncover similar processes in other receptor systems.

Although the genetic knowledge of the olfactory bulb may reduce some of the romance of roses and perfume, it certainly is a comfort knowing that devoted and knowledgeable people are uncovering important biological processes that help explain our overall behavior.

CHAPTER OUTLINE

Objectives

After reading this chapter, you should be able to do the following:

Nature of Our Knowledge of the World

- Describe naïve realism, including the reasons people hold this view and what creates problems for this view.

A Model of Sensation and Perception

- Describe the stages in the general model of perception.
- Describe transduction.

Psychophysics

- Describe the field of psychophysics and some of the main perceptual limitations discovered using psychophysical methods.
- Distinguish between absolute thresholds and difference thresholds, and be able to recognize examples of each.
- Describe sensory adaptation and what sensory adaptation indicates about our sensory systems.

Vision

- Describe what light is, including its physical characteristics and the psychological dimensions related to these characteristics.
- Describe the functions of the pupil, cornea, and lens.
- Describe the structures contained in the retina and the main functions of each of these structures.
- Describe the differences between the rods and cones, and describe how these differences are related to their specific functions.
- Describe the blind spot, including why it occurs and why we are usually unaware of it.

- Explain why the analogy of the visual system as a camera breaks down beyond the receptors.
- Describe the trichromatic and opponent-process theories of color vision, including the phenomena each is able to explain.
- Describe the functions of the two major visual pathways beyond the primary visual cortex.

Hearing

- Describe the main structures of the outer, middle, and inner ear.
- Describe the receptor cells for hearing and how these receptors carry out the process of sensory transduction.
- Describe the different theories of pitch perception.

Perception

- Identify the differences between sensation and perception.
- Describe the main idea of the Gestalt view of perception.
- Describe, and be able to recognize examples of, the Gestalt principles of grouping.
- Distinguish between figure and ground.
- Describe and identify examples of the two binocular cues to distance.
- Describe and identify examples of the monocular cues to distance.
- Describe, and be able to recognize examples of, various types of perceptual constancy.
- Distinguish between, and identify examples of, bottom-up and top-down processing.

PREVIEW

Our perception of the world seems direct and immediate, so we often take it for granted. In this chapter, we will show that perception, rather than being direct and infallible, is a complicated process involving a number of stages. We will describe the kinds of changes information goes through as it moves from the receptors to the brain. We will discuss psychophysics, the study of the relationships between physical characteristics and psychological experience, and we will describe some of the principles associated with this part of perception. We will then discuss our general perception model in detail by applying it to the study of vision. This will be followed by a brief description of the processes involved in hearing and the other senses. Finally, we will move beyond accounting for sensations and discuss how perception typically involves meaningful objects and events. In doing so, we will discuss the Gestalt psychologists' emphasis on the relationships among the parts of a display and the principles they offered to explain how perceptions are organized. We will also describe the sources of information that allow us to see the world as three-dimensional and how both perceptual constancy and visual illusions may reflect the rules we use to process incoming information. Finally, the idea that perception results from a combination of bottom-up and top-down processing will be discussed.

SENSATION AND PERCEPTION

Psychologists who study sensation and perception are interested in how we interpret the external world using our five senses: vision, hearing, smell, taste, and body senses such as touch. Perception of the external world is critical to our survival, and it also provides us with much of the joy we experience in life—from the sounds of our favorite music to the tastes of our favorite foods. The term "sensation" is often used to refer to our experience of basic stimulus qualities, whereas the term "perception" is often used to refer to more holistic and unified experiences of objects and events, although the boundaries between these two terms are not precisely defined. For example, when eating a piece of fruit, we may perceive that the object we are eating is an apple (perception). The qualities that are combined to give rise to our perception of the apple, such as redness, roundness, firmness, and sweetness, are sensations. We will focus primarily on sensation in the first part of this chapter and then move on to perception in the second part, although we will often use the term "perception" to generically refer to both sensations and perceptions.

Although perceiving our world seems simple and straightforward, as you will soon learn, it is actually the end result of a great deal of complicated perceptual processing by the brain and sensory systems. First, we will discuss the everyday, layperson's view of perception and why this view is incorrect.

NAÏVE REALISM

Naïve realism:
The view of perception that says our perception is the way it is because that's the way the world is.

Why do we perceive the world in the way that we do? For many people, this seems like a silly question. Many people would answer that we perceive the world the way we do because that is the way that the world really is. For example, many would say that we perceive grass as green because grass *is* green. This everyday, layperson's view of perception is called **naïve realism**. But, as you will see, naïve realism is incorrect. As an example, there is nothing inherently "green" about green grass. Rather, what we experience as "green" is created in our brains and depends on the wavelengths of light present in the environment, the wavelengths of light reflected by grass, and the characteristics of our particular visual systems. Before discussing evidence that naïve realism is incorrect, let us first discuss likely reasons why people maintain this point of view. For one thing, perception seems immediate and direct, and it occurs without effort. However, psychologists know that perception is the result of a great deal of processing of information in various parts of the brain, although we are not consciously aware of this processing. A second reason for believing in naïve realism is consensual validation—other people experiencing the same situations will generally agree with your perception. Finally, perception usually corresponds with reality. You perceive this book in front of you, and it is actually there when you reach out to touch it. These factors seem to lend support to the idea that we perceive the world as it really is.

However, there are several problems for naïve realism. For one thing, there are individual differences in perception, including developmental changes in perception and differences in perception across species. For example, some people are able to perceive some colors but are unable to see the difference between red and green. Some people, called supertasters, are able to taste substances that many of us cannot taste. Babies are unable to see the fine details that an adult can see, and older people are sometimes unable to hear the same high-pitched tones that younger adults can easily hear. Bees can see ultraviolet light, which the unaided human eye cannot perceive. Dogs can respond to dog whistles because they can hear high-frequency sounds that humans cannot hear, and elephants can hear low-frequency sounds that we cannot hear. The point is, if we perceived the world exactly as it is, then such differences between individuals and across species should not exist.

Sensory adaptation:
The reduced responsiveness of our sensory systems when exposed to prolonged, continuous stimulation.

A second problem for naïve realism is that our perception of something can change even when the stimulus itself is not changing. For example, a common characteristic of all of our senses is **sensory adaptation**—the perceived decrease in the intensity of a continuously presented stimulus. Before reading this sentence,

One of the oldest known illusions is the moon illusion, where the full moon appears to be larger when it is on the horizon than when it is directly overhead.

you were probably not aware of the feel of your shirt on your back, yet you probably noticed it when you first put it on today. Likewise, the smell of your friend's cologne does not seem so overpowering after having been in his presence for a while, and water in a swimming pool that seems ice-cold at first soon feels comfortably cool. Sensory adaptation is often due to a reduction in neural firing with prolonged exposure to a stimulus. It makes sense that our sensory systems have evolved in this way. From a survival standpoint, it is important to detect changes in the environment; stimuli that are not changing are generally not as important. Thus, adapting to unchanging stimuli frees up resources that can be used to process more important information about changes in the environment. **Ambiguous figures** (reversible figures) provide another example of how your perception of an unchanging stimulus can change. A classic example is the Necker cube, shown in Figure 5.1. The line labeled A in **Figure 5.1** appears as part of the back of the cube when the cube appears to have its front face to the left, and appears as part of the front of the cube when the cube appears to have its front face to the right. If naïve realism is correct and we perceive the world exactly as it is, then our perception of something that is not changing should not change.

A third problem for naïve realism is the existence of **illusions**. Illusions are stimuli for which our perception does not agree with the measurable physical characteristics of the stimulus. In other words, when we experience an illusion, we perceive something that does not correspond to physical reality. Examples of several illusions are shown in the box on the next page. Don't get the idea that illusions occur only in drawings; many illusions occur in real-life viewing situations. For example, one of the oldest known illusions is the **moon illusion**. For thousands of years, people have noticed that the full moon appears to be larger when the moon is on the horizon than when it is directly overhead, even though neither the physical size of the moon nor the size of the moon's image in our eyes differs with its changing position in the sky. The fact that we sometimes perceive things that do not correspond to physical reality is a significant problem for naïve realism.

A Model of Sensation and Perception

There are obvious qualitative differences between each of our senses: Vision seems completely different from hearing, which seems completely different from taste, and so on. Our senses also differ in terms of the types of physical stimuli

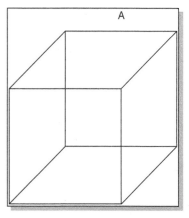

FIGURE 5.1 ▧ The Necker cube.

Ambiguous (reversible) figures: A figure for which perceptions alternate as the observer stares at it...

Illusions: The perception of the stimulus does not agree with the physical characteristics...

Moon illusion: The moon appears to be larger when it is near the horizon...

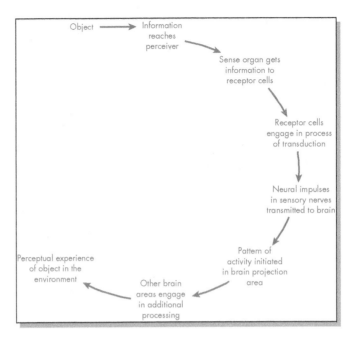

FIGURE 5.2 ■ A general model of perception.

to which they will respond, how they go about transforming physical stimuli into neural impulses, and the areas of the brain used to process information. Despite these differences, commonalities exist among all of our senses in the perceptual process. Thus, we can discuss a general model of perception that describes the stages of perception for all of our senses (**Figure 5.2**), although the case of vision will be used to provide concrete examples.

ILLUSIONS

Many visual illusions exist, with new ones being discovered all the time. For example, the Neural Correlate Society hosts a yearly competition for newly created illusions, and an Internet search for "visual illusions" will lead you to numerous websites showing many interesting illusions. The focus here will be on a few of the classic illusions.

(a) Müller-Lyer Illusion: Ignore the arrowheads and judge the relative lengths of the horizontal lines. Does the top horizontal line appear shorter than the bottom horizontal line? They are actually the same length. (You can verify this with a ruler.)

(b) Ponzo Illusion: Does the top horizontal line appear slightly longer than the bottom horizontal line? Again, they are actually the same length.

(c) Zöllner Illusion: In this illusion, the horizontal lines appear to be tilted with respect to each other, but they are in fact parallel.

(d) Hermann Grid: Do you see grayish spots at the intersections that disappear when you try to look directly at them?

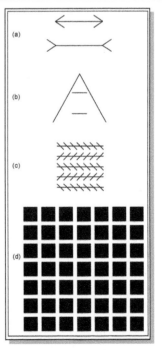

Illusions are not limited to vision—they have been demonstrated for our other senses as well. For example, there are numerous auditory and musical illusions (Bregman, 1990; Deutsch, 1995). One example of a musical illusion is called the scale illusion (Deutsch, 1974). In this illusion, listeners are presented, through headphones, with a pattern of tones that jumps dramatically up and down in pitch in each ear. However, listeners do not hear this jumping pattern and instead perceptually reorganize the tones such that they hear two smooth melodies in each ear. This perceptual reorganization causes listeners to mislocalize the tones such that they hear some of the pitches that are actually presented to the right ear as coming from the left and vice versa.

First, information coming from some object or event in the environment has to reach the sensory organs of the perceiver. In the case of vision, light is reflected from objects into our eyes. The purpose of sensory organs such as the eyes is to get information to specialized cells called receptor cells. Each sense has its own specialized receptor cells that respond to a specific kind of energy. The receptor cells perform a crucial function called transduction. **Transduction** refers to converting one kind of energy to another kind of energy. In perception, environmental energy has to be converted into action potentials, which provide the only means of communication for neurons. For example, if you were to shine a light on a neuron in the brain, it would not respond—neurons respond to electrochemical signals from other cells, not to light (nor to sound, odors, etc.). Thus, we need specialized receptor cells for each sense in order to transduce a particular form of energy from the environment into action potentials. In the case of vision, the receptor cells, called photoreceptors, convert light energy into action potentials. Once transduction has occurred, neural impulses are relayed along sensory nerves, such as the optic nerve in vision, to projection areas in the brain. Projection areas are the parts of the cortex to which information is first sent. In vision, the main projection area is the primary visual cortex, located in the occipital lobes of the brain. The signal is then sent to other parts of the brain, which engage in further processing of the signal. There are thought to be more than 30 distinct cortical areas involved in visual processing (Felleman & Van Essen, 1991), and in many cases, a specific area is specialized for processing a particular perceptual attribute. For example, motion is primarily processed in one part of the brain, shape in another part, and so on. Ultimately, all of these separate sensory attributes are linked together and lead to our perceptual experiences of objects and events. Again, a similar sequence of events occurs for all of our senses.

Transduction:
The process by which receptor cells change environmental energy into neural impulses that can be sent through the nervous system.

Implications of the Model

Based on the preceding model, you can see that perception is not direct. Visual images, sounds, smells, tastes, and so on, are not directly transmitted to the brain. Rather, our perceptions are indirect representations of the world, and external stimuli are represented by neural codes. In other words, when you see something, the visual stimulus leads to particular rates and patterns of neural firing in various parts of the brain, ultimately leading to visual perception. This fact can explain why individual differences exist: They result from physiological differences or changes in either the brain or the sensory systems. For example, older people often lose some of the receptor cells for hearing, resulting in loss of hearing for some frequencies of sound. Bees have photoreceptors that respond to ultraviolet light, which humans do not have. In addition, such a model can account for phenomena such as sensory adaptation (decreased neural firing in response to an unchanging stimulus), ambiguous figures (changes in neural states over time), and illusions (the stimulus leads to a pattern of neural firing that does not accurately represent the stimulus).

If all perception is the result of neural firing, what gives rise to qualitatively different sensory experiences for each of our senses? Why do hearing, vision, taste, smell, and somatosensation seem so completely different from each other? One answer to this question is called anatomical coding. Each of our senses sends information to a different projection area in the cortex, and each sense is largely subserved by different areas of the brain. For example, visual signals are sent to the primary visual cortex, located in the occipital lobes at the back of the brain. However, auditory signals are sent to the primary auditory cortex, located in the temporal lobes on the sides of the brain. Therefore, the particular parts of the brain that are active can give rise to the qualitative differences between the senses. This idea is consistent with the finding that electrical stimulation of the auditory cortex gives rise to auditory sensations, electrical stimulation of the visual cortex leads to visual sensations, stimulation of the somatosensory cortex leads to bodily sensations, and so on. In addition, within a particular area of the brain, the rate and pattern of neural firing, as well as the particular neurons that are active, could give rise to qualitative differences within a sense and allow us to distinguish between different pitches, colors, tastes, and so on. For example, some cells in the visual system show excitation (increased firing) in response to the color red and inhibition (decreased firing) in response to green. As another example, neurons in the medial temporal (MT) visual area respond selectively to both speed and direction of motion (Maunsell & Van Essen, 1983). For instance, some MT neurons might show excitation in response to something moving slowly to the right, but not to stimuli that have other speeds or directions of movement. Different MT neurons might show excitation only in response to a stimulus moving quickly to the left. Thus, the particular cells that are active in the MT cortex could give rise to our perception of the specific direction and speed of a moving stimulus.

PSYCHOPHYSICS

Psychophysics:
The study of the relationship between physical characteristics of stimuli and psychological experience.

Because perception is not direct, we need to distinguish between a physical stimulus and the psychological experience of that stimulus. The area of perception in which psychologists map out the relationships between physical characteristics and psychological experience is called psychophysics. Gustav Theodor Fechner, the founder of psychophysics, was a nineteenth century physicist and philosopher. He published his classic book, *Elements of Psychophysics,* in 1860, before psychology as a field formally existed. Fechner demonstrated that it is possible to objectively measure mental phenomena at a time when most believed it was not possible, and he developed a set of classic psychophysical methods for doing so. Fechner is considered so important that some psychologists who specialize in the study of perception still celebrate "Fechner Day." Fechner's classic psychophysical methods were primarily designed to measure two things: absolute thresholds and difference thresholds.

Absolute Threshold

Absolute threshold:
The smallest amount of stimulus energy required for an observer to reliably detect the stimulus.

Absolute thresholds indicate the minimum amount of a stimulus that can just barely be reliably detected. For example, what is the dimmest light we can just barely see? What is the softest sound we can just barely hear? How much sugar must be added to water before we can just barely detect a hint of sweetness? We are unable to perceive stimuli that fall below our absolute thresholds, even though such stimuli can be physically measured and are known to be physically present. Imagine you added a single grain of sugar to a gallon of water. Although a physically measurable amount of sugar is present, you would not be able to taste any sweetness because the amount of sugar falls below your threshold for detecting the presence of sugar. The same is true for all of our senses: There is always some point below which you are unable to perceive the presence of a stimulus. Absolute threshold and sensitivity are directly related to one another. The inverse of absolute threshold is sensitivity. In other words, if you have a higher threshold, you have lower sensitivity, and vice versa.

If you have ever had your hearing tested, you have some idea of what a psychophysics experiment measuring absolute thresholds is all about. In a typical hearing test, you are presented with a number of tones of different frequencies and intensities (i.e., different pitches and loudnesses) and are asked to indicate when a tone is present. By measuring which tones you can or cannot hear, the person administering the test is able to determine your threshold for hearing various frequencies. In addition, if you have had a hearing test, you may remember that sometimes you were not entirely sure whether or not a tone had been presented. This uncertainty is normal. People do not respond like machines in a consistent way—changes in neural states, fluctuations in attention, and so on, affect your perception. So, for tones that are very near your threshold, you will sometimes hear them and will sometimes not hear them. For this reason, the phrase "reliably detected" was used in the preceding definition of an absolute threshold. Specifically, the absolute threshold is defined as the point at which you will detect a stimulus 50 percent of the time.

In addition to showing the minimum intensity required to detect a stimulus, research on absolute thresholds shows that there is a limited range of stimuli that we can detect regardless of intensity. For example, we are able to see electromagnetic energy with wavelengths between roughly 400 nanometers and 700 nanometers (i.e., visible light). A nanometer is one-billionth of a meter. We are unable to see either shorter (e.g., ultraviolet) or longer (e.g., infrared) wavelengths, no matter how intense. We are able to hear sounds with frequencies roughly between 20 and 20,000 cycles per second and unable to hear sounds outside this range, no matter how intense. Similar findings apply to all of our senses. This limited operating range is due primarily to the nature of our receptor cells, which respond to some stimuli but not to others. Other species can detect energy outside the human range. As discussed previously, bees can see ultraviolet light, which is electromagnetic energy with a wavelength shorter than 400 nanometers; dogs can hear sounds with much higher frequencies than can humans. This difference in perception between species is due to differences in the sense organs and receptors among species.

Despite limitations in the range of stimuli that we can detect, we can be incredibly sensitive to some stimuli. For example, we can detect the equivalent of a candle flame seen from 30 miles away on a clear dark night, and we can detect the equivalent of a watch ticking from a distance of 20 feet in a quiet room (Galanter, 1962). However, we are not always equally sensitive to all stimuli within the range we can detect. For example, we are more sensitive (our thresholds our lower) for sounds that lie in the range of roughly 2,000 to 4,000 cycles per second, the range in which most speech sounds occur, than to either lower- or higher-frequency sounds. Our fingertips and lips are much more sensitive than many other parts of our bodies, such as our backs and legs.

Signal Detection Theory

A newer approach to measuring sensitivity is based on **signal detection theory**, which allows researchers to separate motivational factors from sensitivity. Imagine participating in an experiment designed to determine your threshold for hearing. Unlike the case in the typical hearing test, though, the experimenter always

An example of the limitations of human perception is the elephant, which can hear sounds at a much lower frequency than humans.

Signal detection theory: Techniques that allow a researcher to separate sensitivity to a stimulus from factors that may be affecting a willingness to report the presence of the stimulus.

presents very soft tones that are so close to your threshold that you are never completely sure whether or not a tone is present. So, you sometimes decide that you hear the tone, and sometimes decide that you do not hear the tone. For example, you might report that you hear the tone 50 percent of the time and do not hear the tone 50 percent of the time. Now, imagine the same experiment, but this time the experimenter says you will be paid $1.00 every time you correctly detect the presence of a tone, with no penalty for being wrong. Do you think your responses would change in this situation? If you are like most people, you will try to maximize your money by saying you hear the tone considerably more than 50 percent of the time, perhaps even 100 percent of the time, even though you are often not completely sure if a tone is present. In these examples, your sensitivity does not change. What does change is your criterion for reporting that you hear the tone. Even without being paid, different people naturally have different criteria for responding. Some people are inclined to say they hear a tone even when they are very unsure; other people will not say they hear a tone unless they are fairly certain it is present. Researchers who use signal detection methods conduct experiments such as those just described and calculate two different measures: d′ ("d prime"), which is a measure of your sensitivity, and ß (the Greek letter beta), which represents your criterion for responding (i.e., your willingness to report that you hear a tone).

Difference Threshold

Difference threshold:
The smallest amount of change in a stimulus that can be reliably detected.

Psychophysicists are also interested in how much a stimulus has to be changed before you can just barely notice the difference. Imagine that you have a solution of sugar dissolved in water and that the sugar content is above your absolute threshold such that you can easily detect sweetness. How much more sugar must be added before the solution tastes just barely sweeter? The smallest amount of physical change in a stimulus that can be reliably detected is called the difference threshold. The psychological unit that corresponds to the difference threshold is called the just noticeable difference (jnd).

Just noticeable difference (jnd):
The psychological unit of measurement corresponding to the difference threshold.

In the nineteenth century, Ernst Weber discovered that the amount a stimulus needs to be increased in order to be just noticeably different is not an absolute amount. Rather, the amount of change needed is some proportion of the standard stimulus (i.e., the starting stimulus to which you are comparing). This relationship between the amount of the stimulus required to produce a jnd and the amount of the standard stimulus is called Weber's law, and the particular proportion of change needed to produce a jnd is called Weber's fraction (even though it is often expressed as a proportion or a percentage rather than as a fraction).

Weber's law:
Relationship between the amount of a stimulus required to produce a jnd and the amount of the standard stimulus.

For example, imagine you have two separate 1-gallon containers of water and 10 teaspoons of salt has been dissolved in each container. You can easily determine that the water in each container tastes salty, because the amount of salt is well above your absolute threshold for detecting salt. To one of these containers (the "comparison"), you add 1 teaspoon of salt at a time. With each teaspoon you add to this comparison container, you compare its taste to the water in the other container, to which you are not adding in more salt (called the "standard"). Suppose that you can't taste any difference between 10 and 11 teaspoons of salt, but you find that you can just barely taste a difference between 10 and 12 teaspoons of salt. So, you had to add two additional teaspoons of salt to produce a jnd, and Weber's fraction is 2/10. In other words, you had to increase the amount of salt in the comparison container by 2/10 (or .20, or 20 percent) of the amount in the standard container to produce a jnd. Now, suppose you do the same experiment, but you start with water in which 20 teaspoons of salt has been dissolved (i.e., the standard is 20 teaspoons). If you now add 2 teaspoons of salt to the comparison container (22 teaspoons altogether), will you be able to taste a difference? According to Weber's law, you will not. Instead, you will need to add 4 teaspoons to the comparison container to produce a jnd, because the amount needed to produce a jnd is not an absolute amount (i.e., not 2 teaspoons), but rather some proportion of the standard stimulus (in this case, .20 3 20 teaspoons, which is 4 teaspoons). According to Weber's law, how many teaspoons of salt would you need to add to the comparison container to produce a jnd if the standard contained 50 teaspoons of salt? The answer is .20 of 50, or 10 teaspoons.

Weber's fraction differs for each sensory attribute. For example, Weber's fraction is 1 percent for brightness discrimination and 2 percent for loudness discrimination (Stevens, 1971). Weber's fraction tends to be higher for smell and taste qualities than for visual and auditory qualities, meaning that we are generally less sensitive to intensity differences in smells and tastes than we are to intensity differences in visual and auditory stimuli.

VISION

In this section of the chapter we will use visual perception as an example of how perception works. We will describe, specifically for vision, the various stages of the general model of perception presented earlier. We will begin by describing the information that we use to "see" objects in the environment, and we will then look in some detail at how this information is transformed on its way to the brain. Thus, the starting point of our discussion is the nature of light.

The Stimulus for Vision

The stimulus that provides the visual system with information about objects in the world is light. Light is actually just a very small part of the electromagnetic spectrum. The electromagnetic spectrum, shown in **Figure 5.3**, includes all forms of electromagnetic radiation, from the very short wavelengths called gamma rays

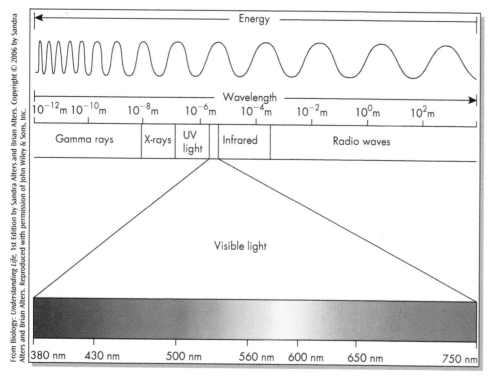

FIGURE 5.3 ■ The electromagnetic spectrum.

to the very long wavelengths used in radio broadcasts. The particular wavelengths, which we call light are just like the rest of the electromagnetic spectrum, except for one crucial difference. The human visual sys-tem has receptor cells that can respond to electromagnetic radiation with wavelengths between roughly 400 and 700 nanometers (nm). Thus, when electromagnetic radiation with wavelengths in this range bounces off objects in the environment and is reflected to a human observer's eye, this radiation has the possibility of initiating a response in the visual system. In this way the electromagnetic radiation provides the observer with information that may allow the object to be seen. Other wavelengths of elec-tromagnetic radiation may also bounce off objects and be re-flected to the observer's eye, but because we lack receptors that will respond to these other wavelengths, they do not initiate a response in the visual system.

The light reaching our eyes can vary in terms of three basic physical characteristics. All of the visual information about objects in the world is transmitted to us in terms of these characteristics. The first physical charac-teristic on which light can vary is wavelength. Wavelength is the major deter-minant of the psychological dimension of vision called **hue**. Hue is what we usually describe in everyday language with the term "color." In other words, hue refers to the dimension that distinguishes among violet, blue, green, yel-low, orange, and red, as shown in the visible light part of the electromagnetic spectrum in **Figure 5.3**.

The second physical dimension on which light can vary is intensity, or the amount of radiation present in the reflected light. **Lightness** is the psychological dimension most closely related to intensity. As the amount of light reaching the eye from an object increases, the apparent lightness of the object increases. (An analogous term "brightness," is used to refer to the perceived intensity of a direct light source such as a light bulb.)

The third physical dimension on which light can vary is the purity of the light, which refers to how many different wavelengths the radiation contains. In a pure light source, all of the radiation is of a single wavelength. Sunlight, or white light, on the other hand, contains all the wavelengths in the visible spectrum. The psychological dimension associated with purity is called **saturation**, which is the dimension that distinguishes vivid colors from washed-out colors. In other words, saturation is an indication of how much of a particular hue appears to be present. Highly saturated colors are very vivid, whereas completely unsaturated colors yield no experience of hue—they appear to be achromatic, or without color (i.e., white, black, or some shade of gray). The complete range of visual perceptions we experience is communicated to us by the light energy reaching particular recep-tors in our eyes. The variations in wavelength, intensity, and purity reaching dif-ferent receptors, and the changes in these patterns of stimulation over time, provide the information from which these experiences are constructed.

The Human Eye

The main function of the eye as a sense organ is to collect the light reflected from objects and get that light to the receptor cells in a usable form. A diagram of the human eye, showing some of the most important structures, is presented in **Figure 5.4**. As shown in the diagram, light reflected from an object first enters the eye through the **cornea**. After passing through the fluid-filled chamber behind the cornea, the light strikes a colored membrane, the iris, the colorful ring in the center of the eye. When we talk about a person having brown or blue eyes, we are talking about the color of the person's irises. In the center of the iris is a hole called the **pupil**.

The pupil, which allows the light to pass through, changes size depending on the amount of light present in the environment. In dimly lit conditions, the

Hue:
The psychological dimension, usually described as color, that is primarily determined by wavelength.

Lightness: The psychological dimension, usually described as varying from dim to bright, that increases as the amount of light reaching the eye increases.

Saturation:
The psychological dimension associated with purity that distinguishes vivid colors from washed-out colors.

Cornea:
The major light-bending structure in the eye; it always bends light the same amount.

Pupil:
The opening in the iris that controls the amount of light entering the eye.

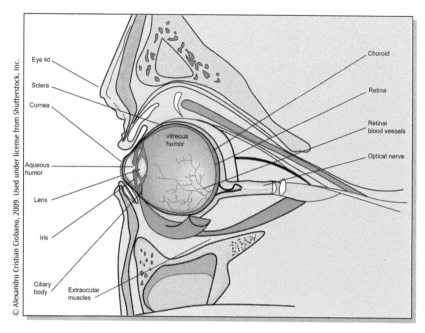

FIGURE 5.4 ■ The human eye and most of it's main components

pupils dilate to allow in as much light as possible, making it easier to see in such conditions. In more brightly lit conditions, the pupils constrict to reduce the amount of light entering the eye. This constriction also increases depth of field, the range of distances over which objects are in focus.

After passing through the pupil, light passes through the **lens**, an important structure in image formation, which we will discuss shortly. After passing through the lens, the light enters a large chamber filled with a fluid called vitreous humor. Finally, after passing through the vitreous humor, the light reaches the **retina**, a multilayered structure at the back of the eye that contains, among other things, the actual photoreceptors. The image formed on the retina must then be transduced by the photoreceptors into the language of the nervous system. Given that the image formed on the retina provides the information used by the photoreceptors, we will look in more detail at how this image is formed.

Forming a Retinal Image

The eye is often compared to a camera, and in terms of image formation, the analogy is quite good. The image formed on your retina, just like the image formed on the film in your camera, must duplicate faithfully the pattern of light present in the part of the external environment at which you are looking. In other words, the image on the retina, like the image in your camera, must be in focus for perception, or your picture, to be clear and accurately detailed. When light is reflected from objects, the light rays diverge, so the rays of light must be refracted, or bent, so that they will come into focus at a single point. How much the rays need to be bent depends on how far away the object is. Thus, in the eye, as in a camera, the goal is to have the light rays from objects at various distances away come into focus at precisely the right place. That place is the retina in the eye and the film in a camera. The two main structures in the eye responsible for the bending, or refraction, of light are the cornea and the lens.

The cornea is a small, spherical-shaped, transparent bulge at the front of the eye (**Figure 5.4**). The cornea is the major light-bending structure in the eye, responsible for about two-thirds of the total bending that occurs. The major limitation of the cornea in terms of image formation is that it is a fixed structure.

Lens:
The structure in the eye able to bend light different amounts; critical for focusing objects close to the observer.

Retina:
The structure at the back of the eye on which images are formed; contains the photoreceptors for transducing light.

Because the cornea always bends light the same amount, it is not able to adjust the amount of bending based on how far away an object is. The amount that the cornea bends light is determined by its shape: The more spherical one's cornea, the more light-bending power it has. In some individuals, the cornea does not have a completely regular, spherical shape. The result of a misshapen cornea is that light entering the eye at different orientations gets bent different amounts, causing the retinal image to be distorted. This condition, called astigmatism, can be corrected by a lens that compensates for the distortion introduced by the cornea.

The structure in the eye able to bend light different amounts is the lens (see **Figure 5.4**). When the ciliary muscles attached to the lens are relaxed, the lens flattens. In this state, which occurs when looking at distant objects, the lens contributes its smallest amount of bending relative to the bending done by the cornea. Light from distant objects does not require as much bending for the light to come to a point of focus on the retina. Thus, in the normal eye, the flattening of the lens will result in distant objects being properly focused. When the ciliary muscles contract, the lens assumes a more spherical shape, which causes the incoming light to be bent more. Light reaching the eye from objects close to the ob-server must be bent more in order to come to a point of focus on the retina. Thus, the bulging of the lens, which causes increased bending of the light, occurs when viewing nearby objects and results in these objects being properly focused. The process by which the lens varies its focusing power by changing shape is called accommodation.

We have been talking about how the combined bending of light by the cornea and lens results in objects at various distances from the observer being in proper focus for a normal observer. However, for many of us, the combined bending of light by our cornea and lens, given the distance from the front of our eye to our retina, does not result in objects at all distances being in proper focus. Some of us are nearsighted (myopic), which means that we can see close-by objects clearly but have trouble with more distant objects. The problem here is that even when our lens flattens to its maximum amount, the light rays from distant objects (which don't require as much bending) are bent too much. Thus, the image comes into focus at a point in front of the retina. Some of us have the opposite problem: We are farsighted (hyperopic), which means we can see distant objects clearly but have problems bringing close-by objects into focus. In this case the problem is that even when our lens bulges as much as it can, the total bending from the cornea and lens together is not enough to bring the light rays from nearby objects into focus on the retina. The point at which the rays would be in focus is actually behind the retina, which means that for the image on the retina to be properly focused, additional bending of the rays would be required. As those of us who wear glasses or contacts know, both of these problems are easily overcome by the addition of a corrective lens. The nearsighted person wears a lens that causes light to diverge before entering the eye, whereas the farsighted person wears a lens that provides additional bending.

Another common problem with forming a clear image on the retina is related to the accommodation ability of the lens. The ability of the lens to change shape begins to decline as early as age 16, as the lens begins to lose its elasticity (Weale, 1986). The effects of this reduced elasticity aren't usually noticeable until people reach their 40s, at which time a decrease in the ability to clearly see objects close to the eye becomes apparent. One of the first signs may be that the person starts holding reading material farther away. Only up-close vision is affected, because only nearby objects require the amount of bending that the less elastic lens can no longer provide. This condition is called presbyopia, which means "old-sight." Presbyopia is responsible for many individuals, who had perfectly normal vision throughout their lives, getting their first set of "reading glasses."

Accommodation: The process by which the lens varies its focusing power by changing shape.

Presbyopia: The condition of reduced elasticity of the lens, which decreases the ability to see clearly objects close to the eye.

The effects of reduced elasticity of the lens usually becomes noticeable in a person's 40s, requiring the use of reading glasses.

Sensory Transduction

So far we have described how light carries information about an object in the world to the eye and how the eye as an optical instrument brings an image of that object into focus on the retina. The retina is the part of the eye that is actually responsible for changing this image into a set of neural impulses and beginning the process of transmitting this transduced information to the brain. A diagram showing the main structures contained in the retina is presented in Figure 5.5. The retina is arranged in layers: one containing the photoreceptors, one containing the bipolar cells, and one containing the ganglion cells. Note that the light passing through the eye must pass through the ganglion cell and bipolar cell layers before reaching the photoreceptors, which are at the back of the retina.

The Photoreceptors

The job of actually converting light into electrical signals is handled by the photoreceptors, which contain chemicals called photopigments. When these photopigments are hit by light, a chemical reaction is initiated in which the photopigment is broken down into simpler molecules. When this happens, neurotransmitters are released by the photoreceptors, causing activity in the bipolar cells connected to the photoreceptors. The bipolar cells in turn relay their signals to the ganglion cells, whose axons form the optic nerve. The breaking down of the photopigment in response to light is the sensory transduction process. You may have noticed that when you first enter a darkened room, such as a movie theater, after having been in bright sunlight, you are unable to see very well. But, after remaining in the darkened room, your ability to make out details gradually improves over a period of about half an hour. This increase in your ability to see in dimly lit conditions over time is called **dark adaptation**, and it is due to the gradual regeneration of photopigments in your photoreceptors as you sit in dimly lit conditions.

The human visual system contains two separate types of photoreceptors, rods and cones, each of which is specialized for specific visual functions. **Rods** are specialized to function in dim light conditions. In fact, animals like the owl, active at night, have retinas that contain primarily rods. In humans, there are about 120 million rods in the retina of each eye. The rods cannot signal information about the wavelength of light stimulating them, so when only the rods are

Dark adaptation: The increased sensitivity of our visual system as we remain in the dark.

Rods: Photoreceptors specialized to function in nighttime or dim light conditions.

© vaklav, 2009. Used under license from Shutterstock, Inc.

Owls, who are active at night, have retinas that are made up primarily of rods.

Cones: Photoreceptors specialized to function in daytime or bright light conditions.

Fovea: The central region of the retina, which contains only cones.

functioning, our perception of the world involves shades of gray rather than colors. You have probably noticed that colors become hard to distinguish and finally fade away as darkness approaches. Cones require much more light to function and thus are primarily responsible for our visual experiences during daylight or bright light conditions. Animals active primarily during the day, such as squirrels and pigeons, have retinas that contain primarily cones. In humans, there are about 5 to 8 million cones in the retina of each eye.

Although cones need more light than the rods to function, there are some advantages to vision controlled by the cones. The cones are able to signal information about the wavelengths of light stimulating them, so the cones are responsible for color vision. Also, the cones are much better able to resolve fine details and thus are responsible for what is called visual acuity. You may have noticed that it is very difficult, if not impossible, to read fine print under dim light conditions, conditions where the amount of light available is insufficient for the functioning of the cones. The specialized functions of the rods and cones each provide advantages and disadvantages. As a result, organisms that have two separate types of receptors, such as humans, are better adapted to function over a wide range of lighting conditions.

The specialized functions of the rods and cones are the result of a number of differences that exist between them. One major difference involves the location of the rods and cones on the retina. The central region of the retina is called the fovea (see **Figure 5.4**). The image of an object you are looking directly at stimulates photoreceptors in the fovea. The fovea contains only cones. Thus, when we want to examine something in detail, we look directly at it so that the information reaches the fovea. In this way the cones, which are specialized for resolving fine detail, are stimulated. As we move away from the fovea toward the peripheral regions of the retina, the number of cones rapidly decreases. In contrast, there are no rods in the fovea, but the rods are found in large numbers throughout the rest of the retina. Thus, as we move away from the fovea, the rods assume a larger role in our visual experience. You may have noticed that if you are looking at the night sky and catch a glimpse of a faint star out of the corner of your eye, when you try to look directly at the star to study it more intently, the star is no longer visible. The initial glimpse of the star resulted from the light hitting rods in the peripheral parts of the retina.

The rods are much more sensitive to small amounts of light than are the cones in the fovea, which were the only receptors stimulated when you tried to look directly at the star. The lesson here is that if you want to maximize your chances of seeing a dim object at night, look off to the side of the object rather than directly at it. In this way the rods, rather than the cones, will be stimulated.

Part of the reason that the rods and cones are specialized for different functions is that they contain different photopigments, the actual chemicals that capture light and begin the transduction process. The photopigments in the rods are much more sensitive to light than the photopigments in the cones, requiring much less light for transduction to occur. However, the way the rods and cones are connected to the bipolar and ganglion cells is also related to their specialized functions. The photoreceptors synapse with the bipolar cells and the bipolar cells synapse with the ganglion cells. One way to make it more likely for light to be detected is to have a number of individual photoreceptors converge and send their messages to a single cell. In this way the individual messages, each of which may be quite weak, can be added together, making it more likely that a message will get sent to the brain. The rods, especially in the peripheral part of the retina, show such connections, with a large number of photoreceptors synapsing with a single bipolar cell and a number of these bipolar cells synapsing with a single ganglion cell.

Although having a number of photoreceptors converge on a single bipolar cell is beneficial for detecting weak light sources, such an arrangement is not conducive to resolving fine details. Detailed vision requires that the responses of neighboring receptors be kept distinct so that differences in the amount of light hitting neighboring regions on the retina can be registered. If neighboring receptors send their messages to the same bipolar cell, the specific location of the receptor receiving stimulation would be lost. Thus, in the fovea, which contains only cones, each individual receptor cell sends its message to a single bipolar cell, which in turn sends its message to a single ganglion cell. Such connections between photoreceptors and ganglion cells, where each cone has its own private line for sending messages to the brain, are well suited to the cones' role in providing good visual acuity.

The Blind Spot

The area where the optic nerve fibers leave the retina is called the optic disc. Because the optic disc contains no photoreceptors, there is no way for visual information from this part of the visual field in each eye to be registered. Thus, the optic disc produces a **blind spot** in the view of the world provided by each eye. You can experience the blind spot by using one eye to view the demonstration provided in **Figure 5.5**. Close your left eye and fixate the cross with your right eye. While remaining fixated on the cross, move Figure 5.6 slowly back and forth. At a given distance, the circle on the right will disappear. At this point the circle will be hitting the blind spot in your right eye. In real-world situations, we are unaware of this hole in each eye's visual field for several reasons. First, a given object does not hit the blind spot in both eyes at the same time. Second, the blind spot lies in the periphery of the visual field, where objects are not in sharp focus, making loss of information less noticeable. The third reason is perhaps the most important. You may have noticed in the demonstration that there was not a gaping hole in the blind spot. Rather, your brain 'filled in' the area containing the circle with the color and pattern that surrounded it. This filling-in process, which has been studied in detail by Ramachandran (1992), is consistent with the view expressed in our model of perception—perception occurs in the brain rather than in the eye.

Blind spot: A hole in each eye's visual field produced by the optic disc, where there are no rods or cones.

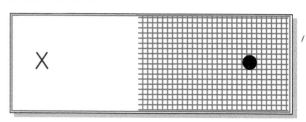

FIGURE 5.5 ■ Locating your blind spot.

Pathways to the Brain

The routes that the visual signals take to various parts of the brain after exiting the eye are called visual pathways. Most of the visual signals are relayed along a primary visual pathway on which we will focus our discussion. However, there are other pathways to various parts of the brain. The optic nerves in each eye, which consist of ganglion cell axons exiting each eye, soon reach a spot called the optic chiasm, at which point half of the nerve fibers from each eye cross over to the other side of the brain (called contralateral projection). The remaining nerve fibers from each eye remain on the same side of the brain (ipsilateral). The end result is that signals from the left visual field from both eyes are represented in the right half of the brain, and the signals from the right visual field from both eyes are represented in the left half of the brain. This contralateral representation of information is a general characteristic of the brain. For example, when you move your right arm, the command originated from the left motor cortex. If you feel something touch your left foot, the signal is relayed to the somatosensory cortex in the right hemisphere. Although there is crossing over of the signal at the optic chiasm, there are no synapses here. The first place along the primary visual pathway at which there are synapses is the lateral geniculate nucleus (LGN), which is located in the thalamus. For all of the different senses, information is relayed through one of the nuclei located in the thalamus. From the LGN, the signal is relayed via the optic radiations to the primary visual cortex, located in the occipital lobes.

Single-cell recordings have been used to study how ganglion cells, cells in the LGN, and cells in the visual cortex respond to various types of visual stimulation. One of the most important conclusions from these studies is that, beyond the receptors, the analogy between the visual system and a camera breaks down. The neurons in the visual system do not, like photographic film, simply passively register areas of dark and light. Rather, neurons in the visual cortex, as was first demonstrated by Hubel and Wiesel (1962), act like **feature detectors**. Some neurons respond best when lines are presented; others, when corners are presented. Some prefer horizontally oriented lines or edges; others, diagonally oriented stimuli. Some respond best to stationary stimuli; others, to stimuli moving in a particular direction. These cells are thus responding to specific features of objects located at particular locations in the visual field, from which a representation of what's out there can be constructed.

Visual processing does not end with the primary visual cortex. As discussed previously, numerous cortical areas are involved in visual processing, and a detailed description of these areas is well beyond the scope of this book. However, many of these visual areas lie along two major pathways after the primary visual cortex: the "What" pathway and the "Action" pathway (Goodale & Humphrey, 1998; Ungerleider & Mishkin, 1982). The "What" pathway conveys information along the lower parts of the temporal lobes and is primarily involved in processing information that leads to object identification. The "Action" pathway travels through the upper parts of the temporal lobes and to the parietal lobes. This pathway is involved in processing information that allows us to interact with our environment, including location, spatial layout, and motion. In addition, at these higher levels of the brain, cells respond to even more complex features than do cells in the primary visual cortex. For example, there are cells in the temporal lobe, along the "What" pathway, that respond best to faces (Damasio, Tranel, & Damasio, 1990). Damage to such brain areas in humans is often associated with a condition called prosopagnosia, which is an inability to identify faces even though vision is otherwise normal.

Feature detectors: Specific neurons respond best to specific features, such as lines, moving stimuli, etc.

Color Vision

One of the most striking aspects of vision is our perception of color. As we described earlier in this chapter, the hue of the objects we experience is primarily determined by the particular wavelengths of light that the objects reflect to our eyes. The question now is how information about wavelengths is communicated to the brain. Two potential answers to this question, which constitute theories of color vision, were originally developed during the 1800s. These two theories have been shown to be complementary rather than contradictory, each explaining a different stage in the processing of color information.

One theory of color vision, usually referred to as the Young-Helmholtz trichromatic theory, was based on the observation that any color a normal human can perceive can be produced by mixing together three different wavelengths of light from separated points along the spectrum. Color television uses small glowing dots of blue, green, and red to produce multicolored pictures. According to the trichromatic (or three-color) theory, the human eye contains three different kinds of receptors, each of which responds best to a particular wavelength of light. Our experience of color is determined by the relative response in each of the three types of receptors.

Physiological research has revealed that, at the receptor level, trichromatic theory is in fact correct. The retinas of humans and other higher primates contain three different kinds of cones, each containing somewhat different photopigments. One type of cone is most sensitive to short wavelengths of light, a second type of cone is most sensitive to medium wavelengths of light, and a third type of cone is most sensitive to long wavelengths of light. Each type of cone responds to a range of wavelengths around their peak sensitivity, these peaks being about 419 nanometers, 531 nanometers, and 558 nanometers (Dartnall, Bowmaker, & Mollon, 1983). Because each cone type responds to a range of wavelengths, the response of any given cone is ambiguous. A given cone could show a large response either by being stimulated by light whose wavelength corresponded to its peak sensitivity or by being stimulated by a brighter light whose wavelength was some distance from its peak sensitivity. Thus, only by comparing the responses of the three cone types can changes in lightness and changes in color be distinguished. Given that our retinas contain only one type of rod, this also explains why we can't see colors in very dim lighting. Problems with color vision are also consistent with trichromatic theory. Total color blindness, in which visual experience consists of black, white, and shades of gray, results from having either only one type of cone or no cones at all. This condition is exceedingly rare. More common is a color deficiency in which the person confuses reds and greens, due to a defect in the photopigments in the medium or long wavelength cones.

The other approach to explaining color vision, called opponent-process theory, was originally proposed by Ewald Hering. A number of facts about color perception, not explainable by trichromatic theory, formed the basis of this alternative approach. First, although certain colors appear to blend, others do not. We can talk about something being bluish green or reddish yellow but not bluish yellow or reddish green. Blue and yellow, and red and green, like black and white, appear to be opposites of each other. Something is either red *or* green, or blue *or* yellow, but not a combination of red *and* green or blue *and* yellow. Also, humans tend to perceive yellow, along with red, green, and blue, as primary colors, with all other colors being mixtures of these four primaries. Finally, there is the phenomenon of color afterimages. Stare at the fixation cross at the center of **Figure 5.6** for one minute without moving your eyes around. After a minute, look at a blank sheet of white paper. You should see faint afterimages. Notice that the afterimage for blue is yellowish, the afterimage for yellow is

FIGURE 5.6 ■ Color after images.

bluish, the afterimage for red is greenish, and the afterimage for green is reddish. In other words, the afterimages are of an opposite color. All of these observations suggest that there is some kind of opposition between red and green and between blue and yellow.

Beyond the receptors, support for an opponent-process theory of color vision has been found (DeValois & DeValois, 1975). The three types of cones found in the retina send their messages to what are called opponent-process cells. Ganglion cells and cells at higher levels in the visual system have been shown to respond in opposite fashion to red and green and to blue and yellow. For example, a red-green cell either increases its rate of response when red is presented and decreases its rate of response when green is presented, or vice versa. Similar patterns are shown for blue-yellow cells. Because these cells signal red or green, and blue or yellow, with opposite responses, it is impossible to perceive a color as reddish green or bluish yellow. A cell cannot increase and decrease its response at the same time. In addition, after a given cell has fired for a period of time, it becomes fatigued and reduces its rate of firing. Thus, if one looks at a colorless patch after looking at a red patch for a period of time, a red-green cell that increases its response to red would be responding at a lower-than-normal level. A decrease in responding from such a redgreen cell is used to code the presence of green. In this way, color afterimages can be explained. Thus, it has been shown that a combination of trichromatic theory at the receptor level and opponent-process theory at later stages of processing is able to account for many aspects of our perception of color.

HEARING

We have just discussed vision in some detail. As you might guess, more research has been done on vision than on any other sense. However, for many people, hearing is just as important, if not more important, than vision. Therefore, we will now briefly cover some of the basics of hearing, which is also called audition. We will begin with a discussion of the nature of sound.

The Stimulus for Hearing

The typical stimulus for hearing is sound. Sound is produced by a vibrating object, such as the bowed string on a violin or your vocal cords, causing the molecules in some medium to move. The usual medium through which sound reaches our ears is the air, although sound can be transmitted through liquids and solids as well. The movements of the air molecules cause changes in air pressure, which result in sound waves that move toward your ears. The simplest type of sound wave we can discuss is called a sine wave. Examples of sine waves are shown in **Figure 5.7a** and **b**. As was the case in vision, we can make a distinction between the physical characteristics of a sine wave and the psychological experience of those characteristics.

One important characteristic of a sine wave is its frequency. Frequency, measured in Hertz (Hz), refers to how many cycles of a wave occur per second. The sine wave in **Figure 5.7a** depicts one cycle, and the sine wave in **Figure 5.7b** depicts two cycles. The sine wave shown in **Figure 5.7a** has a lower frequency (fewer cycles in the same amount of time) than the sine wave in **Figure 5.7b**. The physical property of frequency corresponds to our psychological experience of pitch. Higher-frequency sine waves have a higher pitch than lower-frequency sine waves. Psychophysical studies indicate that humans can generally hear frequencies between roughly 20 and 20,000 Hz but that we are most sensitive in the range of about 2,000 to 4,000 Hz, which is the range in which most speech sounds

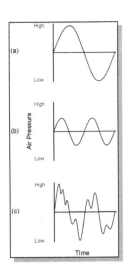

FIGURE 5.7 ■

Examples of sound waves.

lie. As mentioned earlier in this chapter, the range of frequencies that can be perceived differs among species. For example, dogs can hear higher frequencies than can humans, whereas elephants can hear lower frequencies.

A second important property of a sine wave is its amplitude. Amplitude refers to the difference in pressure between the high pressure and low pressure "peaks" in the sine wave. The sine wave in **Figure 5.7a** has twice the amplitude of the sine wave in **Figure 5.7b**. The physical property of amplitude generally corresponds to our psychological experience of loudness. Because we are not equally sensitive to all frequencies, the loudness of a sine wave also largely depends on its frequency. However, for sine waves with the same frequency, larger-amplitude sine waves generally sound louder than smaller-amplitude sine waves. Because we can hear such a large range of amplitudes, we often use a scale called the decibel scale (dB) to indicate sound pressure levels rather than discussing the size of the amplitudes of the sound waves. Humans can hear sounds from about 0 dB up to about 140 dB, which is a 10 million-to-1 range of amplitudes. Sounds that are greater than 140 dB are experienced as pain.

In everyday life, we rarely encounter sine waves in isolation. Instead, we usually hear complex waves, such as musical notes, speech sounds, noises, and so on. A complex wave is illustrated in **Figure 5.7c**. The famous mathematician Fourier demonstrated that any complex wave can be broken down into a number of individual sine wave components, or sinusoids, each of which has its own frequency and amplitude. For example, a single note played on a piano is a complex waveform that can be broken down into a number of sinusoids. However, we do not generally perceive each of these sinusoids individually. As is the case with light, in which we see one unified color rather than a combination of wavelengths, with complex sounds we perceive a unified sound with a particular pitch, loudness, and timbre. Timbre refers to sound quality. Timbre is the characteristic that distinguishes, for example, between a note played on a violin and a note played on a piano or between two different speaking voices. Several physical characteristics give rise to our experience of timbre, including the particular sinusoids that are present and how they change over time.

The Auditory System

When sound waves reach your ears, a complicated series of processes occur that eventually results in neural impulses being generated. The important structures in the ear involved in these processes are shown in Figure 5.8. As sound waves enter the ear, they travel down the auditory canal and cause the eardrum (tympanic membrane) to vibrate. As shown in Figure 5.8, the pinna (the visible part of the ear that sticks out from the side of your head), the auditory canal, and the eardrum make up the outer ear. The vibration of the eardrum causes movement of the three bones that make up the middle ear—the malleus, incus, and stapes, collectively called the ossicles. Based on their appearances, the ossicles are also commonly called the hammer, anvil, and stirrup, respectively. When the stapes is moved, it pushes on the oval window, a thin membrane that transmits vibrations to the fluid of the inner ear.

The inner ear consists of a set of fluid-filled canals called the semicircular canals and the cochlea. The semicircular canals are involved in our sense of balance. The location of the semicircular canals explains why, when we get an ear infection, our equilibrium, or sense of balance, is also sometimes affected. The other fluid-filled canal, the cochlea, is directly involved in transforming the movements of the stapes into messages that can be transmitted to the brain. The movement of the oval window causes the fluid in the cochlea to move. The fluid in the cochlea is contained such that when the oval window pushes in, the round window bulges out (**see Figure 5.8**). How does the movement of fluids in the

Outer ear: Made up of the pinna, auditory canal, and eardrum, its function is to carry sound waves to the eardrum.

Middle ear: Made up of the malleus, incus, and stapes, it connects the eardrum to the oval window.

Inner ear: A set of fluid-filled canals involved in both our sense of balance and sense of hearing.

Cochlea: The fluid-filled canal in the inner ear that contains the organ of Corti.

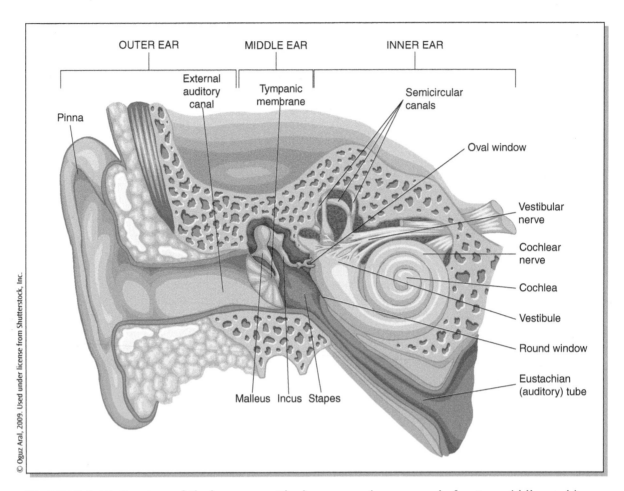

FIGURE 5.8 ■ *Structure of the human ear.* The human ear is composed of outer, middle, and inner sections. The outer ear extends from the pinna to the tympanic membrane (eardrum). The middle ear contains bones that transmit sound vibrations from the tympanic membrane to the cochlea. The cochlea contains the organ of hearing and makes up part of the inner ear. (Not to scale.)

Organ of Corti: Analagous to the retina in vision, it contains the receptor cells for hearing.

Inner hair cells: The receptor cells for hearing.

Basilar membrane: The organ of Corti sits on top of it and its wave-like motion is involved in the bending of the hair cells.

cochlea result in neural impulses being generated and sent by way of the auditory nerve to the brain? To explain this, we must look in detail at a structure that is part of the cochlea, the organ of Corti.

The organ of Corti, is analogous to the retina in vision. In other words, it contains the receptor cells that are responsible for sensory transduction—the changing of the movements of the cochlear fluid into neural impulses. The receptor cells for hearing are the inner hair cells. The inner hair cells are contained in the organ of Corti, which sits on top of the basilar membrane. Like the rods and cones in vision, the inner hair cells are responsible for transduction. The organ of Corti also contains the outer hair cells, which affect the movements of the basilar membrane but are not thought to be involved in transduction. Above the hair cells is the tectorial membrane. As previously mentioned, when the stapes pushes against the oval window, the fluid in the cochlea moves. This movement produces a wave-like, up-and-down motion of the basilar membrane and a back-and-forth motion of the tectorial membrane. The combination of these two movements causes the cilia, or hairs, of the inner hair cells to bend. The result of the bending of the cilia of the hair cells is the release of neurotransmitters that are picked up by the auditory nerve fibers. In this way, neural impulses are generated in the auditory nerve and these neural messages can then be transmitted to the brain. The messages from the auditory nerve eventually reach the primary auditory cortex in the temporal lobes of the brain (the primary projection area for hearing). The activity in the primary auditory cortex in turn causes activity to be initiated in other areas of the temporal lobe (the auditory association cortex). Thus, as in vision, our perceptual experience results from the pattern of activity occurring in particular areas of the brain. This brain activity was initiated by a complicated series of processes, beginning with energy reaching the appropriate sense organ and then being transduced into neural impulses, which were then transmitted to the brain along the appropriate sensory nerves. The only differences are that now the energy providing the information about the environment is sound, the sense organ that collects the sound is the ear, the receptor cells are the inner hair cells, the sensory nerves are the auditory nerves, and the primary projection area is in the temporal lobes.

Coding for Pitch

As just discussed, movements of the basilar membrane cause the cilia of the inner hair cells to bend, which leads to transduction of the auditory signal. In addition, we have seen that higher-frequency sounds are heard as higher in pitch, and lower-frequency sounds are heard as lower in pitch. Thus, an important question is, how does the auditory system code for pitch? There are two categories of theories that attempt to answer this question: (1) temporal theories, such as frequency theory, that depend on the timing of neural activity, and (2) place theories that depend on the place on the basilar membrane that is maximally stimulated.

An example of a temporal theory is frequency theory (rate theory), an early version of which was first proposed by Rutherford (1886). According to frequency theory, sounds of a particular frequency cause the basilar membrane to vibrate uniformly at that same frequency, which causes the cilia of the inner hair cells to bend and fire at that frequency. This in turn causes the fibers in the auditory nerve to fire at that frequency. For example, a 500 Hz sine wave would cause the basilar membrane to vibrate 500 times per second, thereby causing the inner hair cells to fire at 500 times per second, thereby causing the auditory nerve to fire at 500 times per second. However, a major limitation of this theory has to do with how quickly a neuron can fire. Immediately after a neuron generates an action potential, it enters a brief refractory period. During this refractory period, the neuron is hyperpolarized and unable to fire again for a short time. As a result, neurons cannot fire faster than roughly 1,000 times per second. Yet, we can hear frequencies as high as 20,000 Hz. Clearly, frequency theory cannot account for our perception of frequencies higher than approximately 1,000 Hz.

The volley principle, proposed by Wever and Bray (1930), overcame this limitation of the firing rate of neurons. According to the volley principle, even though one neuron by itself cannot signal frequencies above 1,000 Hz, the response of several neurons taken together could signal higher frequencies. Indeed, there is support for the volley principle. Researchers have found neurons that fire in response to high-frequency sounds, but they do not fire with every cycle of the sound wave. Instead, they fire irregularly, but when they do fire, they always fire at the same point in the cycle of the sound wave. This phenomenon is called phase-locking. Thus, groups of neurons that phase-lock could, taken together, signal higher frequencies. Unfortunately, researchers have been unable to find neurons that phase-lock in response to tones above 5,000 Hz.

An alternative theory of how the auditory system codes for pitch is called place theory. According to place theory, the particular place on the basilar membrane that is activated determines the pitch that we will perceive. For example, a 1,000 Hz tone would cause the inner hair cells at one particular location on the basilar membrane to fire vigorously. A 5,000 Hz tone would stimulate hair cells at a different place along the basilar membrane, a 10,000 Hz tone would stimulate hair cells at a third location, and so on. Helmholtz, whose name you should recognize from the trichromatic theory of color vision, proposed an early version of place theory, but many of the specifics of Helmholtz's theory proved to be incorrect. In 1961, Georg von Békésy won a Nobel Prize for his version of place theory. Békésy demonstrated traveling waves on the basilar membrane. Traveling waves are wave-like motions that travel down the length of the basilar membrane, causing the membrane to be bent the most at one particular location; this in turn causes the inner hair cells at that location to fire the most. Furthermore, Békésy demonstrated that high-frequency sounds produce a traveling wave with a peak near the base of the basilar membrane (the part nearest to the oval window) and progressively lower-frequency sounds produce a peak in the traveling wave at progressively more distant parts of the basilar membrane (toward the opposite end of the basilar membrane, called the apex). Additional support for place theory comes from the fact that stimulating auditory nerve fibers exiting the cochlea at different points produces the perception of different pitches, with stimulation near the base leading to perception of higher pitches and stimulation near the apex leading to perception of lower pitches. However, a problem for place theory is that, with tones below roughly 1,000 Hz, there is no single place at which the basilar membrane is bent the most. Instead, low-frequency tones appear to cause uniform vibration, rather than a traveling wave, along the basilar membrane.

So, is pitch coding based on the place that is most active, or is it based on the timing of information? There is still contentious debate among some researchers regarding this issue, and no single theory accounts for all of the data regarding pitch perception. However, many hold the view that place theory does a good job of explaining our perception of higher-frequency sounds (above 1,000 Hz) and that frequency theory and the volley principle do a good job of accounting for our perception of lower-frequency sounds (below 5,000 Hz), with some overlap in these mechanisms between 1,000 and 5,000 Hz.

THE OTHER SENSES

As previously pointed out, the stages in the general model of perception and the implications of such a model are basically the same from one sensory system to another, although the specifics differ for each sense. The goal of this chapter is much more to provide an understanding of how perception in general operates rather than to provide a detailed description of the workings of each of our sensory systems. As a result, taste, smell, and somatosensation will be discussed only briefly.

Somatosensation

The term somatosensation collectively refers to the senses that provide information about our body. Somatosensation includes the vestibular sense, which gives rise to our sense of balance and body position and is mediated by the movement of fluid in the semicircular canals of the inner ear as discussed previously. Somatosensation also includes the kinesthetic sense, which provides information about the position and movement of our limbs and is mediated by receptors in the muscles and tendons. Somatosensation also includes the cutaneous (skin) senses, and we will focus here on these cutaneous senses. The cutaneous senses consist of the qualitatively distinct sensory categories of touch, temperature, and pain. However, even though these sensory characteristics are subjectively different, each of them is mediated by receptors in the skin. There are a variety of different receptor types in the skin that are responsible for transduction, and the different types of receptors respond best to different types of stimuli.

Mechanoreceptors respond to things such as pressure, vibration, and stretch. For example, some mechanoreceptors respond best to slow, steady pressure, such as a gentle touch, whereas others respond best to rapid vibrations, such as those that occur when running your hand across a rough-textured surface. Thermoreceptors respond to temperature. Nociceptors respond to noxious stimuli, such as intense pressure, and give rise to our perception of pain. Receptors throughout the body convey their messages through the peripheral nerves to the spinal cord and then to the brain. The primary receiving area for the skin senses is the somatosensory cortex, located in the parietal lobes. The somatosensory cortex contains a map of the body, with different parts of the body represented in an orderly way on the cortex. However, the size of the body part has little to do with the amount of cortex devoted to it in the brain. you will see that more sensitive areas of the body, such as the fingers and lips, are given more representation in the cortex than are less sensitive areas of the body such as the back.

Some researchers are primarily interested in our perception of pain. Pain serves an important function: It helps us avoid situations that can lead to damage and death. Some people are born without the ability to experience pain and, as a result, often suffer from bizarre injuries, and sometimes early death. Some odd phenomena are associated with pain perception. For example, suppose you were to bang your shin. What is the first thing you might do? For many people, their first impulse is to rub the injured area, and this rubbing does in fact seem to help reduce the pain. As another example, it has long been noted that soldiers on the battlefield with severe injuries may not notice the pain until after the battle has ended; it seems that the brain is able to modify perception of pain. One popular model that accounts for these phenomena is called the gate-control theory of pain (Melzack & Wall, 1965). According to this theory, special cells in the spinal cord are able to inhibit our experience of pain, essentially acting as a gate that closes to partially block the pain signal. Rubbing your banged shin activates these inhibitory cells, as do efferent signals coming from the brain.

Just as signals from the brain can reduce the experience of pain, some pain is thought to be created entirely in the brain, even in the absence of pain-inducing stimuli. In the phantom limb phenomenon, people who have lost a limb report that they feel as if the missing limb is still present. In some cases, people who have lost a limb experience severe pain in the phantom limb, even though the receptors that would signal such pain are gone along with the missing limb. It seems likely that both the experience of the phantom limb itself and the pain in the missing limb are created in the brain (Ramachandran & Hirstein, 1998).

The Chemical Senses: Taste and Smell

Taste (technically called gustation) and smell (technically called olfaction) are chemical senses: The receptors for both taste and smell respond to molecules of chemical substances. Because these receptors are exposed to harsh chemicals, they are constantly regenerated, unlike the receptors for vision or hearing. In taste, the receptors, called taste cells, are located inside the taste buds. Each taste bud contains as many as 100 individual taste cells. Taste buds are located primarily on structures called papillae, which are bumps and ridges on the tongue. The taste cells respond to the basic taste categories: sweet, sour, salty, bitter, and umami. "Umami" is a Japanese word that roughly translates as meaty or savory. The taste cells transduce the taste stimulus and relay the signal via several different nerves to the thalamus and then to areas in the frontal lobes.

There are individual differences in taste abilities. When given a substance called PROP to put on their tongues, supertasters experience an intensely bitter sensation that other people do not experience. It is thought that supertasters are more sensitive to bitter tastes in general, not just to PROP, which may lead them to avoid some healthy foods (Bartoshuk, 2000).

If there are only five basic taste categories, why can we taste so many different nuances in food? Researchers make a distinction between taste and flavor, which depends not only on our sense of taste but quite a bit on our other senses—most importantly, our sense of smell. You may have noticed that food does not taste right when you have a cold, when your sense of smell is impaired. It is to the sense of smell we will now turn.

Humans can identify thousands of different odorants, the chemical molecules that provide the stimuli for our sense of smell. The receptors for olfaction, called simply olfactory receptors or odorant receptors, are embedded in the olfactory epithelium, a patch of skin at the top of the nasal cavity. Chemical substances dissolve in the mucus of the olfactory epithelium, allowing these molecules to activate the receptors and initiate transduction. The signal is relayed to structures called glomeruli in the olfactory bulb, which is a projection of the brain. Several pathways lead from the olfactory bulb to other areas of the brain. One of these pathways goes to the thalamus and then to the frontal cortex; it is thought to be involved in the conscious perception of odors. Other pathways project to the limbic system and are thought to be involved in the emotional response to odors.

Unlike most other sensory receptors, the different types of olfactory receptors are not anatomically distinct, so they were not well understood until relatively recently. In 2004, Axel and Buck won the Nobel Prize in medicine for their work in which they discovered the genes that give rise to the different types of olfactory receptors (Buck & Axel, 1991). More recent work has indicated that humans have hundreds of different types of olfactory receptors (Zhang et al., 2007).

PERCEPTION

Sensation: The registering of information by our sensory systems.

Up to this point, we have been talking about sensation, the registering of information by our sensory systems. Sensations, which include patches of various colors and lightnesses, lines at particular angles, or tones of a particular loudness or pitch, are the raw materials provided by our sensory systems, out of which our experience of the world is constructed. However, we do not generally experience the world solely in terms of these raw, meaningless sensations. Typically, what we experience are organized, meaningful objects and events. The organization and interpretation of sensory information is what is typically referred to as perception. We perceive a rose, or the face of a friend, rather than patches that have a particular color, or brightness, or shape. We perceive a familiar melody, rather than a collection of tones that might differ in pitch or loudness. In this section of the chapter we will examine some of the principles by which we organize and interpret sensations so that our experience of the world contains meaningful, and relatively stable and constant, objects and events. Our emphasis will be on visual perception, although similar principles can be applied to our other senses.

Perception: The organization and interpretation of sensory information.

Gestalt Psychology

The importance of organization to our perception of the world was pointed out early and forcefully by the Gestalt psychologists. The Gestalt psychologists argued that trying to understand perception by breaking stimuli down into their basic elements and analyzing these raw sensations was not likely to be successful, because our perception of the world is based on the patterns or relationships present in sensory inputs. The main Gestalt idea is often summarized as "the whole is different from the sum of the individual parts." What the Gestalt psychologists meant was that there are aspects of our perceptual experience that are not determined by any particular part of the input but that emerge from the relationships that exist among the parts of the input. One example would be transposing a melody. When a melody is transposed from one key to another, all of the individual notes are changed. However, the relationships among the individual notes remain the same, and we can thus perceive the melody as staying the same. Another example is the phi phenomenon, a motion illusion first described by Wertheimer (1912/1961), one of the founders of Gestalt psychology. Wertheimer varied the time between the presentations of two vertical lines separated by a given distance. When the time between presentations was very short, the two lines appeared to go on and off simultaneously; with long delays, one line appeared to go on and off and then the other line appeared to go on and off. However, with intermediate delays between the presentations of the two lines, a single line was perceived as moving smoothly from one location to the other. The same principle applies to movies: A series of still pictures is rapidly presented, yet you perceive smooth and continuous motion. This apparent motion shows that even though the parts of the display stay the same, the perception of the display as a whole changes as the relationships among the parts changes.

Principles of Organization

One important contribution of the Gestalt psychologists was their elaboration of the Gestalt principles of grouping, or principles of perceptual organization. The Gestalt psychologists believed that, of the various ways any stimulus display might be organized, people are most likely to organize the parts of a display in certain predictable ways. In other words, there are rules or principles of organization. According to the Gestaltists, these rules are based on the nature of the physical environment in which we live. We are most likely to organize the elements in a display in particular ways because the parts of objects in the world are in fact organized in these ways.

The Gestalt principles of grouping are presented in **Figure 5.9**. Notice in the principle of proximity (nearness) example that the **O**s on the left are likely to be seen as columns, because the vertical distance between the **O**s is less than the horizontal distance. On the other hand, the **O**s on the right are likely to be seen as rows, because here the horizontal distances are less than the vertical distances. In the example of the principle of similarity, we are likely to group the elements of **O**s and **X**s into alternating columns. We are likely to see the example of the principle of closure as a triangle, even though some of the parts are missing. In the principle of good continuation example, we see two connected upward-pointing angles with a wavy line going across them. In the example of the principle of common fate, if the **O**s were moving in the direction indicated by the arrows, then we would group together the four upward-moving **O**s and the four downward-moving **O**s.

As stated earlier, we tend to group the parts of a display using such principles because these principles reflect the regularities that exist in real-world objects. For example, the parts of real-world objects tend to be close together rather than far apart (proximity), and they tend to be made of similar materials and have similarly shaped and colored parts (similarity). Realworld objects also often have parts of them obscured by other objects and therefore have gaps in their outlines that must be completed (closure). Finally, real-world objects have extended lines and curves (good continuation), and their parts move together when the object

Gestalt Principles of Grouping		
Principle	Statement of Principle	Example
Proximity	Objects close together are more likeley to be grouped into a perceptual unit than objects farther apart.	O O O O O O O O O O O O O O O O O O O O O O O O O O O O
Similarity	Objects that are similar to each other are likely to be grouped together.	O X O X O X O X O X O X O X O X O X O X O X O X
Closure	We tend to see figures as complete, filling in any gaps that may be present when parts are missing or obscured from view.	
Good Continuation	Elements arranged in a straight line or smooth curve are likely to be grouped together.	
Common Fate	When objects move in a similar fashion (at the same time, same speed, same direction), they are grouped together as part of the same figure.	

FIGURE 5.9 ▨ Gestalt principles of grouping.

moves (common fate). These principles of organization do not just apply to vision; they have also been shown to apply to musical stimuli. For example, the explanation for the scale illusion discussed in the box on page 196 is that we perceptually reorganize the tones based on proximity of pitch (Deutsch, 1974).

Figure-Ground Organization

Another important contribution of the Gestalt psychologists regarding how we organize our perception of the world is called figure-ground organization. The information we receive from the environment gets divided into two parts: the figure and the ground.

The figure part of the display has a definite shape; it seems closer to us and occupies a definite location in space, and is more dominant—the object of our attention. The ground, on the other hand, is a shapeless background for the figure, appearing behind the figure at some unspecified location. A picture illustrating figure-ground organization is presented in **Figure 5.10**. Although most often illustrated with visual examples, figure-ground organization also applies to nonvisual perceptions. For many people, when listening to music, the main melody is typically the focus of their attention, standing out against a somewhat formless background of musical accompaniment.

Usually, when looking at a visual input, one part of the scene immediately stands out as the figure and, if we continue to look at the picture, this organization

© Jupiterimages Corporation.

FIGURE 5.10 ▨ An example of figure-ground organization.

Sensation and Perception

remains unchanged. However, when certain types of figures are presented against certain types of backgrounds, the figure and ground appear to reverse after staring at the display for a period of time. **Figure 5.11** presents one of the most famous displays showing ambiguous figure-ground relationships: the goblet-faces figure first presented by Rubin in 1915. In this figure you can see either a white goblet against a black background, or two outlined black faces against a white background. Note that while both organizations are possible, we see only one or the other of them at any given time. If you are familiar with the work of the artist M. C. Escher, you may be aware that he often incorporated ambiguous figure-ground displays in his work.

FIGURE 5.11 ▪ Rubin's goblet-faces reversible figure.

Depth Perception

We not only perceive meaningful objects organized and grouped in predictable ways, but we also perceive these objects as occupying a particular location in three-dimensional space. A classic question in the field of perception asks how we come to perceive the world as three-dimensional, with objects in the world located at various distances away from us, when the retinal images formed by objects in the world are two-dimensional. In other words, what is the basis of our perception of depth or distance? The answer to the question involves the fact that the information reaching our retinas contains a number of sources of information about where in the environment objects are located. These sources of information about the depth or distance of objects, which are referred to as depth cues, are typically divided into two major classes. Those that require the use of both eyes are called binocular cues, and those that require the use of only one eye are called monocular cues. It is to these two sources of depth information that we now turn.

Binocular Cues

One binocular depth cue is convergence, the degree to which the two eyes must turn in toward one another so that the image of the object projects on the fovea of each eye. The degree to which the eyes must converge to accomplish this depends, at least up to a distance of about 20 feet, on how far away the object is located. To appreciate that convergence varies with distance, stare at one of your fingers held at arm's length. Then, keeping both eyes focused on your finger, move your finger slowly toward your nose. You should be aware of the fact that your eyes have to keep turning further inward to maintain your focus as the finger gets closer to your nose. Thus, at least for objects relatively close to us, the degree to which the eyes are converged provides a potential source of information about the distances of objects.

BINOCULAR CUES
1. Convergence: The degree to which the two eyes must turn in toward one another so that the image projects on the fovea of each eye.
2. Retinal Disparity: The difference in the two retinal images from objects at different distances from the observer.

Another binocular cue to distance is based on the fact that, because the two eyes are separated by a given distance, the two eyes receive a slightly different view of objects at any distance different from the distance at which one

© myVector, 2009. Used under license from Shutterstock, Inc.

is focused. How much one eye's view of an object differs from the other eye's view varies as a function of the distance of the object from one's fixation distance. This cue is called retinal disparity, and it is the basis of what is typically called stereoscopic vision. The brain fuses the two images and interprets the degree of retinal disparity as an indication of where the object is located in three-dimensional space. In the nineteenth century, stereoscopes were used to present two slightly different pictures of objects to each eye. The resulting perception was a vivid three-dimensional view of the object or scene presented. A modern version of the stereoscope, with which you are probably familiar, is the Viewmaster viewer. The principle of providing each eye with a slightly different view of a scene is also the basis of three-dimensional movies. Special glasses, which selectively filter out what each eye sees, create retinal disparity when viewing such movies. The result is that objects appear to project out of the screen toward the viewer. Autostereograms, which create impressive three-dimensional effects from disparity presented in a single image, became extremely popular during the 1990s, appearing in books such as the *Magic Eye* (Thomas, 1993).

Monocular Cues

Close one eye and notice what happens. The world continues to maintain its three-dimensional appearance even though the binocular cues just described have been eliminated. This effect indicates that at least some information about depth and distance requires the use of only one eye. There are several monocular distance cues. One cue that may be used at close distances is accommodation. As discussed earlier in this chapter, accommodation is the process in which the lens of the eye changes shape to keep nearby objects in focus. Closer objects

Courtesy of the author

The boys must be in front of the sports car because they are blocking your view of it. This is an illustration of the monocular depth cue, occlusion.

require greater accommodation, which requires more exertion by the ciliary muscles that control the shape of the lens. Thus, the brain may use information about the activity of these muscles as a cue to distance, with more activity indicating focusing at a closer distance. A second monocular cue, motion parallax, involves motion. Objects at different distances from the point of fixation appear to move at different speeds and in different directions when you are in motion. Specifically, objects that are farther than your point of fixation appear to move more slowly and in the same direction in which your head is moving, whereas objects closer than the point of fixation appear to move more rapidly and in the opposite direction in which your head is moving. You may have noticed this effect if you have ever looked out the side window of a car while traveling down the highway (hopefully as a passenger rather than when driving). If you focus at an intermediate distance, objects nearer than your point of fixation, such as brush and street signs near the road, appear to rapidly whiz past in the opposite direction from which you are traveling. Objects farther away than your point of fixation, such as trees way off in the distance, appear to move much more slowly and in the same direction, relative to the point of fixation, in which you are traveling. Motion parallax is a powerful cue—simply moving your head from side to side provides a great deal of information about distance.

MONOCULAR CUES

1. Accommodation: Degree of ciliary muscle tension
2. Motion parallax: Differences in speed and direction of movement relative to fixation point
3. Pictorial cues: Occlusion, relative size, elevation, shading and highlights, linear perspective, texture gradients, and atmospheric perspective

---

A final category of monocular cues are called pictorial depth cues, because they are the same cues used by artists to portray a sense of depth and distance in their paintings. Occlusion (interposition) refers to the fact that objects that are nearer to you tend to block, or occlude, more distant objects. In **Figure 5.12**, we can tell that the younger boy is closer because he occludes the view of the boy behind him, and both of them occlude the view of the more distant background objects and scenery. Relative size refers to the fact that when two similar objects appear together, the one that takes up more space in the field of view (and likewise on the retina) is seen as being closer. In **Figure 5.13**, the nearer trees appear larger than the more distant trees. Another pictorial distance cue is elevation: Objects that are nearer to the horizon line are perceived as being more distant. In **Figure 5.13**, the trees that are nearer to the horizon appear more distant than the trees that are farther from the horizon line. Shading and highlights also provide a cue to depth. In **Figure 5.14**, you can see the pictorial cues of linear perspective and texture gradients. Linear perspective refers to the fact that parallel lines appear to converge (get closer together) toward a vanishing point as they move away from the observer. Notice in **Figure 5.14** that the lines defining the left side of the bridge appear to become closer together as they move farther into the distance. Likewise, the lines defining the right side of the bridge converge, as do the lines defining the floor of the bridge. **Figure 5.14** also illustrates a texture gradient. With increasing distance, textures appear to be more fine-grained, with the textural elements appearing smaller and more densely packed together. In the figure, the visible "pieces" of the vertical posts appear more spread out in the nearer part of the photograph and appear more densely packed

FIGURE 5.12 ■ Occlusion as a distance cue.

© Hydromet, 2009. Used under license from Shutterstock, Inc.

FIGURE 5.13 ■ The distance cues of relative size and distance.

together with increasing distance. The final pictorial cue is atmospheric perspective. Particles in the atmosphere, such as dust and water droplets, differentially scatter light of different wavelengths, which makes more distant objects take on a bluish or purplish tint and appear more blurred. In **Figure 5.15**, the more distant hills appear hazy and somewhat bluish, unlike the nearer parts of the landscape that are green and in sharp focus.

Perceptual Constancy

As we move around in the world, and as objects in the environment move, the information reaching our retinas changes continually. However, our perception is not of an environment inhabited by objects that chaotically change shape, size, color, and lightness. Instead, our perception of the world is relatively stable and constant. The characteristics of the objects we perceive remain relatively unchanged despite the numerous changes taking place in the information reaching our eyes. Such **perceptual constancy** provides another indication that perception takes place in the brain rather than in the eyes. If perception simply depended on the information reaching our eyes at any given moment in time, our experience of the world would be both unstable and quite confusing.

To make the concept of perceptual constancy more concrete, we will describe some examples. Assume a friend approaches you from the opposite side of a room. As he moves toward you, his image on your retina becomes much larger. If he now moves away again, the retinal image gets smaller. However,

Perceptual constancy:
Characteristics of the objects we perceive remain relatively unchanged despite the numerous changes taking place in the information reaching our eyes.

© Virfir, 2009. Used under license from Shutterstock, Inc.

FIGURE 5.14 ■ Linear perspective and texture gradient.

despite such changes in the size of the retinal image of your friend, your perception of his size remains unchanged. The fact that people, and other objects, appear to remain the same size as their distance from you changes is called **size constancy**.

A second example of a perceptual constancy is **shape constancy**. Try the following demonstration: Hold a quarter directly in front of you, perpendicular to your eyes. It will project a circular image on your retina. Now, place the quarter flat on a table and look at it from various angles. As you do so, the image of the quarter on your retina will have various oval shapes depending on the viewing angle. However, you will still perceive the quarter as being circular, rather than as some sort of oval shape.

There are other perceptual constancies, such as **lightness constancy**, in which the perceived lightness of an object remains unchanged despite changes in overall illumination levels, and color constancy, in which the perceived color of objects does not change despite changes in the wavelengths of light being reflected from them in different lighting conditions. For example, both the overall lightness and the color of your shirt will appear the same as you move from indoor lighting to outdoor sunlight, even though there is a dramatic change in both the amount of light being reflected and in the particular wavelengths being reflected from your shirt in these two different lighting conditions.

All of these examples show that we do not simply sense the momentary images projected on our retinas. The retinal images formed on the eye are simply information. Our perception of the world uses all of the information available,

Size constancy: Objects appear to remain the same size as the distance from you changes.

Shape constancy: Perception of an object's shape remains unchanged, despite changes in the shape of the retinal image.

Lightness constancy: The lightness of an object remains unchanged even when the amount of illumination changes greatly.

FIGURE 5.15 ■ Atmospheric perspective.

combining various forms of information to arrive at a consistent interpretation of what's out there in the environment. We perceive the size of objects not simply based on the size of the retinal image present, but based on all the information available about the object. Thus, information about where the object is located, provided by the various distance cues available, may affect how a given size retinal image is interpreted. In a recent study, Granrud (2006) found that even four-month-old infants demonstrate a form of size constancy by taking distance into account. Likewise, whether an object is perceived as being black or white, or light or dark, depends not only on how much light is being reflected to our eyes by that object but also on how much light is being reflected by nearby objects and/or how much total light is actually present.

Rules govern the final interpretation of the information being received. One such rule might be that an object near to us will yield a relatively large retinal image, but the same object, when much farther away, will yield a relatively small retinal image. Another rule might be that an object of constant size covers the same relative amount of the visual field regardless of the distance from the observer to the object. These rules, for interpreting what a given pattern of information represents, are likely in most situations to result in an accurate perception of the nature of our environment. However, occasionally our perceptual systems are fooled by the incoming information, resulting in a misperception of what's out there. Indeed, an incorrect application of the principles that lead to constancy has been proposed for some of the illusions presented earlier in this chapter. Consider, for example, the moon illusion in which the moon appears larger when on the horizon than when it is overhead. One popular explanation of this illusion

(Kaufman & Rock, 1962) is that the moon is perceived as being farther away (even though it is not actually farther away) when it is on the horizon because of the presence of numerous distance cues compared with when it is overhead. Usually, when something that is farther away creates the same size retinal image as an object that is nearer, the more distant object is in fact larger. Thus, some have proposed that the moon illusion results from an incorrect application of the rules that we use to maintain size constancy and that because the moon appears to be more distant when it is on the horizon, it is seen as larger than when it is overhead and appears to be nearer. Likewise, one popular explanation of the Ponzo illusion is that we interpret the figure as three-dimensional because of the distance cue of linear perspective (Gregory, 1970), in which parallel lines appear to converge with increasing distance. Therefore, the top horizontal line is seen as being farther away than the bottom horizontal line; however, because they are actually the same size, they each create retinal images of the same size. As in the moon illusion, if two objects have the same retinal image size but one is farther away than the other, our perceptual system concludes that the more distant object must be larger. It should be noted that there are numerous explanations of these illusions that do not rely on distance cues, and we are not trying to argue that the explanations presented here are the only possible explanations of these illusions. The point here is that the rules used in interpreting illusions are the same rules that usually result in accurate perceptions. Indeed, the reason for studying illusions is that they tell us something about how perception works in everyday situations. The possible effects of misperceiving the distance of objects is simply one example of this point.

Bottom-Up and Top-Down Processing

Our discussion of perception to this point, exemplified in the model of perception presented in Figure 5.2, has focused on **bottom-up processing** in which a stimulus from the environment reaches our sensory organs, is transduced, and is then relayed to progressively higher areas of the brain. However, an important aspect of human perception is left out if we talk about only bottom-up processing. When humans encounter objects and events in the environment, they do so from the perspective of a knowledge base accumulated from past interactions with their environment. As a result, when we encounter incoming information from the environment, we don't have to simply wait passively for bottom-up processing to inform us what is out there. We know from past experience how the world is organized, and we have expectations based on this knowledge about what is likely, and unlikely, to occur in certain situations. Our knowledge and expectations allow us to perceive things based on often incomplete information. This is fortunate because in many real-world situations, the incoming information is incomplete. Imagine you were reading a book in which a bit of ink had been spilled, obscuring the part of the word indicated by * in the following sentence: "He removed the *eel from the orange before he ate it." If perception were based purely on bottom-up processes, you would not be able to interpret the word because there is no stimulus letter present. Yet, you probably had no difficulty determining that the word should be "peel." Likewise, imagine you saw the same stimulus in a different context: "He removed the *eel from the car in order to change the tire." In this case, you would have no difficulty determining that the word should be "wheel." In addition, the same bottom-up information (*eel) is present in both examples, yet you interpret the word differently depending on the context. This phenomenon works for hearing as well and is called the phonemic restoration effect. In an experiment by Warren (1970), listeners heard sentences similar to those just given in which the missing sound (a phoneme) in a word was replaced by a coughing noise. Listeners "heard" the missing phoneme even though it was not physically present; in fact, they did not even notice that

Bottom-up processing: Beginning with low-level analysis and working up to higher levels that occur in the cortex.

Top-down processing: The perceiver's knowledge and expectations may affect perception.

a portion of the word had been missing. The point of these examples is that **top-down processing** has a major influence on perception. Specifically, top-down processing refers to the use of our existing knowledge and expectations, often based on context, in perception. Such processing is called top-down because higher-order cognitive processes affect how the lower-level processes proceed. At times, top-down processing can have undesired effects on perception. For example, if we are expecting an important phone call, we may mistake other sounds for the sound of a phone ringing. However, in general, top-down processing facilitates perception. Both top-down processing and bottom-up processing working together are critical in accounting for our ability to perceive the world quickly and accurately in most situations.

SUMMARY

Our perception of the world is not direct and infallible. It is the result of a complicated series of processes, beginning with the information reaching our sense receptors being transduced into neural impulses and continuing until the resulting pattern of activity in the brain is interpreted. All sensory systems have absolute thresholds and difference thresholds and show sensory adaptation. In vision, light reflected from objects is focused on the retina, where the photoreceptors—the rods and cones—convert it to neural impulses. These neural impulses are then transmitted to the occipital lobes of the brain. Color vision can be accounted for by combining the principles of trichromatic and opponent-process theories.

In hearing, sounds reaching our ears result in our eardrums vibrating, and these vibrations are carried by the ossicles to the inner ear, where they generate movements in the fluid in the cochlea. These movements result in the bending of the inner hair cells, which results in neural impulses being transmitted to the temporal lobes. Place theory and frequency theory account for how the auditory system codes for pitch.

Even though the information reaching our sense organs is continuously changing, we perceive objects and events as relatively stable and constant. The principles of how perceptual experiences are organized were originally described by the Gestalt psychologists. We are able to perceive the world as three-dimensional through the processing of binocular and monocular depth cues. The processing rules our perceptual systems use can result in both perceptual constancies and the experience of illusions. Both bottom-up processing and top-down processing are involved in most real-world situations.

MATCHING

1. jnd
2. Linear perspective
3. Pupil
4. Inner hair cells
5. Convergence
6. Cone
7. Dark adaptation
8. Absolute threshold
9. Lens
10. Sensory adaptation
11. Psychophysics
12. Cornea

A. weakest stimulus that can be detected
B. reduced responsiveness to continuous stimulation
C. increased sensitivity in the absence of light
D. accommodation
E. smallest change in stimulation that can be detected
F. astigmatism
G. receptor cells for hearing
H. relationship between physical and psychological characteristics
I. represents distance in photographs
J. controls amount of light entering the eye
K. photoreceptor
L. binocular depth cue

FILL IN THE BLANKS

1. _____ are receptors in the skin that respond to temperature.
2. The structure of the inner ear, which like the retina in the eye, contains the actual receptor cells is the _____.
3. The Gestalt principle of _____ states that objects close together are more likely to be grouped together than objects far apart.
4. Ambiguous figures and visual illusions create problems for the _____ view of perception.
5. The photoreceptors primarily responsible for vision at night are the _____.
6. The physical characteristic of light that is the main determinant of the psychological dimension of vision called hue is _____.
7. The receptor cells change environmental energy into neural impulses, a process called _____.
8. The theory of color vision that maintains that the human eye contains three different kinds of receptors, each of which responds best to a particular wavelength of light, is the _____ theory.
9. If you need four units of change to notice a difference with a standard stimulus of 20 units, you will need eight units of change if the standard stimulus is 40 units. _____ is being described.
10. The depth cue which forms the basis of three-dimensional movies is _____.

SHORT-ANSWER QUESTIONS

1. Explain why perceptual psychologists consider the study of visual illusions important.

2. Give two reasons why naïve realism is incorrect.

3. Explain what the Gestalt psychologists meant by the idea that "the whole is different from the sum of its parts."

4. Describe three things that the different senses all have in common.

5. Describe, with an example, what is meant by perceptual constancy.

IDENTIFYING DEPTH CUES

For each of the following, indicate the depth cue that is being described.

1. In a photograph of a long stretch of road that moves straight away from the observer, the road far away from the observer is much narrower than the road close to the observer.

2. In the Muppets show at MGM studios in Florida, they give you a special set of glasses to wear during the movie. While wearing the glasses, the characters in the movie appear to be coming out of the screen into the audience.

3. An artist wants to show one set of pine trees in the foreground of a painting and another set of similar pine trees way off in the distance. The artist draws the pine trees in the foreground much larger than she draws the distant pine trees.

4. You just got your vacation photos back. You notice that in your photo of your friends in the mountains, your friends, who were a few feet in front of you, appear clear and distinct. However, the distant mountains don't appear very clear and they appear to have a somewhat bluish color.

5. Your friend just constructed a long walkway made up of individual stones laid out in a very regular pattern. When you are standing at one end of the walkway looking at the part near you, the individual stones making up the pattern are quite distinct and the spaces between the stones appear to be quite wide. However, when you shift your gaze to the far end of the walkway, the individual stones are hard to make out as the stones appear to be very close together, with little space appearing between the stones.

6. You are standing in your living room with your face against the window. You are looking out at a bird that is perched in a tree about 30 feet away. The bird flies right up to the feeder attached to the window, directly in front of you. You notice that you really have to turn your eyes inward to see the bird clearly.

7. As you look at the neighbor's yard across the street, you notice that the person standing in front of the tree in your neighbor's yard partially blocks out some of your view of the tree. You also notice that the tree, which is located in front of the neighbor's house, blocks out part of your view of the house.

ILLUSORY SIZE JUDGMENTS

You will need one friend or family member for this exercise. Tear out the next two pages and give them, one at a time, to the person you selected to carry out this exercise. There is a horizontal line on each page and a dot some distance below the line. When you give the person each page, tell the person you want him or her to draw a line that appears to be the same length as the line on the page. The person must start the line being drawn at the dot. After the person has drawn both lines, measure each line using a millimeter ruler. Record the person's judgments (to the nearest millimeter) in the spaces below. This is an attempt to demonstrate, with quantitative data, the Müller-Lyer illusion described in this chapter. The line with the inward-pointing arrowheads should be judged to be shorter than the line with the outward-pointing arrow feathers. The difference between the lengths of the two lines drawn shows how large the illusion is for this individual. Record the illusion score in the space indicated.

LENGTH OF THE ARROWHEADS LINE: _____ MILLIMETERS

LENGTH OF THE ARROW FEATHERS LINE: _____ MILLIMETERS

ILLUSION SCORE: _____ MILLIMETERS

TOP-DOWN PROCESSING

Tear out the next page and give it to a friend or family member. Have the friend or family member read the messages on the page, one at a time. Ask the reader to read out loud at his or her normal reading speed. DON'T TELL THE PERSON THAT EACH OF THE MESSAGES HAS A FUNCTION WORD REPEATED, BUT NOTE WHETHER OR NOT THEY READ THE REPEATED WORD TWICE. When the person is finished reading both statements, take the sheet away and ask whether he or she noticed anything strange about the statements just read. Record the person's response and whether the person read the extra word in neither of the sentences (0), in one of the sentences (1), or in both of the sentences (2). Write this information on the bottom of this page.

Read each of the following statements, one at a time. Read them out loud at your normal reading speed.

May the joy of the holiday season be with you for all the days of of the coming year.

The grass is always greener on the the other side of the fence.

KEY TERMS

absolute threshold
accommodation
ambiguous (reversible) figures
basilar membrane
blind spot
bottom-up processing
cochlea
cones
convergence
cornea
dark adaptation
difference threshold
feature detectors
fovea

hue
illusions
inner ear
inner hair cells
just noticeable difference (jnd)
lens
lightness
lightness constancy
middle ear
moon illusion
naïve realism
organ of Corti
outer ear
perception
perceptual constancy
presbyopia

psychophysics
pupil
retina
rods
saturation
sensation
sensory adaptation
shape constancy
signal detection theory
size constancy
top-down processing
transduction
Weber's law

Chapter 5: Sensation and Perception

END OF CHAPTER QUIZ

1. The field of study that examines the connection between physical stimuli and human perception is called:
   a. Psychophysics
   b. Signal detection theory
   c. Weber's Law
   d. Memory

2. Which of the following is analyzed so that you get a perception of hue?
   a. Color
   b. Brightness
   c. Wavelength cycle
   d. Wavelength amplitude
   e. Rods

3. Which of the following is MOST CLOSELY linked anatomically to the blind spot?
   a. Fovea
   b. Optic chiasm
   c. Visual cortex
   d. Optic nerve

4. Analysis that begins with the sense receptors and works up to the brain's integration of sensory information is called:
   a. Bottom up processing
   b. Top down processing
   c. Psychophysics
   d. Sensation

5. The minimal stimulus intensity needed to report observing a stimulus 50% of the time is called:
   a. Absolute threshold
   b. Difference threshold
   c. Perception
   d. Signal detection

6. The area of your eye on which light is focused is called the:
   a. Fovea
   b. Blind spot
   c. Iris
   d. Rods

7. Light waves which make you see GREEN are actually green-colored light waves.
   a. True
   b. False

8. Which of the following is a correct opponent-process color pair?
   a. Yellow-green
   b. Blue-red
   c. Yellow-red
   d. Red-green

9. Increases in sound wave amplitude increases:
   a. Pitch
   b. Tone
   c. Loudness
   d. Key

10. Which of the following is the name for your sense of balance?
    a. Sensorineural
    b. Vestibular
    c. Cochlear
    d. Kinesthesis

11. The Cocktail-Party effect and the Necker Cube are both examples of:
    a. Perceptual set
    b. Perceptual adaptation
    c. Form perception
    d. Selective attention

12. Our inability to consciously perceive all the sensory information available to us at any single point in time best illustrates the necessity of:
    a. Selective attention
    b. Perceptual adaptation
    c. Perceptual constancy
    d. The phi phenomenon

13. Which of the following is known as a chemical sense?
    a. Vision
    b. Hearing
    c. Smell
    d. Balance

14. The Muller-Lyer illusion is created by changing:
    a. Line angles
    b. Odor strength
    c. Loudness
    d. Confusion

15. Which of the following is NOT a perceptual grouping factor?
    a. Proximity
    b. Closeness
    c. Shading
    d. Closure

16. Generally, "figure" occupies more area than "ground."
    a. True
    b. False

17. Which of the following does NOT influence binocular depth perception?
    a. Retinal disparity
    b. Distance to the object
    c. Neuromuscular cues from your eye muscles
    d. Interposition

18. With respect to the monocular cues for depth perception, which of the following is FALSE?
    a. Smaller objects are more distant.
    b. Parallel lines converge with distance.
    c. Smaller images seem closer.
    d. Closer objects move more quickly.

19. With respect to the monocular cues for depth perception, which of the following is FALSE?
    a. Closer objects move more quickly.
    b. Smaller objects are more distant.
    c. Higher objects appear more distant.
    d. Hazy objects appear closer.

20. A gestalt is best described as a(n):
    a. Binocular cue
    b. Perceptual adaptation
    c. Organized whole
    d. Perceptual set

21. The idea that your sensations accurately reflect the reality around you is called:
    a. Constancy
    b. Detection theory
    c. Naïve realism
    d. Transduction
    e. Absolute threshold

22. The process by which physical objects and energy are detected and processed by your nervous system is called:
    a. Sensation
    b. Perception
    c. Convergence
    d. Illusions
    e. Constancy

23. Which of the following is the name for the most widely accepted theory/methodology in psychophysics?
    a. Weber's law
    b. Helmholtz's constant
    c. Just-noticeable-difference theory
    d. Signal detection theory
    e. Naïve realism

24. This concept is defined by the point at which the observer shows a fifty percent accuracy in detecting the presence of the stimulus.
    a. Absolute threshold
    b. Difference threshold
    c. Convergence threshold
    d. Psychophysical threshold
    e. Detection theory

25. This concept is defined by the point at which the observer shows a fifty percent accuracy in detecting the presence of a change in a stimulus.
    a. Absolute threshold
    b. Difference threshold
    c. Convergence threshold
    d. Psychophysical threshold
    e. Detection theory

26. The name for when sensory detectors are used continuously and become fatigued and turn off briefly is called:
    a. Basilar threshold
    b. Accommodation
    c. Retinal degradation
    d. Size constancy
    e. Sensory adaptation

27. Without arguing the physics of light energy, psychologists have generally accepted that light is:
    a. A tiny photon ball that travels in a wave pattern
    b. A tine photon ball that travels is a straight line
    c. An energy wave
    d. Not electromagnetic radiation

28. The reason you can see color is because the physical properties of light at different wavelengths have different colors.
    a. True
    b. False ✓

29. Color is a perceptual phenomenon with no physical basis outside of your body except for photon wavelengths.
    a. True ✓
    b. False

30. Which of the following visual phenomena are processed in both the retina as well as the brain?
    a. Line angles
    b. Faces
    c. Color ✓
    d. Motion

31. Which three colors does trichromatic theory involve?
    a. Red, green, blue ✓
    b. Red, orange, yellow
    c. Yellow, green, blue
    d. Orange, yellow, blue
    e. Red, yellow, blue

32. The color of an object is dependent upon the total amount and proportions of the various wavelengths available when you are looking at it.
    a. True ✓
    b. False

33. The fact that you perceive objects as having one color, despite the changing relative proportions of wavelengths projected from it is called:
    a. Illusions
    b. Saturation
    c. Sensory adaptation
    d. Transduction
    e. Color constancy ✓

34. Which of the following colors is the opponent color of red?
    a. Red
    b. Yellow
    c. White
    d. Blue
    e. Green ✓

35. When the amplitude of a sound's wavelength changes you get the perception of a changing:
    a. Pitch
    b. Volume ✓
    c. Treble
    d. Bass
    e. Constancy

36. At the beginning of the auditory canal is the:
    a. Eustachian tube
    b. Stapes ✓
    c. Semicircular canals
    d. Tympanic membrane
    e. Pinna

37. Damage to the pinna, tympanic membrane or the auditory sensory nerves will result in the same symptoms of hearing loss.
    a. True
    b. False ✓

38. Your tactile sense can detect:
    a. Pressure and vibration
    b. Pressure and temperature
    c. Pain and vibration
    d. Pressure, vibration, temperature and pain
    e. Pressure, vibration, tickle, temperature and pain ✓

39. Which of the following pairs constitute the chemical senses?
    a. Sight and hearing
    b. Sight and smell
    c. Taste and smell ✓
    d. Taste and hearing
    e. Balance and sight

40. The difference between your vestibular and kinesthetic senses is your ability to detect:
    a. Balance and limb location ✓
    b. Balance and nausea
    c. Nausea and limb location
    d. Balance, limb location and nausea

41. Which of the following is not an example of selective attention?
    a. Accommodation ✓
    b. Necker cube
    c. Cocktail party effect
    d. Change blindness

42. Which of the following cues has been found to be the most relevant in the understanding of perceptual phenomena?
    a. The stimulus
    b. The context
    c. The stimulus and context
    d. Memory capacity

43. The tendency to pay more attention to visual stimuli as opposed to other types of stimuli is called:
    a. Visual capture
    b. Naïve realism
    c. Detection theory
    d. Saturation theory
    e. Weber's law

44. Which of the following occupies the least area of an image?
    a. Figure
    b. Context
    c. Signal
    d. Ground

45. Which percentage of your depth perception comes from monocular cues?
    a. 10%
    b. 30%
    c. 50%
    d. 90%
    e. Depth perception only comes from binocular cues

46. Which of the following is not related to binocular depth perception?
    a. Retinal disparity
    b. Convergence
    c. Occipital lobe
    d. Interposition

47. Interposition is related to:
    a. When things off the horizon appear to be further away
    b. When things further away appear more blurry
    c. When closer objects cast a larger image on your retina
    d. When close objects block your view of objects that are further away

48. Relative size is related to:
    a. When things off the horizon appear to be further away
    b. When things further away appear more blurry
    c. When closer objects cast a larger image on your retina
    d. When close objects block your view of objects that are further away

49. Relative clarity is related to:
    a. When things off the horizon appear to be further away
    b. When things further away appear more blurry
    c. When closer objects cast a larger image on your retina
    d. When close objects block your view of objects that are further away

50. Relative height is related to:
    a. When things off the horizon appear to be further away
    b. When things further away appear more blurry
    c. When closer objects cast a larger image on your retina
    d. When close objects block your view of objects that are further away

Answers: 1. a; 2. c; 3. d; 4. a; 5. a; 6. a; 7. b; 8. d; 9. c; 10. b; 11. d; 12. a; 13. c; 14. a; 15. c; 16. b; 17. d; 18. c; 19. d; 20. c; 21. c; 22. a; 23. d; 24. a; 25. b; 26. e; 27. a; 28. b; 29. a; 30. c; 31. a; 32. a; 33. e; 34. e; 35. b; 36. b; 37. b; 38. d; 39. c; 40. a; 41. a; 42. c; 43. a; 44. a; 45. d; 46. d; 47. d; 48. c; 49. b; 50. a

6 | *States of Consciousness*

I Feel I've Been Here Before

Have you ever visited a location for the first time and felt like you had already been there before? This feeling, usually named déjà vu, or more specifically, déjà visté, may have some biological underpinnings.

Since 1971, there has been research on the cellular basis of spatial mapping. Many of the studies from that work show that there are cells devoted to locating where you are among the objects in your environment and other cells that help you navigate through those objects. For instance, knowing where you are in the library is generally associated with place cells but your ability to travel through the library without bumping into objects is related to grid cells. Both types of cells signal the hippocampus. The hippocampus then activates memories related to those locations and directions. Of course, knowing that there are brain cells dedicated to spatial mapping does not automatically explain our déjà vu experiences. Rather, we need to add more to our explanation.

Evidence indicates that grid cells influence memory recall of events that occurred in a particular location. Therefore, part of our explanation comes from the activity of brain cells and another part comes from associative learning. All learning involves the association between two different events within some environmental context. Therefore, the next time you feel like you have "been here before," recall that the associations formed between the grid and place cells helping you navigate the world are linked to memories. Those memories of places may be just similar enough to old, forgotten locations to make you feel that you have been there before.

References

Hafting, T., Fyhn, M., Molden, S., Moser, M. B., and Moser, E. I. (2005). Microstructure of a spatial map in the entorhinal cortex. *Nature*, 436, 801–806.

O'Keefe, J., Dostrovsky, J. (1971). The hippocampus as a spatial map. Preliminary evidence from unit activity in the freely-moving rat. *Brain Research*, 34, 171–175.

CHAPTER OUTLINE

TERRY WALLIS—AWAKENED AFTER ALMOST 20 YEARS

Imagine falling asleep at the age of 19 and waking up nearly 20 years later. With no memories of the last 2 decades, you open your eyes to a world that has changed drastically. You see that the people you love have aged, seemingly quite suddenly. Meanwhile, you are oblivious to the fact that they have held a worried vigil at your bedside for weeks and months that turned into years and years.

This story is Terry Wallis's story. He was 19 years old in 1984 when the pickup truck he was driving went through a guardrail and dove off a 25-foot bluff. Terry was found paralyzed and in a coma, unable to communicate. For the next 19 years, he persisted in a state of minimal consciousness, occasionally grunting or nodding, seemingly awake but not communicative. His parents took him home every other week and continued to talk to him, but they never knew if he had any awareness of what was going on. Then, one day in 2003, Terry shocked everyone by answering "Mom" when one of his nursing home caretakers asked him who his visitor was that day.

The last 3 years have seen improvements in Terry's functioning. He is now able to count to 25. But more important, to his family he has become "himself" again, making jokes and expressing joy at being alive. A real-life Rip Van Winkle, Terry Wallis has taken a while to accommodate to his new world. He still believes that Ronald Reagan is president, and until recently he could not imagine that he was 42 years old, not a young adult of 20.

Recoveries such as Terry's are extremely rare. And now, for the first time, scientists have evidence of how he recovered. In the summer of 2006, neuroscientists Henning Voss and his colleagues (2006) published the first proof that Terry's brain had actually rewired itself, allowing him to regain consciousness. Using the new technology of diffusion tensor imaging, or DTI, the researchers showed that nerve cells in Terry's brain (cells that were damaged but not destroyed by his accident) had made new connections, over time restoring him to consciousness. During what seemed like a long wait to everyone who loved him, Terry's brain was engaged in a complex process of healing, with his brain cells slowly forming new connections and finally making enough to form a network. Terry's return to conscious life and his sense that he is himself again are based on the recovery of conscious awareness.

From *The Science of Psychology: an Appreciative View* by Laura King. © 2008 by The McGraw-Hill Companies. Reprinted with permission of The McGraw-Hill Companies.

PREVIEW

Such is the enormous importance of consciousness in human life, the focus of this chapter. We first review the meaning of various states of consciousness. We next explore the intriguing world of sleep and dreams, states in which most of us spend a great deal of time. Then we turn to the topic of hypnosis—a technique that may provide ways to harness altered consciousness—before exploring various altered states of consciousness produced by psychoactive drugs. The chapter closes with a look at the important role of consciousness in health and wellness.

THE NATURE OF CONSCIOUSNESS

Objective 1   **Discuss the nature of consciousness.**

In his entry for *consciousness* in the 1989 *Dictionary of Psychology*, British psychologist Stuart Sutherland gave the following pessimistic assessment: "Consciousness is a fascinating but elusive phenomenon; it is impossible to specify what it is, what it does, or why it evolved. Nothing worth reading has ever been written about it." Although Sutherland dismissed the potential for scientific research on consciousness, this "fascinating but elusive" aspect of life has interested psychologists for centuries, down to the present day, and for good reason: Consciousness is a crucial part of many human experiences (Owen & others, 2006; Pinker, 2007).

On an autumn afternoon, when you see a beautiful tree, vibrant with color, you are not simply perceiving the colors; you are aware as well that you are seeing them. Many emotional experiences also rely on consciousness. You would never feel embarrassment, for example, except that you have conscious awareness of yourself as a social object. *Metacognition* refers to thinking about thinking (Pressley & Harris, 2006). When you think about your thoughts—for example, when you reflect on why you are so nervous before an exam—you are using your conscious awareness to examine your own thought processes. This awareness might even have significance for survival. Recently it has been argued that consciousness is adaptive, because it gives us a feeling that we are truly special, heightening our motivation to survive (Humphrey, 2006).

In the late nineteenth and early twentieth centuries, psychology pioneers such as Sigmund Freud and William James took great interest in the study of the conscious and unconscious mind. However, for much of the twentieth century, psychologists shifted instead to a focus on behaviors and on the rewards and punishments that determined those behaviors (Skinner, 1938; Watson, 1913). In the past decade, though, the study of consciousness has gained widespread respectability in psychology (Mashour, 2006). For the first time in many decades, psychologists from many different fields are interested in consciousness, including its relation to subconsciousness (Hebb, 2002; Lamme, 2006; Wiens, 2006).

Although there is disagreement about a proper definition, we can define consciousness in terms of its two parts: awareness and arousal. **Consciousness** refers to *awareness* of external events and internal sensations, including awareness of the self and thoughts about one's experiences; this awareness occurs under a condition of *arousal*, the physiological state of being engaged with the environment. Thus, a sleeping person is not conscious in the same way as he or she would be while awake.

The contents of our awareness change from moment to moment. Information moves rapidly in and out of consciousness. William James (1890/1950) described the mind as a stream of consciousness—a continuous flow of changing sensations, images, thoughts, and feelings. Our minds can race from one topic to the next: from thinking about the person approaching us to our physical state today to our strategy for the test tomorrow to the café where we are going to have lunch.

Consciousness: Awareness of external events and internal sensations, including awareness of the self and thoughts about one's experiences; this awareness occurs under a condition of arousal.

Stream of consciousness: James's concept that the mind is a continuous flow of changing sensations, images, thoughts, and feelings.

Consciousness and the Brain

One of the great unanswered questions about consciousness involves its location. Does consciousness stand alone (located in what might be called the *mind*), separate in some way from the brain (Livaditis & Tsatalmpasidou, 2007)? Or is it an intrinsic aspect of the brain's functioning? If consciousness is in the brain, is there a particular location that is the seat of consciousness, or is consciousness distributed across different areas (Arshavsky, 2006)?

Most neuroscientists do not believe that a specific location in the brain takes incoming information from one's body and the world and converts it into the conscious world we are aware of and can report on. Rather, it is likely that separate distributed processing systems connect to produce consciousness. Depending on what a person is aware of at a particular point in time, different areas of the brain "light up," or are activated (Nunez & Srinivasan, 2006; Seth & others, 2006).

The two aspects of consciousness, awareness and arousal, are associated with different parts of the brain. Awareness, the subjective state of being conscious of what is going on, typically involves the cerebral cortex, especially its association areas and frontal lobes (Macknik, 2006; Rees, 2007). It may be that the integration of input from the senses, along with information about emotions and memories in the association areas, creates consciousness (Bloom, Nelson, & Lazerson, 2001). Arousal is a physiological state determined by the reticular activating system, a network of structures including the brain stem, medulla, and thalamus. Damage to either of the two areas related to consciousness may cause a coma.

Levels of Awareness

The flow of sensations, images, thoughts, and feelings that William James spoke of can occur at different levels of awareness. Although we might think of consciousness as either present or not, there are in fact shades of awareness, observed in coma patients as well as in everyday life. Here we consider five levels of awareness: higher-level consciousness, lower-level consciousness, altered states of consciousness, subconscious awareness, and no awareness **(Figure 6.1)**.

Higher-Level Consciousness

Controlled processes represent the most alert states of human consciousness, in which individuals actively focus their efforts toward a goal (Tanida & Poppel, 2006). Watch Maria as she struggles to master the unfamiliar buttons on her new 10-function cell phone. She does not hear you humming to yourself or notice the intriguing shadow on the wall. Her state of focused awareness is what is meant by controlled processes.

Controlled processes require selective attention, the ability to focus on a specific aspect of experience while ignoring others (Gunstad & others, 2006).

Lower-Level Awareness

Beneath the level of controlled processes are other levels of conscious awareness. Lower levels of awareness include automatic processes and the familiar state of daydreaming.

Automatic Processes

A few weeks after acquiring her cell phone, Maria flips it open and sends a text message in the middle of a conversation with you. Her fingers fly almost automatically across the buttons. She does not have to concentrate on the keys now and hardly seems aware of the gadget in her hand as she continues to talk to you while finishing her lunch. For her, using her cell phone has reached the point of automatic processing. **Automatic processes** are states of consciousness that require little attention and do not interfere with other

Controlled processes:
The most alert states of consciousness, in which individuals actively focus their efforts toward a goal.

Automatic processes:
States of consciousness that require little attention and do not interfere with other ongoing activities.

Level of Awareness	Description	Examples
Higher-Level Consciousness	Involves controlled processing, in which individuals actively focus their efforts on attaining a goal; the most alert state of consciousness.	Doing a math or science problem; preparing for a debate; taking an at-bat in a baseball game.
Lower-Level Consciousness	Includes automatic processing that requires little attention, as well as daydreaming.	Punching in a number on a cell phone; typing on a keyboard when one is an expert; gazing at a sunset.
Altered States of Consciousness	Can be produced by drugs, trauma, fatigue, possibly hypnosis, and sensory deprivation.	Feeling the effects of having taken alcohol or psychedelic drugs; undergoing hypnosis to quit smoking or lose weight.
Subconscious Awareness	Can occur when people are awake, as well as when they are sleeping and dreaming.	Sleeping and dreaming.
No Awareness	Freud's belief that some unconscious thoughts are too laden with anxiety and other negative emotions for consciousness to admit them.	Having unconscious thoughts; being knocked out by a blow or anesthetized.

FIGURE 6.1 ■ Levels of Awareness.
Each level of awareness has its time and place in human life.

ongoing activities. Automatic processes require less conscious effort than controlled processes (Aarts, Custers, & Holland, 2007; Lieberman, 2007; Moors & De Houwer, 2006). When we are awake, our automatic behaviors occur at a lower level of awareness than controlled processes, but they are still conscious behaviors. Maria pushed the right buttons, so at some level she apparently was aware of what she was doing.

Daydreaming

Another state of consciousness that involves a low level of conscious effort, *daydreaming* lies somewhere between active consciousness and dreaming while we are asleep. It is a little like dreaming while we are awake. Daydreams usually begin spontaneously when we are doing something that requires less than our full attention.

Mind wandering is probably the most obvious type of daydreaming. We regularly take brief side trips into our own private kingdoms of imagery and memory while reading, listening, or working. When we daydream, we drift into a world of fantasy. We imagine ourselves on dates, at parties, on television, in faraway places, at another time in our lives, and so on. Sometimes our daydreams are about everyday events such as paying the rent, going to the dentist, and meeting with somebody at school or work.

The semiautomatic flow of daydreaming can be useful. As you daydream while you shave, iron a pair of pants, or walk to the store, you may make plans, solve a problem, or come up with a creative idea. Daydreams can remind us of important things ahead. Daydreaming keeps our minds active while helping us to cope, create, and fantasize (Klinger, 2000).

Altered States of Consciousness

Altered states of consciousness or awareness are mental states that are noticeably different from normal awareness. They can be produced by drugs, trauma, fatigue, possibly hypnosis, and sensory deprivation (Avner, 2006). In some cases, drug use may create a higher level of awareness (Fields, 2007). The popularity of coffee and other beverages that contain caffeine, a stimulant drug, provides evidence of the widespread belief that caffeine increases alertness. Awareness also may be altered to a lower level. Alcohol has this effect.

Subconscious Awareness

We saw that a great deal of brain activity is going on beneath the level of conscious awareness. Psychologists are increasingly interested in subconscious processing of information, which can take place while we are awake or asleep (Gaillard & others, 2006).

Waking Subconscious Awareness

When we are awake, processes are going on just below the surface of awareness. For example, while you are grappling with a problem, the solution may just "pop" into your head. Such insights can occur when a subconscious connection between ideas is so strong that it rises into awareness, somewhat the way a cork held underwater bobs to the surface as soon as it is released (Csikszentmihalyi, 1995).

Evidence that we are not always aware of the processing of information in our brains comes from studies of individuals with certain neurological disorders. In one case, a woman who suffered neurological damage was unable to describe or report the shape or size of objects in her visual field, although she was capable of describing other physical perceptions that she had (Milner & Goodale, 1995). Yet when she reached for an object, she could accurately adjust the size of her grip to allow her to grasp the object. Thus, she did possess some subconscious knowledge of the size and shape of objects, even though she had no awareness of this knowledge.

Subconscious information processing can occur simultaneously in a distributed manner along many parallel tracks. For example, when you look at a dog running down the street, you are consciously aware of the event but not of the subconscious processing of the object's identity (a dog), its color (black), and its movement (fast). In contrast, conscious processing is *serial*. That is, it occurs in sequence and is slower than much subconscious processing.

Sleep and Dreams

When we sleep and dream, our level of awareness is lower than when we daydream, but sleep and dreams are not best regarded as the absence of consciousness (Zeman, 2006). Rather, they are low levels of consciousness.

Consider the German chemist August Kekulé, who in 1865 developed the insight that the benzene molecule might be shaped like a ring. This idea occurred to him after he fell asleep while watching sparks in the fireplace make circles in the air. If he had remained awake, Kekulé would likely have rejected as ridiculous the notion of a link between the sparks and the shape of the benzene molecule. However, in his subconscious mind rational thought could not censor the connection, so when Kekulé woke up he could not ignore its possibility. It may be that irrelevant connections fade away and disappear but those that are robust survive long enough to emerge eventually into consciousness (Csikszentmihalyi, 1995).

Researchers have found that when people are asleep, they remain aware of external stimuli to some degree. For example, in sleep laboratories, when people are clearly asleep (as determined by physiological monitoring devices), they are able to respond to faint tones by pressing a handheld button (Ogilvie & Wilkinson, 1988). In one study, the presentation of pure auditory tones to sleeping individuals activated auditory processing regions of the brain, whereas participants' names activated language areas, the amygdala, and the prefrontal cortex (Stickgold, 2001). We return to the topics of sleep and dreams in the next section.

Among those who practice altered states of consciousness are Zen monks who explore the Buddha-nature at the center of their beings.

No Awareness

The term *unconscious* generally applies to someone who has been knocked out by a blow or anesthetized, or who has fallen into a deep, prolonged unconscious state (Harden, Dey, & Gawne-Cain, 2007; Valentine & Curl, 2006). However, Sigmund Freud (1917) used the term *unconscious* in a very different way. At about the same time that William James was charting the shifting nature of our stream of consciousness, Freud concluded that most of our thoughts are unconscious. **Unconscious thought**, said Freud, is a reservoir of unacceptable wishes, feelings, and thoughts that are beyond conscious awareness.

Freud's interpretation viewed the unconscious as a storehouse for vile thoughts. Freud believed that some aspects of our experience remain unconscious for good reason, as if we are better off not knowing about them. Although Freud's ideas remain controversial, psychologists now widely accept the notion that unconscious processes do exist (Cramer, 2000). Recently, researchers have found that many mental processes (thoughts, emotions, and perceptions) can occur outside of awareness. Some psychologists term these processes *nonconscious* rather than *unconscious*, to avoid the Freudian connotation (Bargh, 2006).

For further insights on consciousness, see the Intersection, which explores children's beliefs and understanding of how the mind works and the implications of these beliefs and understanding for their social functioning.

Unconscious thought: Freud's concept of a reservoir of unacceptable wishes, feelings, and thoughts that are beyond conscious awareness.

CONSCIOUSNESS AND DEVELOPMENTAL PSYCHOLOGY: HOW DO WE DEVELOP A SENSE FOR THE MINDS OF OTHERS?

Imagine yourself in a conversation with a friend, describing a complex issue you have been thinking about. While talking, you search your friend's face for signs of understanding. Does she nod? Does her brow furrow? As you talk, you watch her face and body for signs of what you think is going on in her head. In a sense, although you may have never thought of it this way, these observations reveal your belief in your friend's consciousness. You

Continued

pause and ask, "Do you see what I mean?" When you do, you are checking in on your conversation partner's mind.

There is perhaps no greater mystery than what is going on behind another person's eyes.

The way human beings interact in a situation such as this gives us clues about how we think others think. It might seem obvious that other people have "minds of their own," but the human ability to recognize the subjective experience of another is a true developmental accomplishment. Developmental psychologists who study children's ideas about mental states use the phrase *theory of mind* to refer to individuals' understanding that they and others think, feel, perceive, and have private experiences (Pressley & Hilden, 2006).

In subtle ways, children reveal very early in life their sense that other people think. For example, if a 6-month-old sees a person talking to someone who is hidden behind a curtain, the child will be surprised if the curtain is opened to reveal an object rather than another person. This outcome suggests that even an infant "knows" that people talk to people (Legerstee, Barna, & DiAdamo, 2000). When a 9-month-old points to something he or she wants, these actions imply that the infant recognizes that the other person can understand that he or she wants something (Tomasello, 2006). If a toddler sees someone express disgust for a particular food, such as a cookie, she will know that the person would prefer some other food over the cookie that she herself prefers (Repacholi & Gopnik, 1997). At around ages 2 and 3, children can talk about mental states—indicating, for example, that they know that someone might feel sad if he or she does not get a hoped-for present (Wellman, Philips, & Rodriguez, 2000). Around that same time, children understand that they can know something someone else does not know, and they start telling fibs (Harris, 2006).

Developmental psychologists have used a clever procedure called the false belief task to examine children's theory of mind (Sabbagh, Moses, & Shiverick, 2006). In one version of the false belief task, the child is asked to consider the following situation (Wellman & Woolley, 1990). Anna is a little girl who has some chocolate that she decides to save for later. She puts it in a blue cupboard and goes outside to play. While Anna is gone, her mother moves the chocolate to the red cupboard. When Anna comes back in, where will she look for her chocolate? Three-year-olds give the wrong answer—they assume that Anna will look in the red cupboard because they know (even though Anna does not) that Anna's mom moved the chocolate to the red one. But 4-year-olds answer correctly—they recognize that Anna does not know everything they do and that she will believe the chocolate is where she left it (Wellman & Woolley, 1990). Success at the false belief task is associated with social competence, and children who perform well at it are better liked by their peers (Cassidy & others, 2003; Leslie, German, & Polizzi, 2005).

Theory of mind is essential to many valuable social capacities, such as empathy and sympathy (Lockl & Schneider, 2007; Volim & others, 2006). We know we have found a true kindred spirit when someone really "gets" us—when a friend can say, "I know exactly what you mean." When we have a problem, we might look to someone we trust to get his or her point of view. Theory of mind means that we know that others *have* a point of view. Our desire that others should know all of what is going on in our head is demonstrated by the use of emoticons in e-mails and instant messages. Why is it important to include a :) or a ;)? These icons fill in the missing pieces of our full intentions for our electronic correspondent.

Simon Baron-Cohen (1995, 2006) is an expert on autism, a disorder that affects communication and social interaction. He has proposed that the emergence of theory of mind is so central to human functioning that evolution would not leave it up to chance. Indeed, Baron-Cohen suggests that we are born with a brain mechanism that is ready to develop a theory of mind. This theory of mind mechanism (or TOMM) accounts for the fact that nearly all children over the age of 4 pass the false belief task, even children with the genetic disorder Down syndrome. Baron-Cohen has proposed that autistic individuals lack the TOMM, a condition that would explain their unique social deficits. Indeed, he has referred to autism as "mind blindness."

Fascinating research has revealed the very social nature of theory of mind. Using a procedure similar to the false belief test, researchers direct children to watch as a photograph is taken of Big Bird sitting on a bed. Before the photograph is developed, the kids observe Big Bird moving to the bathtub. The question for the child is, Where will Big Bird be in the photograph, once it is developed? In this situation, 3-year-olds perform quite poorly, thinking that Big Bird will be in the bathtub. But autistic children of a variety of ages get the answer right (Leslie & Thais, 1992; Zaitchik, 1990). In this situation, success at the task does not require a mental representation of another's mind.

We often use our own internal states as a "default" for judging how another person is feeling or thinking (Royzman, Cassidy, & Baron, 2003), but the autistic individual has no such luxury. Indeed, research has shown that the autistic amygdala has fewer neurons devoted to processing emotion than the non-autistic amygdala (Schumann & Amaral, 2006). Temple Grandin (2006), an accomplished scientist who is autistic, has described in her memoir *Thinking in Pictures* how she has had to memorize and practice the kinds of things that go on effortlessly in other people's heads. For example, she must commit to memory the fact that nonautistic people think in words, not images, and that their facial expressions reveal important information about their feelings. To support individuals who are coping with such challenges, researchers have designed special training programs for people who have Asperger syndrome (a type of autism typically associated with normal levels of IQ) and high-functioning autism (a kind of autism in which individuals are able to function close to or above normal levels in society). The programs aim to help these individuals decode the complex emotional messages conveyed by facial expressions and tone of voice (Golan & Baron-Cohen, 2006). Researchers have found that such training increases activation of the fusiform face area in the brain, which, as discussed in Chapter 3, is vital in human face recognition (Bolte & others, 2006).

But even with our remarkable TOMM in full working order, our intuitions about others are sometimes inaccurate. We might love someone who does not return our feelings. Or we might trust a person who does not have our best interest at heart. There is perhaps no greater mystery than what is going on behind another person's eyes. What another person knows, thinks, believes, and wants—these are questions that have fascinated human beings since the beginning of our species.

■ REVIEW AND SHARPEN YOUR THINKING

Discuss the nature of consciousness.

- ■ Explain the brain's role in consciousness.
- ■ Define consciousness and describe five levels of awareness.

How many different states of awareness have you experienced? In one or two sentences each, describe the nature of your experience in each state.

SLEEP AND DREAMS

Objective 2   **Explain the nature of sleep and dreams.**

Sleep claims about one-third of the time in our lives, more than any other pursuit. What is sleep, and why is it so important? This section explores the answers to these questions, as well as the fascinating world of dreams. First, let's see how sleep is linked to our internal biological rhythms.

Biological Rhythms and Sleep

Biological rhythms:
Periodic physiological
fluctuations in the body.

Biological rhythms are periodic physiological fluctuations in the body. We are unaware of most biological rhythms, such as the rise and fall of hormones and accelerated and decelerated cycles of brain activity, but they can influence our behavior. These rhythms are controlled by biological clocks, which include

- *Annual or seasonal cycles*, such as the migration of birds, the hibernation of bears, and the seasonal fluctuations of humans' eating habits
- *Twenty-eight-day cycles*, such as the female menstrual cycle, which averages 28 days
- *Twenty-four-hour cycles*, such as the sleep/wake cycle and temperature changes in the body

Let's further explore the 24-hour cycles.

Circadian Rhythms

Circadian rhythm: A daily
behavioral or physiological
cycle, such as the
sleep/wake cycle.

A **circadian rhythm** is a daily behavioral or physiological cycle. Daily circadian rhythms involve the sleep/wake cycle, body temperature, blood pressure, and blood sugar level (Skene & Arendt, 2006). The term *circadian* comes from the Latin words *circa*, meaning "about," and *dies*, meaning "day." For example, body temperature fluctuates about 3 degrees Fahrenheit in a 24-hour day, peaking in the afternoon and reaching its lowest point between 2 A.M. and 5 A.M.

**Suprachiasmatic nucleus
(SCN):** A small structure in
the brain that synchronizes
its own rhythm with the
daily cycle of light and dark
based on input from the
retina.

Researchers have discovered that the change from day to night is monitored by the **suprachiasmatic nucleus (SCN)**, a small structure in the brain that synchronizes its own rhythm with the daily cycle of light and dark based on input from the retina (Michel & others, 2006). Output from the SCN allows the hypothalamus to regulate daily rhythms such as temperature and hunger and the reticular formation to regulate daily rhythms of sleep and wakefulness (**Figure 6.2**). Although a number of biological clocks or pacemakers seem to be involved in regulating circadian rhythms, researchers have found that the SCN is the most important one (Buijs & others, 2006).

Many individuals who are totally blind experience lifelong sleeping problems because their retinas are unable to detect light. These people have a kind of permanent jet lag and periodic insomnia because their circadian rhythms often do not follow a 24-hour cycle (National Institute of Neurological Disorders and Stroke, 2001).

Desynchronizing the Biological Clock

Biological clocks can become desynchronized, or thrown off their regular schedules. Among the circumstances of modern life that can introduce irregularities into our sleep are jet travel, changing work shifts, and insomnia. What effects might such irregularities have on circadian rhythms?

If you fly from Los Angeles to New York and then go to bed at 11 P.M. eastern time, you may have trouble falling asleep because your body is still on west

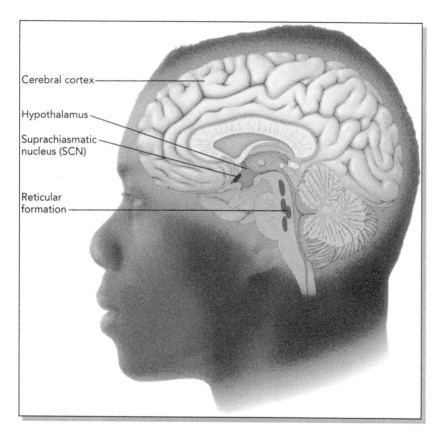

Cerebral cortex

Hypothalamus

Suprachiasmatic
nucleus (SCN)

Reticular
formation

FIGURE 6.2 ■ Suprachiasmatic Nucleus.
The suprachiasmatic nucleus (SCN) plays an important role in keeping our biological clock running on time. The SCN is located in the hypothalamus. It receives information from the retina about light, which is the external stimulus that synchronizes the SCN. Output from the SCN is distributed to the rest of the hypothalamus and to the reticular formation.

coast time. Even if you sleep for 8 hours that night, you may have a hard time waking up at 7 A.M. eastern time, because your body thinks it is 4 A.M. If you stay in New York for several days, your body will adjust to this new schedule.

The jet lag you experience when you fly from Los Angeles to New York occurs because your body time is out of phase, or synchronization, with clock time (Lack & Wright, 2007). Jet lag is the result of two or more body rhythms being out of sync. You usually go to bed when your body temperature begins to drop, but in your new location, you might be trying to go to sleep when it is rising. In the morning, your adrenal glands release large doses of the hormone *cortisol* to help you wake up. In your new geographic time zone, the glands may be releasing this chemical just as you are getting ready for bed at night.

Circadian rhythms may also become desynchronized when shift workers change their work hours (Lee, Smith, & Eastman, 2006). A number of near accidents in air travel have been associated with pilots who have not yet become synchronized to their new shifts and are not working as efficiently as usual (Kim & Lee, 2007).

Shift-work problems most often affect night-shift workers who never fully adjust to sleeping in the daytime after their work shifts. Such workers may fall asleep at work and are at increased risk for heart disease and gastrointestinal disorders (Fujino & others, 2006). But not all shift workers are affected equally (Monk, 1993). Individuals older than 50, those who require more than 9 hours of

Traveling by jet across a number of time zones and changing to a night-shift job can desynchronize our biological clocks and can affect our circadian rhythms and performance. Sleep deprivation has negative implications for academic performance.

sleep a night, and those with a tendency to be "morning types" (get up early, go to bed early) are the most adversely affected by shift work.

Resetting the Biological Clock

If your biological clock for sleeping and waking becomes desynchronized, how can you reset it? With regard to jet lag, if you take a transoceanic flight and arrive at your destination during the day, it is a good idea to spend as much time outside in the daylight as possible. Bright light during the day, especially in the morning, increases wakefulness, whereas bright light at night delays sleep (Oren & Terman, 1998).

Melatonin, a hormone that increases at night in humans, also is being studied for its possible effects in reducing jet lag (Pandi-Perumal & others, 2007). Recent studies have shown that a small dosage of melatonin can reduce jet lag by advancing the circadian clock, which makes it useful for eastward jet lag but not westward jet lag (Waterhouse & others, 2007).

Why Do We Need Sleep?

Everyone sleeps, and when we do not get enough sleep, we often do not function well, physically and mentally. The important benefits of sleep include restoration, adaptation, growth, and memory.

Because all animals require sleep, it seems that sleep is a fundamental mechanism for survival. Examining the evolutionary basis for sleep, scientists have proposed that sleep restores, replenishes, and rebuilds our brains and bodies, which can become worn out or used up by the day's waking activities. This idea fits with the feeling of being worn out or tired before we go to sleep and restored when we wake up.

In support of the restorative function of sleep, many of the body's cells show increased production and reduced breakdown of proteins during deep sleep (National Institute of Neurological Disorders and Stroke, 2001). Protein molecules are the building blocks needed for cell growth and for repair of damages from factors such as stress Also, some neuroscientists believe that sleep gives neurons that are used while we are awake a chance to shut down and repair themselves (National Institute of Neurological Disorders and Stroke, 2001). Without sleep, neurons might become so depleted in energy or so pol-luted by the by-products of cellular activity that they begin to malfunction.

In addition to having a restorative function, sleep has had an adaptive evolutionary function. Sleep may have developed because animals needed to protect themselves. For example, for some animals the search for food and water is easier and safer when the sun is up. When it is dark, it is adaptive for these animals to save energy, prevent getting eaten, and avoid falling off a cliff that they cannot see. In general, animals that serve as food for other animals sleep the least. **Figure 6.3** portrays the average amount of sleep per day of various animals.

Sleep also may be beneficial to physical growth and increased brain development in infants and children. For exam-ple, deep sleep coincides with the release of growth hormone in children (National Institute of Neurological Disorders and Stroke, 2001). The lack of sleep is stressful, and stress hor-mones may interfere with the creation of neurons in the hip-pocampus: the part of the brain most associated with memory (Mirescu & others, 2006).

In fact, the important role of sleep in the consolidation, storage, and maintenance of long-term memory is now recog-nized (Born, Rasch, & Gais, 2006; Walker & Stickgold, 2006). One possible explanation is that during sleep the cerebral cortex is not busy with the processing of sensory input, active aware-ness, and motor functions. Therefore, it is free to conduct activ-ities that strengthen memory associations, so that memories formed during recent waking hours can be integrated into long-term memory storage.

Are you thinking about studying all night for the next test in one of your classes? You might want to think again. In one study, a good night's sleep helped the brain to store the memory of what had been learned during the day (Stickgold & Hobson, 2000). In the study, the memory of individuals who stayed up all night for one of the nights during the study was inferior to the memory of individuals who got a good night's sleep every night during the study. Lost sleep often results in lost memories (Kalia, 2006).

The Effects of Chronic Sleep Deprivation

Testing the limits of his capacity to function without sleep, one 17-year-old high school student, Randy Gardner, went without sleep for 264 hours (about 11 days), the longest observed period of total sleep deprivation. He did it as part of a science fair project (Dement, 1978). Randy, who was carefully monitored by sleep researchers, did suffer some hallucinations, as well as speech and movement problems. However, on the last night, Randy played arcade games with sleep researcher William Dement and consis-tently beat him. Randy recovered fully, as well as could be detected, after a 14-hour, 40-minute restorative sleep. Randy's story is exceptional in that he was able to maintain a high level of physical activity and in that he received national TV coverage, which helped him to stay awake. Even so, he almost fell asleep several times, but his observers would not let him close his eyes. Under more normal circumstances, individuals have far more dif-ficulty staying awake all night, especially between 3 A.M. and 6 A.M.

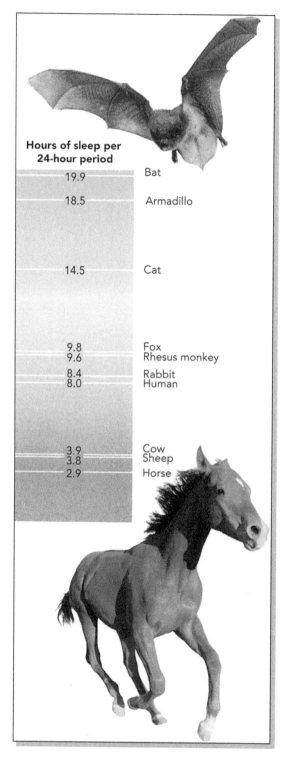

Hours of sleep per 24-hour period

19.9	Bat
18.5	Armadillo
14.5	Cat
9.8	Fox
9.6	Rhesus monkey
8.4	Rabbit
8.0	Human
3.9	Cow
3.8	Sheep
2.9	Horse

FIGURE 6.3 ■ From Bats to Horses: The Wide Range of Sleep in Animals.
We might feel envious of bats, which sleep nearly 20 hours a day, and more than a little in awe of horses, still running on just under 3 hours of rest.

Although Randy Gardner went about 11 days without sleep, the following discussion should convince you that even getting 60 to 90 minutes less sleep than you need at night can harm your ability to perform optimally the next day. Optimal performance is enhanced by sleeping more than 8 hours a night and reduced by sleeping less (Habeck & others, 2004). Lack of sleep is stressful and has impact on our bodies (Goh & others, 2001) and, of course, our brains. For example, in one study, brain scans showed that sleep deprivation decreased brain activity in the thalamus and the prefrontal cortex (Thomas & others, 2001). Alertness and cognitive performance declined, along with brain activity. In another study, sleep deprivation was linked with an inability to sustain attention (Doran, Van Dongen, & Dinges, 2001). Research using EEGs of individuals deprived of sleep for 24 hours revealed a decline in the complexity of brain activity (Jeong & others, 2001). Research using fMRI has shown that when deprived of sleep, the brain must compensate by using other pathways for cognitive work (Drummond & others, 2005) and that interactions among areas of the brain differ during problem solving (Stricker & others, 2006).

Sleep deprivation also can affect decision making, especially dealing with the unexpected, innovation, revising plans, and effective communication (Harrison & Horne, 2000). Sleep can also influence moral judgment. A recent study demonstrated that following 53 hours of wakefulness, participants had more difficulty making moral decisions and were more likely to agree with decisions that violated their personal standards (Killgore & others, 2007).

Sleep, then, is key to optimal performance, both physically and mentally. Yet, many of us do not get sufficient sleep. In a national survey of more than 1,000 American adults conducted by the National Sleep Foundation (2001), 63 percent said that they get less than 8 hours of sleep a night, and 31 percent said that they get less than 7 hours of sleep a night. Many said they try to catch up on their sleep on the weekend, but they still reported getting less than 8 hours on weekend nights. Forty percent of those surveyed said that they become so sleepy during the day that their work suffers at least a few days per month, and 22 percent said their work suffers a few days each week. Seven percent said sleepiness on the job is a daily problem for them. It is estimated that 50 to 70 million Americans chronically suffer from lack of sleep or a sleep disorder (Institute of Medicine, 2006). The Institute of Medicine declared that sleep deprivation is an unmet health problem in the United States (2006).

Why are Americans getting too little sleep? Work pressures, school pressures, family obligations, and social obligations often lead to long hours of wakefulness and irregular sleep/wake schedules (Kiernan & others, 2006). Not having enough hours to do all we want to do in a day, we cheat on our sleep. Most people need to get 60 to 90 minutes more sleep each night than they presently get.

Sleep Deprivation in Adolescents and Older Adults

Might changing sleep patterns in adolescence contribute to adolescents' health-compromising behaviors? Recently there has been a surge of interest in adolescent sleep patterns (Carskadon, 2005, 2006; Carskadon, Mindell, & Drake, 2006; Crowley, Acebo, & Carskadon, 2007; Dahl, 2006).

The National Sleep Foundation (2006) conducted a U.S. survey of 1,602 caregivers and their 11- to 17-year-olds. Forty-five percent of the adolescents got inadequate sleep on school nights (less than 8 hours). Older adolescents (ninth- to twelfth-graders) got markedly less sleep on school nights than younger adolescents (sixth-to eighth-graders)—specifically, 62 percent of the older adolescents got inadequate sleep compared to 21 percent of the younger adolescents. Adolescents who got inadequate sleep (8 hours or less) on school nights were more likely to feel more tired or sleepy, and more cranky and irritable; to fall asleep in school; to be in a depressed mood; and to drink caffeinated beverages than their counterparts who got optimal sleep (9 or more hours).

Many adolescents stay up later at night and sleep longer in the morning than they did when they were children, and this changing timetable has physiological underpinnings. These findings have implications for the hours during which adolescents learn most effectively in school (Carskadon, Mindell, & Drake, 2006; Hansen & others, 2005).

Mary Carskadon and her colleagues have conducted a number of research studies on adolescent sleep patterns (Carskadon, 2005, 2006; Carskadon, Acebo, & Jenni, 2004; Carskadon, Mindell, & Drake, 2006). They found that when given the opportunity, adolescents will sleep an average of 9 hours and 25 minutes a night. Most get considerably less than 9 hours of sleep, especially during the week. This shortfall creates a sleep deficit, which adolescents often attempt to make up on the weekend. The researchers also found that older adolescents tend to be sleepier during the day than younger adolescents. They theorized that this sleepiness was not due to academic work or social pressures. Rather, their research suggests that adolescents' biological clocks undergo a shift as they get older, delaying their period of wakefulness by about 1 hour. A delay in the nightly release of the sleep-inducing hormone melatonin, produced in the brain's pineal gland, seems to underlie this shift. Melatonin is secreted at about 9:30 P.M. in younger adolescents and approximately an hour later in older adolescents.

Carskadon has suggested that early school starting times may cause grogginess, inattention in class, and poor performance on tests. Based on her research, school officials in Edina, Minnesota, decided to start classes at 8:30 A.M. rather than the usual 7:25 A.M. Since then there have been fewer referrals for discipline problems, and the number of students who report being ill or depressed has decreased. The school system reports that test scores have improved for high school students, but not for middle school students. This finding supports Carskadon's suspicion that early start times are likely to be more stressful for older than for younger adolescents.

Sleep patterns also change as people age through the middle-adult (40s and 50s) and late-adult (60s and older) years (Ancoli-Israel, 2006; Dijk, 2006). Many adults go to bed earlier at night and wake up earlier in the morning. Thus, a clear reversal occurs in the time at which individuals go to bed—later to bed as adolescents, earlier to bed in middle age. Beginning in the 40s, individuals report that they are less likely to sleep through the entire night than when they were younger. Middle-aged adults also spend less time in the deepest sleep stage than when they were younger. More than 50 percent of individuals in late adulthood report that they experience some degree of insomnia (Kamel & Gammack, 2006; Wolkove & others, 2007).

Think about your own sleep patterns. Are you getting enough sleep? See the Psychology and Life box.

Developmental changes in sleep patterns during adolescence can influence alertness at school.

Sleep Stages

Have you ever been awakened from your sleep and been totally disoriented? Have you ever awakened in the middle of a dream and gone right back into the dream as if it were a movie running just under the surface of your consciousness? These two circumstances reflect two distinct stages in the sleep cycle.

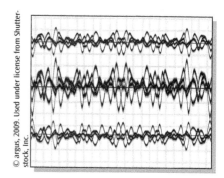

An individual being monitored by an EEG in a sleep experiment.

Stages of sleep correspond to massive electrophysiological changes that occur throughout the brain as the fast, irregular, and low-amplitude electrical activity of wakefulness is replaced by the slow, regular, high-amplitude waves of deep sleep. Using the electroencephalograph (EEG) to monitor the brain's electrical activity, scientists have discovered five distinct stages of sleep and two stages of wakefulness.

When people are awake, their EEG patterns exhibit two types of waves: beta and alpha. *Beta waves* reflect wakefulness. These waves are the highest in frequency and lowest in amplitude. They also are more *desynchronous* than other waves. Desynchronous waves do not form a very consistent pattern. Inconsistent patterning makes sense, given the extensive variation in sensory input and activities we experience when we are awake. When we are relaxed but still awake, our brain waves slow down, increase in amplitude, and become more *synchronous*, or regular. These waves are called *alpha waves*. The five stages of sleep are differentiated by the types of wave patterns detected with an EEG, and the depth of sleep varies from one stage to another.

PSYCHOLOGY AND LIFE

Do You Get Enough Sleep?

Some people seem to take a "do it all" approach to life, pushing and pushing themselves without listening to what their body is telling them about its level of exhaustion (Aziz & Zickar, 2006). In fact, no amount of motivation is going to overcome the physical limits of our bodies. Sleep is an essential restorative element in a healthy life (Zheng & others, 2006).

Imagine how differently such people might view their lifestyle if insufficient sleep had consequences for their interactions with others. Think about it in personal terms: You would not stop brushing your teeth, because you would not want to have bad breath. You would not avoid showering for days on end, because your physical state would be socially unacceptable. What if tired people started to have bad breath or smell funky? Consider how much more support the world might provide for the occasional nap! Even though people generally do not smell bad when they are tired, they owe it to themselves to sleep when sleep is needed. The brain is a remarkable organ, capable of doing an awful lot for us, but it cannot work its best magic without reasonable time for refueling.

Many college students do not get enough sleep (Brown, Buboltz, & Soper, 2006). To evaluate whether you are sleep-deprived, place a check mark next to the following items.

Yes	No	
____	____	I need an alarm clock to wake up at the appropriate time.
____	____	It is a struggle for me to get out of bed in the morning.
____	____	I feel tired, irritable, and stressed out during the week.
____	____	I have trouble concentrating.
____	____	I have trouble remembering.
____	____	I feel slow with critical thinking, problem solving, and being creative.
____	____	I often fall asleep watching TV.
____	____	I often fall asleep in boring meetings or lectures in warm rooms.

_____ _____ I often fall asleep after heavy meals or after low doses
of alcohol.
_____ _____ I often fall asleep within 5 minutes of getting into bed.
_____ _____ I often feel drowsy while driving.
_____ _____ I often sleep extra hours on weekend mornings.
_____ _____ I often need a nap to get through the day.
_____ _____ I have dark circles around my eyes.

According to sleep expert James Maas (1998), who developed this quiz, if you responded "yes" to three or more of these items, you probably are not getting enough sleep.

If you are not getting enough sleep, the following behavioral strategies for what sleep experts call "good sleep hygiene" might help you:

1. Reduce stress as much as possible.
2. Exercise regularly, but not just before you go to bed.
3. Keep mentally stimulated during the day.
4. Become a good time manager.
5. Eat a proper diet.
6. Stop smoking.
7. Reduce caffeine intake, especially in the afternoon.
8. Avoid alcohol, especially near bedtime.
9. Take a warm bath before bed.
10. Maintain a relaxing atmosphere in the bedroom and keep the temperature cool.
11. Clear your mind at bedtime.
12. Before going to bed, use a relaxation technique, such as listening to a CD designed for relaxation.
13. Learn to value sleep.
14. Go to bed and wake up at the same time every day, even on weekends.
15. If necessary, contact the health service at your college or university for advice about your sleeping problem.

Stages 1–4

Stage 1 sleep is characterized by _theta waves_, which are even slower in frequency and greater in amplitude than alpha waves. The difference between just being relaxed and stage 1 sleep is gradual. **Figure 6.4** shows the EEG pattern of stage 1 sleep, along with the EEG patterns for the other four sleep stages and beta and alpha waves.

In _stage 2 sleep_, theta waves continue but are interspersed with a defining characteristic of stage 2 sleep: _sleep spindles_. These involve a sudden increase in wave frequency (Fogel & Smith, 2006). Stages 1 and 2 are both relatively light stages of sleep, and if people awaken during one of these stages, they often report not having been asleep at all.

Stage 3 and _stage 4 sleep_ are characterized by _delta waves_, the slowest and highest-amplitude brain waves during sleep. These two stages are often referred to as _delta sleep_. Distinguishing between stage 3 and stage 4 is difficult, although typically stage 3 is characterized by delta waves occurring less than 50 percent of the time and stage 4 by delta waves occurring more than 50 percent of the time. Delta sleep is our deepest sleep, the time when our brain waves are least like waking brain waves. It is during delta sleep that it is the most difficult to wake sleepers. When they are awakened during this stage, they usually are confused and disoriented.

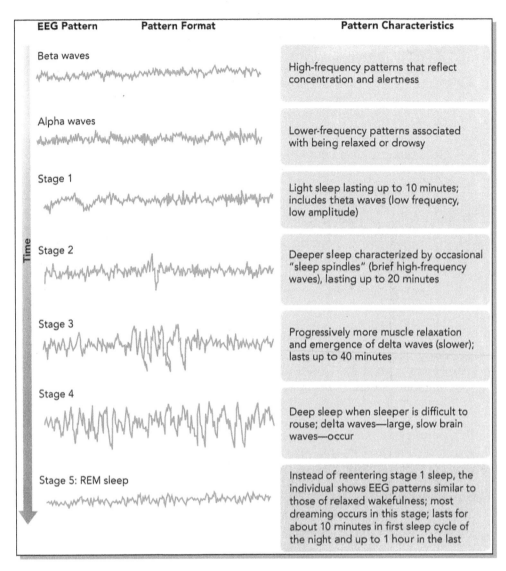

FIGURE 6.4 ■ Characteristics and Formats of EEG Recordings During Stages of Sleep.
Even while we are sleeping, our brains are busy. No wonder we sometimes wake up feeling tired.

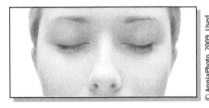

FIGURE 6.5 ■ REM Sleep
During REM sleep, your eyes move rapidly, as if following the images moving in your dreams.

REM sleep: Rapid eye movement sleep; stage 5 of sleep, in which dreaming occurs.

REM Sleep

After going through stages 1–4, sleepers drift up through the sleep stages toward wakefulness. But instead of reentering stage 1, they enter *stage 5*, a different form of sleep called *REM (rapid eye movement) sleep* (Dan & Boyd, 2006). **REM sleep** is an active stage of sleep during which dreaming occurs. During REM sleep, the EEG pattern shows fast waves similar to those of relaxed wakefulness, and the sleeper's eyeballs move up and down and from left to right (**Figure 6.5**).

Stages 1–4 are referred to as *non-REM sleep*. Non-REM sleep is characterized by a lack of rapid eye movement and little dreaming. A person who is awakened during REM sleep is more likely to report having dreamed than when awakened at any other stage (Ogawa, Nittono, & Hori, 2005). Even people who claim they rarely dream frequently report dreaming when they are awakened during REM sleep. The longer the period of REM sleep, the more likely it is that the person will report dreaming. Dreams also occur during slow-wave or

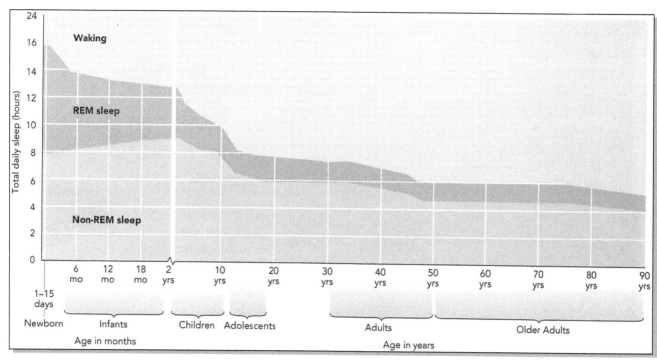

FIGURE 6.6 ▓ Sleep Across the Human Life Span.
With age, human beings require less sleep.

non-REM sleep, but the frequency of dreams in these stages is relatively low (Takeuchi & others, 2001). Reports of dreaming by individuals awakened from REM sleep are typically longer, more vivid, more motorically animated, more emotionally charged, and less related to waking life than reports by those awakened from non-REM sleep (Hobson, 2004).

The amount of time we spend in REM sleep changes over the life span. As shown in **Figure 6.6**, the percentage of total sleep during a 24-hour period that consists of REM sleep is especially large during early infancy (almost 8 hours). Older adults experience less than 1 hour of REM sleep per 24-hour period. Figure 6.6 also reveals how the total amount of sleep changes from approximately 16 hours per 24-hour period for young infants to less than 6 hours for older adults.

These dramatic changes in sleep, especially REM sleep, raise questions about the function of sleep. For young infants, REM sleep may be nature's way of stimulating the brain and contributing to its growth.

REM sleep also likely plays a role in memory (Cipolli & others, 2006). Researchers have presented individuals with unique phrases before they go to bed. When they are awakened just before they begin REM sleep, they remember less the next morning than when they are awakened during the other sleep stages (Stickgold & Walker, 2005).

Sleep Cycling Through the Night

The five stages of sleep described here make up a normal cycle of sleep. As shown in **Figure 6.7**, one of these cycles lasts about 90 to 100 minutes and recurs several times during the night. The amount of deep sleep (stages 3 and 4) is much greater in the first half of a night's sleep than in the second half. Most REM sleep takes place toward the end of a night's sleep, when the REM stage becomes progressively longer. The night's first REM stage might last for only 10 minutes, and the final REM stage might continue for as long as an hour. During a normal night of sleep, individuals will spend about 60 percent of sleep in light sleep (stages 1 and 2), 20 percent in delta or deep sleep, and 20 percent in REM sleep (Webb, 2000).

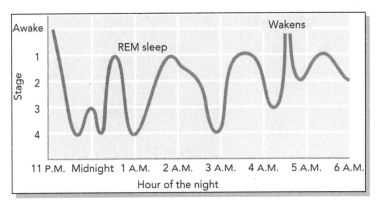

FIGURE 6.7 ■ Cycling Through a Night's Sleep. During a night's sleep, we go through several cycles. Depth of sleep decreases and REM sleep (shown in light blue) increases as the night progresses. In this graph, the person is depicted as awakening at about 5 A.M. and then going back to sleep for another hour.

Sleep and the Brain

The five sleep stages are associated with distinct patterns of neurotransmitter activity initiated in the reticular formation, the core of the brain stem. In all vertebrates, the reticular formation plays a crucial role in sleep and arousal (see Figure 6.2). As previously noted, damage to the reticular formation can result in coma and death.

Three important neurotransmitters involved in sleep are serotonin, epinephrine, and acetylcholine (Kalia, 2006). As sleep begins, the levels of neurotransmitters sent to the forebrain from the reticular formation start dropping, and they continue to fall until they reach their lowest levels during the deepest sleep stage—stage 4. REM sleep (stage 5) is initiated by a rise in acetylcholine, which activates the cerebral cortex while the rest of the brain remains relatively inactive. REM sleep is terminated by a rise in serotonin and norepinephrine, which increase the level of forebrain activity nearly to the awakened state (Miller & O'Callaghan, 2006). You are most likely to wake up just after a REM period. If you do not wake up then, the level of the neurotransmitters begins to fall again, and you enter another sleep cycle.

Another neurotransmitter associated with sleep is adenosine (Landolt & others, 2004). Adenosine builds up during our waking hours. At night, adenosine deaminase (or ADA) breaks down the adenosine, during slow-wave sleep. Caffeine stops adenosine from binding with receptors—and if the adenosine does not bind, you cannot fall asleep (Salin-Pascual & others, 2006).

Sleep and Disease

Sleep plays a role in a large number of diseases and disorders (Costa & Silva, 2006). For example, stroke and asthma attacks are more common during the night and in the early morning probably because of changes in hormones, heart rate, and other characteristics associated with sleep (Teodorescu & others, 2006). Sleeplessness is also associated with obesity and heart disease (Plante, 2006).

Neurons that control sleep interact closely with the immune system (Lange & others, 2006). As anyone who has had the flu knows, infectious diseases make us sleepy. The probable reason is that chemicals called *cytokines*, produced by the body's cells while we are fighting an infection, are powerful sleep-inducing chemicals (Opp, 2006). Sleep may help the body conserve energy and other resources that the body needs to overcome infection (Irwin & others, 2006).

Sleep problems afflict most people who have mental disorders, including those with depression (Agargun & others, 2006). Individuals with depression often awaken in the early hours of the morning and cannot get back to sleep, and they often spend less time in delta wave or deep sleep than do non-depressed individuals.

Sleep problems are common in many other disorders as well, including Alzheimer disease, stroke, and cancer (McEwen, 2006; Wu & Swaab, 2007). In some cases, however, these problems may be due not to the disease itself but to the drugs used to treat the disease.

Sleep Disorders

Many individuals suffer from undiagnosed and untreated sleep disorders that leave them struggling through the day, feeling unmotivated and exhausted (Culpepper, 2005; Ekstedt & others, 2006). Some of the major sleep problems are insomnia, sleepwalking and sleep talking, nightmares and night terrors, narcolepsy, and sleep apnea.

Insomnia

A common sleep problem is *insomnia*, the inability to sleep. Insomnia can involve a problem in falling asleep, waking up during the night, or waking up too early. In the United States, as many as one in five adults have insomnia (Pearson, Johnson, & Nahin, 2006). It is more common among women and older adults, as well as individuals who are thin, stressed, or depressed (Johnson, Roth, & Breslau, 2006). Women are more likely to suffer from insomnia than men, for a variety of factors, including iron deficiencies and hormonal changes (Kotani & others, 2007; Lee, 2006; Sanford & others, 2006). The National Sleep Foundation found that over 70 percent of women from all walks of life (stay-at-home moms, single mothers, working mothers, and so on) reported experiencing sleep problems (2007).

For short-term insomnia, most physicians prescribe sleeping pills (Becker, 2005). However, most sleeping pills stop working after several weeks of nightly use, and their long-term use can interfere with good sleep. Mild insomnia often can be reduced by simply practicing good sleep habits. In more serious cases, researchers are experimenting with light therapy, melatonin supplements, and other ways to alter circadian cycles (Cohen, 2002; Revell & Eastman, 2005). Also, in one study, behavioral changes helped insomniacs to increase their sleep time and to awaken less frequently in the night (Edinger & others, 2001). In this study, insomniacs were restricted from taking a nap during the day, and they were required to set an alarm and to force themselves to get out of bed in the morning. Thus, the longer they stayed awake during the day, the better they were able to sleep at night.

Sleepwalking and Sleep Talking

Somnambulism is the formal term for sleepwalking, which occurs during the deepest stages of sleep (Guilleminault & others, 2006). For many years, experts believed that somnambulists were just acting out their dreams. But somnambulism occurs during stages 3 and 4, usually early in the night, when a person is unlikely to be dreaming. There is nothing really abnormal about sleepwalking. Despite superstition, it is safe to awaken sleepwalkers; in fact, they probably should be awakened, as they may harm themselves wandering around in the dark (Swanson, 1999).

© Dennis Cox, 2009. Used under license from Shutterstock, Inc.

While sleeping, this person may make a sandwich, eat it, go for a drive, rob a grocery store, and return to bed. Once he wakes in the morning, he will have no idea why the police are outside of his house.

Another quirky night behavior is sleep talking (Hublin & others, 2001). If you interrogate sleep talkers, can you find out what they did, for instance, last Thursday night? Probably not. Although sleep talkers will converse with you and make fairly coherent statements, they are soundly asleep. Thus, even if a sleep talker mumbles a response to your question, do not count on its accuracy.

Recently, a few cases of an even rarer sleep behavior have come to light—sleep eating. Ambien is a widely prescribed sleep medication for insomnia. Some Ambien users began to notice odd things upon waking up from a much-needed good night's sleep: candy wrappers strewn around the room, crumbs in the bed, and food missing from the refrigerator. One woman gained 100 pounds without changing her waking, eating, or exercise habits. How could this be? Dr. Mark Mahowald, the medical director of the Minnesota Regional Sleep Disorders Center in Minneapolis, has confirmed that sleep eating may be a side effect of using Ambien (CBS News, 2006). The phenomenon of sleep eating highlights the fact that even when we feel fast asleep, we may be "half awake"—and capable of putting together some unusual late-night snacks, including buttered cigarettes, salt sandwiches, and raw bacon! The maker of Ambien has noted this unusual side effect on the label of the drug. Even more alarming than sleep eating may be recent reports of sleep driving under the influence of Ambien (Saul, 2006). Sleep experts agree that reports of sleep driving while taking Ambien are rare and extreme but are plausible, nonetheless.

Of course, no one should abruptly stop taking any medication without talking to his or her doctor. For individuals who are battling persistent insomnia, a drug that permits them to have a good night's rest may be worth the risk of these unusual side effects.

Nightmares and Night Terrors

A *nightmare* is a frightening dream that awakens a dreamer from REM sleep (Zadra, Pilon, & Donderi, 2006). The nightmare's content invariably involves danger—the dreamer is chased, robbed, raped, murdered, or thrown off a cliff. Nightmares are common. Most of us have had them, especially as young children. Nightmares peak at 3 to 6 years of age and then decline, although the average college student experiences four to eight nightmares a year (Hartmann, 1993). Reported increases in nightmares or worsening nightmares are often associated with an increase in life stressors such as the loss of a relative or a job, conflicts, and other negative events.

A *night terror* is characterized by sudden arousal from sleep and intense fear. Night terrors are accompanied by a number of physiological reactions, such as rapid heart rate and breathing, loud screams, heavy perspiration, and movement (Mason & Pack, 2005). Night terrors are less common than nightmares. Unlike nightmares, night terrors occur during slow-wave non-REM sleep. Night terrors peak at 5 to 7 years of age and decline thereafter.

Narcolepsy

The overpowering urge to sleep is called *narcolepsy*. The urge is so strong that the person may fall asleep while talking or standing up. Narcoleptics immediately REM sleep rather than progressing through the first four sleep stages (Stores, Montgomery, & Wiggs, 2006). Researchers suspect that narcolepsy is inherited. Treatment usually involves counseling to discover potential causes of the excessive sleepiness (Morrish & others, 2004)

Sleep Apnea

Sleep apnea is a sleep disorder in which individuals stop breathing because the windpipe fails to open or because brain processes involved in respiration fail to work properly. People with sleep apnea experience numerous brief awakenings during the night so that they can breathe better, although they usually are not aware of their awakened state. During the day, these people may feel sleepy because they were deprived of sleep at night. A common sign of sleep apnea is loud snoring, punctuated by silence (the apnea)

According to the American Sleep Apnea Association (ASAA), sleep apena affects approximately 12 million Americans (ASAA, 2006). Sleep apnea is most common among infants and adults over the age of 65. Sleep apnea also occurs more frequently among obese individuals, men, and individuals with large necks and recessed chins (ASAA, 2006; Scott & others, 2006). Untreated sleep apnea can cause high blood pressure, stroke, and impotence. In addition, the daytime sleepiness it causes can result in accidents, lost productivity and relationship problems (Hartenbaum & others, 2006).

Dreams

Have you ever had a dream in which you had a fight with someone, and then woken up still angry at the person? Have you had a dream in which you left your long-term romantic partner for a former flame? Would you tell your partner about that dream? Probably not. But you would likely wonder about the dream's meaning. The idea that dreams "mean" something has been with us for a very long time.

Ever since the dawn of language, human beings have imbued dreams with historical, personal, and religious significance. As early as 5000 B.C.E., Babylonians recorded and interpreted their dreams on clay tablets. Egyptians built temples in honor of Serapis, the god of dreams. Dreams are described at length in more than 70 passages in the Bible. Sigmund Freud put great stock in dreams as a key to our unconscious minds. He believed that dreams symbolize unconscious wishes, and that by analyzing dream symbols we could discover our hidden desires. Artists have sometimes incorporated the symbolic world of dreaming in their work (**Figure 6.8**). Because dreams are written in the mind with little or no conscious participation, it is difficult to unravel their mysteries. The most prominent theories that attempt to explain dreams are cognitive theory and activation-synthesis theory.

FIGURE 6.8 ■ The fantasy world of dreams may contain any form of image, bizarre or beautiful. The reasons for dreaming particular images are somewhat understood, however, their interpretation into meaningful knowledge appears to be an idea without any support.

Subconscious Cognitive Processing

The **cognitive theory of dreaming** proposes that dreaming can be understood by applying the same cognitive concepts that are used in studying the waking mind. That is, dreaming involves information processing, memory, and problem solving. In the cognitive theory of dreaming, there is little or no search for the hidden, symbolic content of dreams that Freud sought (Foulkes, 1993, 1999).

From this perspective, dreams might be a mental realm in which we can solve problems and think creatively. For example, the Scottish author Robert Louis Stevenson (1850–1894) claimed that he got the idea for his story about Dr. Jekyll and Mr. Hyde in a dream. Elias Howe, attempting to invent a machine that sewed, reportedly dreamed that he was captured by savages carrying spears with holes in their tips. On waking, he realized that he should place the hole for the thread at the end of the needle, not in the middle. Dreams may spark such gifts of inspiration because, in unique and creative ways, they weave together current experiences with the past.

Criticisms of the cognitive theory of dreaming focus on skepticism about the ability to resolve problems during sleep and the lack of attention to the roles of brain structures and activity in dreaming, the main emphasis of the activation-synthesis theory of dreams.

Cognitive theory of dreaming: Theory proposing that dreaming can be understood by applying the same cognitive concepts that are used in studying the waking mind.

Finding Logic in Random Brain Activity

Activation-synthesis theory states that dreaming occurs when the cerebral cortex synthesizes neural signals generated from activity in the lower part of the brain. In this view, dreams reflect the brain's efforts to make sense out of neural activity that takes place during sleep (Hobson, 1999).

When we are awake and alert, the contents of our conscious experience tend to be driven by external stimuli that result in specific motor behavior. During sleep, according to activation-synthesis theory, conscious experience is driven by internally generated stimuli that have no apparent behavioral consequence. You may have noticed how internal states influence your dreams if you have ever been very thirsty while sleeping and dream that you get a glass of water. A key source of internal stimulation is spontaneous neural activity in the reticular formation of the limbic system (Hobson, 2000).

Proponents of activation-synthesis theory have suggested that neural networks in other areas of the forebrain play a key role in dreaming (Hobson, Pace-Schott, & Stickgold, 2000). Specifically, they believe that the same regions of the forebrain that are involved in certain waking behaviors also function in particular aspects of dreaming (Lu & others, 2006). Thus, the primary motor and sensory areas of the forebrain would be activated in the sensorimotor aspects of the dream; the parietal lobe would be activated in the spatial organization of the dream; the visual aspects of the dream in the visual association cortex; the amygdala, hippocampus, and frontal lobe would be activated in the emotional aspects of a dream; and so on.

The sudden, uncoordinated eye movements of REM sleep make the dream world move in odd ways. For instance, a dream might include magic carpets flying over an undulating landscape. Dreams tend to truncate, dissolve, or shift suddenly in midstream. Freud explained this phenomenon as the dreamer's attempt to elude the unpleasant and the taboo. Activation-synthesis theorists say that this shifting is due to normal cycles of neural activation (Hobson, 2000, 2004). As levels of neurotransmitters rise and fall during the stages of sleep, some neural networks are activated, and others shut down. As a new cycle is activated, a new dream landscape emerges. In sum, in the activation-synthesis view, dreams are merely a glitzy sideshow, not the main event (Hooper & Teresi, 1993).

Like all dream theories, activation-synthesis theory has its critics. Among their criticisms are the beliefs that the brain stem is not the only starting point for neural activity in dreaming and that life experiences stimulate and shape dreaming more than activation-synthesis theory acknowledges (Domhoff, 2001).

Activation-synthesis theory: Theory stating that dreaming occurs when the cerebral cortex synthesizes neural signals generated from activity in the lower part of the brain.

■ REVIEW AND SHARPEN YOUR THINKING

Explain the nature of sleep and dreams.

- ■ Describe the relationship between biological rhythms and sleep.
- ■ Summarize the benefits of sleep and the effects of sleep deprivation.
- ■ Describe the five stages of sleep and changes in the level of activity in the brain during sleep.
- ■ Explain the links between sleep and disease.
- ■ Name and describe five types of sleep disorders.
- ■ Understand the nature of dreams, including theories of why people dream.

Do you know someone who might have a diagnosed or an undiagnosed sleep disorder? What might he or she be able to do about it?

HYPNOSIS

Objective 3 **Describe hypnosis.**

Fifty-three-year-old Shelley Thomas entered a London Hospital for a 30-minute pelvic surgery. Before the operation, with her hypnotherapist guiding her, Shelley counted backward from 100 and entered a hypnotic trance. Her surgery was performed with no anesthesia (Song, 2006); rather, Shelley relied on hypnosis to harness her mind's powers to overcome pain.

You may have seen a hypnotist on TV or in a nightclub, putting people into a trance and then making them act like chickens or pretend to be contestants on *American Idol*. When we see someone in such a trance, we might be convinced that hypnosis involves a powerful manipulation of another person's consciousness. But, what is hypnosis? The answer to this question, is, itself, the source of some debate. Some think of hypnosis as an altered state of consciousness, while others believe that hypnosis is simply a product of more mundane processes such as focused attention and expectation (Lynn, 2007; Raz, 2007). Hypnosis may be defined as an altered state of consciousness or simply a psychological state of altered attention and expectation, in which the individual is unusually receptive to suggestions. Basic hypnotic techniques have been used since the beginning of recorded history in association with religious ceremonies, magic, the supernatural, and many erroneous theories.

In the late nineteenth century, the Austrian physician Friedrich Anton Mesmer cured patients of various problems by passing magnets over their bodies. Mesmer credited his success to "animal magnetism," an intangible force that passes from therapist to patient. In reality, the cures were due to hypnotic suggestion. A committee was appointed by the French Academy of Science to investigate Mesmer's claims. The committee agreed that his treatment was effective. However, they disputed his theory about animal magnetism and prohibited him from practicing in Paris. Mesmer's theory was called "mesmerism," and even today we use the term *mesmerized* to mean hypnotized or enthralled.

Today, hypnosis is recognized as a legitimate process in psychology and medicine, although there is still much to learn about how it works. In addition, there is continuing debate about whether hypnosis truly is an altered state of consciousness (Chaves, 2000; Raz, 2007).

Hypnosis: An altered state of consciousness or simply a psychological state of altered attention and expectation, in which the individual is unusually receptive to suggestions.

The Nature of Hypnosis

A common misconception is that the hypnotic state is much like a sleep state. However, unlike sleepers, hypnotized individuals are aware of what is happening and remember the experience later unless they are instructed to forget it. Evidence from studies involving EEGs documents that individuals show different patterns of brain activity during hypnosis than they do when they are not under hypnosis (Gemignani & others, 2006). Individuals in a hypnotic state display a predominance of alpha and beta waves, characteristic of persons in a waking state, when monitored by an EEG (Williams & Gruzelier, 2001). In one study, hypnotized individuals' EEGs resembled those of a person in a relaxed waking state (Graffin, Ray, & Lundy, 1995). Also, in a recent brain-imaging study, widespread areas of the cerebral cortex—including the occipital lobes, parietal lobes, sensorimotor cortex, and prefrontal cortex—were activated when individuals were in a hypnotic state (Faymonville, Boly, & Laureys, 2006). A similar activation pattern is found in individuals in a nonhypnotic waking state who are engaging in mental imagery.

The Four Steps in Hypnosis

Successful hypnosis involves four steps:

1. Distractions are minimized; the person to be hypnotized is made comfortable.
2. The hypnotist tells the person to concentrate on something specific, such as an imagined scene or the ticking of a watch.
3. The hypnotist tells the person what to expect in the hypnotic state, such as relaxation or a pleasant floating sensation.
4. The hypnotist suggests certain events or feelings he or she knows will occur or observes occurring, such as "Your eyes are getting tired." When the suggested effects occur, the person interprets them as being caused by the hypnotist's suggestions and accepts them as an indication that something is happening. This increase in the person's expectations that the hypnotist will make things happen in the future makes the person even more suggestible.

Individual Variations in Hypnosis

Do you think you could be hypnotized? For as long as hypnosis has been studied (about 200 years), some people have been found to be more easily hypnotized than others. About 65 percent of individuals are moderately hypnotizable, with an additional 15 percent being highly susceptible to hypnosis (Song, 2006). Ten percent or fewer cannot be hypnotized at all, and the remainder fall somewhere in between (Hilgard, 1965).

There is no simple way to tell beforehand who can be hypnotized. But if you have the capacity to immerse yourself in imaginative activities—listening to a favorite piece of music or reading a novel, for example—you are a likely candidate. People susceptible to hypnosis become completely absorbed in what they are doing, removing the boundaries between themselves and what they are experiencing in their environment. Nonetheless, such absorption is best described as a weak rather than a strong predictor of a person's likelihood of being hypnotized (Nash, 2001).

Hypnosis and Will

If you are in a hypnotic state, can the hypnotist make you do something against your will? Individuals being hypnotized surrender their responsibility to the hypnotist and follow the hypnotist's suggestions. However, when in a hypnotic state, they are unlikely to do anything that violates their morals or that is dangerous.

Explaining Hypnosis

Ever since Anton Mesmer proposed his theory of animal magnetism, psychologists have been trying to figure out why hypnosis works. Contemporary theorists are divided on their answers to the question, Is hypnosis a divided state of consciousness, or is it simply a form of learned social behavior?

A Divided State of Consciousness

Ernest Hilgard (1977, 1992) proposed that hypnosis involves a special divided state of consciousness, a sort of splitting of consciousness into separate components. One component follows the hypnotist's commands, while another component acts as a "hidden observer."

In one situation, Hilgard placed one arm of hypnotized individuals in a bucket of ice-cold water and told them that they would not feel any pain but that another part of their minds—the hidden part that is aware of what is going on—could signal any true pain by pressing a key with the hand that was not submerged. The individuals under hypnosis reported afterward that they did not experience any pain, but while their arms were submerged in the ice-cold water, they had indeed pressed the key with their non-submerged hands, and they pressed it more frequently the longer their arms were in the cold water. Thus, in Hilgard's view, in hypnosis, consciousness has a hidden part that stays in contact with reality and feels pain while another part of consciousness feels no pain.

Social Cognitive Behavior

Some experts are skeptical that hypnosis is truly an altered state of consciousness (Chaves, 2000; Lynn & others, 2006). In the social cognitive behavior view of hypnosis, hypnosis is a normal state in which the hypnotized person behaves the way he or she believes that a hypnotized person should behave. The social cognitive perspective frames the important questions about hypnosis around cognitive factors—the attitudes, expectations, and beliefs of good hypnotic participants—and around the social context in which hypnosis occurs (Lynn, 2007; Spanos & Chaves, 1989).

Social cognitive behavior view of hypnosis: Perspective that views hypnosis as a normal state in which the hypnotized person behaves the way he or she believes a hypnotized person should behave.

Applications of Hypnosis

In the United States, where it was first approved for medical use in 1958, hypnosis is used for a wide array of purposes. These include the treatment of alcoholism, somnambulism suicidal tendencies, post-traumatic stress disorder, migraines, over-eating, and smoking (Hammond, 2007; Holt & others, 2006; Lynn & Cardena, 2007; Sandor & Afra, 2005). Among the least effective, but most common, applications of hypnosis are those intended to help people stop overeating or quit smoking. Hypnotists direct individuals to cease these behaviors, but dramatic results rarely are achieved unless the individuals are already motivated to change. Hypnosis is most effective when combined with psychotherapy (Borckardt, 2002).

A long history of research and practice clearly has demonstrated that hypnosis can reduce the experience of pain (Jensen & Patterson, 2006). A fascinating study examined the pain perceptions of individuals who were hypnotized with the goal of changing their pain threshold. In that study, participants' brains were monitored while they received painful electrical shocks (rated 8 or higher on a 1 to 10 pain scale) (Schulz-Stubner & others, 2004). Those who were hypnotized to find the shocks less painful did indeed rate them as lower in pain (giving them a 3 or less). The brain-scanning results were most interesting: The subcortical brain areas (the brain stem and midbrain) of the hypnotized patients responded the same as those of the patients who were not hypnotized, suggesting that these lower brain structures recognized the painful stimulation. However, the sensory cortex was not activated in the hypnotized patients, suggesting that although they sensed pain on some level, they were never conscious of it. In essence, the "ouch" signal never made it to awareness.

Hypnosis is used more widely in Europe than in the United States as a pain-control technique during surgery—specifically, as a replacement for or complement to typical sedation and anesthesia. Hypnosedation involves the combination of hypnosis and administration of a local anesthetic (Pyati & Gan, 2007; Wobst, 2007). In hypnosedation, patients receive less than 1 percent of the typical amount of medication as in traditional surgery and report fewer side effects (Song, 2006). In one study comparing hypnosedation and typical anesthesia for thyroid surgery, individuals in the hypnosedation group returned to work 2 weeks earlier than patients who received standard procedures (Faymonville, Meurisse, & Fissette, 1999).

REVIEW AND SHARPEN YOUR THINKING

Describe hypnosis.

■ Explain what hypnosis is.
■ Discuss two theoretical explanations of hypnosis.
■ Identify some applications of hypnosis.

Do you think you are a good candidate for hypnosis? Why or why not?

PSYCHOACTIVE DRUGS

Objective 4   **Evaluate the uses and types of psychoactive drugs.**

Illicit drug use is a global problem. More than 200 million people worldwide use drugs each year (UNDCP, 2007). Among those, 25 million individuals (or 2.7 percent of the world population) are characterized as problem drug users (UNDCP, 2007). Media images of drug abusers span all segments of society: the urban professional snorting cocaine in a downtown nightclub, the farmer addicted to the opium poppy he grows, the teenage Ecstasy user in a comfortable suburban home.

Drug use among youth is a special concern because of its relation to a variety of other problems, including unsafe sexual practices, sexually transmitted infections, unplanned pregnancy, depression, and school-related difficulties (Eaton & others, 2006; UNDCP, 2007).

What are some trends in drug use by U.S. adolescents? The use of drugs among U.S. secondary school students declined in the 1980s but began to increase in the early 1990s (Johnston & others, 2006). In the late 1990s and early part of the twenty-first century, the proportion of secondary school students reporting the use of any illicit drug has declined (Johnston & others, 2006). The overall decline in the use of illicit drugs by adolescents during this time frame is approximately one-third for eighth-graders, one-fourth for tenth-graders, and one-tenth for twelfth-graders. **Figure 6.9** shows the overall trends in drug use by

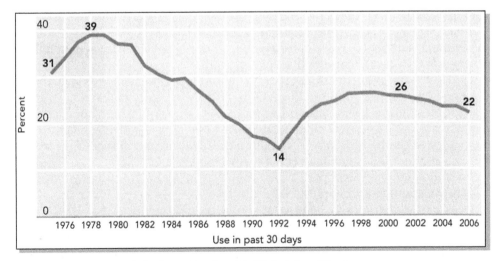

FIGURE 6.9 ■ Trends in Drug Use by U.S. High School Seniors.
This graph shows the percentage of high school seniors who say they have taken an illicit drug in the previous 30 days. Notice the increased use in the latter half of the 1970s, the decrease in the 1980s, the increase in the 1990s, and the recent leveling off.

U.S. high school seniors since 1975 and by U.S. eighth- and tenth-graders since 1991. The most notable declines in drug use by U.S. adolescents in the twenty-first century have occurred for marijuana, LSD, Ecstasy, steroids, and cigarettes. Yet the United States still has the highest rate of adolescent drug use of any industrialized nation (Johnston & others, 2006).

Although drug use is high among U.S. adolescents, it increases further in emerging adulthood. In one national survey, approximately 20 percent of 18- to 25- year-old Americans reported recent illicit drug use compared with 11 percent of adolescents (Substance Abuse and Mental Health Services Administration, 2006).

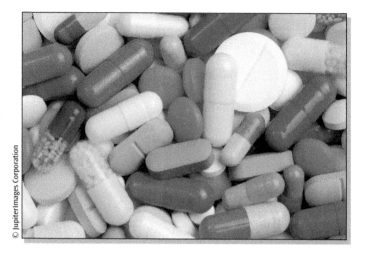

Uses of Psychoactive Drugs

Psychoactive drugs are substances that act on the nervous system to alter consciousness, modify perceptions, and change moods. People are attracted to psychoactive substances because they help them adapt to an ever-changing environment. Drinking, smoking, and taking drugs reduce tension, relieve boredom and fatigue, and in some cases help people to escape from the harsh realities of the world. Some people use drugs because they are curious about their effects. Others may take drugs for social reasons—for example, to feel more at ease and happier in interactions with others.

The use of psychoactive drugs for personal gratification and temporary adaptation can carry a high price tag: drug dependence, personal disarray, and a predisposition to serious, sometimes fatal diseases (Fields, 2007; McKim, 2007). What was initially intended to provide pleasure and adaptation can lead to enormous grief. For example, drinking alcohol may initially help people relax and forget about their worries. But if they turn more and more to alcohol to escape reality, they may develop a dependence that can destroy relationships, careers, and their bodies.

Continued use of psychoactive drugs leads to tolerance, which is the need to take increasing amounts of a drug to get the same effect (Holland, 2007; Ksir, Hart, & Ray, 2008). For example, the first time someone takes 5 milligrams of the tranquilizer Valium, the person feels very relaxed. However, after taking the pill every day for 6 months, the individual may need to consume 10 milligrams to achieve the same calming effect.

Continuing drug use can also result in physical dependence, the physiological need for a drug that causes unpleasant *withdrawal* symptoms, such as physical pain and a craving for the drug, when it is discontinued. Psychological dependence is the strong desire to repeat the use of a drug for emotional reasons, such as a feeling of well-being and reduction of stress. Experts on drug abuse use the term addiction to describe either a physical or psychological dependence, or both, on the drug (Hales, 2007). Physical and psychological dependence mean that the psychoactive drug is exerting a powerful influence over the person's behavior.

Can the brain become addicted? Psychoactive drugs increase dopamine levels in the brain's reward pathways (Schultz, 2006; Zhou & others, 2007). This reward pathway is located in the *ventral tegmental area (VTA)* and *nucleus accumbens* (**Figure 6.10**). Only the limbic and prefrontal areas of the brain are directly activated by dopamine, which comes from the VTA (Koob, 2006). Although different drugs have different mechanisms of action, each drug increases the activity of the reward pathway by increasing dopamine transmission. When a drug

Psychoactive drugs: Substances that act on the nervous system to alter consciousness, modify perceptions, and change moods.

Tolerance: The need to take increasing amounts of a drug to produce the same effect.

Physical dependence: The physiological need for a drug, accompanied by unpleasant withdrawal symptoms, such as pain and craving, when the drug is discontinued.

Psychological dependence: The strong desire to repeat the use of a drug for emotional reasons, such as a feeling of well-being and stress reduction.

Addiction: Either a physical or a psychological dependence, or both, on a drug.

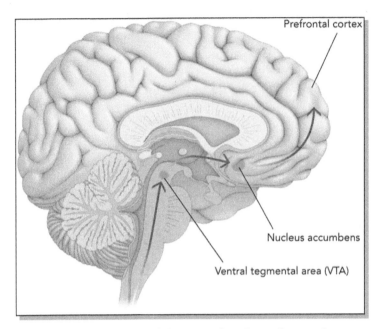

FIGURE 6.10 ■ The Brain's Reward Pathway for Psychoactive Drugs.
The ventral tegmental area (VTA) and nucleus accumbens are important locations in the reward pathway for psychoactive drugs. Information travels from the VTA to the nucleus accumbens and then up to the prefrontal cortex. The VTA is located in the midbrain just above the pons, and the nucleus accumbens is located in the forebrain, just beneath the prefrontal cortex.

mimics a particular neurotransmitter or blocks its reuptake, it is referred to as an *agonist*. Thus, drugs that increase dopamine levels in the brain are agonists. In contrast, when a drug blocks a neurotransmitter or diminishes its release, it is called an *antagonist*.

Types of Psychoactive Drugs

Three main categories of psychoactive drugs are depressants, stimulants, and hallucinogens. All of them have the potential to cause health or behavior problems or both. To evaluate whether you abuse drugs, see **Figure 6.11**.

Depressants

Depressants: Psychoactive drugs that slow down mental and physical activity.

Depressants are psychoactive drugs that slow down mental and physical activity. Among the most widely used depressants are alcohol, barbiturates, tranquilizers, and opiates.

Alcohol.

Alcohol is a powerful drug. It acts on the body primarily as a depressant and slows down the brain's activities. This effect might seem surprising, as people who tend to be inhibited may begin to talk, dance, and socialize after a few drinks. However, people "loosen up" after a few drinks because the areas of the brain involved in inhibition and judgment slow down. As people drink more, their inhibitions decrease even further, and their judgment becomes increasingly impaired. Activities that require intellectual functioning and motor skills, such as driving, become harder to perform. Eventually the drinker falls asleep. With

Respond yes or no to the following items:

Yes	No	
☐	☐	I have gotten into problems because of using drugs.
☐	☐	Using alcohol or other drugs has made my college life unhappy at times.
☐	☐	Drinking alcohol or taking other drugs has been a factor in my losing a job.
☐	☐	Drinking alcohol or taking other drugs has interfered with my studying for exams.
☐	☐	Drinking alcohol or taking drugs has jeopardized my academic performance.
☐	☐	My ambition is not as strong since I've been drinking a lot or taking drugs.
☐	☐	Drinking or taking drugs has caused me to have difficulty sleeping.
☐	☐	I have felt remorse after drinking or taking drugs.
☐	☐	I crave a drink or other drugs at a definite time of the day.
☐	☐	I want a drink or other drug in the morning.
☐	☐	I have had a complete or partial loss of memory as a result of drinking or using other drugs.
☐	☐	Drinking or using other drugs is affecting my reputation.
☐	☐	I have been in the hospital or another institution because of my drinking or taking drugs.

College students who responded yes to items similar to these on the Rutgers Collegiate Abuse Screening Test were more likely to be substance abusers than those who answered no. If you responded yes to just 1 of the 13 items on this screening test, consider going to your college health or counseling center for further screening.

FIGURE 6.11 ■ Do You Abuse Drugs?
Take this short quiz to see if your use of drugs and alcohol might be a cause for concern.

extreme intoxication, the person may lapse into a coma and die. Each of these effects varies with the way the individual's body metabolizes alcohol, body weight, the amount consumed, and whether previous drinking has led to tolerance (Fields, 2007).

How does alcohol affect the brain? Like other psychoactive drugs, alcohol goes to the ventral tegmental area (VTA) and the nucleus accumbens (NIDA, 2001). Alcohol also increases the concentration of the neurotransmitter gamma aminobutyric acid (GABA), which is widely distributed in many areas of the brain, including the cerebral cortex, cerebellum, hippocampus, amygdala, and nucleus accumbens (Krystal & others, 2006; Zhou & others, 2007). Researchers believe that the frontal cortex holds a memory of the pleasure involved in prior alcohol use and contributes to continued drinking. Alcohol consumption also may affect the areas of the frontal cortex involved in judgment and impulse control (Mantere & others, 2002). It is further believed that the basal ganglia, which are involved in compulsive behaviors, may lead to a greater demand for alcohol, regardless of reason and consequences (Brink, 2001).

After caffeine, alcohol is the most widely used drug in the United States. As many as two-thirds of U.S. adults drink beer, wine, or liquor at least occasionally, and in one recent survey approximately 30 percent reported drinking more than five drinks at one sitting at least once in the last year (National Center for Health Statistics, 2005).

Approximately 14 million people in the United States are alcoholics (Brink, 2001). Alcoholism is the third leading killer in the United States. Approximately 20,000 people are killed and 1.5 million injured by drunk drivers each year.

Approximately 34 percent of all fatal crashes and 50 percent of those during holidays involve alcohol (U.S. Department of Transportation, 2005). It may be surprising that the vast majority of offenses for drinking under the influence are committed not by alcoholics but by social drinkers (Caetano & McGrath, 2005). An estimated 3 in 10 Americans will be involved in an alcohol-related crash (National Highway Traffic Safety Administration, 2001). Alcohol is also related to violence and aggression (Dawson & others, 2007). More than 60 percent of homicides involve alcohol use by either the offender or the victim, and 65 percent of aggressive sexual acts against women involve alcohol consumption by the offender.

A special concern is the high rate of alcohol use by U.S. secondary school and college students (Shillington & Clapp, 2006). In a recent national survey of more than 17,000 high school seniors in the United States, 75 percent had tried alcohol, and 41 percent had done so by the eighth grade (Johnston & others, 2007). In this survey, 57 percent of the twelfth-graders and 19 percent of the eighth-graders reported having been drunk at least once in their life. Thirty percent of the high school seniors had engaged in binge drinking (having five or more drinks in a row at least once in the previous 2 weeks) at least once during the previous month.

Two recent longitudinal studies have linked early onset of drinking to later alcohol problems. In one study, individuals who began drinking alcohol before 14 years of age were more likely to become alcohol dependent than their counterparts who began drinking alcohol at 21 years of age or older (Hingson, Heeren, & Winter, 2006). In a second study, individuals were assessed from the time they were 8 years old to 42 years old (Pitkanen, Lyyra, & Pulkkinen. 2005). Early onset of drinking was linked to an elevated risk of heavy drinking in middle age.

Heavy binge drinking often increases during the first 2 years of college, and it can take its toll on students (Park, 2004). Chronic binge drinking is more common among male college students than among females and among students living away from home, especially males residing in fraternity houses (Schulenberg & Zarrett, 2006). In a national survey of drinking patterns on college campuses, almost half

Themselves[1]		and Others[2]	
(% of those surveyed who admitted having had the problem)		(% of those surveyed who had been affected)	
Missed class	61	Had study or sleep interrupted	68
Forgot where they were or what they did	54	Had to care for drunken student	54
Engaged in unplanned sex	41	Were insulted or humiliated	34
Got hurt	23	Experienced unwanted sexual advances	26
Had unprotected sex	22	Had serious argument	20
Damaged property	22	Had property damaged	15
Got into trouble with campus or local police	11	Were pushed or assaulted	13
Had five or more alcohol-related problems in school year	47	Had at least one of the above problems	87

FIGURE 6.12 ■ Consequences of Binge Drinking.
Binge drinking has wide-ranging negative consequences.

[1]Frequent binge drinkers were defined as those who had at least four or five drinks at one time on at least three occasions in the previous two weeks.

[2]These figures are from colleges where at least 50 percent of students are binge drinkers.

of the binge drinkers reported problems that included missed classes, injuries, trouble with police, and unprotected sex (Wechsler & others, 2000; 2002) (**Figure 6.12**). Binge-drinking college students were 11 times more likely to fall behind in school, 10 times more likely to drive after drinking, and twice as likely to have unprotected sex as college students who did not binge drink. Many emerging adults decrease their use of alcohol as they move into adult roles such as a permanent job, marriage or cohabitation, and parenthood (Slutske, 2005).

Alcoholism is a disorder that involves long-term, repeated, uncontrolled, compulsive, and excessive use of alcoholic beverages and that impairs the drinker's health and social relationships. One in nine individuals who drink continues the path to alcoholism. Those who do are disproportionately related to alcoholics. Family studies consistently find a high frequency of alcoholism in the first-degree relatives of alcoholics (Edenberg & Foroud, 2006). Indeed, researchers have determined that heredity likely plays a role in alcoholism, with the gene associated with GABA being most likely implicated (Soyka & others, 2007). An estimated 50 to 60 percent of those who become alcoholics are believed to have a genetic predisposition for it (Quickfall & el-Guebaly, 2006).

> **Alcoholism:** A disorder that involves long-term, repeated, uncontrolled, compulsive, and excessive use of alcoholic beverages and that impairs the drinker's health and social relationships.

One possible explanation is that the brains of people genetically predisposed to alcoholism may be unable to produce adequate dopamine, a neurotransmitter that can make us feel pleasure (Dick & Bierut, 2006). For these individuals, alcohol may increase dopamine concentration and resulting pleasure to the point at which it leads to addiction.

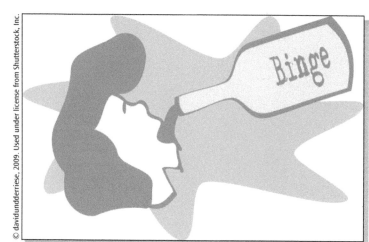

© davidundderriese, 2009. Used under license from Shutterstock, Inc.

Although studies reveal a genetic influence on alcoholism, they also show that environmental factors play a role (Fromme, 2006). For example, family studies indicate that many alcoholics do not have close relatives who are alcoholics (Duncan & others, 2006).

What does it take to stop alcoholism? About one-third of alcoholics recover, whether they are in a treatment program or not. This finding came from a long-term study of 700 individuals over 50 years (Vaillant, 1983, 1992) and has consistently been confirmed by other researchers. George Vaillant formulated the one-third rule for alcoholism: By age 65, one-third are dead or in terrible shape; one-third are still trying to beat their addiction; and one-third are abstinent or drinking only socially. In his extensive research, Vaillant found that recovery from alcoholism was predicted by (1) having a strong negative experience with drinking, such as a serious medical emergency; (2) finding a substitute dependency, such as meditation, exercise, or overeating (which has its own adverse health effects); (3) developing new, positive relationships (such as with a concerned employer or a new spouse); and (4) joining a support group such as Alcoholics Anonymous or Rational Recovery.

Barbiturates

Barbiturates, such as Nembutal and Seconal, are depressant drugs that decrease central nervous system activity. They were once widely prescribed as sleep aids. In heavy dosages, they can lead to impaired memory and decision making. When combined with alcohol (for example, sleeping pills taken after a night of binge drinking), barbiturates can be lethal. Heavy doses of barbiturates by themselves can cause death. For this reason, barbiturates are the drug most often used in suicide attempts. Abrupt withdrawal can produce seizures. Because of the addictive potential and relative ease of toxic overdose, barbiturates have been largely replaced by tranquilizers in the treatment of insomnia.

> **Barbiturates:** Depressant drugs that decrease the activity of the central nervous system.

Tranquilizers

Tranquilizers, such as Valium and Xanax, are depressant drugs that reduce anxiety and induce relaxation. Unlike barbiturates, which often are given to induce sleep, tranquilizers are usually prescribed to calm an anxious, nervous individual. Widely prescribed in the United States, tranquilizers can produce withdrawal symptoms when use is stopped (Voshaar & others, 2006).

Opiates

Narcotics, or opiates, consist of opium and its derivatives and depress the central nervous system's activity. The most common opiate drugs—morphine and heroin—affect synapses in the brain that use endorphins as their neurotransmitter. When these drugs leave the brain, the affected synapses become understimulated. For several hours after taking an opiate, the person feels euphoric and pain-free and has an increased appetite for food and sex. Opiates are highly addictive drugs, leading to craving and painful withdrawal when the drug becomes unavailable.

Another hazardous consequence of opiate addiction is the risk of exposure to HIV, the virus that causes AIDS. Most heroin addicts inject the drug intravenously. When they share needles without sterilizing them, one infected addict can transmit the virus to others.

Stimulants

Stimulants are psychoactive drugs that increase the central nervous system's activity. The most widely used stimulants are caffeine, nicotine, amphetamines, and cocaine.

Caffeine

Often overlooked as a drug, caffeine is the world's most widely used psychoactive drug. Caffeine is a stimulant and a natural component of the plants that are the sources of coffee, tea, and cola drinks. Caffeine also is present in chocolate and in many nonprescription medications. People often perceive the stimulating effects of caffeine as beneficial for boosting energy and alertness, but some experience unpleasant side effects.

Caffeinism refers to an overindulgence in caffeine. It is characterized by mood changes, anxiety, and sleep disruption. Caffeinism often develops in people who drink five or more cups of coffee (at least 500 milligrams) each day. Common symptoms are insomnia, irritability, headaches, ringing ears, dry mouth, increased blood pressure, and digestive problems (Hogan, Hornick, & Bouchoux, 2002).

Caffeine affects the brain's pleasure centers, so it is not surprising that it is difficult to kick the caffeine habit. When individuals who regularly consume caffeinated beverages remove caffeine from their diet, they typically experience headaches, lethargy, apathy, and concentration difficulties. These symptoms of withdrawal are usually mild and subside after several days.

Nicotine

Nicotine is the main psychoactive ingredient in all forms of smoking and smokeless tobacco. Even with all the publicity given to the enormous health risks posed by tobacco, we sometimes overlook the highly addictive nature of nicotine. Nicotine stimulates the brain's reward centers by raising dopamine levels. Behavioral effects of nicotine include improved attention and alertness, reduced anger and anxiety, and pain relief (Knott & others, 2006).

Tolerance develops for nicotine both in the long run and on a daily basis, so that cigarettes smoked later in the day have less effect than those smoked earlier. Withdrawal from nicotine often quickly produces strong, unpleasant symptoms such as irritability, craving, inability to focus, sleep disturbance, and increased appetite. Withdrawal symptoms can persist for months or longer.

Despite the positive short-term effects of nicotine (such as increased energy and alertness), most smokers recognize the serious health risks of smoking and wish they could quit.

Tobacco poses a much larger threat to public health than illegal drugs. A full 28 percent of the world's population between the ages of 15 and 64 smokes (UNDCP, 2007). Today there are approximately 1 billion smokers globally, and estimates are that by 2030, another 1 billion youth will have started to smoke (UN World Youth Report, 2005). In 2005, about 21 percent of U.S. adults smoked—a decline from 1996, when nearly a quarter of surveyed Americans smoked (Centers for Disease Control and Prevention, 2006).

Fortunately, cigarette smoking is decreasing among both adolescents and college students. In a national survey by the Institute of Social Research, the percentage of U.S. adolescents who are current cigarette smokers continued to decline in 2005 (Johnston & others, 2007). Cigarette smoking peaked in 1996 and 1997 and then declined 11 to 15 percent, depending on grade level, from 1998 to 2005 (**Figure 6.13**). The drop in cigarette use by U.S. youth may have several sources, including higher cigarette prices, less tobacco advertising reaching adolescents, more antismoking advertisements, and more negative publicity about the tobacco industry than before. Since the mid-1990s, a rising percentage of adolescents has reported perceiving cigarette smoking as dangerous, disapproving of it, becoming less accepting of being around smokers, and preferring to date nonsmokers (Johnston & others, 2007).

The devastating effects of early smoking were brought home in a research study that found that smoking in the adolescent years causes permanent genetic changes in the lungs and forever increases the risk of lung cancer, even if the smoker quits (Weineke & others, 1999). The damage was much less likely among smokers in the study who started in their 20s. One of the remarkable findings in the study was that the early age of onset of smoking was more important in predicting genetic damage than was how heavily the individuals smoked.

Although cigarette smoking by U.S. adolescents and adults in general has declined considerably in recent years, cigarette smoking by college students has shown a smaller decline, and little change has been revealed in young adults (Johnston & others, 2007). Among college students, the peak rate of smoking occurred in 1999 when 31 percent said they had smoked a cigarette in the past 30 days; this figure declined to 24 percent in 2005. Young adults 19 to 28 years of age

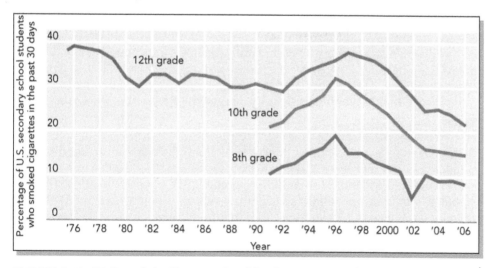

FIGURE 6.13 ■ Trends in Cigarette Smoking by U.S. Secondary School Students. Fortunately, cigarette smoking by American high school students is on the decline.

showed little change in their smoking habits between 1996 and 2005, with approximately 30 percent reporting they had smoked a cigarette in the past 30 days.

Amphetamines

Amphetamines, commonly called "pep pills" or "uppers," are stimulant drugs that people use to boost energy, stay awake, or lose weight. Amphetamines often are prescribed in the form of diet pills. These drugs increase the release of dopamine, which enhances the user's activity level and pleasurable feelings.

Perhaps the most insidious illicit drug for contemporary society is crystal methamphetamine, or crystal meth. Crystal meth (or "tina") is a synthetic stimulant that causes a very strong feeling of euphoria, particularly the first time it is ingested (it can be smoked, injected, or swallowed). Meth is made using household products such as battery acid, cold medicine, drain cleaner, and kitty litter, and its effects have been devastating, particularly in rural areas.

Crystal meth is highly addictive. The drug's extreme high drains the body of endorphins, causing a severe "come down" experience that is associated with strong cravings. The Drug Enforcement Agency (DEA) has committed some $145 million per year to combat methamphetamine (U.S. Department of Justice, 2006). Because the person's very first experience with crystal meth can lead to devastating consequences, the DEA has also started a website, designed by and targeted at teenagers, http://www.justthinktwice.com, to share the hard facts of the horrific effects of this and other illicit substances.

Cocaine

Cocaine is an illegal drug that comes from the coca plant, native to Bolivia and Peru. For centuries, Bolivians and Peruvians have chewed the leaves of the plant to increase their stamina. Generally, however, cocaine is either snorted or injected in the form of crystals or powder. Used this way, cocaine can trigger a heart attack, stroke, or brain seizure.

When animals and humans chew coca leaves, small amounts of cocaine gradually enter the bloodstream, without any apparent adverse effects. However, when extracted cocaine is sniffed or injected, it enters the bloodstream very rapidly, producing a rush of euphoric feelings that lasts for about 15 to 30 minutes. Because the rush depletes the supply of the neurotransmitters dopamine, serotonin, and norepinephrine in the brain, an agitated, depressed mood usually follows as the drug's effects decline. **Figure 6.14** shows how cocaine affects dopamine levels in the brain.

Crack is a potent form of cocaine, consisting of chips of pure cocaine that are usually smoked. Crack is believed to be one of the most addictive substances known, even more addictive than heroin, barbiturates, and alcohol.

Treatment of cocaine addiction has not been very successful (Hser & others, 2006). Cocaine's addictive properties are so strong that, 6 months after treatment, more than 50 percent of cocaine abusers return to the drug. Experts on drug abuse argue that prevention is the best approach to reducing cocaine use.

Inhalants

Although the consumption of illicit drugs generally appears to be declining, inhalant use has increased alarmingly. Inhalants are volatile substances that are intentionally breathed in to produce psychoactive effects. "Huffing" involves inhaling common household chemicals such as gasoline and paint thinner; aerosol sprays such as hairspray and deodorant; medical anesthetics such as ether; or nitrates (also called "poppers"). According to a 2004 survey, nearly 10 percent of the population over age 12 reported using inhalants (SAMHSA, 2005). Indeed, the National Institute on Drug Abuse (NIDA) found that over 17 percent of eighth-graders reported using inhalants, and 3 percent of children have tried inhalants before they reach the fourth grade (NIDA, 2005).

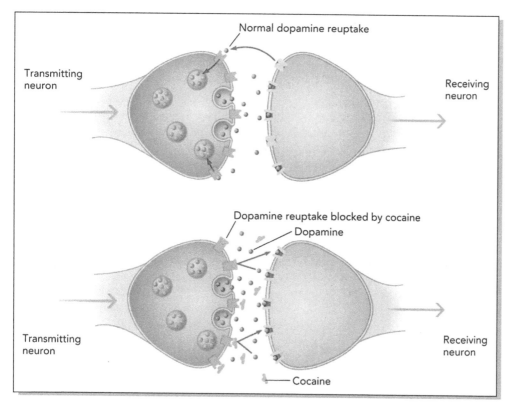

Normal dopamine reuptake

Transmitting neuron

Receiving neuron

Dopamine reuptake blocked by cocaine

Dopamine

Transmitting neuron

Receiving neuron

Cocaine

FIGURE 6.14 ▇

Most inhalants produce a rapid high and have an effect similar to anesthesia. Because the effects are quite short-lived, users may seek to prolong the experience by inhaling more, sometimes bringing on a loss of consciousness. Even a single use of inhalants can result in death by disrupting the person's heart rhythms (NIDA, 2005). These drugs often deprive the brain of oxygen and can produce lingering effects, including headache, lack of motor coordination, difficulty concentrating, memory loss, irritability, and depression (NIDA, 2005).

> **Hallucinogens:** Psychoactive drugs that modify a person's perceptual experiences and produce visual images that are not real.

Hallucinogens

Hallucinogens are psychoactive drugs that modify a person's perceptual experiences and produce visual images that are not real. Hallucinogens are also called psychedelic (from the Greek meaning "mind-revealing") drugs. Marijuana has a mild hallucinogenic effect; LSD, a stronger one (**Figure 6.15**).

Marijuana

Marijuana is the dried leaves and flowers of the hemp plant *Cannabis sativa*, which originated in central Asia but is now grown in most parts of the world. The plant's dried resin is known as hashish. The active ingredient in marijuana is THC (delta-9-tetrahydrocannabinol). Unlike other psychoactive drugs, THC does not affect a specific neurotransmitter. Rather, marijuana disrupts the membranes of neurons and affects the functioning of a variety of neurotransmitters and hormones.

The physical effects of marijuana include increases in pulse rate and blood pressure, reddening of the eyes, coughing, and dryness of the mouth. Psychological

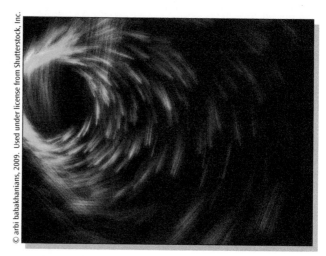

© arbi babakhanians, 2009. Used under license from Shutterstock, Inc.

FIGURE 6.15 ▇ LSD-Induced Hallucination. Under the influence of hallucinogenic drugs, such as LSD, several users have reported seeing tunnel-like images.

Drug Classification	Medical Uses	Short-Term Effects	Overdose Effects	Health Risks	Risk of Physical/ Psychological Dependence
Depressants					
Alcohol	Pain relief	Relaxation, depressed brain activity, slowed behavior, reduced inhibitions	Disorientation, loss of consciousness, even death at high blood-alcohol levels	Accidents, brain damage, liver disease, heart disease, ulcers, birth defects	Physical: moderate Psychological: moderate
Barbiturates	Sleeping pill	Relaxation, sleep	Breathing difficulty, coma, possible death	Accidents, coma, possible death	Physical and psychological: moderate to high
Tranquilizers	Anxiety reduction	Relaxation, slowed behavior	Breathing difficulty, coma, possible death	Accidents, coma, possible death	Physical: low to moderate Psychological: moderate to high
Opiates (narcotics)	Pain relief	Euphoric feelings, drowsiness, nausea	Convulsions, coma, possible death	Accidents, infectious diseases such as AIDS	Physical: high Psychological: moderate to high
Stimulants					
Amphetamines	Weight control	Increased alertness, excitability; decreased fatigue, irritability	Extreme irritability, feelings of persecution, convulsions	Insomnia, hypertension, malnutrition, possible death	Physical: possible Psychological: moderate to high
Cocaine	Local anesthetic	Increased alertness, excitability, euphoric feelings; decreased fatigue, irritability	Extreme irritability, feelings of persecution, convulsions, cardiac arrest, possible death	Insomnia, hypertension, malnutrition, possible death	Physical: possible Psychological: moderate (oral) to very high (injected or smoked)
MDMA (Ecstasy)	None	Mild amphetamine and hallucinogenic effects; high body temperature and dehydration; sense of well-being and social connectedness	Brain damage, especially memory and thinking	Cardiovascular problems; death	Physical: possible Psychological: moderate
Caffeine	None	Alertness and sense of well-being followed by fatigue	Nervousness, anxiety, disturbed sleep	Possible cardiovascular problems	Physical: moderate Psychological: moderate
Nicotine	None	Stimulation, stress reduction, followed by fatigue, anger	Nervousness, disturbed sleep	Cancer and cardio-vascular disease	Physical: high Psychological: high
Hallucinogens					
LSD	None	Strong hallucinations, distorted time perception	Severe mental disturbance, loss of contact with reality	Accidents	Physical: none Psychological: low
Marijuana	Treatment of the eye disorder glaucoma	Euphoric feelings, relaxation, mild hallucinations, time distortion, attention and memory impairment	Fatigue, disoriented behavior	Accidents, respiratory disease	Physical: very low Psychological: moderate

FIGURE 6.16 ■ Categories of Psychoactive Drugs: Depressants, Stimulants, and Hallucinogens. Note that these various drugs have different effects and negative consequences.

effects include a mixture of excitatory, depressive, and mildly hallucinatory characteristics that make it difficult to classify the drug. Marijuana can trigger spontaneous unrelated ideas; distorted perceptions of time and place; increased sensitivity to sounds, tastes, smells, and colors; and erratic verbal behavior. Marijuana can also impair attention and memory. When used daily in large amounts, marijuana also can alter sperm count and change hormonal cycles (Close, Roberts, & Berger, 1990). It may be involved in some birth defects and less effective information processing in children. For example, a recent review of research concluded that marijuana use by pregnant women is related to negative outcomes in memory and information processing in their offspring (Kalant, 2004). On a positive note, researchers have found some medical uses for marijuana, such as treating glaucoma, chemotherapy-caused vomiting, and AIDS-related weight loss.

Marijuana is the illegal drug most widely used by high school students. As many as 32 percent of high school seniors in the United States say that they have used marijuana in the past year (Bureau of Justice Statistics, 2006).

MDMA (Ecstasy)

MDMA is an illegal synthetic drug with both stimulant and hallucinogenic properties. Street names for MDMA include Ecstasy, X, XTC, hug, beans, and love drug. Ecstasy has been referred to as an "empathogen" because under its influence, users tend to feel warm bonds with others.

MDMA has adverse effects on memory and cognitive processing. Individuals who have been heavy users of Ecstasy, for example, show cognitive deficits (Dafters, 2006) that persist even *two years* after they begin to abstain (Ward, Hall, & Haslam, 2006). MDMA kills serotonergic axons, suggesting that repeated use might lead to susceptibility to depression (Guillot & Greenway, 2006).

LSD

LSD (lysergic acid diethylamide) is a hallucinogen that even in low doses produces striking perceptual changes. Objects change their shapes and glow. Colors become kaleidoscopic, and fabulous images unfold. Designs swirl, colors shimmer, and bizarre scenes appear. LSD-induced images are sometimes pleasurable and sometimes grotesque. Figure 6.15 shows one kind of perceptual experience that a number of LSD users have reported. LSD can also influence a user's sense of time. Time seems to slow down dramatically, so that brief glances at objects are experienced as deep, penetrating, and lengthy examinations, and minutes seem to be hours or even days. A bad LSD trip can trigger extreme anxiety, paranoia, and suicidal or homicidal impulses.

LSD's effects on the body can include dizziness, nausea, and tremors. LSD acts primarily on the neurotransmitter serotonin in the brain, though it also can affect dopamine (Nichols & Sanders-Bush, 2002). Emotional and cognitive effects may include rapid mood swings and impaired attention and memory. LSD is one psychoactive drug that has no beneficial effects. Its effects are summarized in **Figure 6.16**, along with the characteristics of the other types of drugs that have been discussed.

The use of LSD peaked in the 1960s and 1970s. Its popularity declined after its unpredictable effects became publicized. However, in the 1990s, the use of LSD by high school students increased, although not to the level in the 1960s and 1970s, and its use has been decreasing in the twenty-first century (Johnston & others, 2007).

A current controversy involves the extent hallucinogenic drugs, such as LSD and marijuana, should be used for medical purposes. To read about this issue, see the Critical Controversy.

CRITICAL CONTROVERSY

Should Psychedelic Drugs Be Legalized for Medical Uses?

During one phase of his career, Sigmund Freud personally experimented with therapeutic uses of cocaine. He was searching for possible medical applications such as the drug's potential use as a painkiller during eye surgery. He found that the drug induced feelings of ecstasy. Writing to his fiancée, he told her how just a small dose produced wonderful, lofty sensations. But as he heard stories about others who had become addicted and suffered overdoses, Freud quit using the drug.

The notion of exploring the use of mind-altering drugs for legitimate purposes is not exclusive to Freud. Psychedelic drugs such as LSD (acid),

Continued

MDMA (Ecstasy), psilocybin (magic mushrooms), mescaline (peyote buttons), and cannabis (marijuana, or pot) all have mind-altering effects. Users sometimes talk about the amazing insights they have experienced under the influence of these substances, and some cultures and religions incorporate the use of hallucinogens in rituals. Could these effects be harnessed to promote healthier functioning in the mentally ill? Could they be used to promote well-being more generally? John Halpern, an associate director of

© Karin Lau, 2009. Used under license from Shutterstock, Inc.

The Supreme Court recently upheld the federal government's right to enforce drug laws strictly, regardless of state regulations such as those permitting medical usage of marijuana. Congress, as recently as June 2006, voted down a proposal that would have blocked drug enforcers' raids on patients using medical marijuana.

addiction research at Harvard University's McLean Hospital, and his colleagues think so (Halpern, 2003; Halpern & Sewell, 2005; Halpern & others, 2005; Sewell, Halpern, & Pope, 2006). They have been leading advocates for research using psychedelic drugs to treat addiction, anxiety, and other disorders.

Of course, these drugs are illegal today, but they were not always. The effects of LSD were discovered by a Swiss chemist who accidentally ingested LSD while working in a pharmaceutical lab. He described his "trip" as both terrifying and thrilling, and his experience led others to consider whether LSD might have a use in psychological treatment. During the 1960s, more than 100 peer-reviewed articles examining the effects and potential benefits of psychedelic drugs were published in scientific journals. During that time, more than 40,000 patients were given LSD for a variety of problems, including schizophrenia, alcoholism, and depression.

The benefits of LSD were championed especially passionately by the late Timothy Leary. In the 1960s, Leary, a Harvard psychologist, embarked on a research program dedicated to unlocking the secrets of consciousness through the use of LSD. Leary believed that LSD could be beneficial in freeing people from addiction, changing the behavior of criminals, and providing entry into mystical experience. Perhaps less interested in science than celebrity, however, Leary ultimately fell out of favor and lost his job over his and his research associates' tendencies to sample the research stimuli, sacrificing scientific rigor in favor of simply promoting the use of LSD (Greenfield, 2006). Certainly, Leary's controversial persona and behavior had a chilling effect on research into the potential applications of psychedelic drugs (Horgan, 2005; Sessa, 2007). By the late 1960s, LSD and other psychedelic drugs were outlawed in the United States, Canada, and Europe. In 1971, the *Journal of the American Medical Association* printed an editorial decrying the negative effects of LSD and warning that among those who had used the drug more than 50 times, only a lucky few escaped without severe "personality deterioration."

Slowly, however, researchers again have begun to consider the potential benefits of these now illegal substances. On the basis of a review of previous studies, Halpern (1996) concluded that LSD may help addicts avoid cravings. During the months following an acid trip, for example, addicts experience an "afterglow" in which they no longer have cravings for heroin or alcohol. Although government restrictions make the research difficult, a variety of scholars are examining the legitimate uses of psychedelic drugs for a broad range of problems. For example, psilocybin is being studied as a treatment for obsessive-compulsive disorder; MDMA, for anxiety and migraine headaches; and ketamin ("vitamin K," a veterinary tranquilizer), for alcoholism (Horgan, 2005). Promising initial results are leading some to consider whether these drugs should be legalized for medical use.

The controversy over medical marijuana illustrates the conflicts that can erupt over the possibility of an illicit drug's legalization. In the late 1970s, it became apparent that marijuana could be used as treatment for glaucoma (American Academy of Ophthalmology, 2003). More recently, marijuana has been recognized as a potential treatment for individuals who suffer from diseases such as AIDS and cancer (as well as the unpleasant side effects of treatments for these illnesses). For such individuals, "medical marijuana" may be a means to promote appetite, to calm anxiety, and to stimulate well-being (Joy, Watson, & Benson, 1999). If marijuana were legalized for medical purposes, would drug use rise more generally, as many believe (Schwartz & others, 2003)?

In 1996, California provided a natural experiment that addressed this very question when voters passed Proposition 215, legalizing the noncommercial possession, cultivation, and distribution of marijuana for medical purposes. Researchers looked at data from a survey of a broad sample of 16- to 25-year-old Californians that was begun before the passage of Proposition 215. The survey, which measured attitudes toward pot and self-reported usage, allowed researchers to gauge the effects of Proposition 215. They concluded that while attitudes about marijuana were more lenient in 1999 than in the years prior to the passage of the proposition, usage did not change (Khatapoush & Hallfors, 2004).

More recently, the U.S. Supreme Court upheld the right of the federal government strictly to enforce drug laws, regardless of state regulations (or lack thereof). The justices ruled that "medical necessity" is not a viable

Continued

legal defense (Aggarwal, Carter, & Steinborn, 2005). As recently as June 2006, the U.S. Congress voted down a proposal that would have prevented drug enforcement officials from conducting raids on patients using medical marijuana in the 11 states in which such use is not illegal (Alaska, California, Colorado, Hawaii, Maine, Montana, Nevada, Oregon, Rhode Island, Vermont, and Washington). Legislators defeated this proposal despite support from both Democrats and Republicans.

Naturally, there are reasons why these drugs have been outlawed, including matters of safety. One issue is the occurrence of *flashbacks*, the experience in which a user is transported back into the hallucinogenic state even without the use of the drug. Another concern centers on the levels at which these drugs can be safely taken. Yet some advocates point out that the safety risks associated with some of the hallucinogenic substances are not different from those posed by alcohol and tobacco (Grinspoon, 2000).

The scientific study of the uses of these drugs is hampered not only by the legal issues involved but also by specific issues of research design. Indeed, drug research has faced a variety of challenges. First, in general, participants in studies of the effects of illegal drugs are by definition participating in illegal behavior, and this fact may make them less representative of the population as a whole. Second, older studies failed to measure preexisting psychiatric conditions, thus leaving the negative effects of drugs potentially attributable to these preexisting factors. In addition, many drug users ingest multiple drugs at the same time—for example, taking LSD or Ecstasy while drinking and smoking—so that teasing apart the specific causes of reactions is difficult. To avoid these pitfalls, some studies have focused on individuals who use psychedelic drugs only in religious contexts; this way, the researchers can examine the effects of specific drugs in the absence of any other substance use and without concern for legal issues (Doering-Silveira & others, 2005).

Another controversial question is whether such drugs ought to be legalized not just for medical purposes but for the enhancement of everyday life. Some people even argue that psychedelic drugs should be legalized because they are an avenue for gaining creative insight. "The illegality of cannabis is outrageous, an impediment to full utilization of a drug which helps produce serenity, insight, sensitivity and fellowship so desperately needed in this increasingly mad and dangerous world." This quote is from the late scientist and author Carl Sagan, writing as "Mr. X" in Lester Grinspoon's *Marihuana Reconsidered* (1994).

Whether hallucinogenic drugs provide us with insight into the great mysteries of life is certainly debatable. One of Timothy Leary's early participants noted that he had solved all the world's problems during an acid trip, yet the next day he could not remember how (Greenfield, 2006). The use of these drugs to help individuals struggling with serious life difficulties is certain to remain a subject of debate for years to come.

What Do You Think?

- Would the legalization of psychedelic drugs for medical purposes "send the wrong message" about drug use? Why or why not?
- Compare the legalization of illicit drugs for medical use versus for the enhancement of daily life. What are the different implications of each of these notions?
- How might the particular characteristics of an individual influence the person's experiences with hallucinogenic drugs? How might these experiences compare with those of others using the drugs?
- Would you support the legalization of drugs for medical purposes? Why or why not?

■ REVIEW AND SHARPEN YOUR THINKING

Evaluate the uses and types of psychoactive drugs.

- ■ Describe the effects of psychoactive drugs.
- ■ Know the characteristics of the three main types of psychoactive drugs: depressants, stimulants, and hallucinogens.

Do you know someone who has a drug problem? If so, describe the nature of the problem. Is he or she willing to admit to having a problem?

CONSCIOUSNESS AND HEALTH AND WELLNESS

Objective 5 **Discuss the role of the conscious mind in constructing a happy and healthy life.**

Positive and Negative Aspects of Our Thoughts

Consciousness is perhaps the central feature of the human mind—our internal running awareness of life's events and our thoughts and feelings. Being alone with our thoughts can be stressful, as when we are thinking about all the things we have to accomplish, the bills we neglected to pay, and the phone calls we forgot to return. But our inner life can also be a powerful tool for constructing a healthy life, as the experience of Melissa Munroe illustrates.

Munroe, a Canadian woman diagnosed with Hodgkin's lymphoma, found herself tormented by excruciating pain. Seeking ways to cope with the agony, Munroe enrolled in a meditation program. She was skeptical at first. "What I didn't realize," she said, "is that if people have ever found themselves taking a walk in the countryside or in the forest or on a nice pleasant autumn day . . . and find themselves in a contemplative state, that's a form of meditation." Monroe worked hard to use meditation to control her pain. Interestingly, the way she harnessed the power of her mind to overcome pain was by concentrating her thoughts on the pain—not trying to avoid it.

Using *mindfulness meditation*, a technique practiced by yoga enthusiasts and Buddhist monks, Monroe focused on her pain. By doing so, she was able to isolate the pain from her emotional response to it and to her cancer diagnosis. She grew to see her physical discomfort as something she could tolerate. Monroe's success shows that, contrary to what a non-meditator might think, meditation is not about avoiding one's thoughts. Indeed, the effort involved in avoiding steers the person away from the contemplative state. Monroe described her thoughts as like people striding by her on the street, walking in the other direction; she explained, "They come closer and closer, then they pass you by."

Jon Kabat-Zinn (2006) has pioneered the use of meditation techniques in medical settings. Research by Kabat-Zinn and colleagues has demonstrated the beneficial effects of mindfulness meditation for a variety of conditions, including depression, panic attacks, and anxiety (Miller, Fletcher, & Kabat-Zinn, 1995), chronic pain (Kabat-Zinn, Lipworth, & Burney, 1985), and stress and the skin condition psoriasis (Kabat-Zinn & others, 1998). Many of these effects have also been shown to be long-lasting.

Richard Davidson and colleagues (including Jon Kabat-Zinn) studied the brain and immune system changes that might underlie

Regular meditation can help you to clarify your goals and purpose in life, strengthen your values, and improve your outlook.

the health and wellness effects of meditation (Davidson & others, 2003). They performed MRIs on the brains of individuals who were in a standard 8-week meditation training program. After the training program and as compared to a control group, those in the meditation program reported reduced anxiety and fewer negative emotions. Furthermore, brain scans revealed that these individuals showed increased activation in the left hemisphere—the "happy brain". In addition, the meditators showed a better immune system response to a flu vaccine (Davidson & others, 2003). These results suggest that our conscious minds may have a role to play in enhancing our psychological and physical health (Arias & others, 2006; Ekman & others, 2005).

The Meditative State of Mind

What actually is the meditative state of mind? As a physiological state, meditation shows qualities of sleep *and* wakefulness, yet it is distinct from both. You may have experienced a state researchers call *hypnogogic reverie*—an overwhelming feeling of wellness right before you fall asleep, the sense that everything is going to work out. Meditation has been compared to this relaxed sense that all is well (Friedman, Myers, & Benson, 1998). In a study of Zen meditators, researchers were interested in examining what happens when people switch from their normal waking state to a meditative state (Ritskes & others, 2003). Using fMRI, the researchers got images of the brain before and after the participants entered the meditative state. They found that the switch to meditation involved initial increases in activation in the basal ganglia and prefrontal cortex (the now familiar area that is often activated during consciousness). However, and interestingly, they also found that these initial activations led to decreases in the anterior cingulate, a brain area that is thought to be associated with acts of will. These results provide a picture of the physical events of the brain that are connected with the somewhat paradoxical state of meditation—controlling one's thoughts in order to let go of the need to control.

Would you like to experience what a state of meditation is like? If so, you can probably reach that state by following some simple instructions. First, you need a quiet place and a comfortable chair. Sit upright in the chair, rest your chin comfortably on your chest, and place your arms in your lap. Close your eyes. Now focus on your breathing. Every time you inhale and every time you exhale, pay attention to the sensations of air flowing through your body, the feeling of your lungs filling and emptying. After you have focused on several breaths, begin to repeat silently to yourself a single word every time you breathe out. The word you choose does not have to mean anything: You can make a word up, you can use the word *one*, or you can try a word associated with the emotion you want to produce, such as *trust, love, patience*, or *happy*. Experiment with several different words to see which one works for you. At first, you will find that thoughts are intruding and that you are no longer attending to your breathing. Just return to your breathing and say the word each time you exhale.

After you have practiced this exercise for 10 to 15 minutes, twice a day, every day for 2 weeks, you will be ready for a shortened version. If you notice that you are experiencing stressful thoughts or circumstances, simply meditate, on the spot, for several minutes. If you are in public, you do not have to close your eyes; just fix your gaze on a nearby object, attend to your breathing, and say your word silently every time you exhale.

Meditation is an age-old practice. Without explicitly mentioning meditation, some religions advocate related practices such as daily

Being alone with our thoughts can be a source of great stress or one of strength.

© Galyna Andrushko, 2009. Used under license from Shutterstock, Inc.

prayer and peaceful introspection. Whether the practice involves praying over rosary beads, chanting before a Buddhist shrine, or simply taking a moment to commune with nature, a contemplative state clearly has broad appeal and conveys many benefits (Kabat-Zinn, 2006). Current research on the contemplative state suggests that there are good reasons why human beings have been harnessing its beneficial powers for centuries.

Being alone with your thoughts can be challenging. But with practice, meditation can help you to develop a clearer picture of your life, a stronger sense of your values, and ultimately a healthier and more positive perspective.

REVIEW AND SHARPEN YOUR THINKING

Discuss the role of the conscious mind in constructing a happy and healthy life.

- Give some positive and negative aspects of "being alone with one's thoughts."
- Describe the meditative state of mind and findings about the benefits of meditation to health and wellness.

Try meditating for just 15 minutes when you finish reading this chapter. What was the experience like? How would you describe the quality of your thoughts? Were you able to "let go"? Why or why not? Is the skill of meditation something you would like to pursue?

SUMMARY

1 THE NATURE OF CONSCIOUSNESS

Discuss the nature of consciousness.

Consciousness and the Brain

Consciousness is the awareness of external events and internal sensations, including awareness of the self and thoughts about experiences. Unanswered questions about consciousness concern its location—in the mind, in the brain?—and, if in the brain, whether there is a seat of consciousness or rather a distribution across different areas. Most experts agree that consciousness is likely distributed across the brain, although the association areas and prefrontal lobes are believed to play important roles in consciousness.

Levels of Awareness

William James described the mind as a stream of consciousness. Consciousness occurs at different levels of awareness that include higher-level awareness (controlled processes and selective attention), lower-level awareness (automatic processes and daydreaming), altered states of consciousness (produced by drugs, trauma, fatigue, and other factors), subconscious awareness (waking subconscious awareness, sleep, and dreams), and no awareness (unconscious thought).

2 SLEEP AND DREAMS

Explain the nature of sleep and dreams.

Biological Rhythms and Sleep

Biological rhythms are periodic physiological fluctuations. The biological rhythm that regulates the daily sleep/wake cycle is the circadian rhythm. The part of the brain that keeps our biological clocks synchronized is the suprachiasmatic nucleus, a small structure in the hypothalamus that registers light. Biological clocks can become desynchronized by such things as jet travel and work shifts. Some strategies are available for resetting the biological clock.

Why Do We Need Sleep?

We need sleep for physical restoration, adaptation, growth, and memory. Research studies increasingly reveal that people do not function optimally when they are sleep-deprived. In general, Americans—and adolescents and aging adults in particular—do not get enough sleep.

Sleep Stages

Stages of sleep correspond to massive electrophysiological changes that occur in the brain and that can be assessed by an EEG. Humans go through four stages of non-REM sleep and one stage of REM sleep, or rapid eye movement sleep. Most dreaming occurs during REM sleep. The amount of REM sleep changes over the life span. A sleep cycle of five stages lasts about 90 to 100 minutes and recurs several times during the night. The REM stage lasts longer toward the end of a night's sleep. The sleep stages are associated with distinct patterns of neurotransmitter activity. Levels of the neurotransmitters serotonin, norepinephrine, and acetylcholine decrease as the sleep cycle progresses from stage 1 through stage 4. Stage 5, REM sleep, begins when the reticular formation raises the level of acetylcholine.

Sleep and Disease

Sleep plays a role in a large number of diseases and disorders. Neurons that control sleep interact closely with the immune system, and when our bodies are fighting infection our cells produce a substance that makes us sleepy. Individuals with depression often have sleep problems.

Sleep Disorders

Many Americans suffer from chronic, long-term sleep disorders that can impair normal daily functioning. These include insomnia, sleep-walking and sleep talking, nightmares and night terrors, narcolepsy, and sleep apnea.

Dreams

There are cultural and gender variations in dreaming. People in primitive cultures more often tie dreaming to reality or to the spiritual than do people in modern cultures. In Freud's view, dreams represented symbols of unconscious wishes. The cognitive theory of dreaming attempts to explain dreaming in terms of the same cognitive concepts that are used in studying the waking mind. In this view, dreams might be an arena for solving problems and thinking creatively. According to activation-synthesis theory, dreaming occurs when the cerebral cortex synthesizes neural signals emanating from activity in the lower part of the brain. In this view, the rising level of acetylcholine during REM sleep plays a role in neural activity in the reticular formation of the limbic system that the cerebral cortex tries to make sense of.

3 HYPNOSIS

Describe hypnosis.

The Nature of Hypnosis

Hypnosis is a psychological state or possibly altered attention and awareness in which the individual is unusually receptive to suggestions. The hypnotic state is different from a sleep state, as confirmed by EEG recordings. Inducing hypnosis involves four basic steps, beginning with minimizing distractions and making the person feel comfortable and ending with the hypnotist's suggesting certain events or feelings that he or she knows will occur or observes occurring. There are substantial individual variations in people's susceptibility to hypnosis. People in a hypnotic state are unlikely to do anything that violates their morals or that involves a real danger.

Explaining Hypnosis

Two theories have been proposed to explain hypnosis. In Hilgard's divided consciousness view, hypnosis involves a divided state of consciousness, a splitting of consciousness into separate components. One component follows the hypnotist's commands; the other acts as a "hidden observer." In the social cognitive behavior view, hypnotized individuals behave the way they believe hypnotized individuals are expected to behave.

Applications of Hypnosis

Hypnosis is widely used in psychotherapy and medicine and has become more popular in Europe as a complement to more standard anesthesia.

4 PSYCHOACTIVE DRUGS

Evaluate the uses and types of psychoactive drugs.

Uses of Psychoactive Drugs

Psychoactive drugs act on the nervous system to alter states of consciousness, modify perceptions, and change moods. Humans are attracted to these types of drugs because they help people adapt to change. Addictive drugs activate the brain's reward system by increasing dopamine concentration. The reward pathway involves the ventral tegmental area (VTA) and nucleus accumbens. The abuse of psychoactive drugs can lead to tolerance, psychological and physical dependence, and addiction—a pattern of behavior characterized by a preoccupation with using a drug and securing its supply.

Types of Psychoactive Drugs

Depressants slow down mental and physical activity. Among the most widely used depressants are alcohol, barbiturates, tranquilizers, and opiates. After caffeine, alcohol is the most widely used drug in America. The high rate of alcohol abuse by high school and college students is especially alarming. Alcoholism is a disorder that involves long-term, repeated, uncontrolled, compulsive, and excessive use of alcoholic beverages that impairs the drinker's health and work and social relationships. Stimulants increase the central nervous system's activity and include caffeine, nicotine, amphetamines, cocaine, and MDMA (Ecstasy). Hallucinogens modify a person's perceptual experiences and produce visual images that are not real. Marijuana has a mild hallucinogenic effect. LSD has a strong one.

5 CONSCIOUSNESS AND HEALTH AND WELLNESS

Discuss the role of the conscious mind in constructing a happy and healthy life.

Positive and Negative Aspects of Our Thoughts

How we think about our lives and experiences plays a role in determining whether we feel stressed and worried or challenged and excited about life. Seeking times of quiet contemplation can have a positive impact on our abilities to cope with life's ups and downs.

The Meditative State of Mind

One powerful tool for managing life's problems is mindfulness meditation. Meditation refers to a state of quiet reflection. Meditation has benefits for a wide range of psychological and physical illnesses. Meditation can also benefit the body's immune system. Research using fMRI suggests that meditation allows an individual to control his or her thoughts in order to "let go" of the need to control.

KEY TERMS

activation-synthesis
    theory
addiction
alcoholism
automatic processes
barbiturates
biological rhythms
circadian rhythm
cognitive theory of
    dreaming
consciousness

controlled processes
depressants
hallucinogens
hypnosis
ior view of hypnosis
opiates
physical dependence
psychoactive drugs
psychological
    dependence
REM sleep

social cognitive
    behavtolerance
stimulants
stream of
    consciousness
suprachiasmatic
    nucleus (SCN)
tranquilizers
unconscious thought

Chapter 6: States of Consciousness

END OF CHAPTER QUIZ

1. The type of brain activity you have while awake.
   a. Alpha waves
   b. Delta waves
   c. Stage four activity
   d. Manifest content

2. The story line of a dream is called the:
   a. Imagination process
   b. Wish fulfillment
   c. Latent content
   d. Manifest content

3. The BEST definition for "States of Consciousness" is:
   a. Unconscious motivational factors
   b. What you are currently aware of
   c. How you feel emotionally
   d. Your physical state

4. Circadian rhythms follow which cycle length?
   a. 12 hours
   b. 24 hours
   c. 28 days
   d. 365 day periods

5. Which of the following is a correct representation of sleep cycle stages?
   a. REM,2,3,4,5,3,2
   b. 1,2,3,4,3,2,1
   c. 1,2,3,4,3,2,REM
   d. REM,4,3,2,1,2,3,4

6. In which sleep period does dreaming occur?
   a. REM
   b. 2
   c. 3
   d. 4

7. REM sleep seems to positively influence:
   a. Memory
   b. Posthypnotic suggestions
   c. Near death experiences
   d. Divided consciousness

8. Which of the following is NOT associated with dreaming?
   a. Body paralysis
   b. Eye movements
   c. Sleep walking
   d. Sexual arousal

9. Which of the following will NOT occur if you are sleep deprived?
   a. General malaise
   b. Weakened immune system
   c. Hallucinations
   d. Increases in semantic memory recognition

10. Which of the following sleep disorders occur during stage 4 sleep?
    a. Sleep apnea
    b. Night terrors
    c. Narcolepsy
    d. Insomnia

11. On average, a newborn infant will dream _____ hours per day.
    a. 4
    b. 8
    c. 12
    d. 16

12. Hypnosis is a combination of:
    a. Social influence and splits in consciousness
    b. Sleep and concentration
    c. Daydreaming and concentration
    d. Splits in consciousness and concentration

13. Hypnotized subjects will behave in a manner similar to people who were only asked to pretend to be hypnotized.
    a. True
    b. False

14. How many general classes of psychoactive drugs are there?
    a. 1
    b. 2
    c. 3
    d. 4

15. A substance that makes you feel less pain that has been used as a anesthetic.
    a. Caffeine
    b. Amphetamine

c. Opiates
d. Marijuana

16. This thing is positively correlated with dependence.
    a. Delta waves
    b. Withdrawal
    c. Detoxification
    d. Seizures

17. Marijuana officially belongs to which drug class?
    a. Depressants
    b. Stimulants
    c. Hallucinogens
    d. Opiates

18. Meditation has been known to improve both mental and physical health due to its calming effect on the person
    a. True
    b. False

19. Hypnosis-based smoking-cessation programs have generally not been associated with great success.
    a. True
    b. False

20. The strong desire to repeatedly use a drug due to emotional reasons is called:
    a. Physical dependence
    b. Tolerance
    c. Psychological dependence
    d. Addiction

21. Which of the following is required to observe a state of awareness?
    a. Language
    b. Consciousness
    c. Automatic processes
    d. Hypnosis
    e. Unconscious thought

22. Which of the following is used to assess the consciousness of nonhumans?
    a. Suprachiasmatic nucleus
    b. Biological rhythms
    c. Controlled processes
    d. Learning and memory
    e. Activation-synthesis theory

23. A basic understanding of what consciousness will reveal the connection between these things:
    a. Attention, language, consciousness
    b. Attention, working memory, language
    c. Working memory, language, automatic processes
    d. Language, unconscious thought, activation-synthesis theory

24. Which of the following uses a "lower-level consciousness?"
    a. Focused attention
    b. Daydreaming
    c. Drugs
    d. Dreaming
    e. Anesthesia

25. Which of the following statements has little or no scientific support?
    a. Probabilistic reasoning dominates psychological theory
    b. Brain circuits control many, if not all, forms of human behavior
    c. Genes and environment each control about 50% of the variability in behavior
    d. Mental conflict in the subconscious is a hidden form of human behavior control

26. Which two cycles are related to sleeping and dreaming?
    a. 365 day and 28 day
    b. 24 hours and 90 minutes
    c. 24 hours and 28 days
    d. 90 minutes and 28 days

27. Which of the following sensations are associated with hypnagogic sensations?
    a. Feelings of fear
    b. Feeling that a hand is grabbing your wrist
    c. Feeling of weightlessness
    d. Feeling that is difficult to breath

28. As an evening of sleep progresses, you are less likely to experience:
    a. Dreaming
    b. Sleep apnea
    c. Alpha waves
    d. Stage 4 sleep

29. Most dreams occur during _____ sleep.
    a. Stage 1 sleep
    b. Stage 2 sleep
    c. Stage 3 sleep
    d. Stage 4 sleep
    e. REM sleep

30. Which of the following events is most likely to influence your nightly dreams?
    a. The fact that you have been waiting for three weeks to see if you get fired in the next round of workplace cutbacks
    b. Your emotional reaction to the wedding you attended yesterday
    c. The emotionally laden thriller you watched at noontime
    d. The funny movie you watched just before going to bed
    e. Both A & D

31. Which of the following lists go together?
    a. Consciousness, cognitive theory of dreaming, hypnosis
    b. Dreams, REM activity, memory consolidation
    c. Tolerance, physical dependence, controlled processes
    d. Biological rhythms, hypnosis, depressants

32. What happens to the amount of REM sleep you experience each night over the course of your lifetime?
    a. It decreases
    b. It does not change
    c. It increases
    d. It changes in topography

33. Which of the following was not mentioned as something sleepwalkers have been known to do?
    a. Eating
    b. Driving
    c. Talking
    d. Paying bills

34. Lucid dreams are characterized by:
    a. Tolerance to nightmares
    b. Your knowledge that you are dreaming
    c. Unconsciousness thoughts expressed during the dream
    d. Automatic processes related to dream integration

35. Franz Mesmer began using a form of hypnosis in the late 18th century; however, it was not until _____ in 1843 do we see the modern form of hypnosis appear.
    a. Braid
    b. Avner
    c. Fields
    d. Holt

36. Which of the following behaviors might a hypnotized person be likely to carry out?
    a. Feel an urge to make a sandwich
    b. Rob a bank
    c. Punch their loving spouse
    d. Spend all the money in their bank account
    e. Work as an assassin

37. What is a major contributor to the fact that hypnotized patients in experiments seem willing to do anything, including acts of violence?
    a. The influence of "stream of consciousness"
    b. Unconscious thoughts
    c. The subject's assumption of safety in the experiment
    d. The role of activation-synthesis theory

38. Which of the following is unlikely to benefit from hypnotherapy?
    a. Smoking cessation program
    b. Pain-management program
    c. Therapy for overcoming social anxiety
    d. Driving instruction

39. Which of the following is not related to recreational drug use?
    a. Reward
    b. Tolerance
    c. Dependence
    d. Biological rhythms
    e. Addiction

40. People are getting addicted to a hypothetical new drug called Quickies. Quickies make you feel awake and talkative. Frequently, people who take Quickies stay awake for two days dancing at raves, talking to everyone and generally feeling very happy and excited. When Quickies addicts start coming to your drug detoxification clinic for treatment, what type of withdrawal symptoms do you expect to see in them?
    a. Convulsions and hallucinations
    b. Hallucinations and vomiting
    c. Extreme weakness and a perception that time is passing slowly
    d. Hallucinations and talkative

41. Which of the following is not a general class of psychoactive drugs?
    a. Muscle relaxants
    b. Stimulants
    c. Depressants
    d. Hallucinogenics

42. Which of the following is not a stimulant?
    a. Methamphetamine
    b. Alcohol
    c. Nicotine
    d. Cocaine

43. Which of the following is not a depressant?
    a. Muscle relaxants
    b. Alcohol
    c. Anti-anxiety medications
    d. Cocaine

44. Which of the following is not a hallucinogenic?
    a. Methamphetamine
    b. LSD
    c. Peyote
    d. Ecstasy

45. Which of the following reasons is generally given as to why meditation may have beneficial psychological effects?
    a. Lowered blood pressure keeps you out of the doctor's office
    b. Meditation is brain training
    c. Reductions in stress may make someone more capable of dealing with future stress
    d. Increased alpha wave activity increases the division of labor across the cerebral hemispheres

46. Déjà vu is:
    a. Proof that consciousness streams can cross physical barriers
    b. A period of reduced stimulus salience
    c. Understood as a situation in which environmental cues are again present but in a weaker state
    d. Related to completely novel environments

47. Out-of-body experiences do not occur from:
    a. Almost dying
    b. Drug use
    c. Insomnia
    d. Prolong extreme stress

48. Which of the following is not a recognized component of near-death experiences?
    a. Permanent death
    b. Progression toward a light
    c. An out-of-body experience
    d. Dreams

49. Substances which make you see things that are not there.
    a. Depressants
    b. Stimulants
    c. Hallucinogenics
    d. Opiates

50. Substances which are frequently used to reduce pain but also influence your thinking processes.
    a. Depressants
    b. Stimulants
    c. Hallucinogenics
    d. Opiates

Answers: 1. A; 2. D; 3. B; 4. B; 5. C; 6. A; 7. A; 8. C; 9. D; 10. B; 11. B; 12. A; 13. A; 14. C; 15. C; 16. B; 17. C; 18. A; 19. A; 20. C; 21. A; 22. D; 23. A; 24. B; 25. D; 26. B; 27. C; 28. D; 29. E; 30. E; 31. B; 32. A; 33. D; 34. B; 35. A; 36. A; 37. C; 38. D; 39. D; 40. C; 41. A; 42. B; 43. D; 44. A; 45. C; 46. C; 47. C; 48. A; 49. C; 50. D

Improving College Grades through Drug Use—Or Not

Wouldn't college be easy if there were some way to immediately learn everything you needed to know and a guarantee that you will retain all that information for later with perfectly accurate recall? This need to learn quickly is omnipresent on college campuses and elsewhere when people frequently need to absorb new information.

We previously reviewed one of the quack attempts to learn quickly when we reviewed the evidence for subliminal messaging. Currently, another technique from dietary supplement manufacturers has become more popular; the use of ginkgo biloba as a cognitive enhancement supplement. Advertisements indicate that ginkgo may increase the ability to concentrate, learn, and remember. Thankfully, these reports may be investigated scientifically so that we can all begin using ginkgo if it really works.

A study conducted at Williams College (Williamstown, MA) conducted a placebo-controlled, double-blind study of 230 healthy volunteers: They were evaluated while taking a 40 mg dose three times per day over the course of six weeks. Standardized, objective tests of learning and memory, attention and concentration, as well as language-skills-use were applied to assess for gingko's cognitive effects.

Results indicated that the experimental group (n = 115) did not differ statistically in any cognitive skill from the control group (n = 115). Therefore, there was no evidence that ginkgo had any beneficial effects on the measured abilities.

The message that one can take away from this study is that this herbal remedy does not improve cognitive skills. I would not be surprised to find that, in a few years, a new substance, touted as all-natural and herbal, will replace gingko biloba as a new cognitive aid. When it does, I'm sure that millions of dollars will be spent on the manufacture, advertisement, and sale of the substance before anyone actually gets around to evaluating it in a placebo-controlled, double-blind study.

References

Solomon, P. R., Adams, F., Silver, A., Zimmer, J., and DeVeaux, R. (2002). Ginkgo for memory enhancement: A randomized controlled trial. *Journal of the American Medical Association*, 288, 835–840.

CHAPTER OUTLINE

DEFINITION OF LEARNING

What is Learning?

The term *learning* is one of those concepts whose meaning is crystal clear until one has to put it in actual words. "Learning is when you learn something." "Learning is learning how to do something." A more useful definition is as follows: *Learning* is any relatively permanent change in behavior brought about by experience or practice.

What does "relatively permanent" mean? And how does experience change what we do? The "relatively permanent" part of the definition refers to the fact that when people learn anything, some part of their brain is physically changed to record what they've learned. This is actually a process of memory, for without the ability to remember what happens, people cannot learn anything. Although there is no conclusive proof as yet, research suggests strongly that once people learn something, it is always present somewhere in memory (Barsalou, 1992). They may be unable to "get" to it, but it's there.

As for the part about experience or practice, think about the last time you did something that caused you a lot of pain. Are you going to do it again? Of course not. You don't want to experience that pain again, so you change your behavior to avoid the painful consequence.* This is how children learn not to touch hot stoves. Of course, if a person does something that results in a very pleasurable consequence, that person is more likely to do that same thing again. This is another change in behavior. Think back to the prologue. Stephanie's experience with the doctor and the nurse changed her behavior from that of a

---

* Consequence: an end result of some action.

friendly, outgoing infant to a frightened, screaming child whenever she saw anyone in a white coat coming near her.

So, is any kind of change learning? Not all change is accomplished through learning. Any kind of change in the way an organism *behaves* is learning. Changes like an increase in height or the size of the brain are another kind of change controlled by a genetic blueprint. This kind of change is called *maturation*, and it is not the same as learning. For example, children learn to walk *when* they do because their nervous systems, muscle strength, and sense of balance have reached the point where walking is possible for them—all factors controlled by maturation, not by how much practice those children have had in trying to walk. No amount of experience or practice will help that child walk before maturation makes it possible—in spite of what some eager parents might wish.

IT MAKES YOUR MOUTH WATER: CLASSICAL CONDITIONING

In the early 1900s, when Freud was just becoming famous in Europe and the structuralists and functionalists were arguing over consciousness in the ivy-covered halls of American universities, research scientists were unhappy with psychology's focus on mental activity. Many were looking for a way to bring some kind of objectivity and scientific research to the field.

It was not a psychologist who accomplished that goal. It was a Russian *physiologist* (a person who studies the workings of the body) named Ivan Pavlov (1849–1936) who accidentally stumbled across the basic principles of a particular kind of learning (Pavlov, 1926).

What is Classical Conditioning and Who First Studied It?

Studying the digestive system in his dogs, Pavlov had built a device that would accurately measure the amount of saliva produced by the dogs when they were fed a measured amount of food. Normally, when food is placed in the mouth of any animal, the salivary glands automatically start releasing saliva to help with chewing and digestion. This is a normal *reflex* (involuntary* response) in both animals and humans. The food causes a particular reaction, the salivation. A *stimulus* can be defined as any object, event, or experience that causes a *response*, the reaction of an organism. In the case of Pavlov's dogs, the food is the stimulus and salivation is the response.

Ivan Pavlov was celebrated on this Russian stamp in 1969.

Pavlov and the Salivating Dogs

What first annoyed and then intrigued Pavlov was that his dogs began salivating when they weren't supposed to be salivating. Some dogs would start salivating when they saw the lab assistant bringing their food, others when they heard clatter of the food bowl from the kitchen, and still others when it was the time of day they were usually fed. Pavlov spent the rest of his career studying what eventually he termed **classical conditioning**, learning to make a reflex response to a stimulus other than the original, natural stimulus that normally produces it.

classical conditioning: learning to make a reflex response to a stimulus other than the original, natural stimulus that normally produces the reflex.

---

* Involuntary: not under personal control or choice.

Elements of Classical Conditioning

Pavlov eventually identified several key elements that must be present and experienced in a particular way for conditioning to take place.

What are the Important Concepts in Classical Conditioning?

Unconditioned Stimulus

unconditioned stimulus (UCS): a naturally occurring stimulus that leads to an involuntary response.

The original, naturally occurring stimulus mentioned in the preceding paragraph is called the unconditioned stimulus (UCS). The term *unconditioned* means "unlearned" or "naturally occurring." This is the stimulus that ordinarily leads to the reflex, involuntary response. In the case of Pavlov's dogs, the food served is the unconditioned stimulus.

Unconditioned Response

unconditioned response (UCR): an involuntary response to a naturally occurring or unconditioned stimulus.

The reflex response to the unconditioned stimulus is called the unconditioned response (UCR) for much the same reason. It is unlearned and occurs because of genetic "wiring" in the nervous system. For example, in Pavlov's experiment, the food given to the dogs is the UCS, and the salivation to that food is the UCR.

Conditioned Stimulus

neutral stimulus (NS): stimulus that has no effect on the desired response.

Pavlov determined that almost any kind of stimulus could become associated with the unconditioned stimulus (UCS) if it is paired with the UCS often enough. In his original study, for example, the sight of the food dish itself became a stimulus for salivation *before* the food was given to the dogs. Every time they got food (to which they naturally salivated), they saw the dish. At this point, the dish was called a neutral stimulus (NS) because it had no effect on salivation. After being paired with the food so many times, the dish came to produce the same salivation response, although a somewhat weaker one, as did the food itself. When a previously neutral stimulus, through repeated pairing with the unconditioned stimulus, begins to cause the same kind of reflexive response, learning has occurred. The neutral stimulus can now be called a conditioned stimulus (CS). (*Unconditioned* means "unlearned," and *conditioned* means "learned.")

conditioned stimulus (CS): stimulus that becomes able to produce a learned reflex response by being paired with the original unconditioned stimulus.

Conditioned Response

The response that is given to the CS is not usually quite as strong as the original unconditioned response (UCR), but it is essentially the same response. However, because it comes as a response to the conditioned stimulus, it is called the conditioned response (CR) or sometimes the *conditioned reflex*.

conditioned response (CR): learned reflex response to a conditioned stimulus.

Putting It All Together: Pavlov's Canine Classic, or Ding, Dong, Bell

What was Pavlov's Classic Experiment in Conditioning?

The whole idea of classical conditioning is not as complex as it sounds. What gets tough is keeping all the letters straight: UCS, UCR, CS, and CR. Pavlov did a classic experiment in which he paired the ringing of a bell with the presentation of food to see if the dogs would eventually salivate to the sound of the bell. Since the bell did not normally produce salivation, it was the neutral stimulus (NS) before any conditioning took place. The repeated pairing of the NS and the UCS is usually called *acquisition*, because the organism is in the process of acquiring learning.

Notice that the responses, CR and UCR, are the same—salivation. They simply differ in what they are the response *to*. An unconditioned stimulus (UCS) is always followed by an unconditioned response (UCR), and a conditioned stimulus (CS) is always followed by a conditioned response (CR).

Is this rocket science? No, not really. Classical conditioning is actually one of the simplest forms of learning. It's so simple that it happens to people all the time without their even being aware of it. Does your mouth water when you merely see an advertisement for your favorite food on television? Does your stomach get upset every time you hear the high-pitched whine of the dentist's drill? These are both examples of classical conditioning.

After all the dog stories, the salivation to the TV ad probably needs no explanation, but what about the dentist's drill? Over the course of many visits, the body comes to associate that sound (CS) with the anxiety or fear (UCR) the person has felt while receiving a painful dental treatment (UCS), and so the sound produces a feeling of anxiety (CR) whether that person is in the chair or just in the outer waiting area.

Although classical conditioning happens quite easily, there are a few basic principles that researchers have discovered:

(1) The CS must come *before* the UCS. If Pavlov rang the bell just after he gave the dogs the food, they did not become conditioned (Rescorla, 1988).

(2) The CS and UCS must come very close together in time—ideally, only several seconds apart. When Pavlov tried to stretch the time between the potential CS and the UCS to several minutes, no association was made. Too much could happen in the longer interval of time to interfere with conditioning (Pavlov, 1926; Wasserman & Miller, 1997).

(3) The neutral stimulus must be paired with the UCS several times, often many times, before conditioning can take place (Pavlov, 1926).

(4) The CS is usually some stimulus that is distinctive* or stands out from other competing stimuli. The bell was a sound that was not normally present in the laboratory and, therefore, distinct (Pavlov, 1926; Rescorla, 1988).

That seems simple enough. But I have to know—did Pavlov's dogs salivate to the doorbell, too? They certainly could have, if the doorbell were similar in sound to the CS bell, and if the dogs were near enough to hear the doorbell, and assuming Pavlov even *had* a doorbell.

© Jamie Wilson, 2011. Used under license from Shutterstock, Inc.

The music from the ice cream truck always precedes the times you eat its ice cream. Therefore, the music from the truck comes to control a salivary response.

Stimulus Generalization and Discrimination

Pavlov did find that similar-sounding bells would produce the same conditioned response from his dogs. He and other researchers found that the strength of the response to the similar bells was not as strong as to the original one, but the more similar the other bell tone was to the original bell tone, the more similar the strength of the response was as well (Siegel, 1969). (See **Figure 7.1**.) The tendency to respond to a stimulus that is only similar to the original conditioned stimulus is called **stimulus generalization**. For example, a person who reacts

> **stimulus generalization:** the tendency to respond to a stimulus that is only similar to the original conditioned stimulus with the conditioned response.

---

* Distinctive: separate, having a different quality from something else.

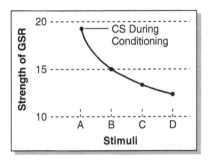

FIGURE 7.1 ■ Strength of the Generalized Response. An example of generalization. The subjects had been conditioned originally to a CS (A) of a given frequency. When tested with the original tone, and with tones B, C, and D of differing frequencies, a clear generalization gradient appeared. The closer the frequency of the test tone to the frequency of tone A, the greater was the magintude of the response to the tone. (Howland, 1937).

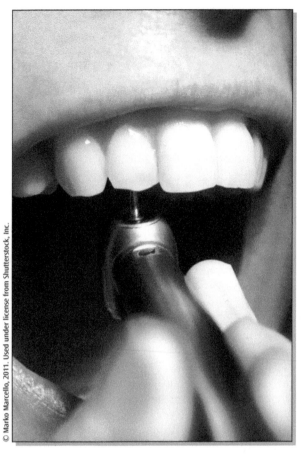

For some readers, the view of this dentist's drill is enough to make you feel squeamish. The reason is that the sight of the drill has previously been associated with pain for you.

stimulus discrimination: the tendency to stop making a generalized response to a stimulus that is similar to the original conditioned stimulus because the similar stimulus is never paired with the unconditioned stimulus.

with anxiety to the sound of a dentist's drill might react with some slight anxiety to a similar-sounding machine, such as an electric coffee grinder.

Of course, Pavlov did not give the dogs any food after the similar bell sounded. They only got food following the correct CS. It didn't take long for the dogs to stop responding (generalizing) to the "fake" bell sounds altogether. Because only the real CS was followed with food, they learned to tell the difference, or *discriminate*, between the "fake" bells and the real one, a process called **stimulus discrimination**. Stimulus discrimination occurs when an organism learns to respond to different stimuli in different ways. For example, although the sound of the coffee grinder might produce a little anxiety in the dental-drill-hating person, after a few uses that sound will no longer produce anxiety because it isn't associated with dental pain.

Extinction and Spontaneous Recovery

extinction: the disappearance or weakening of a learned response following the removal or absence of the unconditioned stimulus (in classical conditioning) or the removal of a reinforcer (in operant conditioning).

What would have happened if Pavlov had stopped giving the dogs food after the real CS? Pavlov did just that, and the dogs gradually stopped salivating to the sound of the bell. When the bell (CS) was repeatedly presented in the absence of the UCS (food, in this case), the salivation (CR) "died out" in a process called **extinction**.

Why does the removal of an unconditioned stimulus lead to extinction of the conditioned response? Once conditioning is acquired, the conditioned stimulus (CS) and conditioned response (CR) will always come *before* the original unconditioned stimulus (UCS). The UCS now serves as a **reinforcer** (strengthener) of the CS–CR association. Remove the reinforcer, and the CR it strengthens will weaken and disappear.

The term *extinction* is a little unfortunate in that it seems to mean that the original conditioned response is totally gone, dead, never coming back, just like the dinosaurs. Remember the definition of learning is any relatively *permanent* change in behavior. The fact is that once people learn something, it's almost impossible to "unlearn" it. People can learn new things that replace it, or lose their way to it in memory, but it's still there. In the case of classical conditioning, this is easily demonstrated.

After extinguishing the conditioned salivation response in his dogs, Pavlov waited a few weeks, putting the bell away. There were no more training sessions and the dogs were not exposed to the bell's ringing in that time at all. But when Pavlov took the bell back out and rang it, the dogs all began to salivate, although it was a fairly weak response and didn't last very long. This brief recovery of the conditioned response proves that the CR is still in there somewhere. It isn't dead and gone, it's just suppressed or inhibited by the lack of an association with the unconditioned stimulus of food (which is no longer reinforcing the CR). As time passes, this inhibition weakens, especially if the original conditioned stimulus has not been present for a while. In **spontaneous recovery** the conditioned response can briefly reappear when the original CS returns, although the response is usually weak and short-lived. See **Figure 7.2** for a graph showing both extinction and spontaneous recovery.

If Pavlov had followed the dogs' spontaneous salivation to the bell with food, their conditioning would have resurfaced in no time at all. This would be an example of retraining. Retraining is made simpler by the fact that the extinguished response isn't really gone, just suppressed.

People experience classical conditioning in many ways. A person who has been hit from behind in a car accident, for example, will spend the next few weeks cringing every time another vehicle gets too close to the rear of the car. That cringing reaction is a conditioned response. The crash itself was the UCS and the closeness of the other cars becomes a CS. People who are allergic to cats sometimes sneeze when they see a *picture* of a cat. One of the recommendations was to avoid reading, working, watching television, or eating in bed. The bed should

> **reinforcer:** any event or object that, when following a response, increases the likelihood of that response occurring again.

> **spontaneous recovery:** the reappearance of a learned response after extinction has occurred.

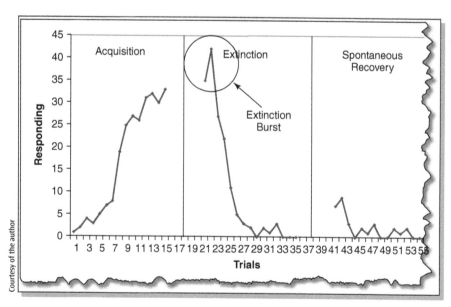

FIGURE 7.2 ■ The acquisition, extinction and spontaneous recovery of a response.

only be used for sleeping (a reflex) and will eventually become a conditioned stimulus for sleeping.

Higher-Order Conditioning

Another concept in classical conditioning is **higher-order conditioning**. This occurs when a strong conditioned stimulus is paired with a neutral stimulus. The strong CS can actually play the part of a UCS, and the previously neutral stimulus becomes a *second* conditioned stimulus.

For example, let's assume that Pavlov has conditioned his dogs to salivate at the sound of the bell. What would happen if just before Pavlov rang the bell, he snapped his fingers? The sequence would now be "snap-bell-salivation," or "NS-CS-CR." If this happens enough times, the finger snap will eventually also produce a salivation response. The finger snap becomes associated with the bell through the same process that the bell became associated with the food originally and is now another conditioned stimulus.

Conditioned Emotional Responses: Rats!

Later scientists took Pavlov's concepts and expanded them to explain not only animal behavior but also human behavior. One of the earliest of these studies showed that even an emotional response could be conditioned.

What is a Conditioned Emotional Response?

Watson and "Little Albert"

In the first chapter of this text, John B. Watson was discussed as the founder of *behaviorism*. He firmly believed that all behavior could be explained in terms of learning, including even the *phobias* (irrational fear responses) that the Freudian camp thought were deeply rooted in the unconscious mind. His classic experiment with "Little Albert" and the white rat was a demonstration of learning a phobia (Watson & Rayner, 1920). It was also a very good example of classical conditioning.

Watson paired the presentation of the white rat to the baby with a loud, scary noise. Although the baby was not afraid of the rat, he was naturally afraid of the loud noise and started to cry. Soon, every time the baby saw the rat, he started to cry. In conditioning terms, the loud noise was the UCS, the fear of the noise the UCR, the white rat became the CS, and the fear of the rat (the phobia) was the CR. (See **Figure 7.4**.) (Of course, no ethics committee today would approve an experiment in which an infant experiences psychological distress like this.)

The learning of phobias is a very good example of a certain type of classical conditioning, the **conditioned emotional response (CER)**. Conditioned emotional responses are some of the easiest forms of classical conditioning to accomplish and our lives are full of them. It's easy to think of fears people might have that are conditioned or learned: a child's fear of the dentist's chair, a puppy's fear of a rolled-up newspaper, or the fear of dogs that is often shown by a person who has been attacked by a dog in the past. But other emotions can be conditioned, too.

The next time you watch television, watch the commercials closely. Advertisers often use certain objects or certain types of people in their ads to generate a certain emotional response in viewers, hoping that the emotional response will become associated with their product. Sexy models, cute little babies, and adorable puppies are some of the examples of stimuli the advertising world uses to tug at our heartstrings, so to speak.

Other television messages are meant to elicit a fear response, such as messages about what drugs will do to your brain. In a classic public service message from the 1980s, a woman holds up an egg and says, "This is your brain." She then drops the egg into a grease-filled, smoking hot skillet and says, "This is your brain on drugs. Any questions?" This spot was supposed to cause disgust by showing the egg being cracked into a filthy-looking skillet and getting immediately fried to a crisp.

It is even possible to become classically conditioned by simply watching someone else respond to a stimulus in a process called **vicarious conditioning** (Bandura & Rosenthal, 1966). Many years ago, children received vaccination shots in school. The nurse lined the children up, and one by one they had to go forward to get a needle in the arm. When some children received their shots, they cried quite a bit. By the time the nurse got near the end of the line of children, they were all crying—many of them before she ever touched needle to skin. They had learned their fear reflex from watching the reactions of the other children.

vicarious conditioning: classical conditioning of a reflex response or emotion by watching the reaction of another person.

Other Conditioned Responses in Humans

Are there any foods that you just can't eat anymore because of a bad experience with them? Believe it or not, your reaction to that food is a kind of classical conditioning.

Many experiments have shown that laboratory rats will develop a **conditioned taste aversion** for any liquid or food they swallow up to six hours before becoming nauseated. Researchers (Garcia et al., 1989; Garcia & Koelling, 1966) found that rats that were given a sweetened liquid and then injected with a drug or exposed to radiation* that caused nausea would not touch the liquid again. (In a similar manner, alcoholics who are given a drug to make them nauseated when they drink alcohol may learn to avoid drinking any alcoholic beverage.)

But I thought that it took several pairings of these stimuli to bring about conditioning. How can classical conditioning happen so fast?

conditioned taste aversion: development of a nausea or aversive response to a particular taste because that taste was followed by a nausea reaction, occurring after only one association.

Biological Preparedness

Conditioned taste aversions are an example of something called **biological preparedness**. Most mammals, who find their food by smell and taste, will learn to avoid any food that smells or tastes like something they are just before becoming ill. It's a survival mechanism, because if they kept on eating a "bad" food, they might die. The mammalian** body seems to be prepared to associate smell and taste with getting sick (Garcia & Koelling, 1966; Seligman, 1970). Although most conditioning requires repeated pairings of CS with UCS, when the response is nausea, one pairing seems to be all that is necessary. Taste aversion conditioning is so effective that it has even been used by renowned psychologist Dr. John Garcia and colleagues as a tool to stop coyotes from killing ranchers' sheep and also to stop the ranchers from wiping out the coyote population entirely (Gustavson et al., 1976). Garcia and his fellow researchers laced sheep meat with lithium chloride and left it for the coyotes to find. The coyotes ate the drugged meat, got extremely sick, and

biological preparedness: referring to the tendency of animals to learn certain associations, such as taste and nausea, with only one or few pairings due to the survival value of the learning.

© Sari Oneal, 2011. Used under license from Shutterstock, Inc.

The Monarch butterfly is poisonous to birds. Therefore, birds will avoid any butterfly or moth that looks similar to the Monarch.

---

* Radiation: beams of energy.

** Mammalian: having to do with mammals (animals with fur or hair who feed their young with milk from milk glands).

avoided eating sheep for quite some time afterwards. The coyotes got to live and the ranchers got to keep their sheep.

It's interesting to note that birds, which find their food by sight, will avoid any object or insect that simply *looks* like the one that made them sick. There is a certain species of moth with coloring that mimics the monarch butterfly. The butterfly is poisonous to birds, but the moth isn't. The moths' mimicry causes birds to avoid eating them, even though they are quite edible. Whereas mammals are biologically prepared to associate taste with illness, birds are biologically prepared to associate visual characteristics with illness (Shapiro et al., 1980).

Why Does Classical Conditioning Work?

There are two ways to explain how one stimulus comes to "stand in" for another. One is the original explanation given by Pavlov, whereas the other is based on a cognitive explanation.

Why Does Classical Conditioning Work?

stimulus substitution: original theory in which Pavlov stated that classical conditioning occurred because the conditioned stimulus became a substitute for the unconditioned stimulus by being paired closely together.

Pavlov believed that the conditioned stimulus, through its association close in time with the unconditioned stimulus, came to activate the same place in the animal's brain that was originally activated by the unconditioned stimulus. He called this process stimulus substitution. But if a mere association in time is all that is needed, why would conditioning *fail to happen* when the CS is presented immediately *after* the UCS?

Robert Rescorla (1988) found that the CS has to provide some kind of information about the coming of the UCS in order to achieve conditioning. In other words, the CS must predict that the UCS is coming. In one study, Rescorla exposed one group of rats to a tone, and just after the tone's onset and while the tone was still able to be heard, an electric shock was administered for some of the tone presentations. Soon the rats became agitated* and reacted in fear by shivering and squealing at the onset of the tone, a kind of conditioned emotional response. But with a second group of rats, Rescorla again sounded a tone, but administered the electric shock only *after* the tone *stopped*, not while the tone was being heard. That group of rats responded with fear to the *stopping* of the tone (Rescorla, 1968).

The tone for the second group of rats provided a different kind of information than the tone in the first instance. For the first group, the tone means the shock is coming, whereas for the second group, the tone means there is no shock while the tone is on. It was the particular *expectancy* created by pairing the tone or absence of tone with the shock that determined the particular response of the rats. Because this explanation involves the mental activity of consciously expecting something to occur, it is an example of an explanation for classical conditioning called the cognitive perspective.

So far, all learning seems to involve reflex behavior. What about how we learn voluntary behavior such as brushing and flossing?

cognitive perspective: modern theory in which classical conditioning is seen to occur because the conditioned stimulus provides information or an expectancy about the coming of the unconditioned stimulus.

WHAT'S IN IT FOR ME? OPERANT CONDITIONING

What is Operant Conditioning and Thorndike's Law of Effect?

There are two kinds of behavior that all organisms are capable of doing: involuntary (reflexive) and voluntary. If Inez blinks her eyes because a gnat flies

---

* Agitated: excited, upset.

close to them, that's a reflex and totally involuntary. But if she then swats at the gnat to frighten it, that's a voluntary choice. She *had* to blink, but she *chose* to swat.

Classical conditioning is the kind of learning that occurs with reflexive, involuntary behavior. The kind of learning that applies to voluntary behavior is called operant conditioning, and it is both different from and similar to classical conditioning.

If Pavlov is the person to associate with classical conditioning, who first studied operant conditioning?

operant conditioning: the learning of voluntary behavior through the effects of pleasant and unpleasant consequences to responses.

Frustrating Cats: Thorndike's Puzzle Box and the Law of Effect

Edward L. Thorndike (1874–1949) was one of the first researchers to explore and attempt to outline the laws of learning voluntary responses, although the field was not yet called operant conditioning. Thorndike placed a hungry cat inside a "puzzle box" from which the only escape was to press a lever located on the floor of the box (see **Figure 7.5**): Cats definitely do *not* like being confined, as anyone who has ever tried to stuff one into a travel box will know (and probably has the scars to prove it), and there's a dish of food *outside* the box, so the cat is highly motivated to get out. Thorndike observed that the cat would move around the box, pushing and rubbing up against the walls in an effort to escape. Eventually, the cat would accidentally push the lever, opening the door. Upon escaping, the cat was fed from a dish placed just outside the box. The lever is the stimulus, the pushing of the lever is the response, and the consequence is both escape (good) and food (even better).

The cat did not learn the connection between the lever and the escape right away. After a number of trials in a box like this one, the cat took less and less time to push the lever to deliberately open the door—it had made an association between pushing the lever and opening the door (see **Figure 7.6**). Each time the cat rubbed and pushed at the part of the box that had led to freedom and food more quickly.

Based on this research, Thorndike developed the Law of Effect: If a response is followed by a pleasurable consequence, it will tend to be repeated. If a response is followed by an unpleasant consequence, it will tend not to be repeated (Thorndike, 1911). This is the basic principle behind learning voluntary behavior. In the case of the cat in the box, pushing the lever was followed by a pleasurable consequence (getting out and getting fed), so pushing the lever became a repeated response.

Who first called it operant conditioning? Thorndike's work began the study of voluntary learning, but the person who has had the greatest influence on the field and who gave it the name *operant conditioning* was B. F. Skinner. He is also known as behaviorism's biggest supporter.

Law of Effect: law stating that if a response is followed by a pleasurable consequence, it will tend to be repeated, and if followed by an unpleasant consequence, it will tend not to be repeated.

B. F. Skinner: The Behaviorist's Behaviorist

What was Skinner's Contribution to Operant Conditioning?

B. F. Skinner (1904–1990) was the behaviorist who assumed leadership of the field after John Watson. He was even more determined than Watson that psychologists should study only measurable, observable behavior. In addition to his knowledge of Pavlovian classical conditioning, Skinner found in the work of Thorndike a way to explain all behavior as the product of learning. He even gave the learning of voluntary behavior a special name: *operant conditioning* (Skinner, 1938). Voluntary behavior is that which people and animals do to *operate* in the

operant: any behavior that is voluntary.

world. When people perform a voluntary action, it is to get something they want or avoid something they don't want, right? So voluntary behavior, for Skinner, is **operant** behavior, and the learning of such behavior is operant conditioning.

The heart of operant conditioning is the effect of consequences on behavior. Thinking back to the section on classical conditioning, learning a reflex really depends on what comes *before* the response—the unconditioned stimulus and what will become the conditioned stimulus. These two stimuli are the *antecedent* stimuli (antecedent means something that comes before another thing). But in operant conditioning, learning depends on what happens *after* the response—the consequence. In a way, operant conditioning could be summed up as this: "If I do this, what's in it for me?"

The Concept of Reinforcement

What are the Important Concepts in Operant Conditioning?

reinforcement: any event or stimulus, that when following a response, increases the probability that the response will occur again.

"What's in it for me" represents the concept of **reinforcement**, one of Skinner's major contributions to behaviorism. The word itself means to strengthen, and Skinner defined reinforcement as anything that, when following a response, causes that response to be more likely to happen again. Typically, this means that reinforcement is a consequence that is in some way pleasurable to the organism, which relates back to Thorndike's Law of Effect. The "pleasurable consequence" is what's in it for the organism—the reward, so to speak.

Going back to Thorndike's puzzle box research, what was "in it" for the cat? We can see that the escape from the box and the food that the cat received after getting out are both *reinforcement* of the lever-pushing response. Every time the cat got out of the box, it got reinforced for doing so. In Skinner's view, this reinforcement is the reason that the cat learned anything at all. In operant conditioning, reinforcement is the key to learning.

Skinner had his own version of a puzzle box called a "Skinner box" or "operant conditioning chamber" (see **Figure 7.3**). His early research often involved placing a rat into one of these chambers and training it to push down on a bar to get food.

Primary and Secondary Reinforcers

The events or items that can be used to reinforce behavior are not all alike. Let's say that a friend of yours asks you to help her move some books from the trunk of her car to her apartment on the second floor. She offers you a choice of $25 or a candy bar. Unless you've suffered recent brain damage, you'll most likely choose the money, right? With $25, you could buy more than one candy bar. (At today's prices, you might even be able to afford three.)

Now pretend that your friend offers the same deal to a 3-year-old child who lives downstairs for carrying up some of the paperback books: $25 or a candy bar. Which reward will the child more likely choose? Most children at that age have no real idea of the value of money, so the child will probably choose the candy bar. The money and the candy bar represent two basic kinds of *reinforcers*, items or events that when following a response will strengthen it. The reinforcing properties of money must be learned, but candy gives immediate reward in the form of taste and satisfying hunger.

© Amanda Tromley, 2012. Used under license from Shutterstock, Inc.

FIGURE 7.3 ■

A reinforcer such as a candy bar that satisfies a basic need like hunger is called a primary reinforcer. Examples would be any kind of food (hunger drive), liquid (thirst drive), or touch (pleasure drive). Infants, toddlers, preschool-age children, and animals can be easily reinforced by using primary reinforcers.

A secondary reinforcer such as money, however, gets its reinforcing properties from being associated with primary reinforcers in the past. A child who is given money to spend soon realizes that the ugly green paper can be traded for candy and treats—primary reinforcers—and so money becomes reinforcing in and of itself. If a person praises a puppy while petting him (touch, a primary reinforcer), the praise alone will eventually make the puppy squirm with delight.

That sounds very familiar. Isn't this related to classical conditioning? Secondary reinforcers do indeed get their reinforcing power from the process of classical conditioning. After all, the pleasure people feel when they eat, drink, or get a back rub is a reflex response, and any reflex can be classically conditioned to occur to a new stimulus. In the case of money, the candy is a UCS for pleasure (the UCR) and the money is present just before the candy is obtained. The money becomes a CS for pleasure, and people certainly do feel pleasure when they have a lot of that green stuff, don't they?

In the case of the puppy, the petting is the UCS, the pleasure at being touched and petted the UCR. The praise, or more specifically the tone of voice, becomes the CS for pleasure. Although classical and operant conditioning often "work together," as in the creation of secondary reinforcers, they are two different processes. **Table 7.1** presents a brief look at how the two types of conditioning differ from each other.

Positive and Negative Reinforcement

Reinforcers can also differ in the way they are used. Most people have no trouble at all understanding that following a response with some kind of pleasurable consequence (like a reward) will lead to an increase in the likelihood of that response being repeated. But many people have trouble understanding that the opposite is also true: Following a response with the *removal* or *escape* from something *unpleasant* will also increase the likelihood of that response being repeated. Reinforcement does not always mean reward.

There are really only two kinds of things people ever experience as consequences in the world: things they like (food, money, candy, sex, praise, and so on) and things they don't like (spankings, being yelled at, and experiencing any kind of pain, to name a few). There are also only two possibilities for experiencing

primary reinforcer: any reinforcer that is naturally reinforcing by meeting a basic biological need, such as hunger, thirst, or touch.

secondary reinforcer: any reinforcer that becomes reinforcing after being paired with a primary reinforcer, such as praise, tokens, or gold stars.

TABLE 7.1 ■ Comparing Classical and Operant Conditioning.

Classical Conditioning	Operant Conditioning
The CS elicits the new response (high probability)	The antecedent sets the occasion for a response (varied probability)
The US may be presented without any response by the subject	The consequence will only occur if a response is made
The CS and US are generally presented across a short duration	The antecedent and consequence may be separated by a long duration
The CS and US are associated	Every combination of the A, B & C are associated
Is often used to influence emotional behavior	Is often used to influence a wide range of social behaviors

Positive reinforcement comes in the form of a college diploma, increased social status and increased attention by others.

these two kinds of consequences: Either people experience them directly (such as getting money for working or getting yelled at for misbehaving) or they don't experience them, such as losing an allowance for misbehaving or avoiding a scolding by lying about behavior.

Getting money for working is an example of **positive reinforcement**, the reinforcement of a response by the *addition* or experience of a pleasurable consequence, such as a reward or a pat on the back. That one everyone understands. But avoiding a scolding by lying about one's behavior is an example of negative reinforcement. **Negative reinforcement** is the reinforcement of a response by the removal, escape from, or avoidance of an unpleasant stimulus. Because the behavior (lying) results in *avoiding* an unpleasant stimulus (the scolding), the likelihood that the person will behave that way again (lie in the future) is increased—just as positive reinforcement will increase a behavior's likelihood. People get confused because "negative" sounds like it ought to be something bad, like a kind of punishment. *Punishment* always decreases the likelihood of a behavior happening again. Punishment *weakens* responses, whereas reinforcement (no matter whether it is positive or negative) *strengthens* responses.

I don't understand—I thought that having a toy removed would be an example of negative reinforcement. What's the difference between negative reinforcement and punishment? That is the heart of the confusion: Negative reinforcement occurs when a response is followed by the *removal* of an *unpleasant* stimulus. If something unpleasant has just gone away as a consequence of that response, wouldn't that response tend to happen again and again? If the response increases, the consequence has to be a kind of *reinforcement*. The problem is that the name sounds like it should be some kind of punishment because of the word *negative*, and that's exactly the problem that many people experience when they are trying to understand negative reinforcement. They get negative reinforcement mixed up with the kind of punishment in which a *pleasant* thing is removed (like having your driver's license taken away because you caused a bad accident). Because something is removed (taken away) in both cases, people think that they will both have the effect of punishment, or weakening a response. The difference between them lies in *what* is taken away: In the case of negative reinforcement, it is an unpleasant thing; in the case of this particular form of

positive reinforcement: the reinforcement of a response by the addition or experiencing of a pleasurable stimulus.

negative reinforcement: the reinforcement of a response by the removal, escape from, or avoidance of an unpleasant stimulus.

If this man gives in to his girlfriend's whinny drama, then he will be negatively reinforced for doing so. She, however, will be positively reinforced for whining. What trajectory do you think this relationship will take?

punishment, it is a pleasant or desirable thing. For a comparison of negative reinforcement and this particular type of punishment by removal, see **Table 7.2**.

Distinguishing between positive reinforcement and negative reinforcement is a little easier. Try to figure out which of the following examples would be positive reinforcement and which would be negative reinforcement:

(1) Arnie's father nags him to wash his car. Arnie hates being nagged, so he washes the car so his father will stop nagging.
(2) Trey learns that talking in a funny voice gets him lots of attention from his classmates, so now he talks that way often.
(3) Allen is a server at a restaurant and always tries to smile and be pleasant because that seems to lead to bigger tips.
(4) An Li turns her report in to her teacher on the day it is due because papers get marked down a letter grade for every day they are late.

The answers are as follows:

(1) Arnie is being negatively reinforced for washing his car because the nagging (unpleasant stimulus) stops when he does so.
(2) Trey is getting positive reinforcement in the form of his classmates' attention.
(3) Allen's smiling and pleasantness are positively reinforced by the customers' tips.
(4) An Li is avoiding an unpleasant stimulus (the marked-down grade) by turning in her paper on time, which is an example of negative reinforcement.

Other Operant Concepts

Operant conditioning is more than just the reinforcement of simple responses. For example, have you ever tried to teach a pet to do a trick?

Yes, it was really hard. How do the circus trainers get their animals to do all those complicated tricks?

Training this horse to jump requires the same operant techniques as it does to teach a dog to sit or a child to speak politely with "please" and "thank you." You simply need to modify the operant technique to fit each situation.

© DaCek, 2011. Used under license from Shutterstock, Inc.

Shaping

When you see an animal in a circus or in a show at a zoo perform tricks, you are seeing the result of applying the rules of conditioning—both classical and operant—to animals. But the more complex tricks are a form of operant conditioning called **shaping**, in which small steps toward some ultimate goal are reinforced until the goal itself is reached.

For example, if Jody wanted to train his dog to jump through a hoop, he would have to start with some behavior that the dog is already capable of doing on its own. Then he would gradually "mold" that starting behavior into the jump—something the dog is capable of doing but not likely to do on its own. Jody would have to start with the hoop on the ground in front of Rover's face, and then call the dog through the hoop, using the treat as bait. After Rover steps through the hoop (as the shortest way to the treat), Jody should give Rover the treat (positive reinforcement). Then he could raise the hoop just a little, reward him for walking through it again, raise the hoop, reward him . . . until Rover is jumping through the hoop to get the treat. The goal is achieved by reinforcing each **successive approximation** (small steps one after the other that get closer and closer to the goal). This process is shaping (Skinner, 1974).

Extinction, Generalization, and Spontaneous Recovery in Operant Conditioning

shaping: the reinforcement of simple steps in behavior that lead to a desired, more complex behavior.

successive approximations: small steps in behavior, one after the other, that lead to a particular goal behavior.

Extinction in classical conditioning involves the removal of the UCS, the unconditioned stimulus that eventually acts as a reinforcer of the CS—CR bond. It should come as no surprise, then, that extinction in operant conditioning involves the removal of the reinforcement. Have you ever seen a child throw a temper tantrum in the checkout line because the little one wanted some candy or toy? Many exasperated* parents will cave in and give the child the treat, positively reinforcing the tantrum. The parent is also being negatively reinforced for giving in, because the obnoxious** behavior stops. The only way to get the tantrum behavior to stop is to remove the reinforcement, which means no candy, no treat, and if possible, no attention from the parent.

Ignoring one's own child's tantrum in public is a lot harder than ignoring it at home, but it can be done. In fact, most of the other people in the store who witness the tantrum will most likely silently applaud a parent who does not give in and groan inwardly when they see the child's tantrum rewarded.

Just as in classical conditioning, operantly conditioned responses also can be generalized to stimuli that are only similar to the original stimulus. For example, what parent has not experienced that wonderful moment when Baby, who is just learning to label objects and people, refers to every man she sees as "Dada" The name "Dada" is a response to the presence of her own father and is reinforced by his delight and attention to her. But in the beginning, she will

---

* Exasperated: irritated or annoyed.
** Obnoxious: highly offensive or undesirable.

generalize her "Dada" response to any man. As other men fail to reinforce her for this response, she'll learn to discriminate between them and her father and only call her father "Dada." In this way, the man who is actually her father becomes a **discriminative stimulus**, which is any stimulus such as a stop sign or a doorknob that provides the organism with a cue for making a certain response in order to obtain reinforcement.

Spontaneous recovery (the recurrence of a conditioned response after extinction) will also happen with operant responses. Remember the hoop-jumping dog? Anyone who has ever trained animals to do several different tricks will say that when first learning a new trick, most animals will try to get reinforcers by performing their old tricks. Rover might very well have tried to roll over, speak, and shake paws to get that treat before finally walking through the hoop.

> **discriminative stimulus:** any stimulus, such as a stop sign or a doorknob, that provides the organism with a cue for making a certain response in order to obtain reinforcement.

The Schedules of Reinforcement: Why the One-Armed Bandit is So Seductive

The timing of reinforcement can make a tremendous difference in the speed at which learning occurs and the strength of the learned response. Skinner (1956) found that reinforcing each and every response was not necessarily the best schedule of reinforcement for long-lasting learning.

What are the Schedules of Reinforcement?

The Partial Reinforcement Effect

Alicia's mother gives her a quarter every night she remembers to put her dirty clothes in the clothes hamper. Bianca's mother gives her a dollar at the end of the week, but only if she has put her clothes in the hamper every night. After a time, the mothers stop giving the girls the money. Which child will stop putting her clothes in the hamper more quickly?

The answer might be surprising. It will more likely be Alicia, who has expected to get a reinforcer (the quarter) after *every single response*. As soon as the reinforcers stop, the behavior extinguishes. Bianca has expected to get a reinforcer only after *seven correct responses*. When the reinforcers stop, Bianca might continue to put the clothes in the hamper for several more days or even another whole week, hoping that the reinforcer will eventually come anyway.

Bianca's behavior illustrates the **partial reinforcement effect** (Skinner, 1956): A response that is reinforced after some, but not all, correct responses will be more resistant to extinction than a response that receives **continuous reinforcement** (a reinforcer for each and every correct response). Imagine being paid for every hamburger you make or every report you turn in. In the real world, people tend to receive partial reinforcement rather than continuous reinforcement for their work.

> **partial reinforcement effect:** the tendency for a response that is reinforced after some, but not all, correct responses to be very resistant to extinction.

Partial reinforcement can be accomplished according to different patterns or schedules. For example, it may be the number of responses that is important, as it would be if one had to sell a certain number of raffle tickets in order to get a prize. On the other hand, it might be a certain interval of time that's important, such as an office safe that can only be opened at a certain time of day. It wouldn't matter how many times one tried to open the safe if the effort didn't come at the right *time*. When it is the number of responses that is important, the schedule is called a *ratio schedule* because a certain number of responses is required for each reinforcer (e.g., 50 raffle tickets for each prize). When the timing of the response is more important, it is called an *interval schedule*.

> **continuous reinforcement:** the reinforcement of each and every correct response.

The other way in which schedules of reinforcement can differ is in whether the number of responses or interval of time is *fixed* (the same in each case) or

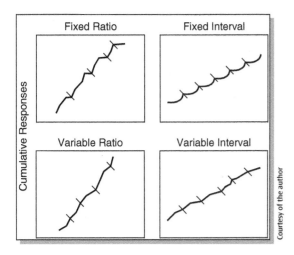

Courtesy of the author

FIGURE 7.4 ■ This figure shows the typical pattern of responding for the four most common schedules of reinforcement. Slash marks show where consequences are presented.

variable (a different number or interval is required in each case). So it is possible to have a fixed ratio schedule, a variable ratio schedule, a fixed interval schedule, and a variable interval schedule (Skinner, 1961).

Fixed Ratio Schedule of Reinforcement

In a fixed ratio schedule of reinforcement, the number of responses required to receive each reinforcer will always be the same number. If Professor Conner were teaching a rat to press a lever to get food pellets, she might require 20 lever pushes for each food pellet, or a fixed ratio of 20:1. If she were to graph the rat's progress, she would end up with something like the graph in the upper left corner of **Figure 7.4**

Notice two things about this graph: The rate of responding is very fast and there are little "breaks" in the response pattern immediately after a reinforcer is given. The rapid response rate occurs because the rat wants to get to the next reinforcer just as fast as possible, and the number of lever pushes counts. The pauses or breaks come right after a reinforcer, because the rat knows "about how many" lever pushes will be needed to get to the next reinforcer because it's always the same. Fixed schedules are predictable, and that allows rest breaks.

In human terms, anyone who does piecework, in which a certain number of items have to be completed before payment is given, is reinforced on a fixed ratio schedule. Some sandwich shops give out punch cards that get punched one time for each sandwich purchased. When the card has 10 punches, for example, the person might get a free sandwich.

Variable Ratio Schedule of Reinforcement

In **Figure 7.4** the graph on the lower left is also very fast, but it's so much smoother. Why? A variable ratio schedule of reinforcement is one in which the number of responses changes from one trial to the next. In the rat example, the rat might be expected to push the bar an *average* of 20 times to get reinforcement. That means that sometimes the rat would push the lever only 10 times before a reinforcer comes, but at other times it might take 30 lever pushes or more.

The graph at the lower left of **Figure 7.4** shows a curve that is just as rapid a response rate as the fixed ratio schedule because the number of responses still matters. But the graph is much smoother because the rat is taking no rest breaks. It can't afford to do so because it *doesn't know* how many times it may have to push that lever to get the next food pellet. It pushes as fast as it can and eats while pushing. It is the *unpredictability* of the variable schedule that makes the responses more or less continuous.

In human terms, people who shove money into the one-armed bandit, or slot machine, are being reinforced on a variable ratio schedule of reinforcement (they hope). They put their coins in (response), but they don't know how many times they will have to do this before reinforcement (the jackpot) comes. People who do this tend to sit there until they either win or run out of money. They don't dare stop because the "next one" might hit that jackpot. Buying lottery tickets is much the same thing, as is any kind of gambling. People don't know how many tickets they will have to buy, and they're afraid that if they don't buy the next one, that will be the ticket that would have won, so they keep buying and buying.

Fixed Interval Schedule of Reinforcement

The kind of reinforcement schedule most people are more familiar with is called a fixed interval schedule of reinforcement, in which a reinforcer is received after a certain, fixed interval of time has passed. If people receive a paycheck

fixed ratio schedule of reinforcement: schedule of reinforcement in which the number of responses required for reinforcement is always the same.

variable ratio schedule of reinforcement: schedule of reinforcement in which the number of responses required for reinforcement is different for each trial or event.

fixed interval schedule of reinforcement: schedule of reinforcement in which the interval of time that must pass before reinforcement becomes possible is always the same.

Whether it be cards, roulette or slot machines, the games at casinos pay off on a variable ratio schedule which always favors the house.

once every two weeks (provided that they show up to work in those two weeks), they are being reinforced on this kind of schedule.

As shown in the upper right corner of **Figure 7.4**, this schedule of reinforcement does not produce as fast a rate of responding as does the fixed ratio schedule. The number of responses doesn't matter in this case, only that at least one response is made during the specific interval of time. In the example with the rat, it might be required to press the lever during a five-minute interval of time. It doesn't have to press the bar fast or even very many times—just once in the five minutes. It is the first correct response after the interval of time has passed that gets reinforced. Eventually, the rat will start pushing the lever only as the interval of time nears its end, causing the scalloping effect you see in the graph. The response rate goes up just before the reinforcer and then drops off immediately after, until it is almost time for the next food pellet.

Paychecks aren't the only kind of fixed schedule that people experience. When do you study the hardest? Isn't it right before a test? If you know when the test is to be given, that's like having a fixed interval of time that is predictable, and you can save your greatest studying efforts until closer to the exam. (Some students save *all* of their studying for the night before the exam, which is not exactly the best strategy.) Another example of a fixed interval schedule would be the way that most people floss and brush their teeth most rigorously* the few days before their next dental exam. In this case, they are probably hoping for negative reinforcement. The cleaner they get their teeth before the appointment, the less time they might have to spend in that chair.

So if a scheduled test is a fixed interval, then would a pop quiz be a variable interval schedule?

Variable Interval Schedule of Reinforcement

Pop quizzes are unpredictable. Students don't know exactly what day they might be given a pop quiz, so the best strategy is to study a little every night just in case there is a quiz the next day. Pop quizzes are good examples of a variable interval schedule of reinforcement, in which the interval of time after which the

> **variable interval schedule of reinforcement:** schedule of reinforcement in which the interval of time that must pass before reinforcement becomes possible is different for each trial or event.

---

* Rigorously: strictly, consistently.

Fishing is rewarded on a variable interval schedule because it is not known how long you have to wait until you catch a fish.

organism must respond in order to receive a reinforcer changes from one time to the next. For example, the rat might receive a food pellet every five minutes *on average*. Sometimes it might be two minutes, sometimes ten, but the rat must push the lever at least once after that interval to get the pellet. Because the rat can't predict how long the interval is going to be, it pushes the bar more or less continuously, producing the smooth graph in the lower right corner of **Figure 7.4**. Once again, the number of responses is not important, so the rate of responding is not as fast as a variable ratio schedule.

Another example of a variable interval schedule might be the kind of fishing in which people put the pole in the water and wait—and wait, and wait, until a fish takes the bait—if they are lucky. They only have to put the pole in once, but they might refrain from taking it out for fear that just when they do, the biggest fish in the world would swim by. Dialing a busy phone number is also this kind of schedule, as people don't know *when* the call will go through, so they keep dialing and dialing.

I've heard that many psychologists don't recommend using punishment. Is that true?

Punishment

How Does Punishment Affect Behavior?

punishment: any event or object that, when following a response, makes that response less likely to happen again.

Although punishment can be effective in reducing or weakening a behavior, it has several drawbacks. **Punishment** is the opposite of reinforcement. It is any event or stimulus, that when following a response causes that response to be less likely to happen again. The job of punishment is much harder than that of reinforcement. In reinforcement, all one has to do is strengthen a response that is already there. But punishment is used to weaken a response, and getting rid of a response that is already well established is not that easy. Many times punishment only serves to temporarily suppress or inhibit a behavior until enough time has passed that the inhibition itself weakens and disappears. As many parents know, punishing a child's bad behavior doesn't always eliminate the behavior

TABLE 7.2 ■ Positive and negative refer to the gain or loss of access to the consequence. Reinforcer and punisher refer to the increase or decrease in future target behavior.

		Consequence's Influence on the Future Probability of the Behavior	
		Increase	**Decrease**
Stimulus Consequence	Gain access to it	*Positive reinforcer*	*Positive punisher*
	Lose access to it	*Negative reinforcer*	*Negative punisher*

completely. As time goes on, the punishment is forgotten and the bad behavior may occur again in a kind of spontaneous recovery.

In trying to understand why punishment works in some cases and not in others, it will be useful to look at **Table 7.2**. Contrast the two types of punishment (Gordon, 1989; Skinner, 1953) represented in the table with the two types of reinforcement discussed earlier in the chapter.

Punishment By Application

On the upper right is **punishment by application**, in which something unpleasant (such as a spanking, scolding, or other unpleasant stimulus) is added to the situation or applied. This is the kind of punishment that most people think of when they hear the word *punishment*. This is also the kind of punishment that many child development specialists strongly recommend parents avoid using with their children because it can easily escalate into abuse (Saunders & Goddard, 1998; Straus, 2000; Straus & Stewart, 1999; Straus & Yodanis, 1994; Trocmé et al., 2001). A spanking might be harmless if it is only two or three swats with a hand, but if done in anger or with a belt or other instrument, it becomes abuse.

> **punishment by application:** the punishment of a response by the addition or experiencing of an unpleasant stimulus.

Punishment by application can be quite severe, and severe punishment does one thing well: It stops the behavior immediately (Bucher & Lovaas, 1967; Carr & Lovass, 1983). It may not stop it permanently, but it does stop it. In a situation in which a child might be doing something dangerous or self-injurious, this kind of punishment is somewhat more acceptable (Duker & Seys, 1995). For example, if a child starts to run into a busy street, the parent might scream at the child to stop and then administer several rather severe swats to the child's rear. If this is not usual behavior on the part of the parent, the child will most likely never run into the street again.

Other than situations of immediately stopping dangerous behavior, severe punishment has too many drawbacks to be really useful. It should also be discouraged because of its potential for leading to abuse (Gershoff, 2000; McMillan et al., 1999; Trocmé et al., 2001):

- Severe punishment may cause the child (or animal) to avoid the punisher instead of the behavior being punished.
- Severe punishment may encourage lying to avoid the punishment (a kind of negative reinforcement).
- Severe punishment creates fear and anxiety, emotional responses that do not promote learning (Baumrind, 1997; Gershoff, 2000; Gershoff, 2002). If the point is to teach something, this kind of consequence isn't going to help.
- Hitting provides a model for aggression (Gershoff, 2000; Milner, 1992).

© DaCek, 2011. Used under license from Shutterstock, Inc.

An effective nonviolent form of punishment is time out. Time out is a form of negative punishment in which the child loses access to their things for a short period.

Punishment by Removal

punishment by removal: the punishment of a response by the removal of a pleasurable stimulus.

On the lower right of **Table 7.3** is a type of punishment called punishment by removal, mentioned earlier in the discussion of positive and negative reinforcement. In this type of punishment, behavior is punished by the removal of something pleasurable or desired after the behavior occurs. "Grounding" a teenager is removing the freedom to do what the teenager wants to do and is an example of this kind of punishment. Other examples would be placing a child in time-out (removing the attention of the others in the room), fining someone for disobeying the law (removing money), and punishing aggressive behavior by taking away television privileges. This type of punishment is far more acceptable to child development specialists, as it involves no physical aggression and avoids the problems caused by more aggressive punishments.

Problems with Punishment

As mentioned earlier, another problem exists when using severe forms of punishment by application. In using an aggressive type of punishment, such as spanking, the adult is actually modeling (presenting a behavior to be imitated by the child). After all, the adult is using aggression to get what the adult wants from the child. Children sometimes become more likely to use aggression to get what they want when they receive this kind of punishment (Bryan & Freed, 1982; Larzelere, 1986).

Punishment by removal is less objectionable to many parents and educators and is the only kind of punishment that is permitted in many public schools. But this kind of punishment also has its drawbacks. Both punishment by removal and punishment by application are usually only temporary in their effect on behavior. After some time has passed, the behavior will most likely return as the memory of the punishment gets weaker, allowing spontaneous recovery.

If punishment doesn't work very well, what can a parent do to keep a child from behaving badly?

How to Make Punishment More Effective

The way to make punishment more effective involves remembering a few simple rules:

(1) **Punishment should immediately follow the behavior it is meant to punish**. If the punishment comes long after the behavior, it will not be associated with that behavior.

(2) **Punishment should be consistent**. This actually means two things. First, if the parent says that a certain punishment will follow a certain behavior, then the parent must make sure to follow through and do what he or she promised to do. Second, punishment for a particular behavior should stay at the same intensity or increase slightly but never decrease. For example, if a child is scolded for jumping on the bed the first time, the second time this behavior happens the child should also be punished by scolding or by a stronger penalty, such as removal of a favorite toy. But if the first misbehavior is punished by spanking and the second by only a scolding, the child learns to "gamble" with the possible punishment.

(3) **Punishment of the wrong behavior should be paired, whenever possible, with reinforcement of the right behavior**. Instead of yelling at a 2-year-old for eating with her fingers, the parent should pull her hand gently out of her plate while saying something such as, "No, we do not eat with our fingers. We eat with our fork," and then placing the fork in the child's hand and praising her for using it. "See, you are doing such a good job with your fork. I'm so proud of you." Pairing punishment (the mild correction of pulling her hand away while saying "No, we do not eat with our fingers") with reinforcement allows parents (and others) to use a much milder punishment and still be effective.

Stimulus Control: Slow Down, It's the Cops

How do Operant Stimuli Control Behavior?

In the beginning of the discussion of operant conditioning, it is stated that there are stimuli associated with learning voluntary behavior, even though it is the consequences of that behavior that create the learning process. These stimuli act as cues in the environment.

Discriminative Stimuli

As stated earlier, a *discriminative stimulus* is any stimulus that provides an organism with a cue for making a certain response in order to obtain reinforcement. For example, a stop sign is a cue for stopping, which is usually followed by negative reinforcement—people don't get a ticket or don't get hit by another vehicle. A doorknob is a cue for where to grab the door in order to successfully open it. In fact, if a door has a knob, people always turn it, but if it has a handle, people usually push it, right? The two kinds of opening devices each bring forth a different response from people, and their reward is opening the door.

Other examples of discriminative stimuli are all around. What do you do when you are out driving and you see a vehicle with flashing lights in the rear view mirror? You slow down and hope the officer is after someone else. The point is that you *slow down*, and you do that any time you see a vehicle that *might* be a police car or a highway patrol car. People are so well conditioned to respond to the sight of a patrol car by slowing down that the Tennessee Highway Patrol once put empty patrol cars in the rather large medians on the interstates, successfully slowing down holiday traffic while conserving labor.

What Kind of Behavior is Resistant to Conditioning?

Raccoons are fairly intelligent animals and are sometimes used in learning experiments. In a typical experiment, a behaviorist would use shaping and reinforcement to teach a raccoon a trick. The goal might be to get the raccoon to pick up several coins and drop them into a metal container, for which the raccoon would be rewarded with food. The behaviorist starts by reinforcing the raccoon for picking up a single coin. Then the metal container is introduced and the raccoon is now required to drop the coin into the slot on the container in order to get reinforcement.

It is at this point that operant conditioning seems to fail. Instead of dropping the coin in the slot, the raccoon puts the coin in and out of the slot and rubs it against the inside of the container, then holds it firmly for a few seconds before finally letting it go. When the requirement is upped to two coins, the raccoon spends several minutes rubbing them against each other and dipping them into the container, without actually dropping them in. In spite of the fact that this dipping and rubbing behavior is not reinforced, it gets worse and worse until conditioning becomes impossible.

How can this be? If a behavior is followed by a reinforcer it should be repeated, yet this raccoon is not only failing to repeat the behavior it is being reinforced to do, but also the raccoon is doing behavior that gets no reward at all. Why has operant conditioning failed?

Keller and Marian Breland found themselves pondering that very question because the raccoon study was one of their attempts to condition an

Raccoons commonly wash their food in water as part of a species-typical pattern of feeding behavior. Generally, it is believed this pattern cannot be overcome with additional operant training.

animal in this manner (Breland & Breland, 1961). The problem wasn't limited to the raccoon, either. They ran into a similar difficulty with a pig that was being trained to pick up a total of five large wooden coins and put them into a "piggy bank." Although at first successful, the pig became slower and slower at the task over a period of weeks, dropping the coin, rooting (pushing) it around with its nose, picking it up, dropping it again, and rooting some more. This behavior became so persistent that the pig actually did not get enough to eat for the day.

The Brelands concluded that the raccoon and the pig were reverting* to behavior that was instinctual for them. Instinctual behavior is genetically determined and not under the influence of learning. Apparently, even though the animals were at first able to learn the tricks, as the coins became more and more associated with food, the animals began to drift back into the instinctual patterns of behavior that they used with real food. Raccoons rub their food between their paws and dip it in and out of water. Pigs root and throw their food around before eating it. The Brelands called this tendency to revert to genetically controlled patterns **instinctive drift**.

In their 1961 paper describing these and other examples of instinctive drift, the Brelands (both trained by Skinner himself) determined that three assumptions in which most Skinnerian behaviorists believed were not actually true. The three false assumptions:

(1) The animal comes to the laboratory a *tabula rasa*, or "blank slate," and can, therefore, be taught anything with the right conditioning.
(2) Differences between species of animals are insignificant.
(3) All responses are equally able to be conditioned to any stimulus.

As became quickly obvious in their studies with these animals, each animal comes into the world (and the laboratory) with certain genetically determined instinctive patterns of behavior already in place. These instincts differ from species to species, with the result that there are some responses that simply cannot be trained into an animal regardless of conditioning. To quote Breland and Breland (1961),

It is our reluctant conclusion that the behavior of any species cannot be adequately understood, predicted, or controlled without knowledge of its instinctive patterns, evolutionary history, and ecological niche (p. 684).

Questions for Further Discussion

(1) What other kinds of limitations do animals have in learning?
(2) What kinds of behavior might people do that would be resistant to conditioning?
(3) How can these research findings about animal behavior be generalized to human behavior?

> **instinctive drift:** tendency for an animal's behavior to revert to genetically controlled patterns.

Applying Operant Conditioning: Behavior Modification

What is Behavior Modification?

Operant conditioning principles such as reinforcement and shaping have been used for many years to change undesirable behavior and create desirable responses in animals and humans—particularly in school children. The term

---

* Reverting: to go back in action, thought, speech, and so on.

behavior modification: the use of operant conditioning techniques to bring about desired changes in behavior.

behavior modification refers to the application of operant conditioning to bring about such changes. People might recall their grade school teacher offering gold stars or some other incentive* as a reward for reading a certain number of books or giving a reward like a wooden stick that could be traded in for a treat.

For example, if a teacher wants to use behavior modification to help a child learn to be more attentive during the teacher's lectures, the teacher may do the following:

(1) Select a target behavior, such as making eye contact with the teacher.
(2) Choose a reinforcer. This may be a gold star applied to the child's chart on the wall, for example.
(3) Put the plan in action. Every time the child makes eye contact, the teacher gives the child a gold star. Inappropriate behavior (such as looking out of the window) is not reinforced with gold stars.
(4) At the end of the day, the teacher gives the child a special treat or reward for having a certain number of gold stars. This special reward is decided on ahead of time and discussed with the child.

token economy: type of behavior modification in which desired behavior is rewarded with tokens.

Both gold stars and wooden sticks can be considered tokens, secondary reinforcers that can be traded in for other kinds of reinforcers. The use of tokens to modify behavior is called a token economy. In the example, the child is collecting gold stars to "buy" the special treat at the end of the day. When one thinks about it, the system of money is very much a token economy. People are rewarded for working for money, which they then trade in for food, shelter, and so on.

Another tool that behaviorists can use to modify behavior is the process of *time-out*. Time-out is a form of mild punishment by removal in which a misbehaving animal, child, or adult is placed in a special area away from the attention of others. Essentially, the organism is being "removed" from any possibility of positive reinforcement in the form of attention. When used with children, time-out should be limited to one minute for each year of age with a maximum time-out of 10 minutes (longer than that and the child can forget why the time-out occurred).

applied behavior analysis (ABA): modern term for a form of behavior modification that uses shaping techniques to mold a desired behavior or response.

Applied behavior analysis (ABA), is the modern term for a form of behavior modification that uses shaping techniques to mold a desired behavior or response. It can be said to have begun with the work of Lovaas (1964) and his associates, although the basic techniques are those first outlined by Skinner. Lovaas used small pieces of candy as reinforcers to teach social skills and language to children with *autism*. (Autism is a disorder in which the person has great difficulty in communicating with others, often refusing to look at another person. People who are autistic may also fail to learn to speak at all, and they normally do not like to be touched. The character played by Dustin Hoffman in the movie *Rainman* was autistic.)

In ABA, skills are broken down to their simplest steps and then taught to the child through a system of reinforcement. Prompts (such as moving a child's face back to look at the teacher or the task) are given as needed when the child is learning a skill or refuses to cooperate. As the child begins to master a skill and receives reinforcement in the form of treats or praise, the prompts are gradually withdrawn until the child can do the skill independently. Applied behavior analysis is a growing field with many colleges and universities offering excellent degrees at both the undergraduate and graduate levels. A person graduating from one of these programs may act as a consultant** to schools or other institutions or may set up a private practice. Typical uses for ABA are: dealing

* Incentive: something that encourages a particular action.
** Consultant: someone who offers expert advice or services.

with children with disorders, training animals, and developing effective teaching methods for children and adults of all levels of mental abilities (Baer et al., 1968).

COGNITIVE LEARNING THEORY

What is Cognitive Learning Theory?

In the early days of behaviorism, the original focus of Watson, Skinner, and many of their followers was on observable behavior. Anything that might be occurring inside a person or animal's head during learning was considered to be of no interest to the behaviorist because it could not be seen or directly measured. But in the 1950s and more intensely in the 1960s, many psychologists were becoming aware that *cognition*, the mental events that take place inside a person's mind while behaving, could no longer be ignored (Kendler, 1985). One of these early cognitive learning scientists was Edward Tolman (1886–1959).

Tolman's Maze-Running Rats: Latent Learning

What was Tolman's Classic Study on Latent Learning?

One of psychologist Edward Tolman's best-known experiments in learning involved teaching three groups of rats the same maze, one at a time (Tolman & Honzik, 1930). In the first group, each rat was placed in the maze and rewarded with food for making its way out the other side. The rat was then placed back in the maze, rewarded, and so on until the rat could successfully solve the maze with no errors—the typical maze-learning experience.

The second group of rats was treated exactly like the first, except that they never received any reinforcement upon exiting the maze. They were simply put back in again and again, until the tenth day of the experiment. On that day, the rats in the second group began to receive reinforcement for getting out of the maze. The third group of rats, serving as a control group, was also not reinforced and was not given reinforcement for the entire duration of the experiment.

A strict Skinnerian behaviorist would predict that only the first group of rats would learn the maze successfully because learning depends on reinforcing consequences. At first, this seemed to be the case. The first group of rats did indeed solve the maze after a certain number of trials, whereas the second and third groups seemed to wander aimlessly around the maze until accidentally finding their way out.

On the tenth day, however, something happened that would be difficult to explain using only Skinner's basic principles. The second group of rats, upon receiving the reinforcement for the first time, *should* have then taken as long as the first group to solve the maze. Instead, they began to solve the maze almost immediately (See **Figure 7.5**).

Tolman concluded that the rats in the second group, while wandering around in the first nine days of the experiment, had indeed learned where all the blind alleys, wrong turns, and correct paths were in the maze. They had simply not *demonstrated* this learning because there was no reason to do so. The learning had remained hidden, or latent, until the rats had a reason to demonstrate their learning by getting to the food. Tolman called this latent learning.

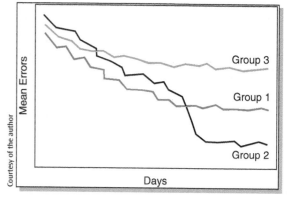

FIGURE 7.5 ■ A stylized replication of Tolman & Honzik's three-group study from 1930.

latent learning: learning that remains hidden until its application becomes useful.

Seligram's Depressed Dogs: Learned Helplessness

What is Learned Helplessness?

Martin Seligman is now famous for founding the field of *positive psychology*, a new way of looking at the entire concept of mental health and therapy. But in the mid- to late 1960s Seligman and his colleagues accidentally discovered an unexpected phenomenon while doing experiments on dogs using classical conditioning (Seligman, 1975). Their original intention was to study escape and avoidance learning. Seligman and colleagues presented a tone followed by a harmless but painful electric shock to one group of dogs (Overmier & Seligman, 1967; Seligman & Maier, 1967). The dogs in this group were harnessed so that they could not escape the shock. The researchers assumed that the dogs would learn to fear the sound of the tone and later try to escape from the tone before being shocked.

These dogs, along with another group of dogs that had not been conditioned to fear the tone, were placed into a special box consisting of a low fence that divided the box into two compartments. The dogs, which were now unharnessed, could easily see over the fence and jump over if they wished—which is precisely what the dogs that had not been conditioned did as soon as the shock occurred. Imagine the researchers' surprise when, instead of jumping over the fence when the tone sounded, the previously conditioned dogs just sat there. In fact, these dogs showed distress but didn't try to jump over the fence *even when the shock itself began.*

Why would the conditioned dogs refuse to move when shocked? The dogs that had been harnessed while being conditioned had apparently learned in the original tone/shock situation that there was nothing they could do to escape the shock. So when placed in a situation in which escape was possible, the dogs still did nothing because they had learned to be "helpless." They believed they could not escape, so they did not try.

I know some people who seem to act just like those dogs—they live in a horrible situation but won't leave. Is this the same thing? Seligman extended this theory of **learned helplessness**, the tendency to fail to act to escape from a situation because of a history of repeated failures in the past, to explain *depression*. Depressed people seem to lack normal emotions and become somewhat apathetic, often staying in unpleasant work environments or bad marriages or relationships rather than trying to escape or better their situation. Seligman proposed that this depressive behavior is a form of learned helplessness. Depressed people may have learned in the past that they seem to have no control over what happens to them (Alloy & Clements, 1998). A sense of powerlessness and hopelessness is common to depressed people, and certainly this would seem to apply to Seligman's dogs as well.

Think about how this might apply to other situations. There are many students who feel that they are bad at math because they have had problems with it in the past. Is it possible that this belief could make them not try as hard or study as much as they should? Isn't this kind of thinking also an example of learned helplessness?

learned helplessness: the tendency to fail to act to escape from a situation because of a history of repeated failures in the past.

Kohler's Smart Chimp: Insight Learning

What is Insight?

Another exploration of the cognitive elements of learning came about almost by accident. Wolfgang Köhler (1887–1967) was a Gestalt psychologist who became marooned* on an island in the Canaries (a series of islands off the coast of North

---

* Marooned: in this sense, being placed on a island from which escape is impossible.

Africa) when World War I broke out. Stuck at the primate research lab that had first drawn him to the island, he turned to studies of animal learning.

In one of his more famous studies (Köhler, 1925), he set up a problem for one of the chimpanzees. Sultan the chimp was faced with the problem of how to get to a banana that was placed just out of his reach outside his cage. Sultan solved this problem relatively easily, first trying to reach through the bars with his arm, then using a stick that was lying in the cage to rake the banana into the cage. As chimpanzees are natural tool users, this behavior is not surprising and is still nothing more than simple trial-and-error learning.

But then the problem was made more difficult. The banana was placed just out of reach of Sultan's extended arm with the stick in his hand. At this point there were two sticks lying around in the cage, which could be fitted together to make a single pole that would be long enough to reach the banana. Sultan first tried one stick, then the other (simple trial and error). After about an hour of trying, Sultan seemed to have a sudden flash of inspiration. He pushed one stick out of the cage as far as it would go toward the banana and then pushed the other stick behind the first one. Of course, when he tried to draw the sticks back, only the one in his hand came. He jumped up and down and was very excited, and when Köhler gave him the second stick, he sat on the floor of the cage and looked at them carefully. He then fitted one stick into the other and retrieved his banana. Köhler called Sultan's rapid "perception of relationships" **insight** and determined that insight could not be gained through trial-and-error learning alone (Köhler, 1925). Although Thorndike and other early learning theorists believed that animals could not demonstrate insight, Kohler's work seems to demonstrate that insight requires a sudden "coming together" of all the elements of a problem in a kind of "aha" moment that is not predicted by traditional animal learning studies. More recent research has also found support for the concept of animal insight (Heinrich, 2000; Heyes, 1998; Zentall, 2000), but there is still controversy over how to interpret the results of those studies (Wynne, 1999).

insight: the sudden perception of relationships among various parts of a problem, allowing the solution to the problem to come quickly.

OBSERVATIONAL LEARNING

What is Observational Learning?

Another type of learning theory that departs from the traditional theories of Pavlov and Skinner and depends at least partly on cognition is that of **observational learning**, the learning of new behavior through the observation of a model (watching someone else who is doing that behavior).

observational learning: learning new behavior by watching a model perform that behavior.

Bandura and the Bobo Doll

What was Bandura's Classic Bobo Doll Study?

Bandura's classic study in observational learning involved having a preschool child in a room in which the experimenter and a model interacted with toys in the room in front of the child (Bandura, et al., 1961). In one condition, the model interacted with the toys in a nonaggressive manner, completely ignoring the presence of a "Bobo" doll (a punch-bag doll in the shape of a clown). In another condition, the model became very aggressive with the doll, kicking it and yelling at it, throwing it in the air and hitting it with a hammer.

When each child was left alone in the room and had the opportunity to play with the toys, a camera filming through a one-way mirror caught the children who were exposed to the aggressive model beating up on the Bobo doll in exact imitation of the model. The children who saw the model ignore the doll did not act aggressively toward the toy. Obviously, the aggressive children had learned

Will these girls want to eat your brains if they watch too many zombie movies?

their aggressive actions from merely watching the model—with no reinforcement necessary.

Ah, but would that child have imitated the model if the model had been punished in the film? Wouldn't the consequences of the model's behavior make a difference? In later studies, Bandura showed a film of a model beating up the Bobo doll. In one condition, the children saw the model rewarded afterward. In another, the model was punished. When placed in the room with toys, the children in the first group beat up the doll, but the children in the second group did not. But, when Bandura told the children in the second group that he would give them a reward if they could show him what the model in the film did, each child duplicated the model's actions. Both groups had learned from watching the model, but only the children watching the successful (rewarded) model imitated the aggression with no prompting (Bandura, 1965). Apparently, consequences do matter in motivating a child (or an adult) to imitate a particular model. The tendency for some movies and television programs to make "heroes" out of violent, aggressive "bad guys" is particularly disturbing in light of these findings. In fact, Bandura began this research to investigate possible links between children's exposure to violence on television and aggressive behavior toward others.

The fact that learning can take place without actual performance (a kind of latent learning) is called the **learning/performance distinction**.

learning/performance distinction: referring to the observation that learning can take place without actual performance of the learned behavior.

The Four Elements of Observational Learning

Are there other elements of observed behavior that make it more or less likely to be learned? Bandura (1986) concluded, from these studies and others, that observational learning required the presence of four elements.

What are the Four Elements of Observational Learning?

Attention

To learn anything through observation, the learner must first pay attention to the model. For example, a person at a fancy dinner party who wants to know which utensil to use has to watch the person who seems to know what is correct.

Certain characteristics of models can make attention more likely. For example, people pay more attention to those people they perceive as similar to them and to people whom they perceive as attractive.

Memory

The learner must also be able to retain the memory of what was done, such as remembering the steps in preparing a dish that was first seen on a cooking show.

Imitation

The learner must be capable of reproducing, or imitating, the actions of the model. A 2-year-old might be able to watch someone tie shoelaces and might even remember most of the steps, but the 2-year-old's chubby little fingers will not have the dexterity* necessary for actually tying the laces. A person with extremely weak ankles might be able to watch and remember how some ballet move was accomplished but will not be able to reproduce it.

Motivation

Finally, the learner must have the desire to perform the action. That person at the fancy dinner, for example, might not care which fork or which knife is the "proper" one to use. Also, if a person expects a reward because one has been given in the past, or has been promised a future reward (like the children in the second group of Bandura's study), or has witnessed a model getting a reward (like the children in the first group), that person will be much more likely to imitate the observed behavior. Successful models are powerful figures for imitation, but rarely would we be motivated to imitate someone who fails or is punished.

(An easy way to remember the four elements of modeling is to remember the letters AMIM, which stands for the first letters of each of the four elements. This is a good example of using a strategy to improve memory.

APPLYING PSYCHOLOGY TO EVERYDAY LIFE: CAN YOU REALLY TOILET TRAIN YOUR CAT?

What is a Real-World Example of the Use of Conditioning?

(This article has been excerpted with permission of the author and cat-trainer extraordinaire, Karawynn Long. Karawynn Long is a published writer and Web designer who lives in Seattle with her family. Sadly, since this article was written, her cat, Misha has passed away. She can be reached at her Web site www.karawynn.net/mishacat/toilet.html. The italicized words in brackets are the author's "editorial" comments.)

There have been more books and articles about toilet-training cats than you'd think. In the summer of 1989, when Misha was a small kitten with big ears and enough meow for five cats, I searched out and read a half-dozen of them. And then tried it myself, and discovered there were a couple of things they all failed to mention . . . here's what worked for me and Misha.

The central idea is that the transition from litter box to toilet should be accomplished in a series of stages. [*This is shaping.*] You make a small change and

---

* Dexterity: skill and ease in using the hands.

then give your cat time to adjust before you make another small change. If at any time Felix gives the whole thing up and goes on the rug instead, you're pushing him too far too fast; back up a stage or two and try again, more slowly.

Ready? First Start By Training Yourself . . .

The very most important thing to remember is: Lid Up, Seat Down. Post a note on the back of the door or the lid of the toilet if you think you (or your house-mates or guests) might forget. And if you are accustomed to closing the bath-room door when it's empty, you'll have to break that habit too. [*In operant conditioning, this is part of "preparing the training arena."*]

Begin by moving the cat's current litter box from wherever it is to one side of the toilet. Make sure he knows where it is and uses it. Rest (this means doing nothing for a period of between a day and a week, depending on how flappable your cat is). Next put something—a stack of newspapers, a phone book, a card-board box—under the litter box to raise it, say, about an inch. (Magazines are too slick; you don't want the litter box sliding around and making your cat feel inse-cure. Tape the litter box down if you need to.) Rest. Get another box or phone book and raise it a little higher. Rest. Continue this process until the bottom of the litter box is level with the top of the toilet seat. (For Misha I raised it about two inches per day.) [*Notice that this is the step-by-step process typically used in shaping.*]

At the beginning of this process, your cat could just step into the litter box; later he began jumping up into it, until at some point he probably started jump-ing up onto the toilet seat first and stepping into the box from there. Lift the seat on your toilet and measure the inside diameter of the top of the bowl at its widest point. Venture forth and buy a metal mixing bowl of that diameter. Do not (I dis-covered this the hard way) substitute a plastic bowl. A plastic bowl will not sup-port the cat's weight and will bend, dropping into the toilet bowl and spilling litter everywhere, not to mention startling the cat.

Now you move the litter box over so that it's sitting directly over the toilet seat. (If your cat has shown reluctance over previ-ous changes, you might want to split this into two stages, moving it halfway onto the seat and then fully over.) Take away the stack of phone books or whatever you used. Rest. [*Again, notice that everything has to be done in small steps. This is the heart of the shaping process—requiring too large a step will stop the process.*]

Here's the cool part. Take away the litter box entirely. (Tada!) Nestle the metal mixing bowl inside the toilet bowl and lower the seat. Fill the bowl with about two inches of litter (all of this is much easier if you have the tiny granules of litter that can be scooped out and flushed).

Naturally, any humans using the toilet at this point will want to remove the metal bowl prior to their own use and replace it afterward. The next week or two the whole process is likely to be something of an annoyance; if you begin to think it's not worth it, just remember that you will never have to clean a litter box again.

Watch your cat using the bathroom in the metal bowl. Count the number of feet he gets up on the toilet seat (as opposed to down in the bowl of litter). The higher the number, the luckier you are and the easier your job is going to be . . .

. . . because next you have to teach him proper squatting posture. Catch him beginning to use the toilet as much of the time as possible and show him where his feet are supposed to go. Just lift them right out of the bowl and place them on the seat (front legs in the middle, hind legs on the outside). If he starts out with three or, heaven forbid, all four feet in the bowl, just get the front two feet out first. Praise him all over the place every time he completes the activity in this position. [*The praise is the positive reinforcement, and should be done with each successful step.*]

(Misha is very doglike in that he craves approval and praise. If your cat is indifferent to this sort of thing, you can also reward him with small food treats and wean him from them later when the toilet behavior has "set." Just keep the treats as small and infrequent as possible—half a Pounce' or similar treat per occasion should be plenty.) [*If treats are too frequent, it will make it difficult to phase out the reinforcer after the behavior is well learned.*]

When he is regularly using the toilet with his front feet out (and some cats naturally start from this position), begin lifting a hind foot out and placing it on the seat outside the front paws. Your cat will probably find this awkward at first and try to replace the foot in the litter. Be persistent. Move that foot four times in a row if you have to, until it stays there. Praise and/or treat.

Repeat with the other hind foot, until your cat learns to balance in that squat. Once he's getting all four feet regularly on the seat, it's all easy from here.

Which is fortunate, because the last bit is also the most unpleasant. I suggest that you postpone this stage until you have at least a weekend, and preferably several days, when you (or another responsible party) will be at home most of the time. I skipped through this part in about two days; I only hope that your cat allows you to move along that fast.

Begin reducing the litter in the bowl. Go as fast as he'll feel comfortable with, because as the litter decreases, the odor increases. You'll want to be home at this point so that you can praise him and dump out the contents of the bowl immediately after he's finished, to minimize both the smell and the possibility that your cat, in a confused attempt to minimize the smell on his own, tries to cover it up with litter that no longer exists and ends up tracking unpleasantness into the rest of the house.

By the time you're down to a token teaspoonful of litter in the bottom of the bowl, your next-door neighbors will probably be aware of the precise instant your cat has used the toilet. This is as bad as it gets. The next time you rinse out the metal bowl, put a little bit of water in the bottom. Increase the water level each time, just as you decreased the litter level. Remember—if at any point Felix looks nervous enough about the change to give the whole thing up and take his business to the corner behind the door, back up a step or two and try the thing again more slowly. [*Shaping takes a lot of patience, depending on the behavior being shaped and the learning ability of the animal—or person.*]

Once the water in the mixing bowl is a couple of inches deep and your cat is comfortable with the whole thing, you get to perform the last bit of magic. Take the mixing bowl away, leaving the bare toilet. (Lid Up, Seat Down.)

Voila! Your cat is now toilet trained.

Some useful books on using operant conditioning to toilet train cats:

Brotman, E. (2001). *How to Toilet Train Your Cat: The Education of Mango*. Sherman Oaks: CA, Bird Brain Press.

Kunkel, P. & Mead K. P. (1991). *How to Toilet Train Your Cat: 21 Days to a Litter-Free Home*. New York: Workman Publishing Company.

Questions for Further Discussion

(1) Why would this technique probably not work with a dog?
(2) Are there any safety concerns with teaching a cat in this way?
(3) Are there any other difficulties that might arise when doing this training?

KEY TERMS

applied behavior analysis (ABA)

behavior modification

biofeedback

biological preparedness

classical conditioning

cognitive perspective

conditioned emotional response (CER)

conditioned response (CR)

conditioned stimulus (CS)

conditioned taste aversion

continuous reinforcement

discriminative stimulus

extinction

fixed interval schedule of reinforcement

fixed ratio schedule of reinforcement

higher-order conditioning

insight

instinctive drift

latent learning

Law of Effect

learned helplessness

learning/performance distinction

negative reinforcement

neurofeedback

neutral stimulus (NS)

observational learning

operant

operant conditioning

partial reinforcement effect

positive reinforcement

primary reinforcer

punishment

punishment by application

punishment by removal

reinforcement

reinforcer

secondary reinforcer

shaping

spontaneous recovery

stimulus discrimination

stimulus generalization

stimulus substitution

successive approximations

token economy

unconditioned response (UCR)

unconditioned stimulus (UCS)

variable interval schedule of reinforcement

variable ratio schedule of reinforcement

vicarious conditioning

Chapter 7: Learning

END OF CHAPTER QUIZ

1. This thing is associated with John Watson.
   a. Behaviorism *(circled)*
   b. Extinction
   c. Operant chamber
   d. Continuous reinforcement
   e. Mirror neurons

2. This thing is associated with B. F. Skinner.
   a. Behaviorism
   b. Extinction
   c. Operant chamber *(circled)*
   d. Continuous reinforcement
   e. Mirror neurons

3. This helps modeled behavior to occur.
   a. Behaviorism
   b. Extinction
   c. Operant chamber
   d. Continuous reinforcement
   e. Mirror neurons *(circled)*

4. When you learn that the previous thing you learned is no longer relevant.
   a. Behaviorism
   b. Extinction *(circled)*
   c. Operant chamber
   d. Continuous reinforcement
   e. Mirror neurons

5. When each response is followed by a reward.
   a. Behaviorism
   b. Extinction
   c. Operant chamber
   d. Continuous reinforcement *(circled)*
   e. Mirror neurons

6. An event that increases the frequency of the behavior that it follows is a(n):
   a. Conditioned stimulus
   b. Punisher
   c. Unconditioned stimulus
   d. Reinforcer *(circled)*
   e. Operant

7. The thing that is sometimes referred to as a neutral stimulus.
   a. Conditioned stimulus *(circled)*
   b. Punisher
   c. Unconditioned stimulus
   d. Reinforcer
   e. Operant

8. The thing that produces a reflexive behavior BEFORE conditioning begins.
   a. Conditioned stimulus
   b. Punisher
   c. Unconditioned stimulus *(circled)*
   d. Reinforcer
   e. Operant

9. When you scream at a child and they do the inappropriate behavior more you know that the screaming functions as a:
   a. Conditioned stimulus
   b. Punisher
   c. Unconditioned stimulus
   d. Reinforcer *(circled)*
   e. Operant

10. When a child refers to all the men he meets as "Daddy"
    a. Observational learning
    b. Discrimination
    c. Punishment
    d. Generalization *(circled)*
    e. Memory

11. When you learn the visual difference between gold, silver and white-gold.
    a. Observational learning
    b. Discrimination *(circled)*
    c. Punishment
    d. Generalization
    e. Memory

12. Which of the following psychologists developed the Law of Effect?
    a. Pavlov
    b. Skinner
    c. Thorndike *(circled)*
    d. Bandura
    e. Watson

13. Rats easily learn to associate nausea-producing radiation treatments with:
    a. Loud sounds
    b. Bright lights
    c. Novel tastes *(circled)*

d. High-pitched sounds

e. Any of the above

14. Studies of latent learning highlight the importance of:

a. Primary reinforcers

b. Respondent behavior

c. Spontaneous recovery

d. Cognitive processes

e. Conditioned reinforcers

15. Children learn to fear spiders more easily than they learn to fear butterflies. This best illustrates the impact of _____ on learning.

a. Spontaneous recovery

b. Conditioned reinforcers

c. Shaping

d. Cognitive processes

e. Biological predispositions

16. Professor Smith tells his students that pop quizzes will be given at unpredictable times throughout the semester. Therefore, the quizzes will come on a _____ schedule.

a. Fixed-interval

b. Fixed-ratio

c. Variable-interval

d. Variable-ratio

17. The idea that any perceivable neutral stimulus can serve as a CS was challenged by:

a. Garcia and Koelling's findings on taste aversion in rats

b. Pavlov's findings on the conditioned salivary response

c. Watson and Rayner's findings on fear conditioning in infants

d. Bandura's findings on observational learning and aggression in children

18. What is the MOST ACCURATE name of the general process you use when training an animal subject to perform a complicated behavior?

a. Learning

b. Negative punishment

c. Reinforcement

d. Conditioning

e. Shaping

19. Which of the following schedules are most likely to explain the behavior of someone using a slot machine?

a. Fixed ratio

b. Variable ratio

c. Fixed time

d. Fixed interval

e. Variable interval

20. When Little Timmy whines to his father for candy, he is reinforced for whining because his father gives him the candy. His irritated father was _____ by getting Timmy to be quiet.

a. Positively reinforced

b. Negatively reinforced

c. Positively punished

d. Negatively punished

e. Pretty annoyed

21. Which of the following terms refers to learning that occurs without any outward sign of behavior change.

a. Cognitive map

b. Intrinsic motivation

c. Latent learning

d. Memory

e. Cognition

22. A fixed-ratio schedule of reinforcement is one in which a response is reinforced only after a(n):

a. Specified time period has elapsed

b. Unpredictable time period has elapsed

c. Specified number of responses have been made

d. Unpredictable number of responses have been made

23. Learning:

a. Always produces an improvement in behavior

b. Requires the ability to think abstractly

c. Enables us to adapt to our environment

d. Does not occur in simple animals

24. Children in abusive households sometimes learn to be aggressive by imitating their parents. This illustrates the importance of:

a. Delayed reinforcement

b. Spontaneous recovery

c. Observational learning

d. Respondent behavior

e. Shaping

25. If your professor only appreciates classroom performance that is flawless, the students may become unmotivated to learn. The professor needs to learn the importance of:

a. Generalization

b. Shaping

c. Latent learning

d. Spontaneous recovery

26. The definition of learning is:

a. A permanent change in behavior

b. The process by which a relatively permanent change in behavior occurs

c. The process by which a permanent change in behavior develops over time

d. Novel behavior patterns developed across time

27. Which of the following scientists developed the school of behaviorism?
    a. Pavlov
    b. Watson
    c. Skinner
    d. Bandura
    e. Garcia

28. Which of the following statements cannot be rephrased through behavioralese?
    a. I had a bad dream last night
    b. I love chocolate ice cream
    c. I feel good
    d. My friends are intelligent
    e. All of the above statements may be converted into behavioralese

29. Ivan Pavlov won the 1904 Nobel Prize for his work in:
    a. Conditioning
    b. Digestion
    c. Cardiac nerve innervation
    d. Learning
    e. Chemistry

30. Pavlov's work gave a scientific basis for the 2,500 year old philosophical tradition that:
    a. Animals learn the same as people
    b. Learning is key to understanding mental activity
    c. Animals learn differently than people
    d. People learn through associations

31. The first stimulus presented in a Pavlovian pairing.
    a. CS
    b. US
    c. CR
    d. UR

32. The second stimulus presented in a Pavlovian pairing.
    a. CS
    b. US
    c. CR
    d. UR

33. Identify which of the following is actually used to assess whether conditioning has developed.
    a. CS
    b. US
    c. CR
    d. UR

34. Which of the following is not an unconditional response?
    a. Startle reflex to a loud unexpected noise
    b. Salivation to sour tastes
    c. Hand withdrawal to electric shock
    d. Brake pressing to a red traffic light
    e. Pupil constriction to bright light

35. It is very unlikely that _____ exist, especially with respect to adult humans.
    a. CS
    b. Learned associations
    c. CR
    d. Complete discriminations
    e. Neutral stimuli

36. Which of the following is related to a reduction in responding to the CS?
    a. Acquisition
    b. Extinction
    c. Spontaneous recovery
    d. Discrimination
    e. Generalization

37. Which of the following will develop during the beginning of an extinction phase in a learning experiment?
    a. Extinction burst
    b. Avoidance learning
    c. Biological preparedness
    d. Partial reinforcement
    e. Spontaneous recovery

38. Whenever untrained stimuli similar to the CS also control the CR.
    a. Generalization
    b. Discrimination
    c. Acquisition
    d. Habituation

39. Whenever untrained stimuli do not control the CR.
    a. Generalization
    b. Discrimination
    c. Acquisition
    d. Habituation

40. This person is associated with the discovery of instrumental conditioning.
    a. Pavlov
    b. Watson
    c. Skinner
    d. Bandura
    e. Thorndike

41. In the original puzzle box experiments, which stimulus served as the antecedent?
    a. The puzzle box
    b. The cat
    c. The food
    d. The cat's hunger

42. In the original puzzle box experiments, which stimulus served as the consequence?
    a. The puzzle box
    b. The cat
    c. The food
    d. The latch

43. In the original puzzle box experiments, which stimulus served as the manipulandum?
    a. The puzzle box
    b. The cat
    c. The food
    d. The latch

44. The Law of Effect specifically refers to the:
    a. Response-consequence relation
    b. Antecedent-consequence relation
    c. Antecedent-response relation
    d. CS-US pairing

45. A response-consequence relation always occurs within a:
    a. Experimental chamber
    b. Puzzle box
    c. Stimulus context
    d. Fixed ration schedule
    e. Response contingency

46. Both Pavlovian and operant conditioning show the phenomena of:
    a. Acquisition, extinction, generalization, discrimination, spontaneous recovery

    b. Extinction, discrimination, spontaneous recovery, blocking
    c. Acquisition, generalization, spontaneous recovery, Law of Effect
    d. Acquisition, extinction, generalization, shaping

47. Which of the following pairs are believed to be conceptually similar across Pavlovian and operant conditioning paradigms?
    a. CS and antecedent
    b. Behavior and CS
    c. US and consequence
    d. US and behavior
    e. Both A & C

48. During this decade, B. F. Skinner developed the experimental chamber that is still in use today.
    a. 1920's
    b. 1930's
    c. 1940's
    d. 1950's

49. Which of the following is not influenced by a schedule of reinforcement?
    a. The rate at which responses occur
    b. The responses' resistance to extinction
    c. The discriminative capacity of stimuli
    d. The likelihood that the subject discriminates schedule changes

50. Which of the following is not an example of a fixed ratio schedule?
    a. Vending machines
    b. Telephone numbers
    c. Pay-per-piece work
    d. Bus schedules

8 | *Memory*

The Story Behind the Neurobiology of Learning and Memory

Eric Kandel shared one-third of the Nobel Prize in medicine with Arvid Carlsson and Paul Greengard in 2000. Kandel tells the story of his life in his autobiography *In Search of Memory*. Kandel took an educationally circuitous route to study the biological bases of learning. His original interests in learning partly came from his experience as a 9-year-old Jewish boy in 1938 Vienna, Austria. He wanted to learn how it was that people joined with the Nazi Party.

After immigrating to the United States with his family, Kandel would eventually attend Harvard University and study European history. He then changed his course of study to Freudian psychoanalysis and finally to the biology of learning. The story of how Kandel passed through these three widely diverse areas reveals how many of our experiences come to influence other portions of our lives.

Kandel first studied European history as a way to understand the German National Socialist, or Nazi party. His connections at Harvard University and his Viennese background ultimately led him to meet Ernst and Marianne Kris, two prominent psychoanalysts from Freud's circle of colleagues. The Kris' psychoanalytic understanding of human behavior seemed to Kandel a more certain way of understanding human behavior than the study of history could provide. At that time, in 1950, the way into a psychoanalysis-training program was through medical school. Consequently, Kandel entered the New York University Medical School with the intent of obtaining his medical degree and obtaining psychoanalytic training.

Kandel became more interested in the biological aspects of learning and memory throughout his medical training. He met many prominent anatomists and neurobiologists of the time and also began to recognize the value of B. F. Skinner's conditioning research.

Little was known of the biological bases of learning and memory in the mid-1950s. Moreover, Kandel was finding out that the techniques to complete such studies were developing in separate areas of experimental medicine. Ultimately, he began studying learning and memory mechanisms in *Aplysia Californica*, a large sea snail found along the coast of California.

Applying the behavioral preparations that you will read about in this chapter, Kandel and his colleagues were able to assess the electrical activity of the cells in the snail's nervous system. This combination of physiological and behavioral research—systematically applied over decades to questions on learning and memory—is what ultimately led to Kandel being awarded the Nobel Prize.

References
Kandel, E. R. (2006). *In search of memory. The emergence of a new science of mind*. New York: W. W. Norton.

CHAPTER OUTLINE

Jimmie, healthy and handsome forty-nine-year-old, was a fine-looking man, with curly gray hair. He was cheerful, friendly, and warm.

"Hi, Doc!" he said. "Nice morning! Do I take this chair here?" He was a genial soul, very ready to talk and to answer any question I asked him. He told me his name and birth date, and the name of the little town in Connecticut where he was born. . . . He recalled, and almost relived, his war days and service, the end of the war, and his thoughts for the future. . . .

With recalling, Jimmie was full of animation; he did not seem to be speaking of the past but of the present. . . . A sudden, improbable suspicion seized me.

"What year is this, Mr. G.?" I asked, concealing my perplexity in a casual manner.

"Forty-five, man. What do you mean?" He went on, "We've won the war, FDR's dead, Truman's at the helm. There are great times ahead."

"And you, Jimmie, how old would you be?"

Oddly, uncertainly, he hesitated a moment as if engaged in calculation.

"Why, I guess I'm nineteen, Doc. I'll be twenty next birthday."

(Sachs, 1970, pp. 21–23)

Jimmie was decades behind the times: He was nearly 50 years old. His amnesia, or memory loss, resulted from Korsakoff's syndrome, a disorder related to chronic alcoholism in which subcortical structures involved in memory deteriorate. Jimmie had no difficulty recalling incidents from World War II, but he could not remember anything that had happened since 1945.

Curiously, though, amnesics like Jimmie are still able to form certain kinds of new memories (Knott & Marlsen-Wilson, 2001; Nadel et al., 2000; Nader & Wang, 2006; Schacter, 1995a). If asked to recall a seven-digit phone number long enough to walk to another room and dial it, they have no difficulty doing so. A minute after completing the call, however, they will not remember having picked up the phone.

Or suppose Jimmie, who grew up before the days of computers, were to play a computer game every day for a week. Like most people, he would steadily improve at it, demonstrating that he was learning and remembering new skills. Yet each day he would likely greet the computer with, "Gee, what's this thing?"

Case studies of neurologically impaired patients and experimental studies of normal participants have demonstrated that memory is not a single function that a person can have or lose. Rather, memory is composed of several systems. Just how many systems and how independently they function are questions at the heart of contemporary research.

The previous chapter was dominated by the behaviorist perspective; this one and the next focus primarily on the cognitive perspective. We begin by considering some of the basic features of memory and an evolving model of information processing that has guided research on memory for over three decades. We then explore the memory systems that allow people to store information temporarily and permanently, and examine why people sometimes forget and misremember. Along the way, we consider the implications of memory research for issues such as the accuracy of eyewitness testimony in court and the existence of repressed memories in victims of childhood sexual abuse.

Two questions form the backdrop of this chapter. The first is deceptively simple: What does it mean to remember? Is memory simply the recollection of "facts"? Or does memory extend to the activation (or reactivation) of goals, emotions, and behaviors—as when we effortlessly "remember" how to drive, even while deeply engrossed in conversation? Second, what is the relation between the kind of learning described in the last chapter, which emphasized behaviors and emotional responses, and memory?

MEMORY AND INFORMATION PROCESSING

Memory is so basic to human functioning that we take it for granted. Consider what was involved the last time you performed the seemingly simple task of remembering a friend's phone number. Did you bring to mind a visual image (a picture of the number), an auditory "image" (pronouncing a series of numbers out loud in your mind), or simply a pattern of motor movements as you punched the numbers on the phone? How did you bring to mind this particular number, given that you likely have a dozen other numbers stored in memory? (More likely, you probably just checked the address book on your cell phone and hit SEND.) Once a number was in your mind, how did you know it was the right one? And were you aware as you reached for the phone that you were remembering at that very moment how to use a phone, what phones do, how to lift an object smoothly to your face, how to push buttons, and who your friend is?

This example suggests how complex the simplest act of memory is. Memory involves taking something we have observed, such as a written phone number, and converting it into a form we can store, retrieve, and use. We begin by briefly considering the various ways the brain can preserve the past—the "raw material" of memory—and an evolving model of information processing that has guided psychologists' efforts to understand memory for the last quarter of a century.

Mental Representations

For a sound, image, or thought to return to mind when it is no longer present, it has to be represented in the mind—literally, *re*-presented, or presented again—this time without the original stimulus. A *mental representation* is a psychological version or mental model of a stimulus or category of stimuli. In neuropsychological terms, it is the patterned firing of a network of neurons that forms the neural "code" for an object or concept, such as "dog" or "sister."

Representational modes are like languages that permit conversation within the mind (see Jackendoff, 1996). The content of our thoughts and memories can be described or translated into many "languages"—images, sounds, words, and so forth—but some languages cannot capture certain experiences the way others can. Fortunately, we are all "multilingual" and frequently process information simultaneously using multiple representational codes (Chapter 3).

Some kinds of representation are difficult to conceptualize and have received less attention from researchers. For example, people store memories of *actions*, such as how to press the buttons on a phone, which suggests the existence of *motoric representations*, or stored memories of muscle movements. The most commonly studied representations are sensory and verbal.

Sensory Representations

Sensory representations: Information that is represented in one of the sense modalities.

Sensory representations store information in a sensory mode, such as the sound of a dog barking or the image of a city skyline (Postle, 2006). The cognitive maps discovered in rats running mazes (Chapter 5) probably include visual representations. People rely on visual representations to recall where they left their keys last night or to catch a ball that is sailing toward them through the air. Visual representations are like pictures that can be mentally scrutinized or manipulated (Kosslyn, 1983).

The auditory mode is also important for encoding information (Thompson & Paivio, 1994). Some forms of auditory information are difficult to represent in any other mode. For instance, most readers would be able to retrieve a tune by Jewel or Celine Dion with little difficulty but would have much more trouble describing the melody than "hearing" it in their minds.

Other types of sensory information have their own mental codes as well. People can identify many objects by smell, a finding that suggests they are comparing current sensory experience with olfactory knowledge (Schab & Crowder, 1995). Olfactory representations in humans are, however, far less reliable than visual representations in identifying even common objects (de Wijk et al., 1995; Herz, 2005). For example, if exposed to the smell of a lemon, people often misidentify it as an orange, whereas people with an intact visual system rarely confuse the two fruits visually.

Verbal Representations

Verbal representations: Information represented in words.

Although many representations are stored in sensory modes, much of the time people think using verbal representations. Try to imagine what *liberty* or *mental representation* means without thinking in words. Other experiences, in contrast, are virtually impossible to describe or remember verbally, such as the smell of bacon. In fact, using words to describe things about which one has little verbal knowledge can actually disrupt sensory-based memory.

Neuroimaging studies confirm that verbal representations are in fact distinct from sensory representations. Consider what happens when researchers present participants with a string of X's versus a word (Menard et al., 1996). Both stimuli lead to activation of the visual cortex, because both are processed visually. Presentation of the word, however, leads to additional activation of a region at the juncture of the left occipital, parietal, and temporal lobes that appears to be involved in transforming the visual representation into a verbal or semantic one.

■ INTERIM SUMMARY

For information to come back to mind after it is no longer present, it has to be represented. **Sensory representations** store information in a sensory mode; **verbal representations** store information in words. People also store knowledge about actions as motoric representations.

Information Processing: An Evolving Model

Psychologists began studying memory in the late nineteenth century, although interest in memory waned under the influence of behaviorism until the "cognitive revolution" of the 1960s. In 1890, William James proposed a distinction between two kinds of memory, which he called primary and secondary memory. *Primary memory* is immediate memory for information momentarily held in consciousness, such as a telephone number. *Secondary memory* is the vast store of information that is unconscious except when called back into primary memory, such as the 10 or 20 phone numbers a person could bring to mind if he wanted to call various friends, family members, and so forth. James's distinction is embodied in the *standard model of memory*. This model has guided research on memory and cognition since the 1960s (Atkinson & Shiffrin, 1968; Healy & McNamara, 1996).

The standard model is predicated on the metaphor of the mind as a computer, which places information into different memory stores (the system's "hardware") and retrieves and transforms it using various programs ("software"). According to this model **(Figure 8.1)**, memory consists of three stores: sensory registers, short-term memory (James's primary memory), and long-term memory (James's secondary memory). Storing and retrieving memories involve passing information from one store to the next and then retrieving the information from long-term memory.

Sensory Registers

Suppose you grab a handful of quarters from your pocket and, while looking away, stretch out your hand so that all of the coins are visible. If you then glance for a second at your hand but look away before counting the change, you are still likely to be able to report accurately the number of coins in your hand because the image is held momentarily in your visual sensory register. **Sensory registers** hold information about a perceived stimulus for a fraction of a second after the stimulus disappears, allowing a mental representation of it to remain in memory briefly for further processing (Sperling, 1960).

Most research has focused on visual and auditory sensory registration. The term **iconic storage** describes momentary memory for visual information. For a brief period after an image disappears from vision, people retain a mental image (or "icon") of what they have seen. This visual trace is remarkably accurate and contains considerably more

Sensory registers: Memory systems that hold information for a very brief period of time.

Iconic storage: A visual sensory registration process by which people retain an afterimage of a visual stimulus.

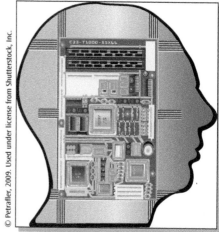

The standard model of memory follows the metaphor of the mind as a computer.

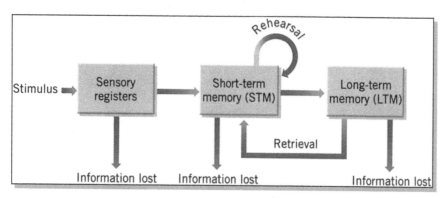

FIGURE 8.1 ■ Standard model of memory. Stimulus information enters the sensory registers. Some information enters STM and is then passed on for storage in LTM. Information can be lost from any of the sensory stores, usually if it is not very important or if a traumatic event has occurred that interferes with memory consolidation or retrieval.

information than people can report before it fades (Baddeley & Patterson, 1971; Keysers et al., 2005). The duration of icons varies from approximately half a second to two seconds, depending on the individual, the content of the image, and the circumstances (Neisser, 1976a; Smithson & Mollon, 2006). The auditory counterpart of iconic storage is called **echoic storage** (Battacchi et al., 1981; Buchsbaum et al., 2005; Neisser, 1967).

Short-Term Memory

According to the standard model, then, the first stage of memory is a brief sensory representation of a stimulus. Many stimuli that people perceive register for such a short time that they drop out of the memory system without further processing, as indicated in Figure 8.1 ("information lost"). Other stimuli make a greater impression. Information about them is passed on to **short-term memory (STM)**, a memory store that holds a small amount of information in consciousness—such as a phone number—for roughly 20 to 30 seconds, unless the person makes a deliberate effort to maintain it longer by repeating it over and over (Waugh & Norman, 1965).

Limited Capacity

Short-term memory has *limited capacity*—that is, it does not hold much information. To assess STM, psychologists often measure participants' *digit span*, that is, how many numbers they can hold in mind at once. On the average, people can remember about seven pieces of information at a time, with a normal range of from five to nine items (Miller, 1956). That phone numbers in most countries are five to seven digits is no coincidence.

Hermann Ebbinghaus (1885) was the first to note the seven-item limit to STM. Ebbinghaus pioneered the study of memory using the most convenient participant he could find—himself—with a method that involved inventing some 2300 nonsense syllables (such as *pir* and *vup*). Ebbinghaus randomly placed these syllables in lists of varying lengths and then attempted to memorize the lists; he used nonsense syllables rather than real words to try to control the possible influence of prior knowledge on memory. Ebbinghaus found that he could memorize up to seven syllables, but no more, in a single trial. The limits of STM seem to be neurologically based, as they are similar in other cultures, including those with very different languages (Yu et al., 1985).

Because of STM's limited capacity, psychologists often liken it to a lunch counter (Bower, 1975). If only seven stools are available at the counter, some customers will have to get up before new customers can be seated. Similarly, new information "bumps" previous information from consciousness. **Figure 8.2** illustrates this bumping effect.

Rehearsal

Short-term memory is not, however, a completely passive process of getting bumped off a stool. People can control the information stored in STM. For example, after looking up a phone number, most people will repeat the information over and over in their minds—a procedure termed **rehearsal**—to prevent it from fading until they have dialed the number. This mental repetition to maintain information in STM is called **maintenance rehearsal**.

Rehearsal is also important in transferring information to long-term memory. As we will see, however, maintenance rehearsal is not as useful for storing information in long-term memory as actively thinking about the information while rehearsing, a procedure known as **elaborative rehearsal**. Remembering the words to a poem, for example, is much easier if the person really understands what it is about, rather than just committing each word to memory by rote.

…torage: An auditory sensory registration process by which people retain an echo or brief auditory representation of a sound to which they have been exposed.

Short-term memory (STM): Memory for information that is available to consciousness for roughly 20 to 30 seconds; also called working memory.

Rehearsal: The process of repeating or studying information to retain it in memory.

Maintenance rehearsal: The process of repeating information over and over to maintain it momentarily in STM.

Elaborative rehearsal: An aid to long-term memory storage that involves thinking about the meaning of information in order to process it with more depth.

(*a*) 7638826

(*b*) 7638826 (20 seconds later)

(*c*) 9188826 (25 seconds later)

FIGURE 8.2 ■ Short-term memory. In an experimental task, the subject is presented with a string of seven digits (*a*). Without rehearsal, 20 seconds later, the representations of the digits have begun to fade but are still likely to be retrievable (*b*). At 25 seconds, however, the experimenter introduces three more digits, which "bump" the earliest of the still-fading digits (*c*).

■ INTERIM SUMMARY

The standard model of memory is predicated on the metaphor of the mind as a computer. It distinguishes three memory stores sensory memory (or sensory registers), short-term memory, and long-term memory. **Sensory registers** hold information about a perceived stimulus for a split second after the stimulus disappears. From the sensory registers, information is passed on to a limited-capacity **short-term memory (STM)**, which holds up to seven pieces of information in consciousness for roughly 20 to 30 seconds unless the person makes a deliberate effort to maintain it by repeating it over and over (**maintenance rehearsal**) **Elaborative rehearsal**, which involves actually thinking about the material while committing it to memory is more useful for long-term than for short term storage.

Long-Term Memory

Just as relatively unimportant information drops out of memory after brief sensory registration, the same is true after storage in STM. An infrequently called phone number is not worth cluttering up the memory banks. More important information, however, goes on to long-term memory (LTM). According to the standard model, the longer information remains in STM, the more likely it is to make a permanent impression in LTM. Recovering information from LTM, known as retrieval, involves bringing it back into STM (i.e., consciousness).

Why did researchers distinguish short-term from long-term memory? One reason was simple: Short-term memory is brief, limited in capacity, and quickly accessed, whereas LTM is enduring, virtually limitless, but more difficult to access (as anyone knows who has tried without success to recall a person's name or a term on an exam).

Another reason emerged as psychologists tested memory using free-recall tasks. In *free-recall tasks*, the experimenter presents participants with a list of words, one at a time, and then asks them to recall as many as possible. When the delay between presentation of the list and recall is short, participants demonstrate a phenomenon known as the serial position effect: a tendency to remember information toward the beginning and end of a list rather than in the middle **(Figure 8.3)**.

Evolution of the Model

Although the standard model provides a basic foundation for thinking about memory, in the last decade it has evolved in four major respects. First, the standard model is a *serial processing model*: It proposes a series of stages of memory storage and retrieval that occur one at a time (*serially*) in a particular order, with information passing from the sensory registers to STM to LTM. For information to get into LTM, it must first be represented in each of the prior two memory stores, and the longer it stays in STM, the more likely it is to receive permanent storage in LTM.

Subsequent research suggests that a serial processing model cannot provide a full account of memory. Most sensory information is never processed consciously (i.e., placed in STM), but it can nevertheless be stored and retrieved—an explanation for the familiar experience of finding oneself humming a tune that was playing in the background at a store without you ever having noticed consciously that it was playing.

Long-term memory (LTM): Memory for facts, images, thoughts, feelings, skills, and experiences that may last as long as a lifetime.

Retrieval: The process of bringing information from long-term memory into short-term, or working, memory.

Serial position effect: The phenomenon that people are more likely to remember information that appears first and last in a list than information in the middle of the list.

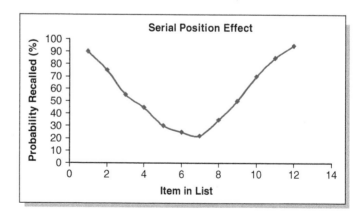

FIGURE 8.3 ■ Serial position effect. Items earlier in a list and those at the end show a heightened probability of recall in comparison to those in the middle.

Further, the process of selecting which sensory information to store in STM is actually influenced by LTM; that is, LTM is often activated *before* STM rather than after it. The function of STM is to hold important information in consciousness long enough to use it to solve problems and make decisions. But how do we know what information is important? The only way to decide which information to bring into STM is to compare incoming data with information stored in LTM that indicates its potential significance (Logie, 1996). Thus, LTM must actually be engaged *before* STM to figure out how to allocate conscious attention.

A second major shift is that researchers have come to view memory as involving a set of **modules**. These modules operate simultaneously (i.e., *parallel*), rather than serially (one at a time) (Fodor, 1983; Rumelhart et al., 1986). This view fits with neuropsychological theories suggesting that the central nervous system consists of coordinated but autonomously functioning systems of neurons.

For instance, when people simultaneously hear thunder and see lightning, they identify the sound using auditory modules in the temporal cortex and identify the image as lightning using visual modules in the occipital and lower (inferior) temporal lobes (the "what" pathway), and they pinpoint the location of the lightning using a visuospatial processing module (the "where" pathway) that runs from the occipital lobes through the upper (superior) temporal and parietal lobes. When they remember the episode, however, all three modules are activated at the same time, so they have no awareness that these memory systems have been operating in parallel.

Similarly, researchers have come to question whether STM is really a single memory store. As we will see shortly, experimental evidence suggests, instead, that STM is part of a *working memory* system that can briefly keep at least three different kinds of information in mind simultaneously so that the information is available for conscious problem solving (Baddeley, 1992, 1995).

Third, researchers once focused exclusively on conscious recollection of word lists, nonsense syllables, and similar types of information. Cognitive psychologists now recognize other forms of remembering that do not involve retrieval into consciousness. An amnesic like Jimmie (whose case opened this chapter) who learns a new skill, or a child who learns to tie a shoe, is storing new information in LTM. When this information is remembered, however, it is expressed directly in skilled behavior rather than retrieved into consciousness or STM. Further, researchers are now paying closer attention to the kinds of remembering that occur in everyday life, as when people remember emotionally significant events (Uttl et al., 2006) or try to remember to pick up several items at the grocery store on the way back home from work.

The fourth change is a shift in the metaphor underlying the model. Researchers in the 1960s were struck by the extraordinary developments in computer science that were just beginning to revolutionize technology, and they saw in the computer a powerful metaphor for the most impressive computing machine ever designed: the human mind. Today, after a decade of similarly extraordinary progress in unraveling the mysteries of the brain, cognitive scientists have turned to a different metaphor: mind as brain.

In the remainder of this chapter we will explore the major components of this evolving model. We begin with working memory (the current version of STM) and then examine the variety of memory processes and systems that constitute LTM.

> **Modules:** Discrete but interdependent processing units responsible for different kinds of remembering.

■ INTERIM SUMMARY

In **long-term memory (LTM)** representations of facts images, thoughts feelings, skills, and experiences may reside for as long as a lifetime. Recovering information from LTM, or **retrieval**, involves bringing it back into STM. The **serial position effect** is a tendency to remember information toward the beginning and end of a list rather than from the middle. Although the standard model still provides a foundation for thinking about memory, in the last decade it has evolved in four major ways. First, the assumption that a serial processing model can account for all of memory no longer seems likely. Second and related, researchers have come to view memory as involving a set of **modules**—discrete but interdependent processing units responsible for different kinds of remembering that operate simultaneously (in parallel) rather than sequentially (one at a time). Third, the standard model overemphasizes conscious memory for relatively neutral facts and underemphasizes other forms of remembering, such as skill learning and everyday remembering. Fourth, the underlying metaphor has changed, from *mind as computer to mind as brain*.

WORKING MEMORY

Because people use STM as a "workspace" to process new information and to call up relevant information from LTM, many psychologists now think of STM as a component of working memory. Working memory refers to the temporary storage and processing of information that can be used to solve problems, to respond to environmental demands, or to achieve goals (see Baddeley, 1992, 1995; Richardson, 1996a,b).

> **Working memory:** Conscious "workspace" used for retrieving and manipulating information, maintained through maintenance rehearsal; also called short-term memory.

Working memory is *active* memory: Information remains in working memory only as long as the person is consciously processing, examining, or manipulating it. Like the older concept of STM, working memory includes both a temporary memory store and a set of strategies, or *control processes*, for mentally manipulating the information momentarily held in that store. These control processes can be as simple as repeating a phone number over and over until we have finished dialing it—or as complex as trying to solve an equation in our heads.

Researchers initially believed that these two components of working memory—temporary storage and mental control—competed for the limited space at the lunch counter. In this view, rehearsing information is an active process that itself uses up some of the limited capacity of STM. Researchers also tended to view STM as a single system that could hold a maximum of about seven pieces of information of *any* kind, whether numbers, words, or images.

Researchers now believe, however, that working memory consists of multiple systems and that its storage and processing functions do not compete for limited space. According to one prominent model, working memory consists of three memory systems: a visual memory store, a verbal memory store, and a "central executive" that controls and manipulates the information these two short-term stores hold in mind (Baddeley, 1992, 1995). We begin by discussing the central executive and then examine the memory stores at its disposal.

Processing Information in Working Memory: The Central Executive

In 1994, Alan Baddeley and Graham Hitch challenged the view of a single all-purpose working memory by presenting participants with two tasks simultaneously, one involving recall of a series of digits and the other involving some kind of thinking, such as reasoning or comprehending the meaning of sentences. They reasoned that if working memory is a single system, trying to remember seven or eight digits would fill the memory store and eliminate any further capacity for thinking.

The investigators *did* find that performing STM and reasoning tasks simultaneously slowed down participants' ability to think. In one study, holding a memory load of four to eight digits increased the time participants took to solve a reasoning task. However, a memory load of three items had no effect at all on reasoning speed, despite the fact that it should have consumed at least three of the "slots" in STM. Further, performing the two tasks simultaneously had no impact on the number of *errors* participants made on the thinking task, suggesting that carrying out processes such as reasoning and rehearsal does not compete with storing digits for "workspace" in a short-term store.

These and other data led Baddeley and his colleagues to propose that storage capacity and processing capacity are two separate aspects of working memory. Processes such as rehearsal, reasoning, and making decisions about how to balance two tasks simultaneously are the work of a *central executive* system that has its own limited capacity, independent of the information it is storing or holding momentarily in mind. Other researchers have found that working memory as a whole does seem to have a limited capacity—people cannot do and remember too many things at the same time—but working memory capacity varies across individuals and is related to their general intellectual ability (Chapter 8) (Cahan, 2007; Daneman & Merikle, 1996; Just & Carpenter, 1992; Logie, 1996).

Visual and Verbal Storage

Most contemporary models of working memory distinguish between at least two kinds of temporary memory: a visual store and a verbal store (Baddeley, 1995; Baddeley et al., 1998). Evidence that these are indeed distinct components comes from several lines of research **(Figure 8.4)**.

The visual store (also called the *visuospatial sketchpad*) is like a temporary image the person can hold in mind for 20 or 30 seconds. It momentarily stores visual information such as the location and nature of objects in the environment, so that, for example, a person turning around to grab a mug at the sink will remember where she placed a tea bag a moment before. Images in the visual store can be mentally rotated, moved around, or used to locate objects in space that have momentarily dropped out of sight.

The verbal (or *phonological*) store is the familiar short-term store studied using tasks such as digit span. Verbal working memory is relatively shallow: Words are stored in order, based primarily on their sound (*phonology*), not their meaning.

Researchers learned about the "shallowness" of verbal working memory by studying the kinds of words that interfere with each other in free-recall tasks (Baddeley, 1986). A list of similar-sounding words (such as *man, mat, cap,* and *map*) is more difficult to recall than a list of words that do not sound alike. Similarity of

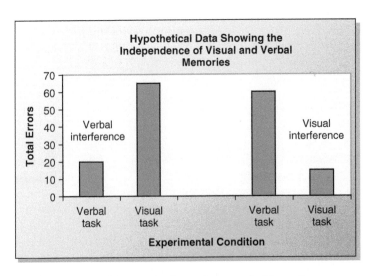

FIGURE 8.4 ■ This graph shows how verbal interference tasks interfere with verbal memory and not visual memory. The converse is also true with visual interference.

meaning (e.g., *large, big, huge, tall*) does not similarly interfere with verbal working memory, but it *does* interfere with LTM. These findings suggest that verbal working memory and LTM have somewhat different ways of storing information.

■ INTERIM SUMMARY

Many psychologists now refer to STM as **working memory**—the temporary storage and processing of information that can be used to solve problems, respond to environmental demands, or achieve goals. Working memory includes both a storage capacity and a processing capacity. According to the model proposed by Baddeley and his colleagues, processes such as rehearsal, reasoning, and making decisions about how to balance two tasks simultaneously are the work of a limited-capacity central executive system. Most contemporary models distinguish between at least two kinds of temporary memory—a visual store (the visuospatial sketchpad) and a verbal store.

The Relation between Working Memory and Long-Term Memory

What can we conclude from these various studies about working memory? First, consistent with the original concept of STM, working memory appears to be a system for temporarily storing and processing information, a way of holding information in mind long enough to use it. Second, working memory includes a number of limited-capacity component processes, including a central executive

---

ONE STEP FURTHER

The Neuropsychology Of Working Memory

Researchers have begun tracking down the neuropsychology of working memory. The emerging consensus is that working memory is "orchestrated," or directed, by the *prefrontal cortex*, a region of the brain long known to be involved in the most high-level cognitive functions (Kane & Engle, 2002). When information is temporarily stored and manipulated, the prefrontal cortex is activated along with whichever posterior regions (i.e., regions toward the back of the brain) normally process the kind of information being held in memory, such as words or images (D'Esposito et al., 1997; Faw, 2003; Goldman-Rakic, 1996; Smith, 2000).

Activation of the prefrontal cortex seems to provide access to *consciousness* to representations normally processed in other parts of the cortex, so that the person can temporarily hold the information in mind and manipulate it. Evidence for the pivotal role of the prefrontal cortex began to accumulate when researchers designed working memory tasks for monkeys and observed the activity of neurons in this region (Fuster, 1989, 1997; Goldman-Rakic, 1995).

Similar studies have now been conducted with humans. In one study, the researchers used fMRI to study the activation of different cortical regions while participants tried to remember faces or scrambled faces (a meaningless visual stimulus) (Courtney et al., 1997). The results were striking. Relatively meaningless visual information activated posterior regions of the occipital lobes involved in the early stages of processing visual stimuli. Facial stimuli activated areas of the visual cortex in the

Continued

occipital and temporal lobes involved in processing and identifying meaningful visual stimuli (and perhaps faces in particular). Anterior regions of the frontal lobes—that is, the prefrontal cortex—were most active during the delay period in which the faces and scrambled faces were removed and had to be held in working memory.

Research also demonstrates the independence of different *components* of working memory. For example, neuroimaging studies confirm that verbal and visual working memory activate different cortical regions (Smith et al., 1996). Studies even document the existence of two distinct kinds of *visual* working memory, processed in different areas of the prefrontal cortex: memory for location and memory for objects (Courtney et al., 1998; Rao et al., 1997). This finding makes sense in light of research, that distinguishes between two visual pathways involved in perception, the "what" pathway (involved in identifying what objects are) and the "where" pathway (involved in identifying where they are in space). Researchers have even begun tracking down the anatomical location of the central executive.

Using fMRI, one team of researchers identified a region of the prefrontal cortex that may be involved in functions such as managing the demands of two simultaneous tasks (D'Esposito et al., 1997). The researchers presented subjects with two tasks that do not involve short-term storage, one verbal (making simple decisions about some words) and the other visual (mentally rotating images).

As expected, the verbal task activated the left temporal cortex, whereas the visual task activated the occipital and parietal cortex. Neither task alone activated the prefrontal cortex. However, when subjects had to complete both tasks at the same time, regions of the prefrontal cortex became active—a suggestion that prefrontal working memory circuits are indeed activated when people have to make "executive decisions" about how to manage the limited workspace in working memory (see also Adcock et al., 2000; Bunge et al., 2000).

system, a verbal storage system, and at least one and probably two or three visual storage systems (one for location, one for identification of objects, and perhaps another that stores both simultaneously). Third, working memory is better conceived as a conscious workspace for accomplishing goals than as a way station or gateway to storage in LTM, because information can be stored in LTM without being represented in consciousness, and information in LTM is often accessed prior to its representation in working memory (Logie, 1996).

How Distinct are Working Memory and Long-Term Memory?

Are working memory and LTM really distinct? In many ways, yes. As we have seen, working memory is rapidly accessed and severely limited in capacity. Imagine if our LTM allowed us to remember only seven pieces of verbal information, seven objects or faces, and seven locations!

Some of the strongest evidence for a distinction between working memory and LTM is neurological. Patients like Jimmie with severe amnesia can often store and manipulate information for momentary use with little trouble. They may be able, for example, to recall seven digits and keep them in mind by rehearsing them. The moment they stop rehearsing, however, they may forget that they were even trying to recall digits, an indication of a severe impairment in LTM. Researchers have also observed patients with the opposite problem: severe working memory deficits (such as a memory span of only two digits) but intact LTM (Caplan & Waters, 1990; Shallice & Warrington, 1970).

Interactions of Working Memory and Long-Term Memory

Working memory and LTM may be distinct, but much of the time they are so intertwined that they can be difficult to distinguish. For example, when people are asked to recall a sequence of words after a brief delay, their performance is better if the words are semantically related (such as *chicken* and *duck*), presumably because they recognize the link between them and can use the memory of one to cue the memory of the other from LTM (Wetherick, 1975). Similarly, words are more easily remembered than nonsense syllables (Hulme et al., 1991). These findings suggest that working memory involves the conscious activation of knowledge from LTM, since, without accessing LTM, the person could not tell the difference between words and nonwords.

Indeed, from a neuroanatomical standpoint, working memory appears to become engaged when neural networks in the frontal lobes become activated along with (and linked to) networks in the occipital, temporal, and parietal lobes that represent various words or images. These mental representations of words or images themselves reflect an interaction between current sensory data and stored knowledge from LTM, such as matching a visual pattern with a stored image of a particular person's face. In this sense, working memory in part involves a special kind of activation of information stored in LTM (see Cowan, 1994; Ericsson & Kintsch, 1995).

Chunking

Perhaps the best example of the interaction between working memory and LTM in daily life is a strategy people use to expand the capacity of their working memory in particular situations (Erickson & Kintsch, 1995). We have noted that the brain holds a certain number of units of information in consciousness at a time. But what constitutes a unit? A letter? A word? Perhaps an entire sentence or idea?

Consider the working memory capacity of a skilled server in a restaurant. How can a person take the order of eight people without the aid of a notepad, armed only with a *mental* sketchpad and a limited-capacity verbal store? One way is to use chunking, a memory technique that uses knowledge stored in LTM to group information in larger units than single words or digits. Chunking is essential in everyday life, particularly in cultures that rely upon literacy, because people are constantly called upon to remember telephone numbers, written words, and lists.

Now consider the following sequence of letters: DJIBMNYSEWSJSEC. This string would be impossible for most people to hold in working memory, unless they are interested in business and recognize some meaningful chunks: *DJ* for Dow Jones, *IBM* for International Business Machines, *NYSE* for New York Stock Exchange, *WSJ* for *Wall Street Journal*, and *SEC* for Securities and Exchange Commission. In this example, chunking effectively reduces the number of pieces of information in working memory from 15 to 5. People tend to use chunking most effectively in their areas of expertise, such as servers who know a menu "like the back of their hands." Similarly, knowledge of area codes allows people to store 10 or 11 digits at a time, since 202 (the area code for Washington, D.C.) or 212 (one of the area codes for Manhattan in New York City) can become a single chunk rather than three "slots" in verbal working memory.

Chunking: The process of organizing information into small, meaningful bits to aid memory.

■ INTERIM SUMMARY

Working memory and LTM are distinct from one another in both their functions and neuroanatomy because patients with brain damage can show severe deficits on one but not the other. Working memory appears to occur as frontal lobe neural networks become activated along with and linked to networks in the occipital, temporal, and parietal lobes that represent various words or images. Working memory clearly interacts with LTM systems, as occurs in **chunking**—using knowledge stored in LTM to group information in larger units than single words or digits and hence to expand working memory capacity in specific domains.

VARIETIES OF LONG-TERM MEMORY

Most readers have had the experience of going into the refrigerator looking for a condiment such as ketchup. Our first pass at "remembering" where the ketchup is seems more like habit than memory—we automatically look in a particular place, such as the side door, where we have found it many times. If the bottle is not there, we typically employ one of two strategies. The first is to think about where we *usually* put it, drawing on our general knowledge about what we have done in the past—do we usually put it on the door or on the top shelf? The second is to try to remember a specific episode, namely the last time we used the ketchup.

This simple example reveals something not so simple: that LTM comes in multiple forms, such as automatic "habits," general knowledge, and memory for specific episodes. Researchers do not yet agree on precisely how many systems constitute LTM, but developments in neuroimaging have made clear that the three different ways of finding the ketchup represent three very different kinds of memory, each with its own neuroanatomy. In this section, we explore some of the major types of LTM.

Declarative and Procedural Memory

In general, people store two kinds of information, declarative and procedural. Declarative memory refers to memory for facts and events, much of which can be stated or "declared" (Squire, 1986). Procedural memory refers to how-to knowledge of procedures or skills.

When we think of memory, we usually mean **declarative memory**: knowledge of facts and events. Remembering that Abraham Lincoln was the sixteenth president of the United States, or calling up a happy memory from the past, requires access to declarative memory.

Declarative memory can be semantic or episodic (Tulving, 1972, 1987). **Semantic memory** refers to general world knowledge or facts, such as the knowledge that summers are hot in Katmandu or that NaCl is the chemical formula for table salt (Tulving, 1972). The term is somewhat misleading because *semantic* implies that general knowledge is stored in words, whereas people know many things about objects, such as their color or smell, that are encoded as sensory representations. For this reason, many psychologists now refer to *semantic memory* as *generic memory*.

Episodic memory consists of memories of particular events, rather than general knowledge. Episodic memory allows people to travel mentally through time, to remember thoughts and feelings (or in memory experiments, word lists) from the recent or distant past, or to imagine the future (Wheeler et al., 1997).

In everyday life, episodic memory is often *autobiographical*, as when people remember what they did on their eighteenth birthday or what they ate yesterday (see Howe, 2000). It is also closely linked to semantic memory, because, when people experience similar episodes over time (such as 180 days a year in school or hundreds of thousands of interactions with their father), they gradually develop generic memories of what those situations were like (e.g., "I used to love weekends with my father").

Declarative memory is the most obvious kind of memory, but another kind of memory is equally important in daily life: **procedural memory**, also referred to as skill or habit memory. People are often astonished to find that even though they have not skated for 20 years, the skills are reactivated easily, almost as if

Declarative memory: Knowledge that can be consciously retrieved and "declared".

Semantic memory: General world knowledge or facts; also called generic memory.

Episodic memory: Memories of particular episodes or events from personal experience.

Procedural memory: Knowledge of procedures or skills that emerges when people engage in activities that require them; also called skill or habit memory.

their use had never been interrupted. When people put a backspin on a tennis ball, speak grammatically, or drive a car, they are drawing on procedural memory. Other procedural skills are less obvious, such as reading, which involves a set of complex procedures for decoding strings of letters and words.

Although procedural memories often form without conscious effort (as in conditioning procedures with rats who presumably do not carefully think out their next move in a maze), at other times procedural memories are "residues" of prior conscious knowledge and strategies that have become automatic and highly efficient. For example, when we first learn to type, we study the layout of the keyboard, trying to form declarative memories. As we are typing our first words, we also hold in working memory the sequence of keys to hit and knowledge about which fingers to use for each key. Over time, however, our speed and accuracy improve, while conscious effort diminishes. This process reflects the formation of procedural memory for typing. In the end, we think only of the words we want to type and would have difficulty describing the layout of the keyboard (declarative memory), even though our fingers "remember." As we will see, this shift from conscious, effortful memory to automatic procedural memory occurs as regions of the cortex "pass the torch" of memory to subcortical regions in the basal ganglia.

Explicit and Implicit Memory

For much of the last century psychologists studied memory by asking participants to memorize word lists, nonsense syllables, or connections between pairs of words and then asking them to recall them. These tasks all tap explicit memory, or conscious recollection. However, psychologists have recognized another kind of memory: implicit memory (Graf & Schacter, 1987; Roediger, 1990; Schacter & Buckner, 1998). Implicit memory refers to memory that is expressed in behavior but does not require conscious recollection, such as tying a shoelace.

Some psychologists use explicit and implicit memory as synonyms for declarative and procedural memory. Although there is clearly some overlap, the declarative–procedural dichotomy refers more to the *type of knowledge* that is stored (facts versus skills), whereas the explicit–implicit distinction refers more to the *way this knowledge is retrieved and expressed* (with or without conscious awareness). As we will see, people's knowledge of facts (declarative knowledge) is often expressed without awareness (implicitly). **Figure 8.5** provides a model of the different dimensions of LTM.

> **Explicit memory:** The conscious recollection of facts and events.

> **Implicit memory:** Memory that cannot be brought to mind consciously but can be expressed in behavior.

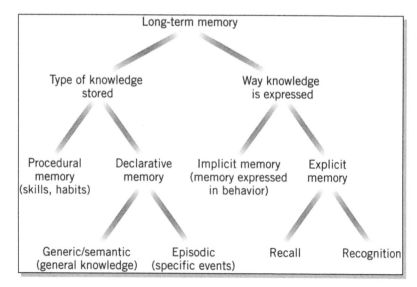

FIGURE 8.5   Key distinctions in long-term memory.

THE NEUROPSYCHOLOGY OF LONG-TERM MEMORY

How distinct are these varieties of long-term memories? Are researchers simply splitting hairs, or are they really "carving nature at its joints," making distinctions where distinctions truly exist?

Some of the most definitive data supporting distinctions among different types of memory are neuroanatomical studies, including case studies of patients with neurological damage, brain imaging with normal and brain-damaged patients, and experimental studies with animals (Gabrieli, 1998; Gluck & Myers, 1997; Squire, 1992, 1995). Researchers discovered the distinction between implicit and explicit memory in part by observing amnesic patients who have trouble storing and retrieving new declarative information (such as their age or the name or face of their doctor) but show minimal impairment on implicit tasks (Schacter, 1995a). Consider the case of H.M., who had most of his *medial temporal lobes* (the region in the middle of the temporal lobes, including the hippocampus and amygdala) removed because of uncontrollable seizures **(Figure 8.6)**. Following the operation, H.M. had one of the deepest, purest cases of amnesia ever recorded, leading to the conclusion that medial temporal structures play a central role in the *consolidation* (i.e., encoding and "solidification") of new explicit memories (Nader et al., 2006). Despite his inability to store new memories, however, H.M. was able to learn new procedural skills, such as writing words upside down. Each new time H.M. was asked to perform this task, his speed improved, but he had no recollection that he had ever performed it before.

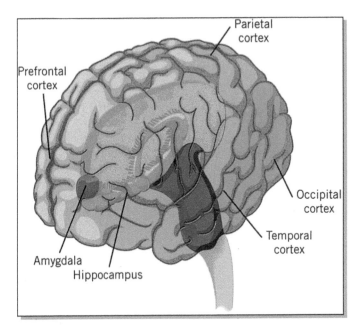

FIGURE 8.6 ■ Anatomy of memory. The medial temporal region (inside the middle of the temporal lobes), particularly the hippocampus, plays a key role in consolidation of explicit, declarative information. The frontal lobes play a more important role in working memory, procedural memory, and aspects of episodic memory, such as dating memories for the time at which they occurred. Posterior regions of the cortex (occipital, parietal, and temporal cortex) are involved in memory just as they are in perception, by creating mental representations.

Lesion research with monkeys and imaging research with humans have demonstrated that the hippocampus and adjacent regions of the cortex are central to the consolidation of explicit memories (Eichenbaum, 1997; McGaugh, 2000; Squire & Zola, 1991). In contrast, the fact that amnesics like H.M. often show normal skill learning and priming effects suggests that the hippocampus is not central to implicit memory.

In daily life, of course, implicit and explicit memory are often intertwined. For example, people learn through conditioning to fear and avoid stimuli that are painful, but they are also frequently aware of the connection between various stimuli or behaviors and their effects. Thus, a child might learn by touching a stove that doing so is punishing (conditioning) but also might be able explicitly to recall the connection between the two events: "If I touch the stove, I get an ouchie!"

Neurologically speaking, however, implicit and explicit memory rely on separate mechanisms (Bechara et al., 1995). For example, fear conditioning and avoidance learning require an intact amygdala. In a classical conditioning procedure in which a particular sound (the conditioned stimulus) is paired with an electric shock (the unconditioned stimulus), patients with an intact hippocampus but a damaged amygdala can explicitly state the connection between the CS and the UCS—that is, they consciously know that the tone is associated with shock. However, their nervous system shows no signs of autonomic arousal (e.g., increased heart rate) or behavioral expressions of fear when exposed to the CS. They *know* the connection but cannot *feel* it. In contrast, patients with an intact amygdala but a damaged hippocampus may have no conscious idea that the CS is associated with electric shock—in fact, they may have no recollection of ever having encountered the stimulus before—but nonetheless they show a conditioned fear response to it, including autonomic arousal.

Subsystems of Implicit and Explicit Memory

Implicit and explicit memory are themselves broad categories that include neurologically distinct phenomena. The two kinds of explicit memory, semantic and episodic, rely on different neural mechanisms. Patients with damage to the frontal lobes have little trouble retrieving semantic knowledge but often show deficits in episodic memory (Shimamura, 1995; Wheeler et al., 1995, 1997). They may, for example, have trouble remembering the order of events in their lives (Swain et al., 1998), or they may vividly recall events that never occurred because they have difficulty distinguishing true from false memories of events (Schacter, 1997). PET studies show greater activation of prefrontal regions when recalling episodic rather than semantic information (Nyberg, 1998).

Implicit memory also likely comprises at least two systems. Patients with damage to the cortex caused by Alzheimer's disease may have normal procedural memory but impaired performance on priming tasks. In contrast, patients with Huntington's disease, a fatal, degenerative condition that affects the basal ganglia, show normal priming but impaired procedural learning (Butters et al., 1990).

Brain-imaging data on normal participants have provided insight into the way knowledge that at first requires considerable effort becomes procedural, as the brain essentially transfers the processing of the task from one network to another (see Poldrack et al., 1998). For example, after practice at reading words backward in a mirror, people show *decreased* activity in visual pathways but *increased* activity in verbal pathways in the left temporal lobe. This switch suggests that they are more rapidly moving from the visual task of mentally turning the word around to the linguistic task of understanding its meaning.

Explicit Memory

Explicit memory involves the conscious retrieval of information. Researchers distinguish between two kinds of explicit retrieval: recall and recognition. **Recall** is the spontaneous conscious recollection of information from LTM, as when a person brings to mind memories of her wedding day or the name of the capital of Egypt. Neuroimaging studies show that recall activates parts of the brain that are also activated during working memory tasks involving the central executive (Nolde et al., 1998). This makes sense given that recall requires conscious effort.

Although recall occurs spontaneously, it generally requires effortful use of strategies for calling the desired information to mind. When efforts at recall fail, people sometimes experience the **tip-of-the-tongue phenomenon**, in which the person knows the information is "in there" but is not quite able to retrieve it (Brown & McNeill, 1966). Research suggests that this phenomenon stems from problems linking the sounds of words (which are arbitrary—a *table* could just as easily have been called a *blah*) with their meanings (Merriman et al., 2000). Thus, using the word *prognosticate* in a conversation with someone who has the word *pontificate* on the tip of his tongue can lead to sudden recall (and a feeling of relief!).

Recognition refers to the explicit sense or recollection that something currently perceived has been previously encountered or learned. Researchers often test recognition memory by asking participants whether a word was on a list they saw the previous day. Recognition is easier than recall (as any student knows who has answered multiple-choice items that simply require recognition of names or concepts), because the person does not have to *generate* the information, just make a judgment about it.

Implicit Memory

Implicit memory is evident in skills, conditioned learning, and associative memory (i.e., associations between one representation and another). It can be seen in skills such as turning the wheel in the correct direction when the car starts to skid in the snow (which skilled drivers in cold regions do before they have even formed the thought "I'm skidding") as well as in responses learned through classical and operant conditioning, such as avoiding a food that was once associated with nausea, whether or not the person has any explicit recollection of the event.

Implicit associative memory emerges in experiments on **priming effects**. Participants in memory experiments show priming effects even when they do not consciously remember being exposed to the prime (Bowers & Schacter, 1990; Tulving et al., 1982). For example, they might be exposed to a list of words that are relatively rarely used in everyday conversation, such as *assassin*. A week later, they may have no idea whether *assassin* was on the list (a test of explicit recognition memory), but if asked to fill in the missing letters of a word fragment such as *A_A_IN*, they are more likely to complete it with the word *assassin* than control subjects who studied a different list the week earlier. Priming effects appear to rely on activation of information stored in LTM, even though the person is unaware of what has been activated.

© Rune Hellestad/CORBIS

An expert guitarist like Eric Clapton can improvise much faster than he can consciously choose the notes he is going to play.

■ INTERIM SUMMARY

Types of LTM can be distinguished by kind of knowledge stored (facts versus skills) and the way this knowledge is retrieved and expressed (with or without conscious awareness). People store two kinds of information, declarative and procedural. **Declarative memory** refers to memory for facts and events; it can be **semantic** (general world knowledge or facts) or **episodic** (memories of particular events). **Procedural memory** refers to how to knowledge of procedures or skills.

Knowledge can be retrieved explicitly or implicitly. **Explicit memory** refers to conscious recollection, whereas **implicit memory** refers to memory that is expressed in behavior. Researchers distinguish between two kinds of explicit retrieval: **recall** (the spontaneous retrieval of material from LTM) and **recognition** (memory for whether something currently perceived has been previously encountered or learned). Implicit memory is evident in skills, conditioned learning, and associative memory (associations between one representation and another).

■ INTERIM SUMMARY

Implicit and explicit memory are neuroanatomically distinct. The hippocampus and adjacent regions of the cortex are centrally involved in consolidating explicit memories. Amnesics with hippocampal damage often show normal skill learning, conditioning, and priming effects, suggesting that the hippocampus is not central to implicit memory. Different kinds of explicit memory, notably episodic and semantic, also appear to constitute distinct memory systems. The same is true of two types of implicit memory, procedural and associative.

Everyday Memory

In designing studies, researchers have to strike a balance between the often conflicting goals of maximizing internal validity—creating a study whose methods are sound and rigorous and can lead to clear causal inferences—and external validity—making sure the results generalize to the real world. Since Ebbinghaus's studies in the late nineteenth century, memory research has tended to emphasize internal validity—by measuring participants' responses as they memorize words, nonsense syllables, and pairs of words,—to try to learn about basic memory processes. Increasingly, however, researchers have begun to argue for the importance of studying everyday memory as well, that is, memory as it occurs in daily life (Ceci & Bronfenbrenner, 1991; Herrmann et al., 1996; Koriat et al., 2000).

> **Everyday memory:** Memory as it occurs in daily life.

In the laboratory, the experimenter usually supplies the information to be remembered, the reason to remember it, and the occasion to remember it (immediately, a week later, etc.). Often the information to be remembered has little intrinsic meaning, such as isolated words on a list. In contrast, in daily life, people store and retrieve information because they need to for one reason or another. The information is usually meaningful and emotionally significant, and the context for retrieval is sometimes a future point in time that itself must be remembered, as when a person tries to remember to call a friend later in the day. Thus, researchers have begun to study everyday memory in its naturalistic setting—such as people's memory for appointments (Andrzejewski et al., 1991)—as well as to devise ways to bring it into the laboratory. Recently, researchers have applied technology to measure everyday memory. In a study measuring the effects of age on everyday memory, participants used a touch screen to move through a virtual street, while completing "event-based shopping errands" (Farrimond et al., 2006).

Everyday Memory is Functional Memory

In their daily lives, people typically remember for a purpose, to achieve some goal (Anderson, 1996). Memory, like all psychological processes, is *functional*. Of all the things we could commit to memory over the course of a day, we tend to remember those that bear on our needs and interests.

The functional nature of memory was demonstrated in a set of studies that examined whether men and women would have better recall for stereotypically masculine and feminine memory tasks (Herrmann et al., 1992). In one study, the investigators asked participants to remember a shopping list and a list of travel directions. As predicted, women's memory was better for the shopping list, whereas men had better memory for the directions.

Does this mean that women are born to shop and men to navigate? A second study suggested otherwise. This time, some participants received a "grocery list" to remember whereas others received a "hardware list." Additionally, some received directions on "how to make a shirt" whereas others received directions on "how to make a workbench." In reality, the grocery and hardware lists were identical, as were the two lists of "directions." For example, the shopping list included items such as *brush, oil, chips, nuts*, and *gum* that could just as easily be interpreted as goods at a grocery store as hardware items. The "directions" were so general that they could refer to almost anything (e.g., "First, you rearrange the pieces into different groups. Of course, one pile may be sufficient . . .").

As predicted, women were more likely to remember details about shirt making and grocery lists. The biases in recall for directions for men were particularly strong. Apparently, "real men" do not make shirts. These findings demonstrate the importance of noncognitive factors such as motivation and interest in everyday memory: What men define as not relevant, not interesting, or threatening to their masculinity does not make a lasting impression on their memory (Colley et al., 2002).

Recent research links some forms of everyday memory to the hippocampus. Researchers tested London taxi drivers' knowledge of the streets of their city. Drivers showed more activation in the hippocampus for a navigation task that required their expertise than for several other memory tasks (Maguire et al., 1997). In fact, the size of the activated regions of the hippocampus was strongly correlated with the number of years they had been driving, a suggestion that the brain devotes more "room" in the hippocampus for frequently used information, just as it does in the cortex (Maguire et al., 2000).

Prospective Memory

Retrospective memory: Memory for events that have already occurred.

Most studies of memory have examined retrospective memory, that is, memory for things from the past, such as a list of words encountered 20 minutes earlier. In everyday life, an equally important kind of memory is **prospective memory**, or memory for things that need to be done in the future, such as picking up some items at the store after work (Brandimonte et al., 1996; Einstein & McDaniel, 2004; Ellis & Kvavilashvili, 2000; McDaniel et al., 1998; Smith, 2003). Prospective memory has at least two components: remembering *to* remember ("be sure to stop at the store after work") and remembering *what* to remember (e.g., a loaf of bread and a sponge). In other words, prospective memory requires memory of *intent* as well as *content* (Kvavilashvili, 1987; Marsh et al., 1998). Experimental studies suggest that intending to carry out certain acts in the future leads to their heightened activation in LTM (Goschke & Kuhl, 1993, 1996).

Although prospective memory is probably not itself a memory "system" with its own properties, it does have elements that distinguish it from other kinds of memory (see McDaniel, 1995). One is its heavy emphasis on time. Part of remembering an intention is remembering *when* to remember it, such as at a specific time (e.g., right after work) or an interval of time (tonight, tomorrow, sometime over the next few days).

Another unique feature of remembered intentions is that the person has to remember whether the action has been performed so the intentions can be "shut off." This facet of prospective memory is obviously more important with some tasks than with others. Inadvertently renting the same video you already watched a month ago is clearly less harmful than taking medication you didn't remember taking an hour earlier.

■ INTERIM SUMMARY

Everyday memory refers to memory as it occurs in daily life. Everyday memory is functional, focused on remembering information that is meaningful. One kind of everyday memory is prospective memory, memory for things that need to be done in the future.

> **Prospective memory:** Memory for things that need to be done in the future.

ENCODING AND ORGANIZATION OF LONG-TERM MEMORY

We have now completed our tour of the varieties of memory. But how does information find its way into LTM? And how is information organized in the mind so that it can be readily retrieved? In this section we explore these two questions. The focus is on the storage and organization of declarative knowledge, because it has received the most empirical attention.

Encoding

For information to be retrievable from memory, it must be encoded. The manner of encoding—how, how much, and when the person tries to learn new information—has a substantial influence on its *accessibility*.

> **Encoded:** Refers to information that is cast into a representational form, or "code," so that it can be readily accessed from memory.

Levels of Processing

Anyone who has ever crammed for a test knows that rehearsal is important for storing information in LTM. As noted earlier, however, the simple, repetitive rehearsal that maintains information momentarily in working memory is not optimal for LTM. Usually, a more effective strategy is to attend to the *meaning* of the stimulus and form mental connections between it and previously stored information.

Some encoding is deliberate, such as studying for an exam, learning lines for a play, or trying to remember a joke. However, much of the time encoding simply occurs as a by-product of thought and perception—a reason why people can remember incidents that happened to them 10 years ago even though they were not trying to commit them to memory.

Deep and Shallow Processing

The degree to which information is elaborated, reflected upon, and processed in a meaningful way during memory storage is referred to as the *depth* or level of processing (Craik & Lockhart, 1972; Lockhart & Craik, 1990). Information may be processed at a shallow, structural level (focusing on physical characteristics of the stimulus); at a somewhat deeper, phonemic level (focusing on simple characteristics of the language used to describe it); or at the deepest, semantic level (focusing on the meaning of the stimulus).

> **Level of processing:** The degree to which information is elaborated, reflected upon, or processed in a meaningful way during encoding of memory.

For example, at a shallow, structural level, a person may walk by a restaurant and notice the typeface and colors of its sign. At a phonemic level, she may read the sign to herself and notice that it sounds Spanish. Processing material deeply, in contrast, means paying attention to its meaning or significance—noticing, for instance, that this is the restaurant a friend has been recommending for months.

Different levels of processing activate different neural circuits. As one might guess, encoding that occurs as people make judgments about the meaning of words (such as whether they are concrete or abstract) leads to greater activation of the left temporal cortex, which is involved in language comprehension, than if they attend to qualities of the printed words, such as whether they are in upper- or lowercase letters (Gabrieli et al., 1996). *Deliberate* use of strategies to remember (such as remembering to buy bread and bottled water by thinking of a prisoner who is fed only bread and water) activates regions of the prefrontal cortex involved in other executive functions such as manipulating information in working memory (Kapur et al., 1996). Research has even shown that the amount of activity in the prefrontal and temporal cortexes predicts the extent to which participants are likely to remember studied material successfully (Brewer et al., 1998; Wagner et al., 1998).

Encoding Specificity

Advocates of depth-of-processing theory originally thought that deeper processing is always better. Although this is *generally* true, subsequent research shows that the best encoding strategy depends on what the person later needs to retrieve (see Anderson, 1995). If a person is asked to recall shallow information (such as whether a word was originally presented in capital letters), shallow encoding tends to be more useful.

The fact that ease of retrieval depends on the match between the way information is encoded and later retrieved is known as the encoding specificity principle (Tulving & Thompson, 1973). For example, a student who studies for a multiple-choice test by memorizing definitions and details without trying to understand the underlying concepts may be in much more trouble if the professor decides to include an essay question, because the student has encoded the information at too shallow a level.

Why does the match between encoding and retrieval influence the ease with which people can access information from memory? According to several theorists, memory is not really a process distinct from perception and thought; rather, it is a by-product of the normal processes of perceiving and thinking, which automatically lay down traces of an experience as it is occurring. When people remember, they simply reactivate the same neural networks that processed the information in the first place (Crowder, 1993; Lockhart & Craik, 1990). If the circumstances at encoding and retrieval are similar, the memory is more easily retrieved because more of the neural network that represents it is activated. To put it another way, a new thought, feeling, or perception is like a hiker who has to create a new trail through the woods. Each time another traveler takes that path—that is, each time a similar event occurs—the trail becomes more defined and easier to locate.

Context and Retrieval

According to the encoding specificity principle, the *contexts* in which people encode and retrieve information can also affect the ease of retrieval. One study presented scuba divers with different lists of words, some while the divers were underwater and others while they were above the water (Godden & Baddeley, 1975). The divers had better recall for lists they had encoded underwater when they were underwater at retrieval; conversely, lists encoded above water were better recalled above water. Another study of Russian immigrants to the United States found that they were more likely to remember events in their lives from Russia when interviewed in Russian and more likely to remember events from their new lives in the United States when interviewed in English (Marian & Neisser, 2000). They retrieved few memories from the period shortly following their immigration, when they were "changing over" languages.

The same phenomenon appears to occur with people's *emotional state* at encoding and retrieval, a phenomenon called *state-dependent memory*: Being in a similar mood at encoding and retrieval (e.g., angry while learning a word list and angry while trying to remember it) can facilitate memory, as long as the emotional state is not so intense that it inhibits memory in general (see Bower, 1981; Keenly, 1997). Having the same context during encoding and retrieval facilitates recall because the context provides retrieval cues.

Encoding specificity principle: The notion that the match between the way information is encoded and the way it is retrieved is important to remembering.

Retrieval cues: Stimuli or thoughts that can be used to stimulate retrieval.

Spacing

Another encoding variable that influences memory is of particular importance in educational settings: the interval between study sessions. Students intuitively know that if they cram the night before a test, the information is likely to be available to them when they need it the next day. They also tend to believe that *massed* rehearsal (i.e., pulling an all-nighter) is more effective than *spaced*, or *distributed*, rehearsal over longer intervals (Zechmeister & Shaughnessy, 1980). But is this strategy really optimal for long-term retention?

In fact, distributed rehearsal is best (Bruce & Bahrick, 1992; Dempster, 1996; Ebbinghaus, 1885). Massed rehearsal *seems* superior because it makes initial acquisition of memory slightly easier, since the material is at a heightened state of activation in a massed-practice session. Over the long run, however, research on the spacing effect—the superiority of memory for information rehearsed over longer intervals—demonstrates that spacing study sessions over longer intervals tends to *double* long-term retention of information.

> **Spacing effect:** The superior long-term retention of information rehearsed in sessions spread out over longer intervals of time.

In one study, the Bahrick family tested the long-term effects of spaced rehearsal on the study of 300 foreign-language vocabulary words (Bahrick et al., 1993). The major finding was that, over a five-year period, 13 training sessions at intervals of 56 days apart increased memory retention rates compared to 26 sessions spaced at 14-day intervals. These results are robust across a variety of memory tasks, even including implicit memory (Perruchet, 1989; Toppino & Schneider, 1999).

These and related findings have important implications for students and teachers (Bruce & Bahrick, 1992; Rea & Modigliani, 1988). Students who want to remember information for more than a day or two after an exam should space their studying over time and avoid cramming. Medical students, law students, and others who intend to practice a profession based on their coursework should be particularly wary of all-nighters.

Moreover, much as students might protest, cumulative exams over the course of a semester are superior to exams that test only the material that immediately preceded them. Cumulative exams require students to relearn material at long intervals, and the tests themselves constitute learning sessions in which memory is retrieved and reinforced. In fact, research on spacing is part of what led the authors of this text to include both interim summaries and a general summary at the end of each chapter, since learning occurs best with a combination of immediate review and spaced rehearsal.

Representational Modes and Encoding

The ability to retrieve information from LTM also depends on the modes used to encode it. In general, the more ways a memory can be encoded, the greater the likelihood that it will be accessible for later retrieval. Storing a memory in multiple representational modes—such as words, images, and sounds—provides more retrieval cues to bring it back to mind (see Paivio, 1991).

For instance, many people remember phone numbers not only by memorizing the digits but also by forming a mental map of the buttons they need to push and a motoric (procedural) representation of the pattern of buttons to push that becomes automatic and is expressed implicitly. When pushing the buttons, they may even be alerted that they have dialed the wrong number by hearing a sound pattern that does not match the expected pattern, suggesting auditory storage as well.

People come to remember phone numbers through rehearsal of numbers, through procedural representations of the appropriate buttons to push, and through auditory associations with particular numbers.

■ INTERIM SUMMARY

For information to be retrievable from memory, it must be **encoded**, or cast into a representational form that can be readily accessed from memory. The degree to which information is elaborated, reflected upon, and processed in a meaningful way during memory storage is referred to as the *depth* or **level of processing**. Although deeper processing tends to be more useful for storing information for the long term, ease of retrieval depends on the match between the way information is encoded and the way it is later retrieved, a phenomenon known as the **encoding specificity principle**. Similar contexts during encoding and retrieval provide **retrieval cues**—stimuli or thoughts that can be used to facilitate recollection. Aside from level of processing, two other variables influence accessibility of memory, the **spacing** of study sessions and the use of multiple representational modes.

Mnemonic Devices

Mnemonic devices: Systematic strategies for remembering information.

The principles of encoding we have just been describing help explain the utility of many mnemonic devices—systematic strategies for remembering information (named after the Greek word *mneme*, which means "memory"). People can use external aids (such as note taking or asking someone else) to enhance their memory, or they can rely on internal aids, such as rehearsal and various mnemonic strategies (Glisky, 2005). Most mnemonic devices draw on the principle that the more retrieval cues that can be created and the more vivid these cues are, the better memory is likely to be. Generally, mnemonic devices are most useful when the to-be-remembered information lacks clear organization.

Method of Loci

Method of loci: A memory aid, or mnemonic device, in which images are remembered by fitting them into an orderly arrangement of locations.

One mnemonic strategy is the method of loci, which uses visual imagery as a memory aid. The ancient Roman writer Cicero attributed this technique to the Greek poet Simonides, who was attending a banquet when he was reportedly summoned by the gods from the banquet hall to receive a message. In his absence, the roof collapsed, killing everyone. The bodies were mangled beyond recognition, but Simonides was able to identify the guests by their physical placement around the banquet table. He thus realized that images could be remembered by fitting them into an orderly arrangement of locations (Bower, 1970).

© Chris Rodenberg Photography, 2009. Used under license from Shutterstock, Inc.

You could easily use the method of loci to learn a list of words by associating each of the words with various places around your bedroom.

To use the method of loci, you must first decide on a series of "snapshot" mental images of familiar locations. For instance, locations in your bedroom might be your pillow, your closet, the top of your dresser, and under the bed. Now, suppose that you need to do the following errands: pick up vitamin C, buy milk, return a book to the library, and make plans with one of your friends for the weekend. You can remember these items by visualizing each in one of your loci, making the image as vivid as possible to maximize the likelihood of retrieving it. Thus, you might picture the vitamin C pills as spilled all over your pillow, a bottle of milk poured over the best outfit in your closet, the book lying on top of your dresser, and your friend hiding under your bed until Friday night. Often, the more ridiculous the image, the easier it is to remember. While you are out doing your errands, you can mentally flip through your imagined loci to bring back the mental images.

SQ3R Method

SQ3R: A mnemonic device designed for helping students remember material from textbooks, which includes five steps: survey, question, read, recite, and review.

As much as authors would like to think that students hang on every word of their textbook, we know that is not the case. In fact, we realize that students often finish reading a portion of a textbook chapter feeling as if they had zoned out the entire time they were reading, and retaining little actual new knowledge. A strategy specifically developed to help students remember information in textbooks is called the SQ3R method, for the five steps involved in the method: survey, question, read, recite, and review (Martin, 1985; Robinson, 1961). The SQ3R method fosters active rather than passive learning while reading. In brief, the steps of this method are as follows:

- *Survey:* Page through the chapter, looking at headings and the summary. This will help you organize the material more efficiently as you encode.
- *Question:* When you begin a section, turn the heading into a question; this orients you to the content and makes reading more interesting. For example, for the subheading, "Encoding and Organization of Long-Term Memory" you might ask yourself, "How does information find its way into LTM? Are some people better than others at organizing information in LTM?"
- *Read:* As you read, try to answer the questions you posed.
- *Recite:* Mentally (or orally) answer your questions and rehearse relevant information before going on to the next section.
- *Review:* When you finish the chapter, recall your questions and relate what you have learned to your experiences and interests.

■ INTERIM SUMMARY

Mnemonic devices are systematic strategies for remembering information. The **method of loci** associates new information with a visual image of a familiar place. The **SQ3R method** helps students study textbook material efficiently by encouraging them to survey, question, read, recite, and review.

Networks of Association

One of the reasons mnemonics can be effective is that they connect new information with information already organized in memory. This makes the new information easier to access because a "trail" blazed in the neural woods by prior knowledge can be more easily spotted than a new, barely worn path. As William James (1890) proposed over a century ago:

> The more other facts a fact is associated with in the mind, the better possession of it our memory retains. Each of its associates becomes a hook to which it hangs, a means to fish it up by when sunk beneath the surface. Together, they form a network of attachments by which it is woven into the entire tissue of our thought. The "secret of a good memory" is thus the secret of forming diverse and multiple associations with every fact we care to retain.
>
> (p. 662)

James's comments bring us back once again to the concept of *association*, which, as we saw in Chapter 5, is central to many aspects of learning. Associations are crucial to remembering because the pieces of information stored in memory form **networks of association**. For example, for most people the word *dog* is associatively linked to characteristics such as barking and fetching **(Figure 8.7)**. It is also associated, though less strongly, with *cat* because cats and dogs are both household pets. The word or image of a dog is also linked to more idiosyncratic personal associations, such as an episodic memory of being bitten by a dog in childhood.

Each piece of information along a network is called a **node**. Nodes may be thoughts, images, concepts, propositions, smells, tastes, memories, emotions, or any other piece of information. That one node may have connections to many other nodes leads to tremendously complex networks of association. One way to think of a node is as a set of neurons distributed throughout the brain that fire together (see Chapter 3). Their joint firing produces a representation of an object or category such as *dog*, which integrates visual, tactile, auditory, verbal, and other information stored in memory. To search through memory

Networks of association: Clusters of inter-connected information stored in long-term memory.

Node: A cluster or piece of information along a network of association.

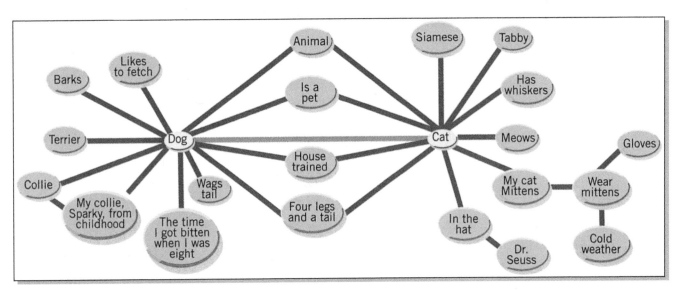

FIGURE 8.7 ■ Networks of association. Long-term knowledge is stored in networks of association, ideas that are mentally connected with one another by repeatedly occurring together.

means you go from node to node until you locate the right information. In this sense, nodes are like cities, which are connected to each other (associated) by roads (Reisberg, 1997).

Not all associations are equally strong; *dog* is more strongly connected to *barks* than to *cat* or *animal*. To return to the cities analogy, some cities are connected by super-highways, which facilitate rapid travel between them, whereas others are connected only by slow, winding country roads. Other cities have no direct links at all, which means that travel between them requires an intermediate link. The same is true of associative networks: In Figure 8.7 *cat* is not directly associated to *cold weather*, but it is through the intermediate link of *my cat Mittens*, which is semantically related to *wear mittens*, which is in turn linked to the *cold weather* node.

From a neuropsychological perspective, if two nodes without a direct link become increasingly associated through experience, a "road" between them is built; and if the association continues to grow, that road will be "widened" to ensure rapid neural transit between one and the other. If, on the other hand, a neural highway between two nodes falls into disuse because two objects or events stop occurring together (such as the link between the word *girlfriend* and a particular girlfriend months after the relationship has ended), the highway will fall into disrepair and be less easily traveled. The old road will not likely disappear completely: Occasionally a traveler may wander off the main road down the old highway, as when a person accidentally calls his new girlfriend by his old girlfriend's name.

Spreading Activation

One theory that attempts to explain the workings of networks of association involves spreading activation (Collins & Loftus, 1975; Collins & Quillian, 1969). According to **spreading activation theory**, activating one node in a network triggers activation in closely related nodes. In other words, presenting a stimulus that leads to firing in the neural circuits that represent that stimulus spreads activation, or energy, to related information stored in memory.

Spreading activation does not always start with a stimulus such as a spoken word. Activation may also begin with a thought, fantasy, or wish, which in turn activates other nodes. For example, a psychotherapy patient trying to decide whether to divorce his wife found the song "Reunited and It Feels So

Spreading activation theory: The theory that the presentation of a stimulus triggers activation of closely related nodes.

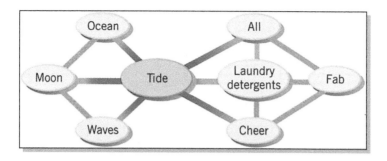

FIGURE 8.8 ▪ Spreading activation. Tide stands at the intersection of two activated networks of association and is thus doubly activated. In contrast, other brands only receive activation from one network. (This experiment, of course, only works in North America and other places where Tide has a substantial market share.)

Good" coming to mind on days when he leaned toward reconciliation. On days when he was contemplating divorce, however, he found himself inadvertently singing a different tune, "Fifty Ways to Leave Your Lover."

Considerable research supports the theory of spreading activation. In one study, the experimenters presented participants with word pairs to learn, including the pair *ocean/moon* (see Nisbett & Wilson, 1977). Later, when asked to name a laundry detergent, participants in this condition were more likely to respond with *Tide* than control subjects, who had been exposed to a different list of word pairs.

The researchers offered an intriguing explanation **(Figure 8.8)**: The network of associations that includes *ocean* and *moon* also includes *tide*. Priming with *ocean/moon* thus activated other nodes on the network, spreading activation to *tide*, which was associated with another network of associations, laundry detergents.

According to many contemporary models, each time a thought or image is perceived, primed, or retrieved from memory, the level of activation of the neural networks that represent it increases. Thus, two kinds of information are likely to be at a high state of activation at any given moment: *recently activated information* (such as a news story seen a moment ago on television) and *frequently activated information* (such as a physician's knowledge about disease). For example, a person who has just seen a documentary on cancer is likely to identify the word *leukemia* faster than someone who tuned in to a different channel; a doctor is similarly likely to identify the word quickly because *leukemia* is at a chronically higher state of activation.

Hierarchical Organization of Information

Although activating a *dog* node can trigger some idiosyncratic thoughts and memories, networks of association are far from haphazard jumbles of information. Efficient retrieval requires some degree of organization of information so that the mind can find its way through dense networks of neural trails.

Some researchers have compared LTM to a filing cabinet, in which important information is kept toward the front of the files and less important information is relegated to the back of our mental archives or to a dusty box in the attic. The filing cabinet metaphor also suggests that some information is filed *hierarchically*; that is, broad categories are composed of narrower subcategories, which in turn consist of even more specific categories.

For example, a person could store information about *animals* under the subcategories *pets, farm animals*, and *wild animals*. Under *farm animals* are *cows, horses*, and *chickens*. At each level of the hierarchy, each node will have features associated with it (such as knowledge that chickens squawk and lay eggs) as well as other associations to it (such as roasted chicken, which is associated with a very different smell than is the generic chicken).

Hierarchical storage is generally quite efficient, but it can occasionally lead to errors. For instance, when asked, "Which is farther north, Seattle or Montreal?" most people say Montreal (Stevens & Coupe, 1978). In fact, Seattle is farther north. People mistakenly assume that Montreal is north of Seattle because they go to their general level of knowledge about Canada and the United States and remember that Canada is north of the United States. In reality, some parts of the United States are farther north than many parts of Canada. A better strategy in this case would be to visualize a map of North America and scan it for Seattle and Montreal.

■ INTERIM SUMMARY

Knowledge stored in memory forms **networks of association**—clusters of interconnected information. Each piece of information along a network is called a **node**. According to **spreading activation theory**, activating one node in a network triggers activation in closely related nodes. Some parts of networks are organized hierarchically, with broad categories composed of narrower subcategories, which in turn consist of even more specific categories.

Schemas

The models of associative networks and spreading activation we have been discussing go a long way toward describing the organization of memory, but they have limits. For example, psychologists have not yet agreed on how to represent propositions like "The dog chased the cat" using network models, because, if *dog* and *cat* are nodes, how is the link between them (*chased*) represented? Further, activation of one node can actually either increase or *inhibit* activation of associated nodes, as when a person identifies an approaching animal as a dog, not a wolf, and hence "shuts off" the *wolf* node.

Psychologists have argued for over a century about the adequacy of principles of association in explaining memory (Bahrick, 1985). Some have argued that we do not associate isolated bits of information with each other but instead store and remember the gist of facts and events. They note that when people remember passages of prose rather than single words or word pairs, they typically remember the general meaning of the passage rather than a verbatim account.

According to this view, when confronted with a novel event people match it against *schemas* stored in memory. Schemas are patterns of thought, or organized knowledge structures, that render the environment relatively predictable. When students walk into a classroom on the first day of class and a person resembling a professor begins to lecture, they listen and take notes in a routine fashion. They are not surprised that one person has assumed control of the situation and begun talking because they have a schema for events that normally transpire in a classroom. Proponents of schema theories argue that memory is an active process of *reconstruction* of the past. Remembering means combining bits and pieces of what we once perceived with general knowledge in a way that helps us fill in the gaps. In this view, memory is not like taking snapshots of an event; it is more like *taking notes*.

Schemas affect the way people remember in two ways: by influencing the information they encode and by shaping the way they reconstruct data they have already stored (Davidson, 1995; Rumelhart, 1984).

Schemas and Encoding

Schemas influence the way people initially understand the meaning of an event and thus the manner in which they encode it in LTM. Harry Triandis (1994)

Now is the time for all good men to to come to the aid of their countrymen. The extra *to* at the beginning of the second line is easily overlooked because of the schema-based expectation that it is not there. Students often fail to notice typographical errors in their papers for the same reason.

relates an account of two Englishmen engaged in a friendly game of tennis in nineteenth-century China. The two were sweating and panting under the hot August sun. As they finished their final set, a Chinese friend sympathetically asked, "Could you not get two servants to do this for you?" Operating from a different set of schemas, their Chinese friend encoded this event rather differently than would an audience at Wimbledon.

Schemas and Retrieval

Schemas not only provide hooks on which to hang information during encoding; they also provide hooks for fishing information out of LTM. Many schemas have "slots" for particular kinds of information (Minsky, 1975). A person shopping for a compact disc player who is trying to recall the models she saw that day is likely to remember the names Sony and Pioneer but not Frank Sylvester (the salesman at one of the stores). Unlike Sony, Frank Sylvester does not fit into the slot "brand names of compact disc players."

The slots in schemas often have *default values*, standard answers that fill in missing information the person did not initially notice or bother to store. When asked if the cover of this book gives the authors' names, you are likely to report that it does (default value = yes) even if you never really noticed because the authors' names normally appear on a book cover. In fact, people are generally unable to tell which pieces of information in memory are truly remembered and which reflect the operation of default values.

One classic study demonstrated the reconstructive role of schemas using a visual task (Brewer & Treyens, 1981). The experimenter instructed college student participants to wait (one at a time) in a "graduate student's office" similar to the one depicted in **Figure 8.9** while he excused himself to check on something. The experimenter returned in 35 seconds and led the student to a different room. There, he asked the participant either to write down a description of the graduate student's office or to draw a picture of it, including as many objects as could be recalled.

The room contained a number of objects (e.g., bookshelves, coffeepot, desk) that would fit most participants' schema of a graduate student's office. Several objects, however, were conspicuous—or rather, inconspicuous—in their absence, such as a filing cabinet, a coffee cup, books on the shelves, a window, pens and pencils, and curtains. Many participants assumed the presence of these default items, however, and "remembered" seeing them even though they had not actually been present.

Without schemas, life would seem like one random event after another, and efficient memory would be impossible. Yet as the research just described shows, schemas can lead people to misclassify information, to believe they have seen what they really have not seen, and to fail to notice things that might be important.

■ INTERIM SUMMARY

One way psychologists describe the organization of LTM is in terms of schemas, organized knowledge about a particular domain. Proponents of schema theories argue that memory involves reconstruction of the past, by combining knowledge of what we once perceived with general knowledge that helps fill in the gaps. Schemas influence both the way information is encoded and the way it is retrieved.

© Lasevsky Pavel, 2009. Used under license from Shutterstock, Inc.

FIGURE 8.9 ■ Your memory of this office is likely to include items that do not exist in it but are part of your office schema.

CROSS-CULTURAL VARIATION IN MEMORY—BETTER, WORSE, OR JUST DIFFERENT?

The account of memory presented thus far is based almost exclusively on studies of individuals in Western, technologically advanced societies. Do the general principles of memory from these samples apply cross-culturally, or do memory and thought differ depending on the cultural, historical, and ecological context?

Studies comparing memory processes across cultures (such as large industrial versus small tribal societies) often produce inconsistent findings, largely because people tend to do better on tasks that resemble the demands of their everyday lives (see Cole et al., 1967). Thus, members of hunter-gatherer societies are better at remembering the location of edible berries than people in industrial societies, who have superior recall for strings of digits (e.g., phone numbers).

Not everyone in a culture is the same, however, and different subgroups confront different ecological or environmental demands. For example, a study in Zambia (Africa) compared the ability of urban schoolboys and rural women to recall information from stories relevant to *time* (Deregowski, 1970). Whereas the day of a Zambian schoolboy is precisely structured by the clock (as in the West), the daily life of rural Zambian women is regulated primarily by cycles of night and day and is not driven by specific units of time. The experimenters found no differences between the two groups in their ability to recall information in general. However, the schoolboys were significantly more likely to recall aspects of the stories related to *when* things happened. Across and within cultures, people tend to remember information that matters to them, and they organize information in memory to match the demands of their environment.

A particularly important influence on memory that varies across cultures is literacy. Literacy increases the role played by verbal representations, because it converts many visual experiences to verbal experiences. In preliterate societies, the human brain is the means of storing memories, and people rely on oral history and tradition, such as storytelling, to pass on collective knowledge. Literate societies, on the other hand, store information in many ways that extend the limits of memory, from magazines, textbooks, and computers, to simple devices such as lists, which can expand memory capacity exponentially (Goody, 1977).

In preliterate societies, oral tradition shapes the way people think and serves as an archive for collective memories.

© veselin gajin, 2009. Used under license from Shutterstock, Inc.

■ INTERIM SUMMARY

Across and within cultures, people tend to remember information that matters to them, and they organize information in memory to match the demands of their environment.

REMEMBERING, MISREMEMBERING, AND FORGETTING

We could not do without our memories, but sometimes we wish we could. According to Daniel Schacter (1999), who has spent his life studying memory, human memory systems evolved through natural selection, but the same mechanisms that generally foster adaptation can regularly cause memory failures. He describes "seven sins of memory" that plague us all:

- *Transience* the fact that memories fade
- *Absent-mindedness* the failure to remember something when attention is elsewhere
- *Misattribution* misremembering the source of a memory—something advertisers rely on when they tell half-truths about competing brands and people remember the half-truth but forget its source

- *Suggestibility* thinking we remember an event that someone actually implanted in our minds
- *Bias* distortions in the way we recall events that often tell the story in a way we would *rather* remember it
- *Persistence* memories that we wish we could get rid of but that keep coming back

Although at first glance these "sins" all seem maladaptive, many stem from adaptive memory processes that can go awry. For example, if memory were not transient or temporary, our minds would overflow with irrelevant information.

Perhaps the cardinal sin of memory is **forgetting**. Over a century ago, Ebbinghaus (1885) documented a typical pattern of forgetting that occurs with many kinds of declarative knowledge: rapid initial loss of information after initial learning and only gradual decline thereafter **(Figure 8.10)**. More recently, researchers have refined Ebbinghaus's forgetting curve slightly to make it more precise—finding, in fact, that the relation between memory decline and length of time between learning and retrieval is logarithmic and hence predictable by a very precise mathematical function (Wixted & Ebbesen, 1991). This logarithmic relationship is very similar to Stevens's power law for sensory stimuli.

This forgetting curve seems to apply whether the period of time is hours or years. For example, the same curve emerged when researchers studied people's ability to remember the names of old television shows: They rapidly forgot the names of shows canceled within the last seven years, but the rate of forgetting trailed off after that (Squire, 1989).

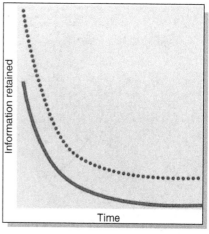

FIGURE 8.10 ▦ Rate of forgetting. Forgetting follows a standard pattern, with rapid initial loss of information followed by more gradual later decline. Increasing initial study time (the dotted line) increases retention, but forgetting occurs at the same rate. In other words, increased study shifts the curve upward but does not change the rate of forgetting or eliminate it.

How Long Is Long-Term Memory?

When people forget, is the information no longer stored or is it simply no longer easy to retrieve? And is some information permanent, or does the brain eventually throw away old boxes in the attic if it has not used them for a number of years?

The first question is more difficult to answer than the second. Psychologists often distinguish between the *availability* of information in memory—whether it is still "in there"—and its *accessibility*—the ease with which it can be retrieved. The tip-of-the-tongue phenomenon, like the priming effects shown by amnesics, is a good example of information that is available but inaccessible.

In large part, accessibility reflects level of activation, which diminishes over time but remains for much longer than most people would intuitively suppose. Memory for a picture flashed briefly on a screen a year earlier continues to produce some activation of the visual cortex, which is expressed implicitly even if the person has no conscious recollection of it (Cave, 1997). And most people have vivid recollections from their childhood of certain incidents that occurred once, such as the moment they heard the news that a beloved pet died. But what about the other hundreds of millions of incidents that they cannot retrieve? To what degree these memories are now unavailable, rather than just inaccessible, is unknown.

Studies of very-long-term memory suggest, however, that if information is consolidated through spacing over long learning intervals, it will last a lifetime, even if the person does not rehearse it for half a century (Bahrick & Hall, 1991). Eight years after having taught students for a single semester, college professors will forget the names and faces of most of their students (sorry!), but 35 years after graduation people still recognize 90 percent of the names and faces from their high school yearbook.

The difference is in the spacing: The professor teaches a student for only a few months, whereas high school students typically know each other for at least three or four years. Similarly, people who take college mathematics courses that require them to use the knowledge they learned in high school algebra show nearly complete memory for algebra 50 years later even if they work as artists and never balance their checkbook. People who stop at high school algebra remember nothing of it decades later.

How Accurate Is Long-Term Memory?

Aside from the question of *how long* people remember is the question of *how accurately* they remember. The short answer is that memory is both functional and reconstructive, so that most of the time it serves us well, but it is subject to a variety of errors and biases.

For example, the normal associative processes that help people remember can also lead to memory errors (see Robinson & Roediger, 1997; Schacter et al., 1998). In one set of studies, the researchers presented participants with a series of words (such as *slumber, nap*, and *bed*) that were all related to a single word that had *not* been presented (*sleep*). This essentially primed the word *sleep* repeatedly (Roediger & McDermott, 1995). Not only did most participants remember having heard the multiply primed word, but the majority even remembered which of two people had read the word to them. Some participants refused to believe that the word had not been presented even after hearing an audiotape of the session!

Emotional factors can also bias recall. The investigators in one study asked college student participants to recall their math, science, history, English, and foreign-language grades from high school and then compared their recollections to their high school transcripts (Bahrick et al., 1996). Students recalled 71 percent of their grades correctly, which is certainly impressive.

More interesting, however, was the pattern of their errors **(Figure 8.11)**. Participants rarely misremembered their As, but they rarely *correctly* remembered their Ds. In fact, a D was twice as likely to be remembered as a B or C than as a D. Approximately 80 percent of participants tended to inflate their remembered grades, whereas only 6 percent reported grades lower than they had actually achieved. (The remaining 14 percent tended to remember correctly.)

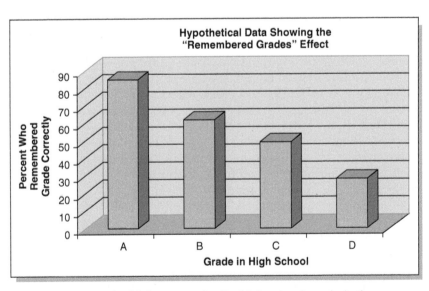

FIGURE 8.11 ■ The higher a particular high school grade is the more likely you will remember it accurately. If the grade is low then you tend to misremember it being higher than it actually is.

RESEARCH IN DEPTH

Eyewitness Testimony

No discussion of the accuracy of memory would be complete without an examination of eyewitness testimony. Indeed, research on the accuracy of memory has an important real-life application in the courtroom: How accurate is eyewitness testimony (see Schacter, 1995b; Sporer et al., 1996)? Numerous studies have explored this question experimentally, usually by showing participants a short film or slides of an event such as a car accident (Wells & Loftus, 1984; Zaragosta & Mitchell, 1996). The experimenter then asks participants specific questions about the scene, sometimes introducing information that was not present in the actual scene, asking leading questions, or contradicting what participants saw. These studies show that seemingly minor variations in the wording of a question can determine what participants remember from a scene. One study simply substituted the definite article *the* for the indefinite article *a* in the question "Did you see the/a broken headlight?" Using *the* instead of *a* increased both the likelihood that participants would recall seeing a broken headlight and their certainty that they had, even if they never actually observed one (Loftus & Palmer, 1974; Loftus & Zanni, 1975).

In a classic study examining the accuracy of people's memories for events, Loftus and Palmer examined the influence of the phrasing of a question related to the speed with which automobiles were traveling when they were involved in an accident. In the first experiment, 45 students viewed seven films, each showing a car accident. After viewing each film, participants completed a questionnaire that asked them to write about what they had seen and to answer questions about the accident. Nine participants were asked the question: "About how fast were the cars going when they hit each other?" All of the other participants were asked a similar question, but using the words *smashed, collided, bumped,* or *contacted* instead of *hit.* Participants' estimates of the speed with which the cars were traveling was highest when the word *smashed* was used and lowest when the word contacted was used.

Thinking that the word choice (e.g., *smashed* versus *contacted*) produces a change in the way participants remember what they actually saw in the film, Loftus and Palmer conducted a second study. One hundred and fifty students watched a film showing a multicar accident. After viewing the film, participants completed a questionnaire similar to that used in the first study. Fifty participants were asked "About how fast were the cars going when they smashed into each other?" Another 50 individuals were asked the same question substituting *hit* for *smashed*. A final group of 50 was not asked about the speed at which the cars were traveling (control condition). A week later, the participants

© Vilena Makarica, 2009. Used under license from Shutterstock, Inc.

An accident can become more severe if a lawyer asks the right questions, such as, "How fast were the cars going when they smashed [rather than hit] each other?"

Continued

completed another questionnaire regarding what they remembered about the accident. Among the questions was "Did you see any broken glass?" Although there was, in fact, no broken glass shown in the film, 16 percent of the respondents in the *smashed* condition answered "yes" compared to 7 percent in the *hit* condition and 6 percent in the control condition.

The results of these two studies illustrate that the wording of information can influence perceptions of and memories for particular events. These findings have clear implications both in the courtroom and in the way police interrogate witnesses. However, individuals vary in their susceptibility to misleading information (Loftus et al., 1992). Further, some aspects of a memory may be more reliable than others. The emotional stress of witnessing a traumatic event can lead to heightened processing of (and hence better memory for) core details of the event but less extensive processing of peripheral details (Christianson, 1992; Reisberg, 2006). A sharp attorney could thus attack the credibility of a witness's entire testimony by establishing that her memory of peripheral details is faulty even though she clearly remembers the central aspects of the event.

In a testament to the sometimes imperfect nature of eyewitness testimony, Father Bernard Pagano was just short of a seemingly airtight conviction for several armed robberies based on the testimony of seven eyewitnesses. Just as the prosecutor concluded his case, however, Ronald Clouser stepped forward and confessed to the crimes. How could seven people have been so mistaken in their identification of the perpetrator? (Loftus & Ketchum, 1991).

EMOTIONAL AROUSAL AND MEMORY

In trying to understand flashbulb memories, Cahill and colleagues (1994) designed an elegant experiment that manipulated both the emotional content of the material to be remembered and adrenaline (the fight-or-flight hormone). First, they developed two series of 12 slides depicting a little boy leaving for school, having an unusual experience, and then returning home. In the middle section of slides, the unusual experience differed for the two series. In the *control*, or neutral, condition, the little boy goes on a field trip to the hospital and sees a disaster drill. In the *experimental*, or arousal, condition, the little boy is in a tragic accident in which his feet are severed from his legs and a concussion leads to bleeding in the brain. Miraculously, the doctors are able to reattach the boy's feet and control the brain bleeding.

Half of the subjects were shown the neutral slide series; the other half were shown the arousal slide series. The second manipulation, that of adrenaline activity, was created by giving a drug that antagonizes the actions of adrenaline (propranolol) to half of the participants in each group. The propranolol blocked any effect of adrenaline that the arousal slides produced. In this *two-by-two design*, two factors were studied: (1) neutral or arousal slide versions, and (2) placebo drug or the adrenaline antagonist propranolol. Thus, there were four groups (see **Figure 8.12** NPl: neutral, placebo drug; NPr: neutral, propranolol; APl: arousal, placebo drug; and APr: arousal, propranolol).

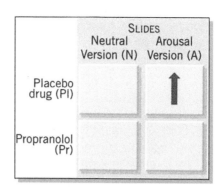

FIGURE 8.12 In an investigation of the relationship between emotional arousal and memory, researchers found that memory was higher for participants in the arousal condition who had not received propranolol, relative to the other three conditions.

The researchers hypothesized that the memory for all groups, when tested one week later, would be the same, *except for* the APl group, for which memory of the middle set of slides (when the boy was in the accident) would be better than the other groups. That is, they hypothesized that the emotionally arousing slides, which triggered adrenaline release, would lead to enhanced memory of those slides. Neither of the neutral groups would have any adrenaline release (thus, the propranolol would not have any adrenaline to antagonize) and the arousal group whose adrenaline activity was antagonized by propranolol would not have enhanced memory, even though they saw the arousing slides. The results supported their hypothesis.

These results support the notion that our flashbulb memories for emotionally arousing events are dependent on the fight-or-flight hormone, adrenaline. It is important to note that memory was enhanced *only* for the arousal slide, not for the neutral beginning and ending slides. Thus, emotional arousal, via adrenaline activity in the brain, leads to enhanced memory (Reisberg, 2006).

Flashbulb Memories

If remembering is more like consulting an artist's sketch than a photograph, what do we make of **flashbulb memories**, that is, vivid memories of exciting or highly consequential events (Brown & Kulik, 1977; Conway, 1995; Winograd & Neisser, 1993)? Many people can recall precisely where and when they first heard the news of the space shuttle *Columbia* disaster in 2003, almost as if a camera had recorded that moment in time. People report similarly vivid memories of the verdict in the O.J. Simpson murder trial in 1995, as well as personal events such as the death of a loved one or a romantic encounter (Rubin & Kozin, 1984).

Flashbulb memories are so clear and vivid that we tend to think of them as totally accurate; however, considerable evidence suggests that they are often not of snapshot clarity or accuracy and can even be entirely incorrect (Neisser, 1991). For example, on the day following the *Challenger* disaster in 1986, people reported where they were when they heard the space shuttle had disintegrated. Three years later when they were again asked where they were, not a single

Flashbulb memories: Especially vivid memories of exciting or highly consequential events.

person recalled with complete accuracy where they had been, and a third of the respondents were completely incorrect in their recall (McCloskey et al., 1988; Neisser & Harsch, 1992).

■ INTERIM SUMMARY

The flipside of memory is **forgetting**. Many kinds of declarative knowledge show a similar forgetting curve, which is initially steep and then levels off. Psychologists often distinguish between the availability of information in memory—whether it is still in there—and its accessibility—the ease with which it can be retrieved. People tend to make memory errors for a variety of reasons some cognitive and some emotional. **Flashbulb memories**—vivid memories of exciting or highly consequential events—are sometimes extremely accurate but sometimes completely mistaken. Eyewitness testimony is also subject to many biases and errors.

Why Do People Forget?

The reconstructive nature of remembering—the fact that we have to weave together a memory from patches of specific and general knowledge—leaves memory open to a number of potential errors and biases. But why do people sometimes forget things entirely? Psychologists have proposed several explanations, including decay, interference, and motivated forgetting.

Decay Theory

Decay theory: The notion that memories are lost as a result of a fading of the memory trace.

Decay theory explains forgetting as a result of a fading memory trace. Having a thought or perception produces changes in synaptic connections, which in turn create the *potential* for remembering if the neural circuits that were initially activated are later reactivated. According to decay theory, these neurophysiological changes fade with disuse, much as a path in the forest grows over unless repeatedly trodden.

The decay theory is difficult to corroborate or disprove empirically. However, it fits with many observed memory phenomena. Further, some studies do show a pattern of rapid and then more gradual deactivation of neural pathways in the hippocampus (which is involved in memory consolidation), which suggests a possible physiological basis for decay (see Anderson, 1995).

Interference Theory

Interference: The intrusion of similar memories on one another.

A prime culprit in memory failure is interference, as when students confuse two theories they learned around the same time or two similar-sounding words in a foreign language. Finding the right path in the neural wilderness is difficult if two paths are close together and look alike. Or to use the filing cabinet metaphor, storing too many documents under the same heading makes finding the right one difficult.

Proactive interference: A phenomenon in which old memories that have already been stored interfere with the retrieval of new information.

Cognitive psychologists distinguish two kinds of interference. Proactive interference refers to the interference of previously stored memories with the retrieval of new information, as when a person calls a new romantic partner by the name of an old one (a common but dangerous memory lapse). In retroactive interference, new information interferes with retrieval of old information, as when people have difficulty recalling their home phone numbers from past residences. One reason children take years to memorize multiplication tables, even though they can learn the names of cartoon characters or classmates with astonishing speed, is the tremendous interference that is involved, because every number is paired with so many others (Anderson, 1995).

Retroactive interference: Interference of new information with the retrieval of old information.

Motivated Forgetting

Another cause of forgetting is motivated forgetting. People often explicitly instruct themselves or others to forget, as when a person stops in the middle of a sentence and says, "Oops—forget that. That's the wrong address. The right one is. . ." (Bjork & Bjork, 1996). At other times, the intention to forget is implicit, as when a person who parks in a different parking space every day implicitly *remembers to forget* where he parked the day before so it does not interfere with memory for where he parked today (Bjork et al., 1998).

Experimental evidence suggests that goal-directed forgetting requires active inhibition of the forgotten information, which remains available but inaccessible. Researchers have demonstrated this by using *directed-forgetting* procedures: Participants learn a list of words but are told midway to forget the words they just learned and remember only the last part of the list. This procedure reduces recall for the words in the first part of the list and decreases proactive interference from them, so that participants can more easily remember words in the last half of the list. This outcome suggests that the procedure is in fact inhibiting retrieval of the to-be-forgotten words. On the other hand, this procedure does *not* decrease recognition of, or implicit memory for, the to-be-forgotten words, and they remain available, just less accessible.

Other studies show that instructing a person not to think about something can effectively keep the information from consciousness but that deliberately suppressing information in this way creates an automatic, unconscious process that "watches out" for the information and hence keeps it available (Wegner, 1992). For example, when people are instructed to suppress an exciting thought about sex, they remain physiologically aroused even while the thought is outside awareness. In fact, they remain just as aroused as subjects instructed to *think about* the sexual thought (Wegner et al., 1990). In a sense, goal-directed forgetting is like a form of prospective memory, in which the intention is to forget something in the future rather than to remember it. In this situation, forgetting is actually a form of remembering!

In real life, people often try to inhibit unpleasant or anxiety-provoking thoughts or feelings (Chapter 12). They often forget things they do not want to remember, such as "overlooking" a dentist appointment. If dentists were handing out $100 bills instead of filling teeth, few people would forget their appointments.

> **Motivated forgetting:** Forgetting for a reason, which leads to inhibition of retrieval.

The string on my finger was to remind me to forget why the string is on my finger!

© Thomas M. Perkins, 2009. Used under license from Shutterstock, Inc.

REPRESSED MEMORIES OF SEXUAL ABUSE

Commentary

The concept of repression has always been controversial in psychology (Holmes, 1990), but it is now the centerpiece of controversy. It is at the heart of claims of childhood sexual abuse and counterclaims of false memories raised by alleged perpetrators. The alleged perpetrators claim that the charges of sexual abuse against them have been invented by incompetent clinicians who have convinced their patients of the existence of events that never occurred (Delmonte, 2001; Howe, 2000; Pezdek & Banks, 1996).

The question of implanting false memories is exceedingly difficult to address scientifically for a number of reasons. First, distinguishing true from false allegations is difficult in all legal circumstances, but it is even more difficult when the events may have occurred 15 years ago.

Continued

Second, a cardinal feature of sexual abuse is that the perpetrator does everything possible to maintain secrecy (including threatening the victim) and to discredit the victim if he or she ever tells the story—a situation not unlike what often occurs with rape, political torture, and genocide (Herman, 1992). Third, some number of innocent people are unfairly accused: Divorcing parents sometimes accuse former spouses as a tactic in custody disputes, and some poorly trained therapists look for (and "find") abuse whenever an adult female patient steps into their office complaining of anxiety or depression (Loftus, 1993).

Evidence of False Memories

Data from numerous laboratory studies suggest that people can sometimes be led to create compelling memories of things that did not happen (Loftus, 1997a; Payne et al., 1997). As we have seen, presenting people with a series of words semantically related to a target word that was *not* presented can produce high rates of false recognition of the target, and people can be quite firm in their beliefs about these false memories. Women reporting a recovered memory of childhood sexual abuse are more likely than other women to recognize a target word (*sweet*) mistakenly as having been present in an earlier list of related words (*sugar, candy, honey*) (Clancy et al., 2000). Women who report remembering abuse all along (as opposed to recovering it) do not show this bias.

In another experimental design that bears on false memories, researchers obtain detailed information from parents of college students about events that actually occurred when their children were younger and then present the students with several real memories and one false one, such as getting lost in a mall at age five and being found by an elderly woman (Loftus, 1997b). The investigators then interview participants about each event, ask them if they remember it, and ask them to recall what they remember. In these studies, roughly 15 to 25 percent of participants can be induced to recall a false memory over the course of two or three interviews.

For most people, however, the vulnerability to recall false memories is not without limit. When one researcher tried to induce memories more like those of sexual abuse victims (in this case, memory of a rectal enema in childhood), *none* of the subjects created a false memory (Pezdek, cited in Loftus, 1997b). There is obviously a need for caution in extending the findings of these experimental studies to the creation of false memories of sexual abuse, a highly traumatic and evocative event.

Evidence of Repressed Memories

Other studies call into question the charge that most psychotherapy patients who believe they have been sexually abused invent these memories. The majority of victims of repeated or severe sexual abuse in childhood have at least some memories of the abuse prior to psychotherapy, although their memories are often fragmented (Herman, 1992). Their recollection of childhood events tends to have gaps of months or years, and the memories of traumatic experiences they do recall frequently come to them in flashbacks, in physical forms (such as the sensation of gagging that initially attended the experience of being forced to perform oral sex), or in nightmares.

Several studies document that periods of amnesia for sexual abuse are common (see Briere & Conte, 1993; Loftus et al., 1994), just as in other traumatic events such as combat or rape (Arrigo & Pezdek, 1997). Perhaps the clearest empirical evidence for repressed memories comes from a study that tracked down women who had been treated at a hospital for sexual molestation when they were children (Williams, 1994). Seventeen years after their documented abuse, 38 percent were amnesic for the incident. When asked if any family members had ever gotten into trouble for their sexual behavior, one person, who denied sexual abuse, reported that before she was born an uncle had apparently molested a little girl and was stabbed to death by the girl's mother. Examination of newspaper reports 17 years earlier found that the subject herself had been one of the uncle's two victims and that the mother of the other victim had indeed stabbed the perpetrator.

Perhaps the moral of the story is that psychologists should always attend both to the phenomenon they are studying—in this case, repressed memories—and to their own needs, fears, and cognitive biases. For example, research demonstrates that people with abuse histories are more likely to see or hear themes of abuse in ambiguous situations (Nigg et al., 1992). Thus, clinicians with painful childhood histories of their own should be particularly careful to avoid jumping to conclusions or subtly influencing patients with leading questions.

On the other hand, researchers who may have had little or no exposure to real sexual abuse victims should be circumspect about overstepping the limits of their vantage point. Researchers and clinicians alike need to look carefully at their own cognitive and motivational biases before attempting to rewrite—or write off—the life histories of others.

■ INTERIM SUMMARY

The **decay theory** explains forgetting as a result of a fading memory trace; disuse of information leads to a gradual decrease in the strength of neural connections. **Interference** of similar information is another cause of forgetting. **Proactive interference** refers to the interference of previously stored memories with the retrieval of new information, whereas **retroactive interference** refers to the interference of new information with retrieval of old information. Another cause of forgetting is **motivated forgetting**, or forgetting for a reason. The final word has not yet been written about repressed memories of childhood sexual abuse, although the data suggest caution on both sides: Memories recovered in therapy cannot be assumed to be accurate, but they also cannot be routinely dismissed as false.

SUMMARY

Memory and Information Processing

1. Case studies of neurologically impaired patients and experimental studies of normal participants have demonstrated that memory is composed of several systems.

2. For information to return to mind after it is no longer present, it has to be put into a mental code, or representation. The major forms of representations studied by psychologists are **sensory representations** and **verbal representations**. People also store memory for actions as motoric representations.

3. The standard model of memory views the mind as a computer, which stores, transforms, and retrieves information. It includes three sequential memory stores or stages of memory. The first is the **sensory register**, the split-second mental representation of a perceived stimulus that remains very briefly after that stimulus disappears. **Iconic storage** describes visual sensory registration; **echoic storage** describes auditory sensory registration.

4. **Short-term memory (STM)** stores information for roughly 20 to 30 seconds, unless the information is maintained through **rehearsal** (repeating the information again and again). This form of rehearsal, which merely maintains information in STM, is called **maintenance rehearsal. Elaborative rehearsal**—thinking about and elaborating on the information's meaning—tends to be superior for storing information in long-term memory.

5. Important information is passed along to **long-term memory (LTM)**, where representations may last as long as a lifetime. Recovering information from LTM, or **retrieval**, brings it back into STM, or consciousness.

6. In recent years this model has been changing substantially. Instead of viewing memory exclusively in terms of serial processing (which assumes that information passes through a series of stages, one at a time and in order), researchers now view memory as involving a set of **modules** that operate simultaneously (in parallel) rather than sequentially (one at a time). Researchers now recognize that not all remembering is expressed by retrieving information into consciousness, or STM, and they rely less on the metaphor of mind as computer than mind as brain.

Working Memory

7. Psychologists now refer to STM as **working memory**, the temporary storage and processing of information that can be used to solve problems, respond to environmental demands, or achieve goals. According to one prominent model, control processes such as rehearsal, reasoning, and making decisions about how to balance two tasks simultaneously are the work of a limited-capacity central executive system; whereas storage involves at least two limited-capacity systems, a visual store (also called the visuospatial sketchpad) and a verbal store.

8. The existence of neurological patients who show deficits in either working memory or LTM but not both suggests that these memory systems are neurologically distinct, although in everyday life they work together, as frontal working memory networks provide a special form of activation to networks in the posterior parts of the cortex that represent current perceptions and information stored in LTM. One way to expand the capacity of working memory in particular domains is **chunking**, that is, grouping information into larger units than single words or digits. The roughly seven pieces of information stored in visual or auditory working memory can represent larger, more meaningful pieces of information.

Varieties of Long-Term Memory

9. Types of long-term memory can be distinguished by the kind of knowledge stored and the way this knowledge is retrieved and expressed. People store two kinds of information, declarative and procedural. **Declarative memory** refers to memory for facts and events and is subdivided into **semantic**, or generic, **memory** (general world knowledge or facts) and **episodic memory** (memories of particular events). **Procedural memory** refers to how-to knowledge of procedures or skills.

10. Information can be retrieved either explicitly or implicitly. **Explicit memory** refers to conscious recollection, expressed through **recall** (the spontaneous retrieval of material from LTM) or **recognition** (memory for whether something currently perceived has been previously encountered or learned). **Implicit memory** is expressed in behavior rather than consciously retrieved.

11. Neurological data suggest that different kinds of memory form discrete memory systems. The hippocampus and adjacent regions of the cortex are central to the consolidation of explicit memories but do not appear to play an important role in either implicit memory or working memory.

12. **Everyday memory**—memory as it occurs in daily life—tends to be functional (focused on remembering information that is meaningful) and emotionally significant. **Prospective memory** is memory for things that need to be done in the future.

Encoding and Organization of Long-Term Memory

13. For information to be retrievable from memory, it must be **encoded**, or cast into a representational form, or code, that can be readily accessed from memory.

14. Among the factors that influence later accessibility of memory are the degree to which information is elaborated, reflected upon, and processed in a meaningful way during encoding (**level of processing**); the presence of **retrieval cues** (stimuli or thoughts that can be used to facilitate recollection); the **spacing** of study sessions (with longer intervals between rehearsal sessions tending to be more effective); and the use of multiple and redundant representational modes to encode the information, which provides more cues for its retrieval. **Mnemonic devices**, or systematic strategies for remembering information, can also be useful for remembering, as can external memory aids such as notes.

15. Information stored in memory forms **networks of association**—clusters of interconnected units of information called **nodes**. According to **spreading activation theory**, activating one node in a network triggers activation in closely related nodes. Some information is organized hierarchically, with broad categories composed of narrower subcategories, which in turn consist of even more specific categories.

16. Schemas are organized knowledge about a particular domain. According to schema theory, memory is an active, reconstructive process that involves reactivation of both the initial representations of an event and general knowledge that helps fill in the gaps. Schemas facilitate memory by organizing information at both encoding and retrieval.

17. Many schemas are shaped by culture, from beliefs about foods that are appropriate to eat to beliefs about the meaning of life.

Remembering, Misremembering, and Forgetting

18. Ebbinghaus discovered a forgetting curve that applies to many kinds of declarative memory, in which considerable information is initially lost but **forgetting** then tapers off.

19. Memory is a reconstructive process that mingles representations of actual experiences with general knowledge. Although memory is functional and tends to work well most of the time, misremembering is common, even in **flashbulb memories** (vivid memories of exciting or highly consequential events) and eyewitness testimony, which can be biased by even seemingly minor changes in the way questions are asked.

20. Three theories attempt to account for forgetting: **decay theory** (which explains forgetting as a result of a fading memory trace); **interference** of new and old information with retrieval of the other; and **motivated forgetting** (forgetting for a reason, which leads to inhibition of retrieval).

KEY TERMS

chunking
decay theory
declarative memory
echoic storage
elaborative rehearsal
encoded
encoding specificity
  principle
episodic memory
everyday memory
explicit memory
flashbulb memories
forgetting
iconic storage
implicit memory
interference
level of processing
long-term memory
  (LTM)

maintenance rehearsal
method of loci
mnemonic devices
modules
motivated forgetting
networks of association
node
priming effects
proactive interference
procedural memory
prospective memory
recall
recognition
rehearsal
retrieval
retrieval cues
retroactive
  interference
retrospective memory

semantic or generic
  memory
sensory registers
sensory
  representations
serial position effect
short-term memory
  (STM)
spacing effect
spreading activation
  theory
SQ3R method
tip-of-the-tongue
  phenomenon
verbal representations
working memory

Chapter 8: Memory

END OF CHAPTER QUIZ

1. When you forget who you are.
   a. Spacing effect
   b. Imagery
   c. Amnesia
   d. Hippocampus
   e. Mood-congruent memory

2. An area of the brain that helps control memory.
   a. Spacing effect
   b. Imagery
   c. Amnesia
   d. Hippocampus
   e. Mood-congruent memory

3. Active/colorful stories to help memorize an event.
   a. Spacing effect
   b. Imagery
   c. Amnesia
   d. Hippocampus
   e. Mood-congruent memory

4. Studying for repeated short periods of time increases memory consolidation in comparison to cramming.
   a. Spacing effect
   b. Imagery
   c. Amnesia
   d. Hippocampus
   e. Mood-congruent memory

5. Who was one of the first memory researchers?
   a. Weber
   b. Muller
   c. Von Helmholtz
   d. Ebbinghaus

6. The persistence of learning over time:
   a. Rehearsal
   b. Encoding
   c. Memory
   d. Retrieval

7. When some event is learned immediately, usually as the result of an emotional event.
   a. Flashbulb memory
   b. Short-term memory
   c. Mnemonics
   d. Long term storage

8. How many general components are there to memory?
   a. 2
   b. 3
   c. 4
   d. 5

9. Automatic processing is when:
   a. Information requires rehearsal
   b. Information is learned without effort
   c. Learning occurs slowly
   d. Memory is decaying

10. Which of the following is NOT going to be analyzed by Automatic Processing?
    a. Space
    b. Time
    c. Semantics
    d. Frequency

11. Information is learned better if it is learned in small pieces over a long period of time.
    a. True
    b. False

12. Which form of meaning will enhance your retrieval of information?
    a. Visual
    b. Auditory
    c. Semantic
    d. Academic

13. Placing to-be-remembered items along a "mental path."
    a. Method of loci
    b. Chunking
    c. Peg words
    d. Body list

14. Remembering items by grouping them together.
    a. Method of loci
    b. Chunking
    c. Peg words
    d. Rescorla's Process

15. Which is the correct order of the types of memory that produce the MOST to LEAST remembered items?
    a. Auditory, visual, semantic
    b. Semantic, visual, auditory
    c. Semantic, auditory, visual
    d. Visual, auditory, semantic

16. On average, you can hold about _____ items in memory.
    a. 5
    b. 6
    c. 7
    d. 8

17. Can stimuli you were exposed to be irretrievable because you never encoded them?
    a. Yes
    b. No

18. Memories are stored in a single location of the brain called the hippocampus.
    a. True
    b. False

19. It is possible to establish a false memory simply by imagining the event so that later on you begin to think that it actually happened.
    a. True
    b. False

20. Working memory:
    a. Processes old memories
    b. Processes new memories
    c. Processes all memories
    d. Is a place that lets memories decay

21. Which of the following is not part of the basic memory model?
    a. Encoding
    b. Attention
    c. Storage
    d. Retrieval

22. In which component of the memory model does rehearsal operate?
    a. Sensory registers
    b. Short-term memory
    c. Long-term memory
    d. Retrieval

23. Which one of the following is the most common encoding factor?
    a. Stimulus duration
    b. Strength/salience
    c. Novelty
    d. Chunking capacity

24. Which of the following clearly exists in humans and nonhumans?
    a. Effortful processing
    b. Declarative memory
    c. Chunking
    d. Automatic processing

25. Which of the following is not related to automatic processing?
    a. Space
    b. Duration
    c. Frequency
    d. Recognition

26. Which of the following is not related to effortful processing?
    a. Effortful processing
    b. Declarative memory
    c. Chunking
    d. Spatial memory

27. Hermann Ebbinghaus did not discover the following phenomena?
    a. "Saving"
    b. Rules of relearning
    c. The spacing effect
    d. Parallel processing

28. Which of the following was most likely used in experiments by Hermann Ebbinghaus?
    a. Colored lights
    b. Buzzing and ticking stimuli
    c. Reaction time measurements
    d. Nonsense syllables

29. Encoding occurs for each of your six sensory systems.
    a. True
    b. False

30. Which of the following is not a form of memory storage?
    a. Sensory
    b. Working
    c. Priming
    d. Short
    e. Long

31. Which of the following is an example of sensory memory?
    a. A blue ball of light appears to float before your face after having your picture taken with a flashbulb
    b. Hearing your name
    c. Recalling your address
    d. Remembering today how bad a spanking felt when you were a child

32. Working memory may also be understood as:
    a. Attention
    b. A retrieval cue
    c. Node
    d. A mnemonic device
    e. Generic memory

33. Which of the following is the typical range of items that can be held in short term memory?
    a. 5-9
    b. 6-10
    c. 7-10
    d. 8-12

34. Long term storage does not show decay.
    a. True
    b. False

35. Which of the following is unlikely a part of the physical storage of memories in your brain?
    a. Neural circuits
    b. mRNA function
    c. Hippocampus
    d. DNA transcription and translation

36. All of the following identified areas influence memory, however, which of them is most closely related to any and all of the basic memory systems?
    a. Limbic system
    b. Hippocampus
    c. Amygdala
    d. Hypothalamus

37. Memories of particular events of your life are categorized as a subcategory of:
    a. Procedural memories
    b. Declarative memories
    c. Implicit memories
    d. Explicit memories

38. The process by which previous experiences are brought back into working memory.
    a. Encoding
    b. Storage
    c. Retrieval
    d. Level of processing
    e. Encoding specificity principle

39. If you want a person to say the word "sleep" and you cue them in by saying "snooze", "slumber" and "rest."
    a. Recognition
    b. Tip-of-the-tongue phenomena
    c. Priming
    d. Mnemonic devices

40. While you are at home you cannot remember a comment your professor made, however, you immediately remember that comment as you walk back into the classroom the following day.
    a. Episodic memory
    b. Elaborate rehearsal
    c. Declarative memory
    d. State dependent memory

41. When your current emotional state affects your recall of memories.
    a. Congruent moods
    b. Encoding specificity principle
    c. Flashbulb memories
    d. Spreading activation theory

42. Which of the following is involved in the serial position effect phenomenon?
    a. Proactive interference
    b. Proactive obstruction
    c. Priming effect
    d. Prospective memory

43. Which of the following is least likely related to false memories?
    a. A dream you had as a child is remembered as a real event in adulthood
    b. A trusted person tells you with certainty about an event from your childhood
    c. A psychotherapist repeatedly asks you questions about something until you begin giving answers other than "I don't know."
    d. Although you have a winning lottery ticket, you are certain you asked the clerk for a different set of numbers than those that are actually on the ticket

44. Is it possible for a lawyer to knowingly ask you leading questions during a court case to control the way your testimony sounds to the jury?
    a. Yes
    b. No

45. How should you think about the concept of repression?
    a. Strong events produce strong memories and weak events produce weak memories
    b. Unconscious processing is a reflection of unexpressed desires
    c. Horrible life events are frequently covered up with mental effort until the person is not even aware of the event any longer
    d. Some opinions expressed by adults are due to repressed life events

383

46. Which of the following is not a mnemonic technique?
    a. Method of loci
    b. Chunking
    c. Peg words
    d. Modules
    e. Organizing

47. Arranging to-be-remembered material so that each unit is a cue for the next unit is called:
    a. Chunking
    b. Peg words
    c. Modules
    d. Organizing

48. Remembering a list of items by placing them along a mental path is called:
    a. Chunking
    b. Peg words
    c. Method of Loci
    d. Organizing

49. Creating a novel word, (e.g., NASA) from a long name such as the National Aeronautic and Space Agency is called a(n):
    a. Chunking
    b. Acronym
    c. Acrostic
    d. Organizing

50. Creating a sentence by using the first letter of each of the words in a lengthy list is called a(n):
    a. Chunking
    b. Acronym
    c. Acrostic
    d. Organizing

UNIT THREE

Combining the
Basic Functions
of Psychology

9 | *Intelligence*

Understanding the Role of Constructs in Intelligence

The discussion of intelligence can get pretty vague. Most of the concepts in the field of intelligence are what scientists call hypothetical constructs. Hypothetical constructs are defined as; *variables which are believed to intervene between the independent and dependent variables*. These constructs may or may not exist as physical entities. Typically, if scientists call something a hypothetical construct, they are not certain that it truly exists. It may only seem to exist given the currently known dataset in the field of study.

One common hypothetical construct is hunger. To understand this construct, suppose that we want to relate food-related changes in the environment to a person's motivation for eating. The environmental changes we can manipulate—our potential set of *independent* variables—are many. A few examples are the time since last feeding, total calories ingested within a 24-hour period, total sugar or fat content of a food item, etc. The behavioral measures we take—our potential set of *dependent* variables—exist as how much effort the subject will expend to obtain food, their verbal statements of their level of hunger and even how long they will wait for food, etc. All of those independent variables can then be associated with each of the dependent variables.

How does all this relate to hunger? Well, hunger is a hypothetical construct, not a known physical entity. Despite all that is known about the physiology of feeding, the concept of hunger simply refers to a wide variety of biological systems, environmental inputs and behavioral outputs that exist for the subject. If we were to link each separate independent variable to each separate dependent variable, we would have an extraordinary mess to deal with. The total number of ways in which to make your subject hungry and the various ways to measure that hunger are too many to deal with in an understandable theory on the psychology of feeding. Instead, it is presumed that each of the various ways to make someone hungry affects the same system, the hypothetical hunger system. Therefore, each independent variable can be packaged under one title; hunger. When a construct is used this way, it simplifies the overall theory. Instead of referring to each independent to dependent variable connection separately, a range of inputs, which are all expected to produce similar effects, are packaged under the same name, that name referring to the construct in question.

Although there will be many, intelligence is the most widely discussed hypothetical construct in the following chapter. There is no known physical basis for intelligence and there is no particular location in the brain in which it is known to reside. Rather, intelligence is a hypothetical construct made up of all the various behavioral outputs that a subject exhibits under certain testing conditions. For example, high intelligence for mathematics indicates that the person does well with equations and calculations, word problems and symbolic manipulation. At this point in the textbook you should be able to posit that each of these skills reside is separate areas of the brain. When pulled together under the category of "mathematical skill," the combined total of all separate abilities adds into the subjects overall measure of mathematical intelligence.

Continued

Understanding the Role of Constructs in Intelligence   *Continued*

Because intelligence is not a physical entity, it makes no sense to "go look for it" in the brain. The wide range of specific skills that go into making up a relevant category of function, such as mathematical skill, may exist in high or low levels. Therefore, two people may each have the same mathematical IQ score; however, they may also have completely different skill sets; one with highly developed word-problem skills and the other with rapid computational abilities.

Often times the concepts in intelligence may become confusing when dealing with the abstract nature of intellectual functioning. A way to help yourself maintain some control of the issue is to change the more difficult topics of intelligence—such as emotional intelligence—into athletic skills. This works because no matter how abstract intelligence becomes, it ultimately will require a behavioral measure. Moreover, athletics has a conceptual connection to intelligence in that both are described in simple terms, athlete or intelligent, but both are constellations of different specific abilities that require a wide range of skills. For example, an intelligent engineer may not make for a successful clinical psychologist and a professional golfer may not make for a great soccer player. The same holds true for psychologists who try to be engineers and soccer players who try to golf.

Remembering that hypothetical constructs are shorthand ways to deal with large amounts of information will make understanding the field of intelligence much easier.

References

Gould, S. J. (1996). *The mismeasure of man.* New York: W. W. Norton

Miller, N. E. (1959). Liberalization of basic S-R concepts: Extensions to conflict behavior, motivation and social learning. In S. Koch (Ed.), *Psychology: A study of a science* (Vol. 2, pp. 196–292). New York: McGraw Hill.

CHAPTER OUTLINE

PREVIEW

THINK

First, think about these questions. Then, as you read, think again. . . .

- Is intelligence one ability or many?
- Is human intelligence related to brain size?
- How do psychologists measure intelligence?
- Are IQ scores stable over time?
- Do IQ tests predict anything useful?
- Is IQ genetically influenced?
- What environmental factors contribute to IQ?
- Are there sex and race differences in mental abilities?
- Are IQ tests biased against certain minority groups?
- Does behaving intelligently involve more than IQ?
- Are all intelligent people creative and are all creative people intelligent?

What would it take to get your face on a piece of German currency? Being a brilliant mathematician would probably help. At least it did the trick for Karl Friedrich Gauss (1777–1855).

Gauss, a great German mathematician, bears two intriguing connections to the concept of intelligence. First, he was the first to come up with the concept of the "bell curve," or normal distribution. Today, we sometimes refer to the bell curve as the "Gaussian distribution" in honor of his mathematical insights. As we'll discover, this statistical concept has played an important—and immensely controversial—role in the history of intelligence and intelligence testing. This simple curve does a surprisingly good job of describing how people differ in their scores on intelligence tests. Yet it's also triggered a bitter debate about the place of intelligence in modern life.

Intelligence quotient (IQ):
Systematic means of quantifying differences among people in their intelligence.

Second, Gauss was an undisputed genius. Historians have estimated his **intelligence quotient**—or IQ—at an astonishing 180, perhaps even higher. As we'll soon discover, the IQ is a systematic means of quantifying differences among people in their intelligence, with the average person's IQ typically falling somewhere around 100. Gauss's extraordinary accomplishments underscore the soaring heights that human intelligence can reach. Yet they also raise fascinating and mysterious questions about the origins of intelligence, and even about what intelligence is.

Like many other geniuses, Gauss was a child prodigy: an individual who displays astounding intellectual achievements at an early age (Morelock & Feldman, 1993). By the time he was about 2 years old, he had taught himself reading and basic arithmetic. At age 3, he caught a calculation error that his father had made when adding up his family's finances. At age 10, his schoolteacher asked his class to add up all of the numbers from 1 to 100. While his classmates were kept busy for half an hour, Gauss stunned his teacher by coming up with the correct answer within a matter of seconds (Hayes, 2006). Gauss immediately recognized a shortcut around this laborious problem: He combined pairs of numbers at both "ends" from 1 to 100: 1 + 100, 2 + 99, 3 + 98, 4 + 97, and on and on. He noticed that each pair summed to 101 and that there were 50 of these pairs, so the answer was 101 multiplied by 50, which is 5050. By age 18, Gauss was already discovering complex mathematical proofs that have stood the test of time. Later in life, he made profoundly important and enduring contributions to electricity, physics, astronomy, and mathematics—including the discovery of his famed bell curve (Dunnington, 1955).

How did Gauss become a genius? We don't know. Both of his parents were poor and uneducated, and neither was distinguished in terms of exceptional intellect. Gauss was also an intensely private individual whom others viewed as cold, even arrogant (Hall, 1970). But we don't know how or even if his personality molded his intellectual accomplishments. Nor do we know what mental raw ingredients set Gauss apart from the rest of us mere mortals. Was it his astonishing speed of processing, his ability to think abstractly, his capacity to catch on quickly to new concepts, his intense intellectual drive, or a combination of all four? Or was it something else? These unresolved questions strike to the heart of what we don't know about intelligence.

Genius Karl Friedrich Gauss, who originated the bell curve, was featured on German currency (prior to Germany's adoption of the Euro as its currency). Note the bell curve to the left of his portrait.

WHAT IS INTELLIGENCE? DEFINITIONAL CONFUSION

As we learned in the Prologue, one of the problems that renders psychology so challenging—and at times exasperating—is the lack of clear-cut definitions for many of its concepts. No area of psychology illustrates this ongoing challenge better than the field of intelligence. Even today, psychologists can't agree on the precise definition of intelligence (Sternberg, 2003; Sternberg & Detterman, 1986).

Special Considerations in Interpreting Intelligence Research

Before proceeding, a word of warning: Many people experience strong negative emotional reactions to certain aspects of intelligence research. That's understandable. For example, the idea that genes play a substantial role in intelligence makes some of us feel uncomfortable. The idea that genes could play a role in differences in intelligence between sexes or across ethnic groups makes many of us feel even more uncomfortable.

When discussing the intense scientific and ethical controversies surrounding intelligence, we must try to avoid *emotional reasoning*, or the affect heuristic, the tendency to judge the validity of an idea by our emotional reactions to it. Just because some of the ideas we'll encounter regarding intelligence may make us feel uneasy or even angry doesn't mean we should dismiss them out of hand. Difficult as it may be, we must try to evaluate these issues objectively and with an open mind to scientific evidence.

Even though not all psychologists agree about what intelligence is, one thing is clear: The way we *think* about intelligence matters. Carol Dweck (2002, 2006) showed that people who believe that intelligence is a fixed entity that doesn't change tend to take fewer academic risks, such as enrolling in challenging classes. According to Dweck, they think, "If I do really poorly in a class, it probably means I'm stupid, and I can't do anything about that." After failing on a problem, they tend to become discouraged and give up, probably because they assume they can't boost their intelligence. In contrast, people who believe that intelligence is a flexible process that can increase over time tend to take more academic risks; they think, "If I do really poorly in a class, I can still do better next time." They tend to persist after failing on a problem, probably because they believe that effort can pay off. Beliefs matter.

Edwin Boring (1923), whom we met in the Prologue, discovered an easy away around the nagging question of what intelligence is. According to *Boring's dictum*, intelligence is whatever intelligence tests measure. Yes, it's that simple. Some modern psychologists have embraced this definition, which lets us off the hook from having to figure out what intelligence is. Yet because this definition sidesteps the central question of what makes some people smarter than others— or whether some people are really smarter than others across the board—it doesn't really get us all that far. The definition of intelligence must go beyond Boring's dictum. With that point in mind, let's examine the most influential attempts to define and understand intelligence.

Intelligence as Sensory Capacity: Out of Sight, Out of Mind

Sir Francis Galton (1822–1911) was a cousin of the great biologist Charles Darwin, codeveloper of the theory of evolution by natural selection. Galton was himself something of a genius in many ways. Like Gauss, he was a child prodigy; he also learned to read by about age 2. Galton invented a host of techniques that are still in widespread use today: the method of studying twins to determine the genetic bases of traits, the correlation as a measure of statistical association, and criminal fingerprinting. Perhaps as a consequence of his accomplishments, he was fascinated by the question of what makes some people especially smart.

Galton proposed a radical hypothesis: Intelligence is the by-product of sensory capacity. He reasoned that most knowledge first comes through the senses, especially vision and hearing. Therefore, he assumed, people with superior sensory capacities, like better eyesight, should acquire more knowledge than other people.

For a 6-year period beginning in 1884, Galton set up a laboratory at a museum in London, England. There, he administered a battery of seventeen sensory tests to more than 9,000 visitors (Gillham, 2001). He measured just about everything under the sun relating to sensory ability: the highest and lowest pitch of sounds that individuals could detect; their reaction times to various stimuli; their ability to discriminate the weights of similar objects; and their capacity to differentiate the smells of various roses. Galton's student James McKeen Cattell shortly thereafter imported Galton's tests to America, administering them to thousands of college students in an effort to find out what they were measuring. Like his teacher, Cattell assumed that intelligence was a matter of raw sensory ability.

Yet later research showed that different measures of sensory capacities, like the ability to distinguish similar sounds from one another or similar colors from one another, are only weakly correlated (Acton & Schroeder, 2001): That is, one exceptional sense, like heightened hearing, doesn't bear much of a relation to other exceptional senses, like heightened vision. Nor are measures of sensory ability highly correlated with assessments of overall intelligence (Li, Jordanova, & Lindenberger, 1998). These findings falsify Galton's and Cattell's claim that intelligence equals sensory ability. Whatever intelligence is, it's more than just good eyesight, hearing, smell, and taste. A moment's reflection reveals that this must be the case: According to Galton, Helen Keller, the blind and deaf woman who became a brilliant author and social critic, would almost by definition have been mentally retarded. Galton's definition can't be right.

Still, as we'll learn later, Galton may have been onto something. Recent research suggests that some forms of sensory ability relate modestly to intelligence, although these two concepts clearly aren't identical.

Intelligence as Abstract Thinking

Early in the last century, the French government wanted to find a way to identify children in need of special educational assistance. In 1904, the Minister of Public Instruction in Paris tapped two individuals, Alfred Binet (pronounced "Bee-NAY") and Henri Simon (pronounced "See-MOAN"), to develop an objective psychological test that would separate "slower" learners from other children without having to rely on the subjective judgments of teachers.

Binet and Simon experimented with many different items designed to distinguish students whom teachers perceived as plodding learners from other students. In 1905, they developed what most psychologists today regard as the first **intelligence test**, a diagnostic tool designed to measure overall thinking ability.

Binet and Simon's items were remarkably diverse in content. They involved naming objects, generating the meanings of words, drawing pictures from memory, completing incomplete sentences ("The man wrote a letter using his _____"), determining the similarities between two objects ("In what way are a dog and a rose alike?"), and constructing a sentence from three words ("woman," "house," and "walked"). Despite the superficial differences among these items, they had one thing in common that Binet and Simon (1905) recognized: *higher mental processes*. These processes included reasoning, understanding, and judgment (Siegler, 1992). In this respect, their items differed sharply from those of Galton, which had relied solely on sensation. Virtually all items on modern intelligence tests have followed in Binet and Simon's footsteps.

Intelligence theorists later built on Binet and Simon's notions. Indeed, most experts agree that whatever intelligence is, it has something to do with **abstract thinking**: the capacity to understand hypothetical concepts, rather than concepts in the here-and-now (Gottfredson, 1997; Sternberg, 2003). In 1921, a panel of fourteen American experts generated a list of definitions of intelligence. They didn't succeed in hammering out a single definition, but they mostly agreed that intelligence consists of the abilities to:

■ reason abstractly
■ learn to adapt to novel environmental circumstances
■ acquire knowledge
■ benefit from experience

Interestingly, research on how laypeople view intelligence yields similar conclusions, at least in the United States. Most Americans view intelligence as consisting of the capacity to reason well and reason quickly ("to think on one's feet"), as well as to amass large amounts of knowledge in brief periods of time (Sternberg, Conway, Ketron, & Bernstein, 1981). In contrast, in some non-Western countries, laypersons view intelligence as reflecting people's wisdom and

Intelligence test:
Diagnostic tool designed to measure overall thinking ability.

Abstract thinking:
Capacity to understand hypothetical concepts.

judgment more than their intellectual brilliance (Baral & Das, 2003). For example, in China people tend to view intelligent individuals as those who perform actions for the greater good of the society and are humble (Yang & Sternberg, 1997). Geniuses who toot their own horns might be showered with fame and fortune in the United States, but they might be viewed as hopeless braggarts in the eyes of many Chinese.

That Controversial Little Letter: g

There was one other crucial way that Binet and Simon's items differed from Galton's. When researchers looked at the correlations among these items, they were in for a surprise. Even though Binet and Simon's items differed enormously in content, the correlations among them were all positive: People who got one item correct were more likely than chance to get the others correct. Admittedly, most of these correlations were fairly low, say .2 or .3, but they were almost never zero or negative. Interestingly, this finding has held up with items on modern IQ tests (Alliger, 1988; Carroll, 1993). Given that some of Binet and Simon's items assessed vocabulary, others assessed spatial ability, and still others assessed verbal reasoning, this finding was puzzling.

The phenomenon of positive correlations among intelligence test items caught the attention of psychologist Charles Spearman (1927). To account for these correlations, Spearman hypothesized the existence of a single common factor across all these aspects—g, or **general intelligence**—that accounted for the overall differences in intellect among people. All intelligence test items are positively correlated, he thought, because they reflect the influence of overall intelligence.

Spearman wasn't sure what produces individual differences in g, although he speculated that it has something to do with "mental energy" (Sternberg, 2003). For Spearman, g corresponds to the strength of our mental engines. Just as some cars possess more powerful engines than others, he thought, some people have more "powerful"—more effective and efficient—brains than others. They have more g.

The meaning of g remains exceedingly controversial (Gould, 1981; Herrnstein & Murray, 1994; Jensen, 1998). All because of this little letter, some intelligence researchers are barely on speaking terms. Why? Because g implies that some people are just plain smarter than others. Many people find this view distasteful, because it smacks of elitism. Later in the chapter, we'll revisit the controversies swirling around g in the context of possible sex and race differences in intelligence.

Spearman didn't believe that g tells the whole story about intelligence. For every intelligence test item, Spearman (1927) also proposed the existence of a factor called s or **specific abilities** that are unique to each item, as shown in **Figure 9.1.** That is, according to Spearman, how well we perform on a given mental task depends not only on our general smarts (g), but also on our particular skills in narrow domains (s). For example, our ability to solve the spatial problem in **Figure 9.2** is due not only to our general problem-solving ability but to our specific talents with spatial tests, tasks examining the location of objects in physical space. Even if we're really smart—high in overall g—we might flunk this item because we have a specific deficiency when it comes to spatial problems. That deficiency may mean that we're inherently not adept at spatial tasks or that we haven't had much experience with them.

Fluid and Crystallized Intelligence

Later researchers found that Spearman's g wasn't as uniform as he'd believed (Carroll, 1993; Vernon, 1971). They discovered that some intelligence test items relate more highly to each other than do other items: These items form clumps.

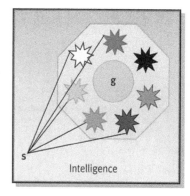

FIGURE 9.1 ■ Schematic of Spearman's Model of g. Spearman's model of intelligence posits the existence of g (general intelligence) along with specific factors (s).

g (general intelligence): Hypothetical factor that accounts for overall differences in intellect among people.

Spearman explained the presence of positive correlations among all IQ test items by hypothesizing the existence of g. What are some other explanations for this finding?

s (specific abilities): Particular ability level in a narrow domain.

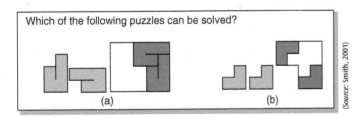

Which of the following puzzles can be solved?

(a)   (b)

(Source: Smith, 2001)

FIGURE 9.2 ■ Spatial Task.
Try it! For each of the two puzzles shown, try to fit the yellow shapes into the white space to complete the red figure.

Fluid intelligence: Capacity to learn new ways of solving problems.

Crystallized intelligence: Accumulated knowledge of the world acquired over time.

Multiple intelligences: Idea that people vary in their ability levels across different domains of intellectual skill.

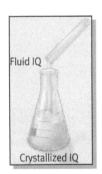

Fluid IQ

Crystallized IQ

FIGURE 9.3 ■ Knowledge "Flowing" into a Flask. According to Cattell and Horn's model, there are two kinds of intelligence, fluid and crystallized. Fluid intelligence "flows" into crystallized intelligence over time.

Among these investigators were Raymond Cattell (no relation to James McKeen Cattell) and John Horn, both of whom distinguished fluid from crystallized intelligence.

Fluid intelligence refers to the capacity to learn new ways of solving problems. We rely on our fluid intelligence the first time we try to solve a puzzle we've never seen or the first time we try to operate a type of vehicle, like a motorcycle, we've never driven. In contrast, **crystallized intelligence** refers to the accumulated knowledge of the world we acquire over time (Cattell, 1971; Horn, 1994). We rely on our crystallized intelligence to answer questions such as "What's the capital of Italy?" or "How many justices sit on the U.S. Supreme Court?" According to Cattell and Horn, knowledge from newly learned tasks "flows" into our long-term memories, "crystallizing" into lasting knowledge (**Figure 9.3**). Most modern researchers don't believe that the existence of fluid and crystallized intelligence undermines the existence of *g*. They view them as "facets" or more specific aspects of *g* (Messick, 1992).

There's some evidence for the fluid—crystallized distinction. Fluid abilities are more likely to decline with age than are crystallized abilities. In fact, some researchers have found that crystallized abilities increase with age, including old age (Salthouse, 1996; Schaie, 1996). In addition, fluid abilities are more highly related to *g* than crystallized abilities (Blair, 2006; Gustafsson, 1988). This finding suggests that of the two abilities, fluid intelligence may better capture the power of the "mental engine" to which Spearman referred.

Multiple Intelligences: Different Ways of Being Smart

Up to this point, we've been talking about "intelligence" as though it were one and only one overarching intellectual ability. But since at least the 1930s, some psychologists have argued for the existence of **multiple intelligences**: different domains of intellectual skill (Thurstone, 1938). According to them, the concept of *g* is wrong, or at least incomplete. These psychologists maintain that we can't simply say that Sally is smarter than Bill, because there are many ways of being smart (Guilford, 1967).

Frames of Mind

Howard Gardner's (1983, 1999) theory of multiple intelligences has been enormously influential in educational practice and theory over the past two decades. According to Gardner, there are numerous "frames of mind," or different ways of thinking about the world. Each frame of mind is a different and fully independent intelligence in its own right.

Gardner (1983) outlined a number of criteria for determining whether a mental ability is a separate intelligence. Among other things, he maintained researchers must demonstrate that different intelligences can be isolated from one another in studies of people with brain damage; people with damage to a specific brain region must show deficits in one intelligence, but not others. In addition, Gardner argued that different intelligences should be especially pronounced in people with exceptional talents. For example, Gardner believed that the presence of *autistic savants*, provides support for the existence of multiple intelligences. These individuals show remarkable abilities in one or two narrow domains, such as knowing the precise batting averages of all active baseball players, but not in most other domains. Gardner also suggested that different intelligences should make sense from an evolutionary standpoint: They should help organisms survive or make it easier for them to.

Gardner (1999) proposed eight different intelligences ranging from linguistic and spatial to musical and interpersonal, as described in **Table 9.1.** He's also tentatively proposed the existence of a ninth intelligence, called *existential* intelligence: the ability to grasp deep philosophical ideas, like the meaning of life.

Gardner's model has inspired thousands of teachers to tailor their lesson plans around children's individual profiles of multiple intelligences, an effort with which Gardner has said he isn't entirely comfortable (Willingham, 2004). For example, in a class of students with high levels of bodily-kinesthetic intelligence, but low levels of logico-mathematical intelligence, a teacher might encourage students to learn arithmetic problems, like 3 + 4 = 7, by dividing them into groups of 3 and 4, having them stand up in front of the class, and all join hands to form a bigger group of 7.

Yet this approach may not be a good idea. After all, if a child has a weakness in a specific skill domain, like vocabulary or mathematics, it may make more sense to try to teach "to" that domain rather than "away" from it. Otherwise, we may allow his already poor skills to decay, much like a weak muscle we elect not to exercise.

The scientific reaction to Gardner's model has been mixed. All researchers agree with Gardner that we vary in our intellectual strengths and weaknesses. Gardner also deserves credit for highlighting the point that intelligent people aren't all smart in the same way. But much of Gardner's model is vague and difficult to test. In particular, it's not clear why certain mental abilities, but not others, qualify as multiple intelligences. According to Gardner's criteria, there should probably also be "humor" and "memory" intelligences (Willingham, 2004). Or, given Gardner's emphasis on evolutionary adaptiveness, why not "romantic" intelligence, the ability to attract sexual partners? It's also not clear that all of Gardner's "intelligences" are genuinely related to intelligence. Some, such as bodily-kinesthetic intelligence, seem much closer to talents that depend heavily on nonmental abilities, like athletic skills (Scarr, 1985; Sternberg, 1988).

Moreover, because Gardner hasn't developed formal tests to measure his intelligences, his model is virtually impossible to falsify (Klein, 1998). In

TABLE 9.1 ◼ Howard Gardner's Multiple Intelligences.

Intelligence Type	Characteristics of High Scorers
Linguistic	Speak and write well
Logico-mathematical	Use logic and mathematical skills to solve problems, such as scientific questions
Spatial	Think and reason about objects in three-dimensional space
Musical	Perform, understand, and enjoy music
Bodily-kinesthetic	Manipulate the body in sports, dance, or other physical endeavors
Interpersonal	Understand and interact effectively with others
Intrapersonal	Understand and possess insight into self
Naturalistic	Recognize, identify, and understand animals, plants, and other living things

According to Gardner, individuals vary in the types of intelligence at which they excel. (a) Martin Luther King Jr. was a great orator with high linguistic (and probably interpersonal) intelligence; (b) Sarah McLachlan is a musician with renowned musical intelligence; and (c) professional tennis player Serena Williams has impressive bodily-kinesthetic intelligence.

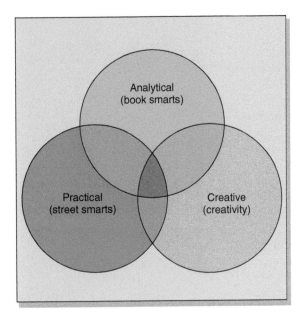

FIGURE 9.4 ■ Sternberg's Triarchic Model of Intelligence.
Sternberg's model proposes three kinds of intelligence: analytical, practical, and creative.

> **Triarchic model:** Model of intelligence proposed by Robert Sternberg positing three distinct types of intelligence: analytical, practical, and creative.

Being a successful politician probably requires a certain degree of practical intelligence, as Illinois Democratic Senator Barak Obama (here chatting pleasantly with **Israeli President Shimon Peres***) demonstrates.*

particular, there's no good evidence that his multiple intelligences are truly independent, as he claims (Lubinski & Benbow, 1995). If measures of these intelligences were all positively correlated, that could suggest that they're all manifestations of *g*, just as Spearman argued. Even research on autistic savants doesn't clearly support Gardner's model, because autistic savants tend to score higher on measures of general intelligence than do other autistic individuals (Miller, 1999). This finding suggests that their highly specialized abilities are due at least partly to *g*.

The Triarchic Model

Like Gardner, Robert Sternberg has argued that there's more to intelligence than *g*. Sternberg's (1983, 1988) **triarchic model** posits the existence of three largely distinct intelligences (see **Figure 9.4**).

(1) *Analytical intelligence:* the ability to reason logically. In essence, analytical intelligence is "book smarts." It's the kind of intelligence we need to do well on traditional intelligence tests and standardized exams. According to Sternberg, this form of intelligence is closely related to *g*. But it's only one component of intelligence, and not necessarily the most crucial. Indeed, Sternberg has long complained about a "*g*-ocentric" view of intelligence, one in which school-related smarts is the only kind of intelligence that psychologists value (Sternberg & Wagner, 1993).

(2) *Practical intelligence:* also called "tacit intelligence"; the ability to solve real-world problems, especially those involving other people. In contrast to analytical intelligence, this form of intelligence is akin to "street smarts." It's the kind of smarts we need to "size up" people we've just met or figure out how to get ahead on the job. Practical intelligence also relates to what some researchers call *social intelligence*, or the capacity to understand others (Guilford, 1967). Sternberg and his colleagues have developed measures of practical intelligence to assess how well employees and bosses perform in business settings, how well soldiers perform in military settings, and so on.

(3) *Creative intelligence:* also called "creativity"; our ability to come up with novel and effective answers to questions. It's the kind of intelligence we need to find new and effective solutions to problems, like composing an emotionally moving poem or exquisite piece of music. Sternberg argues that practical and creative intelligences predict outcomes, like job performance, that analytical intelligence doesn't (Sternberg & Wagner, 1993; Sternberg, Wagner, Williams, & Horvath, 1995).

Our intuitions tell us that these three types of intellect don't always go hand-in-hand. We can all think of people who are extremely book smart but who possess all of the social skills of a block of concrete. Similarly, we can think of people who have high levels of street smarts but who do poorly on school-related tests.

Yet, such anecdotal examples have their limitations. Indeed, many scientists have questioned the bases of Sternberg's claims. In particular, Sternberg hasn't demonstrated convincingly that practical intelligence is independent of *g* (Gottfredson, 2003; Jensen, 1993). Like crystallized intelligence, it may merely be one specialized subtype of *g*. Furthermore, Sternberg's work-related measures of practical intelligence may actually be measures of job knowledge. Not surprisingly, people who know the most about a job tend to perform it the best (Schmidt & Hunter, 1993). Moreover, the causal direction of this correlation isn't clear. Although more practical knowledge may lead to better job performance, better job performance may lead to more practical knowledge (Brody, 1992).

Thus, the concept of multiple intelligences remains controversial. Unquestionably, we all possess different intellectual strengths and weaknesses, but it's not clear that they're as independent of each other as Gardner and Sternberg assert. So there may still be a general intelligence dimension after all.

> Is Spearman's concept of *g* incompatible with the theory of multiple intelligences? Why or why not?

NEW FRONTIERS

HOW AWARE ARE WE OF OUR INTELLECTUAL LIMITATIONS?

Effective functioning in everyday life hinges crucially on our ability to gauge our intellectual limitations. If we enroll in an advanced physics course for which we have little background knowledge or aptitude, the results could be disastrous. If we're an inexperienced pilot and overestimate our capacity to navigate a plane in hazardous weather, the results could be fatal. Knowing what we are—and aren't—good at is terribly important for our effective functioning, even our survival.

Yet there's good reason to believe that most of us don't know much about our intellectual capacities: Self-estimates of IQ correlate only .2 to .3 with objective measures of intelligence (Hansford & Hattie, 1982). Making matters more complicated, recent evidence suggests that people with poor cognitive skills are especially likely to overestimate their intellectual abilities, a phenomenon called the *double curse of incompetence* (Dunning, Heath, & Suls, 2004; Kruger & Dunning, 1999). This curse may explain why some people perform poorly in school and on the job, even though they're convinced they're performing well. It may also explain the embarrassing behavior of our Uncle Ernie, who keeps telling jokes that aren't funny—and keeps laughing at them (Goode, 1999).

Although it's probably going too far to proclaim that "ignorance is bliss," there may be a kernel of truth to the notion that knowing our intellectual limitations makes us more keenly aware of what we don't know. Conversely, not knowing our intellectual limitations may render us overconfident in our knowledge (Kruger & Dunning, 1999). For example, undergraduates who scored in the bottom 25 percent on a psychology exam walked out of the exam certain they'd done better than their average classmates (Dunning, Johnson, Ehrlinger, & Kruger, 2003). Similarly, members of debate teams who scored in the bottom 25 percent of a tournament thought they were better than most other teams (Ehrlinger, Johnson, Banner, Dunning, & Kruger, 2004). The message is clear: We shouldn't necessarily trust our intuitions about how well we've performed. If our abilities in a domain are weak, we're often the last to know about it.

Researchers are still debating how to interpret these findings (Krueger & Mueller, 2002). One possibility is that *metacognitive skills* play a key role in the double curse of incompetence (Koriat & Bjork, 2005). Metacognition refers to knowledge of our own knowledge. People with poor metacognitive skills in a given domain may overestimate their performance, because they don't know what they don't know (Sinkavich, 1995).

Continued

The layperson's stereotype of the alien consistently features a large head and large eyes, presumably indicators of advanced intelligence. Why?

Myth: Albert Einstein had dyslexia.

Reality: Scores of popular psychology sources, including many organizations for dyslexia, claim that Albert Einstein suffered from this learning disability, which is marked by difficulties with word recognition and reading in the absence of other intellectual deficits. Although there's some anecdotal but inconsistent evidence that Einstein was an abnormally late talker, there's no good evidence that he had dyslexia or any other learning disability (Thomas, 2004).

Ironically, the best means of improving these students' performance may be to help them become *less* confident of their knowledge, in part by providing them with crystal-clear feedback about what they do and don't know (Dunning et al., 2004). Such feedback may allow them to adjust their perceived knowledge to their actual knowledge.

Revisiting Karl Friedrich Gauss, whom we met at the beginning of this chapter, we can see how Spearman, on the one hand, and Gardner and Sternberg, on the other, would conceptualize his genius. Spearman would have viewed Gauss as possessing extremely high *g*. Even though Gauss excelled at math, physics, and other "hard" sciences, Spearman would probably have guessed that Gauss was above average in language and other skills. In contrast, Gardner and Sternberg, while acknowledging that Gauss had remarkable analytical powers, might emphasize that he appeared to possess poor social skills and to be below average in interpersonal (Gardner) or practical (Sternberg) intelligence.

Biological Bases of Intelligence

One popular notion about intelligence is that it's related positively to brain size. We speak of smart people as "brainy" or having "lots of marbles upstairs." When researchers have asked people to draw pictures of aliens—who supposedly have high levels of extraterrestrial "intelligence"—they've found that depictions of these otherworldly creatures share surprisingly similar features, like big heads, big eyes, and tiny bodies (Blackmore, 1998).

It's almost as though large heads—and large brains—are central to our stereotype of intelligent creatures, whether they inhabit Earth or some faraway planet. Galton, who equated sensory perception with intelligence, would surely have been delighted that we perceive intelligent aliens as possessing big eyes! But to what extent is intelligence related to the brain's size and efficiency?

Brain Size and Intelligence in Humans

For years, almost all psychology textbooks informed students that although brain size correlates with intelligence *across* species, it's uncorrelated with intelligence *within* species, including humans. But several studies demonstrate that brain volume, as measured by structural MRI scans, correlates positively—between .3 and .4—with measured intelligence (McDaniel, 2005; Willerman, Schultz, Rutlege, & Bigler, 1991). So when we refer to the super smart kid in class who gets 100s on all of his exams without studying as a "brain," we aren't entirely off base.

Still, we don't know whether these findings reflect a direct causal association. Perhaps bigger brains lead to higher intelligence. Or perhaps some third variable, like better nutrition before or shortly after birth, leads to both. Moreover, a correlation of less than .4 tells us that the association between brain size and intelligence is far less than perfect. For example, Albert Einstein's brain actually weighed about 1,230 grams, slightly less than the average brain. Interestingly, though, the lower part of Einstein's parietal cortex, an area that becomes active during mathematical reasoning tasks, was 15 percent wider than normal (Witelson, Kigar, & Harvey, 1999). Further complicating matters, Karl Friedrich Gauss's brain appears to have been completely normal in size and shape (Wittman, Frahm, & Haenicke, 1999).

Recent studies on brain development suggest that there may be more to the story. A study using structural MRI revealed that highly intelligent (IQs in the top 10 percent) 7-year-olds have a *thinner* cerebral cortex than other children. The cortexes of these children then thicken rapidly, peaking at about age

12 (Shaw et al., 2006). We don't yet know what these findings mean, and independent investigators haven't replicated them. But they may indicate that, like fine wines, intelligent brains take longer to mature than others.

Intelligence and the Brain in Action

Functional brain imaging studies and laboratory studies of information processing offer intriguing clues regarding what intelligence is and where in the brain it resides. Over the span of about a month, Richard Haier and his colleagues (Haier, Siegel, MacLachlan, Soderling, Lottenberg, & Buchsbaum, 1992) taught a group of eight undergraduates to play the computer video game Tetris. All subjects improved over time, and those with the highest scores on a measure of intelligence improved the most. Surprisingly, subjects with higher levels of intelligence exhibited *less* brain activity in many areas than subjects with lower levels of intelligence (Haier et al., 2005). Haier's explanation? The brains of the more intelligent students were especially efficient. Much like well-conditioned athletes who barely break a sweat while running a 5-mile race, they could afford to slack off a bit while learning the task. Admittedly, not all researchers have replicated Haier's findings (Fidelman, 1993), but they raise the possibility that intelligence in part reflects efficiency of mental processing.

Intelligence and the Brain in Reaction

When speaking loosely, we sometimes refer to people who don't seem as intelligent as other people as "slow." Psychologists have brought this folk belief to the laboratory by studying the relation of intelligence to *reaction time*, or the speed of responding to a stimulus (Jensen, 2006). Imagine being seated in front of the reaction time box shown in **Figure 9.5** (Hick, 1952), which features a semicircle of eight buttons, with lights alongside of them. On each trial, anywhere from one to eight of the lights turn on, and then one of them suddenly turns off. Your job is to hit the button next to the light that turned off, and to do so as quickly as possible. The results of numerous studies indicate that measured intelligence correlates negatively (about–.3 to –.4) with reaction time on this task (Deary, Der, & Ford, 2001; Detterman, 1987): People with higher intelligence react more quickly than other people when the light turns off. There's also evidence that this gap widens as the number of lights that turn on increases, although this finding hasn't been entirely consistent (Brody, 1992). So Galton may not have been completely wrong in believing that speed of sensory processing contributes to intelligence, although these two concepts clearly aren't identical.

Intelligence and Memory

Intelligence also bears an intimate connection to memory capacity. Many researchers have examined the relation of tasks that assess "working memory" to intelligence. This type of memory is closely related to short-term memory. A typical working memory task might require that subjects perform a test of digit span while trying to figure out the meaning of a proverb (such as "What does the saying 'A bird in the hand is worth two in the bush mean'?"). Scores on working memory tasks are moderately correlated (about .5) with scores on intelligence tests (Ackerman, Beier, & Boyle, 2005; Engle, 2002; Kane, Honbrick, & Conway, 2005).

The Location of Intelligence

Where in the brain is intelligence located? This may seem like a silly question, as it's unlikely that a neurosurgeon can point to a specific region of the brain and say "Right there . . . that's what makes us smart." Yet intelligence is more localized to certain areas of the cortex than others. One group of investigators administered a number of reasoning tasks that are highly "*g*-loaded," meaning they're

FIGURE 9.5 ■ Reaction-Time Apparatus. Psychologists have used a reaction-time box to study the relation between intelligence and response to simple stimuli. Typically, the red lights light up and then, as soon as one goes out, the participant tries as quickly as possible to press the blue button next to the unlit light.

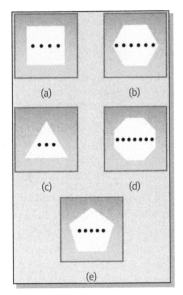

FIGURE 9.6 ■ Sample Task (a Highly *g*-Loaded Item). This sample item is similar to items that researchers have identified as highly "*g*-loaded," meaning that it's a good predictor of general intelligence. In this item, one of the five choices differs from the others. Can you figure out which one it is? (Turn your page upside down to find out.)

Answer to Figure 9.6: d

The popularity of the eugenics movement of the early twentieth century led the name "Eugene" to become one of the most frequently used boys' names in the United States.

substantially related to general intelligence (see **Figure 9.6**). They found that these tasks all activated the same area: the prefrontal cortex (Duncan et al., 2000). The prefrontal cortex is intimately involved in planning and impulse control, as well as in short-term memory.

Pulling It All Together

How can we make sense of all of these findings? If there's one central theme, it's that intelligence is related to efficiency or speed of information processing (Vernon, 1987). So common sense may be partly correct: People who are quick thinkers tend to be especially intelligent. Still, the associations are far less than a perfect correlation of 1.0, which tells us that intelligence is more than quickness of thinking. These results also suggest that the capacity to recall short-term information is related to intelligence, although the causal direction of this association isn't clear.

■ ASSESS YOUR KNOWLEDGE: FACT OR FICTION?

(1) Most research suggests that intelligence is almost entirely a function of sensory ability. (True/False)
(2) Almost all items on modern intelligence tests tend to be positively correlated with each other. (True/False)
(3) According to Sternberg, practical intelligence is essentially the same thing as book smarts. (True/False)
(4) Within humans, brain size tends to be moderately positively correlated with measured intelligence. (True/False)
(5) Intelligence is unrelated to reaction time. (True/False)

Answers: (1) F (p. 383); (2) T (p. 385); (3) F (p. 388); (4) T (p. 390); (5) F (p. 391)

INTELLIGENCE TESTING: THE GOOD, THE BAD, AND THE UGLY

When Binet and Simon created the first intelligence test more than a century ago, they had no inkling that they'd alter the landscape of psychology. Yet their invention has changed how we select people for schools, jobs, and the military; it's changed schooling and social policies; and it's changed how we think about ourselves. The history of intelligence testing begins where Binet and Simon left off.

Two More Controversial Letters: *IQ*

Shortly before World War I, German psychologist Wilhelm Stern (1912) invented the formula for the intelligence quotient, which will forever be known by two letters: *IQ*. Stern's formula for computing IQ was simple: Divide *mental age* by *chronological age* and multiply the resulting number by 100. **Mental age** is the age corresponding to the average person's performance on an intelligence test. A girl who takes an IQ test and does as well as the average 6-year-old has a mental age of 6, regardless of her actual age. Her chronological age is nothing more than her actual age. So, if a 10-year-old child does as well on an IQ test as the average 8-year-old, his IQ according to Stern's formula would be 80 (a mental age of 8 divided by a chronological age of 10, multiplied by 100). Conversely, if an 8-year-old child does as well on an IQ test as the average 10-year-old, his IQ according to Stern's formula would be 125 (a mental age of 10 divided by a chronological age of 8 multiplied by 100).

Deviation IQ: Rescuing Adults from Declining Intelligence

Some popular sources still refer to Stern's formula for computing IQ. For children and early adolescents, this formula does a respectable job of estimating intelligence. But it soon became evident that Stern's formula contains a critical flaw. Mental age scores increase progressively in childhood, but start to level out at around age 16 (Eysenck, 1994). Once we hit 16 or so, our performance on IQ test items doesn't increase by much. Because our mental age levels off but our chronological age increases with time, Stern's formula would result in everyone's IQ getting lower and lower as they get older.

That's why almost all modern intelligence researchers rely on a statistic called deviation IQ when computing IQ for adults (Wechsler, 1939). Basically, the deviation IQ expresses each person's IQ relative to his or her same-aged peers. An IQ of 100, which is average, means that a person's IQ is exactly typical of people of his age. An IQ of 80 is a standard amount below average for any age group, and an IQ of 120 is a standard amount above. In this way, the deviation IQ gets rid of the problem posed by Stern's formula, because it doesn't result in IQ decreasing after age 16.

Mental age: Age corresponding to the average individual's performance on an intelligence test.

Deviation IQ: Expression of a person's IQ relative to his or her same-aged peers.

The Eugenics Movement: Misuses and Abuses of IQ Testing

Soon after French psychologists Binet and Simon had developed their test, researchers in other countries began translating it into various languages. Among the first was American psychologist Henry Goddard, who translated it into English in 1908. In only a matter of years, IQ testing became a booming business in the United States. It was no longer merely a vehicle for targeting schoolchildren in need of special help, however, but a means of identifying adults deemed intellectually inferior.

The IQ testing movement quickly spiraled out of control. Examiners frequently administered these tests in English to new American immigrants who barely knew the language. It's hardly surprising, then, that about 40 percent of new immigrants to the United States received IQ scores placing them in the mentally retarded—or what was then called "feebleminded"—range. Moreover, Goddard and others adapted childhood tests for use in testing adults, without fully understanding how the IQ scores applied to adults (Kevles, 1985). As a consequence, legions of adults given his tests, including prison inmates and delinquents, scored in the mentally retarded range. In one especially embarrassing episode, a psychologist administered Goddard's IQ test to the mayor of Chicago, as well as to his running mates and opponents. Almost all scored in the mentally retarded range, creating a public relations disaster for Goddard when the newspapers found out about it (Wood, Garb, & Nezworski, 2006).

Eventually, concern with the low IQs of many immigrants and even many Americans led to a social movement called eugenics (meaning "good genes"), a term coined by none other than Sir Francis Galton (Gillham, 2001). Eugenics was the effort to improve a population's "genetic stock" by encouraging people with "good genes" to reproduce (*positive eugenics*), by discouraging people with "bad genes" from reproducing (*negative eugenics*), or both. Galton had been a proponent of only positive eugenics, but many later psychologists advocated negative eugenics.

Although eugenics was by no means unique to America, it became immensely popular there in the early twentieth century, especially from 1910 to 1930. Dozens of universities, among them Harvard, Cornell, Columbia, and Brown, offered courses in eugenics to approximately 20,000 undergraduates (Selden, 1999). Most high school and college biology texts presented eugenics as a scientific enterprise.

Eugenics came to be associated with at least two disturbing practices. First, beginning in the 1920s, the U.S. Congress passed laws designed to restrict

Eugenics: Movement in the early twentieth century to improve a population's genetic stock by encouraging those with good genes to reproduce, preventing those with bad genes from reproducing, or both.

© 2009 by margol. Used under license of Shutterstock, Inc.

Association fallacy: Error of confusing a claim's validity with the people who advocate it.

Is there an ethical difference between positive and negative eugenics? If so, why?

We can find dozens of informal "Test Yourself" IQ tests on the Internet, in magazines, or in self-help books. Most of these tests haven't been validated, so we shouldn't put much stock in the IQ scores they yield.

Wechsler Adult Intelligence Scale (WAIS): Most widely used intelligence test for adults today, consisting of fourteen subtests to assess different types of mental abilities.

immigration from other countries supposedly marked by low intelligence, especially those in eastern and southern Europe (Gould, 1981).

Second, beginning in 1907, thirty-three U.S. states passed laws requiring the sterilization of low-IQ individuals. Some of the surgeons who performed these sterilizations tricked their patients into believing they were undergoing emergency appendectomies (removal of their appendices) (Leslie, 2000). The assumption behind mandatory sterilization was that IQ was genetically influenced, so preventing low-IQ individuals from reproducing would halt the supposed deterioration of the population's intelligence. When all was said and done, about 66,000 North Americans, many of them African Americans and other poor minorities, underwent forced sterilizations (Reynolds, 2003). Disturbingly, the U.S. Supreme Court upheld these sterilization practices in 1927 in a famous case called *Buck v. Bell*. Ruling to uphold the sterilization of 18-year-old Carrie Buck, who'd come from two generations of purportedly "feeble-minded" ancestors, Justice Oliver Wendell Holmes wrote that "three generations of imbeciles are enough." Fortunately, the practice of sterilization slowed in the 1940s and had subsided almost completely by the early 1960s, although involuntary sterilization laws remained on the books in America for years. Virginia became the last state to repeal them in 1974.

A variety of other troubling practices were perpetuated on individuals in the United States and Europe as a result of early IQ testing. In 1917, psychologist Robert Yerkes joined forces with the U.S. Army to launch an IQ testing program that helped determine who'd serve as officers and who'd serve on the front lines in battle during World War I. Not surprisingly, recent immigrants and underprivileged minorities were the most frequently relegated to hazardous duty.

We can still feel the impact of the eugenics movement today. Many people are understandably suspicious of claims regarding IQ and its genetic bases, as these claims remind them of the unethical efforts by eugenics advocates to "purge" low-IQ individuals from the gene pool. Still, we must be careful to avoid the **association fallacy** (Harris, 2000): the error of confusing a claim's validity with the people who advocate it (otherwise known as the error of "guilt by association"). It's true that many eugenics supporters were strong proponents of IQ testing and research on the genetic bases of IQ. But this fact doesn't, by itself, imply that we should dismiss the science of IQ testing or research on genetic bases of IQ. Although it's entirely appropriate to be dismayed by the tragic history of the eugenics movement in America, the two issues are logically separable.

IQ Testing Today

Today, the IQ test stands as one of psychology's best-known, yet most controversial, accomplishments. In 1989, the American Academy for the Advancement of Science listed the IQ test as one of the twenty greatest scientific achievements of the twentieth century (Henshaw, 2006). Whether or not we agree with this assessment, there's no question that IQ testing has been remarkably influential. Although psychologists have developed dozens of IQ tests, a mere handful have come to dominate the modern testing scene. We'll discuss these tests next, along with standardized tests like the SAT and measures of infant intelligence.

Commonly Used Adult IQ Tests

The IQ test administered most widely to assess intelligence in adults is the Wechsler Adult Intelligence Scale, or WAIS (see **Figure 9.7** as an example) (Watkins, Campbell, Nieberding, & Hallmark, 1995), now in its third version (the WAIS-III; Wechsler, 1997). Ironically, David Wechsler, a psychologist who developed this test,

Wechsler Adult Intelligence Scale (WAIS) Sample Items		
Test	**Description**	**Example**
Verbal Scale		
Information	Tabs general range of information	On which continent is France?
Comprehension	Tests understanding of social conventions and ability to evaluate past experience	Why do people nead birth certificates?
Arithmetic	Tests arithmetic reasoning through verbal problems	How many hours will it take to drive 150 miles at 50 miles per hour?
Similarities	Asks in what way certain objects or concepts are similar: measures abstract thinking	How are a calculator and a typewriter alike?
Digit span	Tests attention and rote memory by orally presenting series of digits to be repeated forward or backward	Repeat the following numbers backward: 2 4 3 5 1 8 6
Vocabulary	Tests ability to define increasingly difficult words	What does repudiate mean?
Performance scale		
Digital symbol	Tests speed of learning through timed coding tasks in which numbers must be associated with marks of various shapes	Shown: Fill in:
Picture completion	Tests visual alertness and visual memory through presentation of incompletely drawn figure: the missing part must be discovered and named	Tell me what is missing
Block design	Tests ability to perceive and analyze patterns presenting designs that must be copied with bloks.	Assemble blocks to match this design:
Picture arrangement	Tests understanding of social situations through a series of comic-strip-type pictures that must be arranged in the right sequence to tell a story	Put this picture in the right order:
Object assembly	Tests ability to deal with part/whole relationships by presenting puzzle pieces that must be assembled to form a complete object	Assemble the pieces into a complete object:

FIGURE 9.7 ■ Sample Items from WAIS.
Eleven of fourteen subtests of the WAIS-III, along with items similar to those on the test. (*Source:* Harcourt Assessment, Inc.)

was a Romanian immigrant to the United States who was among those classified as feebleminded by early, flawed IQ tests. The WAIS-III consists of fourteen "subtests," or specific tasks, designed to assess mental abilities such as vocabulary, arithmetic, spatial ability, reasoning about proverbs, and general knowledge about the world. We can find sample items from eleven of the fourteen subtests in **Figure 9.7**. The WAIS-III yields three major scores: (1) an overall IQ score, (2) a verbal IQ score, and (3) a performance (non-verbal) IQ score. Verbal IQ relates primarily to crystallized intelligence, and performance IQ relates primarily to fluid intelligence.

Commonly Used Childhood IQ Tests

Two widely used IQ tests for children are the Wechsler Intelligence Scale for Children (WISC) and the Wechsler Primary and Preschool Scale of Intelligence (WPPSI; pronounced "WHIP-see"), both also in their third editions. Both measures are versions of the WAIS adapted for older children and adolescents (the WISC-III) or younger children aged 2½ to 7 years old (the WPPSI-III) (Kaplan & Sacuzzo, 2005).

Shortly after Binet and Simon introduced their test to France, Lewis Terman of Stanford University developed a modified and translated version called the **Stanford-Binet IQ test**, which psychologists still use today. The Stanford-Binet consists of a wide variety of tasks like those Binet and Simon used, such as tests of vocabulary, memory for pictures, naming of familiar objects, repeating sentences, and following commands.

> **Stanford-Binet IQ test:** Intelligence test based on the measure developed by Binet and Simon, adapted by Lewis Terman of Stanford University.

Culture-Fair IQ Tests

One major criticism of IQ tests is that they rely heavily on language. Test takers who aren't fluent in the native language may do poorly on IQ tests largely because they don't comprehend the test instructions or the questions themselves. Moreover, cultural factors can affect people's familiarity with test materials, and in turn their performance on intellectual tasks (Neisser et al., 1996). In one study, a researcher asked school-children in England and Zambia (a country in southern Africa) to reproduce a series of visual patterns using both paper and pencil—a medium with which British children tend to be familar—and wire—a medium with which Zambian children tend to be familiar. The British children did better than the Zambian children when using paper and pencil, but the Zambian children did better than the British children when using wire (Serpell, 1979).

As a consequence of these problems, psychologists have developed a variety of **culture-fair IQ tests**, which consist of abstract-reasoning items that don't depend on language (Cattell, 1949). Presumably, these tests are less influenced by cultural differences than standard IQ tests are.

> **Culture-fair IQ tests:** Abstract reasoning items that don't depend on language and are often believed to be less influenced by cultural factors than other IQ tests.

Standardized Tests: What Do They Measure?

The odds are high you've taken at least one, and perhaps many, standardized tests in your life. In fact, to get into college you may have endured the misery of either the Scholastic Assessment Test (SAT), once known as the Scholastic Aptitude Test, or the American College Test (ACT). The SAT now consists of three sections—Mathematics, Reading, and Writing—with the score on each ranging from 200 to 800.

Standardized Tests and IQ

Standardized tests are designed either to test overall competence in a specific domain or to predict academic success. For many years, the Educational Testing Service apparently collected data on the correlation between the SAT and IQ, but didn't release them until recently (Seligman, 2004). Until that time, we knew little or nothing about the SAT-IQ relationship. Murphy Frey and Douglas Detterman (2004) found that the SAT correlated highly (between about .7 and .8) with two standard measures of intelligence, including the Raven's Progressive Matrices. So the SAT is clearly linked to measured intelligence.

Coaching on Standardized Tests

You've probably heard of companies, such as Princeton Review or Kaplan, that prepare students for the SAT and other standardized tests. These companies charge sizable chunks of money and make some pretty lavish claims. For example, Princeton Review has guaranteed 100 point increases on the SAT, and Kaplan has asserted that more than a quarter of students improve by 170 points or more when taking the SAT a second time (Powers & Rock, 1999).

Do these courses really work? The answer isn't clear (DerSimonian & Laird, 1983), which is surprising given how long these programs have been around. Still, the evidence suggests that commercial coaching improves SAT scores only slightly, probably by 10 to 15 points on average per section (Kulik, Bangert-Drowns, & Kulik, 1984; Powers, 1993).

Are the companies deliberately exaggerating? Not necessarily. It's true that some people improve by 100 points or more after taking SAT preparation courses. But the companies are probably neglecting to consider an alternative explanation for these increases: practice effects (Shadish, Cook, & Campbell, 2002). By *practice effects*, we mean that people frequently improve on tests as a result of practice alone. So the companies may be concluding mistakenly that people who take their courses are improving *because* of these courses rather than merely *after* them. When researchers have controlled for practice effects by including a control group of people who take the SAT a second time but haven't taken an SAT preparation course, the improvements resulting from these courses has been much smaller than claimed by the companies (Powers & Rock, 1999). So if you want to gain a slight edge on the SAT or similar standardized tests, by all means consider enrolling in one of these courses, or buy some practice tests of your own. But if you're looking for a 200- or 300-point increase, you'd do best to hold onto your money.

PSYCHOMYTHOLOGY

DO STANDARDIZED TESTS PREDICT GRADES?

Psychologists designed the SAT, ACT, Graduate Record Exam (GRE), and other standardized tests to forecast performance in college courses. Yet the correlations between these tests and college grades are often below 0.5 and in a few cases close to zero (Morrison & Morrison, 1995). Moreover, although SATs and GREs tend to predict first-year grades at reasonable levels, they generally do a worse job of predicting performance in later years of college (Kuncel & Hezlett, 2007).

These low correlations have prompted many critics to conclude that the SAT and GRE aren't helpful for making predictions about grades (Oldfield, 1998; Sternberg & Williams, 1997). More than one-fourth of major liberal arts colleges in the United States no longer require the SAT, and these numbers are growing (Lewin, 2006). Ralph Nader, a consumer advocate and former presidential candidate, argued that the SAT is so invalid that it should be banned (Kaplan, 1982; Nairn, 1980).

Is Nader right? Yes and no. He's right that the SAT and GRE are highly imperfect predictors and that they don't correlate highly with future grades. But he's wrong that this fact renders the tests useless. To understand why, let's look at the graph in **Figure 9.8a.** We call this graph a *scatterplot*, because it's a plot of the correlation between two variables, in this case between SAT scores and grade point average (GPA) in college. As we can see, the SAT scores (combined across all three subtests) range from 700 to 2,300, and GPA ranges from 1.5 to almost 4.0. The correlation in this scatterplot is .65, which is fairly high. High positive correlations display a pronounced upward tilt.

Continued

Technically, you can receive a score of 0 on the SAT if you answer every question incorrectly (you'll receive a score of 200 if you answer the questions randomly). Nevertheless, because the Educational Testing Service, which administers and scores the SAT, doesn't report scores below 200, you'll receive a score of 200 on your SAT just for signing your name.

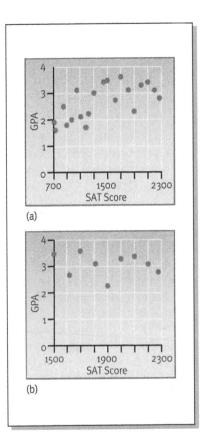

(a)

(b)

FIGURE 9.8 ■ Scatterplot of Correlation between SAT Scores and College GPA.
In the graph depicted in (a), SAT scores are clearly correlated with GPA. We can see an upward slant to the data points as we move from lower to higher scores. In the graph depicted in (b), the same data are depicted but only for the narrow range of higher SAT scores (1,500–2,300). As we can see, there is no clear correlation between SAT scores and GPA in this range.

But let's now look at **Figure 9.8b,** which is a close-up of the dots that are 1500 or higher on the x (horizontal) axis. As we can see, the range of SAT scores is now only between 1,500 and 2,300 combined. This range is typical of what we find at many highly competitive colleges. That's because few people with SAT scores much below 1500 combined get into these colleges. What does the correlation look like now? As we can see, it's much lower than that in Figure 9.8a; in fact, the correlation is close to zero (it's even slightly negative). The upward tilt of this correlation has clearly disappeared.

These two scatterplots illustrate a crucial phenomenon overlooked by many critics of the SAT and GRE (for example, Sternberg & Williams, 1997): restriction of range. *Restriction of range* refers to the fact that correlations tend to go down when we limit the range of scores on one or both variables (Alexander, Carson, Alliger, & Carr, 1987). To understand restriction of range, think of the relation of height to basketball playing ability. In a group of ordinary people playing a pickup basketball game on a Saturday afternoon, height will correlate highly with who scores more points. But in a game of professional basketball players, height barely matters, because almost everyone who makes it to a professional basketball team is tall.

Restriction of range helps to explain why the SAT and GRE aren't highly predictive of scores in college and graduate school: Colleges and graduate schools rarely admit low scorers. Indeed, when two researchers examined the validity of the GRE in a graduate department that admitted applicants regardless of their GRE scores, the GRE correlated highly (between .55 and .70) with measures of graduate GPA (Huitema & Stein, 1993). So when we remove restriction of range, the GRE becomes highly predictive of later grades. Restriction of range also probably accounts for why SATs and GREs are less predictive of later grades than of first-year grades. When students get to pick the classes in which they do well, they tend to obtain higher grades, thereby limiting the range of GPAs.

To return to the question we posed at the outset—Do standardized tests predict grades?—the answer is, "When we measure the full range of scores, yes, although by no means perfectly."

Reliability of IQ Scores: IS IQ Forever?

We often think of people's IQ scores in much the same way we think of their social security numbers: as sticking with them for life. Joe's a 116, Maria a 130, and Bill a 97. Yet IQ scores aren't fixed. They almost never remain exactly the same over time; in fact, they occasionally shift within the same person by as much as 10 points or more over a matter of months.

Stability of IQ in Adulthood

IQ scores usually remain reasonably stable in adulthood. *Reliability* refers to consistency of measurement. As we also learned, one important type of reliability is *test-retest reliability*, which refers to the extent to which scores on a measure remain stable over time. For adult IQ tests like the WAIS-III, test-retest reliabilities tend to be about .95 over a several week interval (Weschler, 1997). As you'll recall, .95 is an extremely high correlation, nearly but not quite perfect. Even across long stretches of time, IQ scores tend to be reasonably stable. In one study of 101 Scottish schoolchildren followed up over time, IQ scores obtained at age 11 correlated .73 with their IQ scores at age 77 (Deary, Whalley, Lemmon, Crawford, & Starr, 2000).

Stability of IQ in Infancy and Childhood

There's a key exception to the rule regarding the high test-retest reliability of IQ tests. Prior to age 2 or 3, IQ tests aren't stable over time. In fact, IQ measured in the first 6 months of life correlates just about zero with adult IQ (Brody, 1992). Nor do IQ scores obtained in the first few years of life do a good job of forecasting outcomes, unless they're extremely low, such as under 50; such scores tend to be predictive of later mental retardation. That's probably because IQ tests designed for very young children assess the sensory abilities that Galton and Cattell emphasized, which bear little association with intelligence. In contrast, IQ tests designed for older children and beyond assess the abstract reasoning emphasized by Binet, Simon, and others. This reasoning, as we've seen, lies at the heart of what we call intelligence.

Some measures of infant intelligence are slightly more promising when it comes to predicting later IQ. One is speed of habituation. Habituation refers to the tendency to stop responding to repeated presentations of the same stimulus. Infants who habituate to a visual stimulus (like a red circle) more quickly—as measured by how long they stare at it—turn out to have higher IQs in later childhood and adolescence, with correlations typically in the .3 to .5 range (McCall & Ganringer, 1993; Slater, 1997).

It's not entirely clear why this is so. Perhaps this correlation reflects a direct causal association between intelligence and habituation: Infants who are smart "take in" information from novel stimuli quickly, so they're ready to move on to new things. Alternatively, this correlation may reflect the influence of a third variable, like interest in new stimuli (Colombo, 1993). Perhaps infants who are more interested in new things both habituate more quickly *and* learn more things, resulting in higher intelligence later on.

A related approach presents babies with pairs of pictures, like photos of faces. For many trials, the two faces are the same. Then suddenly, a novel face appears along with the familiar face. Infants who attend more to the new face later tend to have higher IQs in childhood and adolescence than other infants (DiLalla et al., 1990; Smith, Fagan, & Ulvund, 2002). Still, this measure has its problems. In particular, its test-retest reliability is fairly low (Benasich & Bejar, 1992).

It remains to be seen whether researchers will develop even better measures of infant intelligence. Ultimately, these measures may yield clues regarding how intelligence develops and perhaps even what intelligence is.

Among professional basketball players, height isn't an especially good predictor of who scores the most points, because the range of heights is dramatically restricted.

Why do you think IQ predicts performance better in more mentally demanding jobs than in less mentally demanding ones? How could you test your hypothesis?

Bell curve: Distribution of scores in which the bulk of the scores fall toward the middle, with progressively fewer scores toward the "tails" or extremes.

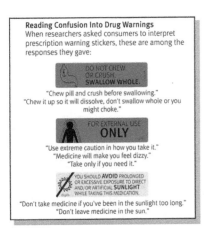

Reading Confusion Into Drug Warnings
When researchers asked consumers to interpret prescription warning stickers, these are among the responses they gave:

DO NOT CHEW OR CRUSH. SWALLOW WHOLE.
"Chew pill and crush before swallowing."
"Chew it up so it will dissolve, don't swallow whole or you might choke."

FOR EXTERNAL USE ONLY
"Use extreme caution in how you take it."
"Medicine will make you feel dizzy."
"Take only if you need it."

YOU SHOULD AVOID PROLONGED OR EXCESSIVE EXPOSURE TO DIRECT AND/OR ARTIFICIAL SUNLIGHT WHILE TAKING THIS MEDICATION.
"Don't take medicine if you've been in the sunlight too long."
"Don't leave medicine in the sun."

Low levels of health literacy, which are associated with IQ, can lead to dangerous misunderstandings of medication instructions. On the top are actual warning labels attached to certain medications; underneath each warning label are actual interpretations of these warnings by some subjects in a published study (Davis et al., 2006).
(*Source:* Franklin, 2005)

Validity of IQ Scores: Predicting Life Outcomes

Whatever we think of IQ tests, there's little question that they're valid for at least some purposes. *Validity* refers to the extent to which a test measures what it purports to measure. One important indicator of a test's validity is its capacity to forecast future outcomes (or what psychologists call "predictive" validity).

IQ scores do a good job of predicting academic success; they correlate about .5 with grades in high school and college (Neisser et al., 1996). Still, because this correlation is considerably lower than 1.0, it tells us there's more to school success than IQ. Motivation, intellectual curiosity, and effort also play crucial roles.

IQ scores also predict performance across a wide variety of occupations, with the average correlation again being about .5 (Ones, Viswesveran, & Dilchert, 2005). By comparison, the correlation between ratings of how well people do in job interviews and job performance is only about .15, which is ironic given that many employers place heavier weight on interviews than on IQ when selecting job applicants (Hunter & Hunter, 1984). The correlation between IQ and job performance is higher in more mentally demanding occupations, such as physician or lawyer, than in less mentally demanding occupations, like clerk or newspaper delivery person (Salgado et al., 2003).

IQ also predicts a variety of important real-world behaviors outside the classroom and workplace. For example, IQ is associated with health-related outcomes, including sickness and car accidents (Gottfredson, 2004; Lubinski & Humphreys, 1992). At least some of the negative correlation between IQ and illness may be attributable to *health literacy*, the ability to understand health-related information, such as instructions from doctors or on drug labels. People with low health literacy may have difficulty maintaining good health behaviors, such as getting enough exercise, eating the right foods, or taking the right dosage of their medications. IQ is also associated with criminal tendencies: The IQs of delinquent adolescents are about 7 points lower than those of other adolescents (Wilson & Herrnstein, 1985).

But there's a potential confound here. IQ is negatively associated with social class, as poorer people tend to have lower IQs. So poverty, rather than IQ, may explain at least some of the associations we've discussed. Researchers have tried to address this rival hypothesis by determining whether the correlations hold up even when accounting for social class. In most cases, including health outcomes and crime, they do (Herrnstein & Murray, 1994; Neisser et al., 1997).

A Tale of Two Tails: From Mental Retardation to Genius

As we promised at the chapter's outset, we'll now revisit the **bell curve** discovered by Gauss. In a bell curve distribution, the bulk of the scores fall toward the middle, with progressively fewer scores toward the "tails" or extremes, forming the shape of a bell.

Figure 9.9 shows that the bell curve fits the distribution of IQ scores in the population fairly well, with one minor exception. The bulk of scores fall in the broad middle of the distribution; about 95 percent of people have IQs between 70 and 130. The curve contains a small bump on the left, indicating that there are more very low IQ scores than we'd expect from a perfect bell curve. These extreme scores are probably the result of *assortative mating* (Mackintosh, 1998): the tendency of individuals with similar genes to have children. In this case, individuals with mental retardation are especially likely to parent a child with other individuals with mental retardation, probably because they frequent the same locations (such as special schools), then develop a relationship, and have children.

Let's now look at what we know about the two tails of the IQ score distribution: mental retardation and genius.

Mental Retardation

Psychologists define **mental retardation** by three criteria, all of which must be present: (1) onset prior to adulthood, (2) IQ below approximately 70, and (3) inadequate adaptive functioning, as assessed by difficulties with dressing and feeding oneself, communicating with others, and other basic life skills (Greenspan & Switzky, 2003). The adaptive functioning criterion largely explains why about two-thirds of children with mental retardation lose this diagnosis in adulthood (Grossman, 1983); as individuals acquire life-functioning skills, they no longer qualify for this diagnosis. Some experts have also recently placed heightened emphasis on *gullibility* (the susceptibility to being duped by others) as a criterion for mental retardation, in part for social policy reasons. A diagnosis of mental retardation qualifies individuals for additional government services. For this reason, the inability to protect oneself from being taken advantage of by others should be weighted heavily in determining whether a person is mentally retarded (Greenspan, Loughlin, & Black, 2001).

About 1 percent of persons in the United States, most of them males, fulfill the criteria for mental retardation (American Psychiatric Association, 2000). The current system of psychiatric diagnosis classifies mental retardation into four categories: mild (once called "educable"), moderate (once called "trainable"), severe, and profound. Contrary to popular conception, most mentally retarded individuals—at least 85 percent—fall into the "mild" category. In most cases, mildly retarded children can be integrated or *mainstreamed* into classrooms along with nonretarded individuals. Still, the term "mild mental retardation" is misleading, because individuals in this category still have significant deficits in adaptive functioning.

Contrary to what we might expect, the more severe the mental retardation, the *less* likely it is to run in families (Reed & Reed, 1965). Mild forms of mental retardation are typically due to a mix of genetic and environmental influences that parents pass on to their children. In contrast, severe forms of mental retardation are more often the result of rare genetic mutations or accidents during birth, neither of which tend to be transmitted within families.

There are at least 200 different causes of mental retardation. Two of the most common genetic conditions associated with mental retardation are fragile X syndrome, which is produced by a mutation on the X chromosome (females have two copies of this chromosome, males only one), and Down syndrome, which is the result of an extra copy of chromosome 21. Most children with Down syndrome are either mildly or moderately retarded. Nevertheless, a subset of individuals with Down syndrome known as *mosaics* (so called because only some of their cells contain an extra chromosome 21) have relatively normal IQs. People with Down syndrome typically exhibit a distinctive pattern of physical features, including a flat nose, upwardly slanted eyes, a protruding tongue, and a short neck. The prevalence of Down syndrome rises sharply with the birth mother's age; at age 30, it's less than 1 in 1,000, but by age 49, it's about 1 in 12 (Hook & Lindjso, 1978).

Societal attitudes toward individuals with mental retardation have improved dramatically over the past century. Today, if we want to insult

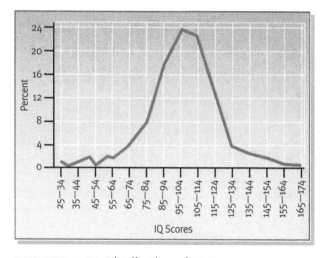

FIGURE 9.9 Distribution of IQ Scores in General Population.
The bell curve roughly approximates the distribution of IQ scores in the general population.

Mental retardation:
Condition characterized by an onset prior to adulthood, an IQ below about 70, and an inability to engage in adequate daily functioning.

Most individuals with Down syndrome are mildly or moderately mentally retarded. Nevertheless, many have been successfully mainstreamed into traditional classrooms.

someone's intelligence, we might refer to him as a "moron," "idiot," or "imbecile." Yet few of us realize that these terms originally described different classes of individuals with mental retardation: "moron" referred to the mildly retarded, "idiot" to the moderately and severely retarded, and "imbecile" to the profoundly retarded (Scheerenberger, 1983). Thankfully, our views are far more enlightened today. The Americans with Disabilities Act (ADA), passed in 1990, outlawed job and educational discrimination on the basis of mental and physical disabilities, and the Individuals with Disabilities Education Act (IDEA), passed in 1996, provided federal aid to states and local educational districts for accommodations to mentally and physically disabled youth. Both ADA and IDEA have helped bring the mentally retarded out of institutions and into our workplaces and schools. As we increase our regular contact with the mentally retarded, such laws may further erode the lingering stigma that some Americans feel toward these members of society.

Genius and Exceptional Intelligence

Let's now turn to the opposite tail of the bell curve. If you're fortunate enough to score in the top 2 percent of the IQ range, you'll qualify for membership in an organization called Mensa. A large proportion of individuals with IQs at or near this range populate certain occupations, such as doctors, lawyers, engineers, and college professors (Herrnstein & Murray, 1994). Yet we know relatively little about the psychological characteristics of individuals with high IQs or their academic, occupational, and social performance over time. Several research studies offer tantalizing clues.

The stereotype of intelligent nerds being uncoordinated weaklings is not supported by the data. In fact, nerds are actually a race of super beings from outer space occupying low-paying jobs on earth until the main space assault begins.

In the 1920s, Lewis Terman and his colleagues (Terman & Oden, 1959) initiated one of the classic studies of intellectually gifted individuals. From some 250,000 junior high school students in California, Terman selected about 1,500 who scored in the top 1 percent on the Stanford-Binet and similar IQ tests, that is, who had IQs of about 135 or higher. He tracked these individuals, known affectionately as Terman's "Termites," for several decades (some are still alive today). Although Terman's study was flawed, in part because he didn't recruit a control group of individuals with average or low IQs, it refuted three common misconceptions regarding people with high IQs.

First, his study refuted the popular stereotype of the "nerd" or "98-pound weakling"—the highly intelligent individual who is physically frail and nonathletic. We all remember the skinny kid in high school with a calculator in his belt who was always the last guy to be picked for the sports team. Yet Terman found that his Termites were above average in physical health and were taller and heavier than individuals in the general population.

Second, Terman's study raised doubts about the common claim that almost all child prodigies "burn out" in adulthood ("early ripe, early rot," so the saying goes). Terman's subjects became a highly distinguished group: ninety-seven earned doctoral degrees, fifty-seven medical degrees, and ninety-two law degrees (Leslie, 2000). An additional seventy-four became college professors, and collectively they published nearly 100 books and about 2,000 journal articles. These numbers are all considerably higher than what we'd expect from the general population. A later study of an even more select group—young adolescents who scored in the top .001 percent (that's 1 in 10,000) on tests of verbal or mathematical ability—generated similar results. By their early twenties, these individuals were attending graduate school at a rate more than fifty times higher than that in the general population, and many had already published scientific or literary articles (Lubinski, Benbow, Webb, & Bleske-Rechek, 2006).

Third, Terman's results disputed the popular notion that there's an intimate link between genius and insanity. Although the absence of a control group makes it difficult to know for certain, his findings pointed to slightly lower rates of mental illness and suicide among his adult Termites compared with the general population. Later researchers have generally found similar results, although some have reported that exceedingly intelligent children, such as those with IQs over 180, may be at heightened risk for selected mental health problems, especially loneliness and depression (Janos & Robinson, 1985; Winner, 1999). These negative outcomes may be a consequence of the greater ridicule and isolation that these children experience. Still, there's scant evidence that high intelligence is associated with high levels of severe mental illness.

What's the recipe for creating a genius, like Karl Friedrich Gauss? We don't know, although as we'll soon discover, genetic factors probably play a significant role. Still, as the brilliant inventor Thomas Edison said famously, "genius is 1% inspiration, 99% perspiration." Becoming a genius in one's chosen field takes many years of hard work. Gauss was no exception; his biographers describe him as intensely dedicated to mathematics, routinely toiling away for many hours in complete isolation when solving proofs (Dunnington, 1955).

Here common wisdom is correct: Practice makes perfect, or at least pretty darned good. The best predictor of exceptional career success in violin, piano, ballet, chess, and sports is the sheer amount of time we spend in practice. The most talented musicians practice twice as much as the less talented ones (Ericsson, Krampe, & Tesch-Romer, 1993). Of course, the causal arrow here isn't clear. Greater amounts of practice could be causing greater success, or greater levels of initial talent could be causing greater amounts of practice. We won't spend ten hours a day perfecting our guitar playing unless we're decent at it to begin with. In addition, research shows that across many domains, such as science, art, and music, individuals almost never attain remarkable intellectual accomplishments until they've dedicated themselves intensely for at least 10 years in that domain (Simonton, 1997). So the familiar Hollywood stereotype of the teenager or young adult who achieves astonishing intellectual brilliance with virtually no effort is exceedingly unrealistic.

Many Hollywood movies, like the 1997 movie Good Will Hunting (starring Matt Damon, shown here, as Will Hunting), portray childhood or adolescent geniuses as requiring minimal effort to make astonishing intellectual discoveries. Yet research shows that such discoveries almost always require a decade or more of hard, concentrated work in a specific area.

■ ASSESS YOUR KNOWLEDGE: FACT OR FICTION?

(1) Today, IQ is measured as mental age divided by chronological age, multiplied by 100. (True/False)
(2) Standard IQ tests administered in infancy tend not to be highly predictive of later IQ scores. (True/False)
(3) Although IQ scores predict school achievement, they are almost useless for predicting occupational success. (True/False)
(4) The most prevalent form of mental retardation is mild retardation. (True/False)
(5) Most highly intelligent people tend to be physically weak and underdeveloped. (True/False)

Answers: (1) F; (2) T; (3) F; (4) T; (5) F

GENETIC AND ENVIRONMENTAL INFLUENCES ON IQ

Up to this point, we've talked at length about what intelligence is and how we measure it. But we've said little about its causes, or about the relative roles of nature and nurture in its development. Fortunately, over the past few decades, psychologists have obtained a much better handle on the genetic and environmental contributors to IQ. As we'll discover, however, significant flash points of controversy remain.

Exploring Genetic Influences on IQ

Scientists can study genetic influences on psychological characteristics in three major ways: family studies, twin studies, and adoption studies. They've done so for intelligence, with surprisingly consistent results.

Family Studies

Family studies allow us to examine the extent to which a trait "runs" or goes together in intact families, those in which all family members live together in the same home. Sir Francis Galton, who coined the phrase "nature and nurture" (Galton, 1876), conducted one of the first family studies of intelligence. Intrigued by the possibility that intellectual brilliance runs in families, Galton (1869) gathered data on the extent to which persons renowned for their intellectual accomplishments—as gauged by their obituaries in newspapers—had biological relatives who were also renowned for their intellectual accomplishments. He found that the proportion of relatives who'd achieved intellectual greatness declined steadily with increasing biological distance. Intellectually brilliant individuals had many first-degree relatives (parents, siblings, and children) who were also brilliant, but fewer second-degree relatives (such as cousins), and still fewer third-degree relatives (such as second cousins) who were brilliant. Later studies have confirmed that IQ runs in families: The correlation of IQ for brothers and sisters raised in the same family is about .5, whereas for cousins it's about .15 (Bouchard & McGue, 1981). Galton concluded that these findings demonstrated a genetic basis to intellectual greatness, but he overlooked two alternative explanations.

First, he neglected to consider a potential confound: wealth. People who come from rich families are more likely to acquire fame and to be memorialized in newspaper obituaries. And of course, the closer the relatives biologically, the more likely they are to have a similar income level.

Second, Galton largely ignored a crucial limitation that applies to all family studies: *Studies of intact families don't allow us to distinguish the effects of genes from those of the environment.* That's because individuals in these families share both genes and environment. As a consequence, when a trait runs in families, we don't know whether it's for genetic reasons, environmental reasons, or both.

Twin Studies

Because family studies don't permit investigators to disentangle the effects of nature from those of nurture, they've turned to more informative research designs. These include *twin studies*, which as we've seen compare correlations in a trait in two types of twins: identical (monozygotic) and fraternal (dizygotic).

The logic of the twin design is straightforward. Because identical twins share twice as many of their genes on average as fraternal twins, we can compare the correlations in IQ in these two different twin types. Given a handful of assumptions, higher identical than fraternal twin correlations strongly suggest genetic influence. In almost all cases, studies of twins reared together have offered evidence of considerably higher identical than fraternal twin correlations for IQ (Bouchard & McGue, 1981; Loehlin, Willerman, & Horn, 1988). In typical studies of IQ, identical twin correlations have been in the .7 to .8 range, whereas fraternal twin correlations have been in the .3 to .4 range. Nevertheless, in all studies of twins raised together, identical twin correlations have been lower than 1.0.

These findings tell us two things. First, the higher identical than fraternal twin correlations tell us that IQ is influenced by genetic factors. The best estimate for the heritability of IQ lies somewhere between 40 and

Twin studies of intelligence compare the mental performance of identical (top) versus fraternal (bottom) twins raised together.

70 percent (Brody, 1992; Devlin, Daniels, & Roeder, 1997). Interestingly, the heritability of IQ seems to increase from childhood to adulthood (McClearn et al., 1997), perhaps because people become less influenced by their environments, especially their parents, as they move away from home. Although the twin findings don't tell us which genes are relevant to intelligence, the past decade has witnessed progress in identifying specific genes for intelligence. These genes appear to cut across multiple domains of mental ability, including attention, working memory, and perhaps even risk for Alzheimer's disease (Plomin & Kovas, 2005; Posthuma & de Gues, 2006).

Second, these twin findings provide convincing evidence for environmental influences on IQ. Why? Because the identical twin correlations for IQ are less than perfect. Given that identical twins share 100 percent of their genes, they would correlate 1.0 if genetic influences alone were operative (assuming the IQ tests are reliable). The fact that they correlate less than 1.0 tells us that environmental influences also play a role, although the studies don't tell us what these influences are.

Note that up to this point, we've discussed only studies of twins raised together. These studies are vulnerable to a rival hypothesis; perhaps identical twins are more similar than fraternal twins because they spend more time together. To exclude this possibility, investigators have conducted studies of identical and fraternal twins reared apart since birth or shortly after birth. Thomas Bouchard and his colleagues at the University of Minnesota conducted the landmark study of twins reared apart in the 1980s and 1990s. Remarkably, the results of this study revealed that a sample of over forty identical twin pairs reared apart were just as similar on three measures of IQ (including the WAIS and Raven's Progressive Matrices) as identical twins reared together (Bouchard, Lykken, McGue, Segal, & Tellegen, 1990). Other investigators have replicated these findings (Pederson, Plomin, Nesselroade, & McClearn, 1992), although because twins reared apart are extremely rare, the sample sizes of these studies are relatively low.

Adoption Studies

Studies of intact family members are limited because they can't disentangle genetic from environmental influences. To address this shortcoming, psychologists have turned to *adoption studies*, which examine the extent to which children adopted into new homes resemble their adoptive versus biological parents. Adoption studies allow us to separate environmental from genetic effects on IQ, because adoptees are raised by parents with whom they share an environment, but not genes. One potential confound in adoption studies is *selective placement:* Adoption agencies frequently place children in homes similar to those of the biological parents (DeFries & Plomin, 1978). This confound can lead investigators to mistakenly interpret the similarity between adoptive children and adoptive parents as an environmental effect. In adoption studies of IQ, researchers often try to control for selective placement by correcting statistically for the correlation in IQ between biological and adoptive parents.

Adoption studies have established a clear contribution of the environment in IQ. For example, adopted children who come from extremely deprived environments show an increase in IQ when adopted into homes that provide more enriched environments (Capron & Duyme, 1989). In one study of French children raised in an extremely deprived environment, children who were adopted showed an average 16-point IQ edge over children who weren't (Schiff et al., 1982).

But do adopted children's IQs resemble their biological parents' IQs? The results of adoption studies indicate that the IQs of adopted children tend to be similar to the IQs of their biological parents offering evidence of

Many children adopted from environments of severe deprivation show increases in IQ after immersion in a healthier and more attentive adoptive environment.

genetic influence. As young children, adoptees tend to resemble the adoptive parents in IQ, but this resemblance dissipates once these children become older and approach adolescence (Loehlin, Horn, & Willerman, 1989; Phillips & Fulker, 1989; Plomin, Fulker, Corley, & Defries, 1997).

Exploring Environmental Influences on IQ

As we've learned, twin and adoption studies paint a consistent picture: Both genes and environment affect IQ scores. But these studies leave a mysterious question unanswered: What environmental factors influence IQ? Psychologists don't know for sure, although they've made significant inroads toward identifying promising candidates. As we'll see, environmental influences can include not only the *social* environment, such as school and parents, but also the *biological* environment, such as the availability of nutrients and exposure to toxic substances, such as lead. We'll also see that the evidence for some of these environmental influences is more convincing than for others.

Birth Order: Are Older Siblings Wiser?

In the 1970s, Robert Zajonc (whose name, oddly enough, rhymes with "science"), created a stir by arguing that later-born children tend to be less intelligent than earlier-born children (Zajonc, 1976). According to Zajonc, IQ declines steadily with increasing numbers of children in a family. He even authored an article in the popular magazine *Psychology Today* entitled "Dumber by the Dozen" (Zajonc, 1975).

In one respect, Zajonc was right: later-born children tend to have slightly lower IQs (on the order of a few points) than earlier-born children (Kristensen & Bjerkedal, 2007). But it's not clear that he interpreted this correlation correctly. Here's the problem. Parents with lower IQs are slightly more likely to have many children than are parents with higher IQs. As a consequence, when we look across families, birth order is associated with IQ, but only because low-IQ families have a larger number of later-born children than do high-IQ families. In contrast, when we look *within* families, the relationship between birth order and IQ becomes smaller and may even vanish (Michalski & Shackelford, 2001; Rodgers et al., 2000). So a more accurate way to state the correlation is that children who come from larger families have slightly lower IQs than do children who come from smaller families.

Does Schooling Make Us Smarter?

Number of years in school correlates between .5 and .6 with IQ scores (Neisser et al., 1995). Although some authors have interpreted this correlation as meaning that schooling leads to higher IQ, it's equally possible that the causal arrow is reversed. Indeed, there's evidence that individuals with high IQ scores enjoy taking classes more than individuals with low IQ scores (Rehberg & Rosenthal, 1978). As a consequence, they may be more likely to stay in school and go on to college and beyond. This wouldn't be terribly surprising given that individuals with high IQ scores tend to do better in their classes.

Still, several lines of evidence suggest that schooling exerts a causal influence on IQ (Ceci, 1991; Ceci & Williams, 1997):

1. Researchers have examined pairs of children who are almost exactly the same age, but in which one child attended an extra year of school because he was born just a few days earlier (say, August 31 as opposed to September 2). This can occur because public schools often have hard-and-fast cutoff dates for how old children must be to begin

Children's IQs tend to drop significantly during summer vacations, suggesting an environmental influence on IQ.

The federal Head Start program was launched in the 1960s to give disadvantaged preschoolers a jump-start on their education. Studies show that Head Start programs typically produce short-term increases in IQ, but that these increases fade with time.

school. In such cases, children who've attended an extra year of school tend to have higher IQs, despite being nearly identical in chronological age.

2. Children's IQs tend to drop significantly during summer vacations.
3. Students who drop out of school end up with lower IQs than students who stay in school, even when they start out with the same IQ.

Boosting IQ by Early Intervention

In a controversial article in the late 1960s, Arthur Jensen contended that IQ was highly heritable and therefore difficult to modify by means of environmental intervention (Jensen, 1969). In making this argument, Jensen fell prey to a logical error we debunked earlier in this book: namely, that heritability implies that a trait can't be changed. Yet he raised an important question: Can we boost IQ with early educational interventions?

Some of the best evidence comes from studies of *Head Start*, a preschool program launched in the 1960s to give disadvantaged children a "jump start" by offering them an enriched educational experience. The hope was that this program would allow them to catch up intellectually to other children. Dozens of studies of Head Start programs have yielded consistent results, and they've been largely disappointing. Although these programs produce short-term increases in IQ, these increases don't typically persist after the programs end (Caruso, Taylor, & Detterman, 1982; Royce, Darlington, & Murray, 1983). Similar results emerge from studies of other early-intervention programs (Brody, 1992; Herrnstein & Murray, 1994). At the same time, these programs may not be entirely worthless. Several studies indicate that Head Start and other early-intervention programs result in lower rates of high school dropout and of being held back a grade compared with control conditions (Campbell & Raney, 1995; Darlington, 1986; Neisser et al., 1995).

A Self-Fulfilling Prophecy: Expectancy Effects on IQ

In the 1960s, Robert Rosenthal and Lenore Jacobson wanted to examine the effects of teacher expectancies on IQ. The *experimenter expectancy effect* refers to the tendency of researchers to unintentionally influence the outcome of studies. In this case, Rosenthal and Jacobson (1966) looked at the expectancies of teachers rather than researchers. They administered an IQ test to students in the first through sixth grades, disguising it with a fake name ("The Harvard Test of Inflected Acquisition"). Then they gave teachers the results, which indicated that 20 percent of their students would show remarkable gains in intelligence during the subsequent 8 months: These students were "bloomers" who'd soon reach their full intellectual potential. But Rosenthal and Jacobson misled the teachers. They had *randomly* selected these 20 percent of students to be classified as bloomers, and these students' initial scores didn't differ from those of other students. Yet when Rosenthal and Jacobson retested all students a year later with the same IQ test, the 20 percent labeled as bloomers scored about 4 IQ points higher than the other students. Expectations had become reality.

This effect has now been replicated in a number of studies, although the size of the effect isn't large (Rosenthal, 1994; Smith, 1980). We don't know how this effect occurs, although there's evidence that teachers more often smile at, make eye contact with, and nod their heads toward students they incorrectly believe are smart compared with other students (Chaiken, Sigler, & Derlega, 1974). As a consequence, they may positively reinforce these students' learning. Nevertheless, the effects of expectancy on IQ have their limits. These effects are substantial only when teachers don't know their students well; when teachers have worked with students for at least a few weeks, the effects often disappear (Raudenbush, 1984). Once teachers form definite impressions of how smart their students are, it's hard to persuade them their impressions are off base.

Lead exposure can arise from many sources in everyday life and may contribute to decreased IQ. Nevertheless, the causal association between lead intake and IQ remains controversial.

Poverty and IQ: Socioeconomic and Nutritional Deprivation

It's difficult to put a firm number on the effects of poverty, but there's reason to believe that social and economic deprivation can adversely affect IQ. Arthur Jensen (1977) studied a group of families in an extremely poor area of rural Georgia. For African American (but not Caucasian) children, he found evidence for a *cumulative deficit*, a difference that grows over time. Older siblings consistently had lower IQs than younger siblings, with a steady decrease of about 1.5 IQ points per year. Jensen's explanation was that siblings in this impoverished region experienced progressively more intellectual deprivation as they aged, leading them to fall further behind other children (Willerman, 1979).

Along with poverty often comes inadequate diet. Studies from poor areas in Central America suggest that malnutrition in childhood, especially if prolonged, can lower IQ (Eysenck & Schoenthaler, 1997). In one investigation, researchers gave nutritional (protein) supplements to preschool children from an impoverished region of Guatemala. These children's school-related test scores were significantly higher than those of similar children who didn't receive supplements (Pollitt, German, Engle, Martorell, & Rivera, 1993).

Poor children are also especially likely to be exposed to lead as a result of drinking lead-contaminated water, breathing lead-contaminated dust, or eating lead paint chips. Such exposure is also associated with intellectual deficits (Bellinger & Needleman, 2003; Canfield et al., 2003; Ris, Dietrich, Succop, Berger, & Bornschein, 2004). Nevertheless, it's unclear how much of this correlation is due to the direct effects of lead itself as opposed to poverty or other factors, like malnutrition.

Scientific controversy has swirled around another potential nutritional influence: breast-feeding. On the one side are researchers who claim that infants who are breast-fed end up with higher IQs—perhaps on the order of a few points—than children who are bottle-fed (Mortonsen, Michaelson, Sanders, & Reinisch, 2002; Quinn et al., 2001). Indeed, mothers' milk contains about 100 ingredients absent from milk formula, including several that speed up the myelinization of neurons. On the other side are researchers who contend that this IQ difference is due to one or more confounds: For example, mothers who breast-feed their babies tend to be somewhat higher in social class and IQ than mothers who bottle-feed their babies (Der, Batty, & Deary, 2006; Jacobson, Chiodo, & Jacobson, 1999). These confounds could account for the seeming effect of breast-feeding on IQ. The debate rages on. (Caspi et al., 2007).

Getting Smarter All the Time: The Mysterious Flynn Effect

Flynn effect: Finding that average IQ scores have been rising at a rate of approximately 3 points per decade.

In the 1980s, while looking at changes in IQ scores over time in the United States and Europe, political scientist James Flynn noticed something very odd (Dickens & Flynn, 2001; Flynn, 1981, 1987). Mysteriously, IQ scores were rising at a rate of about 3 points per decade, a phenomenon later dubbed the **Flynn effect** (Herrnstein & Murray, 1994). The magnitude of the Flynn effect is mind-boggling. It suggests that, on average, our IQs are a full 15 points higher than those of our grandparents who lived 50 years ago (see **Figure 9.10**). With a few exceptions (Mingronin, 2007; Rushton, 1999), most researchers agree that the Flynn effect is a result of unidentified environmental influences on IQ, because it's unlikely that genetic changes could account for such rapid rises in IQ over brief time periods.

What could these environmental influences be? Psychologists have proposed at least four explanations:

1. *Increased test sophistication.* According to this explanation, the rise in IQ scores results from people becoming more experienced at taking tests. This hypothesis implies that the Flynn effect reflects an increase in IQ scores but not in underlying intelligence (Flynn, 1998). There may be some truth to the test sophistication hypothesis, but there's a fly in the ointment. The Flynn

effect is most pronounced on "culture-fair" tests, such as Raven's Progressive Matrices, to which people have had the least exposure (Neisser, 1998).

2. *Increased complexity of the modern world.* With television, e-mail, the Internet, fax machines, cell phones, and the like, we're forced to process far more information far more quickly than our parents and grandparents ever did. So the modern information explosion may be putting pressure on us to become more intelligent (Greenfield, 1998; Schooler, 1998).

3. *Better nutrition.* Most evidence suggests that the Flynn effect is affecting primarily the lower, but not the upper, tail of the bell curve. One potential explanation for this finding is diet. People are better fed than ever before, and the rates of severe malnutrition in many (although not all) parts of the world are declining (Lynn, 1998; Sigman & Whaley, 1998). As we've already learned, there's good evidence that nutrition can affect IQ.

4. *Changes at home and school.* Over the past several decades in the United States, families have become smaller, allowing parents to devote more time to their children. Parents also have more access to intellectual resources than ever. In addition, children and adolescents spend more years in school than in previous generations (Bronfenbrenner, McClelland, Wethington, Moen, & Ceci, 1996).

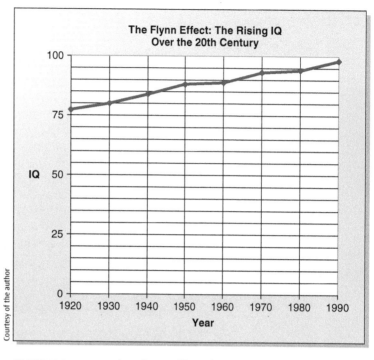

FIGURE 9.10 ■ The Flynn Effect shows that mean IQ scores have been increasing in society by about three points each decade since the 1920s.

We don't fully understand the causes of the Flynn effect, and there may be some truth to several of these explanations. But the mystery doesn't end here. Recent data suggest that the Flynn effect may be subsiding or even reversing, at least in Europe (Sundet, Barlaug, & Torjussen, 2004). Some investigators have suggested that children's decreasing amounts of play with other children, perhaps resulting from greater computer and video game use, may be the culprit (Schneider, 2006), but no one knows for sure. The causes of the apparent end to the Flynn effect are as puzzling as the causes of its beginning. Yet it's a safe bet that the rise and fall of the Flynn effect holds the key to unlocking much of the mystery of environmental influences on IQ.

> Let's imagine that psychologists discover the Flynn effect is due primarily to increasing test sophistication. What would that tell us about the validity of IQ tests as measures of intelligence?

■ ASSESS YOUR KNOWLEDGE: FACT OR FICTION?

(1) Identical twins reared apart appear to be about as similar on IQ tests as identical twins reared together. (True/False)

(2) Children adopted at birth bear almost no resemblance in IQ to their biological parents. (True/False)

(3) There's good evidence that being removed from school can lower IQ scores. (True/False)

(4) Head Start programs produce lasting increases in IQ scores. (True/False)

(5) People's average performance on IQ tests have remained virtually unchanged over the past several decades. (True/False)

Answers: (1) T; (2) F; (3) T; (4) F; (5) F

GROUP DIFFERENCES IN IQ: THE SCIENCE AND THE POLITICS

Thus far, we've focused almost entirely on the thorny question of *individual differences* (see Prologue) in IQ: Why does measured intelligence differ among people within a population? If you think that what we've discussed so far is controversial, fasten your seat belts. The topic of *group differences* in IQ is perhaps the most bitterly disputed in all of psychology. Here we'll look at what the research says about two group differences in IQ: (1) differences between men and women and (2) differences among races.

As we'll discover, the issues are as emotionally charged as they are scientifically complex. They've also become deeply entangled with politics (Hunt, 1998), with people on differing sides of these debates accusing each other of biases and bad intentions. When evaluating these issues, it's crucial that we try our best to be as objective as possible. That's not always easy, as it requires us to put aside our understandable emotional reactions to examine the scientific evidence.

Sex Differences in IQ and Mental Abilities

In January 2005, then Harvard University President Lawrence Summers created a furor. Speaking at an informal meeting of university faculty from around the country, Summers wondered aloud why there were so few women in the "hard" sciences, like physics, chemistry, and biology. He tentatively proposed a few reasons, one involving discrimination against women and a second involving women's preference for raising families rather than for competing in grueling, cutthroat occupations. But it was Summers's third reason that really got people going. Summers conjectured that perhaps women enter the world with a genetic disadvantage in science and mathematics. Many people were appalled. One prominent woman biologist from the Massachusetts Institute of Technology stormed out of Summers' talk in protest. Within days, hundreds of Harvard faculty members were calling for his head (he resigned shortly thereafter). A firestorm of controversy regarding sex differences in mental abilities followed on the heels of Summers's provocative statements. In this section, we'll do our best to take a scientifically balanced look at the evidence.

Sex Differences in IQ

Do men and women differ in overall IQ? A handful of researchers have recently reported that men have slightly higher IQs than women—perhaps between 3 and 5 points (Jackson & Rushton, 2005; Lynn & Irwing, 2004)—but these claims are controversial, to put it mildly. Indeed, most researchers have found few or no average sex differences in IQ (Jensen, 1998). The best current scientific bet is that males and females are extremely similar, if not identical, in IQ.

Yet average differences don't tell the whole story. Numerous studies indicate that men are more *variable* in their overall IQ scores than women (Hedges & Nowell, 1995). So although men don't appear to have higher average IQs than women, there are more men at both the low and the high ends of IQ bell curve (see **Figure 9.11**). We don't know the reason for this difference; researchers have, not surprisingly, proposed both genetic and environmental explanations.

Sex Differences in Specific Mental Abilities

Even though there's little, if any, difference in overall IQ between men and women, the picture becomes more interesting—and more complicated—when we get to specific mental abilities. Men and women are quite similar when it comes to most intellectual abilities (Hyde, 2005; Maccoby & Jacklin, 1974), but a

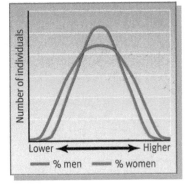

FIGURE 9.11 ■ Distributions of Men and Women in IQ Tests.
The IQ distribution of men is wider than the distribution of women. As a consequence, there are more men than women with both low and high IQ scores and more women with scores in the middle.

closer look reveals some consistent sex differences (Block, 1976; Halpern, 1992; Halpern et al., 2007; Pinker, 2005).

Women tend to do better than men on some verbal tasks, like spelling, writing, and pronouncing words (Feingold, 1988; Halpern et al., 2007; Kimura, 1999). This sex difference may have a hormonal component; even within women, verbal ability seems to ebb and flow along with the level of estrogen, a sex hormone that's more plentiful in women than men. In one study, women were best at quickly repeating tongue twisters (like "A box of mixed biscuits in a biscuit mixer") when their estrogen levels were at their peak (Hampson & Kimura, 1988). On average, females also do better than males in arithmetic calculation, like adding or subtracting numbers, although this difference is present only in childhood (Hyde, Fennema, & Lamon, 1990). Finally, females tend to be better than males in detecting and recognizing feelings in others, especially when they reach adulthood (Hall, 1978; McClure, 2000). For example, they're usually better than men at distinguishing among faces that display different emotions, such as fear and anger. Incidentally, despite popular stereotypes (Brizendine, 2006), there's no good evidence that women talk more than men. A recent study that tracked six samples of men and women in the United States and Mexico found that both sexes speak about 16,000 words per day (Mehr, Vazire, Ramirez-Esparza, Slatcher, & Pennebaker, 2007).

In contrast, men tend to do better than women on most tasks requiring spatial ability (Halpern et al., 2007). Interestingly, one of the largest reported psychological sex differences is in geography, an area of study that relies heavily on spatial ability. Among the 5 million children who've participated in the National Geography Bee, 77 percent have been boys (Zernicke, 2000). Males also tend to do better than females on mathematics tasks that involve complicated reasoning, like deriving proofs in geometry (Benbow & Stanley, 1980). This difference doesn't emerge until adolescence (Hyde et al., 1990). At the extreme tails of the bell curve, this difference is magnified. For example, in one study of students who received scores of 700 or above on the SAT math section, males outnumbered females by 13 to 1 (Benbow & Stanley, 1983). But there are more males than females in the low tail of the test too.

So what's the bottom line? On the one hand, it's possible that some sex differences in mental abilities, such as women's higher scores on certain verbal tasks and men's higher scores on spatial and complex math-solving tasks, are rooted in genes. Indeed, despite many changes in men's and women's roles over the past several decades, sex differences in spatial ability haven't decreased over time (Voyer et al., 1995). Moreover, some studies indicate that excess levels of prenatal testosterone, a hormone of which males have more than females, is associated with better spatial ability (Hampson, Rovert, & Altman, 1998), although not all researchers have replicated this finding.

On the other hand, there's ample reason to suspect that some, perhaps even most, of the sex differences in science and math ability are environmental (Levine, Vasilyera, Lourenco, Newcombe, & Huttenlocker, 2006). For one thing, male and female infants show few or no differences in spatial or counting ability (Spelke, 2005). Even when sex differences in these abilities emerge later in life, they may be due more to sex differences in problem-solving strategies than in inherent abilities. For example, when researchers have encouraged both men and women to solve math problems using spatial imagery (which men usually prefer) rather than verbal reasoning (which women usually prefer), the sex difference in math performance becomes noticeably smaller (Geary, 1996). From 1966 to 2001, the percentage of women entering the "hard" sciences has been increasing steadily. This finding makes us wonder how much of the traditional underrepresentation of women in the "hard" sciences is the result of

Myth: Women are worse drivers than men.

Reality: Men's better average spatial ability than women may have contributed to the popular belief that men are better—and safer—drivers than women. In fact, even when controlling for the fact that men drive more miles than women, men get into about 70 percent more car accidents than women (Meyer, 2006), perhaps because they take more risks when driving.

Men and women tend to differ in how they solve spatial problems.

© Phase4Photography, 2009. Used under license from Shutterstock, Inc.

Earlier in the chapter we learned that heritability doesn't imply that a trait can't be changed. How might this fact bear on Lawrence Summer's comments?

societal factors, such as discrimination and society's expectations concerning women's intellectual strengths and weaknesses. It also makes us wonder what this graph will look like in 10 years. Stay tuned.

Racial Differences in IQ

Perhaps one of the most controversial and troubling findings in the study of intelligence is that average IQ scores differ among races. The differences vary in size but have been replicated multiple times (Loehlin, Lindzey, & Spuhler, 1977). On average, African Americans and Hispanic Americans score lower than Caucasians on standard IQ tests (Hunt & Carlson, 2007; Lynn, 2006; Neisser et al., 1995), and Asian Americans score higher than Caucasians (Lynn, 1996; Sue, 1993). Among Caucasians in the United States, the IQs of Jews are slightly higher than those of non-Jews (Lynn, 2003). The average IQ difference between Caucasians and African Americans, which some researchers have estimated to be as high as 15 points, has received the most attention. What do these differences tell us about the abilities and potential of individuals from different races, and why these differences exist?

Over the years, some sectors of society have attempted to use these findings in a misguided, and at times even malicious, attempt to argue that some races are innately superior to others. There are several serious problems with this claim. First, claims of inherent racial "superiority" lie outside the boundaries of science and can't be answered by data. Scientists can determine only the origins of racial differences, namely, whether they're genetic, environmental, or both. Second, the IQ differences among races may be narrowing over recent decades (Dickens & Flynn, 2006; Hauser, 1998). Third, the variability *within* any given race tends to be considerably larger than the variability *between* races (Nisbett, 1995). This finding means that the distributions of IQ scores for different races overlap substantially (see **Figure 9.12**). As a result, many African Americans and Hispanic Americans have higher IQs than many Caucasians and Asian Americans. The bottom line is clear: We can't use race as a basis for inferring any given person's IQ.

For Whom the Bell Curve Tolls

In 1994, Richard Herrnstein and Charles Murray touched off a bitter dispute among scientists and politicians alike. In their explosive book, *The Bell Curve*, they argued that IQ plays a much more important role in society than most people are willing to admit. People at the upper tail of the IQ bell curve, they maintained, tend to "rise to the top" of the social ladder, because they possess high levels of cognitive skills. As a consequence, they make more money, assume more positions of leadership, and enter more powerful occupations than people at the lower tail.

Had Herrnstein and Murray (1994) stopped there, their book would probably have attracted scant public attention. But they went further, conjecturing that at least some of the IQ gap between races might be genetic in origin. Herrnstein and Murray were hardly the first to make this suggestion (Jensen, 1973; Rushton & Bogaert, 1987). Nevertheless, their claims received unprecedented press coverage, reawakening a bitter debate that had arisen in the 1960s when Arthur Jensen proposed a genetic basis for racial differences in IQ. Jensen's work aroused widespread suspicions of racism, and was even interpreted by some White supremacists as supporting claims that Caucasians are genetically superior to Blacks. J. Phillippe Rushton (1995) also became a controversial figure in the 1980s and 1990s when he offered an evolutionary explanation for racial differences in IQ. Although some researchers have advanced strong arguments for a genetic basis for

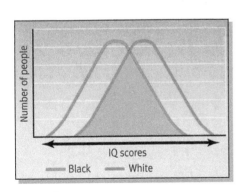

FIGURE 9.12 ■ Diagram of African American and Caucasian Distributions for IQ.
African American and Caucasian IQ distributions differ by an average of 15 IQ points—but they show substantial overlap, as indicated by the shaded area.

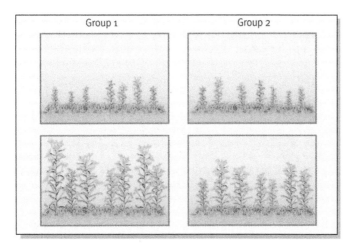

FIGURE 9.13 ▪ Drawings of Two Groups of Plants. These two groups of plants are well matched in height to start, but one outstrips the other over time due to different environmental conditions. This demonstrates how group differences in IQ could be "real" but completely environmentally determined. (*Source:* Based on Lewontin, 1970)

racial differences in IQ, we'll soon discover that the preponderance of evidence supports the idea that racial differences in IQ are largely or entirely environmental in origin. Most likely, these differences stem primarily from the different resources and opportunities available to individuals from different races.

Reconciling Racial Differences

To see why racial differences in IQ don't necessarily imply genetic differences in intelligence or learning potential, let's look at the two groups of plants in the upper panel of **Figure 9.13** (Lewontin, 1970). As we can see, in this "thought experiment" the plants within each group differ in height. These differences in height reflect (at least in part) genetic influences on plants' tendencies to grow and flourish. Note, however, that at this point in the growth cycle, the plants in the two groups are, on average, roughly equal in height. Now let's imagine that we provide one of these groups of plants, in this case the one on the left, with plenty of water and light, but provide the other group with minimal water and light. We twiddle our thumbs and wait a few weeks, and then voila: We now find that the plants on the left are, on average, much taller than the plants on the right. Although the two groups each had equal potential to grow and flourish, environmental influences resulted in one group growing taller than the other.

So what's the take-home message? The difference in height between these groups is *entirely environmental*—it's due to watering and light—so we can't explain the difference between the two groups in genetic terms. In other words, the between-group differences aren't at all heritable. If we think of children as little "human plants" (after all, the word "kindergarten" means "child garden" in German), we can easily imagine that different races begin life with no average genetic differences in IQ. But over time, the cumulative effects of factors such as social deprivation and prejudice may produce a notable difference in IQ between racial groups, one that's entirely environmental in origin.

It's also important to point out that although one group of plants in our example grew taller than the other, one or two individual plants in the shorter group actually grew taller than some plants from the taller group. This point highlights the overlapping distributions of heights in the two groups, demonstrating that

Test bias: Tendency of a test to predict outcomes better in one group than another.

even within a relatively "deprived" group, some plants exceed the growth of some members of the more "privileged" group. This point reminds us why we can't use group differences in IQ to infer the IQ of any given person. Although this example demonstrates that racial differences in IQ *could* be entirely environmental in nature, it doesn't demonstrate that they *are*. We need to look at the scientific evidence for answers to that question.

Test Bias

One popular explanation for race differences in IQ is that the tests are biased against some groups and in favor of others. *Test bias* has a specific meaning for psychologists, which differs from the popular use of the term. In scientific terms, a test isn't biased merely because some groups perform better on it than others. Psychologists don't regard a tape measure as biased, even though men obtain higher average scores than women when we use it to measure height. When psychologists refer to test bias, they mean that a test predicts outcomes—such as grades or occupational success—better in one group than in another (Anastasi & Urbina, 1996). Putting it a bit differently, a biased test means different things in one group than in another. Let's suppose that the correlation between IQ scores and college grade point average (GPA) in Caucasians was .7, as shown in **Figure 9.14a**, but only .25 for Asian Americans, as shown in **Figure 9.14b**. This finding would imply that IQ was a better predictor of GPA in Caucasians than in Asian Americans. In this case, the IQ test would be biased *against* Asian Americans, even though the average IQ scores for that group were higher than those of Caucasians. Thus, average differences between groups *do not* necessarily indicate test bias.

So are IQ tests racially biased? The answer seems to be no (Brody, 1992; Neisser et al., 1995). In almost all studies, researchers have found that the correlations between IQ tests and both academic and occupational achievement are about equal across races (Brody, 1992; Herrnstein & Murray, 1984; Hunter, Schmidt, & Hunter, 1979). This finding leads to the conclusion that IQ differences among races go hand-in-hand with differences in average *achievement* among races. Unfortunately, in U.S. society some races tend to do better in school and have higher-ranking and higher-paying jobs than others. According to some psychologists, the most likely explanation for why both IQ and achievement vary across races is that *society*, not IQ tests themselves, is biased, leading both to differences in IQ test performance and to differences in grades and career achievement among races. For example, African Americans and Hispanic Americans may receive lower scores on IQ tests because of prejudice, inferior schooling, and other environmental disadvantages. These disadvantages, in turn, leave many African and Hispanic Americans less prepared to compete in higher education and the job market. Nevertheless, the finding that IQ tests are also equally correlated with reaction time measures across races suggests that this explanation may not tell the whole story, because these measures are unlikely to be affected by social disadvantage (Jensen, 1980).

Although IQ tests don't appear to be biased in the technical sense, some questions do seem to be biased against people of certain racial or cultural backgrounds. For example, the answer to the question "Who was the prime minister of England during the Second World War?" may be more relevant to some ethnic

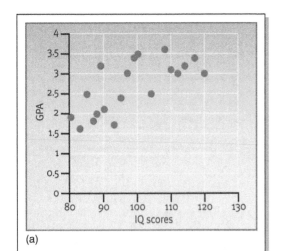

(a)

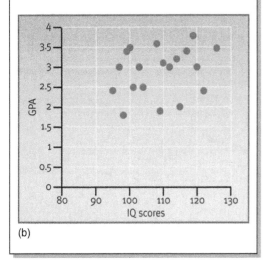

(b)

FIGURE 9.14 ■ Two Scatterplots Representing Test Bias.
These two scatterplots display a made-up example of test bias. In (*a*) IQ scores correlate highly with GPA for Caucasians (.7 correlation), whereas in (*b*) correlations between IQ scores and GPA are much lower for Asian Americans (.25). Even though Asian Americans display higher IQs on average in this example, the test is biased against them because it's a weaker predictor of GPA in that group.

groups than others, especially those in Europe. But surprisingly, we can't always tell whether a test item is biased just by looking at it (Jensen & McGurk, 1987). For example, a number of years ago, test developers adapting an American IQ test for Canadians removed an item asking them to name four U.S. presidents and replaced it with an item asking them to name four Canadian prime ministers. There was only one problem with this reasonable-sounding idea: Canadians did worse on the new question than the old one (Stanovich, 2006).

Some researchers have tried to develop IQ tests that erase or even reverse the racial IQ gap. For example, African American psychologist Robert Williams (1972) developed the Black Intelligence Test of Cultural Homogeneity (BITCH), a measure designed to assess knowledge specific to African American culture. As Williams predicted, African Americans not only did better on the BITCH than on standard IQ tests, but they did better than Caucasians. Although the BITCH received a good deal of attention in the popular press (Williams, 1974), later research showed that it didn't correlate positively with other measures of intelligence (Matarazzo & Weins, 1977).

What Are the Causes of Racial Differences in IQ?

The finding that IQ tests aren't biased means we can't blame the tests for the race gap in IQ, but it doesn't address the question of what's producing this gap. Some researchers have pointed out that IQ is heritable and have argued from this finding that racial differences must be due at least partly to genetic influences. However, this is a faulty conclusion based on a misunderstanding of how the heritability of a trait among individuals *within* a group relates to the heritability of this trait *between* groups.

Within-group heritability is the extent to which a trait, like IQ, is heritable within groups, such as Asian Americans or women. Between-group heritability is the extent to which the difference in this trait between groups, such as between Asian Americans and Caucasians or between men and women, is heritable. It's critical to keep in mind that *within-group heritability doesn't necessarily imply between-group heritability*. That is, just because IQ is heritable within groups doesn't imply that the difference between these groups has anything to do with their genes. Some researchers have confused within-group and between-group heritability, assuming mistakenly that because IQ is heritable within any group such as a race or gender, racial differences in IQ must themselves be heritable (Lilienfeld & Waldman, 2000; Nisbett, 1995). To return to our plant analogy, we must remember that within each, some plants grew taller than others. These differences were caused by differences in the heartiness of the genetic strain of the individual plants within each group. Nevertheless, the differences between the two groups of plants were due entirely to environmental factors, even though within-group differences were due entirely to genes.

So what's the evidence that racial differences in IQ result from environmental and *not* genetic factors? Most of this research comes from analyses of differences between African Americans and Caucasians, and it largely points away from a genetic explanation of racial IQ gaps.

One study conducted in Germany shortly after World War II compared the IQ scores of children of African American soldiers and Caucasian German mothers with the children of Caucasian American soldiers and Caucasian German mothers. In both groups, mothers raised the children, so the societal environment was approximately the same. The IQs of these two groups of children didn't differ (Eyferth, 1961). Thus, the differing race-related genes appeared to have no bearing on children's IQ when environment was roughly equated. Other studies have examined whether African Americans with Caucasian European ancestry obtain a "boost" in IQ relative to those with few European ancestors, which would be expected if racial differences were genetic. The research shows that African Americans with more ancestors of Caucasian descent don't differ significantly in

Within-group heritability: Extent to which the variability of a trait within a group is genetically influenced.

Between-group heritability: Extent to which differences in a trait between groups is genetically influenced.

IQ from those with few or no such ancestors (Nisbett, 1995; Scarr, Pakstis, Katz, & Barker, 1977; Witty & Jenkins, 1934). One group of researchers even found a slight tendency in the opposite direction: African Americans with more Caucasian European ancestry had *lower* IQs (Loehlin, Vandenberg, & Osborne, 1973). In any case, these findings provide no evidence for a genetic explanation of the IQ gap between African Americans and Caucasians.

Another study examined the effect of cross-racial adoption on IQ. This study showed that the IQs of African American children adopted by middle-class Caucasian parents were higher at age 7 than those of either the average African American or Caucasian child (Scarr & Weinberg, 1976). This finding suggests that what appears to be a race-related effect may actually be more related to socio-economic status, because a much higher percentage of African and Hispanic Americans than Caucasians and Asian Americans are living in poverty. A follow-up of these children revealed that their IQs declined over a 10-year period (Weinberg, Scarr, & Waldman, 1992), which may mean that the effects of socioeconomic status are short-lived. Or it may mean that the negative effects (such as discrimination) of being a member of an ethnic minority group in a predominantly Caucasian community gradually counteracts the effects of a changed environment.

Stereotype Threat

> **Stereotype threat:** Fear that we may confirm a negative group stereotype.

One environmental factor that may affect how individuals perform and achieve is **stereotype threat**. Stereotype threat refers to the fear that we may confirm a negative group stereotype, such as a stereotype of our group as less intelligent or less athletic than others. Stereotype threat can create a self-fulfilling prophecy, in which those who are anxious about confirming a negative stereotype actually increase their likelihood of doing so. According to Claude Steele, stereotype threat can impair individuals' performance on IQ tests and standardized tests, like the SAT. Here's his reasoning: If we're members of a group that has a reputation for doing poorly on IQ tests, the mere thought that we're taking an IQ test will arouse stereotype threat. We think, "I'm supposed to do really badly on this test." This belief, Steele (1997) contends, can itself influence behavior, leading some people who would otherwise do well to display reduced performance.

Steele has shown that stereotype threat can indeed depress African Americans' IQ scores, at least in the laboratory. When researchers gave African Americans items from an IQ test but told them the items were measuring something other than IQ, like "the ability to solve puzzles," they performed better than when told the items were measuring IQ (Steele & Aronson, 1995). Also, giving African Americans and Caucasians an in-class writing assignment designed to boost their personal identity—by asking them to identify their most important personal value, like friends, family, or expressing themselves through art—reduced the racial gap in academic performance by 40 percent (Cohen, Garcia, Apfel, & Master, 2006). The meaning of these intriguing findings isn't clear. One possibility is that thinking about what's important to us, or focusing on ourselves as individuals rather than as members of a group, renders us less vulnerable to stereotype threat. The extent to which stereotype threat findings extend beyond the laboratory and generalize to the real world remains an active area of investigation and debate (Stricker & Ward, 2004).

Some researchers (McCarty, 2001) and writers in the popular media (Chandler, 1999) have gone so far as to suggest that racial differences between African Americans and Caucasians on IQ tests are due completely to stereotype threat and self-fulfilling prophecies (Brown & Day, 2006). Nevertheless, most studies suggest that the effects of stereotype threat aren't large enough to account fully for this gap (Sackett, Hardison, & Cullen, 2004).

Research suggests that stereotype threat can lead African American students to perform worse on tests on which they believe members of their race tend to do poorly.

Our discussion leads us to the unsettling conclusion that broader societal differences in resources, opportunities, attitudes, and experiences are probably responsible for much, if not all, of the racial differences in IQ. The encouraging news, however, is that nothing in the research literature implies that racial differences in IQ are unchangeable. If environmental disadvantages can contribute to IQ differences, then eradicating the disadvantages may eliminate these differences.

■ ASSESS YOUR KNOWLEDGE: FACT OR FICTION?

(1) There are few or no sex differences on spatial tasks, such as mental rotation. (True/False)
(2) The IQ difference between African Americans and Caucasians is smaller than the IQ difference within each group. (True/False)
(3) Average differences between groups on a test don't necessarily indicate that the test is biased. (True/False)
(4) Within-group heritability necessarily implies between-group heritability. (True/False)
(5) Stereotype threat may account for part of the IQ difference between African Americans and Caucasians. (True/False)

Answers: (1) F; (2) T; (3) T; (4) F; (5) T

THE REST OF THE STORY: OTHER DIMENSIONS OF INTELLECT

IQ, IQ, and still more IQ. Pretty much everything we've discussed in this chapter presumes that IQ is a good measure of intelligence. Although there's strong evidence that IQ tests are valid indicators of what psychologists call intelligence, it's clear that there's far more than high IQ to living our lives intelligently. Many people without sky-high IQs are wise and thoughtful citizens of society, and many people with sky-high IQs behave in foolish, even disastrous ways. If you have any doubt about the latter, just look at the string of high-profile corporate scandals over the past 10 years, in which well-educated and highly intelligent CEOs got caught red-handed doing remarkably dumb things. We'll conclude the chapter with a survey of other psychological variables that can make us act intelligently—and not so intelligently.

Creativity

By age 54, German composer Ludwig van Beethoven was almost completely deaf. Yet when he reached that age in 1824, he somehow managed to compose his monumental Ninth Symphony, even though while conducting the orchestra performing its world premiere, he couldn't hear a note of it.

"Beethoven's Ninth," as musicologists call it, was astonishing in its originality and brilliance: It was completely unlike any piece of music ever written. No one had thought of composing a symphony more than an hour long (most symphonies were less than half that long), let alone including singers and a full chorus in a musical form that had always been purely instrumental. Nor had anyone been so daring—or brash—as to switch the long-established order of the symphony's traditional four movements, with the slow movement coming third instead of second. As is often the case in response to works of music, art, and literature that break the mold, some critics condemned Beethoven's

© Jeff Mitchell/Reuters/CORBIS

The string of high-profile corporate scandals over the past decade is evidence enough that high IQ doesn't prevent smart and successful people, like the late Enron CEO Ken Lay, from doing foolish and illegal things.

Ninth as too abrasive, too reckless, and too "different." One wrote that the piece "sounds to me like the upsetting of a bag of nails, with here and there also a dropped hammer" (Goulding, 1992). Yet today, many experts consider Beethoven's Ninth Symphony the greatest piece of music ever written.

Beethoven's music personifies creativity. But like Supreme Court Justice Potter Stewart, who defined obscenity by saying, "I know it when I see it" (*Jacobellis v. Ohio*, 1964), psychologists have found creativity easier to identify than define. Nevertheless, most psychologists agree that creative accomplishments consist of two features: they are *novel* and *successful*. When we hear an exceptionally creative piece of music, like Beethoven's Ninth, or see an exceptionally creative painting, we nod our heads and say "Wow, that's amazing. He—or she—got it exactly right."

Psychologists often measure creativity using tests of **divergent thinking** (Guilford, 1967; Razoumnikova, 2000): the capacity to generate many different solutions to problems. For this reason, psychologists sometimes call it "outside the box" thinking. For example, in the "Uses for Objects" test, subjects must generate as many uses for an ordinary object, like a paper clip or a brick, as they can (Hudson, 1967). It's likely, though, that tests of divergent thinking don't capture everything about creativity. To be creative, we also need to be good at **convergent thinking**: the capacity to find the single best answer to a problem (Bink & Marsh, 2000). As two-time Nobel Prize winner Linus Pauling said, to be creative we need to first come up with lots of ideas, and then toss out all the bad ones.

We shouldn't confuse intelligence with creativity: Measures of these two capacities are only weakly or moderately associated, with correlations often in the .2 or .3 range (Furnham, Zhung, & Chamorro Premuzio, 2006; Willerman, 1979). Many intelligent people aren't especially creative, and vice versa.

Highly creative people are an interesting lot. They tend to be emotionally troubled while possessed of high self-esteem. In short, they're not always the easiest folks in the world to get along with (Barron, 1969; Cattell, 1971). Creative individuals also tend to be bold and willing to take intellectual risks (Sternberg & Lubart, 1992). When the Kaufman family asked architect Frank Lloyd Wright to build a house in rural Pennsylvania overlooking a waterfall, they assumed that it would be just another pretty house with a view of flowing water. To their amazement, Wright designed the house not overlooking the waterfall but *over* it, with the water running

Myth: Most creative ideas arrive in sudden flashes of insight.
Reality: Studies of brain activity indicate that well before people report a sudden creative answer to a problem brain areas involved in problem solving (particularly those in the frontal and temporal lobes) have already been active (Kounios et al., 2006).

Divergent thinking: Capacity to generate many different solutions to a problem.

Convergent thinking: Capacity to generate the single best solution to a problem.

Frank Lloyd Wright's architectural masterpiece, "Fallingwater," is a prime example of a remarkable creative achievement. It still stands proudly in rural Pennsylvania.

beneath it! Today, Wright's "Fallingwater," completed in 1937, stands as perhaps the greatest accomplishment in modern American architecture.

There's evidence of a link between creativity and *bipolar disorder*. People with bipolar disorder (once called manic depression) experience episodes of greatly elevated exuberance, energy, self-esteem, and risk taking. They frequently report that their thoughts race through their heads more quickly than they can speak them, and they can go for days without much sleep. During these dramatic bursts of heightened mood and activity (called manic episodes), individuals with bipolar disorder who have artistic talents may become especially productive. Nevertheless, there's not much evidence that their work increases in quality, only quantity (Weisburg, 1994).

Biographical evidence suggests that many great painters such as Vincent van Gogh, Paul Gauguin, and Jackson Pollack; great writers such as Emily Dickinson, Mark Twain, and Ernest Hemingway; and great composers such as Gustav Mahler, Peter Iylich Tchaikovsky, and Robert Schumann, suffered from bipolar disorder (Jamison, 1993; McDermott, 2001). Moreover, studies show that highly creative individuals in artistic and literary professions have higher than expected levels of bipolar disorder and closely related conditions (Andreasen, 1987; Jamison, 1989).

Because they're willing to take intellectual risks, creative people typically fall flat on their faces more often than do uncreative people. Even Beethoven composed a few notable clunkers. Probably the best predictor of the *quality* of a person's creative accomplishments is the *quantity* of that person's output (Simonton, 1999). Extremely creative artists, musicians, and scientists produce far more stuff than other people. Some of it isn't especially good, but much of it is. And every once in a while, some of it is truly great.

Personality, Interests, and Intellect

Think of a friend with strong mathematical and engineering skills, perhaps a classmate who's a wizard with computers. Then think of a friend with a strong penchant for literature, perhaps someone who's a poet or even a fiction writer in her spare time. Do they differ in their personalities and interests? Odds are they do. Research shows that people with different intellectual strengths tend to exhibit different personality traits and interest patterns (Ackerman & Beier, 2003).

Although IQ isn't related to most personality traits, it's moderately and positively associated (a correlation of about .3) O*penness to experience* (DeYoung, Peterson, & Higgins, 2005; Gignac, Stough, & Lovkonitis, 2004). People high in openness to experience are imaginative, intellectually curious, and excited about exploring new ideas, places, and things (Goldberg, 1993). Nevertheless, the link between IQ and openness is more associated with crystallized than fluid intelligence (Ackerman & Heggestad, 1997). We don't fully understand the causal direction here. Higher crystallized intelligence could give rise to greater openness to experience, as people who know more things to begin with may find learning new things to be easier and therefore more enjoyable. Alternatively, greater openness to experience could give rise to greater crystallized intelligence, as people who are intellectually curious may expose themselves to more knowledge and learn more things.

When we get to the level of specific mental abilities, we find that people with different intellectual strengths typically display different intellectual interests. People with high levels of scientific and mathematical ability tend to be especially interested in investigating the workings of nature and often describe themselves as enjoying the practical deeds of everyday life, like balancing checkbooks or fixing things around the house. People with high levels of verbal ability tend to be interested in art and music. And people who are poor at math and spatial ability tend to be especially interested in going into professions that involve helping others (Ackerman & Heggestad, 1997; Ackerman, Kanfer, & Goff, 2005). What we're good at—and not good at—tells us quite a bit about what we like to do.

Emotional Intelligence: Is EQ as Important as IQ?

Emotional intelligence:
Ability to understand our own emotions and those of others, and to apply this information to our daily lives.

Emotional intelligence—the ability to understand our emotions and those of others, and to apply this information to our everyday lives (Goleman, 1995; Salovey & Mayer, 1990)—is one of hottest topics in popular psychology today. People with high "EQs" (emotional quotients) know themselves and know others. Most proponents of emotional intelligence maintain that this ability is just as important as traditional intelligence for effective functioning in the world.

Some items on emotional intelligence tests ask subjects to report how good they are at handling their emotions under stress. Others ask subjects to identify which emotion a face is expressing (a skill on which women usually outperform men, as we've already seen). Still others ask subjects to predict what emotion a person will experience in a given situation, like meeting future in-laws for the first time or being asked an embarrassing question during a job interview (**Figure 9.15**). Many American companies now provide their employees and bosses with formal training for boosting their emotional intelligence (Locke, 2005). Among other things, EQ training seminars teach workers to "listen" to their emotions in making decisions, find better means of coping with stressful job situations, and express empathy to coworkers.

Few would dispute the claim that these are helpful skills on the job. Still, the emotional intelligence concept has its critics. In particular, it's not clear that this concept offers much beyond personality (Matthews, Zeidner, & Roberts, 2002). Most measures of emotional intelligence assess personality traits, such as extraversion, agreeableness, and openness to experience, at least as much they do intelligence (Conte, 1995). Moreover, although advocates of emotional intelligence claim that this concept predicts job performance beyond general intelligence, research suggests otherwise (Van Rooy & Viswesvaran, 2004). Nor is there much evidence that different measures of emotional intelligence are highly correlated (Conte, 1995). The most parsimonious hypothesis is that emotional intelligence isn't anything new, and that it's instead a mixture of personality traits that psychologists have studied for decades.

Why Smart People Believe Strange Things

High levels of intelligence afford no guarantee against beliefs for which there's scant evidence (Hyman, 2002). People with high IQs are at least as prone as other people to beliefs in conspiracy theories, such as the belief that President Kennedy's assassination was the result of a coordinated plot within the U.S. government (Goertzel, 1994) or that the Bush administration orchestrated the September 11 attacks (Molé, 2006). Moreover, the history of science is replete with examples of brilliant individuals holding strange beliefs. Two-time Nobel Prize—winning chemist Linus Pauling, whom we encountered when discussing

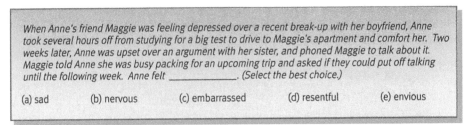

When Anne's friend Maggie was feeling depressed over a recent break-up with her boyfriend, Anne took several hours off from studying for a big test to drive to Maggie's apartment and comfort her. Two weeks later, Anne was upset over an argument with her sister, and phoned Maggie to talk about it. Maggie told Anne she was busy packing for an upcoming trip and asked if they could put off talking until the following week. Anne felt _____. (Select the best choice.)

(a) sad   (b) nervous   (c) embarrassed   (d) resentful   (e) envious

FIGURE 9.15 ■ Item Similar to That on a Test of Emotional Intelligence. How would you do on a test of emotional intelligence? Try your hand at this item, modeled after those on actual emotional intelligence measures. The correct answer is upside-down at the bottom of this page.

Answer to Figure 9.15: d

Even some highly intelligent individuals continue to believe that the Kennedy assassination was the product of an organized conspiracy by the U.S. government despite compelling evidence against this claim.

creativity, insisted that high levels of vitamin C can cure cancer, despite overwhelming evidence to the contrary.

In many cases, smart people embrace odd beliefs because they're adept at finding plausible-sounding reasons to bolster their opinions (Shermer, 2002). IQ is correlated positively with the ability to defend our positions effectively, but correlated negatively with the ability to consider alternative positions (Perkins, 1981). High IQ may be related to the strength of the **ideological immune system:** our defenses against evidence that contradicts our views (Shermer, 2002; Snelson, 1993). We've all felt our ideological immune systems kicking into high gear when a friend challenges our political beliefs (say, about capital punishment) with evidence we'd prefer not to hear. First we first feel defensive, and then we frantically search our mental knowledge banks to find arguments that could refute our friend's irksome evidence. Our knack for defending our positions against competing viewpoints can sometimes lead to confirmation bias, blinding us to information we should take seriously.

Robert Sternberg (2002) suggested that people with high IQs are especially vulnerable to the *sense of omniscience* (knowing everything). Because intelligent people know many things, they frequently make the mistake of thinking they know just about everything. For example, the brilliant writer Sir Arthur Conan Doyle, who invented the character Sherlock Holmes, got taken in by an embarrassingly obvious photographic prank (Hines, 2003). In the 1917 "Cottingley fairies" hoax, two young British girls insisted that they'd photographed themselves along with dancing fairies. Brushing aside the criticisms of doubters, Conan Doyle wrote a book about the Cottingley fairies and defended the girls against accusations of trickery. He'd forgotten the basic principle that extraordinary claims require extraordinary evidence. The girls eventually confessed to doctoring the photographs after someone discovered they'd cut the fairies out of a book (Randi, 1982). Conan Doyle, who had a remarkably sharp mind, may have assumed that he couldn't be duped. Yet, as we've learned throughout this book, none of us is immune from errors in thinking. When intelligent people neglect the safeguards afforded by the scientific method, they'll often be fooled.

Ideological immune system: Our psychological defenses against evidence that contra-dicts our views.

Wisdom

Being intelligent isn't the same as being wise. Indeed, measures of intelligence are only moderately correlated with measures of wisdom (Helson & Srivastava, 2002). Robert Sternberg (2002) defined **wisdom** as the application of intelligence

Wisdom: Application of intelligence toward a common good.

toward a common good. Wise people have learned to achieve a delicate balance among three often-competing interests: (1) concerns about oneself (self-interest), (2) concerns about others, and (3) concerns about the broader society. Wise persons channel their intelligence into avenues that benefit others. To accomplish this end, they come to appreciate alternative points of view, even as they may disagree with them. To a substantial extent, wisdom is marked by an awareness of our biases and cognitive fallibilities (Meacham, 1990). Wisdom sometimes, but by no means always, comes with age (Erikson, 1968).

Abraham Lincoln, although an emotionally troubled man prone to bouts of severe depression (Shenk, 2005), was a wise person who's justifiably regarded as one of America's greatest presidents. He managed to balance his own views about slavery with those of his citizens, rarely making bold political moves until he'd successfully mobilized public opinion in his favor. Lincoln also bent over backward to solicit the views of those who disagreed with him, going so far as to include former opponents in his cabinet (Goodwin, 2005). In all of these cases, Lincoln kept his eye on the ball: the long-term unity of the country. Thanks at least in part to his wisdom, we can today proudly include the word "United" when we say "United States of America."

■ ASSESS YOUR KNOWLEDGE: FACT OR FICTION?

(1) Intelligence and creativity are highly correlated. (True/False)
(2) The work of highly creative people is almost always high in quality. (True/False)
(3) Intelligence and personality aren't entirely independent. (True/False)
(4) People with high IQs are almost always better at considering alternative points of view than people with low IQs. (True/False)

Answers: (1) F; (2) F; (3) T; (4) F

KEY TERMS

Abstract reasoning
Adaptive behavior
   skills
Association fallacy
Bell curve
Between-group
   heritability
Construct
Convergent thinking
Crystallized
   intelligence
Culture-fair IQ tests
Deviation IQ

Divergent thinking
Emotional Intelligence
Eugenics
Fluid intelligence
Flynn effect
g (General intelligence)
Ideological immune
   system
Intelligence quotient
Intelligence test
Mental age
Mental retardation
Multiple intelligences

s (Specific abilities)
Stanford-Binet IQ test
Stereotype threat
Test bias
Triarchic model
Wechsler Adult
   Intelligence Scale
   (WAIS)
Wisdom
Within-group
   heritability

Chapter 9: Intelligence

END OF CHAPTER QUIZ

1. This is a statistical procedure used to make sure everyone is measured on a normal distribution.
   a. Factor Analysis
   b. WAIS
   c. Standardization
   d. Stereotype Threat

2. This IQ test was originally created in the 1950's.
   a. Stanford-Binet
   b. WAIS
   c. Slosson
   d. MMPI

3. This thing is often a factor in gender bias.
   a. Factor Analysis
   b. WAIS
   c. Stanford-Binet
   d. Stereotype Threat

4. This was the first American IQ test.
   a. SAT
   b. WAIS
   c. Stanford-Binet
   d. Army Alpha test

5. A statistical technique used to eliminate social bias from intelligence testing.
   a. Factor Analysis
   b. WAIS
   c. Stanford-Binet
   d. Stereotype Threat

6. The SAT and GRE are forms of intelligence tests.
   a. True
   b. False

7. Psychologists dropped the concept of mental age because it loses its meaning when dealing with adults.
   a. True
   b. False

8. About _____ percent of WAIS scores fall between 85 and 115.
   a. 30
   b. 50
   c. 68
   d. 96

9. Males are most likely to outperform females in a(n):
   a. Spelling bee
   b. Total-number-of-friends in your network test
   c. Short story writing competition
   d. Mental rotation of images test

10. All the men and all the women of the world are going to have a gender-competition. There will be a boxing match, volleyball tournament and a marathon followed by a short story writing contest, spelling bee and EQ test. Who will win, the men or women of the world?
    a. Men
    b. Women
    c. It will be a tie

11. Mary claims that she is intellectually gifted because her IQ is 160. Consequently, she is committing the _____ error.
    a. Heritability
    b. Flynn effect
    c. Reification
    d. Naturalistic fallacy
    e. Savant syndrome

12. Which pair of individuals is most likely to receive similar intelligence test scores?
    a. Same sex fraternal twins
    b. Ordinary siblings of the same sex
    c. A mother and daughter
    d. A father and daughter
    e. Identical twins

13. This term refers to the idea that testing for intelligence and sterilizing those individuals with low IQ scores will improve the overall gene pool.
    a. Eugenics
    b. Social Darwinism
    c. Medical progress
    d. Gene therapy

14. If a test yields consistent results every time it is used, it has a high degree of:
    a. Standardization
    b. Predictive validity
    c. Reliability
    d. Content validity
    e. Heritability

15. The ability to control one's impulses and delay immediate pleasures in pursuit of long-term goals is most clearly a characteristic of:
    a. Emotional intelligence
    b. Heritability
    c. Mental age
    d. Savant syndrome
    e. The g factor

16. What is the Flynn effect?
    a. The rising mean IQ across the 20th century
    b. A failure to measure IQ properly
    c. A validity issue
    d. A reliability issue

17. If your IQ is less than 70 then you AUTO-MATICALLY receive the diagnosis of mental retardation.
    a. True
    b. False

18. IQ will generally increase across years of schooling
    a. True
    b. False

19. Once they are adults, adopted children that lived together will have the same similarity in IQs that unrelated children from different families have.
    a. True
    b. False

20. Psychologists tend to believe that IQ is about:
    a. 0% genetic and 100% environmental
    b. 25% genetic and 75% environmental
    c. 50% genetic and 50% environmental
    d. 75% genetic and 25% environmental

21. Distinguishing that people have different levels of "smartness" is purely a modern concept.
    a. True
    b. False

22. Who coined the terms "eugenics" and "nature versus nurture"?
    a. Darwin
    b. Binet
    c. Galton
    d. Simon
    e. Terman

23. Which of the following people were not involved in the measurement of IQ, the development of IQ tests or the measurement of human intelligence?
    a. Galton
    b. Binet
    c. Terman
    d. Goddard

24. Which of the following people used the original Binet-Simon test to assess the genetic contribution of intelligence?
    a. Goddard
    b. Yerkes
    c. Terman
    d. Galton
    e. A, B & C are correct

25. Which of the following people were not involved in the eugenics movement?
    a. Terman
    b. Goddard
    c. Galton
    d. Binet
    e. Yerkes

26. Eugenics programs were intended to:
    a. Help the sick
    b. Make people physically stronger and more disease proof
    c. Eliminate the weak, sick and diseased
    d. Reduce the need for medical research
    e. Both B & C

27. Just as in our previous discussions of Nature/Nurture, intelligence researchers focus on the ____ of intellectual capacity.
    a. "How much" and "what type"
    b. Biology
    c. Environmental control
    d. Genetic contribution
    e. Learning capacity

28. Which of the following was not given as a definition of intelligence in class or in the textbook?
    a. The measurement of intellectual functioning
    b. The ability to process sensory experiences
    c. The ability to think flexibly with a large information set
    d. The measure from the intelligence test

29. The concept of general intelligence was developed at about:
    a. 1897
    b. 1907
    c. 1917
    d. 1927

30. Which of the following is negatively correlated with age?
    a. Crystallized intelligence
    b. Fluid intelligence
    c. Long term memory
    d. Language ability

31. Most intelligence tests pull information directly from:
    a. Creativity measures
    b. Tests of social functioning
    c. Academic learning
    d. Memory function

32. Which statistical test was used to establish much of modern intelligence theorizing?
    a. ANOVA
    b. T-test
    c. F-test
    d. Factor analysis
    e. Pearson's correlation coefficient

33. At about what time did intelligence testing begin in the U.S.?
    a. 1892
    b. 1902
    c. 1912
    d. 1922

34. Ten-year-old Timmy is as smart as a 15-year-old. What is Timmy's IQ?
    a. 50
    b. 100
    c. 150
    d. 200
    e. 250

35. Why was the mental age measure of IQ eliminated?
    a. Because it does not seem to make any sense with respect to adults
    b. Because the IQs become overly specific in older people
    c. Because the IQs become overly vague in older people
    d. Because they do not work with the mentally retarded

36. Why do most modern IQ tests have a mean of 100?
    a. To give room enough to move up or down
    b. Because the mental age scale set average IQs at 100
    c. It was an arbitrary selection unrelated to anything
    d. Because when you do well on an academic test you get a "100"

37. Which of the following tests was not created by David Wechsler?
    a. Stanford-Binet
    b. WAIS
    c. WIAT
    d. Wonderlic
    e. Both A & D

38. The Wonderlic IQ test only takes about ____ minutes to complete.
    a. 5
    b. 15
    c. 30
    d. 45

39. Which of the following tests measures the likelihood that you will do well in a particular area of endeavor?
    a. WAIS
    b. Wonderlic
    c. Aptitude
    d. Achievement

40. Essentially, the process of test standardization today is the same process used nearly 100 years ago.
    a. True
    b. False

41. Which range of IQ scores below reflects typical "average" intelligence?
    a. 95–105
    b. 85–115
    c. 70–130
    d. 55–145

42. An accurately measured IQ of 110 at age 16 essentially guarantees that at age 70 this person will have an IQ of 110.
    a. True
    b. False

43. Most savants have a broad range of severe intellectual deficits.
    a. True
    b. False

44. The idea that physical or behavioral traits may be acquired through genetics.
    a. Nurture
    b. Eugenics
    c. Heritability
    d. Intelligence

45. Which of the following would constitute a family-study of intelligence?
    a. Measuring the similarity in intelligence between adoptees
    b. Measuring the similarity in intelligence between twins only
    c. Measuring the similarity in intelligence between siblings, first cousins and second cousins
    d. None of the above

46. Twin studies of intelligence attempt to determine the:
    a. Degree of similarity of intelligence between twins and adoptees
    b. Degree of similarity of intelligence between twins, triplets, etc.
    c. Degree of genetic similarity between twins and adoptees
    d. None of the above

47. Which of the following would constitute a twin-study of intelligence?
    a. Measuring the similarity in intelligence between adoptees
    b. Measuring the similarity in intelligence between triplets
    c. Measuring the similarity in intelligence between siblings, first cousins and second cousins
    d. None of the above

48. Adoption studies of intelligence attempt to determine the:
    a. Degree of similarity of intelligence between twins and adoptees
    b. Degree of similarity of intelligence between adoptees and the members of their adoptive families
    c. Degree of genetic similarity between twins and adoptees
    d. None of the above

49. Which of the following would constitute an adoption-study of intelligence?
    a. Measuring the similarity in intelligence between adoptees and their non-biological siblings
    b. Measuring the similarity in intelligence between twins
    c. Measuring the similarity in intelligence between siblings, first cousins and second cousins
    d. None of the above

50. Which of the following statements is TRUE?
    a. Parents with lower IQs tend to have larger families
    b. Parents with higher IQs tend to have larger families
    c. Parents with lower IQs tend to have smaller families
    d. None of the above

Answers: 1. c; 2. b; 3. d; 4. c; 5. a; 6. a; 7. a; 8. c; 9. d; 10. c; 11. c; 12. e; 13. a; 14. c; 15. a; 16. a; 17. b; 18. a; 19. a; 20. c; 21. b; 22. c; 23. b; 24. e; 25. d; 26. e; 27. a; 28. a; 29. d; 30. b; 31. c; 32. d; 33. c; 34. c; 35. a; 36. b; 37. e; 38. b; 39. c; 40. a; 41. b; 42. b; 43. b; 44. c; 45. c; 46. b; 47. b; 48. b; 49. c; 50. a

10 *Personality*

The Spread of Psychological Constructs through Society

In the public dissemination of scientific theories, you sometimes hear about wormholes in space or alternate dimensions populated with evil versions of ourselves. These concepts are often presented as though it were certain they existed. Do they exist? Well, if you ask your physics professor, I think you will get a more carefully balanced view of wormholes and alternate dimensions. Both wormholes and alternate dimensions are constructs; things which may exist only if a very select set of theorized conditions truly exists. Constructs exist in all areas of science. Just like physics, psychology is full of constructs. If the mainstream media popularizes those constructs then it may come to pass that people will begin to believe they are things that truly exist.

Many of the most popularized psychological constructs come from the field of personality psychology. Personality has been a psychological construct since the end of the 19th century. Sigmund Freud popularized personality before his death in 1939. Freud's influence on the field of personality—and psychology in general—cannot be understated. Many psychological constructs people use in everyday speech have come from Freud's theory of development. Such terms include id, ego, superego, repression, sublimation, complex, and fixation. Probably the most commonly used phrase is "being anal" which generally implies that you are obsessive about doing something (e.g., Susan is really anal about keeping her house clean).

Other concepts that also come from early 20th century psychologists are related to projective personality tests. The test you most likely recognize is the Rorschach test. Hermann Rorschach first developed this test in 1921. It consists of ten inkblots that are shown to the subject in succession. The subject is expected to look at this abstract image and give their opinion of what it looks like to them. There are no correct or incorrect answers in the Rorschach test. Rorschach expected that the answers given by his subjects simply reflected their personality. Therefore, the Rorschach is known as a projective personality test. If the test worked the way it was envisioned to, then the same inkblot would cause a fearful subject to imagine bats and devils whereas a happy person imagines flowers and sunshine.

The attempts of Freud and Rorschach to understand personality must be understood within the context of their time period. The early 20th century included a much smaller database of knowledge than exists today and so their ideas may seem simplistic and sometimes rather bizarre. One issue to keep in mind, however, is that Freud and Rorschach were dealing with psychological constructs. Constructs do not necessarily exist; they depend on the validity of the theoretical assumptions that created them. One way to understand these odd constructs is through a quote by Lewis Carroll, the author of *Alice in Wonderland*; "If there were an invisible cat in that chair, the chair would look empty; but the chair does look empty. Therefore there is an invisible cat in it." Well, maybe personality is not a *thing* after all.

References
Carroll, L. (1865/1993). Alice's Adventures in Wonderland. New York: Dover.

Myers, D. G. (2007). *Psychology*. New York: Worth.

CHAPTER OUTLINE

Objectives

After reading this chapter, you should be able to do the following:

What Is Personality?

- ▨ Identify the characteristics of the trait approach, psychoanalytic approach, phenomenological approach, and social learning approach to personality.
- ▨ Understand Salvatore Maddi's definition of personality.

The Trait Approach

- ▨ Identify the differences between the idiographic and nomothetic approaches.
- ▨ Distinguish between cardinal, central, and secondary traits.
- ▨ Discuss L-data, Q-data, and T-data.
- ▨ Explain the basic logic of factor analysis.
- ▨ Describe introversion-extroversion, emotionality-stability, and psychoticism.
- ▨ Identify the "big five" personality traits.

Heredity and Traits

- ▨ Identify the research strategies used to study the role heredity plays in personality.
- ▨ Understand how social anxiety could have evolved as a trait.
- ▨ Recognize how birth order could be an environmental factor influencing personality.

Do Traits Predict Behavior?

- ▨ Discuss the concept of traits.
- ▨ Understand Mischel's concept of personality coefficient.

The Origins of Freud's Theory

- Identify and describe the three systems of personality.
- Explain why Freud's theory is called psychodynamic.

Freud's Model of the Mind

- Describe conscious, preconscious, and unconscious.

Personality Development

- Identify the stages of psychosexual development.
- Explain the concept of fixation and describe the oral, anal, and phallic stages.
- Define defense mechanism, and explain the concepts of repression, denial, projection, reaction formation, and rationalization.

Rogers and the Phenomenological Perspective

- Describe the phenomenological approach.
- Define self-actualization.
- Describe what Rogers meant by the self-concept.

Social Learning Theory

- Describe the locus of control and reciprocal determinism.

Personality Tests

- Describe the Thematic Apperception Test (TAT).
- Identify the differences between objective and projective tests.

PREVIEW

One of the most fascinating and intriguing topics to people are the personalities of the people with whom we interact. All of us can undoubtedly recall discussing, or at least thinking about, the personalities of people we work with, go to school with, are neighbors with, and so forth. In fact, one of the more exquisite pleasures in life is the excitement in discovering the personality of someone we're attracted to. This process may not always lead to what we had dreamed of or hoped for, but it is fun nonetheless. It doesn't take a genius to recognize why people are so fascinated with the personalities of others—they have an important impact on our lives. But beyond that, people are interesting in their own right, at least it seems so to most of us. Talk show hosts count on it to make a living.

For psychologists, the concept of personality leads to several interesting questions. Psychologists have put considerable effort into trying to define it and understand how it is developed, how it should be measured, how it can be molded, and even whether or not it exists. Psychologists, like ordinary people, also find it useful to study personality as a way to better understand, predict, and control the behavior of others. You may have had the very same motivations when trying to understand the personality of someone you knew. The questions you and psychologists have about personality are essentially the same, although psychologists will attempt to answer these questions more systematically and with more precision.

This chapter will describe four orientations that psychologists use to address the issues mentioned above in some detail, as well as a fifth approach, the behavioral approach, in less detail. The challenge you face in reading this chapter is to understand how the psychological terms that psychologists use represent experiences you have already had. If you can learn to describe those experiences with the psychological terms discussed in this chapter, you will begin to sound more like a psychologist and an educated person in the field.

WHAT IS PERSONALITY?

This chapter is about personality. But what do psychologists mean when they talk about the concept of personality? To try to get a grip on the way psychologists think about personality I am going to ask you to use your imagination and memory a little—don't worry; this won't be hard. Take a moment and think about your professors. What comes to mind? Now be careful; keep it clean. Maybe I should be more specific.

If you compare your professors' similarities and differences, do they seem more similar than different, or do their differences seem greater than their similarities? As you think about their characteristics, undoubtedly some qualities about each stand out, distinguishing them from each other (energy level, friendliness, leniency, etc.), whereas other qualities seem to overlap and are more or less common to all the professors you have (boring, knowledge-able, nerdy, etc.).

As we work toward an understanding of personality, it is important to note that there are alternative explanations other than personality alone that could account for the differences and similarities we see among people. The age of your professors could account for differences in energy levels and friendliness; some of your professors are in their 20s; others are in their 60s. Thus, it may not be so much their internal personal characteristics as their age that led to the differences.

In regard to the similarities, they are, after all, professors, and scholarship is their business—hardly an arena in which a person's sensation-seeking, rugged physical adroitness is going to be highlighted, but who knows? I'll bet there are professors who roller blade, scuba dive, and skydive.

Because age and occupation could account for the differences and similar-ities you observed among your professors, let's draw another sample of people who are similar in age but not in the same occupation. Think of your friends and acquaintances from high school. I'll bet there were some real characters there—people you will never forget (and no one else would either). There were people you really liked, admired, respected, wanted to be like, and so forth, as well as people you loathed, others you avoided, and still others you just couldn't understand. When you think of these people you can see similarities and differences among them.

My guess is that your recollection of your high school classmates provides you with a rich source of diverse personalities. You recall certain people because one or two characteristics really stand out when you think of them. They may have been very loud and pushy, or so shy and retiring that you're not sure that you ever heard them speak. Others you recall as having some unique quality that set them apart from your classmates in a subtler, more endearing way. For example, maybe there was someone in a totally different social group (clique) from your own. Imagine further that you had little or no respect for what this clique represented, but you had one experience with a person from that clique that set this person apart and above the other members, causing you to wonder why he or she would ever hang out with "those people." For some individuals, the thought of a trait, like sincerity or cruelty, brings a person to mind because that is what he or she "is." In other words, the essence of the person is captured by this trait.

The unique characteristics of some of your high school classmates make them easy to remember.

There may have been others who just seemed to have it all together; they had a balance and symmetry to their personality. It is not that they possessed any single outstanding quality, but their personality seemed so well organized and integrated that you couldn't help but think they were cool. At the other extreme, there were those who made you wonder if they ever had any insight or awareness as to what was motivating their actions.

Some of your old high school friends probably haven't changed since grade school. They have seemed to like, act, and do the same things as long as you have known them. And yet there are others where the changes are so great that it is hard to comprehend. Hopefully, as you thought about your former classmates, it not only put a nostalgic smile on your face, but, at an intuitive level, you began to see that there are many ways to think about and approach the concept of personality. In fact Gordon Allport (1937) reported there were 50 different definitions of personality.

For our purposes we are going to group the concepts and definitions of personality into four major approaches: (1) trait approach, (2) psychodynamic approach, (3) phenomenological approach, and (4) social learning approach.

The Psychodynamic Approach

The psychodynamic approach is not concerned with identifying traits that distinguish us from each other, but how a common core to personality provides a foundation and starting point from which an individual's personality emerges. Freud's theory is such an approach. The common core from which personality develops is the life-sex and death instincts. Instinctual frustration and gratification mold personality, particularly early in life; that is, how our basic biological needs for food, sex, and nurturing are satisfied or frustrated in childhood determines what we are like as adults. Instincts provide an integrating and organizational force within the person and give coherence to our actions. Ultimately, all of our actions are in some way tied to instinctual gratification. Instincts are so basic and fundamental, however, that sometimes it is hard to see the deeper meaning and roots of our actions. It may be unclear how any specific action could be tied to anything other than the immediate situation, but more often than not, actions are ultimately a reflection of internal instinctual processes, operating below our awareness in the unconscious. Often there is a struggle among competing forces within our unconscious to determine which force will be expressed in our behavior. The interpretation of these unconscious processes is what Freud called psychoanalysis.

The Phenomenological Approach

Personality is what makes us unique, not like anyone else. Our experiences are unique to us and can never be experienced in exactly the same way by anyone other than ourselves. Our experiences don't come to us—we choose them, and with this freedom comes the opportunity to make the wrong choice. I don't mean "wrong" in the sense that the choice worked out badly, like a bad date or investment, but "wrong" in the sense that the choice did not complement or fit your uniqueness. In other words, it wasn't "you." The wise choice is the one that allows people to be themselves and move toward becoming who they really are; this is often referred to as self-actualization. If people live a life that is inconsistent with who they really are for too long, they become distressed and anxious, as well as confused about their identity and what they want out of life. For example, imagine a mother who, out of a sense of duty to her family or to get the attention of her husband and children, subordinates her choices to those of her family members. In other words, she lives for them, not herself. She does things they like to do, goes places they like to go, and avoids activities that would be uninteresting to them, even though she might like them. If she does this long enough, her sense of self is at odds with her experience, and the resulting confusion about the true nature of who she is can be quite distressing. However, she can regain the capacity to make choices that feel right for her. To do so she needs to experience what Rogers (1965) calls unconditional positive regard. In this atmosphere of approval, the person feels free to explore the choices that optimize his or her experiences and thus provide insight into his or her identity. This approach, referred to as the humanistic approach, emphasizes free will, phenomenology (i.e., immediate experience), and the movement toward your identity or self (i.e., self-actualization).

The Social Learning Approach

The social learning approach emphasizes how people think about their behavior. It is frequently referred to as the social cognitive approach to personality. While social learning theory can trace its roots back to behaviorism, it is in some ways a reaction to it. Social learning theorists argue that not only do people think about their behavior, but in many instances behavior follows from the person's thoughts. Social learning theorists concentrate not only on how our thinking affects behavior but also on how the thoughts and actions of people shape their environments.

Personality: A Definition

For those of us who are compelled in such ways we will offer a single definition of personality before we proceed on to the discussion of different approaches. The definition we have chosen—and remember there are many others—is that of Salvatore Maddi. His definition is as follows: "Personality is a stable set of characteristics and tendencies that determine those commonalities and differences

Working in a job or career that is inconsistent with who you are can be distressing.

in the psychological behavior (thoughts, feelings, and actions) of people that have continuity in time and that may or may not be easily understood in terms of the social and biological pressures of the immediate situation alone" (1972, p. 9). For Maddi, personality can be what is left after the effects of the situation and biology have been accounted for; it is the person, or at least the person's personality, devoid of environmental and biological influence. He believes personality is relatively stable, which gives consistency to a person's behavior, and that it changes rather slowly. Further, he believes personality is represented through behavioral tendencies that create differences and similarities among individuals.

THE TRAIT APPROACH

The first approach we want to talk about is the trait approach. This is the common-sense approach to personality, the approach we use when we talk about other people. If someone asks you about your teacher, you are likely to say she or he is charming, witty, charismatic, intelligent, and a snappy dresser, or something like that. (Hey, it could happen!) The point is, you are describing the person in terms of his or her traits. Traits serve as summaries for behavior. The differences are in terms of degree (some of us are more sociable, some of us are harder workers, etc.), but the qualities themselves are possessed by all of us; we just differ in the amount we possess. The observations you have made of your teacher's behavior have led you to conclude that she or he possess the characteristics mentioned previously, or some others similar to them. These qualities and characteristics give our behavior continuity and consistency across situations and over time. For example, if we are generous, we are so with friends, strangers, money, time, and other commodities. Furthermore, we tend to be generous throughout our lives—as children we shared our toys, as adults we lent our tools to neighbors, and in old age we were generous with our grandchildren.

Traits, like personality itself, are **theoretical constructs**. They don't actually exist in a physical, tangible sense but rather are shorthand summaries for describing behavior. It is easier to say that someone is easy-going than to

Theoretical constructs: Inferred concepts used to explain behavior.

describe several specific instances when an individual did not react with anger or anxiety to a mild calamity. Besides, most people aren't going to want to take the time to listen to a step-by-step description of the details of each incident. Allport (1966) disagrees with the idea that traits don't exist in a real physical sense, believing that, they are, in fact, real. Who knows? It may be that he turns out to be correct. As more knowledge about both brain structure and function are obtained, specific areas of the brain may be identified and related to specific traits. It is already known that the left hemisphere plays a more active role in positive emotions and the right hemisphere in negative emotions (Davidson, 1993). Eventually we may know what area of the brain is responsible for various traits such as shyness.

Allport: The Idiographic and the Nomothetic Approaches

Idiographic approach:
Studying individuals intensely rather than trying to find universal traits possessed by everyone.

G.W. Allport, an early trait theorist, is distinguished from many of the later trait theorists and researchers in his choice of methodology. He argued for the idiographic approach. Allport felt that by focusing on individual subjects, he could identify the traits unique to the individual that wouldn't necessarily apply to all people. Although he made use of the questionnaire and large samples, he advocated research methods similar to those used in a study he conducted with Vernon on expressive behavior (Allport & Vernon, 1933). In that study, Allport and Vernon used many subtle measures, like writing pressure and gesturing during speech, to examine the intensity with which people expressed themselves. He believed this idiographic methodology provided a deeper and better understanding of the individual than did the nomothetic approach.

Nomothetic approach:
Measuring large numbers of people to see where they are different and where they are similar.

The nomothetic approach assumes individuals all possess essentially the same traits, just to varying degrees; that is, some people are high on a trait, others are low, and most people are somewhere in between. The nomothetic approach focuses on discovering those traits common to all people, albeit to varying degrees.

Allport believed traits were not equally applicable to all people. Some traits were unique to the individual and possessed by only him or her, and other traits were insignificant or nonexistent in their influence on behavior. He did believe, however, that the universe of possible traits could be determined from our vocabulary. Allport and Odbert (1936) found 18,000 words that could be used to describe people. With so many ways of describing a person, it's possible that intense scrutiny of a single individual might yield some traits applicable only to that individ-ual, and not to others. In an attempt to explain how traits were organized within the individual, Allport (1937) developed a categorization scheme to classify personality traits based on a trait's relative influence on personality:

Cardinal traits: Almost everything a person does is tied to this trait.

Cardinal traits are so dominating that almost everything the person does is tied to that trait. For example, a political leader may be so consumed with getting and holding on to power that every activity engaged in is done in the service of power. Whether the leader acts friendly or distant is not the result of sincere feeling, but because of some advantage to be gained from who his or her friends are. Recreational activities are chosen, not because of the inherent enjoyment in these activities, but for the photo opportunity to ensure she or he remains in the public eye. Very few people possess cardinal traits.

Central traits: Highly characteristic of the person.

Central traits are the 5 to 10 traits that are highly characteristic of the individual. As Carducci (1998) points out, it is what you might see in a letter of recommendation or hear in the description of a potential blind date. These are the most salient characteristics and are the backbone traits of an individual's personality.

Secondary traits are less important because they generally do not show up in a person's behavior. They appear only in very specific situations, for instance, weepiness and melancholy when a person is tired.

Secondary traits: Show up only in specific instances.

Cattell and the Factor Analytic Approach

R.B. Cattell was also a trait theorist, but unlike Allport, he emphasized the nomothetic method. He attempted to discover the universal traits that are part of everyone's personality. Differences among people, he believed, were not due to the operation of unique traits possessed by different individuals but to variations in the amount of a trait possessed by all individuals. That is, one person may be more reserved, serious, and trusting than another, but these are differences in degree, not in the traits possessed by the individuals.

Cattell's goal was to "discover" the basic traits that are an inherent part of everyone's personality. He called these basic traits source traits, because they were the source of behavioral differences among people. To determine these source traits, Cattell advocated the use of three kinds of data:

Source traits: Basic traits inherent in everyone's personality.

1. **L-data:** subject's life record
2. **Q-data:** subject's self-ratings on various questionnaires
3. **T-data:** subject's response to created/contrived situations

Cattell would analyze these various forms of data, sometimes in combination with the other forms and sometimes by themselves, with a technique called factor analysis. The correlation coefficient that you learned about earlier is the basic workhorse of this method. The logic of factor analysis is to try to identify which traits cluster together in distinct groups, such that all of the traits in a group are related to one another but not to any of the traits in another group. By examining the correlations among several variables, a researcher can tell which group of variables have positive correlations (change in the same direction), which group of variables have a negative correlations (change in the opposite direction), and which variables are uncorrelated (show no predictable pattern of change).

A trait such as sociable has a positive correlation with other traits like outgoing and talkative.

For example, if a teacher was asked to rate her students on a trait questionnaire, some students might receive high ratings on the following group of variables: loud, domineering, talkative, and sociable. Each of these traits would be positively correlated with each of the others, so a high rating on one would be indicative of a high rating on the others. As you might expect, when ratings on these traits were correlated with the ratings on the traits shy, quiet, deferent, and aloof, negative correlations were obtained. People receiving high scores on loud, domineering, talkative, and sociable were getting low scores on shy, quiet, deferent, and aloof. When the correlations among shy, quiet, deferent, and aloof are examined, we see they are all positive. People getting a high score on one trait, like shyness, tend to get high scores on the traits deferent, aloof, and quiet as well. So it appears that two groups of traits tend to go together. One group of traits—loud, domineering, talkative, and sociable—are positively correlated with each other, as are the group shy, quiet, deferent, and aloof. But the traits from these two groups are negatively correlated with each other. Both groups of traits were uncorrelated with traits like neatness and artistic ability.

Factor analysis: Allows the researcher to see if variables share enough in common that they could be summarized with a single label.

© 2009 by Yuri Arcurs. Used under license of Shutterstock, Inc.

It appears that each group of positively related traits share something in common that set them apart from traits that they are either uncorrelated or negatively correlated with.

If you list the two groups of traits that are positively correlated with one another, do you think you could come up with a name that would summarize and represent each list reasonably well?

List 1	List 2
loud	shy
talkative	quiet
domineering	deferent
sociable	aloof

How about the trait names of extrovert for list 1 and introvert for list 2? They seem to capture, in a general way, the traits clustering together in each of the lists. This is the logic of factor analysis, and it was the technique Cattell (1973) used to identify the 16 underlying source traits he believes distinguish people from each other. After identifying these 16 traits, Cattell went on to develop what is called the Sixteen Personality Factors Questionnaire (16PF) to measure these traits precisely. His approach was atheoretical in the sense that he had no preconceived notions as to what traits would be found when he factor analyzed his data.

The next theorist/researcher we want to briefly cover, Hans Eysenck, started with some beliefs about what factors/traits are fundamental to the study of individual differences.

He used factor analysis to refine his measurements of these basic traits, rather than discover them.

Extroverts are more likely to seek the company of others, enjoy talking, and are more spontaneous, outgoing, and willing to take risks.

© Yuri Arcurs, 2009. Used under license from Shutterstock, Inc.

Eysenck's Three-Factor Solution

Following the lead of ancient thinkers and physicians (e.g., Hippocrates and Galen), Eysenck (1967) believed three major factors underlie all variations in personality. Summaries of these three factors follow:

1. **Introversion-extroversion**—Those who are introverted tend to show less social interest and are more reserved and controlled, whereas extroverts are more likely to seek the company of others, enjoy talking, and are more spontaneous, outgoing, and willing to take risks.
2. **Emotionality-stability**—Neuroticism is often substituted for emotionality. A person high in emotionality is apprehensive, self-doubting, troubled, self-conscious, insecure, and moody. The stable person is relaxed, not easily rattled, flexible, and comfortable with himself or herself.
3. **Psychoticism**—Psychoticism is the tendency toward insensitiveness, cruelty, and lack of caring toward others.

Eysenck (1967) has argued that the differences observed in those who are introverted and those who are extroverted can be tied to their level of brain arousal. Introverts' level of brain stimulation is much higher than that of extroverts; they avoid external sources of stimulation (e.g., wild parties and noisy crowds), which are overwhelming given their already high state of arousal. Extroverts, because they are starting at a lower point of internal arousal, don't find other people and lively circumstances overwhelming, but instead find them stimulating and thus seek them out.

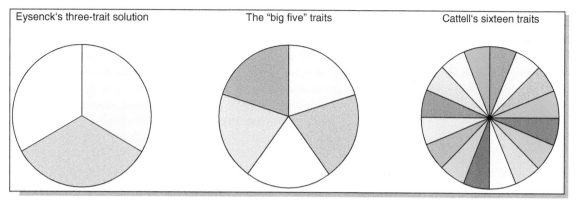

FIGURE 10.1 ▓ The number of traits Eysenck, the "big five" theorists, and Cattell believe are needed to describe personality.

The "Big Five"

How many traits are needed to describe a person? Cattell believes 16, Eysenck says 3, and Allport doesn't specify a number because he believes some traits can be unique to the individual and thus the number can vary from person to person **(Figure 10.1)**. Many current trait theorists who rely on the factor analytic method believe the number is five. This number is not arbitrarily chosen; it is based on the consistency with which they appear across a wide range of studies. Carver and Scheier (1996) point out that five factors have emerged in the following situations:

1. Different measures of personality have been used.
2. Diverse samples have been studied.
3. Different cultures have been tested.

This evidence has led to the conclusion that openness, conscientiousness, extroversion, agreeableness, and neuroticism are the "big five" of personality (Goldberg, 1981). **Table 10.1** lists the "big five" personality factors and some of the characteristics associated with each of the factors.

Heredity and Traits

There has been a long history of linking personality to biological characteristics. Hippocrates argued that body fluids were the determinant of temperament. He believed, for example, that an excessive amount of blood was related to cheerfulness. Gall, a German physician, believed that different bump patterns on the skull were indicative of different personalities. More recently, Sheldon (1942) reported very strong correlations between body type and personality. Thin, frail bodies (ectomorph) were often associated with nervous introverts; soft, round bodies (endomorph) with relaxed, comfort-seeking sociable individuals; and muscular strong bodies (mesomorph) with adventurous risk-seeking types. These approaches have pretty much fallen by the wayside and are not given much credence today.

TABLE 10.1 ▓ The "Big Five" Personality Factors and Associated Characteristics

1. **Openness:** intellectual interest, nonconforming, imaginative, curious
2. **Conscientiousness:** organized, thorough, responsible, persevering
3. **Extroversion:** sociable, talkative, assertive, energetic
4. **Agreeableness:** sympathetic, appreciative, kind, considerate
5. **Neuroticism:** guilt-prone, troubled, apprehensive, vulnerable

Some breeds of dog are known for their aggressive behavior.

Research Strategies Relating Heredity to Personality

The role heredity plays in shaping our personality has become an important and prominent area of research in modern-day psychology. An obvious example of the role genes play in the expression of personality can be seen from the effects of selective breeding in dogs. Dogs can be bred not only to achieve specific physical characteristics (e.g., size, speed) but also to achieve certain behavioral or personality characteristics. In fact, some dog breeds are known as much for their personality/behavioral characteristics as for their physical attributes. For example, Labrador Retrievers are known for their friendly, cheerful disposition; pit bulls, for their aggressiveness; and so forth. Although no one would want to selectively breed humans to examine the role genes play in determining personality, other methods can be used to address this issue.

One strategy involves comparing pairs of identical twins (twins with exactly the same genetic makeup), with fraternal twins (twins who, on average, share half of their genetic material) on an attitude or personality measure. (It is important to keep in mind that for each pair of twins it is assumed that their environments are very similar because they are growing up in the same household.) The scores on a personality measure for each group of twins are then correlated. If the identical twins have a statistically significant higher correlation than do the fraternal twins, it is argued that it must be due to their similar genetic structure. After all, the only difference between the groups was the proportion of genes they shared. As it turns out, identical twins are much more likely to hold the same attitudes toward sex, religion, and the death penalty than are fraternal twins (Tesser, 1993). Their vocational and personal interests are more similar, as are their chances for divorce (Lykken, Bouchard, McGue, & Tellegen, 1993; McGue & Lykken, 1992, respectively).

Other strategies have compared how well the personality scores of adopted children correlate with those of their adoptive parents and their biological parents. If the scores correlate higher with their adoptive parents, it is argued that environment played a larger role in shaping personality, but if they correlate higher with their biological parents, heredity must have played the more important role. Loehlin, Willerman, and Horn (1985) found that adopted children were more similar to their biological parents and siblings than to their adoptive parents and siblings, on measures of sociability and activity level.

A somewhat related strategy is when identical twins raised apart are compared with identical and fraternal twins raised together. It would be expected that identical twins raised together should be more similar because they shared the same environment as well as the same genes. But, as it turns out, identical twins raised together are no more similar on measures of personality than twins raised apart. Also both groups of identical twins are more similar than fraternal twins raised together (Carver & Scheier, 1996). Examination of the studies using all these methods suggest that about 40 to 50 percent of the difference in personality is genetically determined (Bouchard, 1994; Loehlin, 1992; Tellegen et al., 1988). To the extent that traits are inherited, what mechanism determines what traits are there to inherent? In other

Identical twins are much more likely to hold the same attitudes toward sex, religion, and the death penalty than fraternal twins.

words, what is the source from which human traits emerge? Many argue (Baumeister & Tice, 1990; Hogan, 1983) that evolution is the source and mechanism by which human traits emerge. Personality theorists with an evolutionary perspective point to anxiety as an evolved trait.

At first it might be hard to fathom how such a disruptive experience as anxiety could be useful for survival. Recall that evolutionary theory argues that traits (physical or psychological) that increase the chances of survival are more likely to be passed on and be spread into the population. Some psychologists have argued that one of the primary causes of anxiety is social exclusion (Baumeister & Tice, 1990). It has been argued that in order to survive, humans need to be accepted by others for their mutual protection, to cooperate with each other for their mutual benefit, and to share resources, responsibilities, and so forth. Therefore, anything that would threaten a person's social status or acceptance would create anxiety. Recall, for example, in middle school or high school how concerned you were with appearance and popularity, or on the first few days of a new job how concerned you were with identifying the social position or status of your fellow employees, as well as the rules appropriate conduct. Even in ancient times, one of the worst punishments was to be banished from the tribe, city-state, or group. Therefore, people have become sensitive to the cues that signal rejection and social disapproval, because at some primitive level, people recognize that social ostracism is a threat to survival.

It is easy to overestimate the role of heredity when examining the findings of these studies. The environment does appear to play a large role in shaping personality, but a surprisingly small effect is exerted from the family in creating similarity among siblings. This may not come as that much of a surprise to parents who have marveled at the differences in their offspring. Despite the best efforts of parents to treat their children the same with regard to issues of discipline and fairness, the children, nonetheless, differed greatly from each other. This may not be that surprising to you; just think how different you seem from your brothers and sisters. It appears that the family has little impact in creating similarity among children.

Birth order appears to influence personality development.

The impact of the environment is at the individual level (Carver & Scheier, 1996). Siblings have different friends; different school experiences; and different kinds of relationships with their parents, teachers, and each other. These are the environmental influences that appear to affect personality, so the assumption that growing up in the same family will make people similar is a fallacy.

Birth order is a perfect example. You have siblings who are from the same family, but the order of their birth acts to create differences in their personalities—not similarities (Sulloway, 1996). According to Sulloway, siblings are placed in competition with each other for survival; maybe in modern times, it's not so much to survive but to thrive. To do so, they need the support and attention of their parents. Firstborns use different strategies than laterborns to capture their parent's approval and interest. In some respects, firstborns have a ready-made advantage in this regard. Parents are naturally engaged with the first child; not only are they proud of their achievement and fascinated with the future prospects of this child (e.g., seeing a future astronaut or professional athlete), but they are unsure of the parenting process and thus focusing more attention to it to ensure the baby's survival. Therefore, firstborns seek to maintain their close ties to the parents by conforming to parental wishes, identifying with parental values and interests, and in general, not jeopardizing their relationship by rocking the boat or creating problems. Laterborns, on the other hand, need to create a new niche that sets them apart from their older sibling and allows them to shine in their own right. They may often choose pursuits in which the older sibling has not already established a dominant superiority. In an effort to establish an area of accomplishment that separates them from the older sibling, the later child may not follow the example of the parents so closely. Instead, laterborns may seek unique ways to draw attention to themselves. Sulloway characterizes laterborns as "born to rebel." He says, "Laterborns typically culti-vate openness to experience—a useful strategy for anyone who wishes to find a novel and successful niche in life" (Sulloway, 1996, p. 353). In an effort to test his hypothesis, Sulloway examined the extent to which firstborns and laterborns supported 23 new and innovative theories in science—not whether they created the new theory, but whether they were willing to accept the new ideas. Later-borns were much more likely to support the new scientific theories than were firstborns. This finding was consistent with Sulloway's argument that laterborns have a greater openness to new experiences than do firstborns.

Do Traits Predict Behavior?

In 1968 Walter Mischel mounted a serious challenge to the whole notion of traits. Mischel pointed out that the typical correlation between a measure of personal-ity and behavior was between .20 and .30, which is surprisingly low when you take into consideration that this means that less than 10 percent of the variabil-ity we see in people's behavior can be accounted for by their personality traits. Mischel referred to this low correlation as the **personality coefficient**. This finding was very serious for the trait theorists, because it was a direct attack on what traits were supposed to do—predict behavior consistently across situations. The trait approach survived this challenge, albeit with several qualifications and refinements.

> **Personality coefficient:** The low correlation between a measure of personality and behavior.

It would seem, then, that if so little of behavior can be predicted from per-sonality tests, then situational factors must be the important determinants of behavior. But a study by Funder and Ozer (1983) would suggest otherwise. They pointed out that the correlations used by personality psychologists may seem low, but when the significance tests used by psychologists studying situational influences on behavior are translated into the proportion of variance accounted for, the values are no higher than those obtained by the personality psychologist. Thus, situational factors don't seem to be influencing behavior any more than personality factors.

Several other authors argued that you could increase the predictability of personality tests if you measured behavior more accurately. Epstein (1979, 1980) pointed out that in many personality studies, the behavior you are trying to pre-dict is measured only one time. This would be like basing your entire psychology grade on your answer to only one question at the end of the semester. My guess is that you would question the accuracy of such a procedure; it would seem more a matter of luck whether you knew one item after a whole semester of material. That's why many items are included in a test—so your knowledge can be mea-sured more reliably. Epstein argued we should do the same thing when trying to predict behavior from a personality test. Behavior should be measured several times, not just once; this would be more accurate and would lead to higher cor-relations between the personality test and behavior.

Fishbein and Ajzen (1974) add that the behavior a personality test is try-ing to predict should be measured in several different ways, not in just one way. Often your professors measure your knowledge of course material in many dif-ferent ways. For example, you may have multiple-choice tests, essay questions, class presentations, and group projects. With so many different measures, your professor gains a more accurate picture of your knowledge than if only one of these methods was used. The same idea can be applied to a personality test.

Suppose a personality test is designed to measure helpfulness, but the only behavioral measure of helpfulness you create is whether or not a person will donate money. The personality test may not look all that accurate, if this is the only behavioral measure you try to predict from the test. There may be some people who score high on the test but just don't donate money. However, if you also measure how much time the person spends doing charity work, helping the little old lady next door, caring for stray animals, and so on, you may find that the test predicts more accurately. Incorporating many different ways of measuring the same personality trait should increase the predictive capacity of the test.

Other psychologists have argued that there are some people who behave consistently across situations, but some who are less consistent. Research by Bem and Allen (1974) has confirmed this idea. They were able to identify people who rated themselves as behaving consistently with regard to a set of traits and people who rated themselves as behaving inconsistently with regard to those same traits. Independent observations of these subjects' behavior confirmed their self-reports. Apparently, some people are more prone to trait-like consistency than are others. In a related piece of work, Kendrick and Stringfield (1980) have shown that most people have some traits that consistently influence their behavior and other traits that have an inconsistent influence.

Finally, it has been argued that personality traits and situations interact. The argument here is that certain personality traits don't emerge unless the situation brings them out. For example, highly stressful situations bring out depression in individuals who are predisposed to suffer depression, whereas stressful situations are less likely to induce depression in individuals who are not depression-prone (Abramson, Seligman, & Teasdale, 1978).

THE PSYCHODYNAMIC APPROACH

The Origins of Freud's Theory

When one first reads or hears about the concepts of Freud's theory, they seem so far-fetched and bizarre that it is easy to dismiss them as the crazed ravings of a lunatic. However, when you understand the context from which they emerged, regardless of whether you still disagree, his ideas at the very least seem to be an honest attempt to deal with a medical problem that was, and still is, quite baffling. Nonetheless, there is some disagreement about whether Freud represented his cases accurately (Masson, 1984).

As a neurologist, Freud dealt with disorders of the nervous system, the paralysis of a limb, and the loss of sense (vision, hearing, and feeling). Some of these cases, although severe in terms of their symptoms (loss of feeling or paralysis), had no apparent physical basis. These patients were said to be suffering from hysteria. Freud initially tried to treat these patients with hypnosis after being taught the technique by Jean Charcot, a French neurologist, but found the effects provided only temporary relief. He then developed a talking-out technique (1895) with Breuer, which later evolved into psychoanalysis.

Unconscious Conflicts

It was in discussions with his patients that Freud came to believe the cause of many of his patients' problems stemmed from unconscious conflicts. These two concepts, unconscious and conflicts of opposing forces, later became important

© 2009 by Liz Van Steenburgh. Used under license of Shutterstock, Inc.

Decision paralysis may occur when you are motivated to eat these donuts but stop because you also want to avoid gaining weight.

underpinnings of his personality theory. To get a sense of how Freud might have applied these ideas, think about a time when you simultaneously wanted and did not want something, like a big piece of chocolate cake. It looked so good, but the thought of eating it made you anxious about your weight. Situations like this often result in a decision paralysis: wanting and not wanting to do something at the same time. Although this example involved a trivial issue, think of the paralysis that might follow from an issue of much greater magnitude, like the sexual longing for an inappropriate person, such as a relative. The longing could be so disgusting that the patients couldn't even admit it to themselves and yet so strong that it wouldn't go away. The paralysis that may result is not indecisiveness but a physical paralysis. The person's struggle between the "wanting" and detesting themselves for what they want is too much to deal with, and best not be recognized. But it is too strong to be ignored, so it emerges in physical symptoms that allow the patient to escape the conflict. From cases like this, Freud developed a comprehensive theory of personality—comprehensive in the sense that it applies to all people, not just those who are suffering psychological problems. This point has often led to criticisms of Freud's theory, because he has overgeneralized or applied his theory to the general population when it was based on, or generated from, a clinical population. It is comprehensive in another sense in that it attempts to explain all behavior and organize the entire personality of an individual, leading to the criticism that it is overextended and tries to explain too much.

It's hard to know where to begin when describing Freud's theory. The parts are so interrelated and connected that describing them as stand-alone concepts falsely ignores the coherence and organization that make the theory what it is. If you visualize a glob of green JELL-O, and gently wiggle one corner of the JELL-O with the underside of your spoon, you notice that the whole square undulates and wiggles throughout. The same is true of Freud's theory; when you talk about part of the theory, it resonates through the entire structure. The theory is in many ways seamless, just like JELL-O. Each concept is a blend and a mixture of all the others.

Instincts

Let's start our description of Freud's theory with his conception of instinct or drive. Instincts give our behavior direction or purpose. For example, a physiological need for nourishment energizes the wish for food, which eventually manifests itself in activity that has as its goal obtaining something to eat. "All the instincts taken together constitute the sum total of psychic energy available to personality" (Hall, Lindzey, & Campbell, 1998, p. 39).

Freud described two major categories of instincts: life and death. The life instincts serve to ensure our individual survival as well as the survival of the human race. They include things such as hunger, thirst, and sex. Collectively, the energy of the life instincts is known as **libido**. Freud focused much more of his attention on the sex instinct than on the other life instincts.

Freud wrote much less about the death instinct, called **thanatos**, but argued that it is as natural as the life instincts, evidenced by the fact that everyone does eventually die. Its goal is to return to a state of least tension and greatest stability, accomplished presumably through decomposition into inorganic matter. When turned outward, it is directed toward others and could explain the cruel and harmful things people do to each other. When turned inward, it could explain self-inflicted pain and suicide.

Libido: Sexual and life preservation instincts.

Thanatos: Death instinct.

These instincts are constantly motivating us and cannot be shut off, at least not until death. If an instinct is blocked from expression, the tension only becomes stronger and the need for release greater. Imagine the disappointment and anger you felt when the piece of pie you were counting on was gone, eaten by someone else in the house. My guess is that you wanted it more than ever after you couldn't have it. These instinctual drives are in a constant state of flux, increasing and decreasing depending on which instincts are being satisfied and which blocked. The longer an instinct or drive is blocked, the greater the tension built up behind it. If a person is unable to find a suitable object or activity to release the tension, more and more energy is required to keep the drive in check and prevent it from bursting through. This can create a high state of anxiety, as the fear of losing control and acting impulsively increases. People suffering this way often seem stiff and inflexible and are often referred to as "repressed" because they lack personality. Most of their psychic energy is being spent holding their instincts in check, so they fail to show much spontaneity or enjoyment in life.

It is important to note that instincts can work against each other. The reason we don't do more harmful things to ourselves is because our life instincts are usually stronger and block the expression of the death instincts. The death instincts are still there and seek expression, but alternative forms of expression can be pursued even though they may only symbolically allow the expression of the death instinct (for example, the enjoyment people get when hearing about someone else's misfortune or from seeing someone slip on a banana peel). The death instinct has been turned outward, away from us, blocked by the life instincts, but we are able nonetheless to receive indirect satisfaction of this instinct.

The Structure of Personality

Three systems provide a structure to personality: the id, ego, and superego. Ideally these three components work together to satisfy the needs of the person. When the interplay between these systems is organized toward achieving the same end, and there is a suitable balance between them in terms of their relative influence, the person is well adjusted and mentally healthy. When these systems are out of balance and/or are working against each other, the person is psychologically unhealthy, inefficient, and unhappy with himself or herself and the world (Hall, 1954).

Id

Taken together, the instincts are called the id. The id is extremely intolerant of tension and seeks its immediate removal. As bodily needs generate tension (hunger, sexual arousal), the id takes steps to reduce this tension. This reduction of tension is pleasurable. Freud believed the id is slave to the pleasure principle. The **pleasure principle** is the motivation behind almost everything a person does, according to Freud.

Pleasure principle: Reduction of tension.

The means by which the id tries to reduce tension is through reflexive actions, like sneezing to reduce the irritants in the nose, and primary process thinking. **Primary process** refers to the idea that the id is so primitive that it can't tell the difference between the real physical world and the imaginary world of subjective experience. As far as the id is concerned, wishing for something is as good as actually having it. The id cannot tell the difference between the real object and the image of the object. To reduce tension the id uses what is called wish-fulfillment. **Wish-fulfillment** is a type of primary process thinking. For example, as hunger tension starts to build, you imagine or wish for food and, as far as the id is concerned, you have food. This occurs in the unconscious, so you don't even realize that it happens, but similar conscious examples will help you get an idea of how this could work.

Primary process: Thinking confusing fantasy for reality.

Wish-fulfillment: Reducing tension by imagining you have what you need.

I am sure you can recall a time when you were hungry, so you began to imagine a nice big piece of strawberry shortcake with whipped cream on top. As you savored each imaginary bite you undoubtedly experienced some pleasure, and at least momentarily forgot about your hunger.

In another example, you may have daydreamed about how nice it would be to go out on a date with a particular individual. You may have thought about where you would go and what you would talk about and so forth. Going out on the fantasy date and eating the strawberry shortcake are nice substitutes, but they don't actually reduce your sex drive or hunger drive. To obtain companionship and food, a mechanism for dealing with the real, external world must be engaged.

Ego

The ego is the system Freud described that deals with the real world, the external world, not the world in your imagination. The ego functions to obtain what will satisfy the id instincts, real food or companionship, not their images. The ego operates on the basis of the reality principle, which means it can distinguish real food from nonfood, so a pacifier that once was a satisfactory substitute for real food would be rejected, as would other inedible objects.

The **reality principle** gives us the capacity to wait and delay gratification until the needed object, which will reduce the tension, is found. The reality principle operates on the basis of the secondary processes, which are the cognitive and intellectual skills people use to solve problems. If you are hungry, you think about where you last obtained food and develop a plan for how you might get it now. The rational skills like memory, problem solving, planning, and decision making are all part of the **secondary process**. They enable us to get through our daily lives and to obtain what we need to survive. Without them you wouldn't even remember where the refrigerator is or how to find your way home from school.

The ego gains all of its energy from the id and operates to serve the id. It would do so in the most direct, expedient manner possible, if it were not for the fact that doing so would lead to trouble and raise the level of tension rather than lowering it.

The ego has no conscience. It would pursue the person's interests without regard to how they would affect anybody else. Rules of conduct are irrelevant to the satisfaction of drives, but people don't operate this way, at least if there is a

Reality principle: The ability to distinguish reality from fantasy.

Secondary process: Rational skills that enable us to get through our daily lives and survive.

If this boy receives praise for sharing his ice cream then sharing food may become part of his ego-ideal.

chance of getting caught. Freud posited another system, the superego, which acts to keep the ego in check and make sure that the way it satisfies the id instincts conforms to societal rules and law.

Superego

The superego has two subparts: the conscience and the ego-ideal. Both of these subsystems are developed from interactions with the parents.

Scolding and punishment lead to the development of the conscience, whereas praise and instruction about what is right and proper lead to the ego-ideal. For example, if a child is caught pushing a younger sibling down to steal a toy and receives a harsh scolding, the child eventually comes to believe that such behavior is wrong and bad. It becomes part of the conscience. On the other hand, if a child shares a toy with a younger sibling and receives praise and love for doing so, these actions come to be seen as right and good and become part of the ego-ideal. After enough experiences like these, the child comes to see the actions themselves as right or wrong. When the child refrains from doing "bad" things because it is wrong, not from a fear of punishment, or does "good" things because it is right, and not for praise, the child has identified with the value system of the parents. Freud called the process of accepting and identifying with the value system taught by the parents introjection.

Introjection enables the person to experience pride in the case of the ego-ideal; shame, embarrassment, and guilt in the case of the conscience. When you have done well on a test, remember the sense of satisfaction and prideful feelings you had about yourself? This is the ego-ideal operating. When you have done poorly, the shame and embarrassment you felt was due to the conscience operating. These feelings arise because you have come to believe they are good or bad things in and of themselves. In other words, you have introjected these values.

Freud believed the superego could also induce self-punishing accidents or mistakes. A person might break or lose something or do something that would lead to embarrassment or punishment to unconsciously punish themselves for some moral transgression. You might think of it as simply a mistake, but outside of your awareness, in the unconscious, a wrong was being punished.

Just as the id could be likened to a demanding and impatient child, the superego could be likened to an equally harsh, righteous parent. The superego functions

1. to totally and completely inhibit any action that would be disapproved of by society (particularly sexual and aggressive impulses)
2. to control the ego so that it works toward moral rather than realistic goals
3. to strive for perfection rather than settle for merely good enough.

The ego is placed in the middle of these two opposing forces trying to reduce the tension of the id instincts, but within the constraints of the superego, and all the while trying to avoid being overwhelmed or dominated by either side. Sometimes the ego may momentarily succumb to one or the other. For example, our impulsive, irrational, and selfish qualities may dominate for a while when the id is in control. Other times we may agonize for perfection and demand unrealistically high levels of performance when the superego has control.

In some people, the ego permanently surrenders control to either the id or superego. We probably all know self-centered, impulsive individuals who are always getting themselves into trouble. They may assume others are there to serve them and are shocked when preferential treatment is not forthcoming. It would seem that the personality of these individuals is permanently dominated by the id. At the other extreme is the rigid, tightly controlled superego individual obsessing over doing the right thing, worrying about what others will think, vigilant against moral transgression, and ready to mete out punishment to the offender.

Conscience: Knowing and feeling guilt when a person has done wrong.

Ego-ideal: Knowing and feeling pride when a person has done right.

Introjection: The process of accepting and identifying with the value system taught by the parents.

It is the competition of these forces and the waxing and waning of their relative influence that give the theory its dynamic quality. In fact, the theory is often referred to as a psychodynamic theory. People are not static and neither are their personalities. Freud tried to account for the fluidity and variability of behavior both within and across people by the competition and conflict among the id, ego, and superego. Actions flow smoothly from one to the next based on how well these structures are blended and integrated. If the balance and blend of the id, ego, and superego is thorough and complete, we see an integrated, balanced individual, capable of expression and spontaneity. If the blend is not so good, we see a more disjointed individual, somewhat out of control and prone to extremes.

Freud's Model of the Mind

Freud divided the mind into three parts:

1. The **conscious** mind is whatever you are currently thinking about. At this moment it is the words you are reading from the text.
2. The **preconscious** mind is anything that you know and could bring into your conscious mind, like the color of your bedroom or the name of your psychology professor. When you need this information, you bring it from the preconscious to the conscious mind, and then it slips back until it's needed again.
3. The **unconscious** part of the mind holds thoughts, feelings, desires, and drives that can be brought into conscious awareness through psychoanalysis, the form of therapy Freud used with his patients. These things are kept from our awareness because if consciously experienced, they would disgust us, frighten us, and cause us pain or anxiety.

Much of our personality is influenced by the unconscious. Slips of the tongue, mistakes, attraction, and humor all have their unconscious elements. Freud believed that many of the symptoms demonstrated by his patients were due to unconscious conflicts. For example, a woman might have a paralysis in a limb because she has a powerful sexual attraction to a relative. She never experiences the attraction consciously because it is kept in the unconscious. Further, the paralysis prevents her from impulsively acting on her desires; thus, the attraction stays unrecognized.

Freud is said to have described the mind as being similar to an iceberg. The smallest portion, the part sticking out of the water, would be the conscious mind. The part just below the surface, but still visible through the water, is the preconscious. The largest portion, too far under the water to see, is the unconscious.

Freud compared the states of consciousness to an iceberg, with the conscious mind out of water, the preconscious just below the water, and the unconscious being the largest and deepest part.

Personality Development

Freud believed that the sex instinct was not a single instinct but rather many instincts. Specifically, he identified the oral, anal, and genital regions as erogenous zones. These are areas that provide pleasure through stimulation. "Each of the principal zones is associated with the satisfaction of a vital need: the mouth with eating, the anus with elimination, and the sex organs with reproduction" (Hall, 1954, p. 103). The idea here is that stimulating the lip and mouth area generally and specifically with food is pleasurable because it helps sustain us. The reduction of tension following elimination is pleasurable because it helps cleanse the body. Stimulation of the sex organs is pleasurable because it is necessary to maintain the species.

Each of the erogenous zones plays an important role in determining adult personality. Associated with each of the erogenous zones are conflicts that need to be resolved. The way in which these conflicts are resolved determines your adult personality. These conflicts represent much more than what appears on the surface, and they occur early in life, so much of your personality is determined by the time you are six years of age.

Freud believed we move through these conflicts sequentially, starting with the oral stage and then progressing to the anal, phallic, latency, and finally, the genital stage. Collectively, he called these stages the psychosexual stages of development. Your ability to pass through the later stages is determined by how well you pass through the preceding stages. In other words, you can become fixated at a stage and not have enough psychic energy to work through the later stages. Thus, your adult personality could be fixated at the oral, anal, or phallic stages and never completely attain the genital stage.

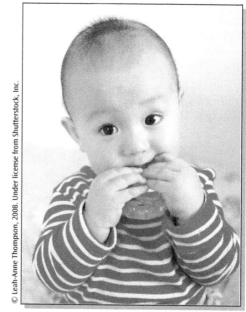

During the oral stage, a child will put just about anything in her mouth.

Oral Stage

Naturally the primary dilemma a newborn faces is survival. The baby needs to take in food and nourishment, and the pleasure obtained from oral stimulation encourages feeding responses by the child, making it more likely the baby will put food in his or her mouth and at least not die from starvation. Because the oral area is the major erogenous zone at this time, the child seems to be constantly seeking oral stimulation, putting many things in the mouth besides food (e.g., toes, toys, blocks) because it feels good.

But taking in food represents more than just taking in the nourishment one needs to survive; it represents being loved and taken care of. Nurturing, loving care, symbolized by suckling at the mother's breast, can lead to a sense of trust and optimism.

Failure to receive adequate care can lead to an adult who is compelled to seek the love and nurturance missed as an infant. These individuals may eat, smoke, or drink in excess to provide the comfort and oral stimulation they missed earlier. They may be gullible in the sense they are still trying to "take in" or "swallow" what others "feed" them, trying to satisfy their hunger for love. A person who has these qualities could be fixated at the oral incorporative stage. Many of us have experienced something similar in the idea of "comfort food." When feeling rejected or anxious, many people seek the comfort and security of a favorite food or drink.

Other fixations are also possible, like the oral sadistic stage. When the child develops teeth, he or she can use them to bite and tear things apart, thus satisfying the aggressive instincts. As an adult, the mouth may continue to be used to satisfy aggressive instincts through verbal attacks like "biting" sarcasm. The average oral stage ends at about 18 months.

Freud theorized that toilet training success influenced personality development. It turns out that he was completely wrong.

Anal Stage

The major issue during the second stage of psychosexual development is defecation and toilet training. The release of tension at elimination is the erogenous pleasure in defecation. Until the onset of toilet training, when and where this tension is released was up to the child. Toilet training focuses attention on this erogenous zone because now external demands are placed on the child to "go" at certain times and in certain places not of his or her own choosing.

Oral incorporative stage: A person who desperately needs to feel loved because he or she didn't get enough love as a child, symbolically achieved through oral stimulation.

Oral sadistic stage: A person who uses his or her mouth (words) to hurt others.

Freud believed that if toilet training is based on praise and reward, the child not only learns how to control and produce bowel movements but symbolically learns to be a creative, productive person. As adults, these individuals are capable of creating and producing products at work and at home, because as children they were rewarded for producing feces, when requested.

If the toilet training is overly harsh or severe and the emphasis is on punishment for making a mess, the child may become fixated at either the anal-expulsive or anal-retentive stage.

Anal expulsive fixation: An adult who is rebellious toward authority, irresponsible, disorderly, and wasteful.

An adult who is rebellious toward authority, irresponsible, disorderly, and wasteful characterizes the **anal expulsive fixation**. These traits are a reaction to harsh toilet training. Just as the child created as big a mess as possible at the most inconvenient time, the adult acts irresponsibly in other ways, creating adult messes.

The **anal retentive fixation** is characterized by an adult who is meticulous, orderly, rigid, and frugal. Just as the child tried to avoid harsh treatment by holding on to feces, so as not to make a mess, the adult holds on to messy feelings. They are clean and orderly and try to keep a tight hold on their money and schedule. The average anal stage ends in the third year of life.

Anal retentive fixation: An adult who is meticulous, orderly, rigid, and frugal.

Phallic Stage

During the phallic stage, children become fascinated with genitals. They begin masturbating and manipulating their own genitals but are also curious about the genitals of members of the opposite sex. Children discover that people are not all the same and are filled with questions about the differences. They may ask why there are differences and seek answers to questions like, "How do they go to the bathroom?" "Does it hurt if they wear pants?" and so forth.

Freud assumed that most children received most of their care from their mothers and, as a result, were quite attached to them. During the phallic stage, however, males and females come to regard their mothers differently. Freud referred to this change in the boys as the Oedipus Complex and in the girls as the Electra Complex.

Oedipus Complex: Male child's love for his mother takes on sexual overtones.

In the **Oedipus Complex**, the male child's love for his mother takes on sexual overtones. He may want to cuddle and caress her out of a sexual attraction to her. He also becomes jealous of the father and comes to view him as a competitor for the mother's affection. The problem is, he is no match for the father. In this rivalry, he surely would be the loser and comes to see himself as in danger. The child's fear stems from the belief that just as he would like to do away with the father, the father must want to do away with him. Freud referred to this fear as **castration anxiety**. This fear is made all that more intense when he recognizes that girls lack protruding genitals and thus appear castrated. Castration anxiety induces the child to repress his desire for the mother, that is, push it into his unconscious, and stop the competition with the father, at least consciously.

Castration anxiety: The fear of a male child that his father would like to do away with him.

Now that the child is no longer consciously competing with the father and has repressed his attraction toward the mother, you would think he would feel safe, but he takes one further step. He identifies with the father. The boy tries to become the father, or at least an extension of the father. The boy believes that father would never hurt himself, thinking that "the closer I become to being Father, the less likely I am to be harmed." The process of identification paves the way for the development of the superego as the boy adopts his father's values.

Identifying with the father also allows the boy symbolic or vicarious access to the mother. That is, he can still, if only through fantasy, continue to sexually enjoy the mother via the father.

© Vasaleks, 2011. Used under licence from Shutterstock, Inc.

Freud believed that boys try to emulate their fathers.

The Electra Complex is somewhat more complicated. The initial bond girls have with their mother weakens for a number of reasons:

1. They develop a sexual attraction for the father, as evidenced by wanting to be Daddy's little girl, sitting in his lap and being the center of his attention.
2. They recognize they have no penis, while boys (specifically their father) do.
3. They suspect or blame their mother for their castrated condition.
4. They envy their fathers for having a protruding organ, rather than a cavity, and what that represents.

In Freud's time, being male provided access to power, status, and wealth, which was not true for women. Thus Freud came to believe that girls develop what he called penis envy. **Penis envy** represents a girl's desire to have a penis and the societal benefits that accompany it. Freud believed that one way a woman could symbolically acquire a penis was by having a baby. As with boys, the emotional conflict is resolved through the process of identification. By becoming more like her mother, the girl gains vicarious access to her father and increases the chances that she'll marry someone just like him.

> **Penis envy:** A girl's desire to have a penis and the societal benefits that accompany it.

Fixations at this stage can result in men trying to seduce as many women as possible to show that they haven't been castrated. Men may also try to assert their masculinity by being extremely successful. Some men, however, out of guilt over competing with their fathers, fail in their sexual and occupational lives. Women fixated at the phallic stage may exhibit a seductive flirtatious interaction style toward men but deny its sexual overtones. The average phallic stage ends at about age five or six.

Latency Stage

The child is less influenced by sexual and aggressive instincts partly because of the development of the superego. The child's attention is focused on forming friendships (predominately same-sexed), attending school, and learning about the world outside the family. The child may come to identify with sports heroes or movie stars. The average latency stage ranges from about 6 to 13 years of age.

Genital Stage

In adolescence, sexual instincts reassert themselves. During this stage, sexuality and pleasure are not as self-centered. In fact, if the person has successfully passed through the preceding stages, he or she also develops an interest in the sexual gratification of another person. The person develops the capacity to love someone beside himself or herself in the fullest sense, that is, emotionally as well as sexually. Better control over sexual and aggressive instincts allows the person to work constructively and thus be an asset to the community. The two fundamental characteristics of the genital personality are being able to

1. love someone other than yourself
2. do constructive work in your society

This stage lasts from the late teens till senility.

Displacement and Sublimation

Satisfaction of the id instincts or the desires associated with the psychosexual stages of development cannot always be directly satisfied, and substitute forms of satisfaction have to be made. To put it more simply, we can't always have what we want, so we have to make do with the next best thing. In general, this is referred to as **displacement**, but when the substitution is approved of and valued by the culture, it is called **sublimation**.

Examples of displacement include smoking to satisfy the need for oral stimulation; yelling at the dog, rather than a co-worker, to satisfy aggressive urges; and applying lipstick from a tube because it resembles a penis and thus helps cope with penis envy.

Examples of sublimation include producing works of art or literature as a substitute for strong sexual longing, practicing surgery or dentistry to satisfy aggressive instincts, achieving in an area that would be approved of by your father to reduce castration anxiety, and surpassing your father's accomplishments to better him in the Oedipal conflict.

Displacements and sublimations occur because society will not allow more direct satisfaction. The specific object or activity chosen is based on its resemblance to what is really desired. Freud believed that displacement is one of the mechanisms for creating differences among people since different people substitute different choices when trying to satisfy their instincts. He also felt that displacement and sublimation could explain the development and progression of civilization. If it weren't for displacement and sublimation, we would still be operating at a primitive level of instinctual urges.

> Displacement: Any object or activity that is a symbolic substitute for what is really desired. This substitution occurs unconsciously.

> Sublimation: When the displacement is approved of and valued by the culture. This substitution occurs unconsciously.

Most alcoholics deny that they have a drinking problem.

© Monkey Business Images, 2011. Used under licence from Shutterstock, Inc.

Defense Mechanisms

When threatening or anxiety-provoking thoughts or feelings threaten to burst through and become expressed, the ego can take steps to prevent this from happening. Defense mechanisms are used to keep thoughts, desires, and feelings that would be upsetting out of awareness.

Repression

Repression is the most basic and fundamental defense mechanism. It simply blocks urges or thoughts from getting into consciousness; thus, you are never aware of them. For example, people are generally not aware of the incestuous desires they had during the phallic stage. Repression is also relevant to more ordinary life events. People often forget the embarrassing or ridiculous things they said or did in an argument. Pushy, self-centered people may never recognize that these qualities stem from feelings of inadequacy. Unpopular individuals often don't see how unpopular they actually are. All of these examples occur because of repression.

Repression: Blocking urges or thoughts from getting into consciousness.

Denial

In denial, you shift your attention away from the threat and ignore what is upsetting. Obvious examples of denial are alcoholics who believe they don't have a drinking problem and smokers who don't apply the warnings about smoking to themselves. Often, denial is simply not recognizing the unpleasant.

Denial: Ignoring, or not recognizing, what is unpleasant.

Projection

Projection occurs when people place an unacceptable feeling, thought, or desire of their own onto somebody else. For example, when people don't get along, it is much easier for most of us to say the other side is being hostile and difficult than it is to admit this about ourselves. Sometimes people feel insecure about the attraction they feel for another. Consequently, they project their attraction onto the other person and talk about the other party as if it were the other party who was smitten. For example, a guy might say with a great deal of bravado, "Oh, she really wants me," or "She is really hot for me," when in fact, he is the one with the crush on her.

Projection: Placing an unacceptable thought, feeling, or desire onto someone else.

Reaction Formation

Reaction formation is expressing the opposite of what you feel. If what you feel is too upsetting or threatening to recognize, you express the opposite. For example, to reduce feelings of rejection a person might say, "I don't care if they like me," when, in fact, he or she does care. Or a woman may resent the child of her sister, but find it intolerable to feel this, so expresses the opposite. She may say things like, "I love you to death," as she smothers the child in bone-crushing hugs. Freud says you can tell the difference between a sincerely motivated action and one coming from reaction formation because in reaction formation the display is over-the-top, too much, excessive, attempting to cover up the true feeling.

Reaction formation: Expressing the opposite of what you feel.

Rationalization

Rationalization is finding an excuse or reason to justify your actions or outcomes. A person who cheats on a test may say to herself or himself, "I will never use this information, anyway, so it is OK to cheat."

Rationalization: Finding an excuse or reason to justify your actions.

ROGERS AND THE PHENOMENOLOGICAL APPROACH

Carl Rogers (1965), like Freud, developed much of his personality theory through interaction with clients. Unlike Freud, however, Rogers focused on the person's immediate experience, that is, his or her subjective reality. Two people in the exact same situation can experience it very differently, having very different thoughts

Carl Rogers theorized that each of these people will perceive their social time differently.

Phenomenological approach: Relies on the immediate experience of the person to understand him or her.

Unconditional positive regard: Accepting a person for who he or she is.

Conditional positive regard: The conditions others place on a person for acceptance and approval.

and feelings. In discussing where to spend a Friday night, one person might view a particular nightclub as exciting and adventurous, while the other person views it as dangerous and threatening. When the focus is on the immediate, subjective experience of the person, it is referred to as the **phenomenological approach**.

Besides deemphasizing the unconscious and focusing on the immediate experience of the person, Rogers, unlike Freud, believed that people have considerable choice in their lives. They are not slave to id instincts or unconscious conflicts but rather have the opportunity to choose the direction for their lives. Rogers would believe people have free will.

The most compelling force in our lives, according to Rogers, is a natural tendency to express who we are, to become our true selves. People often prefer to be with others who make it easy for them to be themselves. When we are being ourselves, we feel complete, whole, absorbed in the moment, and natural. Movement toward this state is referred to as the tendency toward self-actualization. The self-concept and moving toward it are important concepts in Rogers' theory. This would seem straightforward enough; aren't we always who we are? Ideally, yes, Rogers would say, but unfortunately, external demands don't always make it easy. Rogers believed that we strive to be ourselves, but we also strive for the regard, acceptance, and approval of others, particularly the approval of others who matter to us (see Carver & Scheier, 1996). Other people can place conditions of worth on us that are inconsistent with who we are. Instead of loving and accepting us for being ourselves (**unconditional positive regard**), conditions are placed on their love (**conditional positive regard**). In conditional positive regard, to be loved, you have to be or do what others want. Unfortunately, this may not fit with who you are.

If you were to adopt a condition of worth imposed by others in order to get positive regard, you might find yourself living a lie. The lie is believing you are somebody you're not and living a life that really is not you. Eventually, this deception takes its toll. You become unsettled, distressed, anxious, or depressed. For example, imagine a woman whose real interest is in the arts, but she decides against a career in that area because she believes she won't be able to make a lot of money. It's not that a lot of money was very important to her, but her family members and friends seemed to value it so highly that she adopted their view for the sake of their acceptance and approval. Eventually, living a life in the pursuit of money may grow stale and seem rather empty, and the woman may question what she really wants out of life. All people struggle with dilemmas like this, because unconditional positive regard, except for newborns, is not the norm. All of us would like to be prized for who we are, not what we are, but for the most part, the world does not work that way. Furthermore, there is no road map or set of instructions to self-actualization. The path toward self-actualization is something each person must discover for himself or herself. Through trial and error, we discover what experiences are satisfying and completing and feel natural.

The Self

For Rogers, the self-concept is made up of the traits, attributes, and abilities that a person believes he or she possesses (e.g., imaginative, attractive, good dancer). Rogers distinguished two kinds of discrepancies that can occur with the self-concept. One discrepancy involves a difference between the way you view yourself (actual self) and your experience. If you think of yourself as a pleasant person but behave rather coldly toward someone, an incongruency exists between the actual self and your experience. Another way your experience can be incongruent with the actual self is when you think of yourself as being a certain kind of person but others don't acknowledge it. For example, you might think of yourself as a good student but others treat you like an idiot.

A second type of discrepancy can exist; this discrepancy is between the actual self and the ideal self. That is, the kind of person you are is different from what you would like to be. The greater the discrepancies between what you are and what you would like to be, the more unsettled you are. An obvious example is weight or appearance. What a person actually weighs may not be close to the ideal weight. The closer one moves toward self-actualization, the less the discrepancy between the actual self and the ideal self. Furthermore, our experiences become more consistent with both the ideal and actual self. That is, we behave in ways that are consistent with the actual self, which is not far from our ideal self.

THE BEHAVIORAL APPROACH

According to the learning or behavioral perspective, personality is learned. People are who they are not because of inherited traits, unconscious conflicts, or striving to be themselves, but because they have learned to feel certain emotions and behave in certain ways. Most people assume that personality is something inside the person, but not the behaviorist. Behaviorists argue that the assumption of an internal personality is wrong, and the leap from behavior to personality is not necessary. Behaviorists argue that psychologists should focus on the reinforcers and punishers in the external environment, because they lead to differences in behavior, which observers mistakenly assume are due to personality.

Remember the case of little Albert? He was not a particularly nervous or fearful child, but he was afraid of many furry animals. The origin of this fear was outside little Albert, not from within him. He was afraid of furry animals because he had been classically conditioned to fear them. When a loud, unexpected noise was paired with a white rat, he began to fear the animal. This fear was learned and not the result of unconscious conflicts, traits, or striving for self-actualization.

Operant conditioning is just as important as classical conditioning, if not more so, in determining an individual's personality. People differ from each other based on which behaviors have been reinforced and which have resulted in punishment. For example, one person may be outgoing and pushy because this orientation has been successful in many situations, whereas another person may have had little luck with pushy behavior and may have even been punished for it. Instead of being pushy, this person has learned to obtain what is wanted by using humor to get on the good side of other people, who are then willing to accommodate his or her interests.

A behaviorist would argue that the behavior of these two individuals is under **stimulus control**. This means that certain behaviors are likely to follow when an individual's behavior is triggered by cues in the environment. In the past, certain behaviors have resulted in reinforcement in the presence of these cues; therefore, whenever the cues are present, the behaviors are performed. In the case of the pushy individual described earlier, he or she may have been more successful in dealing with a college

> **Stimulus control:** Certain behaviors are likely to follow when an individual's behavior is triggered by cues in the environment.

© Alexander Raths, 2011. Used under licence from Shutterstock, Inc.

Psychologists applying the methods of learning principles believe that social interactions can be understood through the scientifically derived principles of behavior. Therefore, there is no need for the use of internal mental events to make sense of human behavior.

administrator by being pushy, whereas the second individual may have been more successful with the college administrator by ingratiating himself or herself with humor. In each case, however, the behavior of the two individuals was under stimulus control of the situation. One person had learned to be pushy when dealing with college administrators, while the other had learned to be humorous. In each case the behavior performed by the individual was determined by stimulus cues outside the person and had nothing to do with internal personality characteristics.

The idea that our personality is nothing more than a set of stimuli—response connections (that is, a stimulus is presented, which is then followed by a response void of any thought, cognition, or mental processes)—struck many researchers (Bandura, 1999; Mischel, Shoda, & Smith, 2004) as deficient. Specifically, these researchers believe that thoughts not only accompany behavior but also often guide and direct it. In the next section we will describe some ideas from the social learning perspective that make use of mental processes when trying to explain personality.

SOCIAL LEARNING THEORY

Make no mistake, the social learning perspective does not disagree with the basic premise of the behavioral point of view, which believes that personality is the sum total of learned behavior. Instead, this perspective sees humans as playing a greater role in determining their own personality, as well as emphasizing the thinking of people as they interact with the world. In fact, the ideas under the heading "social learning theory" are often described under the heading "social cognitive perspective" (Mischel et al., 2004). The first idea (locus of control) described in the next section emphasizes how people think about and interpret their outcomes. The second idea (reciprocal determinism) argues that the environment, the thinking, and the behavior of a person interact such that the individual has an impact on the environment, as well as the environment having an impact on the person.

Locus of Control

Experiences with the world (i.e., people, machines, situations) teach us what we like and don't like, as well as what we can expect when dealing with someone or something we have dealt with in the past. Rotter (1966) argued that from our experiences we gain expectations about what is likely to happen if we behave in a particular way; he also pointed out that a behavior will not be performed unless some benefit or something of value is seen as following from the behavior. For example, a person will not study for a test unless these two conditions are met:

1. The person expects studying will increase his or her chances of passing.
2. The person values or believes it is important to pass the test.

If either one of these conditions is not met, the person is not likely to study for the test. If he or she doesn't believe studying will make any difference or do any good, the person will be less likely to study and may say something like, "What's the use of studying? It won't do any good, anyway." If the person does not care whether he or she passes or fails, an A or F is irrelevant. For example, the person may have decided college isn't the right choice or may have hit the lottery and is planning to drop all classes. Grades have lost their value, so rather than spend time studying, the person will do something that has higher value, like playing video games or sleeping. Both the *expectancy* of an outcome and the *value* of the outcome have to be high before a person will pursue any given outcome

Rotter proposed that people generalize their experiences so that some people come to see themselves as typically able to determine their outcomes;

This girl would not be studying unless she believed it increases her odds of passing the test and passing is important to her.

© Getty Images

he called these internals. Others do not see any connection between their actions and what happens; he called these externals. Internals are likely to believe that outcomes are under their control, believing effort, motivation, intention, and ability make a difference with regard to what happens. Externals are more likely to believe luck, fate, or whether the teacher or boss likes them determines what happens; that is, outcomes are beyond their control. In other words, a person's belief about the locus of control as to what happens to the person can reside inside the individual (internal) or outside the person (external).

In the next section we see that how a person interprets his or her experiences can influence that person's general orientation about life events and that people actively shape the type of experiences they have in the world by contributing to the creation of their own environments, by actively choosing some settings over others, and by reacting to environmental events. The interplay of these types of influences reveal and shape personality.

Internals: People who generally think they are able to determine their outcome.

Externals: People who don't see any connection between their actions and what happens.

Reciprocal Determinism

Bandura (1986) argues that not only are we shaped by our environment but we shape our environment as well. Bandura believes there is a system of mutual influence among a person's thoughts, behavior, and environment, with each component influencing the other two and it in turn being influenced by them. Bandura calls this system of mutual influence reciprocal determinism. For example, the way you think about someone affects the way you behave toward him or her, and the way you behave toward him or her also affects the way you think about him or her. For example, during a class break you perceive (cognition) someone as a safe recipient of a friendly overture; that is, the break (environmental setting) has provided the opportunity for conversation (behavior), so you strike up a conversation. The mere attempt of making conversation (behavior) also helps convince you (cognition) that the other person is friendly, and because your friendly, pleasant actions (behavior) make the other person comfortable, the other person responds in a friendly manner; the resulting compatibility between the two of you (environment) fosters further friendly exchanges **(Figure 10.2)**. Bandura points out that we are not simple pawns of environmental experience and argues that people choose their environments. Some have an affinity for the pool hall; others, the library. Furthermore, we shape our environments through our actions and from the interpretation we impose on those experiences. Bandura believes people not only are products of their environment but are producers of their environment through their thoughts and actions—thus the term "reciprocal determinism."

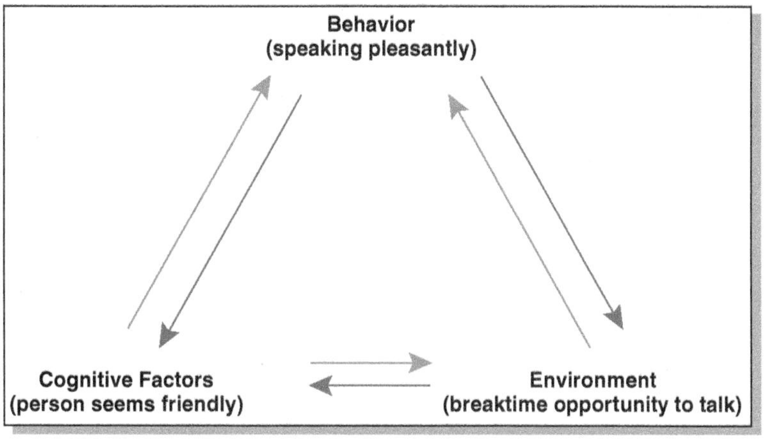

FIGURE 10.2 ■ Reciprocal determinism.

Self-efficacy: Believing you can do what is required to achieve a successful outcome.

Self-efficacy is another concept described by Bandura (1997). Self-efficacy is similar to Rotter's (1966) notions about expectancy, in that both concepts are concerned with a person's belief about what outcomes are likely to follow from his or her actions. Bandura, however, places greater emphasis on the person's belief that he or she knows what steps to take and is capable of performing those steps to bring about a successful outcome. Self-efficacy has been found to be related to actual task accomplishments and to whether people will initiate and improve in psychotherapy (Longo, Lent, & Brown, 1992).

PERSONALITY TESTS

Projective tests: Ambiguous stimuli that require interpretation and thus reveal elements of the unconscious.

The goal of **projective tests** is to subtly get a person to reveal unconscious wishes, motives, or conflicts. The belief is that these aspects of personality have to be assessed indirectly because they are beyond the person's awareness, and even a person's focused efforts to reveal them would be unsuccessful.

In order to delve into the unconscious, Herman Rorschach began asking people, in 1921, to describe what they saw in blots of ink. He reasoned that an ink stain would provide an irregular, ambiguous stimulus that would reveal people's unconscious wishes and conflicts as they tried to describe and make sense out of what they saw in the inkblot. Because there is no right or wrong answer as to what the inkblot represents, it is the person who is being revealed as he or she describes what the inkblot means. In other words, subjects are projecting their unconscious wishes and conflicts onto the ambiguity of the inkblot.

Thematic Apperception Test (TAT): A real-world picture in which unconscious motivation is revealed in the person's story about the picture.

Although many clinicians (Ephraim, 2000) vigorously defend the Rorschach as a means of finding leads for further exploration into an individual's personality, the scientific community has frequently criticized the test's reliability and validity (Lilienfeld, Wood, & Garb, 2000). To be a reliable instrument, the Rorschach should lead to similar evaluations by different clinicians of the same client, but it fails to do so. Its validity is challenged because it fails to predict what it is intended to measure, that is, who will become depressed, violent, withdrawn, and so on—in general, who will have psychological problems.

© Marilyn Volan, 2011. Used under licence from Shutterstock, Inc.

A projective test that does have higher reliability and validity scores is the **Thematic Apperception Test (TAT)**, developed by Henry Murray and Christina Morgan in the 1930s. The assumptions as to how the test works are similar to that of the Rorschach, in that people are projecting their unconscious motives—but onto pictures of real people in real situations rather than inanimate blots of ink, as in the Rorschach. With the TAT, a person tells a story about the picture, including what events led up to the situation, what the characters are feeling and thinking, and what happens to the characters in the picture. Considerable research has shown that the TAT is very good at predicting achievement motivation (McClelland, 1987), which has been its primary use, rather than assessing psychological disorders.

Inkblots do not have right or wrong answers; however, the answers are standardized to people with various mental illnesses. When your set of answers matches one of those categories, it is used to support the therapists's evaluation of your problem. Unfortunately, contemporary research has shown very little support for this idea.

Objective Personality Test

Personality tests, which ask you to describe yourself by answering true or false or by indicating the degree to which a statement does or does not describe you, are often referred to as objective personality tests. The objectivity of the test comes from the test scoring. The administrator of the test doesn't interpret each individual item or the total test score; rather, a tally of the items reveals something about the person, and the same score means the same thing for everyone who has obtained that score.

Many objective personality tests have face or content validity. For example, an item such as "I feel sad most of the time" would be used to measure depression. It is assumed the person will answer truthfully and not try to fake being better or worse than she or he really feels. Unfortunately, sometimes people are motivated to respond in a way that makes them appear better than they really are; this is referred to as the social desirability response bias. Attempting to respond in a socially desirable manner in order to look good can obviously interfere with the validity of the test. One way to avoid this problem is to use empirically keyed tests. The content of an item in an empirically keyed test does not have to represent the concept being measured; it simply has to be answered differently by different groups of people. This is how the Minnesota Multiphasic Personality Inventory (MMPI) was developed. Groups of people with psychological problems, like depression, anxiety disorder, schizophrenia, and so on, were asked to indicate whether a statement was true or false about them. A group of people without psychological problems responded to the same items; those items that distinguished people with psychological problems were kept in the scale. A statement with no face or content validity such as "I like to recite poetry" would be kept in the scale if an abnormal population responded to it differently from the normal population. The MMPI was developed this way and was revised in 1989 (MMPI-2). The scale has several clinical scales to measure characteristics like paranoia, depression, schizophrenia, and hypochondria, just to name a few **(Table 10.2)**. It also has several validity scales to make sure the person taking the test is not faking good or bad, or answering haphazardly **(Table 10.3)**.

Face or content validity: The content of the item is taken at face value and means what it says.

Social desirability response bias: Responding in a way that makes a person appear better than he or she really is.

Empirically keyed tests: Tests that use items consistently answered differently by two groups so as to distinguish between them.

TABLE 10.2   Clinical Scales Of The MMPI

Diagnosis	Characteristics
Hypochondriasis	Concern with bodily functions and physical complaints
Depression	Hopeless, pessimistic, slowed functioning
Hysteria	Uses physical or emotional symptoms to avoid problem
Psychopathic Deviate	Rebellious, inability to profit from experience
Masculinity/Femininity	Typical interests of men and women
Paranoia	Suspicious and resentful of others
Psychasthenia	Worry, guilt, anxiety, indecisiveness
Schizophrenia	Bizarre thoughts, withdrawn
Hypomania	Flight of ideas, impulsive, overactive
Social Introversion	Shy, insecure, self-effacing

TABLE 10.3   Validity Scales Of The MMPI

Diagnosis	Indication
L (lie)	Projects a perfect image
F (confusion)	Answers are contradictory
K (defensiveness)	Minimizes social and emotional complaints
? (cannot say)	Many items unanswered

SUMMARY

In this chapter we learned that the concept of traits is both historically important and currently popular. Traits presumably give our behavior consistency across time and situations and are often measured with paper-and-pencil tests. Furthermore, the scores on these tests are often factor analyzed to distinguish what traits are most relevant for distinguishing individuals from each other. Differences in personality are due to the different scores people receive on a trait. It is possible that some traits are genetically determined and that, under the right conditions, traits can accurately predict behavior.

Freud argued that much of our behavior comes from unconscious instincts. Unconscious instincts are often not satisfied directly but rather are often fulfilled symbolically. Freud taught that much of our adult personality is tied to childhood conflicts. As adults, we continue to try to work through these conflicts, although we are unaware of their childhood origin. The id, ego, and superego metaphorically represent three distinct human capacities, total and complete self-absorption in the case of the id, the pragmatic manager in the case of the ego, and the self-righteous judge in the case of the superego.

Rogers looked at personality from the perspective of our immediate experience or phenomenology. From his way of thinking, we are all on a quest of self-discovery. Self-discovery does not lead to a level of maturity at a particular point in time but rather is a process of being the person you are. Rogers called this self-actualization. Many people are distracted away from the process of self-actualization. The need for approval from others can sidetrack a person away from self-actualization as he or she tries to become the person others will approve of. A supportive person who provides unconditional positive regard can help an individual identify choices that offer greater self-actualizing potential, and thus greater life satisfaction.

Behaviorists argue that the personality of an individual is not something inside the person that is displayed through his or her behavior. Instead, personality is the person's behavior. Furthermore, a person's behavior is controlled by the rewards and punishments in the person's external environment. Social learning theorists point out that human beings are not automatons responding mindlessly to stimulus cues. People apply forethought with regard to whether an action is likely to have a desired effect, and in fact, they shape their environment as much as their environment shapes them. The chapter concluded with a discussion of projective (Rorschach and TAT) and objective personality tests (MMPI).

KEY TERMS

anal expulsive fixation
anal retentive fixation
cardinal traits
castration anxiety
central traits
conditional positive
    regard
conscience
denial
displacement
ego-ideal
empirically keyed tests
externals
face or content validity
factor analysis
idiographic approach
internals

introjection
libido
nomothetic approach
Oedipus Complex
oral incorporative stage
oral sadistic stage
penis envy
personality coefficient
phenomenological
    approach
pleasure principle
primary process
projection
projective tests
psychodynamic theory
rationalization
reaction formation

reality principle
repression
secondary process
secondary traits
self-efficacy
social desirability
    response bias
source traits
stimulus control
sublimation
thanatos
Thematic Apperception
Test (TAT)
theoretical constructs
unconditional positive
    regard
wish-fulfillment

MATCHING

For Questions 19 and 20 you should create the correct matches yourself. Write the name of a concept in the number column and a correct match in the letter column.

____ 1. Unconditional positive regard	A. between .20 and .30
____ 2. Self-actualization	B. libido
____ 3. Internals and externals	C. repression, projection, denial, etc.
____ 4. Idiographic approach	D. pleasure principle
____ 5. Achievement motivation	E. Allport
____ 6. Eysenck	F. reality principle
____ 7. The "big five"	G. conscience
____ 8. Personality coefficient	H. openness: intellectual, imaginative
____ 9. Life instincts	I. what a person is currently thinking
____ 10. Id	J. TAT
____ 11. Ego	K. oral, anal, phallic, latency, genital
____ 12. Superego	L. loving someone as he or she is
____ 13. Conscious	M. phallic stage
____ 14. Psychosexual stages of development	N. defense mechanism
____ 15. Oedipus Complex	O. stimulus control
____ 16. Reaction formation	P. introversion-extroversion
____ 17. Defense mechanisms	Q. realizing or becoming yourself
____ 18. Behavioral approach	R. locus of control
____ 19.	S.
____ 20.	T.

SHORT-ANSWER QUESTIONS

1. Define and give an example of a theoretical construct.

2. Describe a research strategy to determine the relative influence of genetics versus the environment on personality. Describe how the method allows for a comparison of these influences.

3. Describe a method that would increase the accuracy of a personality measure to predict behavior.

4. What does it mean to be fixated at a stage of psychosexual development?

5. What does Rogers mean by "self-actualization"?

6. Describe reciprocal determinism.

FILL IN THE BLANKS

1. The _____ approach to personality is concerned with the immediate experience of the person and what makes us unique from everyone else.
2. The _____ approach, as compared with the idiographic approach, involves measuring large numbers of people on a paper-and-pencil test to see where they are different and where they are similar.
3. _____ is a technique that allows the researcher to see if several variables share enough in common that they could be summarized with a single label.
4. Considerable evidence has led to the conclusion that openness, conscientiousness, extroversion, agreeableness, and neuroticism are the _____ _____ of personality.
5. Examination of several sources of evidence suggest that about _____ percent of the difference in personality is genetically determined.
6. Mischel pointed out that the typical correlation between a measure of personality and behavior was between _____ and _____.
7. The origin of Freud's theory emerged from his attempts to treat patients suffering from _____.
8. Taken together, the instincts are called the _____.
9. The _____ _____ fixation is characterized by an adult who is meticulous, orderly, rigid, and frugal.
10. The defense mechanism of _____ blocks urges or thoughts from getting into consciousness; thus, a person is never aware of them.
11. When certain requirements are placed on an individual to be approved of, loved, and respected, it is called _____ positive regard.
12. The closer one moves toward self-actualization, the less the discrepancy between the _____ self and the _____ self.
13. _____ are likely to believe that outcomes (i.e., what happens to them) is under their control, whereas _____ are likely to believe what happens to them is more a matter of luck.
14. Bandura refers to the system of mutual influence of a person's thoughts, behavior, and environment as _____.
15. A well-known projective test where a person is asked to describe inkblots is called the _____ test.
16. The _____ was developed using an empirically keyed approach.

Read the following story, paying attention to different aspects of thoughts, feeling, and action. Based on what you read in this chapter and as discussed in class, list the key elements of the story that you would pay attention to for each of the major personality theories. When answering Questions 1–3 focus *only* on the aspects that are relevant to the *specific* personality theory mentioned. This exercise is designed to show you that each theory focuses on a different aspect of the same person/event.

Santana is an 18-year-old college student. He is always the first one to volunteer to do fun activities and always tends to live on the edge. He likes to be with people, especially ones who like to do exciting things, like skydiving. It seems as if he is never able to get enough. When he was younger, his parents moved from state to state and his mother and father were not home very often. He did not mind the absence of his father, but he really missed his mother. He always felt he had to work hard to get their attention and often felt neglected. More often than not, he had to work hard to get compliments and love. In college he works hard to keep friends and goes out of his way to please them. He now has a girlfriend, Britney, who actually resembles his mother very much. Britney likes Santana but hates some of his habits: He is always chewing and sucking on pencils and chewing off the tops. He is organized but very insecure and anxious.

1. As a trait theorist, how would you describe Sanatana (high on what, low on what, based on what you just read)?

2. As a humanistic or phenomenological theorist, why do you think his personality is as it is, and what suggestions would you give his girlfriend in regard to how he should be treated?

3. As a psychodynamic theorist, what aspects of Santana would draw your attention, and what "Freudian" ideas do you see in the story?

PERSONALITY PSYCHOLOGISTS AT LUNCH

Imagine that four psychologists are having lunch together and that you are eavesdropping on their conversation. There is a Freudian (F), a trait theorist (T), a theorist with a phenomenological perspective (P), and a social learning theorist (SL). Put the letter representing each kind of psychologist next to the statement he or she would make.

_____ 1. To understand someone you need to understand the thoughts and feelings of the person from his or her point of view.

_____ 2. I believe the quality most important in personality is introversion-extroversion.

_____ 3. The adults' personality is a product of unconscious childhood conflicts.

_____ 4. I just heard of a new factor analytic technique; I can't wait to use it to determine the essential number of personality qualities.

_____ 5. I had a client the other day who expressed to me that she had been living her life for other people so long that she really didn't know who she was and what she wanted out of life.

_____ 6. Most people don't understand the reasons behind their actions; they just think they do.

_____ 7. Sometimes the hardest thing to do is to convince people they have the freedom to change their lives.

_____ 8. What personality is all about is identifying the qualities in a person's makeup that create consistency in his or her behavior.

_____ 9. The sex drive is so fundamental it is with us from birth.

_____ 10. To determine whether a questionnaire can accurately predict a behavior, such as helpfulness, it is best to measure several different types of helping behavior.

_____ 11. What I use to predict whether someone will apply himself or herself to a task is that person's expectancy of success and the value he or she places on that success.

_____ 12. I always believed we have as much influence on the situation as the situation has on us.

Chapter 10: Personality

END OF CHAPTER QUIZ

1. The definition of personality is:
   a. A person's typical manner of thinking, feeling and acting
   b. How you think
   c. Your genetic code for life-long behavior
   d. The way you see the world

2. Which personality theory is associated with Carl Rogers?
   a. Phenomenological approach
   b. Psychoanalysis
   c. Trait approach
   d. Factor Analysis

3. Sigmund Freud was originally trained as a:
   a. Psychologist
   b. Minister
   c. Physician
   d. Biologist

4. This technique requires you to relax and say whatever comes to mind.
   a. Hypnosis
   b. Free association
   c. Therapy
   d. Manifest analysis

5. Which item did Freud associate with the unconscious?
   a. Steam engine
   b. Train
   c. Iceberg
   d. Plants

6. This conceptual part of Freud's theory was supposed to manage both your need for personal excess and order.
   a. Id
   b. Ego
   c. Superego
   d. Sublimation

7. When you try to become like your "rival" parent.
   a. Identification
   b. Conflict resolution
   c. Oedipus complex
   d. Electra complex

8. Which of the following is NOT a Freudian defense mechanism?
   a. Repression
   b. Projection
   c. Displacement
   d. Sublimation

9. Which of the neo-Freudians attempted to develop a more female-friendly version of psychoanalysis?
   a. John Kinsey
   b. Alfred Adler
   c. Karen Horney
   d. Abraham Maslow

10. This theoretician's model involved rising through a hierarchy of needs.
    a. Maslow
    b. Freud
    c. Adler
    d. Allport

11. Carl Rogers believed that to have a good therapeutic process there was needed genuineness, empathy, and:
    a. Confidence
    b. Awareness
    c. Positive emotions
    d. Acceptance

12. Reciprocal determinism is part of which personality theory?
    a. Freudian
    b. Phenomenological
    c. Social learning
    d. Trait

13. Social learning theory involves the use of the _____ model.
    a. Biopsychosocial model
    b. Trait
    c. Factor analysis
    d. Adlerian

14. Which person is more likely to become depressed? The person with the:
    a. Internal locus of control
    b. External locus of control
    c. Conscientious personality trait
    d. Overactive super ego

15. This thing appears to be a learned behavior that can weaken with repeated use.
    a. Self-control
    b. Kindness
    c. Love
    d. Hate

16. The Trait approach to personality was first started by:
    a. Freud
    b. Cattell
    c. Allport
    d. Skinner

17. The Factor Analysis approach to personality was first started by:
    a. Cattell
    b. Allport
    c. Skinner
    d. Rogers

18. Which theorist developed the 16PF test?
    a. Eysenck
    b. Cattell
    c. Allport
    d. Rogers

19. How many personality classifications are currently believed to sufficiently describe all personality types?
    a. Two
    b. Four
    c. Five
    d. Eighteen

20. Personality traits become more _____ over your lifetime.
    a. Changeable
    b. Unstable
    c. Flexible
    d. Stable

21. This thing is defined as a person's typical manner of thinking, feeling, and acting.
    a. Externals
    b. Ego-ideal
    c. Projection
    d. Personality
    e. Source traits

22. Which of the following personality theories is based on a statistical approach?
    a. The psychodynamic approach
    b. The phenomenological approach
    c. The social learning approach
    d. The trait approach

23. Before he began to develop psychological theories, Freud was a:
    a. Butcher
    b. Academic physiologist
    c. Medical doctor specializing in neurological disorders
    d. Medical doctor specializing in sexual disorders
    e. Biologist

24. Which of the following were used in Freud's psychoanalysis therapy sessions?
    a. Free association and hypnosis
    b. Free association and introjection
    c. Hypnosis and nomothetics
    d. Conditional positive regard and self-efficacy

25. Slips-of-the-tongue are associated with:
    a. Freud
    b. Bandura
    c. Skinner
    d. Eysenck

26. Which of the following was not part of Freud's personality theory?
    a. Id
    b. Ego
    c. Self-efficacy
    d. Denial
    e. Displacement

27. In psychoanalysis, trying to become like the "rival" parent is called:
    a. Fixation
    b. Oedipus complex
    c. Genital stage of development
    d. Identification

28. Which of the following is not a Freudian defense mechanism?
    a. Repression
    b. Regression
    c. Reaction formation
    d. Projection
    e. Introjection

29. Who was responsible for developing the "inferiority complex?"
    a. Carl Jung
    b. Sigmund Freud
    c. Karen Horney
    d. Alfred Adler

30. Who was responsible for developing the concepts of "self-esteem" and "self-actualization?"
    a. Carl Rogers
    b. Sigmund Freud
    c. Abraham Maslow
    d. Alfred Adler
    e. Karen Horney

31. The Phenomenological approach was developed by:
    a. Freud
    b. Bandura
    c. Skinner
    d. Eysenck
    e. Maslow

32. This person believed that for psychological growth to occur one must show genuineness, acceptance and empathy.
    a. Rogers
    b. Bandura
    c. Skinner
    d. Eysenck
    e. Maslow

33. Who is responsible for developing the term "self-concept" as a psychological construct?
    a. Rogers
    b. Bandura
    c. Skinner
    d. Eysenck
    e. Maslow

34. All your thoughts and feelings in answer to the question, "Who am I?"
    a. Rationalization
    b. Projection
    c. Self-concept
    d. Response bias
    e. Face validity

35. Reciprocal determinism is associated with which psychological theory?
    a. The psychodynamic approach
    b. The phenomenological approach
    c. The social learning approach
    d. The trait approach

36. Which of the following factors is LEAST LIKELY going to influence your personality development according to Biopsychosocial theory?
    a. Social learning at a kindergarten
    b. An inherited disorder which depletes a person's serotonin levels
    c. The death of a grandparent when you are 6-months old
    d. Always having the best birthday parties compared to any of your friends

37. The _____ factor refers to a person's individual life events.
    a. Biological
    b. Psychological
    c. Educational
    d. Social

38. Which of the following is most closely related to an INTERNAL locus of control?
    a. Your grandparents
    b. Your group of friends
    c. Your grammar school
    d. The presence of Swine flu

39. Which of the following is most closely related to an EXTERNAL locus of control?
    a. The supermarket you shop at
    b. Your test grades
    c. The lunch you eat
    d. The historical time period you live within

40. People with a high INTERNAL locus of control are more likely to:
    a. Become depressed
    b. Stop planning for the future
    c. Control impulses and delay gratification
    d. Wait for a problem before acting

41. Which of the following answers is NOT associated with an EXTERNAL locus of control?
    a. Delaying gratification
    b. Becoming depressed
    c. Not planning for the future
    d. Only addressing issues once they become immediately important

42. Which of the following statements is most likely true?
    a. Exerting self-control comes from internal will power
    b. Will power is a trait you are born with
    c. Showing self-control never makes you feel uncomfortable
    d. Self-control is a learned behavior

43. Which of the following statements is most likely false?
    a. Continually exerting your self-control results in a strengthening of your ability to do so again
    b. Self-control is a learned trait
    c. Exhibiting self-control is sometimes difficult
    d. Self-control increases in strength with practice

44. Circa _____, Allport developed his theory that ultimately included _____ adjectives of human personality characteristics.
    a. 1920's, 3500
    b. 1930's, 4500
    c. 1940's, 5500
    d. 1950's, 6500

45. Which personality theorist is most closely associated with the first applications of factor analysis?
    a. Freud
    b. Allport
    c. Cattell
    d. Eysenck

46. Eysenck's three-factor PEN solution included:
    a. Psychoticism, extroversion, neuroticism
    b. Personality, ego-ideal, nomothetics
    c. Projection, externals, neuroses
    d. Penis envy, extroversion, factor analysis

47. Which of the following titles is NOT part of the Big Five personality characteristics?
    a. Conscientiousness
    b. Agreeableness
    c. Neuroticism
    d. Openness
    e. Ego-ideal

48. Which of the following statements is NOT true regarding the Big Five personality characteristics?
    a. They become more stable over time
    b. Heritability accounts for 50% of their variability

    c. They apply across cultures
    d. These traits first become evident at about the age of puberty
    e. Some traits correlate well with other traits

49. Which of the following tests would be your best choice for evaluating personality?
    a. Thematic apperception test
    b. Draw a person test
    c. Finish a sentence test
    d. Rorschach inkblot test
    e. None of the above tests does a very good job of evaluating personality.

50. Which of the following tests is objective?
    a. Thematic apperception test
    b. Draw a person test
    c. Finish a sentence test
    d. Rorschach inkblot test
    e. Minnesota Multiphasic Personality Inventory

11 *Psychological Disorders*

Current Developments in Understanding Schizophrenia

The many forms of mental illness known may be split into two general categories: those with a clear biological basis and those without. It may be argued that the biologically-based illnesses are more frequently associated with severe psychoses and long-term psychiatric care. One of these illnesses is schizophrenia.

It has been estimated that schizophrenia affects between one and two percent of the world's population, which accounts for a mean estimate of ninety million current cases of schizophrenia worldwide. It is a debilitating disease with no known cure. Generally, individuals are in their early twenties when they are first diagnosed with it. The afflicted individual will then show symptoms for the remainder of their life. In rare cases, the symptoms will reduce to a low level although the person will still carry the specific diagnosis of residual schizophrenia.

The understanding that schizophrenia is a biologically-based disorder comes from familial genetic studies. Such studies reveal that symptoms of the disorder will most likely appear in individuals closely related genetically to an afflicted individual. This correlation holds regardless of whether the family members live together or live apart, as in the case of adoption.

How the genetic component of schizophrenia causes the disorder to initiate twenty years after birth is not well understood. One recent advance in the understanding of the disorder comes at the close of the Human Genome Project; the large-scale project to map all the genes in the human genome.

The Human Genome Project was completed around 2004. At about this time, evidence began to mount showing that the genetic copy number variations (CNV) in about twenty different genes were different between those with and without the disorder. These CNVs reflect the number of times a gene repeats itself on the human genome. The base rate of CNVs in the unafflicted population was about 5 percent, whereas the afflicted group showed about a 15 percent CNV rate. Higher CNV measures were correlated with an earlier onset of the disease. Moreover, those CNVs were most closely associated with genes controlling cellular communication within and between neural cells.

In this chapter, you will see evidence that schizophrenia has an environmental component as well. That, of course, will complicate the understanding of this disease. It is widely accepted that, despite the strong genetic link in schizophrenia, there is also an environmental component to its etiology. That is, no one without the disrupted genes develops the disorder and not all those with the genes develop the disorder, however, persons with the genes and socially troubled lives (i.e., highly stressed) are most likely to develop symptoms.

References

Walsh, T., McClellan, J. M., McCarthy, S. E., Addington, A. M., Pierce, S. B., Cooper, G. M., Nord, A. S., Kusenda, M., Malhotra, D., Bhandari, A., Stray, S. M., Rippey, C. F., Roccanova, P., Makarov, V., Lakshmi, B., Findling, R. L., Sikich, L., Stromberg, T., Merriman, B., Gogtay, N., Butler, P., Eckstrand, K., Noory, L., Gochman, P., Long, R., Chen, Z., Davis, S., Baker, C., Eichler, E. E., Meltzer, P. S., Nelson, S. F., Singleton, A. B., Lee, M. K., Rapoport, J. L., King, M. C., and Sebat, J. (2008). Rare Structural Variants Disrupt Multiple Genes in Neurodevelopmental Pathways in Schizophrenia. Science, 320, 539–543.

CHAPTER OUTLINE

*M*ary's troubles first began in adolescence. She began to miss curfew, was frequently truant, and her grades declined sharply. During family counseling sessions, it was discovered that Mary also had been promiscuous and had prostituted herself several times to get drug money. . . . She quickly fell in love and overly idealized new friends. But when they quickly (and inevitably) disappointed her, she would angrily cast them aside. . . . Mary's problems, coupled with a preoccupation with inflicting pain on herself (by cutting and burning) and persistent thoughts of suicide, eventually led to her admittance to a psychiatric hospital at age 26 (Davison, Neale, & Kring, 2004, pp. 408–409).

Jim is a third-year medical student. Over the last few weeks, he has been noticing that older men appear to be frightened of him when he passes them on the street. Recently, he has become convinced that he is actually the director of the Central Intelligence Agency and that these men are secret agents of a hostile nation. Jim has found confirmatory evidence for his idea in the fact that a helicopter flies over his house every day at 8:00 a.m. and at 4:30 p.m. Surely, this surveillance is part of the plot to assassinate him (Bernheim & Lewine, 1979, p. 4).

Both Mary and Jim have severe psychological problems, and both of their stories raise interesting questions. What caused their difficulties? Was there something in their early backgrounds to explain their later behaviors? Is there something medically wrong with them? What about less-severe forms of abnormal behavior? What is the difference between being eccentric and being disordered?

In this chapter, we discuss how psychological disorders are identified, explained, and classified, and we explore six major categories of psychological disorders: anxiety disorders, mood disorders, schizophrenia, substance-related disorders, dissociative disorders, and personality disorders. Finally, we look at how gender and culture affect mental disorders.

STUDYING PSYCHOLOGICAL DISORDERS

LEARNING OBJECTIVES

List the four criteria for identifying abnormal behavior.

Review how views of abnormal behavior have changed through history.

Explain how the DSM-IV-TR is used to classify psychological disorders.

Identifying Abnormal Behavior: Four Basic Standards

On the continuum ranging from normal to abnormal behavior, people can be unusually healthy or extremely disturbed.

Mental health professionals generally agree on four criteria for abnormal behavior: statistical infrequency, disability or dysfunction, personal distress, and violation of norms **(Figure 11.1)**. However, as we consider these criteria, remember that no single criterion is adequate for identifying all forms of abnormal behavior.

- *Statistical infrequency.* A behavior may be judged abnormal if it occurs infrequently in a given population. Statistical infrequency alone does not determine what is normal—for example, no one would classify Albert Einstein's great intelligence or Lance Armstrong's exceptional athletic ability as abnormal.
- *Disability or dysfunction.* People who suffer from psychological disorders may be unable to get along with others, hold a job, eat properly, or clean themselves. Their ability to think clearly and make rational decisions also may be impaired.
- *Personal distress.* The personal distress criterion focuses on the individual's judgment of his or her level of functioning. Yet many people with psychological disorders deny they have a problem. Also, some serious psychological disorders (such as antisocial personality disorder) cause little or no emotional discomfort. The personal distress criterion by itself is not sufficient for identifying all forms of abnormal behavior.
- *Violation of norms.* The fourth approach to identifying abnormal behavior is violation of social norms, or cultural rules that guide behavior in particular situations. A major problem with this criterion, however, is that cultural diversity can affect what people consider a violation of norms (Lopez & Guarnaccia, 2000).

Abnormal behavior: Patterns of emotion, thought, and action that are considered pathological (diseased or disordered) for one or more of these reasons: statistical infrequency, disability or dysfunction, personal distress, or violation of norms (Davison, Neale, & Kring, 2004).

Explaining Abnormality: From Superstition to Science

What causes abnormal behavior? Historically, evil spirits and witchcraft have been blamed (Millon, 2004). Stone Age people, for example, believed that abnormal behavior stems from demonic possession; the "therapy" was to bore a hole in the skull so that the evil spirit could escape. During the European Middle Ages, a troubled person was sometimes treated with exorcism, an effort to drive the Devil out through prayer, fasting, noise-making, beating, and drinking terrible-tasting brews. During the fifteenth century, many believed that some individuals chose to consort with the Devil. Many of these supposed witches were tortured, imprisoned for life, or executed.

FIGURE 11.1 ■ Rather than fixed categories, both "abnormal" and "normal" behaviors exist along a continuum (Hansell & Damour, 2005).

As the Middle Ages ended, special mental hospitals called *asylums* began to appear in Europe. Initially designed to provide quiet retreats from the world and to protect society (Millon, 2004), the asylums unfortunately became overcrowded, inhumane prisons.

Improvement came in 1792 when Philippe Pinel, a French physician in charge of a Parisian asylum, insisted that asylum inmates—whose behavior he believed to be caused by underlying physical illness—be unshackled and removed from their unlighted, unheated cells. Many inmates improved so dramatically that they could be released. Pinel's **medical model** eventually gave rise to the modern specialty of **psychiatry**.

Medical model: The perspective that diseases (including mental illness) have physical causes that can be diagnosed, treated, and possibly cured.

Unfortunately, when we label people "mentally ill," we may create new problems. One of the most outspoken critics of the medical model is psychiatrist Thomas Szasz (1960, 2000, 2004). Szasz believes that the medical model encourages people to believe that they have no responsibility for their actions. He contends that mental illness is a myth used to label individuals who are peculiar or offensive to others (Wyatt, 2004). Furthermore, labels can become self-perpetuating—that is, the person can begin to behave according to the diagnosed disorder.

Despite these potential dangers, the medical model—and the concept of mental illness—remains a founding principle of psychiatry. In contrast, psychology offers a multifaceted approach to explaining abnormal behavior.

Psychiatry: The branch of medicine that deals with the diagnosis, treatment, and prevention of mental disorders.

Classifying Abnormal Behavior: The Diagnostic and Statistical Manual IV-TR

Without a clear, reliable system for classifying the wide range of psychological disorders, scientific research on them would be almost impossible, and communication among mental health professionals would be seriously impaired. Fortunately, mental health specialists share a uniform classification system, the text revision of the fourth edition of the *Diagnostic and Statistical Manual of Mental Disorders (DSM-IV-TR)* (American Psychiatric Association, 2000).

Each revision of the *DSM* has expanded the list of disorders and changed the descriptions and categories to reflect both the latest in scientific research and changes in the way abnormal behaviors are viewed within our social context (First & Tasman, 2004; Smart & Smart, 1997). For example, take the terms **neurosis** and **psychosis**. In previous editions, the term *neurosis* reflected Freud's belief that all neurotic conditions arise from unconscious conflicts. Now, conditions that were previously grouped under the heading *neurosis* have been formally redistributed as anxiety disorders, somatoform disorders, and dissociative disorders.

Unlike neurosis, the term *psychosis* is still listed in the *DSM-IV-TR* because it is useful for distinguishing the most severe mental disorders, such as schizophrenia and some mood disorders.

Diagnostic and Statistical Manual of Mental Disorders (DSM-IV-TR): The classification system developed by the American Psychiatric Association used to describe abnormal behaviors; the *IV-TR* indicates that it is the text revision (*TR*) of the fourth major edition (*IV*).

THE INSANITY PLEA—GUILTY OF A CRIME OR MENTALLY ILL?

On the morning of June 20, 2001, Texas mother Andrea Yates drowned her five children in the bathtub, then calmly called her husband to tell him he should come home. At Yates's trial, both the defense and prosecution agreed that Yates was mentally ill at the time of the murders, yet the jury

© Aaron M. Sprecher/epa/CORBIS

Continued

still found her guilty and sentenced her to life in prison. (An appellate court later overturned this conviction. In 2006, Yates was found not guilty by reason of insanity and committed to a state mental hospital in which she will be held until she is no longer deemed a threat.) How could two juries come to such opposite conclusions? *Insanity* is a complicated legal term. In most states it refers to a person who cannot be held responsible for his or her actions, or is judged incompetent to manage his or her own affairs, because of mental illness. Despite high profile cases like that of Andrea Yates, it's important to keep in mind that the insanity plea is used in less than 1 percent of all cases that reach trial, and when used, it is rarely successful (Kirschner, Litwack, & Galperin, 2004; Steadman, 1993).

SEVEN PSYCHOLOGICAL PERSPECTIVES ON ABNORMAL BEHAVIOR

Each of the seven major perspectives in psychology emphasizes different factors believed to contribute to abnormal behavior, but in practice they overlap. Consider the phenomenon of compulsive hoarding. Everyone sometimes makes an impulse purchase, and most people are reluctant to discard some possessions

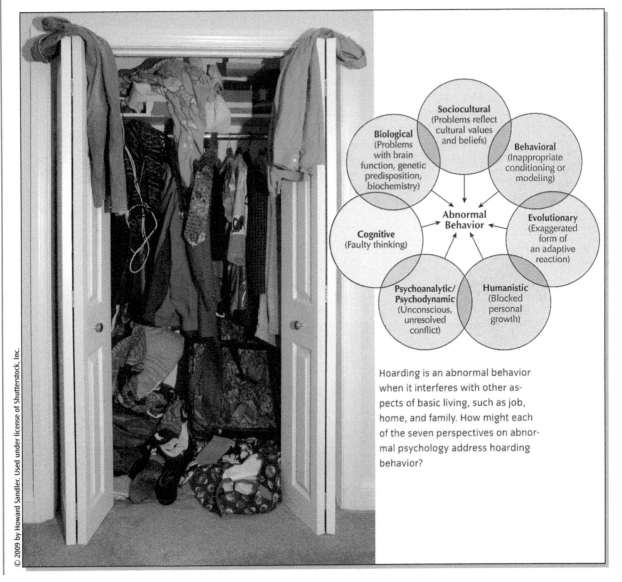

What a Scientist Sees

© 2009 by Howard Sandler. Used under license of Shutterstock, Inc.

Hoarding is an abnormal behavior when it interferes with other aspects of basic living, such as job, home, and family. How might each of the seven perspectives on abnormal psychology address hoarding behavior?

that are of questionable value. But when the acquisition of and inability to discard worthless items becomes extreme, it can interfere with basic aspects of living, such as cleaning, cooking, sleeping on a bed, and moving around one's home. This abnormal behavior is associated with several psychological disorders, but it is most commonly found in people who have obsessive-compulsive disorder, or OCD (an anxiety disorder discussed later in this chapter). How might each of the seven major perspectives explain compulsive hoarding?

Understanding the DSM-IV-TR

The *DSM-IV-TR* is organized according to five major dimensions called *axes*, which serve as guidelines for making decisions about symptoms. Axis I describes **state disorders** (the patient's current condition, or "state"), such as anxiety, substance abuse, and depression. Axis II describes **trait disorders** (enduring problems that seem to be an integral part of the self), including long-running personality disorders and mental retardation.

The other three axes are used to record important supplemental information. Medical conditions (Axis III) and psychosocial and environmental stressors (Axis IV) could contribute to moods and emotional problems. Finally, Axis V evaluates a person's overall level of functioning, on a scale from 1 (serious attempt at suicide) to 100 (happy and productive).

The *DSM-IV-TR* contains more than 200 diagnostic categories grouped into 17 subcategories **(Table 11.1)**.

In this chapter, we focus on only the first 6 of the 17 categories shown in Table 11.1. Before we go on, note that the *DSM-IV-TR* classifies disorders, not people. Accordingly, we use terms such as *a person with schizophrenia*, rather than describing people as *schizophrenic*.

TABLE 11.1 ■ The 17 Main Categories of the Diagnostic and Statistical Manual of the American Psychiatric Association (DSM-IV-TR)

1. Anxiety disorders
2. Mood disorders
3. Schizophrenia and other psychotic disorders
4. Dissociative disorders
5. Personality disorders
6. Substance-related disorders
7. Somatoform disorders
8. Factitious disorders
9. Sexual and gender identity disorders
10. Eating disorders
11. Sleep disorders
12. Impulse control disorders (not elsewhere classified)
13. Adjustment disorders
14. Disorders usually first diagnosed in infancy, childhood, or early adolescence
15. Delirium, dementia, amnestic, and other cognitive disorders
16. Mental disorders due to a general medical condition (not elsewhere classified)
17. Other conditions that may be a focus of clinical attention

Evaluating the DSM-IV-TR

The *DSM-IV-TR* has been praised for carefully and completely describing symptoms, standardizing diagnoses and treatments, facilitating communication, and serving as a valuable educational tool. Critics, however, suggest that it relies too heavily on the medical model and unfairly labels people (Cooper, 2004; Mitchell, 2003; Roelcke, 1997). The *DSM-IV-TR* has also been criticized for its possible cultural bias. The manual does provide a culture-specific section and a glossary of culture-bound syndromes, such as amok (Indonesia), genital retraction syndrome (Asia), and windigo psychosis (Native American cultures), which we discuss later in this chapter. However, the classification of most disorders still reflects a Western European and American perspective (Dana, 1998; Matsumoto, 2000; Smart & Smart, 1997).

■ CONCEPT CHECK STOP

Why isn't any single criterion adequate for classifying abnormal behavior?
How does psychology diverge from the medical model?
What are the purposes of the five axes of the *DSM-IV-TR*?

ANXIETY DISORDERS

LEARNING OBJECTIVES

Describe the symptoms of generalized anxiety disorders, panic disorder, phobias, and obsessive-compulsive disorder.

Summarize how psychological, biological, and sociocultural factors contribute to anxiety disorders.

> Anxiety disorder: A type of abnormal behavior characterized by unrealistic, irrational fear.

Anxiety disorders—which are diagnosed twice as often in women as in men—are the most frequently occurring mental disorders in the general population (National Institute of Mental Health, 1999; Swartz & Margolis, 2004). Fortunately, they are also among the easiest disorders to treat and have one of the best chances for recovery.

Four Major Anxiety Disorders: The Problem of Fear

Symptoms of anxiety, such as rapid breathing, dry mouth, and increased heart rate, plague all of us during stressful moments. But some people experience anxiety that is so intense and chronic it seriously disrupts their lives. They feel threatened, unable to cope, unhappy, and insecure in a world that seems dangerous and hostile. In this section, we consider four anxiety disorders: generalized anxiety disorder, panic disorder, phobias, and obsessive-compulsive disorder **(Figure 11.2)**. Although we discuss these disorders separately, people often have more than one anxiety disorder (Barlow, Esler, & Vitali, 1998).

Generalized anxiety disorder

This disorder affects twice as many women as it does men (Brawman-Mintzer & Lydiard, 1996, 1997). **Generalized anxiety disorder** is characterized by chronic, uncontrollable, and excessive fear and worry that lasts at least six months and that is not focused on any particular object or situation. Because of persistent

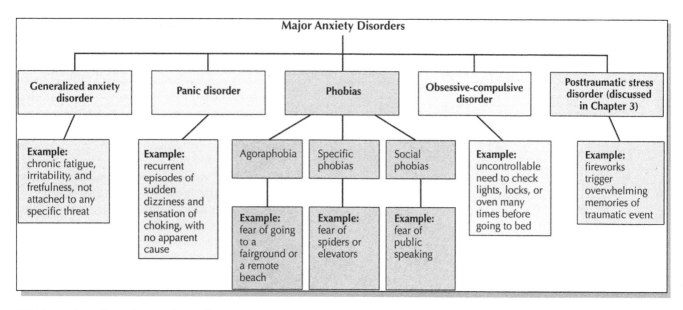

FIGURE 11.2 ■ Major anxiety disorders.

muscle tension and autonomic fear reactions, people with this disorder may develop headaches, heart palpitations, dizziness, and insomnia, making it even harder to cope with normal daily activities.

Panic disorder

Sudden, but brief, attacks of intense apprehension that cause trembling, dizziness, and difficulty breathing are symptoms of **panic disorder**. Panic attacks generally happen after frightening experiences or prolonged stress (and sometimes even after exercise). Panic disorder is diagnosed when several apparently spontaneous panic attacks lead to a persistent concern about future attacks. A common complication of panic disorder is agoraphobia (Craske, 2000; Gorman, 2000).

Phobias

Phobias involve a strong, irrational fear and avoidance of objects or situations that are usually considered harmless (fear of elevators or fear of going to the dentist, for example). Although the person recognizes that the fear is irrational, the experience is still one of overwhelming anxiety, and a full-blown panic attack may follow. The *DSM-IV-TR* divides phobic disorders into three broad categories: agoraphobia, specific phobias, and social phobias.

People with *agoraphobia* restrict their normal activities because they fear having a panic attack in crowded, enclosed, or wide-open places where they would be unable to receive help in an emergency. In severe cases, people with agoraphobia may refuse to leave the safety of their homes.

A *specific phobia* is a fear of a specific object or situation, such as needles, heights, rats, or spiders. Claustrophobia (fear of closed spaces) and acrophobia (fear of heights) are the specific phobias most often treated by therapists. People with specific phobias generally recognize that their fears are excessive and unreasonable, but they are unable to control their anxiety and will go to great lengths to avoid the feared stimulus **(Figure 11.3)**.

People with *social phobias* are irrationally fearful of embarrassing themselves in social situations. Fear of public speaking and of eating in public are the most common social phobias. The fear of public scrutiny and potential humiliation may become so pervasive that normal life is impossible (den Boer, 2000; Swartz & Margolis, 2004).

© 2009 by Cheryl Casey. Used under license of Shutterstock, Inc.

FIGURE 11.3 ▢ Spider phobia.
Can you imagine how it would feel to be so frightened by a spider that you would try to jump out of a speeding car to get away from it? This is how a person suffering from a phobia might feel.

© 2009 by Phase4Photography. Used under license of Shutterstock, Inc.

FIGURE 11.4 ▢ Faulty thinking patterns.
People who suffer from social phobia are excessively concerned about others' evaluations, hypersensitive to any criticism, and obsessively worried about potential mistakes. This intense self-preoccupation leads these people to perpetually believe they have failed. What changes in thinking patterns might lessen this anxiety?

Obsessive-compulsive disorder (OCD)

This disorder involves persistent, unwanted fearful thoughts (obsessions) or irresistible urges to perform an act or repeated ritual (compulsions), which help relieve the anxiety created by the obsession. In adults, this disorder is equally common in men and women. However, it is more prevalent among boys when the onset is in childhood (American Psychiatric Association, 2000).

Imagine what it would be like to worry so obsessively about germs that you compulsively wash your hands hundreds of times a day until they are raw and bleeding. Most sufferers of OCD realize that their actions are senseless. But when they try to stop the behavior, they experience mounting anxiety, which is relieved only by giving in to the urges.

Causes of Anxiety Disorders

The causes of anxiety disorders are debatable. Research has focused on the roles of psychological, biological, and sociocultural processes (the *biopsychosocial model*).

Psychological contributions to anxiety disorders are primarily in the form of faulty cognitive processes and maladaptive learning.

Faulty cognitions

People with anxiety disorders have habits of thinking, or cognitive habits, that make them prone to fear. They tend to be hypervigilant—they constantly scan their environment for signs of danger and ignore signs of safety. They also tend to magnify ordinary threats and failures and to be hypersensitive to others' opinions of them **(Figure 11.4)**.

Maladaptive learning

According to learning theorists, anxiety disorders generally result from conditioning and social learning (Bouton, Mineka, & Barlow, 2001; King, Clowes-Hollins, & Ollendick, 1997; Thomas & Ayres, 2004).

During classical conditioning, for example, a stimulus that is originally neutral (e.g., a harmless spider) becomes paired with a frightening event (a sudden panic attack) so that it becomes a conditioned stimulus that elicits anxiety. The person then begins to avoid spiders in order to reduce anxiety (an operant conditioning process known as negative reinforcement).

Some researchers contend that the fact that most people with phobias cannot remember a specific instance that led to their fear and that frightening experiences do not always trigger phobias suggests that conditioning may not be the only explanation. Social learning theorists propose that some phobias are the result of modeling and imitation.

Phobias may also be learned vicariously (indirectly). In one study, rhesus monkeys viewed videos showing another monkey apparently experiencing extreme fear of a toy snake, a toy rabbit, a toy crocodile and flowers (Cook & Mineka, 1989). The "viewing" monkeys were later afraid of the snake and crocodile but not of the rabbit or flowers, suggesting that phobias have both learned and biological components.

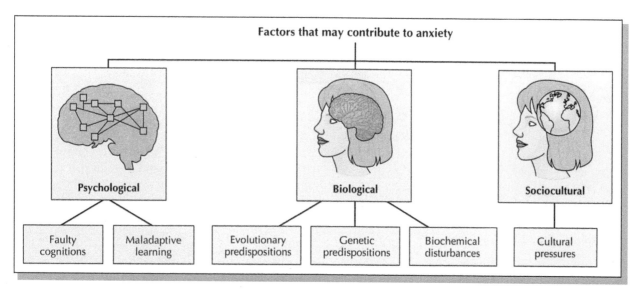

FIGURE 11.5 ■ Factors that may contribute to anxiety.

Some researchers believe that phobias reflect an evolutionary predisposition to fear that which was dangerous to our ancestors (Mineka & Oehman, 2002; Rossano, 2003). Some people with panic disorder also seem to be genetically predisposed toward an overreaction of the autonomic nervous system, further supporting the argument for a biological component. In addition, stress and arousal seem to play a role in panic attacks, and drugs such as caffeine or nicotine and even hyperventilation can trigger an attack, all suggesting a biochemical disturbance.

In addition to psychological and biological components, sociocultural factors can contribute to anxiety. There has been a sharp rise in anxiety disorders in the past 50 years, particularly in Western industrialized countries. Can you see how our increasingly fast-paced lives—along with our increased mobility, decreased job security, and decreased family support—might contribute to anxiety? Unlike the dangers that humans faced in our evolutionary history, today's threats are less identifiable and immediate, which may lead some people to become hypervigilant and predisposed to anxiety disorders **(Figure 11.5)**.

Further support for sociocultural influences on anxiety disorders is that anxiety disorders can have dramatically different forms in other cultures. For example, in a collectivist twist on anxiety, the Japanese have a type of social phobia called *taijin kyofusho* (TKS), which involves morbid dread of doing something to embarrass others. This disorder is quite different from the Western version of social phobia, which centers on a fear of criticism.

■ **CONCEPT CHECK STOP**

How do generalized anxiety disorders and phobias differ?
What are examples of the faulty cognitions that characterize anxiety disorders?

MOOD DISORDERS

LEARNING OBJECTIVES

Explain how major depressive disorder and bipolar disorder differ.

Summarize research on the biological and psychological factors that contribute to mood disorders.

Major depressive disorder: Long-lasting depressed mood that interferes with the ability to function, feel pleasure, or maintain interest in life (Swartz & Margolis, 2004).

Bipolar disorder: Repeated episodes of mania (unreasonable elation and hyperactivity) and depression.

Understanding Mood Disorders: Major Depressive Disorder and Bipolar Disorder

As the name implies, **mood disorders** (also known as affective disorders) are characterized by extreme disturbances in emotional states. There are two main types of mood disorders—major depressive disorder and bipolar disorder.

We all feel "blue" sometimes, especially following the loss of a job, end of a relationship, or death of a loved one. People suffering from major depressive disorder, however, may experience a lasting and continuously depressed mood without a clear trigger.

Clinically depressed people are so deeply sad and discouraged that they often have trouble sleeping, are likely to lose (or gain) weight, and may feel so fatigued that they cannot go to work or school or even comb their hair and brush their teeth. They may sleep constantly, have problems concentrating, and feel so profoundly sad and guilty that they consider suicide. Depressed individuals have a hard time thinking clearly or recognizing their own problems.

When depression is *unipolar*, the depressive episode eventually ends, and the person returns to a "normal" emotional level. People with bipolar disorder, however, rebound to the opposite state, known as *mania* **(Figure 11.6)**.

During a manic episode, the person is overly excited, extremely active, and easily distracted. The person exhibits unrealistically high self-esteem, an inflated sense of importance, and poor judgment **(Figure 11.7)**. The person is hyperactive and may not sleep for days at a time yet does not become fatigued. Thinking is speeded up and can change abruptly to new topics, showing "rapid flight of ideas." Speech is also rapid ("pressured speech") and it is difficult for others to get a word in edgewise.

A manic episode may last a few days or a few months, and it generally ends abruptly. The ensuing depressive episode generally lasts three times as long as the manic episode. The lifetime risk for bipolar disorder is low—somewhere between 0.5 and 1.6 percent—but it can be one of the most debilitating and lethal disorders, with a suicide rate between 10 and 20 percent among sufferers (Goodwin et al., 2004; MacKinnon, Jamison, & DePaulo, 1997).

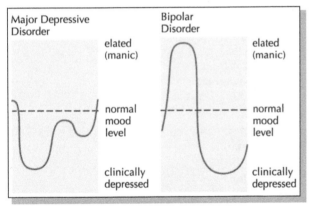

FIGURE 11.6 ■ Mood disorders. If major depressive disorders and bipolar disorders were depicted on a graph, they might look something like this.

Causes of Mood Disorders: Biological Versus Psychosocial Factors

Biological factors appear to play a significant role in both major depression and bipolar disorder. Recent research suggests that structural brain changes may contribute to these mood disorders (Almeida et al., 2003; Lyoo et al., 2004; Steffens et al., 2003). Other research points to imbalances of the neurotransmitters serotonin, norepinephrine, and dopamine (Delgado, 2004; Owens, 2004; Southwick, Vythilingam, & Charney, 2005). Drugs that alter the activity of these neurotransmitters also decrease the symptoms of depression (and are therefore called antidepressants) (Chuang, 1998).

Some research indicates that mood disorders may be inherited (Baldessarini & Hennen, 2004; Horiuchi et al., 2004; Sequeira et al., 2004). For example, when one identical twin has a mood disorder, there is about a 50 percent chance that the other twin will also develop the illness (Swartz & Margolis, 2004). However, it is important to remember that relatives generally have similar environments as well as similar genes.

Finally, the evolutionary perspective suggests that moderate depression may be a normal and healthy adaptive response to a very real loss (such as the death of a loved one). The depression helps us to step back and reassess our goals (Neese, 2000). Clinical, severe depression may just be an extreme version of this generally adaptive response.

Psychosocial theories of depression focus on environmental stressors and disturbances in the person's interpersonal relationships, thought processes, self-concept, and history of learned behaviors (Cheung, Gilbert, & Irons, 2004; Hammen, 2005; Mathews & McLeod, 2005). The psychoanalytic explanation sees depression as anger (stemming from feelings of rejection) turned inward when an important relationship is lost. The humanistic school says that depression results when a person demands perfection of him- or herself or when positive growth is blocked.

According to the **learned helplessness** theory (Seligman, 1975, 1994), depression occurs when people (and other animals) become resigned to the idea that they are helpless to escape from something painful. Learned helplessness may be particularly likely to trigger depression if the person attributes failure to causes that are internal ("my own weakness"), stable ("this weakness is long-standing and unchanging"), and global ("this weakness is a problem in lots of settings") (Chaney et al., 2004; Gotlieb & Abramson, 1999; Peterson & Vaidya, 2001).

Suicide is a major danger associated with depression. Because of the associated shame and secrecy with suicide, many fail to get or give help.

FIGURE 11.7 ■ No limits.
Poor judgment is common during manic episodes. A person may give away valuable possessions, go on wild spending sprees, or make elaborate plans for becoming rich and famous.

■ **CONCEPT CHECK STOP**

What are the key characteristics of a manic episode?
How might major depression be an exaggeration of an evolutionary adaptation?

SCHIZOPHRENIA

LEARNING OBJECTIVES

Describe some common symptoms of schizophrenia.

Compare the traditional (four-group) system for classifying different types of schizophrenia with the (two-group) system that has recently emerged.

Summarize the biological and psychosocial factors that contribute to schizophrenia.

Imagine that your daughter has just left for college and that you hear voices inside your head shouting, "You'll never see her again! You have been a bad mother! She'll die." Or what if you saw live animals in your refrigerator? These experiences have plagued "Mrs. T" for decades (Gershon & Rieder, 1993).

Schizophrenia: A group of psychotic disorders involving major disturbances in perception, language, thought, emotion, and behavior. The individual withdraws from people and reality, often into a fantasy life of delusions and hallucinations.

Mrs. T suffers from schizophrenia (skit-so-FREE-nee-uh). Schizophrenia is often so severe that it is considered a psychosis, meaning that the person is out of touch with reality. People with schizophrenia have serious problems caring for themselves, relating to others, and holding a job. In extreme cases, people with schizophrenia require institutional or custodial care.

Schizophrenia is one of the most widespread and devastating mental disorders. Approximately 1 out of every 100 people will develop schizophrenia in his or her lifetime, and approximately half of all people who are admitted to mental hospitals are diagnosed with this disorder (Gottesman, 1991; Kendler et al., 1996; Kessler et al., 1994; Regier et al., 1993). Schizophrenia usually emerges between the late teens and the mid-30s. It seems to be equally prevalent in men and women, but it's generally more severe and strikes earlier in men than in women (Salyers & Mueser, 2001).

Many people confuse schizophrenia with dissociative identity disorder, which is sometimes referred to as *split* or *multiple personality disorder*. Schizophrenia means "split mind," but when Eugen Bleuler coined the term in 1911, he was referring to the fragmenting of thought processes and emotions, not personalities (Neale, Oltmanns, & Winters, 1983). As we discuss later in this chapter, dissociative identity disorder is the rare condition of having more than one distinct personality.

Symptoms of Schizophrenia: Five Areas of Disturbance

Schizophrenia is a group of disorders characterized by a disturbance in one or more of the following areas: perception, language, thought, affect (emotions), and behavior.

Perceptual symptoms

The senses of people with schizophrenia may be either enhanced or blunted. The filtering and selection processes that allow most people to concentrate on whatever they choose are impaired, and sensory stimulation is jumbled and distorted.

Hallucinations: Imaginary sensory perceptions that occur without an external stimulus.

People with schizophrenia may also experience hallucinations—most commonly auditory hallucinations (hearing voices and sounds).

On rare occasions, people with schizophrenia will hurt others in response to their distorted perceptions. But a person with schizophrenia is more likely to be self-destructive and suicidal than violent toward others.

Language and thought disturbances

For people with schizophrenia, words lose their usual meanings and associations, logic is impaired, and thoughts are disorganized and bizarre. When language and thought disturbances are mild, the individual jumps from topic to topic. With more severe disturbances, the person jumbles phrases and words together (into a "word salad") or creates artificial words.

The most common—and frightening—thought disturbance experienced by people with schizophrenia is the lack of contact with reality (psychosis).

Delusions: Mistaken beliefs based on misrepresentations of reality.

Delusions are also common in people with schizophrenia. We all experience exaggerated thoughts from time to time, such as thinking a friend is trying to avoid us, but the delusions of schizophrenia are much more extreme. For example, Jim (the med student in the chapter opener) was completely convinced that others were trying to assassinate him (a *delusion of persecution*). In *delusions of grandeur*, people believe that they are someone very important, perhaps Jesus Christ or the queen of England. In *delusions of reference*, unrelated events are given special significance, as when a person believes that a radio program is giving him or her a special message.

MENTAL ILLNESS IN PUBLIC VIEW

What could be more terrifying than performing at a final audition for *American Idol*? How about doing so just moments after announcing—to Simon Cowell, the show's notorious "celebrity judge"—that you have a mental illness? It's a moment that few people would relish. In fact, fear of ridicule and discrimination leads many people with psychological disorders to keep their condition secret. But singer and songwriter Tracy Moore, who was diagnosed with schizophrenia at age 21, has taken the opposite approach. Even as she combats paranoia and delusional thoughts, Moore has worked to raise public awareness and develop support networks for people with schizophrenia. And she continues to nourish her longtime dream of succeeding as a performing artist.

Source: Roberts, M. (2006, March). Idol dreams. *Schizophrenia Digest*, 30–33.

Emotional disturbances

Changes in emotion usually occur in people with schizophrenia. In some cases, emotions are exaggerated and fluctuate rapidly. At other times, emotions become blunted. Some people with schizophrenia have *flattened affect*—almost no emotional response of any kind.

THE JERUSALEM SYNDROME

Every year, dozens of tourists to Jerusalem are hospitalized with symptoms of *Jerusalem syndrome*, a psychological disturbance in which a person becomes obsessed with the significance of Jerusalem and engages in bizarre, deluded behavior while visiting the city. For example, the person might come to believe that he or she is Jesus Christ or some other Biblical character, transform hotel linens into a long, white toga, and publicly deliver sermons or recite Bible verses. Although scholars disagree about the explanations for this "religious psychosis" and the extent to which it is a distinct psychological disorder, the symptoms themselves provide a classic example of delusional thought disturbances. Can you see how delusions of persecution, grandeur, and reference might all play out in Jerusalem syndrome?

© 2009 by mforrell. Used under license of Shutterstock, Inc.

Behavioral disturbances

Disturbances in behavior may take the form of unusual actions that have special meaning. For example, one patient massaged his head repeatedly to "clear it" of unwanted thoughts. People with schizophrenia may become *cataleptic* and assume a nearly immobile stance for an extended period.

Types of Schizophrenia: Recent Methods of Classification

For many years, researchers divided schizophrenia into five subtypes: paranoid, catatonic, disorganized, undifferentiated, and residual **(Table 11.2)**. Although these terms are still included in the *DSM-IV-TR*, critics contend that this system does not differentiate in terms of prognosis, cause, or response to treatment and that the undifferentiated type is merely a catchall for cases that are difficult to diagnose (American Psychiatric Association, 2000).

For these reasons, researchers have proposed an alternative classification system:

1. **Positive schizophrenia symptoms** involve additions to or exaggerations of normal thought processes and behaviors, including bizarre delusions and hallucinations.
2. **Negative schizophrenia symptoms** involve the loss or absence of normal thought processes and behaviors, including impaired attention, limited or toneless speech, flattened affect, and social withdrawal.

Positive symptoms are more common when schizophrenia develops rapidly, whereas negative symptoms are more often found in slow-developing schizophrenia. Positive symptoms are associated with better adjustment before the onset and a better prognosis for recovery.

In addition to these two groups, the latest *DSM* suggests adding another dimension to reflect *disorganization of behavior*, including rambling speech, erratic behavior, and inappropriate affect.

Causes of Schizophrenia: Nature and Nurture Theories

Because schizophrenia comes in many different forms, it probably has multiple biological and psychosocial bases (Walker et al., 2004). Let's look at biological contributions first.

TABLE 11.2   Subtypes of schizophrenia

Paranoid	Dominated by delusions (persecution and grandeur) and hallucinations (hearing voices)
Catatonic	Marked by motor disturbances (immobility or wild activity) and echo speech (repeating the speech of others)
Disorganized	Characterized by incoherent speech, flat or exaggerated emotions, and social withdrawal
Undifferentiated	Meets the criteria for schizophrenia but is not any of the above subtypes
Residual	No longer meets the full criteria for schizophrenia but still shows some symptoms

Prenatal viral infections, birth complications, immune responses, maternal malnutrition, and advanced paternal age all may contribute to the development of schizophrenia (Beraki et al., 2005; Cannon et al., 2002; Dalman & Allebeck, 2002; Sawa & Kamiya, 2003; Zuckerman & Weiner, 2005). However, most biological theories of schizophrenia focus on genetics, neurotransmitters, and brain abnormalities.

- *Genetics.* Although researchers are beginning to identify specific genes related to schizophrenia, most genetic studies have focused on twins and adoptions (Crow, 2004; Davalos et al., 2004; Elkin, Kalidindi, & McGuffin, 2004; Hulshoff Pol et al., 2004; Lindholm et al., 2004; Petronis, 2000). This research indicates that the risk for schizophrenia increases with genetic similarity; that is, people who share more genes with a person who has schizophrenia are more likely to develop the disorder.

- *Neurotransmitters.* Precisely how genetic inheritance produces schizophrenia is unclear. According to the **dopamine hypothesis**, overactivity of certain dopamine neurons in the brain causes schizophrenia (Ikemoto, 2004; Paquet et al., 2004). This hypothesis is based on two observations. First, administering amphetamines increases the amount of dopamine and can produce (or worsen) some symptoms of schizophrenia, especially in people with a genetic predisposition to the disorder. Second, drugs that reduce dopamine activity in the brain reduce or eliminate some symptoms of schizophrenia.

- *Brain abnormalities.* The third major biological theory for schizophrenia involves abnormalities in brain function and structure. Researchers have found larger cerebral ventricles (fluid-filled spaces in the brain) in some people with schizophrenia (DeLisi et al., 2004; Gaser et al., 2004).

Also, some people with chronic schizophrenia have a lower level of activity in their frontal and temporal lobes—areas that are involved in language, attention, and memory. Damage in these regions might explain the thought and language disturbances that characterize schizophrenia. This lower level of brain activity, and schizophrenia itself, may also result from an overall loss of gray matter (neurons in the cerebral cortex) (Gogtay et al., 2004; Hulshoff Pol et al., 2004).

Clearly, biological factors play a key role in schizophrenia. But the fact that even in identical twins—who share identical genes—the heritability of schizophrenia is only 48 percent tells us that nongenetic factors must contribute the remaining percentage. Most psychologists believe that there are at least two possible psychosocial contributors.

According to the **diathesis-stress model** of schizophrenia, stress plays an essential role in triggering schizophrenic episodes in people with an inherited predisposition (or diathesis) toward the disease (Corcoran et al., 2003; Schwartz & Smith, 2004; Walker et al., 2004).

Some investigators suggest that communication disorders in family members may also be a predisposing factor for schizophrenia. Such disorders include unintelligible speech, fragmented communication, and parents' frequently sending severely contradictory messages to children. Several studies have also shown greater rates of relapse and worsening of symptoms among hospitalized patients who went home to families that were critical and hostile toward them or overly involved in their lives emotionally (Hooley & Hiller, 2001; Lefley, 2000).

How should we evaluate the different theories about the causes of schizophrenia? Critics of the dopamine hypothesis and the brain damage theory argue that those theories fit only some cases of schizophrenia. Moreover, with both theories, it is difficult to determine cause and effect. The disturbed-communication theories are also hotly debated, and research is inconclusive. Schizophrenia is probably the result of a combination of known and unknown interacting factors.

■ CONCEPT CHECK STOP

How do hallucinations and delusions differ?

How do positive and negative symptoms of schizophrenia differ?

What is the diathesis-stress model of schizophrenia?

OTHER DISORDERS

LEARNING OBJECTIVES

Explain how substance abuse and substance dependence differ.

Describe the types of dissociative disorders.

Identify the major characteristics of personality disorders.

Substance-Related Disorders

Substance-related disorders: Abuse of or dependence on a mood- or behavior-altering drug.

The category of substance-related disorders is subdivided into two general groups: substance abuse and substance dependence **(Table 11.3)**. When alcohol or other drug use interferes with a person's social or occupational functioning, it is called *substance abuse*. Drug use becomes *substance dependence* when it also causes physical reactions, including *tolerance* (requiring more of the drug to get the desired effect) and *withdrawal* (negative physical effects when the drug is removed).

Some people can use alcohol and other drugs and not develop a problem. Unfortunately, researchers have not been able to identify ahead of time those who can use drugs without risk of becoming abusers versus those who are likely to become abusers. Complicating diagnosis and treatment is the fact that substance-related disorders commonly coexist with other mental disorders, including anxiety disorders, mood disorders, schizophrenia, and personality disorders (Bates & Rutherford, 2003; Green et al., 2004; Teesson, Hodder, & Buhrich, 2004). This co-occurrence of disorders is called **comorbidity (Figure 11.8)**.

TABLE 11.3 ■ *DSM-IV-TR* substance abuse and substance dependence

Criteria for Substance Abuse (alcohol and other drugs)	Criteria for Substance Dependence (alcohol and other drugs)
Maladaptive use of a substance shown by one of the following:	*Three or more of the following:*
■ Failure to meet obligations	■ Tolerance
■ Repeated use in situations where it is physically dangerous	■ Withdrawal
■ Continued use despite problems caused by the substance	■ Substance taken for a longer time or greater amount than intended
■ Repeated substance-related legal problems	■ Lack of desire or efforts to reduce or control use
	■ Social, recreational, or occupational activities given up or reduced
	■ Much time spent in activities to obtain the substance
	■ Use continued despite knowing that psychological or physical problems are worsened by it

What causes comorbidity? Perhaps the most influential hypothesis is **self-medication**—individuals drink or use drugs to reduce their symptoms (Batel, 2000; Goswami et al., 2004; Green, 2000). Regardless of the causes, it is critical that patients, family members, and clinicians recognize and deal with comorbidity if treatment is to be effective.

FIGURE 11.8 ■ Comorbidity complicates treatment.
Can you see how comorbidity can cause serious problems? How can the appropriate cause, course, or treatment be identified for someone dealing with a combination of disorders?

Dissociative Disorders: When the Personality Splits Apart

The most dramatic psychological disorders are dissociative disorders. There are several types of dissociative disorders, but all involve a splitting apart (a *dis*-association) of significant aspects of experience from memory or consciousness. Individuals dissociate from the core of their personality by failing to remember past experiences (*dissociative amnesia*) **(Figure 11.9)**, by leaving home and wandering off (*dissociative fugue*), by losing their sense of reality and feeling estranged from the self (*depersonalization disorder*), or by developing completely separate personalities (*dissociative identity disorder*).

Unlike most other psychological disorders, the primary cause of dissociative disorders appears to be environmental variables, with little or no genetic influence (Waller & Ross, 1997).

The most severe dissociative disorder is **dissociative identity disorder (DID)**—previously known as multiple personality disorder—in which at least two separate and distinct personalities exist within a person at the same time. Each personality has unique memories, behaviors, and social relationships. Transition from one personality to another occurs suddenly and is often triggered by psychological stress. Usually, the original personality has no knowledge or awareness of the alternate personalities, but all of the personalities may be aware of lost periods of time. The disorder is diagnosed more among women than among men. Women with DID also tend to have more identities, averaging 15 or more, compared with men, who average 8 (American Psychiatric Association, 2000).

> **Dissociative disorders:** Amnesia, fugue, or multiple personalities resulting from avoidance of painful memories or situations.

DID is a controversial diagnosis. Some experts suggest that many cases are faked or result from false memories and an unconscious need to please the therapist (Kihlstrom, 2005; Loftus, 1997; McNally, 2004; Stafford & Lynn, 2002). Other psychologists accept the validity of multiple personality and contend that the condition is underdiagnosed (Brown, 2001; Lipsanen et al., 2004; Spiegel & Maldonado, 1999).

Personality Disorders: Antisocial and Borderline

What would happen if the characteristics of a personality were so inflexible and maladaptive that they significantly impaired someone's ability to function?

FIGURE 11.9 ■ Dissociation as an escape.
The major force behind all dissociative disorders is the need to escape from anxiety. Imagine witnessing a loved one's death in a horrible car accident. Can you see how your mind might cope by blocking out all memory of the event?

This is what happens with **personality disorders**. Several types of personality disorders are included in this category in the *DSM-IV-TR*, but here we will focus on antisocial personality disorder and borderline personality disorder.

Antisocial personality disorder

The term **antisocial personality disorder** is used interchangeably with the terms *sociopath* and *psychopath*. These labels describe behavior so far outside the ethical and legal standards of society that many consider it the most serious of all mental disorders. Unlike with anxiety, mood disorders, and schizophrenia, people with this diagnosis feel little personal distress (and may not be motivated to change). Yet their maladaptive traits generally bring considerable harm and suffering to others (Hervé et al., 2004; Kirkman, 2002; Nathan et al., 2003). Although serial killers are often seen as classic examples of antisocial personality disorder **(Figure 11.10)**, many sociopaths harm people in less dramatic ways—for example, as ruthless businesspeople and crooked politicians.

The four hallmarks of antisocial personality disorder are egocentrism (preoccupation with oneself and insensitivity to the needs of others), lack of conscience, impulsive behavior, and superficial charm (American Psychiatric Association, 2000).

Unlike most adults, individuals with antisocial personality disorder act impulsively, without giving thought to the consequences. They are usually poised when confronted with their destructive behavior and feel contempt for anyone they are able to manipulate. They also change jobs and relationships suddenly, and they often have a history of truancy from school and of being expelled for destructive behavior. People with antisocial personalities can be charming and persuasive, and they have remarkably good insight into the needs and weaknesses of other people.

Twin and adoption studies suggest a possible genetic predisposition to antisocial personality disorder (Bock & Goode, 1996; Jang et al., 2003). Biological contributions are also suggested by studies that have found abnormally low autonomic activity during stress, right hemisphere abnormalities, and reduced gray matter in the frontal lobes (Kiehl et al., 2004; Raine et al., 2000).

Evidence also exists for environmental or psychological causes. Antisocial personality disorder is highly correlated with abusive parenting styles and inappropriate modeling (Farrington, 2000; Pickering, Farmer, & McGuffin, 2004). People with antisocial personality disorder often come from homes characterized by emotional deprivation, harsh and inconsistent disciplinary practices, and antisocial parental behavior. Still other studies show a strong interaction between both heredity and environment (Paris, 2000; Rutler, 1997).

FIGURE 11.10 ■ The BTK killer.
In 2005, Dennis Rader, known as the "BTK killer" for his method of binding, torturing, and killing his victims, pleaded guilty and was sentenced to life in prison for his crimes. Between 1974 and 1991, Rader murdered 10 women in and around Wichita, Kansas. After his killings, he sent taunting letters to police and local media, boasting of the crimes in graphic detail. Despite having a normal outward appearance—he was a husband, father, Cub Scout leader, and church council president—Rader's egocentrism and lack of conscience are primary characteristics of antisocial personality disorder.

© epa/CORBIS

Borderline personality disorder

Borderline personality disorder (BPD) is among the most commonly diagnosed personality disorders (Markovitz, 2004). The core features of this disorder are impulsivity and instability in mood, relationships, and self-image. Originally, the term implied that the person was on the borderline between neurosis and schizophrenia (Davison, Neale, & Kring, 2004). The modern conceptualization no longer has this connotation, but BPD remains one of the most complex and debilitating of all the personality disorders.

Mary's story of chronic, lifelong dysfunction, described in the chapter opener, illustrates the serious problems associated with this disorder. People with borderline personality disorder experience extreme difficulties in relationships. Subject to chronic feelings of depression, emptiness, and intense fear of abandonment, they also engage in destructive, impulsive behaviors, such as sexual promiscuity, drinking, gambling, and eating sprees (Chabrol et al., 2004; Trull et al., 2000). They may attempt suicide and sometimes engage in self-mutilating behavior (Bohus et al., 2004; McKay, Gavigan, & Kulchycky, 2004; Paris, 2004).

People with BPD tend to see themselves and everyone else in absolute terms—perfect or worthless (Mason & Kreger, 1998). They constantly seek reassurance from others and may quickly erupt in anger at the slightest sign of disapproval. The disorder is also typically marked by a long history of broken friendships, divorces, and lost jobs.

People with borderline personality disorder frequently have a childhood history of neglect; emotional deprivation; and physical, sexual, or emotional abuse (Goodman & Yehuda, 2002; Helgeland & Torgersen, 2004; Schmahl et al., 2004). Borderline personality disorder also tends to run in families, and some data suggest it is a result of impaired functioning of the brain's frontal lobes and limbic system, areas that control impulsive behaviors (Schmahl et al., 2004; Tebartz van Elst et al., 2003).

Although some therapists have had success treating BPD with drug therapy and behavior therapy (Bohus et al., Markovitz, 2004), the general prognosis is not favorable. In one study, seven years after treatment, about 50 percent of the original group still had the disorder (Links, Heslegrave, & van Reekum, 1998).

■ CONCEPT CHECK STOP

Why does the presence of comorbid disorders complicate the diagnosis and treatment of substance-related disorders?

Which is more important in the development of dissociative disorders, environment or genetics?

How do personality disorders differ from the other psychological disorders discussed in this chapter?

HOW GENDER AND CULTURE AFFECT ABNORMAL BEHAVIOR

LEARNING OBJECTIVES

Identify the biological, psychological, and social factors that might explain gender differences in depression.

Explain why it is difficult to directly compare mental disorders across cultures.

Explain why recognizing the difference between culture-general and culture-bound disorders and symptoms can help prevent ethnocentrism in the diagnosis and treatment of psychological disorders.

Among the Chippewa, Cree, and Montagnais-Naskapi Indians in Canada, there is a disorder called *windigo—or wiitiko—psychosis*, which is characterized by delusions and cannibalistic impulses. Believing that they have been possessed by the spirit of a windigo, a cannibal giant with a heart and entrails of ice, victims become severely depressed (Barnouw, 1985). As the malady begins, the individual typically experiences loss of appetite, diarrhea, vomiting, and insomnia, and he or she may see people turning into beavers and other edible animals.

In later stages, the victim becomes obsessed with cannibalistic thoughts and may even attack and kill loved ones in order to devour their flesh (Berreman, 1971).

If you were a therapist, how would you treat this disorder? Does it fit neatly into any of the categories of psychological disorders that you have learned about? We began this chapter discussing the complexities and problems with defining, identifying, and classifying abnormal behavior. Before we close, we need to add two additional confounding factors: gender and culture. In this section, we explore a few of the many ways in which men and women differ in how they experience abnormal behavior. We also look at cultural variations in abnormal behavior.

Gender and Depression: Why Are Women More Depressed?

In the United States, Canada, and other countries, the rate of severe depression for women is two to three times the rate for men (Angst et al., 2002; Nolen-Hoeksema, Larson, & Grayson, 2000; Ohayon & Schatzberg, 2002; Parker & Brotchie, 2004).

Why is there such a disparity between men and women? Research explanations can be grouped under biological influences (hormones, biochemistry, and genetic predisposition), psychological processes (ruminative thought processes), and social factors (greater poverty, work-life conflicts, unhappy marriages, and sexual or physical abuse) (Cheung, Gilbert, & Irons, 2004; Garnefski et al., 2004; Kornstein, 2002; Parker & Brotchie, 2004).

According to the *biopsychosocial model*, some women inherit a genetic or hormonal predisposition toward depression. This biological predisposition combines with society's socialization processes to help reinforce behaviors—such as greater emotional expression, passivity, and dependence—that increase the chances for depression (Alloy et al., 1999; Nolen-Hoeksema, Larson, & Grayson, 2000). At the same time, focusing only on classical symptoms of depression (sadness, low energy, and feelings of helplessness) may cause large numbers of depressed men to be overlooked **(Figure 11.11)**.

© 2009 by Fresnel. Used under license of Shutterstock, Inc.

FIGURE 11.11
Depression in disguise? In our society, men are typically socialized to suppress their emotions and to show their distress by acting out (showing aggression), acting impulsively (driving recklessly and committing petty crimes), and engaging in substance abuse. How might such cultural pressures lead us to underestimate male depression?

Culture and Schizophrenia: Differences Around the World

Peoples of different cultures experience mental disorders in a variety of ways. For example, the reported incidence of schizophrenia varies within different cultures around the world. It is unclear whether these differences result from actual differences in prevalence of the disorder or from differences in definition, diagnosis, or reporting (Kleinman & Cohen, 1997; Lefley, 2000).

The symptoms of schizophrenia also vary across cultures (Stompe et al., 2003), as do the particular stresses that may trigger its onset **(Figure 11.12)**.

Finally, despite the advanced treatment facilities and methods in industrialized nations, the prognosis for people with schizophrenia is actually better in non-industrialized societies. This may be because the core symptoms of schizophrenia (poor rapport with others, incoherent speech, etc.) make it more difficult to survive in highly industrialized countries. In addition, in most industrialized nations, families and other support groups are less likely to feel responsible for relatives and friends with schizophrenia (Brislin, 2000; Lefley, 2000).

© 2009 by Kiselev Andrey Valerevich. Used under license of Shutterstock, Inc.

© 2009 by palms. Used under license of Shutterstock, Inc.

FIGURE 11.12 ■ What is stressful?
A Some stressors are culturally specific, such as feeling possessed by evil forces or being the victim of witchcraft.
B Other stressors are shared by many cultures, such as the unexpected death of a spouse or loss of a job (Al-Issa, 2000; Browne, 2001; Neria et al., 2002; Torrey & Yolken, 1998).

Avoiding Ethnocentrism

Most research on psychological disorders originates and is conducted primarily in Western cultures. Such a restricted sampling can limit our understanding of disorders in general and lead to an ethnocentric view of mental disorders.

Fortunately, cross-cultural researchers have devised ways to overcome these difficulties (Draguns & Tanaka-Matsumi, 2003). For example, Robert Nishimoto (1988) has found several **culture-general symptoms** that are useful in diagnosing disorders across cultures **(Table 11.4)**.

In addition, Nishimoto found several **culture-bound symptoms**. For example, the Vietnamese Chinese reported "fullness in head," the Mexican respondents had "problems with [their] memory," and the Anglo-Americans reported "shortness of breath" and "headaches." Apparently, people learn to express their problems in ways that are acceptable to others in the same culture (Brislin, 1997, 2000; Widiger & Sankis, 2000).

This division between culture-general and culture-bound symptoms also helps us understand depression. Certain symptoms of depression (such as

TABLE 11.4 ■ Across cultures there is a general set of mental health symptoms.

1. Nervous
2. Weak all over
3. Feel alone
4. Low spirits
5. Restless
6. Hot all over
7. Insomnia
8. Extensive worrying
9. Worry about personal issues
10. The feeling you cannot get along
11. The feeling you cannot do anything worthwhile
12. The feeling that nothing turns out right

intense sadness, poor concentration, and low energy) seem to exist across all cultures (Green, 1999). But there is also evidence of some culture-bound symptoms. For example, feelings of guilt are found more often in North America and Europe. And in China, *somatization* (the conversion of depression into bodily complaints) occurs more frequently than it does in other parts of the world (Helms & Cook, 1999).

Just as there are culture-bound and culture-general symptoms, researchers have found that mental disorders are themselves sometimes culturally bound **(Figure 11.13)**. The earlier example of windigo psychosis, a disorder limited to a small group of Canadian Indians, illustrates just such a case.

Psychiatric Disorders Limited to Specific Cultures	
Geographic Locations	**Name of disorder and symptoms**
Western Countries	DISORDER: *Anorexia nervosa* SYMPTOMS: *Symptoms include a preoccupation with thinness so that the patient may eat little and exercise extensively*
United States	DISORDER: *Multiple Personality Disorder* SYMPTOMS: *Symptoms include the belief that multiple personalities exist within oneself and that they may appear at random times to cause shifts in a person's attitudes and behavior*
Latin Cultures	DISORDER: *"Ataque de nervios" Attack of nerves* SYMPTOMS: *Trembling and heart palpitations after the death of a family member or after a bad accident*
West Africa	DISORDER: *Brain fog* SYMPTOMS: *The main symptom is "brain tiredness" and is associated with difficulties in academic learning*
Ethiopia	DISORDER: *Possession by the Zar* SYMPTOMS: *Involuntary movements, mutism and incomprehensible speech*
Southeast Asia	DISORDER: *Running amok* SYMPTOMS: *Out of control aggression with attempts to harm others*
South China and Vietnam	DISORDER: *Koro* SYMPTOMS: *The belief that your penis is retracting into your abdomen and when it does you will die*

FIGURE 11.13 ■ Some forms of mental illness are specific to a particular geographic location in the world.

As you can see, culture has a strong effect on mental disorders. Studying the similarities and differences across cultures can lead to better diagnosis and understanding. It also helps mental health professionals who work with culturally diverse populations understand both culturally general and culturally bound symptoms.

■ CONCEPT CHECK STOP

Why might depression be frequently overlooked in men?
How does schizophrenia differ from one culture to another?
What are some examples of culture-bound disorders?

SUMMARY

1 Studying Psychological Disorders

1. Criteria for **abnormal behavior** include statistical infrequency, disability or dysfunction, personal distress, and violation of norms. None of these criteria alone is adequate for classifying abnormal behavior.
2. Superstitious explanations for abnormal behavior were replaced by the **medical model**, which eventually gave rise to the modern specialty of **psychiatry**. In contrast to the medical model, psychology offers a multifaceted approach to explaining abnormal behavior.
3. The *Diagnostic and Statistical Manual of Mental Disorders*, fourth edition, text revision (*DSM-IV-TR*) is organized according to five major axes, which serve as guidelines for making decisions about symptoms.

2 Anxiety Disorders

1. Major **anxiety disorders** include generalized anxiety disorder, panic disorder, phobias (including agoraphobia, specific phobias, and social phobias), and obsessive-compulsive disorder (OCD).
2. Psychological (faulty cognitions and maladaptive learning), biological (evolutionary and genetic predispositions, biochemical disturbances), and sociocultural factors (cultural pressures toward hypervigilance) likely all contribute to anxiety.

3 Mood Disorders

1. Mood disorders are characterized by extreme disturbances in emotional states. People suffering from **major depressive disorder** may experience a lasting depressed mood without a clear trigger. In contrast, people with **bipolar disorder** alternate between periods of depression and mania (hyperactivity and poor judgment).
2. Biological factors play a significant role in mood disorders. Psychosocial theories of depression focus on environmental stressors and disturbances in interpersonal relationships, thought processes, self-concept, and learning history (including learned helplessness).

4 Schizophrenia

1. **Schizophrenia** is a group of disorders, each characterized by a disturbance in perception (including **hallucinations**), language, thought (including **delusions**), emotions, and/or behavior.

2. In the past, researchers divided schizophrenia into multiple subtypes. More recently, researchers have proposed focusing instead on positive versus negative symptoms. The latest *DSM-IV-TR* also suggests adding another dimension to reflect disorganization of behavior.

3. Most biological theories of schizophrenia focus on genetics, neurotransmitters, and brain abnormalities. Psychologists believe that there are also at least two possible psychosocial contributors: stress and communication disorders in families.

5 Other Disorders

1. **Substance-related disorders** fall into two general groups: substance abuse and substance dependence. Substance-related disorders commonly coexist with other mental disorders (comorbidity), which complicates their diagnosis and treatment.

2. **Dissociative disorders** include dissociative amnesia, dissociative fugue, depersonalization disorder, and dissociative identity disorder (DID). Environmental variables appear to be the primary cause of dissociative disorders.

3. **Personality disorders** occur when inflexible, maladaptive personality traits cause significant impairment of social and occupational functioning. The best-known type of personality disorder is antisocial personality disorder, characterized by egocentrism, lack of conscience, impulsive behavior, and superficial charm. The most common personality disorder is borderline personality disorder (BPD). Its core features are impulsivity and instability in mood, relationships, and self-image. Although some therapists have success with drug therapy and behavior therapy, prognosis is not favorable.

6 How Gender and Culture Affect Abnormal Behavior

1. Men and women differ in how they experience and express abnormal behavior. For example, in North America severe depression is much more common in women than in men. Biological, psychological, and social factors probably combine to explain this phenomenon.

2. Peoples of different cultures experience mental disorders in a variety of ways. For example, the reported incidence of schizophrenia varies within different cultures around the world, as do the disorder's symptoms, triggers, and prognosis.

3. Some symptoms of psychological disorders, as well as some disorders themselves, are culture-general, whereas others are culture-bound.

KEY TERMS

abnormal behavior
antisocial personality disorder
anxiety disorders
bipolar disorder
borderline personality disorder (BPD)
comorbidity
culture-bound symptoms

culture-general symptoms
delusions
Diagnostic and Statistical Manual of Mental Disorders (DSM-IV-TR)
diathesis-stress model
dissociative disorders

dissociative identity disorder (DID)
dopamine hypothesis
generalized anxiety disorder
hallucinations
learned helplessness
major depressive disorders
medical model

mood disorders
negative schizophrenia
    symptoms
neurosis
obsessive-compulsive
    disorder (OCD)
panic disorder

personality disorders
phobias
positive schizophrenia
    symptoms
psychiatry
psychosis
schizophrenia

self-medication
state disorders
substance-related
    disorders
trait disorders

CRITICAL AND CREATIVE THINKING QUESTIONS

1. Can you think of cases where each of the four criteria for abnormal behavior might *not* be suitable for classifying a person's behavior as abnormal?

2. Do you think the insanity plea, as it is currently structured, makes sense?

3. Why do you suppose that anxiety disorders are among the easiest to treat?

4. Have you ever felt depressed? How would you distinguish between "normal" depression and a major depressive disorder?

5. Culture clearly has strong effects on mental disorders. How does that influence how you think about what is normal or abnormal?

6. Most of the disorders discussed in this chapter have some evidence for a genetic predisposition. What would you tell a friend who has a family member with one of these disorders about his or her chances of developing the same disorder?

(Check answers in Appendix B.)

1. Your textbook defines *abnormal* behavior as _____.
   a. a statistically infrequent pattern of pathological emotion, thought, or action
   b. patterns of emotion, thought, and action that are considered pathological
   c. a pattern of pathological emotion, thought, or action that causes personal distress, or violates social norms
   d. all of these options

2. _____ is the branch of medicine that deals with the diagnosis, treatment, and prevention of mental disorders.
   a. Psychology
   b. Psychiatry
   c. Psychobiology
   d. Psychodiagnostics

3. Label the five axes of the *Diagnostic and Statistical Manual of Mental Disorders (DSM-IV-TR)* on the figure below.

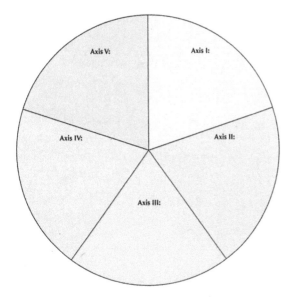

4. Anxiety disorders are _____.
   a. characterized by unrealistic, irrational fear
   b. the least frequent of the mental disorders
   c. twice as common in men as in women
   d. all of these options

5. Label the 5 major anxiety disorders on the figure below.

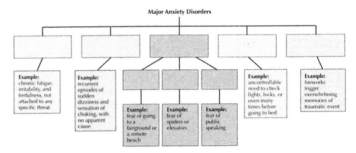

6. The two main types of mood disorders are _____.
   a. major depression and bipolar disorder
   b. mania and depression
   c. SAD and MAD
   d. learned helplessness and suicide

7. Someone who experiences repeated episodes of mania or cycles between mania and depression has a _____.
   a. disruption of circadian rhythms
   b. bipolar disorder
   c. manic-depressive syndrome
   d. cyclothymia disorder

8. According to the theory known as _____, when faced with a painful situation from which there is no escape, animals and people enter a state of helplessness and resignation.
   a. autonomic resignation
   b. helpless resignation
   c. resigned helplessness
   d. learned helplessness

9. A psychotic disorder that is characterized by major disturbances in perception, language, thought, emotion, and behavior is _____.
   a. schizophrenia
   b. multiple personality disorder
   c. borderline psychosis
   d. neurotic psychosis

10. Perceptions for which there are no appropriate external stimuli are called _____, and the most common type among people suffering from schizophrenia is _____.
    a. hallucinations; auditory
    b. hallucinations; visual
    c. delusions; auditory
    d. delusions; visual

11. Label the 5 subtypes of schizophrenia on the table below.

Subtypes of schizophrenia
Dominated by delusions (persecution and grandeur) and hallucinations (hearing voices)
Marked by motor disturbances (immobility or wild activity) and echo speech (repeating the speech of others)
Characterized by incoherent speech, flat or exaggerated emotions, and social withdrawal
Meets the criteria for schizophrenia but is not any of the above subtypes
No longer meets the full criteria for schizophrenia but still shows some symptoms

12. Failure to meet obligations may be indicative of alcohol or drug _____ whereas tolerance and withdrawal may be indicative of alcohol or drug _____.
    a. use; abuse
    b. abuse; dependence
    c. abuse; abuse
    d. dependence; abuse

13. The disorder that is an attempt to avoid painful memories or situations, and is characterized by amnesia, fugue, or multiple personalities is _____.
    a. dissociative disorder
    b. displacement disorder
    c. disoriented disorder
    d. identity disorder

14. Inflexible, maladaptive personality traits that cause significant impairment of social and occupational functioning is known as _____.
    a. nearly all mental disorders
    b. the psychotic and dissociative disorders
    c. personality disorders
    d. none of these options

15. Which of the following are examples of culture-general symptoms of mental health difficulties, useful in diagnosing disorders across cultures?
    a. trouble sleeping
    b. can't get along
    c. worry all the time
    d. all of the above

Chapter 11: Psychological Disorders

END OF CHAPTER QUIZ

1. This illness has a medical cause and is related to REPETITION.
   a. Medical Model
   b. OCD
   c. PTSD
   d. DID

2. This disorder has a Freudian history and is rarely applied any longer.
   a. Medical Model
   b. OCD
   c. PTSD
   d. DID

3. This approach to mental illness asks the scientist to look for physical causes of the disorder.
   a. Medical Model
   b. OCD
   c. Behavior Therapy
   d. DID

4. Survivors of a plane crash are more likely to develop this disorder.
   a. QED
   b. OCD
   c. PTSD
   d. DID

5. The place to go if you want to be a psychiatrist today.
   a. Medical School
   b. Ph.D. Psychology program
   c. Ph.D. Medical Anthropology program
   d. Psychoanalysis Certification program

6. Beginning in the early 1800's, scientists began to believe that mental illnesses resulted from:
   a. Demon possession
   b. Biological disorders
   c. Poor parental upbringing
   d. Learned behavior

7. Which of the following books only lists the known psychological disorders?
   a. ICD-10
   b. DSM-IV
   c. Goodman and Gilman's Reference
   d. Merck's Index

8. Labeling a person as "mentally ill" may affect others perceptions of their normal behavior as "crazy."
   a. True
   b. False

9. Strong anxiety that occurs without warning, lasts for a few minutes, and is not related to any known stimulus in the environment?
   a. Generalized anxiety disorder
   b. Panic attack
   c. Obsessive-compulsive disorder
   d. Bipolar affective disorder

10. Extreme anxiety resulting from exposure to a particular object or event.
    a. Hallucination
    b. Mania
    c. Panic attack
    d. Phobia

11. Repeating THOUGHTS in your head is called:
    a. An obsession
    b. A compulsion
    c. Recursive thinking
    d. Iterative thoughts

12. People in cities repeatedly bombed during WW II generally did NOT develop phobias of airplanes or bombs. This is an example of how a poor biological predisposition protects people from developing phobias.
    a. True
    b. False

13. Mood disorders are characterized by:
    a. Sociopathic behavior
    b. Emotional extremes
    c. Hallucinations
    d. Word salad

14. Which of the following is NOT a characteristic of Major Depressive Disorder?
    a. Depressed mood
    b. Hyperactivity
    c. Feelings of worthlessness
    d. Diminished interest in social activities

15. Which of the following is NOT a characteristic of the manic stage of Bipolar Affective Disorder?
    a. Feelings of worthlessness
    b. Wild optimism
    c. Few inhibitions
    d. Over-talkative

16. Linkage analysis has established a genetic etiology of mood disorders.
    a. True
    b. False

17. Which of the following is NOT a characteristic of Schizophrenia?
    a. Disorganized thinking
    b. Disturbed perceptions
    c. Inappropriate emotions and actions
    d. Feelings of worthlessness

18. There are different types of Schizophrenia.
    a. True
    b. False

19. There are both familial genetic links and biological abnormalities associated with Schizophrenia.
    a. True
    b. False

20. Luke suffers from acrophobia, a fear of high places. Luke's therapist suggests that his reaction to heights is a generalization of the fear triggered by a childhood playground accident in which he fell off a sliding board. The therapist's suggestion reflects a _____ perspective.
    a. Learning
    b. Trait
    c. Humanistic
    d. Biological

21. Which of the following is NOT a delusion of reference?
    a. Listening to the "secret messages" sent to you on the radio
    b. Realizing that you have secret knowledge to cure cancer
    c. Hearing voices inside your stomach
    d. Believing that space aliens are sending messages into you brain

22. Which of the following is NOT a delusion of reference?
    a. Listening to the "secret messages" sent to you on the radio
    b. Realizing that you have secret knowledge to cure cancer
    c. Smelling the dead bodies under the floor

23. The symptoms of schizophrenia may include:
    a. Lowered emotional responding
    b. Heightened emotional responding
    c. Flattened affect
    d. All of the above

24. Which of the following is NOT a behavioral disturbance of schizophrenia?
    a. Massaging you head to get rid of unwanted thoughts
    b. Walking backwards to go back in time
    c. Wearing a tin foil hat to avoid the space alien's messages to you
    d. Knowing that you are going to be assassinated

25. Which of the following is NOT a subtype of schizophrenia?
    a. Obsessed
    b. Catatonic
    c. Disorganized
    d. Undifferentiated
    e. Residual

26. Which of the following is NOT a subtype of schizophrenia?
    a. Paranoid
    b. Cataleptic
    c. Disorganized
    d. Undifferentiated
    e. Residual

27. Which of the following is NOT a subtype of schizophrenia?
    a. Paranoid
    b. Catatonic
    c. Disordered
    d. Undifferentiated
    e. Residual

28. Which of the following is NOT a subtype of schizophrenia?
    a. Paranoid
    b. Catatonic
    c. Disorganized
    d. Abstract
    e. Residual

29. Which of the following is NOT a subtype of schizophrenia?
    a. Paranoid
    b. Catatonic
    c. Disorganized

d. Undifferentiated
e. Persistent

30. Which of the following is NOT a subtype of schizophrenia?
    a. Catatonic
    b. Disorganized
    c. Undifferentiated
    d. Residual
    e. None of the above

31. Which of the following terms refers to the exaggeration of normal thought processes which create symptoms of schizophrenia?
    a. Positive schizophrenia symptoms
    b. Negative schizophrenia symptoms
    c. Affirmative schizophrenia symptoms
    d. Deconstructive schizophrenia symptoms

32. Which of the following terms refers to the loss or absence of normal thought processes which create symptoms of schizophrenia?
    a. Positive schizophrenia symptoms
    b. Negative schizophrenia symptoms
    c. Affirmative schizophrenia symptoms
    d. Deconstructive schizophrenia symptoms

33. Which of the following is NOT a classification of schizophrenic symptoms?
    a. Positive schizophrenia symptoms
    b. Negative schizophrenia symptoms
    c. Deconstructive schizophrenia symptoms
    d. None of the above

34. Which of the following is a classification of schizophrenic symptoms?
    a. Positive schizophrenia symptoms
    b. Deconstructive schizophrenia symptoms
    c. Affirmative schizophrenia symptoms
    d. None of the above

35. Which of the following is a classification of schizophrenic symptoms?
    a. Negative schizophrenia symptoms
    b. Confirmatory schizophrenia symptoms
    c. Deconstructive schizophrenia symptoms
    d. None of the above

36. A slowly developing form of schizophrenia is more likely associated with:
    a. Positive schizophrenia symptoms
    b. Negative schizophrenia symptoms
    c. Emotional disturbances
    d. Language and thought disturbances

37. A rapidly developing form of schizophrenia is more likely associated with:
    a. Emotional disturbances
    b. Language and thought disturbances
    c. Positive schizophrenia symptoms
    d. Negative schizophrenia symptoms

38. Paranoid schizophrenia is most likely to contain symptoms of:
    a. Delusions and persecution
    b. Motor disturbances and echo speech
    c. Emotional disturbances and social withdraw
    d. None of the above

39. Catatonic schizophrenia is most likely to contain symptoms of:
    a. Delusions and persecution
    b. Motor disturbances and echo speech
    c. Emotional disturbances and social withdraw
    d. None of the above

40. Disorganized schizophrenia is most likely to contain symptoms of:
    a. Delusions and persecution
    b. Motor disturbances and echo speech
    c. Emotional disturbances and social withdraw
    d. None of the above

41. Undifferentiated schizophrenia is most likely to contain symptoms of:
    a. Delusions and persecution
    b. Motor disturbances and echo speech
    c. Emotional disturbances and social withdraw
    d. None of the above

42. Residual schizophrenia is most likely to contain symptoms of:
    a. Delusions and persecution
    b. Motor disturbances and echo speech
    c. Emotional disturbances and social withdraw
    d. None of the above

43. A form of schizophrenia which does not fit any of the standard subtype categories is called:
    a. Paranoid
    b. Catatonic
    c. Disorganized
    d. Undifferentiated
    e. Residual

44. The name for a form of schizophrenia which no longer shows the criteria of the disorder, however, symptoms still persist is called:
    a. Paranoid
    b. Catatonic

c. Disorganized
d. Undifferentiated
e. Residual

45. Which of the following is NOT positively correlated with the development of schizophrenia?
   a. Prenatal viral infections
   b. Birth complications
   c. Advanced maternal age
   d. Maternal malnutrition
   e. Advanced paternal age

46. Which of the following is a current model of schizophrenia?A
   a. Dopamine hypothesis
   b. Diathesis-stress model
   c. Communication disorders model
   d. A and B
   e. None of the above

47. Which personality disorder involves the diagnosis of numerous personalities within a single individual?
   a. Borderline personality disorder
   b. Antisocial personality disorder
   c. Dissociative identity disorder
   d. Paranoid personality disorder

48. The terms sociopath and psychopath are synonymous with the term:
   a. Dissociative identity disorder
   b. Borderline personality disorder
   c. Antisocial personality disorder
   d. Paranoid personality disorder

49. Running amok, an out of control aggression is a form of mental illness specific to:
   a. Latin cultures
   b. Southeast Asia
   c. United States
   d. Ethiopia
   e. Western countries

50. Multiple personality disorder is a form of mental illness specific to:
   a. Latin cultures
   b. Southeast Asia
   c. United States
   d. Ethiopia
   e. Western countries

Answers: 1. b; 2. d; 3. a; 4. c; 5. a; 6. b; 7. b; 8. a; 9. b; 10. d; 11. a; 12. a; 13. b; 14. b; 15. a; 16. a; 17. d; 18. a; 19. a; 20. a; 21. c; 22. c; 23. d; 24. d; 25. a; 26. b; 27. c; 28. d; 29. e; 30. e; 31. a; 32. b; 33. c; 34. a; 35. a; 36. b; 37. c; 38. a; 39. b; 40. c; 41. d; 42. d; 43. d; 44. e; 45. c; 46. d; 47. c; 48. c; 49. b; 50. c

510

UNIT FOUR

PEOPLE INTERACTING WITH PEOPLE

Psychology, Decision Making and Economics

In 2002, the Nobel prize for economics was shared by an economist and a psychologist. This might seem odd to many people. Why would a psychologist be studying economics? The reason for this is that for years Daniel Kahneman had studied the cognitive processes involved in how people make decisions. He initially began to explore how people make rational and irrational judgments about their lives. Eventually, he found that his research had great appeal for economists because they need to make assumptions about why and when people spend their money.

Kahneman, along with Vernon L. Smith, an economist, won the prize "for having integrated insights from psychological research into economic science, especially concerning human judgment and decision-making under uncertainty" (Nobelprize.org).

Kahneman was developing a model of decision making that suggested the models applied by economists were flawed. Economists have a long history of assuming that humans behave rationally with respect to their money. They assume that people review their options before making purchases and—in the context of a rational thought process—reach the best conclusion regarding what and when to buy. The data collected by psychologists tends to disfavor such assumptions. Yes, people may act rationally at times; however, the field of psychology offers overwhelming evidence that people also act irrationally even when they are making decisions calmly.

One way to view this irrational behavior is to test people in decision scenario experiments. In one experiment, people were asked to play the role of a public health official and to make a decision regarding which public health policy to follow. In scenario 1, the subjects were told that a new disease will soon cause 600 people to die. If treatment option A is adopted, 200 people will be saved. If treatment option B is adopted then there is a one-third chance that all 600 people will be safe and a two-thirds chance that no one will be saved.

In scenario 2, a different group of subjects is asked the same questions but with a different phraseology. They were told that if option A is adopted then 400 people will die. If option B is adopted then there is a one-third probability that no one will die and a two-thirds probability that 600 people will die.

The likelihood of people living or dying is the same in scenarios 1 and 2. The main difference between them is the way in which the problems are worded (saving 200 versus letting 400 die). In scenario 1, people tend to choose option A. In scenario 2, people tend to choose option B. What Kahnemans's research has shown is that the guaranteed events (saving 200; letting 400 die) are often over weighted in importance by the subjects. In scenario 1, the certainty of saving 200 lives is disproportionately more attractive and in scenario 2, the guaranteed loss of life is disproportionately aversive.

What this work shows is that the cognitive processes in decision-making may not always make rational sense. If one applies these irrational human responses to the field of economics, then one may be better able to understand the many oddities of human purchasing patterns.

Continued

Psychology, Decision Making and Economics   *Continued*

Kahnemans's work, known as Prospect Theory, helps explain why people are willing to drive many miles to save a few dollars on an inexpensive purchase whereas they would not go to such great effort if the purchase were very expensive.

Psychologists may clarify issues in economics by highlighting the principles involved in decision-making. In fact, if everything a living creature does—especially humans—is controlled by psychological principles, then psychologists may be able to explain and affect much broader portions of human society than just mental illness and personality. Therefore, Kahnemans's work drives further interest into human decision-making processes.

References

http://nobelprize.org/nobel_prizes/economics/laureates/2002/

CHAPTER OUTLINE

Social Cognition

Impression Formation

Attribution Theory

Social Influence

Social Norms

Social Roles

Conformity

Compliance

Obedience

Interpersonal Attraction

Proximity

Similarity

Gain/loss Theory

Physical Attractiveness

Altruistic Behavior

Norm of Social Responsibility

Norm of Reciprocity

Cost-Reward Approach to Altruism

Emergency Situations

Other variables in Helping

Aggression

Explaining Aggression

Aggression as an Innate Behavior

Aggression as a Learned Behavior

Objectives

After reading this chapter, you should be able to do the following:

Social Cognition

■ Define attitudes and discuss the origin of attitudes.

■ Understand the link between attitudes and behavior.

■ Recognize the role of cognitive dissonance in behavior and attitude change.

■ Explain why we form impressions of people the way we do.

■ Define the primacy effect and stereotypes as they apply to person perception.

■ Understand the attribution process and distinguish different attributional biases.

Social Influence

- Discuss the social influence of social norms and social roles.
- Discuss criteria that make people likely to change their behavior based on the behavior of others, such as conformity and compliance.
- Define obedience and understand the significance of Milgram's research on obedience.

Positive and Negative Social Behaviors

- Identify factors that influence feelings of attraction, such as proximity, similarity, reward/cost, and physical attractiveness.
- Explain distinctions between liking and loving.
- Describe different theories of love.
- Define different types of conformity.
- Describe different definitions of aggression, and distinguish sources of aggression, both innate and learned.
- Describe the frustration aggression hypothesis and environmental variables of aggression.
- Describe variables associated with altruistic behavior, such as norms, the bystander effect, and the diffusion of responsibility.

PREVIEW

In the final chapter of this book, we will examine several interesting aspects of social psychology. We will begin with social cognition—how we perceive, form, and maintain our thoughts of other people, objects, and ideas—and then delve into social influence. Social influence is a two-way street; we not only influence others but are influenced by them as well.

One interesting fact about humans is that we are capable of both wonderful positive behaviors and horrible negative behaviors. The twentieth century witnessed those extremes of good in the lives of people like Mother Teresa and Albert Schweitzer on one hand, and Adolph Hitler and Joseph Stalin on the other, more evil side. We will examine the positive side of human social behavior when we consider the dynamics of attraction and loving. We will also see the goodness of humans demonstrated when they help each other.

The negative side of human behavior will also be explored as we consider the topic of aggression. We will explore the possible explanations for human aggression and examine how it is learned and under what circumstances it is more likely displayed.

Humans are social animals. We live in groups, work in groups, and play in groups. Much of our day-to-day behavior takes place in a social context. It is this social world that we live in that social psychology investigates. Social psychology focuses on how we relate to other people, and how they, in turn, influence what we do, what we think, and how we feel. These influences can affect our behavior in different social contexts—both internally, in our cognitive processes, and externally, in our outward behaviors. This social context includes the real or imagined presence of other people and the interaction and influence of people upon one another in a wide range of social settings.

Although much of what we have dealt with in this book has examined the broad range of human behaviors and the remarkable capabilities of our senses and central

Humans are social animals who live, work, and play in groups.

nervous system, one fact remains. We are social animals that "think" and "do." Through thinking and doing, we exist in a social reality. Most of our social behavior is logical and predictable, but sometimes it is prone to bias and error.

SOCIAL COGNITION

Social psychology: The study of the ways in which humans use thoughts, perceptions, motives, feelings, and behavior when interacting with each other.

Attitudes: Predispositions or tendencies to act.

We shall begin our exploration of social psychology by considering the processes that are part of our social cognitions—how we think about and try to understand the world. Included in this world are many people, objects, and ideas. And for many of those people, objects, and ideas, we hold positive or negative evaluations.

You may feel positively toward nuns, your favorite chair, and universal human rights while also feeling negatively toward telephone solicitors, a burger made from dog meat, and communism. These positive or negative evaluations (or even neutral ones) form predispositions or tendencies to act and are called attitudes.

Attitudes are important because they influence behavior. They are often at the root of why we do what we do, be it smiling at the nun we pass by at the mall, seeking out our favorite chair when it's naptime, or signing a petition urging legislation strengthening human rights. Where do these attitudes come from? We are not born with them. You certainly weren't born favoring cow meat and rejecting dog meat as a dinnertime choice. Remember, there are cultures in the world that view cows as sacred and reject them as a food source, while other cultures regularly dine on dogs.

Attitudes are learned. We learn to like; we learn to dislike. That learning may be acquired through classical conditioning (Pavlovian) as in the case of anger directed at telephone solicitors trying to sell us dance lessons who call and interrupt our dinner or through our parents repeatedly pairing emotionally charged words such as "bad," "evil," or "inhuman" when talking about communism. We learn those negative associations.

Classical conditioning may cause us to direct anger at telephone solicitors.

In other instances, we learn attitudes through the reward and punishments of operant conditioning (Skinnerian), as when our parents reward us for expressing beliefs in line with theirs or behaving in ways that please them. Negative attitudes such as prejudice and hate can be passed from generation to generation.

In addition, social learning theory argues we may learn by watching as well as by doing. Children may learn attitudes by observing and imitating the behavior of others around them. Those "others around them" may be parents, friends, or the mass media, particularly television in our culture.

Regardless of how we acquire our attitudes, the next question we can ask is how those attitudes affect our behavior. Three types of information are relevant to an attitude:

1. cognitions—the thoughts and beliefs about the attitude that we hold
2. feelings—the affective response, either positive or negative (liking versus disliking) that the attitude evokes
3. behaviors—what we are likely to do in response to our attitude

Consider pizza. You may have cognitive, affective, and behavioral responses to pizza. Cognitively, you may believe pizza tastes good, pizza is relatively nutritious for a "fast food," pizza is fattening, pizza is better from one pizzeria than from another, and so on. These are all thoughts and beliefs you carry with you based on your experience with pizza. Many of these thoughts and feelings are based on personal experience—you think back to all your encounters with pizza. You also have the experience of others that you've seen or heard from in regard to pizza.

Simpler to deal with is the affective or feeling component of your attitude toward pizza. You either like it or you don't. Your liking or disliking may be mild or extreme. You may hate pizza, you may love pizza, or be somewhere in between. The last component, the behavioral, is the trickiest. Here we look for a link between an attitude and behavior. Just because you like pizza doesn't necessarily mean you eat it all the time. And even if you are not a fan of pizza, that doesn't mean that you wouldn't eat it if you were very hungry and pizza was your only choice.

Some attitudes are more important to us, and the stronger the attitude, the more likely it is to predict behavior. That strength may come from a variety of factors. In general, factors such as direct experience, accessibility, and specificity seem to make attitudes more predictive of behavior. Higher levels of direct experience with the object of an attitude make the link between attitudes and behavior stronger. People who have sampled different types of pizza usually have favorites and feel more strongly about pizza than people who have little experience with it. Accessibility refers to how important the attitude is to you and the ease with which it comes to mind. If you own a pizzeria, you likely think about pizza quite a bit and your attitudes are important to you. Finally, there is specificity. If we want to know your attitude toward deep dish triple cheese pizza, we are much more likely to predict behavior if we find out your specific attitude toward deep dish triple cheese pizza as opposed to just asking about pizza in general.

Many smokers continue to smoke even though they are aware of the long-term risks to their health.

The link between attitudes and behavior (what you think and what you do) is sometimes easy to see, and other times, not so easy. Even if you love pizza, you may choose not to eat it because you are out of cash or in a restaurant where it is not available. You may have had pizza the last two days and are looking for some variety, so you go for seafood instead. There may be times that even when we know someone's attitude (including our own!), the match between that attitude and subsequent behavior may not be present.

One of the most common assumptions we tend to make is that attitudes will be consistent over time (Fabrigar, MacDonald, & Wegner, 2005). This striving for consistency was examined in Festinger's (1957) theory of **cognitive dissonance**. We may act in ways that go against our attitudes and what we know. Many people smoke (a behavior) yet also know that smoking causes lung cancer (a cognition). The "I'm doing something harmful to myself" feeling is uncomfortable and we are motivated to either change our beliefs ("smoking really doesn't hurt me"), change our behavior (stop smoking), or add other cognitions (smoke low-tar cigarettes or smoke less). Any of these outcomes may reduce the uncomfortable dissonance we feel. The stronger the attitude, presumably, the stronger the need to reduce this discomfort.

Cognitive dissonance: Unpleasant state of conflict that we experience when our behavior does not match our attitudes.

Besides forming attitudes about behaviors and ideas, we also form attitudes about objects. One of those objects we encounter is people. When we encounter people, especially for the first time, we form impressions of them. Social psychologists have examined how we do this, and this is our next topic, impression formation.

Impression Formation

There are a lot of people in the world. Most of them we will never know or even meet. We see people every day, face-to-face, on television, and through other media sources. Something interesting happens when we see and interact with other people. We form impressions. We make judgments about them from what they do and what they look like. We use such cues as what clothes they're wearing, how old they are, what gender they are, how they speak—in fact, anything that can be perceived may result in the formation of our impressions (Willis & Todorov, 2006).

These impressions form what are called schema. A schema is a set of beliefs or expectations about other people based on experience. The experience may be personal, the result of direct interaction with that person or similar persons. Or it may be the result of stereotypes and biases that we have learned through secondary experience. These beliefs and expectations are important not only for how we think about other people but also for how we act toward other people (Moskowitz, 2005).

For example, let me introduce you to John. John is a young man of about 20 with long blond hair and an athletic physique. He is tanned and wears a T-shirt with the logo of a surfboard company. He is wearing baggy shorts and sandals. When John speaks, he often uses phrases like "dude" and "far out." Assume this introduction took place in the student union of a large state university in northeast Ohio. Based on this information, what state do you think John calls home? Most people would probably say California. John fits the stereotype in the way he looks and acts, so our first hunch is that he is a long way from home.

Is John from California? He might be, but when you think about it, it is much more probable that John is from Ohio. After all, the vast majority of people who attend a large state university in northeast Ohio are probably from Ohio. If not Ohio, then they are likely from Pennsylvania or some other neighboring state. The fact remains that most of us are most comfortable seeing John as being from California regardless of the statistical fact that it is a long shot.

What we're talking about now is the formation of perceptions, in this case, perceptions about people. When we talk about impressions, common sense tells us that first impressions are important. Upon meeting someone for the first time, we often try to create a good impression. Arriving at a job interview, we are likely to be neatly groomed and well dressed. Our behavior in that interview will be such that the interviewer hopefully has a good first impression of us. There is a television commercial that stresses "You never get a second chance to make a first impression." Let's look at one study from more than 50 years ago that supports that notion.

In 1946, Solomon Asch provided evidence for what he called the primacy effect. He gave experimental participants a list of traits describing a fictitious someone they were supposedly going to meet. The total list of traits was the same for all participants but their order of presentation differed. Some participants read a list that began with positive traits followed by negative traits. Other participants read a list that began with negative traits followed by positive ones. Asch found that the person described with positive traits first and negative traits later was liked more than the person described by the exact same traits but in reverse order.

For instance, suppose you are looking out your classroom window and see a young man at a street corner. This young man helps a little old lady across the street. After doing that, you notice that he vigorously starts picking his nose. What is your impression of that young man? The next day, looking out your classroom window again, you see another young male. This fellow is standing on the street corner picking his nose with great gusto. A little old lady walks up to the

Schema: A set of beliefs or expectations about other people based on experience.

Asch's primacy effect concludes that first impressions carry more weight than later information. What is your impression of this man?

Primacy effect: The theory that early information about someone may weigh more heavily on impressions of others than later information.

street corner and he helps her across the street. What is your impression of the second young man? If you are like most people, young man #1 is seen in a slightly more positive light than young man #2.

It may be that the first young man is seen as a helpful guy who just happened to do something disgusting, while the second fellow strikes us as a disgusting person who just happens to do something helpful. Our first impression influences our later perceptions, providing the context in which future behavior is rated and understood.

Stereotypes

With experience, many of our impressions may come to form what are known as stereotypes. Social category and stereotype may be based on ethnicity, gender, age, religion, language, occupation, or dress. In fact, any variable or difference can be the basis for a stereotype. Stereotypes exist because it is our fundamental nature to make sense of and to simplify a complex world (Macrae, Stangor, & Hewstone, 1996). The problems associated with stereotypes arise when we simplify too much.

> **Stereotypes:** Set of characteristics believed to be shared by all members of a social category.

For instance, consider how you feel about the elderly. Common stereotypes about senior citizens include assumptions that they are sickly and frail, suffer memory defects, are not interested in sex, and live in nursing homes. Some of those characteristics may apply to some of the individuals in the broad class of people we call the elderly. The fact is that most elderly citizens in our culture live at home, are in good health both physically and mentally, and enjoy the same activities that they did when they were younger. You probably know a number of senior citizens who do not fit the stereotype at all. Nonetheless, most of us still hold these expectations (Dion, 2003).

Obviously, the use of stereotypes is unfair; groups targeted by and affected by them are quick to point out that fact. Elderly people do not like to be "lumped together" by others in the same way that people with blond hair resist being seen as frivolous because of their hair color, and males recoil when they hear statements such as "all men are pigs." Stereotypes are resistant to change because breaking down stereotypes means that we have to look beyond easily identifiable traits and treat people as individuals. We may view exceptions to stereotypes as somehow being a confirmation of that stereotype: "My friend from West Virginia is very sophisticated even though most West Virginians are hillbillies."

> **Kernal of truth:** Small amount of truth.

At times there may even be what is called a Kernal of truth (Kulik, 2005) to our stereotypes. For instance, we may hold the stereotype that all senior citizens are concerned about the well-being of the Social Security system. While not "all" senior citizens are concerned about Social Security, most likely are (at least more so than college students are), so this stereotype might indeed be somewhat true. Similarly, believing that males are more prone to physical violence than are females is another stereotype that might have some validity.

Another important consideration is that we may behave toward others in different ways depending on the stereotypes we hold of them. Stereotypes persist, in part, because people tend to see what they expect to see when they interact with groups they view with prejudice. Those stereotypes may have long-lasting impact and even come to change the behavior of those we perceive. This

Although it is not uncommon to see an elderly person engaging in activities such as exercising, many people still hold on to the stereotype that senior citizens are sickly, are frail, and live in nursing homes.

© Feverpitch, 2009. Used under license from Shutterstock, Inc.

may be the most important aspect of stereotypes. Societies can outlaw discrimination toward stereotyped groups. Civil rights legislation and human rights legislation do just that. Laws cannot change what people think, but they can decrease acts of discrimination, which may ultimately lead to diminished stereotypes.

Attribution Theory

In addition to perceiving other people, we also try to make sense of their behavior. Humans are curious and the more we understand the reasons for the behavior of others (and ourselves), the better our predictions of behavior will be in the future. More accurate predictions of behavior make a complex world a little more understandable and less threatening (Brehm, Kassin, & Fein, 2005).

Consider the impeachment proceedings against former President Bill Clinton. He was accused of not telling the truth about a sexual liaison with a White House intern. Let's assume that the charges were true and that you were a member of the impeachment committee. Your job is to figure out what is going on. Why did he do that? Was it because he is an amoral man? Did he lie because he was just doing what many men in power do to maintain their positions of power? Was the opposition party just out to get him?

A behavior or event makes sense only when we think we understand why it happened. Attaching a reason for a behavior makes it meaningful and guides our future behavior. You might decide that Clinton was amoral, a man with few scruples who blatantly broke the law. As a member of the impeachment committee, you would have likely voted to have Clinton impeached. On the other hand, if you viewed the entire impeachment process as an attack by rival politicians attempting to undermine Clinton's authority and political power, you would have presumably voted not to impeach him. Your perception of the cause or reason for his behavior would guide your behavior toward him.

SELF-FULFILLING PROPHECY

Most of us, with one quick glance, can easily classify just about anyone as being male or female. Once we have made that classification, we may rely more on the stereotype of that gender that we carry around in our head than on the actual behavior of the person. For instance, women have traditionally been viewed in our culture as more expressive, emotional, and submissive than men (Franzoi, 2003). So when first meeting a female, we may expect her to hold those qualities and be somewhat perplexed if she does not.

Stereotypes can lead to what is called a self-fulfilling prophecy. This can occur when our expectations about other people elicit the very behaviors we expect, confirming those expectations. They start to act in ways we assumed they would. A classic demonstration of the self-fulfilling prophecy involves teachers' expectations of students and how those expectations may influence student performance. More than 40 years of scientific research and more than 400 studies show that teacher expectations do influence student performance (Kenrick, Nueberg, & Cialdini, 2005). When teachers expect higher levels of performance from some students (in some studies, students were simply randomly selected by experimenters without teachers knowing this), subtle changes in teacher behavior result.

Teachers tend to be more supportive of high-expectancy students. Those students are smiled at more and given more positive feedback by teachers. Teachers also give high-expectancy students more challenging tasks. Unfortunately, the reverse is true when teachers have low expectations of students' behavior. This may be especially harmful for students inaccurately perceived as having low ability. To the degree that stereotypes held by teachers about their students exist, this self-fulfilling prophecy may be an important part of the educational climate. Teachers who expect

What a teacher believes to be true about a student can affect the academic achievement of that student.

higher levels of performance from their students tend to find that those students do indeed perform to a higher level of competence. Teachers who expect less from their students may find those expectations met, as well. When President George W. Bush signed the No Child Left Behind legislation in 2002, he referred to the self-fulfilling prophecy as "the soft bigotry of low expectations."

This process of attaching causes to behavior is called the attribution process. The theories in social psychology that describe this process are called **attribution theories**. These theories (Heider, 1958; Jones & Davis, 1965; Kelley, 1972) start with a fundamental decision. Is the behavior in question (be it Clinton's not telling the truth, a friend's outburst of anger, the friendliness of a stranger) the result of something inside the person or outside the person? By inside the person, we mean a personal trait or enduring characteristic of that person. By outside the person, we refer to the environment or the situation within which the behavior occurred.

> **Attribution theories:** People look for an explanation of behavior by associating either internal or external causes to behavior.

Imagine that your friend performs poorly on an exam. What does that behavior tell you? If you attribute the poor behavior to something inside your friend, you might see the poor performance as a result of his or her low intelligence (presumably a stable trait) or a result of lack of effort. Effort is an internal cause but it is not stable—your friend did not study for this exam but usually studies for other ones. In either case, the reason for the behavior of doing poorly is attributed to something going on "inside" your friend.

You also could see the cause of the poor performance as attributable to variables outside your friend. External factors such as exam difficulty or just simply bad luck may be seen as the explanation of why the behavior occurred. Exam difficulty is a stable variable, while luck is an unstable variable. Sometimes we guess on an exam and get lucky. Our guesses are mostly correct. Sometimes the opposite occurs. Is your friend not very bright, or was the exam unfairly difficult? Did your friend not study, or was he or she just very unlucky?

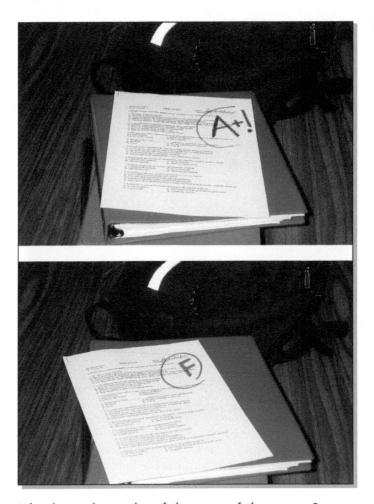

What is your impression of the owner of these exams?

Answering those questions is a complex cognitive process that social psychologists continue to explore. Factors, such as how your friend has performed in the past and how the other students in the class did on the same exam, provide important additional information as we go about the process of attributing meaning to our friend's poor performance.

We also make attributions about the behavior of someone very near and dear to us—ourselves. There are times we look back on our own behavior and say, "Why did I do that?" Students are often eager to see the distribution of grades after an exam is handed back. Social comparison processes of self-attribution might argue that receiving a B when most other students get an A might make you unhappy, whereas receiving the same B on an exam where most other students received a D might just make your day. The first B might make you feel unlucky, the second makes you feel smart.

Many of these processes are quite logical, but others are harder to understand. Our thought processes, when it comes to attributing the causes of behavior, are quite remarkable, but they are not infallible. We may make mistakes in the process of attributing causes of behavior.

Biases in Attribution

Illusions and misperceptions may fool our senses. The moon may appear larger in the sky when it's nearer to the horizon. We may think we smell strawberries when in fact the odor is from cherries. We may hear noises in the night that are harmless, but scare us nonetheless. The same is true of attributions; we may make them in ways that are not always correct or even logical. Our attributions about the causes of behavior in others or in ourselves may, at times, be biased. Those attributions may reflect ways in which we characteristically think, rather than reflecting a "true state of affairs."

One such bias is the **fundamental attribution error** (Moskowitz, 2005) and is detailed in Box below. We may see the behavior of other people as being more determined by internal, dispositional forces rather than by the forces of the environment. We are more likely to attribute our own behaviors as being a reflection of the situation in which we find ourselves.

Another bias that may exist when we make attributions involves how we evaluate our own successes and failures. This is referred to as **self-serving bias** (Moon, 2003). Suppose you take a test and receive an A "What caused that? Was it because you are smart? Now you take another test and get an F" What caused that? Was it because you are not intelligent?

Fundamental attribution error: Overestimating internal causes for someone else's behavior while underestimating external causes.

Self-serving bias: The tendency to assign internal causes for successes and external causes for failures.

FUNDAMENTAL ATTRIBUTION ERROR

Imagine the following scenario. You go to the supermarket one day to buy a half gallon of milk. You are in a hurry and pick up the milk and head over to the express checkout line where it is clearly stated on a sign that this line is for customers purchasing 12 items or less, cash only. You get in line and notice that the person in front of you has more than the maximum number of items. You count the items in their cart . . . one, two, three . . . all the way up to 18. You look at the sign above the checkout—it says 12 items maximum, and cash only. You recount the items, all 18 of them, as the person behind the cash register starts scanning the items. Then you see the person in front of you pulling out a checkbook. What do you think? Why would someone with one and a half times the maximum number of items be in the express line? Can't they read? Can't they count? Most of us would be a little irritated—especially when a person pulls out a checkbook instead of cash only, as the sign required.

In this scenario we have to figure out why the person with 18 items is in the express line. There are options we have at our cognitive disposal as we go about the process of figuring that out. We could see their behavior is determined by the situation. Something about the circumstances might have led this person, in fact any person, to be in a 12-item-only checkout line with 18 items. We look at the person; we look at the 18 items; we look at the sign. We say to ourselves, "This person is rude. This person is inconsiderate. I have to wait because the person in front of me is a jerk." All these thoughts (and others!) indicate that you see this person's behavior as evidence of the person's inner traits and motives. You make a dispositional attribution—bad things are done by bad people. What they did was bad, hence they are bad. You are making the fundamental attribution error—overestimating dispositional causes for someone else's behavior while underestimating situational causes.

Now imagine a different scenario. The semester is coming to an end. Being the wonderful person that you are, you have invited the entire class to your place for a spaghetti dinner. You set up the dinner for 6:00 p.m. a week from Thursday. Time goes by and you're so busy you forget the dinner.

On Thursday at about 5:00 p.m., someone calls you and asks for directions to your place, and suddenly you remember that you are hosting the dinner. You rush to the supermarket to get what you need. You buy four extra large jars of spaghetti sauce, four big boxes of spaghetti, two boxes of grated cheese, five loaves of garlic bread, two giant bags of prepared

Continued

tossed salad, and a jumbo bottle of salad dressing. You now have 18 items and you rush to the checkout lines only to find that the regular checkout lines are jammed with people and their overflowing carts. It looks like these people are buying all the food they'll need for the rest of their lives. You'll never get out of the supermarket in time! You glance at the express checkout and see it's empty. So you rush over and quickly start putting your items on the belt. The checkout person scans the first couple of items and just then five people show up behind you with one or two items each.

Now, you know they're counting your items—all 18 of them. You know they're looking at the sign—12 items maximum. And you know they're making attributions about your behavior. Because you are aware of the fundamental attribution error, you know they're thinking you are an inconsiderate, rude jerk. But are you? Why are you doing this? The answers to these questions are easy for you. You have made an attribution about the causes of your behavior. You know that circumstances have conspired to work against you. You are a good person. You feel bad, so you might even explain to the people behind you that you are very late, the line was empty when you got here, the normal checkout lines were clogged, and so on. You tell those behind you that you have never done this before—you always respect the express lane item limit. Why are you doing this now? It's not your fault.

And, of course, while you are making it perfectly clear that you are not the jerk you appear to be, the other customers behind you continued to think "What a jerk!" The point is that when we look for the causes of our own behavior, we (correctly) consider our previous experiences (ordinarily we never would be in the express lane with more than 12 items) and the situation at present (we're running very late and the regular checkouts are jammed). We don't do the same when we look for causes of behavior in others. We jump to the personal cause, the dispositional cause as for why they do what they do: Bad things are done by bad people. We don't make the fundamental attribution error when examining our own behavior.

If you are like most people, you will take credit for the good grade and find some external reason for the bad grade. You failed the test because it was unfair, the instructor didn't like you, you didn't get a chance to study, the person next to you during the test needed a bath badly and distracted you during the test, or you were sick. There are many possible reasons for poor performance that don't threaten one's self-image. You can see evidence of this when people are quick to sue whenever something bad happens to them. Spill hot coffee in your lap? Sue McDonalds. Slip on the ice in a parking lot? Sue Wal-Mart. Struck by lightning in a National Park? Sue the government. There may be a generalized feeling in our society that whenever something bad happens to us, we should seek out an attorney. We deserve compensation because "it's not my fault, and someone's going to pay."

While self-serving bias is a bias, it may at times be beneficial to one's self-image. Taking credit for successes and looking for nonpersonal causes when things go wrong may lead you to avoid failure in the future by not attributing failure to some unchangeable personal trait or characteristic. Instead of "I failed because I'm stupid," we are likely better off if we can say, "I will study more next time, and the outcome will be better." One's mental health may be strengthened if one avoids attributing negative (particularly unchangeable negative) traits or characteristics to one's self.

Another reason we might not see other people's negative behaviors as being caused by chance or circumstance may be that we're not comfortable admitting that chance or circumstance might affect us in the same way: "It might happen to me." This is called a **defensive attribution** (Goerke, Moller, Schulz-Hardt, Napiersky, & Frey, 2004).

Let's say a student named Matt decided to make some microwave popcorn in his apartment. He put the popcorn in the microwave in the kitchen and set the timer. He heard his phone ring and went back to his bedroom, where he answered the phone and talked with his parents for 10 minutes. Unfortunately, by the time he returned to the kitchen, for some reason the microwave was on fire. He could not put out the fire, and the resulting blaze burned down half the apartment complex.

Most of us would say Matt should have known better than to leave a working microwave unattended. Matt should have not answered his phone, or if he did, he should have called his folks back after his popcorn was done. He didn't do any of those things that now seem so reasonable, and we blame Matt for the fire. After all, we would never do anything so stupid. We are responsible, and we wouldn't have had an out-of-control fire to deal with. We see the results of Matt's behavior and think (hope, even), "That won't happen to me." The error in attribution here is a self-protective one.

Finally, there is an attribution bias that stems from what has been called a **belief in a just world** (Lerner, 1980). Most of us assume (and hope) that good things happen to good people and that sooner or later, bad things happen to bad people. The religious concepts of heaven and hell echo this belief. This may again lead us to overestimate the internal, personal characteristics of people when we view the results of their behavior. If something bad happens, we are quick to see their personal shortcomings and attach blame to them.

A logical outcome of this just-world belief is that when good things happen to bad people or when bad things happen to good people, the fundamental fairness of the world is in doubt. When cheaters prosper or when goodness is struck down, "That just shouldn't happen," and we say, "It's not fair." You can see this belief in a just world operating whenever someone looks to the heavens after a random catastrophe befalls them and cries, "Why me, God? What did I do to deserve this?" We shall see that notions of a just world will arise again when we consider helping behavior later in this chapter. For now, on to the topic of social influence.

> **Defensive attribution:** Not attributing someone's behavior to external attributes because you may react the same way in a similar situation.

> **Belief in a just world:** The belief that good things happen to good people, and bad things, to bad people.

SOCIAL INFLUENCE

Other people may influence us in a number of ways. They influence us by what they do, by what they say, and even by their very presence. Think back to elementary school when the principal or some other authority figure came into your class to observe. The principal likely said something like, "Don't mind me. Just do what you normally do."

Although the principal did not say another word for the entire class time, everyone in the room changed their behavior. The teacher was more focused, and the students were on their best behavior. The mere presence of the principal changed everything.

Fast-forward to today. Would you change your behavior if a video crew followed you around 24 hours a day for the next three days, taping you while you were in class, while you ate your meals, while you slept, even when you went to the bathroom?

The answer is obviously yes. In the same way that even an empty police car sitting next to the road slows down drivers, the real or imagined presence of other people affects us. Part of that effect may be based on evaluation apprehension; we know other people who watch us may be judging us in some way. The presence of other people also reminds us that there are certain social expectations about our behavior.

Violating social norms such as driving laws may lead to unpleasant consequences.

Social Norms

Social norms are taught to us as we grow up (Cialdini & Goldstein, 2004). They are standards of conduct that are culture-specific. Some of these social norms involve expectations about social manners. They tell us what is acceptable behavior in certain situations and what is not acceptable. Many of them are unwritten codes of conduct that everyone in society is expected to observe. Break a social norm and you pay the price of being seen as eccentric, rude, and maybe even mentally ill. Social norms make everyone's behavior more predictable despite individual differences.

Some of these social norms are so important to society that they become laws. In our society, social norms dictate that when we are walking, we usually pass oncoming people to the right. Watch people coming and going in the airport or on crowded campus walkways, and you will see this norm in effect. Although walking to the right is not a law, most people observe this norm. Head out on the highway in our culture, and you'll see (hopefully!) drivers obeying the law that mandates driving to the right on two-way streets. Travel to England and you will quickly see that travel to the left side of the roadway is the norm (and the law) there.

> **Social norms:** Expectations about how we should act.

Social Roles

Social roles are somewhat like social norms except that they are related to expected behaviors based on one's position in society. Like roles in a play or movie, each of us plays many "parts" as we go about our daily activities. One person may be a son or daughter, a parent, a student, a worker, a patient, a customer, and so on, all in one day. Each of those roles has expected behaviors. As a student in a large class, you are expected to be reasonably quiet, take notes, and raise your hand if you have a question. If you were the instructor in that class, you would be expected to arrive on time, present material relevant to the course, and answer questions posed by students. Although those roles are different and the behaviors expected are different as well, those roles are complementary in that without students, the role of an instructor is meaningless, and without an instructor, the role of a student in a large class is undefined. Doctors need patients just as much as patients need doctors, for each of them to "play their respective roles."

There will be times when two or more roles that the same person plays come into conflict. This is known as **inter-role conflict**. A mother who is attending a university may find that at times the different roles of "mother" and "university student" clash, such as when her child becomes sick during finals week when she had hoped to prepare for her finals. She may be torn between being a "good mother—bad student" by not studying and taking care of her child or being a "good student—bad mother" by neglecting her child and diligently preparing for her finals. Hopefully, she will find some compromise that allows her to be successful in both roles.

There is also a predicament involving roles known as **intra-role conflict**. The single role of "parent" may present conflicts when expectations of that role clash. A child who has misbehaved may present a conflict in the parental role. On one hand, parents are supposed to love their children and keep them from harm's way. On the other hand, parents may have to discipline their children in hopes that the child's behavior changes. When a parent decides to discipline a child and says, "This will hurt me more than it does you," they may be describing an intra-role conflict.

> **Social roles:** Expected behavior based on your position in society.

> **Inter-role conflict:** When two or more roles that the same person plays comes into conflict.

> **Intra-role conflict:** When one role makes different demands.

Social roles are important because they allow us to be more predictable in our behavior and to more easily predict the behavior of others in many different social situations (Megarry, 2001). When teachers act like teachers, police officers act like police officers, sales clerks act like sales clerks, and so on, the world is a more predictable and orderly place. When social roles are known and observed, we can expect certain behaviors from others in specific social settings, and they can expect certain behaviors from us.

Social norms and social roles are potent sources that make the behavior of others and the behavior of ourselves more predictable. There are also social influences on our behavior beyond norms and roles. Other people influence us by what they do. We shall examine some of these influences next, starting with conformity.

Conformity

Conformity implies that there is a conflict between an individual and group. It occurs when group norms or a group's social reality are at odds with an individual's free choice of behaviors. Conformity is felt as the pressure to "go along with the group." People may conform because of fear of rejection, or they may go along because they are uncertain as to how to respond. The pressure to conform may be subtle or more obvious.

Conformity may be a response that follows the desire to fit in socially and to be seen as "one of the crowd." When we choose to do something, like wear a baseball cap turned around, we may do so because we see other people doing that. There is no intrinsic advantage to wearing a ball cap reversed; in fact, we lose the shading of the sun that the bill of the hat affords. If other people are doing it, particularly high-visibility role models like Barry Bonds or LeBron James, then we might feel normative pressure to conform.

We may also conform because we are not sure what to do, so we look to others who may have more information than we do. Imagine you wake up one morning and have no idea what the weather forecast is for today. You look outside, and although skies are clear and cloudless, everyone is walking around with an umbrella tucked under their arm. You decide to take your umbrella along today and are rewarded for this conforming behavior when the clouds roll in during the afternoon and there is a heavy rainstorm. You remain relatively dry under your umbrella because you "went along with what others were doing." This could be referred to as an **informational conformity effect** as opposed to the ball cap wearing just described, which is a **normative conformity effect**.

> **Informational conformity effect:** Going along with others if it appears they have more information than you do.

> **Normative conformity effect:** Going along with others because of a desire to fit in socially.

Wearing the same type of clothes as your peers in an effort to fit in socially is the normative conformity effect.

In a group setting, the individual has the opportunity to observe the behavior of others. We realize that different people do different things, and the world as we see it might not be exactly the same as the world as seen by others. At times, the individual has to choose between a social reality as defined by the group and a physical reality as defined by the individual.

That is precisely the choice faced by participants in a series of classic studies by Solomon Asch in the 1950s. In a series of experiments, Asch (1955) placed individuals in a situation in which they had to choose whether to conform to group pressure and deny obvious physical evidence or to trust their own senses. In a group setting of five or six people, people were asked to choose from several lines of differing lengths the one line most similar to a comparison line **(Figure 12.1)**.

The lines were deliberately drawn so that the task was not difficult. Unknown to the participants, all the other members of the group were accomplices of the experimenter. At first, all went well. All of the accomplices made the obviously correct answer. For instance, they would say "B" to the lines in Figure 12.1. The subject invariably went along with this answer—likely because it was the correct one. Then, on certain trials the accomplices would all give a deliberately incorrect answer. They might all say "C" to the lines in Figure 12.1.

After hearing four or five people say "C," what does the person do? Do they go along with the others even though it is pretty clear they are wrong, or do they go "against the tide" and respond based on what they actually see? The answer is that, overall, participants conformed to the incorrect answer roughly 35 percent of the time. This was an average; some conformed more often and some less often.

The size of the unanimous group the person was confronted with was also a variable. Conformity rates increased as the group of accomplices increased to four in number; groups larger than five did not increase conformity rates beyond that level. Higher rates of conformity were also found if the lines were all closer in length, making the task more ambiguous. Here, the right answer was not so obvious and perhaps participants were more willing to go along with the group as a result.

In addition, if any of the accomplices "broke rank" with the others and provided the participant with even a small amount of support, conformity was lowered from that 35 percent to about 25 percent. That "ally" didn't even need to confirm the person's viewpoint. The ally might have chosen another obviously incorrect choice (for instance, "A" to the problem presented in Figure 12.1), but it was enough for the subject to experience less of the pressure to conform.

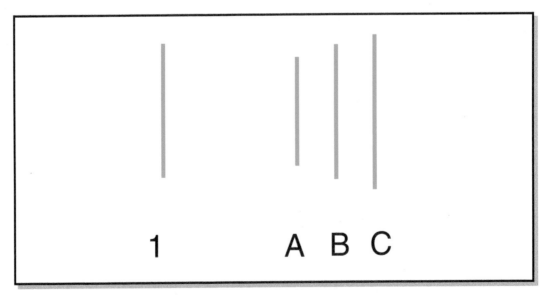

FIGURE 12.1 ■ Sample of lines used by Solomon Asch in studies of conformity.

Compliance

There are times when we change our behavior because we feel the pressure of the group. That response to pressure we have called conformity. There are also times when we change our behavior in response to a direct request. The change in behavior in this instance is called compliance. People may ask us to hold the door open for them when they are carrying an armload of books. Another person might ask you for change for a dollar or directions to the library. Yet another person may ask you to sign a petition.

The classic example of compliance is the salesperson who is eager for us to comply with his or her request to purchase something. The salesperson may use any number of strategies to both persuade us to buy and to buy at a higher price. One strategy is called the lowball procedure (Cialdini, 2001). Pretend you are in the market for a new bed and you see an ad for the wonderful Raftmatic bed—"like sleeping on a raft in the ocean." You go to the showroom and the beds look and feel comfortable. The first step in the lowball procedure is to have the customer make a commitment, any commitment. The salesperson offers you a bed at half price and has you sign your name to a tentative deal. Once you have done that, the terms of the sale abruptly change. That price was just for the mattress. You'll need a box spring, that's extra. You'll need a special frame; that's extra too. The price balloons, and many customers will follow through on their initial agreement to buy and purchase an expensive Raftmatic bed. After all, they made a commitment (at the lower price) and may feel obligated to continue the arrangement, even at a higher cost.

Another technique our Raftmatic salesperson might use is called the door-in-the-face-effect (Cialdini, 2001). Let's say you are in the Raftmatic showroom for an hour or so and the salesperson has shown you all the different models. Finally, you are shown the top-of-the-line model, one costing $5,000. The salesperson asks you to buy this one, and you say, "No, it's too expensive." The price is way too high, but you feel a bit guilty about turning down the salesperson. You agree to buy a less costly bed.

You might feel the same way if someone asked you to make a five-year commitment to Big Brothers/Big Sisters. You are a good person. You want to help, but five years is just too much time to commit. After turning down the five-year plan, you might be more likely to help out Big Brothers/Big Sisters next weekend for an overnight camping trip than you would have been if you had not been asked for an unreasonably large commitment first. This would allow you to maintain your self-impression of being a good person even though you had turned down an initial request to help.

A third variation of compliance is somewhat similar. Instead of being asked for a large (even unreasonable) request first, followed by a smaller one to which one complies, the foot-in-the-door effect requires the first request to be small, followed by a second, much larger, request. The classic study in this area (Freedman & Fraser, 1966) concerned homeowners being approached by people posing as members of the "Committee for Safe Driving," who asked if they could erect a large, ugly sign in their front yards. Only about one in six of the homeowners allowed that sign to be put in their yard. Other homeowners were also asked to allow the sign to be erected in their front yards, but only after they had signed a petition a few days earlier supporting driving safety. Having made the small commitment by signing the petition earlier, over half (more than three times the first group) agreed to have the sign put in their front yards.

Why did they do that? Burger and Cornelius (2003) argue that it may well be that the first small act realigns the homeowner's self-perception as someone who cares about traffic safety. The larger request of sign placement in their yard is seen as just a further step in their commitment, and they feel obligated to comply.

Compliance: Changing behavior in response to a direct request.

Lowball procedure: Compliance strategy that starts low, with something easily agreed to, and then raises the commitment.

A salesperson may employ the door-in-the-face strategy by asking the customer to buy the most expensive item first, making it easier to get a smaller commitment.

Door-in-the-face-effect: Compliance strategy that asks for the most first, so it's easy to agree to a smaller commitment.

Foot-in-the-door effect: Compliance strategy that gets a small commitment first, making the chances of a large commitment later much greater.

Obedience

Obedience: Compliance in the form of a direct demand or order from someone in authority.

A special form of compliance is called obedience. Obedience is compliance in the form of a direct demand or order from someone in authority (Blass, 2004). That person in authority may be a parent, a police officer, or a teacher—someone who can back up the demand with legitimate power. From childhood on, we learn that certain other people (like those just listed) have the power to both reinforce us and punish us.

In some of the most remarkable and controversial studies ever performed in social psychology, Stanley Milgram (1974) demonstrated how far ordinary people will go in obeying a legitimate authority. Milgram set up a laboratory experiment where participants believed they were part of a memory and learning experiment. The experiment was designed so that all the participants played the role of "teachers" while an accomplice of the experimenter was always the "learner." Learners were given a list of word pairs to memorize and teachers then quizzed them. Teachers punished wrong answers by means of an electrical shock generator **(Figure 12.2)**. The generator had switches to deliver shocks from 15 to 450 volts in 15-volt increments.

In reality, no shocks were ever given. The learner's right and wrong answers were preprogrammed and on a rigid schedule that was consistent for all participants. The teachers believed they were really giving shocks, and the intensity of those shocks increased with each wrong answer. As the shock levels went higher, teachers began to hear protests and yelps of pain coming from the learner in the next room. Once again, those behaviors were predetermined and played on a tape recorder.

Many participants in Milgram's study hesitated when the person in the other room seemed to be in pain. A white-coated experimenter then told them that the experiment required the teacher to continue and ordered them to continue giving shocks even when the learner stopped answering and eventually even stopped responding with cries of pain.

Prior to his experiment, Milgram asked 40 psychiatrists to predict how many people would continue delivering shocks to the highest level (one where it appeared to the "teacher" that the learner may have even passed out or been killed). The psychiatrists believed that fewer than 4 percent would deliver shocks

FIGURE 12.2 ■ Stanley Milgram's original shock apparatus is on display at the Archives of the American Psychological Association in Akron, Ohio.

at 300 volts or higher and that less than .01 percent would deliver the maximum 450-volt shock.

Remarkably, 65 percent of participants obeyed the experimenter and delivered the maximum shock. Those results stunned even Milgram himself. People seem likely to obey authority figures they believe are legitimate ones. The ability to "follow orders" and "do what one is told" is a pervasive influence and one that has potential for abuse. Although we hope that the orders that parents give to children, teachers give to students, and officers give to military personnel are all positive and hopefully in the best interests of those who obey, Milgram's results are a bit scary. War crime trials from World War II, the Vietnam conflict, and more recently the war in Iraq have in common the fact that those accused of horrendous war crimes typically argue that they were only "following orders."

Zimbardo (2007) summarized more than 30 years of research on why "good" people may engage in "evil" actions. He argued that social circumstances have the possibility to overwhelm and influence anyone to commit acts that he or she, or anyone who knows that person, would not predict. Zimbardo coined the term "the Lucifer effect" (Lucifer was once God's favorite angel who turned to evil and became a devil) to describe this negative outcome of social influence.

INTERPERSONAL ATTRACTION

We are born into a world full of people. All of them are strangers at first, but we soon come to know our parents and family. Eventually our social world expands as we venture out into the neighborhood and then to school. Our social world continues to widen as we meet and interact with more and more people. We will not meet everyone on the planet, only a small subset. That subset will still be comprised of a lot of people whose paths we will cross. Some of the people we meet along the way will become friends. Some will be merely acquaintances. A few have the potential to become lovers. One or two might become "best friends" as well.

Social psychologists agree that there are differences between the experienced feelings of liking and loving. As seen in Box below, loving involves fundamentally different attitudes to the object of our desire than does liking. It is not simply the case that we like more and more until we finally cross some imaginary psychological line and begin to love. The experience of love is an important one to humans. The need to give love and receive love in return is personally fulfilling and seen in all cultures. The attachment seen in friendships and interpersonal attraction also reflects this need.

What determines whether someone we meet and interact with becomes a friend or merely an acquaintance? Why do some of the people we encounter through life's journey become important and special to us? Is the answer that there is something special about them to which we are attracted? Or is it something special about us that draws us toward them? It may even be both. Social psychologists have long been interested in the phenomenon of interpersonal attraction. The answer to the question of why we like specific people more than others is complex, and there are a number of factors to consider.

SOCIAL PSYCHOLOGY OF LOVE

I love chocolate.
I love Fridays.
I love my mom.
I love America.
I love baseball.
I love God.
I love it when you do that.

Continued

I love my new puppy.

I love that song.

I love you.

Few words in the English language are used with such widely differing motives and recipients as the word "love." Most of us find "being in love" a delightful, if confusing, experience. The loss of love, by whatever means, is painful, and our sense of loss is strong and enduring. "Love makes the world go round."

What is love? To poets and philosophers, love is magical and mysterious. To psychologists, love is a dependent variable. Few, if any, topics in social psychology deal with such a perplexing, joyous, complex, and bewildering emotion. The study of love as a psychological variable has not been without criticism. Some critics have argued that love should be off-limits to researchers who might somehow diminish the impact of this feeling by learning too much about it. Others contend that love is inherently unknowable, and any attempts to quantify it are doomed to failure.

What we do know from the social psychological study of love is that it is different from liking and that there are different kinds of love. Our love for our parents may be different from our love for a new puppy. And our love for a romantic partner may be different from either of these. Research on the difference between liking and loving (Rubin, 1973) has argued that liking implies a positive attitude toward another. Love, on the other hand, is a more emotionally charged concept with three main aspects: attachment, caring, and intimacy.

Attachment is the desire to be in the physical presence of another and to value how he or she thinks and feels about you. *Caring* implies the desire to give of one's self for the benefit of the loved other. *Intimacy* indicates the close bond of communication and trust between two people that may or may not include physical intimacy.

We may both like and love someone at the same time, or we may hold just one or the other feeling. It is possible to love someone that you don't really like, just as we may like someone without holding the feeling of love for that person.

Companionate love can be a very rewarding feeling.

Love can take many forms, as illustrated in the opening examples. Psychologists have generated lists of different kinds of romantic love; we shall focus on two here. Berscheid and Walster (1978) divided romantic love into what they call passionate love and companionate love. *Passionate love* is the love we usually see depicted in movies, soap operas, and popular music. It is the intense, all-consuming "can't keep my hands off of you" fascination with the object of one's desire. This "red-hot" emotion of passionate love is accompanied by an intense physiological arousal. As with all high levels of psychological and physiological arousal, the agony and the ecstasy of passionate love does not seem to be maintained forever. Perhaps it is that we cannot afford to expend vast amounts of energy for very long without becoming exhausted that leads to "the honeymoon being over." Perhaps it is the need for the partners to invest some of that attention on offspring that may have resulted from the original passion. Whatever the reason, studies have shown that couples' passionate love is likely to cool off in a year or two (Sternberg, 1988).

That's not to say that the couple is doomed to go separate ways. It may be that as the passionate love dims a bit, it is replaced and added to by what is called *companionate love*. Less volatile and longer lasting than passionate love, companionate love may be based on shared life experiences and strong feelings of long-term commitment. It is a love that is warm, trusting, and tolerant. The couple celebrating their 50th wedding anniversary may not be in a rush to get back to their bedroom for some sexual heroics. However, any observer can see in the way the couple looks at each other or holds each other's hand that they are very much in love, and those feelings of love are deeply rewarding. They have been through life's ups and downs and have survived—even thrived. We should all be so lucky.

Sternberg (1988) argues that love is composed of three components: intimacy, passion, and decision/commitment. The *intimacy component* is made up of connectedness, closeness, sharing, and affection. The *passion component* encompasses drives associated with physiological arousal, romance, and sex. Last, the *decision/commitment component* is the cognitive realization that one loves the other person along with the long-term determination to maintain the relationship despite difficulties and interpersonal costs.

Different combinations of these factors produce different kinds of love according to Sternberg. These factors may appear singly or in combinations, such as "infatuation," where only passion exists, or "romantic love," where intimacy and passion but not decision/commitment are there. When all three components are present, "consummate love" exists. Nonlove is defined as a relationship when none of these components is present. Relationships are dynamic; they may change over time. These different components of love may emerge or recede over the years in ways that are beneficial or detrimental to the partners involved, and ultimately to the relationship between them.

Proximity

We are most likely to be attracted to people who live or work near us. The same holds true for whom we become friends with and whom we marry. That fact should not be surprising, since we have more opportunity to interact with those who are close by to us. **Proximity** is a powerful factor (Berscheid & Reis, 1998).

Proximity: Physical nearness.

More interactions lead to more attraction for the most part, but more interactions can also lead to increased disliking (Ebbesen, Kjos, & Konecni, 1976). Students randomly paired to become dorm roommates may find that they become best friends for life, or they may come to hate each other. What explains this seeming contradiction? The nearness of proximity likely intensifies feelings of people for one another. If those feelings are positive, they may lead us to greater attraction; we may actually marry the boy or girl next door. If those feelings are negative, we may come to dislike to greater and greater degrees. Statistics have shown that the most likely person to murder a woman is her husband or boyfriend (Straus & Gelles, 1990).

Similarity

We tend to be attracted to people who are similar to us—similar to us in attractiveness, socioeconomic status, education, ethnicity, attitudes, and so on. "Birds of a feather" do attract (Rushon & Bons, 2005). Part of that appeal might be based on the fact that if you are with someone who holds similar views, interests, and values, you simply have less to fight about. Furthermore, the fact that they hold these similar views might provide validation for your views, a sort of psychological pat on the back. We like what is familiar, be it our favorite pillow, a trusted pair of jeans, or another person. While we look forward to vacations and travel, there is something very comforting about returning from one's travels to the safety and familiarity of home.

What about the saying "opposites attract"? A dominant person and a submissive person might make a fine pair. They should have less tension than two dominant people, who might be prone to power struggles, or two submissive people, who might be frustrated by inertia. What may occur in the dominant-submissive pair is that while the two people are different, they both are similar in believing who should play which role in the relationship. This is a **complementarity of needs** (Davis & Rusbult, 2001). Each individual's personality and needs are met by the other. Remember that needs and attitudes are different. The dominant and submissive have different needs but similar attitudes when it comes to deciding how their relationship works best for them.

> **Complementarity of needs:** Each individual's personality and needs are met by the other.

Reward/Cost Theory of Attraction

People prefer being rewarded to being punished. Is there anyone who would rather be struck in the face by a fist than receive a tender kiss? Likely not. One group of theories as to why we are attracted to certain people revolves around the general theme of reinforcement. The assumption is that we learn to like others who are associated with some pleasant turn of events. It may be classical conditioning that teaches us as babies to associate the favorable outcomes (getting fed, getting comfort) with certain people (primary caregivers) that leads us to want to be in their company. Operant conditioning may also be functioning as we learn to make the stimulus-response pairing one of an association of "another person present" and "something good happening."

However we acquire these associations, it is plausible to think that we would like people who reward us better than those who do not. Perhaps that is why friends give each other gifts. It may be why you enjoy spending time with friends. The value we place on spending time and interacting with friends and family is based on the positive feelings we associate with those particular people.

The value we place on spending time and interacting with friends is based on the positive feelings we associate with those particular people.

The idea of rewards and costs affecting attraction can be seen in the dynamic exchange of positives and negatives that mark relationships. If the question is, "Which specific people do I like most?" the answer may be, "Whoever provides me the most rewards at the least cost." Because any interaction between people is an ongoing "give and take," both people may be calculating their relative returns versus their relative investments. Those costs and rewards can change over time. A "good deal" today may turn out to be a "bad deal" tomorrow.

Although it's often said that relationships should be "50-50," in the real world, that is likely a rare event. Nonetheless, both partners in a relationship will likely feel most at ease if both are getting a good return on their investment of time, effort, and emotional involvement. If one partner "puts in" twice the effort, then it would only be fair for him or her to "take out" twice the benefits.

This assessment of attraction based on costs and rewards defines those costs and rewards broadly. Rewards may be thought of as any sort of pleasure, gratification, or good feelings. Costs can include time wasted, money spent, embarrassment, options not taken, or even physical or psychological misery. The economics involved in rating the pluses and the minuses may lead people to stay in a relationship that is bad (to an outside observer) if they believe that all other potential relationships (or even no relationship at all) are worse. In other words, people might remain in abusive, destructive relationships simply because they fear that leaving that relationship would lead to an even worse outcome.

One last note on a reward-cost explanation for liking involves the notion of **reciprocity of attraction**. One reason we may like other people is because they like us (Peretti & Abplanalp, 2004). People who show the extreme good taste to find us attractive might be seen as more favorable or desirable in our eyes. The reciprocal nature of liking can be seen in the behavior of a mythical junior high school boy whom we will call Carlos.

> **Reciprocity of attraction:** We may like someone because they like us.

Not wanting to be rejected, Carlos asks his friend, Ali, to "go find out if she likes me" before he takes the chance of inviting Juanita to the eighth grade dance. If Ali comes back and tells him that she would be thrilled to escort Carlos to the dance, it is likely that Carlos will find Juanita even more beautiful than she was before. However, if the "scout" returns with the bad news that "she wouldn't go out with Carlos if he were the last boy on earth," it is likely that Carlos will respond with a lowered evaluation of the fair young Juanita. He might even say something like "I really didn't want to go out with her anyway. She is ugly." It would not just be "sour grapes" on his part. Carlos might actually see her as less attractive.

Gain/Loss Theory

There is an interesting variation on reinforcement predictions called **gain/loss theory** (Aronson & Linder, 1965). This theory predicts that it is not only the total amount of reinforcement we receive from another that makes him or her attractive, but also the direction of that reinforcement over time.

> **Gain/loss theory:** It is not only the total amount of reinforcement we receive from another that makes him or her attractive, but also the direction of that reinforcement over time.

Imagine you are at a big party and meet a fellow named Richard for the first time. After a few minutes, you move on, but then you overhear Richard talking about you to someone else. Richard is saying very nice things about you. You also meet Tony for the first time, and as luck would have it, you overhear Tony talking to someone else about you. Tony is describing you in negative terms. Reinforcement theory predicts you will like Richard more than Tony, and most research backs that up. What would happen if, later, you get a second opportunity to talk with Richard and with Tony, and then once again overhear them talking about you to a third person? Both Richard and Tony have switched their opinion of you. Tony now is describing you in glowing terms, while Richard is saying bad things about you. Reinforcement theory might argue that you would now like them equally—the sum of positive and negative comments is the same for both Richard and Tony, only the order of presentation is different.

Research approximating this situation finds a very different outcome (Aronson & Linder, 1965). You will probably like Tony much more than Richard. There has been a "gain" in Tony's evaluation of you; there has been a "loss" in how Richard sees you. In fact, you might even like Tony more than Richard even if Richard had made positive comments about you during both of your eavesdropping experiences. Conversely, you are likely to feel more negatively toward Richard, who changed his opinion downward, than to Tony if he had been consistently negative.

Let's take a trip down memory lane. Think of the one nonrelative with whom you have been most in love in your life. That person may be part of your life now or may not be. Now go back in time to when you first met that person and gauge your first impression of him or her. When large groups of people do this, roughly half have a negative first impression of the "love of their life."

The same holds true for the other end of the spectrum. When asked to give their first impression of the "hate of their life," even more than half describe their first impressions as positive. Often it is a former friend or lover who somehow betrayed a person's trust who now is remembered in highly negative ways. And for many people, it is the same person who is their main love and hate focus!

Physical Attractiveness

Dozens of social psychology studies have found that the most powerful variable, at least in the initial phases of relationships, is physical attractiveness. We like to look at pretty people. We like to be around pretty people. This has troubled social psychologists. Are humans so superficial that we make assessments of people based only on their "looks"? We pay lip service to the unfairness of this when we make statements such as "don't judge a book by its cover" and "beauty is only skin deep." The fact of the matter is that we are used to judging people's physical characteristics. We rate people on scales much like the judges' rating in the Miss America pageant. "She's so beautiful, she is definitely a 10."

The entire entertainment industry is built around the public's desire to watch beautiful people. Even if we are not "totally beautiful," there are the multimillion dollar cosmetics and clothing industries to help us look the best we can. "Accentuate the positive, hide the negative." We are taught that looks count—that looking attractive make us more desirable to others. And even though the outward appearance should not be a measure of the inner characteristics of a person, people still are attracted to the beautiful and tend to move away from the not so beautiful.

Most of us have had the experience of being drawn to someone simply because of his or her good looks. After we get to know that person, we may find that he or she continues to be interesting to us because of his or her wonderful personality, or we may shy away because underneath all that outward beauty was a "dud." Live and learn. But what of the poor ugly people? If we move away from them initially, we may never get the chance to know if they are kind, wonderful people or not. We may miss out on the opportunity of getting to know excellent, interesting, "beautiful on the inside" people because those people repel us at first glance. That is unfair to the less attractive and unfair to us, but people do seem to be drawn to the beautiful and drawn away from those not endowed with physical beauty.

And, if that weren't enough, we tend to give physically attractive people credit for much more than their beauty. There is a "what is beautiful is good" stereotype called the **halo effect** (Dion, 1972) that presumes that good-looking people also possess superior personal traits and characteristics. They are expected to be more intelligent, happy, kind, and successful. We believe that beauty is a positive attribute, a valuable asset that can be exchanged for other things in social interactions. In making these assumptions, we may be applying something akin to a "marketplace" mentality to the value of different levels of physical attractiveness.

There is a **matching hypothesis** (Yela & Sangrador, 2001) that states that people will tend to pair up with others of similar physical attractiveness. Beautiful people pair up with beautiful people,

Halo effect: Assumes that good-looking people also possess superior personal traits and characteristics.

Matching hypothesis: People tend to pair up with others of similar attractiveness.

© 2009, by coka. Used under license of Shutterstock, Inc.

The attractiveness of these women would lead many people to believe they are more socially skilled and less likely to commit harm to anyone.

average-looking folks pair up with average-looking others, and unattractive persons find other unattractive persons. Just as we feel better and more attractive when we get "all dressed up," we may feel more attractive when our date is better looking. We may even find that it is to our advantage to hang around with others who are less attractive so as to look better by comparison.

Certainly "beauty is in the eye of the beholder," but our society provides models (in fact, there is an occupation called just that) of what one should look like to be a handsome man or a beautiful woman. The criteria of beauty change over time and across cultures. Looking back at your parents' or grandparents' high school yearbook will illustrate the changes in the criteria of beauty over the years. Before you laugh at who was voted "Best Looking" by their high school peers in 1950 or 1960, remember that your children and grandchildren will be doing the same when they see pictures of you and your friends when you graduated.

One last point provides hope and comfort to those of us who are not "drop-dead beautiful." The powerful influence of physical attractiveness decreases over time as we get to know people beyond just what they look like. As we get to know people better, they tend to become better looking in our eyes, and we become better looking in theirs (Buss, 2005). Those facts still do not diminish the fact that physical attractiveness is a potent factor in how other people see and behave toward each other.

ALTRUISTIC BEHAVIOR

Human societies depend on our willingness to work together, respect one another, and sometimes, to help other people. Cooperation and mutual assistance are important traits of the human species that have aided in our thriving as a species over thousands of years. Starting from infancy, where the individual human baby is completely dependent on the good intentions and care from others, we live in a world that is full of instances of helping. Social psychologists call these helpful acts altruistic behavior or altruism.

Altruistic behavior/ altruism: Helpful acts not linked to personal gain.

A strict definition of altruism would include only helpful behaviors that are not linked to personal gain. Lending a neighbor a tool, in the hopes of having the favor returned at a later date, may be motivated by self-interest. Making a donation to a charity because you will pay less taxes as a result of that donation also seems to involve self-interest. True altruism is behavior that is motivated by the positive outcome for someone else with no expectation of recognition or reward in return. Even when we make an anonymous donation or help a stranger who we will never see again, we still may have an inner feeling of having "done the right thing." So it may be best to loosen our definition to allow for some self-interest and define altruism as behavior that is primarily (but not exclusively) other-motivated.

Norm of Social Responsibility

There are social norms that address helping behavior. There is the norm of social responsibility (Grusec, Davidov, & Lundell, 2002) that stresses that we should help people who are in need. Society has an obligation to the less fortunate among us, and although we may not be able to completely reverse unfortunate circumstances that befall people, we do have an obligation to help. When natural disasters such as tsunamis or earthquakes strike, there arises a feeling that we all should pitch in and help. Helping the less fortunate is also a strong part of the Judeo-Christian ethic in our society. Many charities invoke the norm of social responsibility to persuade us to help. We see the starving children covered with flies in the "Save the Children" ads or watch as television telethons

Norm of social responsibility: Society's expectation that we help people in need.

present us with children with birth defects or incurable diseases, and we may feel motivated to help these victims.

One important point to remember is that the norm of social responsibility is much stronger when the victims played no part in achieving their status as victims. You may lend $10 to a friend who has lost his wallet while volunteering at the orphanage. You will be less likely to lend $10 to someone who told you that he had spent all his money on a drug and alcohol binge. This norm weakens considerably when the people in need are viewed as having had some active part in their own downfall. The belief in a just world would make us more likely to help a person who was not responsible for his or her neediness than a person who we thought brought about his or her need through irresponsible behavior.

Wearing a pink ribbon is an attempt to make people aware of breast cancer as a social issue in need of financial funding.

Norm of Reciprocity

Norm of reciprocity: Help others now so as to receive help, if needed, in the future.

Another norm that relates to altruism is the norm of reciprocity (Batson & Ahmad, 2001). The Golden Rule from the New Testament of the Bible states, "Do unto others as you would have them do unto you." Reciprocity implies that we may help others now so as to receive help, if needed, in the future. You may give to the Heart Fund or United Way today with the hope that you will never need the aid they provide. If you do need them later in your life, your hope is that they will still be around to help you in the future, because you helped them today.

Although a "you scratch my back and I'll scratch yours" reciprocity may be implied in some forms of helping, there may be broader implications. While driving, you might allow another car to enter the roadway from a side street during rush hour. It is unlikely that you do this because you expect the favor to be returned to you by this same driver. You may do it out of simple courtesy, and in doing so, make the highways a little more civil so that down the road that courtesy will come back to you from whomever.

Cost-Reward Approach to Altruism

Cost-reward approach: Helping only when the reward is greater than the cost.

Another way of looking at whether or not to provide help is in a cost-reward approach to altruism. We may help when rewards are more than costs and not help when the opposite is how we view the situation. One reason that rewards may be offered for help in solving everything from criminal cases to lost puppies is that people are more likely to offer help if a clear incentive is provided. Looking around your neighborhood for a stranger's lost pet may not be something you are inclined to spend a lot of time doing. If there is a reward of $10,000 offered, everyone in the entire neighborhood is likely to be out and about searching for poor, lost Fido.

Norm of noninvolvement: By not being involved you may save yourself potential hassles.

The norm of noninvolvement (Matsui, 1981) states that you should "mind your own business" and that if you don't heed this norm, you may find yourself in trouble based on your meddling. The hassles potentially involved in stopping and helping might outweigh norms that direct you to provide help.

Emergency Situations

What about helping in emergency situations? Emergency situations are by definition rare and ambiguous (Latané & Darley, 1968). Is the couple quarreling next door in need of someone to break up the fight before someone gets killed? Or is it just a little family spat? Is the person who has just fallen into the bushes the victim of a heart attack and in need of immediate assistance, or just a drunk who needs to sleep it off?

Intuition might tell you that the more people present at the scene of a potential emergency, the more likely help would be given. Intuition is wrong in this case. The social psychological study of the decision to help or not in an emergency situation was triggered by the sad case of Kitty Genovese. Kitty was walking toward her apartment building in New York City when a man attacked her with a knife. She screamed out and was left lying in a pool of blood. The attacker left briefly but returned to resume his attack. She cried out repeatedly and the attacker left, thinking she was dead. She somehow survived the repeated knife wounds and was scratching her way across a parking lot when the attacker returned 10 minutes later. This third attack was fatal (Dowd, 1984).

At least 38 of Kitty Genovese's neighbors saw or heard the crime. Nearly 20 watched all three attacks from their windows in the apartment building where Kitty lived. Not one of them came to her aid. Not one of them called the police until a half an hour after she died. Why did these witnesses act the way they did? What were they thinking? The murder of Ms. Genovese led two social psychologists (Bibb Latané and John Darley) to the laboratory to answer these questions.

They found evidence for what is called the **bystander effect**—as the number of potential bystanders (witnesses) increases, the likelihood that any one of them will help someone in trouble decreases (Darley & Latané, 1968). The bystander effect is based in part on the fact that when we see a potential emergency in the presence of others, we may feel that surely someone else will help. Or, we may feel the weight of responsibility to help less firmly on our shoulders when others are present. A **diffusion of responsibility** may occur when we feel only one-tenth the total responsibility for helping when there are nine others around. Had we witnessed the emergency alone, all the responsibility would be ours and ours alone.

The presence of other people may even lead us to be less likely to define a situation as an emergency. If we are involved and interacting with other people, we may not even see the emergency situation because the others distract us. Noticing a fan having a heart attack on the other side of a crowded baseball stadium is unlikely. Being on a nearly deserted beach with one other person fifty yards away having a heart attack might be difficult to miss.

Assuming we notice a possible emergency situation, the presence of other people may still lead us to not help. One norm we learn as children is not to overreact. We hear the stories of Chicken Little who thought the sky was falling and "the boy who cried wolf" when, in fact, no wolf was present. The moral of those stories is not to overreact to situations or bad things might happen. The townspeople eventually stopped responding to the boy who cried wolf and all the sheep were lost when the wolf really did show up.

We are taught to "remain cool," to keep our wits about us, and to make an assessment of the situation by looking at how others around us are responding. If you are walking across campus one night with four friends and an older man headed toward you falls into the bushes, you may keep your cool and look at your friends for their reactions to this possible emergency. If all five of you maintain the "I'm not sure what's going on but unless someone else reacts, I'll stay cool" attitude (a mind-set referred to as **pluralistic ignorance**) (Miller & Prentice, 1994; Taylor, 1982), all five of you are likely to define the situation as a nonemergency. Hence no help is needed, and none is given. When we are by ourselves, we do not have to worry about "saving face" and may be more likely to define the situation as an emergency and check the guy slumped in the bushes to see how he is. If it turns out he is drunk, perhaps no help is needed; if he has had a heart attack, we will call 911.

Other Variables in Helping

Social psychologists have been unsuccessful in determining a specific set of personality traits associated with more helpful people. Some folks are more

Bystander effect: As the number of bystanders increases, the likelihood that any of them will help decreases.

Diffusion of responsibility: Feel less responsible with other people around.

Pluralistic ignorance: Not reacting to a situation unless someone else does first.

helpful than others are, but there does not seem to be a set of characteristics that identify them. Even seminary students on their way to deliver a lecture on the "Parable of the Good Samaritan" were likely to pass by a bleeding victim of some mishap if the seminary students believed that they were late for the lecture (Darley & Batson, 1973).

Moods play a part in our decisions to help or not. Sometimes we are in a good mood; sometimes we are in a bad mood. A person in a good mood is more likely to stop and help another in need than is someone in a neutral or bad mood. If someone found change in the scoop of a payphone (that experimenters had preloaded), the result was that the person was more likely to soon thereafter help an experimental accomplice who dropped a folder full of papers (Isen & Levin, 1972).

Finally, we can look at helping behavior as a function of modeling. Shoppers directly behind people who toss change in a Salvation Army kettle at Christmas time are more likely to toss in change than if the person in front of them did not make a donation. Drivers are more likely to stop and render aid to a stranded motorist if those drivers had just witnessed someone else who stopped to help a few miles before (Bryan & Test, 1967). The "tote boards" on the television charity telethon provide potential helpers with feedback about what to do, and also how many other people are doing so.

AGGRESSION

Humans are an aggressive group. History has been shaped by the armed conflict and sometimes brutal aggression displayed by one nation against another. Large groups of people have been singled out for extermination at the hands of a ruling government. Lest we feel smug that the horrors of the holocaust in Nazi Germany did not happen in America, one need only go back a few generations in the United States to witness the near extermination of the indigenous American peoples (Native Americans) and the enslavement of Africans.

Human beings are the only animals that regularly kill members of their own species. We do so using sophisticated weapons (all the way up to the atomic bomb) and not-so-sophisticated weapons (rocks and even hands). Children and teenagers are taking high-powered weaponry to school and using it to kill. In Chicago several years ago, two boys, aged 11 and 12, killed a 5-year-old boy by tossing him out of a 14th story window because he would not steal candy for them.

Aggression is very much a part of current entertainment as seen in the movies, television shows, and video games that are the most popular in our culture (Huesmann, Moise-Titus, Podolski, & Eron, 2003). People like sports with violence as well. There is a penalty in football for unnecessary violence that implies that some violence is necessary. Football players have been rendered totally paralyzed by "clean hits." Ice hockey is a game that is regularly punctuated by fists and sticks flying—and blood on the ice. Boxing is perhaps the truest blend of aggression in sports, where the stated purpose of each combatant is to render their opponent temporarily unconscious, usually by repeated, damaging blows to the head. The increasing popularity of "sports entertainment," as epitomized by the brand of WWE professional wrestling events, are based on violence and threats of violence (Box below).

Although this animal has no personal need to be lassoed, the cowboys will do so anyway to the cheers of an adoring crowd.

RESEARCH REPORT: IS PROFESSIONAL WRESTLING BECOMING MORE VIOLENT?

In the wake of perceived increases in societal violence, particularly that perpetrated by young people with guns (such as the April 1999 Columbine massacre killing 12 and wounding 24 and the April 2007 Virgina Tech massacre killing 32 and wounding 25), a number of media sources have bemoaned increases in the violent content of entertainment available to children and teenagers. Media targets usually include television, motion pictures, the Internet, and video games.

A number of media reports after the 1999 Columbine incident also singled out professional wrestling for its depiction of simulated violence. The television program *Inside Edition* (February 1999), *USA Today* (February 1999), the Knight-Ridder Newsservice (April 1999), and U.S. News and World Report (May 1999) have all pointed to undocumented increases in this form of self-described "sports entertainment."

Research was undertaken (Kather, Chesnut, & Ellyson, 2000), not to establish a link between youth violence and professional wrestling, but to determine:

1. if college students perceive violence to be increasing in professional wrestling
2. if professional wrestling has indeed become more violent over the years

To answer these two questions, two research phases were undertaken. The first involved a questionnaire given to a large sample of undergraduates, asking, among other things, if they viewed violence in professional wrestling as being on the increase. The second project had trained raters coding 15 years of the World Wrestling Entertainment, Inc.'s (WWE) Wrestlemania. Wrestlemania is the annual showcase pay-per-view event that has been described as the "Super Bowl of wrestling." It has become the most popular pay-per-view event on cable/satellite television in the United States and Canada, and sales of videotapes and DVDs of these events have topped 500,000 copies each.

Phase One
Method: A total of 508 undergraduates (203 males and 305 females) enrolled in Introductory Psychology at two large state universities in Ohio (Youngstown State University and Bowling Green State University) completed a questionnaire. The questionnaire asked them the degree to which they agreed or disagreed with 14 statements concerning wrestling's popularity, the reality of the violence portrayed, increases in violence, and the degree to which violence is imitated by children, teenagers, and adults.

Results: Overall, respondents believed that the level of violence in professional wrestling has been increasing. In the study, 35 percent "totally agreed" and 34 percent "agreed somewhat" with the statement "The violence in professional wrestling is increasing." Only 8 percent of respondents agreed totally or somewhat with the statement that the violence in professional wrestling is real. When asked about the potential for imitation of the violence in professional wrestling, 75 percent agreed totally or somewhat that children might imitate, 62 percent agreed totally or somewhat that teens might imitate, while only 32 percent agreed totally or somewhat that adults might imitate the violence they see in professional wrestling.

Phase Two
Method: Prior to content analysis, a coding system was developed and pretested, using random segments taken from the first 15 Wrestlema-

Continued

nias. Individual videotapes of each of these 15 Wrestlemanias (1985 through 1999) were coded by three separate raters for four categories of physical assault:

1. by hand or arm (as in a hit or choke)
2. by leg (as in a kick or trip)
3. by body (as in a body slam)
4. by weapon or object (as by a chair or stick)

Two categories of overt threat (physical or verbal) were also coded. Total incidents of each coded behavior were then averaged across three raters.

Results: Frequencies of physical assault and overt threat for each of the past 15 Wrestlemanias were consistent and relatively unchanged over the years. There were no significant differences between the total number of depicted physical assaults or overt threats over the 15 Wrestlemanias. The mean physical assault rate was 900.07 (SD = 70.42). The mean overt threat rate was 59.07 (SD = 18.07).

Discussion

According to the data, there was a clear distinction between the perception of increased violence and the actual levels of violence coded in the first 15 years of WWE's Wrestlemanias. It simply may be that respondents to the questionnaire had both heard and believed the media reports of increases in violence. Actual levels of simulated violence depicted in the last 15 years of this annual event studied, although certainly high, were relatively consistent year to year. Interestingly, the National Television Violence Study, the largest study of media content ever undertaken, released its findings in April 1998. One of those findings was that there was no change in the overall level of violence in reality programming across the three years studied. That study, however, did not examine cable/satellite programming, the outlet of most professional wrestling.

Despite concerns about steroid abuse (as in the June 2007 murder/suicide involving wrestler Chris Benoit), the popularity of professional wrestling remains strong. The WWE presents approximately 200 live events each year in major arenas and produces nine hours of original content each week (Smackdown, RAW, and ECW). Even with the increasing popularity of "Ultimate Fighting," cable/satellite ratings of WWE programming are still high, to the point that professional wrestling draws more than 35 million viewers each week. Pay-per-view television sales have increased dramatically over the years as well, with more than 900,000 purchases of the live 2007 Wrestlemania.

Once again, the aim of this study was not to link televised simulated violence and real-world violent behavior. Although there is impressive evidence that exposure to violent models increases aggressive behavior in young children, there is less consensus as to its effect on older children and adults. Classic theories based on arousal (Tannenbaum & Zillman, 1975), disinhibition (Berkowitz, 1962), and social learning (Bandura, 1973) have competed with the aggression reduction (or catharsis hypothesis) work of Feshbach (1984), who argued that under certain conditions, exposure to television violence might reduce subsequent aggression.

The fact remains that the level of simulated physical violence depicted across the first 15 years of Wrestlemanias was fairly consistent and displayed no systematic increases in the recent past. Comparing the mean level of physical violence in Wrestlemanias 13, 14, and 15 to the mean level of physical violence in the 12 prior Wrestlemanias reveals an increase of less than 1 percent. Popularity of professional wrestling has clearly increased while violence levels portrayed in this "entertainment" have remained fairly constant.

Explaining Aggression

Before we can look for explanations for aggressive behavior, we must define it. That has not been an easy task for social psychologists (Mak & de Koning, 1995). If we choose a behavioral definition of aggression, then we might consider any act that brings harm (physical and/or psychological) to another person or living thing as being an aggressive behavior. Consider the tennis player who smashes his racquet into pieces after a bad shot. Is that aggression, even though no living thing was hurt? What about the physician who administers an injection to vaccinate a baby against common childhood illnesses? The baby screams; the baby is hurt. Is the physician guilty of aggressive behavior?

On the other hand, what if someone shoots a gun at you and misses? No harm, no foul? The legal system doesn't think so; it is against the law to attempt murder as well as to commit murder. This leads us to a motivational definition of aggression where the key factor is intent (Lysak, Rule, & Dobbs, 1989). Was the behavior intended to bring harm to another? Even unsuccessful aggression is still seen as aggression. The missed punch may not score points in boxing matches, but it certainly counts as aggression in a bar fight. We shall define aggression as the intentional attempt to injure or harm another.

Remember that aggression may take forms other than physical assault. When you were a child, you most likely heard the saying, "Sticks and stones may break my bones, but words can never hurt me." You surely know that is not true. There is such a thing as verbal aggression. Words can hurt and hurt badly. "I don't love you anymore" may cause more pain than getting punched very hard in the stomach. And there is passive aggression as well, where the lack of behavior is an aggressive act. Your spouse refusing to discuss why he or she is mad at you is an example of passive aggression.

There is also aggression that is instrumental in nature; the main purpose of the aggression is to gain something other than the suffering of the victim. Instrumental aggression has the goal of obtaining something of value. The mugger who says, "Just hand over the money and no one will get hurt," is primarily interested in the money. Faced with the threat of aggression, hopefully the money is handed over and no further aggression results.

Some aggression is the result of unchecked emotions. Almost uncontrollably, some people seem to "see red" in certain circumstances, and they act out violently. We call this type of aggression emotional aggression. There is also random and senseless aggression. Turning over gravestones in a cemetery is aggression toward property that would seem to gain the aggressor very little satisfaction other than some grotesque sense of control over the environment.

Why are humans such an aggressive species? Are we just born that way, the result of evolution? Or is aggressive behavior learned? Do we acquire these behaviors because they are in some way reinforcing? As with most human behavior, the question is one of nature versus nurture. Let us look at the possibilities and the evidence.

Aggression as an Innate Behavior

Sigmund Freud (1920) theorized that all humans possessed an unconscious thanatos—a death instinct. Countered by a life force called eros, thanatos was assumed to be a self-directed destructive force. Freud argued that it might also be other-directed, explaining why humans display aggression toward others. Like most of Freudian theory, the evidence in support of Freud's ideas about these unconscious forces is weak.

Konrad Lorenz (1974) suggests that humans, like all animals, may have developed aggressive behaviors as a survival technique over tens of thousands of years. The presence of aggressive instincts would have evolutionary benefits because aggressive behavior (or the threat of aggressive behavior) would allow for animals to preserve territories, weed out the weaker members of the species, and provide more access to food, water, and mates to the strongest animals. Lorenz extended this research on animals to include humans and suggested that present-day humans may also have aggressive and fighting instincts as a result of the natural selection process inherent in evolution. Just as racehorses can be selectively bred for speed, or collie dogs for long, pointy noses, nature may have selectively "bred" humans for aggression.

There are problems with any definition for human behavior that asserts instinctual or innate explanation. Humans are different from other animals, primarily in the cortical areas of our brains. Very few behaviors in humans are "prewired." Even newborn babies begin replacing the few reflexive behaviors they possess at birth with purposeful, self-directed ones. The cortex of the human brain, vast and powerful, fine-tunes its directives for behavior based on the situations and environment into which it is born.

If human aggression were inborn or innate, then we would not see the vast variety of expressions of that aggression across cultures, across time, and across individuals. Animals within one species use threats and fighting behavior that is usually very similar. If you've seen two rats fight, you have seen all rats fight. The aggression behavior of nonhuman animals is consistent, stereotypical, and released by specific stimuli. Specific behaviors by members of a species automatically bring out aggressive responses by other members of that species (Tinbergen, 1951).

Human aggression, on the other hand, is none of those. There are dramatic differences in the way any two people aggress and whether or not they will aggress. Those differences are cultural, familial, and personal. Crime rates for aggressive behaviors such as assault, rape, and murder vary tremendously from culture to culture. Even in nontechnological societies, one might find a tribe of cannibalistic headhunters living not so far from another tribe living in peace and harmony who never seem to exhibit aggressive behaviors (Turnbull, 1961). The point is that not all humans are equally aggressive. When humans become aggressive, they do so in many, many different ways. There are not any specific stimuli that release aggressive responses in humans.

Aggression as a Learned Behavior

The alternative explanation to why there is aggression is that it is a learned response. You might remember on learning that any response that creates a positive outcome (reinforcement) is more likely to be repeated. If aggression (or even the threat of aggression) produces something favorable, we might expect aggression to increase. A toddler who wants another toddler's toy and obtains it through a quick slap to the other would find that the aggression "paid off" (especially if there were no witnesses). If aggressive behaviors are successful in obtaining rewards, they will become learned behaviors.

Courtesy of the author

If the observation of rewarded violence leads to behavior that is more violent, then why are sports programs never identified as the root of all aggression in society?

Not only do we learn by doing, but we can also learn by watching others perform behaviors and noticing what happens to them. Those others we watch are called models. This "learning by imitation" is a key element of social learning theory. In a classic social psychological study on social learning, Bandura, Ross, and Ross (1963) involved four- to five-year-old children who watched an adult male or female play with and eventually attack a large inflatable clown-like "rock-em, sock-em" type of doll named Bobo. The live adult model sat on the doll, hit the doll in the head with a mallet, and shouted statements like, "hit Bobo," "kick him," and "sock him in the nose." Other children witnessed the adults attacking Bobo on videotape instead of watching live aggression. Still others watched a cartoon depicting the same behaviors. A final group of children saw no violence toward Bobo and went directly to the second phase of the study.

In this second phase, all children had an opportunity to interact with a Bobo doll. Those children who had not viewed aggressive behaviors toward Bobo did not aggress toward the doll. However, children who had witnessed aggression toward Bobo (and it mattered not whether they witnessed live or taped, human or cartoon characters) imitated this aggression toward Bobo. The children even mimicked specific behaviors such as whacking Bobo with a hammer and repeated the phrases they had previously heard associated with aggression. Clearly, these children had learned to be aggressive by watching the aggressive behavior of others. Just as clearly, children in our culture are presented with many models of aggressive behavior, from fairy tales and cartoons, to television shows and movies. It's not surprising that they learn aggression.

One last point about the Bandura study. A follow-up study by Bandura and Walters (1963) had children once again watching a model aggressing toward Bobo. Some children then witnessed the model being rewarded for the aggressive behavior, some watched the model being punished for beating up Bobo, and a third group saw the model receive no consequences. When later given a chance to play with the doll, children were less likely to imitate aggressive behavior if they were in the group that saw the model punished. The children in the other two groups (reward or no consequences) beat up poor Bobo. It is likely that all three groups "learned" aggression toward Bobo, but the "punishment" group inhibited their aggression when shown the possible outcome of that behavior. Additional learning had taken place.

Another way the environment may trigger aggression describes aggression as a predictable response. More than 70 years ago, a simple but elegant theory was proposed (Dollard, Doob, Miller, Mowrer, & Sears, 1939) called the **frustration-aggression hypothesis**. Dollard and his colleagues made two assumptions. The first was that frustration always leads to aggression. The second was that aggression is the direct response to frustration. Frustration was defined in learning theory terms as a "blocked goal response": Something you thought was going to happen and hoped would happen, does not happen. Does all frustration result in aggression?

Consider the following scenario. You may wake up one morning and realize your alarm clock failed to work and now you're late. You spring out of bed only to find that your puppy has left a fragrant monument because you forgot to take him out for a walk before you went to bed. You make this discovery by stepping right in it. You head for the shower, but there's no hot water. So you skip taking a shower knowing you might be emitting a foul odor the rest of the day. You head to your car to drive to school, and your car has a flat tire. That's not as frustrating as the fact that your car battery is dead as well and you have to ask a neighbor for a jump-start.

You are finally on your way. Arriving on campus minutes before your class, you see that there's absolutely no place near campus to park. So you have to walk a mile in a driving rainstorm to get to class. Arriving there 15 minutes late and completely soaked, you walk in just as the instructor gives a pop quiz for which you are totally unprepared.

By every definition of frustration, you have had more than your fair share. Does that mean you will be aggressive to someone or something? Life is full of frustrations: some little; some large. We learn to cope with problems and do not necessarily aggress in response to them.

Frustration-aggression hypothesis: Theory that frustration leads to aggression, and all aggression is the result of frustration.

The problem with the original frustration-aggression hypothesis was that it was too rigid. Not all frustration leads to aggression, and not all aggression is the result of frustration. If you were walking toward the library and someone walked up and took a swing at you and you swung back, what would be the "blocked goal response"? Could we say you had hoped to walk to the library without anyone taking a swing at you? And that your "goal response" of making it to the library unharmed was "blocked" by your attacker? That seems a stretch in logic.

It wasn't long after the original frustration-aggression hypothesis was proposed that the shortcomings of such a simple, direct link were discovered. The frustration-aggression hypothesis was eventually modified (Berkowitz, 1989) to state that frustration leads to a "tendency" to aggress. This tendency might be modified by the situation (you are less likely to end up fighting in church than you are in a bar) or by cues in the environment (the presence of weapons tends to increase the aggression of frustrated people).

The environment may also contain specific factors that reduce the restraining forces on aggression. Most of us know that it is not socially acceptable to be aggressive in most circumstances. Most of us also will feel guilty about aggressive behavior because we have incorporated the society's standards of what is right and wrong into our own set of values. What if those external and internal checks on our behavior are altered? We refer now to **environmental variables of aggression**.

> **Environmental variables of aggression:** External situations that may suspend our checks on aggression.

If the chances of getting caught or punished for socially unacceptable behavior are lowered, might people aggress more? Think about what happens on Halloween or at Mardi Gras in New Orleans. Children may become vandals for a night in October, and adults may lose all self-control at a seven-day party in Louisiana. Riots and looting have followed legal decisions and power outages in urban areas in the United States. What do all these situations have in common? They share a common assumption by the people involved that "the social rules are suspended," or "they can't catch us all." People in these situations may experience what is known as **deindividuation**, that is, a mental state of being less aware of their own individuality, less constrained by social checks and balances, and more likely to feel the crowd is the main actor. Reduce the chances of having to account for your behavior, and aggression increases. Even prolonged exposure to violent video games may have the effect of desensitizing individuals to the type of physiological responses normally associated with real-life violence (Carnagey, Anderson, & Bushman, 2007).

> **Deindividuation:** A mental state of being less aware of your own individuality and therefore less constrained by social checks and balances.

As suggested earlier, we may choose not to be aggressive because we feel it is not the moral thing to do. Every day, men and women in the military are trained in ways to be aggressive, and police officers all over the country are fighting the "bad guys." Overcoming the guilt associated with aggression can occur in a number of ways. We may become convinced that our aggression is morally right, for example, when we are defending our nation or the people we care about. Historically, it is not uncommon at all for soldiers to believe "God is on our side" as they march into battle to make the world safe. World War I was described as "the war to end all wars"—certainly a moral-sounding objective.

We may also believe that the decision to aggress is out of our hands. "I was only following orders" implies that one is not morally responsible for the result of aggressive behavior. Soldiers are taught to obey orders given to them by superior officers. In fact, any armed force that does not have soldiers following orders is likely to be ineffective. Military law requires soldiers to obey an officer's order. Disobeying a legitimate order from an officer under combat conditions is a serious offense. On the battlefield, an officer even has the legal right (although rarely used) under military law to summarily execute the disobeyer on the spot.

In modern technological societies, the results of one's aggression may be difficult to see. Weaponry allows us to kill at a distance. We can drop bombs from miles up in the sky and never see the human damage we are doing below. We can launch missiles from one continent to another at the flip of a switch. This long-range, indirect aggression may cause broad devastation, but the one who aggresses may never see the result of his or her behavior. Men and women who might not be morally able to kill another human being in hand-to-hand combat may not have a problem dropping a bomb or randomly shooting into the general direction of the enemy.

SUMMARY

Social psychology is the scientific study of how the thoughts, feelings, and behaviors of one person are influenced by the real or imagined presence of others. Social cognition refers to the ways we organize and make sense of our social environment. We form attitudes and stereotypes toward people and objects in our environment and form impressions by the use of schemas. We make attributions (sometimes biased ones) about the causes of behavior in others and in ourselves. Social influence occurs when we alter our behavior through the dynamics of conformity, compliance, or obedience. Social norms and social roles are also influential in shaping our behavior in different circumstances. Social actions may be positive or negative. The area of inter-personal attraction deals with why and how we come to like other people, perhaps even to love specific others. Altruism refers to helping behavior directed toward other people with little or no reward expected. Last, the negative side of social actions can be seen in aggression, the intentional attempt to bring harm or suffering to another.

Social psychologists, for the most part, have not assumed that human behavior is good or bad. What they do believe, as evidenced by the variety of behaviors they study, is that humans are highly adaptable, intelligent animals that have the ability to perform behaviors that are both positive and negative. When it comes to social behavior and social interaction, very little, if anything, is "written in stone." Unlike other animals, we have evolved highly complex brains and a rich variety of societies in which to use those brains. More than any other creature on the planet, humans have the capacity to change themselves and to change their environments. Examining the ways we think and behave in a social context is one of the more exciting areas in the modern science of psychology.

As we come to the end of this book on general psychology, the authors' hope is that you, the student of modern psychology, have an appreciation of the scientific field that studies human behavior, in all its complexity and diversity. The many discoveries and advances that mark the discipline of psychology are matched by the many more unanswered questions that psychology has yet to resolve.

> "I expect to pass through this world but once. Any good thing, therefore, that I can do or any kindness that I can show to any fellow human being, let me do it now. Let me not defer nor neglect it, for I shall not pass this way again."
>
> —Stephen Grellet (1773-1855), French-born Quaker Minister

KEY TERMS

altruistic behavior/
    altruism
attitudes
attribution theories
behavioral aggression
belief in a just world
bystander effect
cognitive dissonance
complementarity of
    needs
compliance
cost-reward approach
defensive attribution
deindividuation
diffusion of
    responsibility
door-in-the-face effect
emotional aggression
environmental variables
    of aggression

foot-in-the-door effect
frustration-aggression
    hypothesis
fundamental attribution
    error
gain/loss theory
halo effect
informational
    conformity effect
instrumental
    aggression
inter-role conflict
intra-role conflict
kernel of truth
lowball procedure
matching hypothesis
motivational aggression
norm of
    noninvolvement
norm of reciprocity

norm of social
    responsibility
normative conformity
    effect
obedience
passive aggression
pluralistic ignorance
primacy effect
proximity
reciprocity of attraction
    schema
self-serving bias
social norms
social psychology
social roles
stereotypes
verbal aggression

True/False

_____ 1. Attitudes are learned behaviors.

_____ 2. The primacy effect refers to the fact that later information about someone may weigh more heavily on impressions of others than earlier information.

_____ 3. The matching hypothesis states that people will tend to pair up with others of similar physical attractiveness.

_____ 4. Diffusion of responsibility occurs when people believe they are less responsible when no one else is around.

_____ 5. The mental state of being less aware of our own individuality and less constrained by social checks and balances is called deindividuation.

Fill in the Blanks

1. The unpleasant state of conflict that we experience when our behavior does not match our attitudes is called _____.

2. A set of beliefs or expectations about other people based on experience is called a/an _____.

3. If we tend to see the behavior of other people as being more determined by internal disposition forces than by the environment, then we show the _____.

4. Aggressive behavior may be learned by imitating the behavior of a model. This is the key to _____.

5. The _____ argues that, in an emergency, as the number of potential helpers increases, the likelihood that any one of them will help decreases.

Matching

1. Belief in a just world
2. Companionate love
3. Compliance
4. Conformity
5. Halo effect
6. Motivational definition shared by group members of aggression
7. Norm of reciprocity
8. Norm of social
9. Obedience
10. Stereotype

A. a request to change behavior
B. "bad things happen to bad people"
C. "bad things happen to good people"
D. behavior based on long-term commitment
E. behavior intended to harm
F. characteristics believed to be shared by group members
G. following an order by a legitimate authority
H. helping behavior based on favors owed
I. helping behavior based on moral imperatives
J. subtle pressure to change behavior
K. "what is beautiful is good"

BREAKING A SOCIAL NORM

Social norms operate below our level of awareness most of the time. We have learned what are expected behaviors based on where we are and whom we're with.

This assignment will require you to break a social norm and report the reactions of other people and yourself. You are to find a social norm and break it. You may choose to stand facing the rear of an elevator, to answer the phone by saying "good-bye," or pick your nose in public. Use your imagination, but *do not* break the law.

You may not report on a breaking of a social norm you did in the past. This must be a new behavior, and it must be witnessed by others to qualify as a norm violation. It's probably a good idea to tell the witnesses why you behaved this way after you observe their reactions. For instance, if you break a social norm by eating a spaghetti dinner using no tableware but only your hands, you should tell your dining companions about the assignment afterward. It might not be possible to "debrief" witnesses if, for example, you stood on the street corner and waved to every car as it passed by.

Fill in the information on the other side of this page and turn in this page by the date given in class by your instructor.

Remember, *do not* break the law, but *do* have fun.

Social norm that I broke:

The reactions of others when I broke this norm:

My own reactions as I broke this norm:

Comments:

SIXTEEN TRAITS, PART 1

For each of the following 16 pairs of traits, circle the one trait in each pair which is most characteristic of **BILL GATES**, president of Microsoft Corporation.

    If neither of the traits in a trait pair is the most characteristic, indicate that by circling "depends on the situation." Work quickly and go with your first impression.

1. serious.. fun-loving.................................. depends on the situation

2. subjective...................................... analytic...................................... depends on the situation

3. future-oriented............................. present-oriented..................... depends on the situation

4. energetic.. relaxed...................................... depends on the situation

5. unassuming.................................... self-asserting.......................... depends on the situation

6. lenient.. firm.. depends on the situation

7. dignified... casual... depends on the situation

8. realistic.. idealistic................................... depends on the situation

9. intense.. calm... depends on the situation

10. skeptical....................................... trusting..................................... depends on the situation

11. quiet.. talkative.................................... depends on the situation

12. sensitive....................................... tough-minded.......................... depends on the situation

13. self-sufficient.............................. sociable.................................... depends on the situation

14. dominant...................................... deferential............................... depends on the situation

15. cautious.. bold... depends on the situation

16. uninhibited................................... self-controlled........................ depends on the situation

Now, turn the page and complete Part 2.

SIXTEEN TRAITS, PART 2

For each of the following 16 pairs of traits, circle the one trait in each pair which is most characteristic of YOURSELF.

If neither of the traits in a trait pair is the most characteristic, indicate that by circling "depends on the situation." Work quickly and go with your first impression.

 1. serious.. fun-loving.............................. depends on the situation

 2. subjective.................................... analytic................................. depends on the situation

 3. future-oriented........................... present-oriented................... depends on the situation

 4. energetic.................................... relaxed................................. depends on the situation

 5. unassuming................................ self-asserting....................... depends on the situation

 6. lenient....................................... firm...................................... depends on the situation

 7. dignified.................................... casual................................... depends on the situation

 8. realistic...................................... idealistic............................... depends on the situation

 9. intense....................................... calm..................................... depends on the situation

10. skeptical..................................... trusting................................ depends on the situation

11. quiet.. talkative............................... depends on the situation

12. sensitive..................................... tough-minded....................... depends on the situation

13. self-sufficient.............................. sociable................................ depends on the situation

14. dominant.................................... deferential............................ depends on the situation

15. cautious...................................... bold...................................... depends on the situation

16. uninhibited................................. self-controlled...................... depends on the situation

Name: _____ Date: _____

Aggression in Children's Television Programming

Television programming aimed at children has been criticized for providing too much exposure to violence and aggression. Your assignment is to measure the aggressive behavior displayed in current television programming by watching one hour of cartoons. Watch an hour of *Bugs Bunny*, or *Roadrunner*, or *Loony Tunes*, etc. You may also watch two half-hour shows. Do not consider cartoon shows aimed at older audiences, such as *The Simpsons*.

Use the space below to keep track of the number and type of aggressive behaviors seen by checking off each time you see one of the different forms of aggression. Add up the check marks in the final summary at the bottom.

NAME OF SHOW: _____ DATE SEEN: _____ TIME: _____

NAME OF SHOW: _____ DATE SEEN: _____ TIME: _____

Physical aggression:

Verbal aggression:

Threatened aggression:

Physical aggression total: _____
Verbal aggression total: _____
Threatened aggression total: _____

Chapter 12: Social Psychology

END OF CHAPTER QUIZ

1. The personal idea that "you get what you deserve."
   a. Normative Social Influence
   b. Deindividuation
   c. Just-World Phenomenon
   d. Mere Exposure Effect

2. When you begin to like someone's company just because you work near that person.
   a. Normative Social Influence
   b. Deindividuation
   c. Just-World Phenomenon
   d. Mere Exposure Effect

3. Gender bias exists because it gives you someone to blame for your own problems.
   a. Normative Social Influence
   b. Informational Social Influence
   c. Just-World Phenomenon
   d. Scapegoat Theory

4. Television media is related to:
   a. Social Responsibility Norm
   b. Informational Social Influence
   c. Just-World Phenomenon
   d. Scapegoat theory

5. Attribution theory was designed to account for:
   a. The process of revealing intimate aspects of ourselves to others
   b. Social facilitation and social loafing
   c. The loss of self-awareness that occurs in group situations
   d. How people explain others' behavior

6. Sharon insists that her father's car accident resulted from his carelessness. Her explanation for the accident shows:
   a. The bystander effect
   b. Deindividuation
   c. The foot-in-the-door phenomenon
   d. A dispositional attribution

7. The fundamental attribution error refers to our tendency to underestimate the impact of _____ and to overestimate the impact of _____ in explaining the behavior of others.
   a. Normative influences; informational influences
   b. Informational influences; normative influences
   c. Personal dispositions; situational influences
   d. Situational influences; personal dispositions

8. The impact of our actions on our attitudes is best illustrated by the:
   a. Bystander effect
   b. Fundamental attribution error
   c. Foot-in-the-door phenomenon
   d. Mere exposure effect

9. When a salesperson visits your home and asks you to try a free sample of a cleaning fluid, you agree. When he returns the following week and asks you to purchase an assortment of expensive cleaning products, you make the purchase. The salesperson appears to have made effective use of:
   a. The bystander effect
   b. The fundamental attribution error
   c. The foot-in-the-door phenomenon
   d. Deindividuation

10. After he obtained the executive banking job he always wanted, Matthew developed very strong conservative political ideas. This best illustrates the impact of:
    a. Deindividuation
    b. Role-playing
    c. The Johnson-Woodworth Effect
    d. The bystander effect

11. The discomfort we feel when our thoughts and behaviors are inconsistent is called:
    a. Cognitive dissonance
    b. Deindividuation
    c. The foot-in-the-door phenomenon
    d. The fundamental attribution error

12. Which theory best explains why our actions can lead us to modify our attitudes?
    a. Equity theory
    b. Scapegoat theory
    c. Cognitive dissonance theory
    d. Social exchange theory

13. Solomon Asch reported that individuals conformed to a group's judgment regarding the lengths of lines:
    a. Only when the group was composed of at least six members
    b. Even when the group judgment was clearly incorrect
    c. Only when the group was unsure
    d. Only when members of the group were of high status

14. CEO and President Tonya Jones is most likely to vote in favor of a bad business plan if:
    a. The other committee members are unanimous in their opinion
    b. She stated her personal opinion early in the committee's discussion
    c. Committee voting is done by private ballot
    d. She personally dislikes the other committee members

15. A culture that promotes individualism is most likely to encourage:
    a. Nonconformity
    b. In-group bias
    c. Groupthink
    d. Superordinate goals

16. Most people are likely to be surprised by the results of Milgram's initial obedience experiment because:
    a. The "learners" made so few learning errors under stressful circumstances
    b. The "teachers" actually enjoyed shocking another person
    c. The "teachers" were more obedient than most people would have predicted
    d. The "learners" obediently accepted painful shocks without any protest

17. Deindividuation refers to:
    a. Lack of critical thinking due to a strong desire for social harmony within a group
    b. The tendency to overestimate the impact of personal dispositions on another's behavior
    c. The failure to give aid in an emergency situation observed by many onlookers
    d. A loss of self-awareness and self-restraint in group situations that foster arousal and anonymity

18. A social trap is a situation in which:
    a. There are not enough resources to satisfy all members of a social group
    b. False stereotypes influence how people interpret the behavior of others
    c. The pursuit of self-interest leads to collective harm
    d. All people in a conflict situation suffer, no matter how cooperatively they behave

19. Rosita is a pretty 21 year-old college student. Consequently, most of her acquaintances will assume that she:
    a. Is more socially skilled
    b. Has lower levels of self-esteem
    c. Has more difficulty securing employment
    d. Has fewer friends

20. Prejudice is best defined as:
    a. The tendency to favor members of one's own group
    b. A fearful suspicion of people one has never met
    c. A pre-judgment toward a group and its members
    d. A perceived incompatibility of actions or goals

21. The study of how people interact and influence each other is called:
    a. Clinical psychology
    b. Social psychology
    c. Personality psychology
    d. Intelligence research

22. Primacy-of-cognition refers to the idea that:
    a. Thinking precedes behavior
    b. Behavior precedes thinking
    c. You have to think before making decisions
    d. Thinking processes are a main concern in social psychology

23. Which of the following is NOT an example of behavior affecting thinking?
    a. Role playing
    b. Foot-in-the-door phenomenon
    c. Halo effect
    d. Cognitive dissonance

24. When a salesperson keeps talking to you while you are window shopping, it is likely because the salesperson has learned in their training to apply (the):
    a. Role playing techniques
    b. Foot-in-the-door technique
    c. Halo effect
    d. Cognitive dissonance

25. Which of the below processes are most likely to be used when resolving cognitive dissonance?
    a. Verbal aggression
    b. Defensive attribution
    c. Changing your behavior
    d. Changing your attitude about your behavior

26. According to the Fundamental Attribution Error, each time you see someone else make a mistake you tend to attribute their problem to:
    a. Their personality
    b. Their life circumstance
    c. Their environment
    d. Their confusion

27. According to the Fundamental Attribution Error, which of the following scenarios are you likely to highlight INTERNAL attributions?
    a. Your success; others success
    b. Your success; others failures
    c. Others success; your failures
    d. Others failures, your failures

28. According to the Fundamental Attribution Error, which of the following scenarios seems likely to occur? You hate your job and state:
    a. "I'm such an idiot for taking this job."
    b. "Taking this job is going to help me learn patience and emotional reserve."
    c. "My boss has to be tough on me because he has a lot of pressure from his superiors to support the financial bottom line."
    d. The only reason I took this job is to pay the bills. I'll be out of here as soon as something better opens up."

29. Which of the following will the Fundamental Attribution Error NOT DO for you?
    a. Help you think logically
    b. Help you persevere
    c. Help you avoid depressive states
    d. Help you regulate your emotions
    e. Maintain your self-concept

30. Which of the following will the Fundamental Attribution Error do to HELP you?
    a. Give you a positive perception of others
    b. Help you treat others with respect
    c. Help you avoid depressive states
    d. Give you a rational world view

31. The presence of a large group of people is NOT likely to:
    a. Improve someone's athletic performance
    b. Interfere with someone's ability to give a public speech

    c. Make someone less influenced by cognitive dissonance
    d. Allow some people to become anonymous and therefore avoid punishing consequences

32. Which of the following is an example of social facilitation?
    a. John can deliver a really good speech when no one is watching
    b. Mary is more friendly when her best friend is around
    c. Matthew purchases a vacation timeshare because he feels pressured from the salesman
    d. Karen plays basketball best when her boyfriend is watching

33. Which of the following scenarios is likely to lead to social loafing?
    a. The restaurant manager brings in twice the number of employees than is generally recommended during a single shift
    b. Your teacher gives you a grade-competitive assignment and there are three people assigned to each group. There are seventeen groups
    c. John and Mary spend eight hours per day together
    d. The real estate agent you are working with keeps showing you homes that are more expensive than you can afford

34. When President Obama discussed Health Care during his 2009 State of the Union address, a congressman from South Carolina called out "You lie!" Yelling out in this scenario is likely a result of (the) _____ due to the large hall the speech was given in.
    a. Conformity effect
    b. Stereotypes
    c. Verbal aggression
    d. Deindividuation

35. What is it called when you change your behavior or attitude to match that of others?
    a. Attitudes
    b. Gain/loss theory
    c. Conformity
    d. Stereotypes

36. Which of the following does NOT support conformity?
    a. There are at least three people in the group
    b. You admire the group
    c. Group members can watch your actions
    d. Except for you, everyone in the group is unsure of what to do

37. John, a dishwasher at Burger King, believes that the American economic bailout plan has only helped in making the rich richer. His opinion is likely a result of:
    a. Diffusion of responsibility
    b. Informational social influence
    c. Self-serving bias
    d. Normative social influence

38. Once accepted into medical school, you are invited to an afternoon tea party given by the graduate college. While you are there, you are unsure of how to act so you try to copy everyone else as best as you can. Your behavior would be said to be currently influenced by:
    a. Normative social influence
    b. Informational social influence
    c. The norm of reciprocity
    d. Stereotypes

39. Which of the following is MOST LIKELY to induce conformity?
    a. Easy decisions in a small group
    b. Difficult decisions in a small group
    c. Easy decisions of great importance
    d. Difficult decisions of great importance

40. Psychologist's focus on the topic of Obedience was caused by the:
    a. Research completed on conformity
    b. Results of the Nuremberg trials
    c. Historical background of Attribution Theory
    d. Milgram's research

41. Which of the following is TRUE?
    a. The subjects in Milgram's experiment received electric shocks
    b. An experimental confederate delivered fake shocks to a subject in the next room
    c. No one was truly given an electric shock
    d. The study took place during the 1930's at Yale University

42. If prejudice is a pre-judgment of something or some-one, then where does that prejudgment come from?
    a. Normative social influence
    b. Informational social influence
    c. The norm of reciprocity
    d. Stereotypes

43. Which of the following is NOT related to social prejudice?
    a. Inter-role conflict
    b. Real or perceived social inequality
    c. A lack of interaction with other groups
    d. Group polarization

44. The belief that "people get what they deserve" is called:
    a. Just-world phenomenon
    b. Defensive attribution
    c. Informational conformity effect
    d. Norm of social responsibility

45. Physical attraction is generally determined by cultural attributes and:
    a. Reproductive success
    b. Muscularity
    c. Universal gender attributes
    d. Weight

46. Which of the following does NOT support attraction between new romantic partners?
    a. Proximity
    b. Obedience
    c. Physical attractiveness
    d. Similarity

47. Which of the following does NOT influence bystander intervention?
    a. You must notice an event
    b. You must perceive it as an emergency
    c. You must take responsibility
    d. You must be with others to help

48. Which of the following is true regarding bystander intervention?
    a. The likelihood of helping is negatively correlated with the number of people present
    b. The likelihood of helping is positively correlated with the number of people present
    c. The chance of someone accepting help is negatively correlated with how hurt they are
    d. The chance of someone accepting help is positively correlated with how hurt they are

49. Which of the following is NOT a predictor of aggression?
    a. Y-chromosome
    b. Amygdala function
    c. Testosterone level
    d. Defensive attribution

50. Which of the following does predict aggression?
    a. Defensive attribution
    b. Modeled behavior
    c. Testosterone level
    d. Similarity

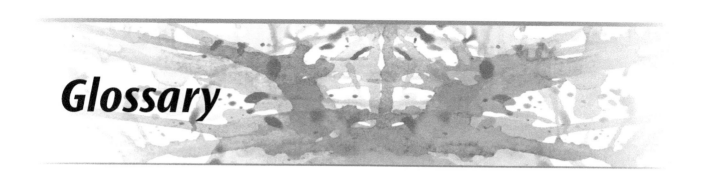

Glossary

CHAPTER 1: INTRODUCTION

Ablation: A technique developed in the mid 19th century in which a portion of the brain is removed so that its function can be assessed through the impairment that the subject develops.

Alchemy: Although usually associated with superstitious attempts to turn base metals into gold, alchemy also attempted to understand the basic medical properties of plants and minerals. It is a prescientific form of chemistry.

Aldini, Giovanni: The nephew of Luigi Galvani who essentially used the application of electricity as a cure-all medical treatment. He also used electricity in an attempt to revive human corpses after they had been executed by hanging or beheading.

Animal electricity: The name given to the belief that electricity ran through the nervous system. It is generally associated with Luigi Galvani in the 18th century.

Aristotle: An ancient Greek philosopher who described knowledge as being reducible to simple sensory associations.

Behavior: Any objective overt action made by a living organism.

Behavioral correlate: Any form of behavior which correlates with some other behavior.

Case studies: An early form of experimental approach which has the researcher focus their attention on a single subject.

Central limit theorem: The mathematical principle that shows that the greater the sample size measured, the more likely an accurate the population mean will be estimated.

Confound: A confound is when an extraneous variable changes at the same time that the independent variable changes. This eliminates the experimenter's ability to argue that the manipulated variable has a functional relationship with the dependent variable.

Control: A particular group in an experiment that is not exposed to the experimental manipulation.

Correlation: A statistical measure of the likelihood that if one variable is observed in a particular state that another variable will also be observed.

Correlation does not mean causation: The logical understanding that the correlation of two variables does not guarantee there will be a cause and effect relationship between them.

Correlational methodology: The application of an experimental technique that is analyzed through a correlational test.

Darwin, Charles: British biologist who published his theory of evolution in The Origin of the Species in 1859.

Deductive: The application of logic that allows one to successively rule out competing ideas until only the correct idea remains.

Democritus: Ancient Greek philosopher who suggested that all matter is reducible to tiny atoms that can not be further reduced in size.

Dependent variable: The variable that an experimenter measures. This measure is said to be "dependent upon" the independent variable.

Descriptive methodologies: Any form of experimental methodology that only describes events. This methodology does not attempt to control the subject matter in question.

Directly measured: Refers to any measure of behavior that is observed directly. Examples such as counting the number of words a person uses or measuring the time it takes to walk across the room. These data contrast with many traditional indirectly measured forms of data such as dreams, thoughts and feelings.

Donders, Franciscus: 19th century Dutch medical doctor who developed a method to assess the time it took to make a decision. His work developed the field of mental chronometry.

Double blind procedure: An experimental control methodology in which the experimenter uses a research assistant—who is unaware of the experimental conditions—to apply the independent variable to the research subjects. The name comes from the idea that the (a) research assistant and (b) subjects are both unaware of the experimental conditions.

Equal and independent: These conditions are required to establish a random process. Each selection or event in the process must have an (a) equal chance to occur relative to all other events and (b) have a selection which is independent (unaffected by) any other selection.

Expectation effects: A social variable in human experiments in which the subject believes that the experiment is being conducted for a particular reason.

Experiment: The systematic manipulation of a variable to assess its influence on another variable is called an experiment.

Experimental methodology: The particular methods used in an experiment.

Fechner, Gustav: A 19th century German researcher who further developed Ernst Weber's finding on psychophysics.

Flourens, Pierre: 19th century French biologist who developed the ablation technique for brain mapping studies.

Folk psychology: The understanding of human behavior using culturally defined beliefs about people (e.g., Birds of a feather flock together).

Fritsch, Gustav: A 19th century biologist most famous for early studies of brain mapping circa 1850. He worked primarily with Eduard Hitzig.

Galvani, Luigi: An 18th century researcher who observed that electricity can make the legs of a dead frog move. He later proposed that electricity travels through the nervous system.

Group designs: A form of experimental methodology in which multiple groups are used to assess the role of an independent variable.

Hitzig, Eduard: A 19th century biologist most famous for early studies of brain mapping circa 1850. He worked primarily with Gustav Fritsch.

Hypothesis: This thing is part of scientific reasoning. It is a testable question derived from a theoretical understanding of your subject matter.

Illusory correlation: An observer perceives this correlation due to their bias in what they expect to observe. This is not a true statistical correlation.

Independent variable: Experimenters manipulate this variable during experiments. It is expected to influence the dependent variable.

Internal mental events: These are the perceived experiences of a subject that cannot be measured directly. The most common ones that psychologists attempt to study are thoughts and feelings.

Kratzenstein, Christian Gottlieb: Biological researcher in the late 18th century who attempted to bring dead animals back to life by electrocuting their bodies. He is believed by some medical historians to be the basis for Mary Shelley's Dr. Frankenstein.

Law of large numbers: A statistical phenomenon in which an increasing population size makes the raw count of extremely unlikely events more common is described by the law of large numbers.

Linear input-output: A type of relationship in which each unit of input results in a consistent measure of output is a linear input-out system. These systems are common in the physical sciences and very uncommon in the behavioral sciences.

Malleus Maleficarum: this term means "Witches Hammer" in Latin. It became the most respected text on the characteristics of witches and evil spirits in the late medieval period. The text describes how to try a witch for heresy.

Muller, Ernst: 19th century German researcher who established that sensory perceptions were a result of anatomical wiring and not of differing forms of brain matter.

Naturalistic observation: The scientific methodology in which the researcher only observes their subjects with no attempt to manipulate the environment is called naturalistic observation.

Negative correlation: The inverse relationship between two variables is called a negative correlation. A common way to describe this is to state that when one variable increases the other variable decreases.

Normal Distribution: A distribution of collected data that matches a particular mathematical form referred to as a bell curve. In general, most statistical tests in the behavioral sciences rely on this form of distribution to make predictions from the data.

Objective definition: A description of a stimulus or behavior that is (a) publicly observable and (b) directly measured. It cannot involve any reference to vague or immeasurable qualities.

Operational definition: An objective definition of a behavior describes it in clear enough terms that anyone can reading the description would measure the same activity.

Paracelsus: Paracelsus was a medical doctor and alchemist who began to study the effects of drugs through trial and error. He also wrote extensively on human psychology during the late medieval period.

Pearson product moment correlation: The Pearson product moment correlation is a mathematical test that determines the degree of correlation between two variables. The value from this test has a range of $-1.0 \leq r \leq +1.0$ and is typically identified by the letter r.

Placebo: A placebo is an inert substance given to a control group in a drug study. The substance is intended to control for any effects of expectation or experimental procedure that may influence the behavior of the subjects.

Polls: This is one of the forms of the descriptive methodology. It essentially requires one to record the opinions of others.

Population characteristics: This generally refers to the various characteristics of the hypothetical population you are trying to measure. Often times, researchers use the term even when discussing the characteristics of a sample group.

Positive correlation: The covarying relationship between two variables is called a positive correlation. When one variable increases the other variable also increases (e.g., height and weight).

Prediction: The ability to determine what will happen in the future based upon a knowledge of current events.

Psychophysics: This is a crossover field between physics, biology and psychology. It examines your ability to detect and perceive energy sources affecting your receptors.

Random assignment: The process by which subjects, or experimental conditions, are given equal and independent chances of being selected for use.

Reactivity: The changed behavior of a research subject due to their knowledge—or belief—that they are being evaluated, usually through deception.

r-value: The specific value ranging from $-1.0 \leq r \leq +1.0$ that identifies the degree of correlation between two variables.

Science of behavior: The understanding that psychology should study behavior only and never topics that cannot be measured directly.

Script: The particular set of interactions—usually verbal interactions—that the experimenter applies to each subject in the experiment are called scripts. A script is used to produce consistency in the experiment.

Skinner, Burrhus Frederick (B. F.): Skinner was an American psychologist known for developing the modern experimental chamber and for advancing the school of behaviorism.

Somatosensory: somatosensory refers to the sense of touch.

Subject population: The specific sample group that is used in an experiment. It is often assumed that it will show characteristics similar to the more important—and theoretical—true population which can never be completely measured.

Subtraction method: The process developed by Franciscus Donders that allows one to infer the duration it takes someone to make a decision or perform some other mental function.

Theory: Theories are part of the scientific process. It is generally an abstracted understanding of your subject matter that allows an experimenter to derive a testable hypothesis. Theories must always be falsifiable or they are not productive.

Trepanning: This is the name given to the process of boring a hole into a skull. It is generally believed that the reason for trepanning was to let the supposed evil spirits out of the head.

Triple blind procedure: The triple blind procedure is an experimental control methodology in which the experimenter uses two research assistants—both of whom are unaware of the experimental conditions—to intervene in the experimental process between the experimenter and the research subjects. The name refers to the three individuals who are "blind" to the independent variable conditions, the (a) first research assistant, (b) second research assistant and (c) subjects.

Verbal descriptions: Verbal descriptions refer to the use of human language behavior as a data source in psychological experiments.

von Helmholtz, Hermann: A mid 19th century German scientist. He conducted valuable research in the fields of medicine, physics and psychology.

Watson, John: An American psychologist who developed the school of Behaviorism.

Weber, Ernst: Early 19th century German researcher who established that a constant proportional increase in the intensity of a stimulus determined how much a stimulus has to change before being detected by the subject.

Wundt, Wilhelm: Founded the first psychological laboratory in 1879 at the University of Leipzig, Germany.

Young-Helmholtz theory of color vision: Thomas Young proposed in 1802 that there were only three-color receptors in the eye. In 1850, Hermann von Helmholtz determined that those receptors were sensitive to the blue, green and red color ranges.

Zero correlation: When there is no correlation between two variables. When one variable increases the other may increase, decrease or do both at different times.

CHAPTER 2: NEUROSCIENCE AND BEHAVIOR

Ablation: The intentional destruction of neural tissue is called ablation.

Acetylcholine (ACh): The primary neuromuscular neurotransmitter is acetylcholine. It is also present in the brain.

Acetylcholinesterase (AchE): Acetylcholinesterase is an enzyme residing in any synaptic gap using acetylcholine. It destroys the acetylcholine neurotransmitter while it is in the synapse and helps maintain the proper concentration of acetylcholine at the postsynaptic receptors.

Action potential: An action potential is the formal name for the packet of electrical activity that travels through a neuron. The action potential is always a +40 mV and strength.

Adrenal glands: The adrenal glands reside on top of the kidneys and release epinephrine.

All-or-none law: The rule that suggests a neuron either fires in one manner based upon its anatomical makeup or it does not fire.

Amperes: Amperes is a measure of the number of electrons passing a point per unit time.

Amygdala: A brain area that is generally associated with the processing of fear and aggression.

Anandamide: A naturally occurring substance in the brain that alleviates anxiety. It has a similar molecular structure to delta-9-tetrahydrocannabinoid (THC), the active ingredient in cannabis.

Antianxiety drug: Any drug that alleviates anxiety is an anti-anxiety drug.

Aphasia: Language impairment that results from brain damage.

Arachnoid membrane: The middle layer of the meninges.

Arachnoid trabeculae: Legs extending from the arachnoid membrane to the top of the pia mater.

Association cortex area: Any area secondary to the initial evaluation of sensory stimuli that is involved in the housing of memories.

Autonomic nervous system: The portion of the nervous system that controls glandular activity and muscles that are not connected to the skeletal system. For example, it regulates the volume of blood in the digestive system, dilates pupils and affects hormonal releases.

Axon: The axon is the section of the neuron that produces an action potential, houses neurotransmitters and is responsible for sending signals away to other neurons.

Axon hillock: The axon hillock is where new action potentials are formed within the cell after signal integration.

Barbiturate: A drug that has been used clinically as an anti-anxiety agent, anti-seizure agent and muscle relaxant.

Basal ganglia: An internal section of the brain involved in the processing of motor behavior. Destruction of cells in the basal ganglia are partly responsible for the symptoms of Parkinson's disease.

Benzodiazepine: A drug that has been used clinically as an anti-anxiety agent, anti-seizure agent and muscle relaxant. It was developed as a replacement for the more highly addictive barbiturates.

Biological electricity: Biological electricity is the name given to the electricity within your nervous system.

Biological psychology: The study of how biological principles influence behavior is called biological psychology.

Black widow spider venom: This substance functions as an acetylcholine (ACh) agonist. Its action will produce muscle cramping and possible seizures.

Blindsight: Blindsight is a disorder in which a person perceives themselves blind and is unaware that they have a limited visual ability.

Blood-brain barrier: This system is created from three anatomical components. They are the endothelial cells, cerebrospinal fluid and skeletal structure covering the central nervous system (CNS).

Bone encasement: Bone encasement is one third of the blood-brain barrier system.

Botulinum toxin: This is a neurotoxin derived from the bacterium *Clostridium botulinum*. It functions as an acetylcholine (ACh) blocker at neuromuscular junctions and therefore produces a loss of motor control, breathing and possibly coma or death.

Brain lesion: A brain lesion is an area of dead tissue in the brain. It will most often refer to a naturally occurring state; however, the term may sometimes be used to refer to an experimental ablation.

Brain stem: The first part of the brain after the spinal cord ends. It includes the medulla and pons.

Broca's area: An area of the language center that manages speech production.

Calcium (Ca^{2+}): Calcium is a charged particle that affects neuronal activity.

Cardiac muscle: Cardiac muscle is another name for your heart.

Cell membrane: The outer surface of a neuron that is made from two layers of fat (lipid bilayer).

Central nervous system (CNS): The portion of a nervous system comprised of the brain and spinal cord.

Central sulcus: The central sulcus is the laterally oriented fissure that separates the parietal lobe from the frontal lobe.

Cerebellum: The cerebellum is also known as the little brain because it looks like a brain itself. It has a primary role in the processing of balance and coordination.

Cerebral cortex: The cerebral cortex is the outer surface of the brain. It is comprised of six layers of cells and would spread out to cover an area of about four standard sheets of paper if it were laid out flat.

Cerebral hemispheres: The left and right sides of the brain are called the cerebral hemispheres.

Cerebral ventricle: The fluid filled areas within the brain that produce and distribute the cerebrospinal fluid.

Cerebrospinal fluid (CSF): This substance is produced near the center of the brain and flows through channels to completely cover the outside of the brain and spinal cord. It serves to cushion the brain and to block outside substances from reaching the central nervous system. Therefore, it is part of the blood brain barrier.

Chlorine (Cl-): Chlorine functions as an inhibitory charged particle in neurons.

Chromosome: A chromosome is a folded string of DNA visible to the naked eye.

Computed tomography (CT): The CT scan is a simulated three-dimensional image of the brain formed by taking x-rays in each of the three planes.

Contralateral: This term refers to the opposite side of the brain or body.

Corpus callosum: The area of neurons that connect the left and right hemispheres of the brain is called the corpus callosum. It is made from myelinated axons crossing between the two hemispheres.

Cortex: The outer surface of the brain which is made from six layers of neurons.

Cranial nerve: There are twelve nerves which extend from the base of the brain and extend to sensorimotor locations of the face and head. Only one cranial nerve—the vagus nerve—travels down into the trunk of the body.

Curare: A substance derived in South America that may cause complete paralysis. The native American population in Peru traditionally placed curare onto the tips of their spears to hunt monkeys.

Dendrite: The portion of a neuron that generates an action potential due to the activity of neurotransmitters affecting its receptors is called the dendrite. This section of the neuron sends the action potentials toward the soma.

Dendritic spine: The spine is a small nub on the side of a dendrite. It serves as a separate location for interconnections between neurons.

Deoxyribonucleic acid (DNA): A very long double helix molecule created by stringing together a series of genes.

Diffusion: Diffusion is the distribution of atoms from areas of high concentration to areas of lower concentration.

Diffusion tensor imaging: A form of brain scan technology that tracks the direction water flows along myelinated axons.

Dopamine (DA): A neurotransmitter commonly associated with emotional responding as well as hallucinations.

Dura mater: The dura mater is the outermost tissue level of the meninges.

Electroencephalogram (EEG): The reading of electrical activity from the brain through small, flat metal pads (electrodes) glued to the scalp.

Electrostatic pressure: Electrostatic pressure is the force of diffusion generated by housing ions of a similar type with in one area.

Endocrine gland: Any gland that releases hormones is called an endocrine gland. The endocrine system is another name for the hormonal system.

Endogenous cannabinoid: A naturally occurring substance in the brain that has a molecular structure similar to delta-9-tetrahydrocannibinol, the activity ingredient in cannabis is an endogenous cannabinoid. The name of one such known substance is *Anandamide*. Its role is to reduce anxiety.

Endogenous opioid: A naturally occurring substance in the brain that has a molecular structure similar to morphine is cold and endogenous opioid. There are a variety of such substances and they generically go by the name *endorphins*.

Endorphins: Any of a series of innate opiate-like substances in the nervous system are called endorphins.

Endothelial cells: The tightly packed cells creating the capillaries of the brain are called endothelial cells. They are part of the blood brain barrier because they stop large molecules from crossing from the blood supply into the central nervous system tissue.

Excitatory postsynaptic potential (EPSP): The EPSP is the proper name for an action potential derived at the dendrite.

Fissures: The fissures are large grooves on the surface of the brain. They are contrasted with the small grooves of the brain called sulci.

Forebrain: The outermost third of the brain. It accounts for more brain tissue than the hindbrain or midbrain.

Frontal lobe: The most anterior lobe of the brain is the frontal lobe. It is most generally known for processing motor behavior as opposed to analyzing sensory input.

Functional magnetic resonance imaging (fMRI): Functional magnetic resonance imaging is the same as magnetic resonance imaging (MRI) except that the image is taken multiple times per second so that a pattern of activity over time may be determined.

Functional measures (brain scan): Functional measures are any measure taken over time.

Functional unit of heredity: The functional unit of heredity is a name given to describe one of the primary functions of a gene. It obtained that name because genes cannot be changed without affecting their function.

Fusiform face area: The fusiform face area is an area of the brain that received its name because it is active while recognizing human faces.

GABA: Gamma-amino-butyric acid is a universally inhibitory neurotransmitter found in the brain and spinal cord.

Gene: The gene is a single section along a DNA molecule.

Gene knockout: The knockout process is a biotechnology used to eliminate the gene of a research animal as a way to determine its use.

Gene replacement: Gene replacement is the removal of an existing gene and its replacement with a new copy. Gene replacement therapy is predicated upon the idea that medical science will be able to perform this treatment to eliminate any disorder resulting from the activity of a corrupted gene.

Glia: The alternative name for myelin is glia. It is the fatty insulating cover around an axon.

Glutamate: This is a universally excitatory neurotransmitter found in the brain and spinal cord.

Gray matter: The common name given to the brain or any neural tissue with a grayish appearance. Neural tissue appears gray when it is not myelinated. The cortex appears gray because the outer surface of the brain is comprised primarily of neural cell bodies.

Hindbrain: The hindbrain is the section of the brain closest to the spinal cord. It primarily controls functions related to basic life sustaining activities such as breathing and heart rate.

Hippocampus: The hippocampus is a section at the end of the limbic system involved in the formation and retrieval of memories.

Homeostasis: The stable level of activity or function of the body.

Hormone: A chemical substance created in neural tissue. It is usually released into the blood supply so that it can reach its site of action at some relatively great distance away.

Hypothalamus: An area of the brain that is frequently associated with hormonal activity.

Inhibitory postsynaptic potential (IPSP): The IPSP is not an action potential but rather a negative voltage applied to a neuron making it more difficult for an EPSP to occur.

Intercellular communication: Communication between two neurons is referred to as intercellular communication.

Interneuron: Any neuron that is not specifically a sensory or motor neuron is called an interneuron. They connect other neurons together and comprise the most common form of neural cell in the brain.

Ion: An ion is a charged particle. These substances are generally associated with intercellular and extracellular fluids.

Ion channel: The channel pathway that ions take to cross a cell membrane is called an ion channel.

Ion transporter: A special protein molecule embedded in the cell membrane that transfers particular charged particles across the cell membrane. One of the most well studied ones is the sodium-potassium pump.

Ipsilateral: When connections between two areas of the brain remain within the same hemisphere, it is an ipsilateral connection.

Kinesthetic system: The kinesthetic system is made from sensory neurons in your muscles that allow you to determine where your body parts are without the addition of sight.

Lateral fissure: The largest fissure on the side of the brain is the lateral fissure. The auditory cortex is located along the inside of the lateral fissure.

Lesion: A destroyed section of brain tissue is called a lesion.

Limbic system: The section of the forebrain that processes emotions is the limbic system.

Lipid bilayer: A molecular double-layer of fat molecules is called a lipid bilayer. It is used to create the vesicles within axons as well as the cell membrane of neurons.

Lysergic Acid Diethylamide (LSD): A hallucinogenic drug.

Magnetic resonance imaging (MRI): A brain scan technique that passes a strong magnetic wave through the body of the subject is called an MRI. Through the additional use of a radio wave, the scanning machine can read how the radio frequency bounces back differently and uses that information to produce an image of the inside of the scanned object.

Magnetoencephalography (MEG): A brain scan technique that measures the differences in magnetic properties of a subject's blood and brain and converts that to an image.

Medulla oblongata: The first section of the brain after the spinal cord. The medulla is generally associated with basic life sustaining functions (e.g., heart rate, breathing, blood pressure).

Meninges: A three layer covering that surrounds the complete central nervous system. It is comprised of the dura mater, arachnoid membrane and the pia mater. The pia mater is the layer closest to the brain tissue.

Microdialysis: A procedure using thin metal cannulae that are inserted into the brain of a research subject. The cannulae extract out chemicals from the local area to determine the concentration of various substances (e.g., neurotransmitters, hormones) during psychological or biological manipulations.

Microelectrode: An extremely thin electrode device that may be used to deliver electric current to the brain or to read the electric current in the brain.

Midbrain: The midbrain is essentially the center section of the brain. It primarily processes hormonal activity and sensory integration.

Mirror cells: Mirror neurons refer to a series of circuits within the forebrain that allow one to duplicate the behavior of others. Learning by observation would be impossible without mirror neurons.

Monoamines: These substances are one of two categories of the biogenic amines; neurotransmitters commonly associated with psychologically relevant brain processing. They include dopamine, norepinephrine and epinephrine.

Monosynaptic stretch reflex: The monosynaptic stretch reflex is a basic spinal reflex that helps maintain one's balance based upon the stretching of calf muscles in the leg.

Motor association cortex: The motor association cortex is located laterally along the posterior section of the frontal lobe. It lays along the central sulcus.

Motor neuron: Any neuron directly connected to muscle. These neurons universally use acetylcholine at the neuromuscular junction.

Myelin: Myelin is the alternative name for glia. Myelin is the fatty insulating cover around an axon.

Naloxone: Naloxone is an opiate blocker. It has previously been used to control opiate drug overdoses by emergency responders. Today, it is more commonly used by research scientists studying the opiates.

Natural ablation: The destruction of neural tissue through natural processes such as a stroke or head injury is call a natural ablation.

Neostigmine: An acetylcholine agonist that specifically destroys acetylcholinesterase. It has been used to treat myasthenia gravis, a muscle weakness disorder that results from too few acetylcholine receptors.

Nerve: A bundled cable of neurons is called a nerve. Nerves are bundled and insulated by a combination of the dura mater and pia mater from the central nervous system's meninges.

Nervous system: The entire conglomeration of your brain, spinal cord and peripheral nerves makes up your nervous system.

Neural networks: The theoretical suggestion that information encoded in the brain is designed to maximize efficiency.

Neural reflex arc: A neural reflex arc refers to the circuitry of any motor reflex.

Neurogenesis: Neurogenesis refers to the development of new neural cells. There is some evidence that new neural cells may develop in adulthood but more research is still needed before fully understanding this issue.

Neuromodulator: A neurotransmitter-like substance that is released from a neuron but is distributed to all the other neurons in the general vicinity. They do not only travel to the next neuron along a pathway in the same manner as neurotransmitters, but also travel in all directions.

Neuron: A single cell of the nervous system is called a neuron. It has three major components; the dendrite, soma and axon.

Neurotransmission: Neurotransmission is the name given to the chemical signaling that occurs between two neural cells.

Neurotransmitter receptor: A large protein molecule embedded in the cell membrane of a dendrite. This embedded molecule receives the neurotransmitter from the preceding cell in the neural pathway.

Neurotransmitter: A neurotransmitter is the chemical that crosses from the end of an axon (presynaptic terminal) to a dendrite (postsynaptic terminal) of the next cell in a pathway.

Nicotine: A drug derived from tobacco that functions as a cholinergic agonist (an agonist of acetylcholine).

Nodes of Ranvier (ROW vee ay): The nodes of Ranvier are tiny gaps in between each successive myelin cell along an axon. These nodes produce salutatory conduction that speeds the rate at which the action potential travels.

Norepinephrine (NE): Norepinephrine is a neurotransmitter that is part of the monoamine family. One of its commonly known functions is to control vigilance; your ability to pay attention for long periods.

Occipital lobe: The posterior lobe of your brain is called the occipital lobe. Vision is analyzed in the occipital lobe.

Ohms: ohms is a measure of electrical resistance.

Oligrodendrocyte cell: Oligrodendrocyte cells are the glial cells in the central nervous system.

One-hundred billion: The number of cells estimated to exist in the adult human brain is one-hundred billion.

Parasympathetic nervous system: The autonomic nervous system can be subdivided into two sections; the sympathetic nervous system and the parasympathetic nervous system. The parasympathetic nervous system controls the operation of your internal organs when you are at rest (compare with the sympathetic nervous system).

Parietal lobe: The parietal lobe is under the crown of your head. The parietal lobe has a primary function in analyzing the somatosenses (e.g., touch).

Parkinson's disease: Parkinson's disease is a progressive neurodegenerative disease that disrupts motor behavior and cognitive skills. Many of its symptoms come from the destruction of the basal ganglia in the forebrain.

Peptide: These chemical signals in the brain are generally neuromodulators. The enkephalins are one of the most common peptide neuromodulators. They help regulate pain sensitivity.

Periaqueductal gray area: The periaqueductal gray area is a group of circuits in the midbrain that are involved in pain perception.

Peripheral nervous system (PNS): The PNS is any part of a nervous system that is not the brain or spinal cord. The PNS can be subdivided into the somatic nervous system (muscular control) and autonomic nervous system (internal organs and glands).

Phantom limb: A phantom limb is the perception of the presence of a limb that had been amputated. Sometimes individuals born without limbs also have phantom limb sensations.

Pia mater: The pia mater is the innermost tissue of the three layers of the meninges. It is the softest and most flexible tissue of the three and lies along the brain and spinal cord.

Pituitary gland: This gland is centrally located on the ventral side of the brain—the middle-lower area just below the hypothalamus. It is considered a master gland that releases hormones and controls the release of hormones in other glands. It has a wide range of effects (e.g., growth, reproduction, water retention).

Plasticity: The ability of neurons to connect and disconnect from other neurons is called plasticity. Applications of plasticity and neurogenesis are at the forefront of neuroscientific research.

Polysynaptic reflexes: Polysynaptic reflexes come from complex spinal circuitry that are often involved in flexion and extension motor behaviors.

Pons: The pons is an area of the hindbrain just above the medulla (first section of the brain beyond the spinal cord). The pons holds circuitry that controls sleep, breathing, hearing and balance.

Positron emission tomography (PET): PET is a brain scan technique that uses radioactive glucose. As select areas of the brain become more active during intellectual tasks, the PET scanner reads where the radioactive glucose accumulates. Higher concentrations of radiation indicate that those areas of the brain are more active because they are in more need of glucose as an energy source.

Postsynaptic neuron: The postsynaptic neuron is the dendritic side of a synapse. It is the location of the neurotransmitter receptors.

Post-traumatic stress disorder (PTSD): PTSD is a psychological disorder in which previous memories involving fear or aggression return as flashbacks to the patient.

Potassium (K+): Potassium is a positively charged ion that exists in high concentrations within the intercellular fluid of neurons.

Prefrontal cortex: The prefrontal cortex is the anterior section of the frontal lobe. It primarily controls behavior related to prepared actions.

Presynaptic neuron: The axonic side of a synapse contains the presynaptic neuron. It is the location where neurotransmitters are housed.

Primary auditory cortex: The primary auditory cortex is located inside the lateral fissure.

Primary cortex area: Primary cortex areas are the first locations within the parietal, occipital and temporal lobes that sensory information is analyzed. Within the output system of the frontal lobe, the primary cortex area is the last place signals are analyzed before exiting the cortex.

Primary motor cortex: The area of the brain located laterally across the posterior section of the frontal lobe. It is one of the final locations along the cortex to process motor behavior before signals are sent to the muscles.

Primary somatosensory cortex: The primary somatosensory cortex is located along the anterior section of the parietal lobe. This area is the first location on the cortex to begin processing the sense of touch.

Primary visual cortex: The primary visual cortex is located along the occipital lobe. This area is the first location on the cortex to begin processing the sense of sight.

Prosopagnosia: Prosopagnosia is a neurological disorder in which the patient can no longer identify individuals by their face. Patients with prosopagnosia cannot detect or remember human faces.

Psychopharmacology: Psychopharmacology is the study of how drugs influence behavior.

Reflex: A reflex is a biologically hardwired response to a particular stimulus.

Resting potential: The name refers to the level of voltage in a cell at rest. The voltage is equal to -70 mV.

Reticular formation: The reticular formation controls general arousal in the hindbrain.

Reuptake: Reuptake is the process by which neurotransmitters return to the axon that released them.

Salutatory conduction: Salutatory conduction refers to the process by which action potentials can only transfer ions across the axonal membrane at the nodes of Ranvier. It increases the speed at which the action potential can pass down the axon.

Sensory association: A sensory association is the association between two stimuli.

Sensory neuron: Any neuron that sends information into the nervous system is called a sensory neuron. Typically, sensory neurons detect stimulate from the external environment or internal bodily states (e.g., temperature, stretched muscle, nausea).

Serotonin: Serotonin is a neurotransmitter from the biogenic amine family. It is the only neurotransmitter metabolized from tryptophan and therefore is the only neurotransmitter classed as an indolamine.

Signal integration: Signal integration refers to the integration of voltages of the various EPSPs that reach the soma within a neural cell.

Skeletal muscles: Skeletal muscles are those muscles attached to the skeletal system. They are the muscles that allow us to move around our bodies. The somatic branch of the peripheral nervous system controls skeletal muscles. They are also referred to as striated muscle because they have visual striations to their appearance.

Smooth muscles: Smooth muscles are those controlled by the autonomic branch of the peripheral nervous system. They are in various locations around the body such as the arteries, bladder, iris of the eye, intestines and uterus. Their anatomy contrasts with striated skeletal muscle.

Sodium (Na+): Sodium is a charged particle that resides in its highest concentration in the extracellular fluid around a neural cell. It's movement into the neuron initiates an action potential.

Soma: The soma is another name for the cell body. The soma houses the genetic material of a neural cell.

Somatic nervous system: The somatic nervous system is one subdivision of the peripheral nervous system. It controls motor behavior.

Somatotopic organization: Somatotopic organization refers to the organizational layout of the primary motor cortex and the primary somatosensory cortex. The arrangement of areas along these cortexes changes similarly with movements across the body.

Species-typical behavior: Species-typical behavior is a form of responding that is unique to a particular creature under a specific set of conditions. For example, ducklings will imprint to the first moving object they see after hatching.

Spinal cord: The spinal cord is central nervous system tissue that runs from the base of the brain to two-thirds down the vertebral column.

Spinal foramen: The spinal foramen is the opening in the center of a vertebra that allows the spinal cord to be encased in bone as it runs down the back.

Spinal nerve: Spinal nerves are any bundled set of nerves that exit the spinal cord at the junctions between vertebrae and variously extend into the trunk and limbs.

Split brain: A split brain is one that has had the corpus callosum surgically severed thereby producing two independent brain hemispheres.

Static measure (brain scan): A static measure is a snapshot image of the brain. The image does not show change over time.

Stem cells: Stem cells are cells that reside in an undifferentiated form; therefore, researchers can make them grow into any type of cell they wish (e.g., skin, liver, blood, etc.). They are abundantly present during the early stages of development but are scarce in adulthood. Their existence presents an opportunity to find new ways to regenerate central nervous system tissue and therefore treat brain and spinal cord injuries.

Stereotaxic apparatus: A mechanical device used to hold in place the head of a human or animal during brain surgery.

Subarachnoid space: The subarachnoid space is the location that cerebrospinal fluid flows through within the meninges.

Sulci: Sulci are the small fissures on the surface of the brain.

Sympathetic nervous system: The sympathetic nervous system is one of two subsections of the autonomic nervous system. The sympathetic branch becomes active during the fight or flight syndrome (compare with the parasympathetic nervous system).

Synapse: The synapse is a small interconnecting gap between two neurons (compare with synaptic cleft). The synapse is also known as a synaptic cleft.

Targeted mutation: A targeted mutation is the application of a genetic procedure that changes the function of a particular gene.

Temporal lobe: The temporal lobe runs along the sides of the head near the temples.

Ten trillion: It is estimated that 10 trillion neural cells make up the adult nervous system.

Terminal button: The terminal button is another name for the axon terminal. It is the very end of an axon where the neurotransmitters are housed in the vesicles.

Thalamus: The thalamus is a centrally located area of the brain that helps to direct sensory input and motor output signals to their target locations.

Three-cell reflex: The three-cell reflex is the simplest type of spinal reflex that exists. It involves one sensory neuron, an interneuron in the spinal cord and a motor neuron extending back to muscles near the location of stimulation.

Threshold: The +10 mV change in a neuron before an action potential is generated is its threshold.

Tolerance: Tolerance is the reduced effect of a drug over time. It is due to the nervous system's compensatory responding to the drugs frequent presence at synaptic receptor sites.

Transcranial magnetic stimulation (TMS): Transcranial magnetic stimulation is the application of a handheld device that emits a magnetic wave through the surface of the brain and elicits activity from the stimulated cortex areas.

Transcription: Transcription is the process by which a gene is decoded within the nucleus of the soma. For the gene to be converted into a useful protein, the process of translation must then take place.

Translation: Translation is the process by which a decoded gene is moved outside the nucleus and decoded by ribosomes into a protein. The translation process follows the transcription process.

Vertebra: Vertebra are the bones covering the spinal cord.

Ventricles: Four hollow chambers in the brain are filled with cerebrospinal fluid (CSF)

Vesicles: Vesicles are the fatty bubbles present in the axon terminal (terminal button) that houses the neurotransmitters.

Visual agnosia: Visual agnosia is a form of brain damage that eliminates one's ability to name objects by sight.

Voltage: Voltage is an electrical measurement.

Wernicke's area: Wernicke's area is an area of the language center that manages language comprehension.

White matter: The presence of white shading on neural tissue indicates that the cells are myelinated axons.

Withdrawal symptom: The symptoms of a malfunctioning nervous system that occur once the drug is removed.

CHAPTER 3: NATURE AND NURTURE WORKING TOGETHER

Adoption studies: An Adoption study is the name given to the study of heritability in adopted and non-adopted children.

Aggression: Aggression is a verbal or physical attack against another person or thing.

Antimiscegenation laws: Antimiscegenation laws restricted interracial marriages in the United States. The idea was supported by the early 20th century eugenicists who suggested that mixing races would result in an overall decrease in intelligence levels throughout the gene pool.

Artificial selection: Artificial selection refers to the human controlled development of heritable properties. Artificial selection has been practiced on farms for millennia as farmers have attempted to breed larger animals for food sources. It has also been practiced in biology labs as ways to test genetic theories.

Behavioral genetics: Behavioral genetics is the subfield of psychology that attempts to study how genes can influence behavior.

Behavioral endocrinology: Behavioral endocrinology refers to the study of how hormones influence behavior.

Behavioral geneticists: Researchers that attempt to study how genes can influence behavior are called behavioral geneticists.

Biopsychosocial model of psychology: The biopsychosocial model psychology suggests that all human behavior is a combination of biology, personal history and cultural influences.

Chromosomes: Long bundled strands of DNA that reside in the nucleus of a cell are called chromosomes.

Collectivism: Collectivism is a social approach to life in which sharing is the norm. Generally there are clear family hierarchies in these cultures.

Culture: Culture is the general view of the world from a whole society.

DNA: Deoxyribonucleic acid is a lengthy double helix molecule comprised of genes.

Environment: Any input into your body—especially your nervous system.

Eugenics: Eugenics is the application of artificial selection to human beings.

Evolution: Evolution is the process by which creatures change their form and function because of natural selection pressures over long periods.

Evolutionary biology: Evolutionary biology is the study of biology with an evolutionary perspective.

Evolutionary psychology: Evolutionary psychology is the study of psychology with an evolutionary perspective. It examines how traits common across all humans today may have developed because of evolutionary pressures.

Fraternal twins: Twins derived from the fertilization of two eggs by two separate sperm cells during the same gestation period.

Gender identity: Gender identity is a person's perception of their identified sex role.

Gender role: A characteristic pattern of behavior that is associated with a gender is called a gender role.

Gender: Gender is determined by the biological and social factors that determine whether one is male or female.

Gender-typing: The development of a traditional gender role is called gender typing.

Genes: Genes are subsections along the DNA molecule that can be replicated. The replication of genes takes place through the processes of transcription and translation. The result of these processes is a protein.

Genes, hormones and learning: Genes, hormones and learning are the three primary factors establishing one's psychological traits.

Genome: The entire set of genes of a species is called the genome.

Heritability: Heritability refers to the likelihood that a genetic trait will be inherited by offspring.

Identical twins: A set of twins derived from a single fertilized egg spitting into two separate individuals. Identical twins are more similar genetically than any other two individuals.

Individualism: Individualism is a cultural approach to life in which each person strives to be as autonomous as possible with respect to the confines of their culture.

Interaction: Interactions are seen when the combination of two separate experimental variables produces an unexpectedly higher or lower result than is predicted through a simple addition of both effects.

Molecular genetics: This term refers to the understanding of genetics from a molecular basis. For example, rather than referring to a broad heritable effect, a molecular approach will discuss what specifically happens with respect to DNA molecules in their biochemical environment.

Mutation: Mutations are irregular changes in genes that are often caused by external factors such as exposure to radiation.

Natural selection: Natural selection is the process by which genetically controlled characteristics that increase the probability of survival and reproduction for a species appear more frequently in the gene pool over time.

Nature: Nature is the general term that refers to biological influences on psychology.

Nature versus nurture: This phrase was developed by Sir Francis Galton in the 1880's and refers to the possibility that biological influences or environmental influences are the basis for human psychology. Currently, it is believed that both nature and nurture influence all psychological traits.

Negative eugenics: This term refers to the application of artificial selection processes to human populations in which killing undesirable members of society is practiced.

Norm: This term generally refers to the common pattern of behavior within a context.

Nurture: Nurture is the general term that refers to environmental influences on psychology.

Ontogeny (ontogenetic): Ontogeny refers to the influences that occur across an organism's life.

Personal space: This term refers to a culturally defined characteristic that controls the physical distance between individuals in different social contexts.

Phylogeny (phylogenetic): Phylogeny refers to the influences that affect heritable traits over generations.

Positive eugenics: This term refers to the application of artificial selection processes to human populations in which killing undesirable members of society is not practiced. In a positive eugenics program, such as in the United States during the early 20th century, undesirables were sterilized but not murdered.

Proportion of variation: This term refers to the amount of variance accounted for in a statistical correlation.

Psychoneuroimmunology: This term refers to the overall influence of learning, neural biology and the immune system.

Role: Roles refer to the general pattern of behavior that is expected from a person in a given social context.

Selection by consequences: This term refers to the change in behavior that occurs over time because of the consequences obtained for behaving.

Social influences: This term generically refers to the individual life history and cultural influences on the psychological makeup of an individual.

Social learning theory: This term refers to the theoretical approach that all social behavior develops through learning.

Temperament studies: Temperament studies are heritability studies on emotional reactivity traits.

Temperament: Temperament refers to one's overall level of emotional reactivity.

Testosterone: Testosterone is present in both males and females; however, it is often referred to as the male hormone. Its presence is associated with male sexual responsiveness and aggression.

Twin studies: A twin study is the generic name given to the study of heritability in children born into the same family, especially twins, triplets etc.

X chromosome: The X chromosome is present in both males and females. The XX and XY chromosomal patterns identify females and males respectively.

Y chromosome: The Y chromosome is only present in males. The XY chromosomal pattern identifies males.

CHAPTER 4: DEVELOPMENTAL PSYCHOLOGY

Accommodation: The process by which a child adjusts their previously established cognitive structure to integrate new information.

Activity theory: The idea that elderly people will be happier if they remain active intellectually or socially.

Adolescence: The period between puberty and adulthood.

Andropause: Also known as male menopause. It is the time in late mid-life during which males will experience a reduction in testosterone production.

Assimilation: The process by which a child integrates new information into a previously established cognitive structure.

Attachment: The emotional connection between two individuals. It generally refers to the relationship between mother and child.

Autonomy versus shame and doubt: Erikson's second stage of development in which a child attempts to become independent.

Bereavement: The experience of missing a loved one and wishing for their company.

Centration: Then phenomenon in which a child attends to only some of the relevant features of an object.

Chromosome: A single long strand of DNA.

Cognitive development: The development of thinking skills throughout the lifespan.

Conception: The period in which an egg becomes fertilized.

Concrete operations stage: The Piagetian stage during which basic logical skills and mathematical abilities begin to emerge.

Conservation: The name of a skill set children develop when they learn to attend to the three-dimensions of objects such as length, width and height or the volume of a liquid.

Conventional morality: The second stage of Kohlberg's stages of morality. This stage refers to a time during which a child focuses on following rules exactly.

Critical periods: A time period during which a behavior may be learned with ease due to a temporary biological development designed to help process that behavior.

Cross-sectional design: An experimental design that assesses the behavior of people of differing ages all at the same time. This methodology allows for a cohort confound.

Cross-sequential design: This is the same as a cross-sectional design; however, the subjects are also measured across time as well. This methodology eliminates the cohort confound that exists in the cross-section al design.

Dizygotic twins: Twins that are a result of two separate eggs being fertilized by two separate sperm cells. Dizygotic twins are more frequently referred to as fraternal twins. Genetically, they are no more similar than typically siblings. Their shared uterine environment, however, results in increased similarities compared to typical siblings.

DNA (deoxyribonucleic acid): The molecules that make up genes.

Dominant: A type of gene that will control genetic expression regardless of the gene contributed by the other parent.

Egocentrism: The technical term—usually applied to children—during a period of their early life in which they cannot perceive of situations from another person's perspective.

Embryo: The period of prenatal development from approximately 2-8 weeks post-fertilization.

Embryonic period: The period of prenatal development from approximately 2-8 weeks post-fertilization. This period of development contains the stage known as organogenesis.

Fertilization: The process by which a sperm and egg combine to begin the process of development.

Fetal period: The period of prenatal development from approximately 9-36 weeks post-fertilization.

Fetus: The prenatal infant during weeks 9-36.

Formal operations: The Piagetian stage that identifies the final stage of cognitive development. It is generally associated with the onset of puberty at around 12-years of age.

Gender: The biologically and socially derived characteristics that determine whether one is female or male.

Gender identity: A person's perception of their identified sex role.

Gender roles: The culturally determined roles of both males and females.

Gene: A subsection of a chromosome that has the function of being translated into a protein.

Generativity: Providing guidance to the next generation.

Genetics: The field of study that examines the role of DNA on biological structure and function.

Germinal period: The first period of prenatal existence during which the fertilized egg becomes a blastocyte. This period runs for the first two weeks after fertilization.

Grief: The distressed feeling one gets after losing a loved one.

Human development: The study of biological, psychological and social changes across the life of a human.

Identity versus role confusion: The fifth Eriksonian stage of development during which a person must attempt to develop a consistent sense of self.

Imaginary audience: A concern seen primarily in adolescents in which the person believes that others are as concerned about their thoughts as they are as well.

Industry versus inferiority: The forth Eriksonian stage of development during which a person attempts to find a sense of purpose in life.

Initiative versus guilt: The third Eriksonian stage of development during which the person attempts to develop emotional and psychological independence.

Integrity: A sense of wholeness that comes from living a good life. It is the final stage of development of the ego.

Intimacy: The psychological ability to trust others as well as to share with them and truly care about them.

Irreversibility: This term comes from Piagetian theory. It refers to the inability for a child to reverse an action.

Longitudinal design: Methodological procedure used to study the same subjects over time. This design allows for a cohort confound which reduces the quality of the data it produces.

Maturation: Changes in development that are believed to be the result of genetic programming.

Menopause: The period for women during which menstruation ends and the opportunity to produce children ceases. This often produces a feeling of liberation in middle-aged women.

Monozygotic twins: Twins produced from the splitting of a single fertilized egg.

Moral dilemma: A scenario in which both morally good and bad options exist within each known alternative path of behavior.

Nature: The biological causes of any physical or psychological trait.

Nurture: The environmental causes of any physical or psychological trait.

Object permanence: A Piagetian concept in which a child learns that objects not directly seen may still exist.

Ovum: An egg used for fertilization.

Personal fable: A type of thinking seen most frequently in adolescents in which the person feels unique and protected from harm.

Postconventional morality: Kohlberg's final stage of moral development in which decisions may be made that conflict with societal norms.

Preconventional morality: Kohlberg's first stage of moral development in which a child determines good and bad by gauging whether they will be punished or rewarded.

Preoperational stage: Piaget's stage of development during which language—and more generally—symbol manipulation develops.

Private speech: When children prompt particular behaviors by speaking to themselves.

Psychosocial development: The effects of both biology and environment on the development of personality and relationships.

Puberty: The period of increased hormonal release in children approximately 12-years of age. This is also the period in which secondary sexual characteristics are established.

Recessive: The name given to a type of gene that can have its effects replaced by a different gene controlling a variation of the same trait (e.g., hair color).

Scaffolding: The process by which a more experienced person helps a less experienced person learn some task. The amount of help is reduced as the less experience person develops their skill set.

Scheme (plural schemas): The way in which a person thinks about a particular object or social interaction.

Self-concept: The attitudes and beliefs that define a particular person to him or herself.

Sensorimotor stage: Piaget's first stage of development during which a child learns about basic sensations and how to perform simple motor behaviors.

Separation anxiety: The anxiety produced in a child while separated from their primary caregiver.

Temperament: One's level of emotional reactivity.

Teratogen: Any chemical or biological agent that causes defects in the development of a prenatal child.

Theory of mind: The development of the ability to distinguish one's thoughts from others thoughts.

Trust versus mistrust: The first Eriksonian stage during which the consistency of a child's care teaches her to trust or mistrust others.

Zone of proximal development (ZPD): The theoretical range of ability of what a child can do alone (low range) versus what a child can do with the help of an adult (high range).

Zygote: A fertilized egg.

CHAPTER 5: SENSATION AND PERCEPTION

Absolute threshold: The measure of the strength of an energy source just strong enough to be detected by a subject under a specific set of conditions.

Accommodation: The adjustment of the eyes to seeing from far to near—or reverse—and the term is also used refer to adjusting from light to dark or dark to light.

Ambiguous (reversible) figures: Images that are observed as one thing or another. It is expected that the subject cannot experience both perceptions at the same time but can only reverse their image back and forth.

Basilar membrane: The location of the receptor cells for audition.

Blind spot: The section of your retina in which there are no photoreceptors.

Bottom-up processing: The theoretical process by which biological processes control perception without any influence or prior learning.

Cochlea: The curled bony structure which incorporates the receptors for hearing and balance.

Cones: The photoreceptors which are sensitive to light wavelengths.

Convergence: The process by which your eyes rotate toward each other to view something which is coming closer.

Cornea: The lens of the eye.

Dark adaptation: The ability to adjust to lower light conditions.

Difference threshold: The measure of the strength of an energy source just strong enough to be detected by a subject at some point above or below a previous level of energy; also known as the just-noticeable difference (jnd).

Feature detectors: These are brain circuits which analyze particular aspects of stimuli.

Fovea: The point on the retina where light is always focused from the lens.

Hue: The stimulus dimension which changes as light wavelength changes; also known more commonly as color.

Illusions: The perception of things or the perception of the inter-relation of things that are not really there.

Inner ear: The section of the auditory system which includes the cochlea and the auditory receptors.

Inner hair cells: The row of single hair cells along the Organ of Corti which analyze sounds in the primary range of normal speech.

Just noticeable difference (jnd): The measure of the strength of an energy source just strong enough to be detected by a subject at some point above or below a previous level of energy. It is also known as the difference threshold.

Lens: The transparent lens of the eye.

Lightness constancy: The perceptual illusion that a changing level of illumination is remaining constant.

Middle ear: The section of the auditory system that contains the ossicles; the bones of the middle ear.

Moon illusion: The illusion that the moon appears larger when it is near the horizon and smaller when it is at a higher angle to the ground.

Naïve realism: The philosophical approach in which it is believed that all perceptions are essentially accurate representations of the physical world's reality.

Organ of Corti: The location of the hair cell receptors of the auditory system.

Outer ear: The pinna.

Perception: The mixture of sensory experience coupled with previous learning.

Perceptual constancy: The perceptual illusion that things appear to be the same despite the fact that they are actually changing.

Presbyopia: The medical term given to the loss of close-vision because of the eye's natural tendency to become less flexible at middle age.

Psychophysics: The scientific study of the relationship between physical stimuli and the sensations they elicit.

Pupil: The opening of your eye through which light passes to you retina.

Retina: The inside back of your eyeball. It is the location of your photoreceptors.

Rods: The photoreceptors which detect the brightness of a light stimulus.

Saturation: The term that refers to how many different wavelengths of light are mixed into a single light stimulus. Highly saturated light has a consistent single wavelength.

Sensation: The biologically-based experience elicited from a stimulus.

Sensory adaptation: The reduction in any experience as a result of being exposed to an unchanging stimulus.

Sensory transduction: The process by which physical stimuli are converted into action potentials at the receptor organ.

Shape constancy: The perceptual illusion that shapes appear to be the same despite the fact that they are actually changing.

Signal detection theory: The primary methodology used to study psychophysics.

Size constancy: The perceptual illusion that the sizes of objects appear to be the same despite the fact that they are actually changing.

Top-down processing: A general cognitive event during which previous learning and memory influence the current perception of a stimulus.

Weber's law: The relationship between the need for physical stimuli to increase at an exponential rate in order to produce a subject's experience of equal size changes in perception.

CHAPTER 6: STATES OF CONSCIOUSNESS

Activation-synthesis theory: This theory proposes that dreaming occurs when the cerebral cortex analyzes signals that reach it from the lower areas of the brain.

Addiction: The presence of tolerance and physical dependence at the same time.

Alcoholism: The state of tolerance and physical dependence to alcohol.

Automatic processes: A state of consciousness which requires little effort. It does not interfere with other processes.

Barbiturates: Addictive substances originally prescribed to treat seizure disorders but later used to control anxiety.

Biological rhythms: Cycles of biological activity.

Circadian rhythm: Cycles of behavioral or biological activity that repeat on a 24 hour cycle.

Cognitive theory of dreaming: This theory proposes that dreaming can be studied and understood through the same processes and databases as for subjects who are not asleep.

Consciousness: The state of being aware.

Controlled processes: The name given to the most alert state of consciousness during which a subject is aware of their behavior and may be working toward a goal.

Depressants: Drug substances that reduce behavioral activity.

Hallucinogens: Substances which produce hallucinations.

Hypnosis: An altered state of consciousness during which the hypnotized subject is sensitive to suggestions from the hypnotherapist. The subject, however, will not generally perform any action that they would not do if they were conscious.

Opiates: Addictive substances derived from morphine which are generally used to reduce pain perception.

Physical dependence: The biological state in which the nervous system has changed its activity levels sufficiently that the removal of the drug results in the experience of an altered nervous system. This process is responsible for withdrawal symptoms.

Psychoactive drugs: Any drug which influences psychological states.

Psychological dependence: The emotional craving for a drug during a period in which physical dependence does not occur.

REM sleep: REM stands for Rapid Eye Movement. It is the stage of sleep during which the subject's eyes roll about in their eye sockets. It is correlated with the presence of dreaming in approximately 90% of the times that the sleeper is awoken and questioned about their experiences.

Social-cognitive behavior view of hypnosis: The theory that hypnotized subjects are only acting the way they believe hypnotized subjects should believe.

Stimulants: Drug substances that increase behavioral activity

Stream of consciousness: A concept put forth by William James that suggests that what is in your consciousness is always changing.

Suprachiasmatic nucleus (SCN): A brain structure near the hypothalamus (endocrine system) that is influenced by the daily cycle of light and dark.

Tolerance: The biological state in which a drug has to be given in increasingly higher doses to produce the same effect it did with its initial administration.

Tranquilizers: Addictive substances which are used to make the subject fall asleep faster.

Unconscious thought: Sigmund Freud's hypothetical construct which suggests that all unacceptable wishes are stored in a reservoir beyond conscious awareness.

CHAPTER 7: LEARNING

Acquisition: The name given to the process by which a subject comes under control of a new three term contingency.

Applied behavior analysis: A field of psychological therapy based on conditioning principles.

Avoidance learning: The process of learning to avoid a stimulus.

Behavior modification: The general term given to the clinical application of conditioning principles.

Biofeedback: A type of psychological therapy based upon computer-controlled feedback of physiological responses.

Cognitive perspective: A theoretical approach in which conditioning principles operate through thought processes in the brain.

Biological preparedness: The increased susceptibility to a particular form of conditioning.

Classical conditioning: Also known as Pavlovian conditioning. It is the form of stimulus-stimulus conditioning originally discovered by Ivan Pavlov.

Cognitive learning: Learning involving logical rules or language in general.

Conditioned emotional response (CER): The learning of an emotional response to the presence of a Pavlovian unconditioned stimulus that elicits emotional behavior.

Conditioned response (CR): The learned elicited response to a conditioned stimulus.

Conditioned stimulus (CS): The first stimulus in a classical conditioning paradigm.

Conditioned taste aversion: The application of Pavlovian principles to the aversion of certain tastes.

Continuous reinforcement: A separate name given to the fixed ratio (FR) 1 schedule in operant conditioning.

Contrapreparedness: The biologically controlled process through which a subject has difficulty associating two stimuli together.

Delayed reinforcement: The process of placing a time delay between a subject's response and the consequence it produces.

Discrimination: The learned ability to distinguish between two objects.

Discriminative stimulus: A stimulus used in a discrimination task.

Extinction (in classical conditioning): The removal of the US after the CS is presented.

Extinction (in operant conditioning): The removal of the consequence after a response has been made.

Fixed interval (FI) schedule: This is an operant schedule during which the first response after a constant time period passes will produce the programmed consequence.

Fixed ratio schedule: An operant schedule during which a set number of responses must occur before a consequence can be delivered.

Food aversion (taste aversion): The result of associating a flavor (CS) with illness (US) so that the flavor elicits the illness CR. This arrangement causes the subject to avoid the CS.

Generalization: The process by which a conditioned stimulus influences other similar stimuli to produce similar responses.

Habituation: This is another term for sensory adaptation. It is the process by which a subject responds less and less to the same stimulus.

Higher order conditioning: The process by which a CS is used as a US to control the development of a second CS.

Immediate reinforcement: The acquisition of a consequence with no delay after the response is made.

Insight learning: Learning that occurs very rapidly and usually as a result of combining together various pieces of information in a novel manner.

Instinctive drift: The tendency for an animal to revert to genetically controlled patterns of behavior.

Interval schedule: An operant schedule during which the first response after a predetermined time period passes will produce the programmed consequence.

Latent learning: Conditioning that is not evident in the dependent variable you are taking from a subject but is revealed once an alternative—correct—dependent variable is measured.

Law of Effect: The name Edward Thorndike gave to the process he discovered in which a subject's behavior is controlled by its consequences.

Learned helplessness: Through exposure to uncontrolled aversive stimuli, the subject's escape behavior will stop.

Learning: This is another name for conditioning.

Learning/performance distinction: The observation that learning can take place without actual behavior occurring.

Negative punishment: This is when a response causes the subject to lose access to a stimulus and that effect makes it less likely that the subject will behave in that same manner.

Negative reinforcement: This is when a response causes the subject to lose access to a stimulus and that effect makes it more likely that the subject will behave in that same manner.

Neural feedback: A type of biofeedback that focuses upon brain activity as the primary variable for change.

Neutral stimulus: A stimulus that is not associated with any other cue and does not control any behavior.

Observational learning: Rather than learning the relation between stimuli by responding to them, you are observing others responding to the stimuli and then learn the relation between them.

Operant: A response controlled by consequences.

Operant conditioning: The form of conditioning in which an antecedent-behavior-consequence contingency is the primary unit of analysis.

Partial reinforcement: Any operant schedule during which a consequence is not obtained for each cycle through the schedule.

Phobia: A strong aversion to an identifiable stimulus.

Positive punishment: This is when a response causes the subject to gain access to a stimulus and that effect makes it less likely that the subject will behave in that same manner.

Positive reinforcement: This is when a response causes the subject to gain access to a stimulus and that effect makes it more likely that the subject will behave in that same manner.

Primary reinforcer: This is another name for a reinforcing consequence (see also secondary reinforcer).

Punishment: A consequence to behavior that reduces its future probability.

Ratio schedule: An operant schedule during which a set number of responses must occur before the consequence will be presented.

Reinforcement: The general term given to an instance of the delivery of a positive or negative reinforcer.

Reinforcer: The reinforcing consequence itself.

Response contingency: The response requirement to obtain a particular consequence.

Secondary reinforcer: This is a stimulus associated with a primary reinforcer that is used to consequent a behavior once the response contingency has been met. (see also primary reinforcer).

Shaping: The application of reward for meeting successive approximations to a final goal response.

Spontaneous recovery (in classical conditioning): When a conditioned response appears to return independently in Pavlovian extinction after previously being extinguished.

Spontaneous recovery (in operant conditioning): When a conditioned response appears to return independently in operant extinction after previously being extinguished.

Stimulus discrimination: When two different stimuli control two different responses.

Stimulus generalization: When two different stimuli control the same response after only one of them was trained with an association.

Stimulus substitution: Pavlov's original theoretical approach to classical conditioning that suggests the CS becomes a substitute for the US.

Successive approximations: The process of training a series of responses in a hierarchical manner which are simpler than a final goal response.

Token economy: A therapeutic approach designed around the acquisition of tokens that serve as secondary reinforcers that may be exchanged for primary reinforcers.

Trace conditioning: Pavlovian conditioning in which the offset of the conditional stimulus follows a period of no stimuli before the unconditional stimulus is presented.

Unconditioned response (UR): A response which is reflexively made in the presence of the unconditional stimulus.

Unconditioned stimulus (US): A stimulus which causes a reflexive response to occur.

Variable interval schedule: An operant schedule in which the time that must pass before a consequence can be obtained is varied in length.

Variable ratio schedule: An operant schedule in which the number of responses that must occur before a consequence can be obtained is varied in size.

Vicarious conditioning: The classical conditioning of a reflexive response through observational learning.

CHAPTER 8: MEMORY

Chunking: The process of grouping pieces of information that can be more easily remembered together and using these groups as the basis for recall.

Decay theory: The idea that memories are lost because of a fading memory trace.

Declarative memory: This is memory which is related to basic facts that can be stated such as "The country just south of the U.S. and bordering Texas is ____."

Echoic storage: Storage of information which related to auditory stimuli.

Elaborative rehearsal: The type of rehearsal which requires the subject to think about the information and connect it to other forms of information.

Encoded: The term used for having formed a memory.

Encoding specificity principle: This term refers to the way in which a stimulus is encoded (e.g., by it visual, auditory or echoic characteristics).

Episodic memory: This refers to the memory for events in your life.

Everyday memory: This is a memory form which focuses on the common information of daily life.

Explicit memory: The conscious remembering of facts and events.

Flashbulb memories: Memories with a strong emotional content which were created through a highly emotional event.

Forgetting: The inability to recall a memory because of a problem retrieving the information or because the information was lost.

Iconic storage: The storage of visual information.

Implicit memory: The memory for things that you do not have to consciously be aware of (e.g., how to walk).

Interference: Any disruption in retrieving a memory.

Level of processing: The degree to which information is being processed by the memory system. It is influenced by the amount of elaboration, reflection and meaningfulness of the information.

Long-term memory (LTM): Any memory which presumably will last your full lifetime.

Maintenance rehearsal: The process of repeating information to yourself so that it stays in your short term memory.

Method of loci: A mnemonic procedure in which a series of items are remembered by associating them with a set of locations along a mental pathway.

Mnemonic devices: Procedures for improving your memory.

Modules: The idea that memory is processed by separate and independent components of the brain which work in parallel (at the same time) rather than serial (one after the other).

Motivated forgetting: This is the process by which people intentionally cause themselves to forget information. It appears to require an active inhibition process.

Networks of association: This is the concept that information is stored in a hierarchical system which creates nodes. Each node relates to a specific component of a concept and drives memory along the networks of association to engender a particular memory.

Node: This is the hypothetical central location of a concept in the brain.

Priming effects: The process of cueing a memory to be retrieved in a particular manner.

Proactive interference: The process by which any stimulus remembered now can influence the processing of memories in the near future.

Procedural memory: The memory for how to do something (e.g., how to fix a flat tire).

Prospective memory: The memory for what to do in the future (e.g., preparing yourself to complete a set of chores one hour in the future). It is contrasted with retrospective memory.

Recall: The retrieval of information with little cueing.

Recognition: The retrieval of information with a great deal of cueing.

Rehearsal: The process of repeating information to yourself to increase the chance that it will be remembered.

Retrieval: The general term for bringing back a memory.

Retrieval cues: Stimuli which facilitate retrieval.

Retroactive interference: The phenomenon during which information learned now will adversely affect a memory you just previously formed.

Retrospective memory: The memory for things which have already occurred. It is contrasted with prospective memory.

Semantic or generic memory: Knowledge for general facts.

Sensory registers: The theoretical location which holds stimuli for a brief time after the receptor has been stimulated.

Sensory representations: A stored memory for a sensory experience.

Serial position effect: The phenomenon which shows that the beginning and end of a list of items are always retrieved more accurately than the items in the middle of the list.

Short-term memory (STM): Memory for stimuli which last approximately 30 seconds in duration.

Spacing effect: This is the phenomenon of enhanced memory retrieval as a result of information being learned in small bits with lengthy durations between remembering periods.

Spreading activation theory: The theory that a stimulus activates closely related nodes in the networks of association.

SQ3R method: A study technique which enhances the retrieval of information. It includes the five steps of survey, question, read, recite & review.

Tip-of-the-tongue phenomenon: The feeling that you are about to say something that you are actually unable to remember.

Verbal representations: This refers to encoded verbal information.

Working memory: This is the type of memory that is functioning when you are consciously aware of an object or event.

CHAPTER 9: INTELLIGENCE

Abstract reasoning: The ability to understand hypothetical concepts.

Adaptive behavior skills: The ability to perform the normal functions of everyday life within your culture (e.g., tying your shoes, cooking your food, driving a car, paying your bills, etc.).

Association fallacy: The fallacy of confusing a claim's validity with the person who makes that claim.

Bell curve: Another name for the normal distribution.

Between-group heritability: The extent to which the differences between groups are due to genetic changes. Compare this with within-group variability.

Construct: A hypothetical entity describing the relationships between a wide variety of factors. Scientists generally use constructs when they are dealing with large multi-factored problems.

Convergent thinking: The ability to create the one best solution to a problem (compare with divergent thinking).

Crystallized intelligence: Knowledge of facts. It is frequently associated with declarative memory (see Memory chapter).

Culture-fair IQ tests: Intelligence tests that are less influenced by language or culture and more weighted toward abstract reasoning skills.

Deviation IQ: A person's IQ score relative to others of the same age.

Divergent thinking: The ability to create many different solutions to a problem (compare with convergent thinking).

Emotional Intelligence: The ability to detect and display emotions in ourselves and others.

Eugenics: A political process that suggests that those with genetic "disorders" not be allowed to reproduce so that the gene pool will contain fewer diseases.

Fluid intelligence: The ability to repeatedly adjust your thinking and solve problems creatively.

Flynn effect: The phenomenon of rising IQ scores across the 20th century.

g (General intelligence): A form of intelligence which reflects a single form or speed of mental processing.

Ideological immune system: Defensive reactions that deflect information contradicting our world view.

Intelligence quotient: The name given to the test score of an intelligence test.

Intelligence test: A test to measure thinking ability.

Mental age: The original basis for an IQ scale of measurement. It was created by Wilhelm Stern (1912) and required one to compare the age-level of one's correct set of IQ responses to the subject's chronological age (mental age / chronological age X 100 = IQ).

Mental retardation: The name given to the intellectual deficit which is characterized by a measured IQ two standard deviations below the mean before age 18 with the addition of adaptive behavior sills deficits.

Multiple intelligences: The concept that a person has multiple skill levels across a variety of intellectual domains.

s (Specific abilities): A particular ability in a specific area of intelligence.

Stanford-Binet IQ test: The current version of Lewis Terman's translated and modified version of the original Binet-Simon test from 1905.

Stereotype threat: The anxiety produced during a testing procedure resulting from the possibility that you may verify a stereotype based on your demographic makeup.

Test bias: Tendency of a standardized test to better predict the results for one group over another.

Triarchic model: A model of intelligence which suggest there are three forms of intelligence; analytical, practical and creative.

Wechsler Adult Intelligence Scale (WAIS): Currently, the most widely used test for intelligence.

Wisdom: The application of intelligent reasoning toward a common good.

Within-group heritability: The extent to which the differences within a group are due to genetic changes. Compare this with between-group variability.

CHAPTER 10: PERSONALITY

Anal expulsive fixation: A Freudian concept in which a person hates authority and is also sloppy and disorganized.

Anal retentive fixation: A Freudian concept which makes a person orderly, inflexible and structured.

Cardinal traits: Traits which are assumed to affect almost everything that you do.

Castration anxiety: A Freudian concept which suggests a male child is afraid that his father will get rid of him during a competition for the love of the child's mother.

Central traits: Traits that appear frequently in an individual.

Conditional positive regard: Accepting a person only if they meet they demands you place on them (compare with unconditional positive regard).

Conscience: Feeling bad when you believe you have done something wrong (compare with ego-ideal).

Denial: A Freudian concept in which one ignores or does not recognize unpleasant events.

Displacement: A Freudian concept which in which an unconscious substitution for something desired (see also sublimation).

Ego-ideal: Feeling good when you believe you have done something right (compare with conscience).

Empirically keyed tests: This is the name give to tests that use questions which are consistently answered differently across groups so that members of those groups can be easily identified.

Externals: People who believe that they cannot control their experience with the world (compare with internals).

Face or content validity: These are terms from the field of measurement and testing. They refer to the idea that a test question is measuring just what it appears to be testing and not some hidden psychological construct.

Factor analysis: A statistical technique that allows a researcher to determine whether different patterns of behavior tend to correlate with each other.

Idiographic approach: The study of individuals in the field of personality rather than studying groups and looking for general principles of personality.

Internals: People who believe that they can control their experience with the world (compare with externals).

Introjection: Internalizing the value system which your parents taught you.

Libido: A Freudian concept referring to the energy of life instincts.

Nomothetic approach: The name given to the study of groups of people in the field of personality so as to uncover their general personality traits.

Oedipus complex: A Freudian concept which suggests a male child will have sexual feelings for his mother.

Oral incorporative stage: A Freudian stage in which the person exhibits an oral fixation due to a need for love.

Oral sadistic stage: A Freudian stage in which a person uses words (oral expression) to hurt others.

Penis envy: A Freudian concept in which a female desires to have a penis so as to access the societal benefits associated with being male.

Personality coefficient: The term that Walter Mischel created in 1968 to describe the low correlation between personality traits and behavior.

Phenomenological approach: An approach which relies on an understanding the immediate experience of a person as a way to explain their behavior.

Pleasure principle: The Freudian concept of the motivation to eliminate any tension the person feels.

Primary process: The Freudian concept that the Id is so primal it cannot tell the difference between reality and fantasy.

Projection: A Freudian concept in which a person places their own unacceptable thoughts or feelings onto others.

Projective tests: A form of personality test in which ambiguous stimuli are presented to a subject. The subject is then asked to interpret what they see. The interpretation of the ambiguous stimuli is taken as a measure of the subject's unconscious state.

Psychodynamic theory: The interrelationships of the id, ego and superego across time.

Rationalization: A Freudian concept in which a person has to find a reason to justify their socially inappropriate behavior.

Reaction formation: A Freudian concept in which a person reacts in the opposite way in which they truly feel.

Reality principle: The Freudian concept which describes one's ability to distinguish fantasy from reality.

Repression: A Freudian concept in which one blocks thoughts or feelings from getting into their conscious awareness.

Secondary process: The Freudian concept of the capacity to use logical thinking to help us survive on a daily basis.

Secondary traits: Personality traits which only some up under specific circumstances.

Self-efficacy: The belief that you can perform the functions necessary to be successful.

Social desirability response bias: The tendency for people to answer questions in a socially acceptable manner.

Source traits: Personality traits that come up in almost all people.

Stimulus control: Control by stimuli in the environment.

Sublimation: A Freudian concept which in which an unconscious substitution for something desired and it is also socially desirable to do so (see also displacement).

Thanatos: The Freudian concept of the death instinct.

Thematic Apperception Test (TAT): A form of personality test in which images of people and places presented to a subject. The subject is then asked to interpret what they see. The interpretation of the ambiguous stimuli is taken as a measure of the subject's unconscious state.

Theoretical constructs: Hypothetical constructs used to explain behavior through a multitude of combined factors.

Unconditional positive regard: Accepting a person for who he or she is (compare with conditional positive regard).

Wish-fulfillment: The Freudian concept of reducing mental tension by imagining that you have the things or experiences that you want to have.

CHAPTER 11: PSYCHOLOGICAL DISORDERS

Abnormal behavior: Observed behavioral patterns that are considered pathological because they are statistically infrequent, cause dysfunction, personal distress and violate social norms.

Antisocial personality disorder: A form of personality disorder which is primarily characterized by a lack of empathy for others.

Anxiety disorders: A type of disorder which includes an irrational fear of some object or situation.

Bipolar disorder: A mental disorder which produces cycles of depression and mania.

Borderline personality disorder (BPD):

Comorbidity: The name given to the time in which a person has more than one disorder.

Culture-bound symptoms: The symptoms of a mental disorder are specific to a particular culture.

Culture-general symptoms: Symptoms of a mental disorder which are general across cultures.

Delusions: A disordered thought process in which a person comes to believe things that are not real.

Diagnostic and Statistical Manual of Mental Disorders (DSM-IV-TR): A text showing the full range of mental disorders identified by the psychiatric community.

Diathesis-stress model: The theoretical suggestion that stress plays a central part in establishing the symptoms of schizophrenia for those that have a genetic predisposition (diathesis) for the disease.

Dissociative disorders: A mental disorder in which a person comes to either forget who they are or believe they are someone else.

Dissociative identity disorder (DID): A mental disorder in which it appears that a person develops multiple personalities.

Dopamine hypothesis: A general theory which suggests that excessive dopaminergic activity is partly responsible for schizophrenia.

Generalized anxiety disorder: A disorder characterized by a low grade feeling of anxiety that is always present and cannot be attributed to any particular life event.

Hallucinations: Imagined experiences that are associated with any of your six sensory systems.

Learned helplessness: Learning to stop responding due to repeated failure to obtain a reward.

Major depressive disorder: An intense depression that may be life threatening if not treated.

Medical model: A theoretical approach to medial and mental illness which suggests all disorders have physical causes that can be diagnosed and treated.

Mood disorders: A mental disorder characterized by either depression or depression and mania.

Negative schizophrenia: Symptoms of schizophrenia which involve the loss of normal thought processes, flat affect, toneless speech, and social withdrawal (compare with positive schizophrenia).

Neurosis: This is the term given to a level of mental disorder which is not strong enough to stop a person from living independently and taking care of him or herself (compare with psychosis).

Obsessive-compulsive disorder (OCD): A form of anxiety disorder

Panic disorder: A form of anxiety disorder characterized by extreme fear and panic that occurs at random times.

Personality disorders: Entrenched maladaptive behavior patterns which cause significant impairment of social functioning.

Phobias: A type of anxiety disorder in which a specific stimulus elicits a great deal of anxiety and fear in the subject.

Positive schizophrenia: The symptoms of schizophrenia which include the addition of bizarre delusions and hallucinations (compare with negative schizophrenia).

Psychiatry: The field of medicine which deals with mental illnesses.

Psychosis: This is the term given to a level of mental disorder which is strong enough to stop a person from living independently and taking care of his or herself (compare with neurosis).

Schizophrenia: A psychotic disorder which contains hallucinations as well as disturbances in thought, perceptions and language.

Self-medication: The process by which a person with a mental disorder takes psychoactive substances (e.g., alcohol) in an attempt to control the symptoms of the mental disorder (e.g., mania).

State disorders: Another name for Axis 1 of the DSM.

Substance-related disorders: The abuse or dependence on an addictive substance.

Trait disorders: Long standing disorders which seem to be characteristic of an individual.

CHAPTER 12: SOCIAL PSYCHOLOGY

Altruistic behavior/altruism: When someone performs helpful acts that are not related to their own personal gain.

Attitudes: Predispositions in the way that one thinks or acts.

Attribution theories: The name given to the explanations for people trying to associate internal or external explanations to everyone's behavior.

Behavioral aggression: Any act that causes physical or emotional harm to another living being.

Belief in a just world: The belief that good things happen to good people and that bad things happen to bad people.

Bystander effect: The empirical finding that as the number of people present at an emergency increases the less likely that any one person will help.

Cognitive dissonance: A feeling of anxiety that occurs when our attitudes do not match our behavior.

Complementarity of needs: When each person's needs are met by another with whom they have a relationship.

Compliance: When one changes their behavior due to a request by another (compare with Obedience).

Cost-reward approach: Helping others only when the reward is greater than the cost.

Defensive attribution: The process by which someone avoids giving external attributions to another's negative behaviors because they are afraid that they might act the same way under similar conditions.

Deindividuation: A mental state in which one becomes less aware of themselves as an individual and conforms more to the group.

Diffusion of responsibility: When someone feels less responsibility for things when others are around.

Door-in-the-face effect: A compliance strategy which initially requests large—unlikely accepted—demands from a subject with the expectation that a later lesser demand will be more likely accepted (compare with Foot-in-the-door effect).

Emotional aggression: Aggression elicited by emotional responding.

Environmental variables of aggression: Environmental events which cause us to lose our self-evaluations of our aggressive behavior.

Foot-in-the-door effect: A compliance strategy which makes small—likely accepted—demands from a subject which build up to much larger demands (compare with Door-in-the-face effect).

Frustration-aggression hypothesis: A theoretical understanding of aggression in which it is believed that all aggression comes from frustration.

Fundamental attribution error: The name given to the process by which someone tends to give internal explanations for others behavior.

Gain/loss theory: When we like or are attracted to another due to the reward we obtain from the relationship as well as the gain vs. loss of reward over time.

Halo effect: The name given to the phenomenon by which people assume that attractive individuals also have positive behavioral characteristics.

Informational conformity effect: When you go along with others because it appears that they have more information than you do about something important.

Instrumental aggression: Aggression directed with the intention of obtaining something.

Inter-role conflict: Times during which there is conflict between two or more roles that a person plays.

Intra-role conflict: When one role places competing responsibilities on a person.

Kernel of truth: A small amount of truth in some information.

Lowball procedure: A procedure to make someone agree to a difficult request by first asking getting their compliance on a series of minor requests which increase in difficulty.

Matching hypothesis: The process by which people tend to pair up with others of the same level of attractiveness.

Motivational aggression: The intention to cause physical or emotional harm to another living being.

Norm of noninvolvement: The process of avoiding involvement with others so that you can avoid any potential troubles.

Norm of reciprocity: The process of helping others now with the expectation that you will be helped in the future.

Norm of social responsibility: Social expectations that we should help others in need.

Normative conformity effect: Doing the same things as others so you fit into the group.

Obedience: When one changes their behavior due to a request or demand from another person in authority (compare with Compliance).

Passive aggression: Causing emotional harm to another by not acting.

Pluralistic ignorance: The name given to the scenario in which one does not help unless someone else helps first.

Primacy effect: The idea that the first information you gain about someone may be more valued than information obtained later.

Proximity: The regular physical proximity between two people which has a bearing on their attractiveness to each other.

Reciprocity of attraction: When one likes someone else because that person likes them.

Schema: An attitude or expectation about others that is based on previous experience.

Self-serving bias: The tendency to assign internal causes for your own successes and external causes for your own failures.

Social norms: The social expectations which control how we should act in a particular scenario.

Social psychology: The study of human-human interaction.

Social roles: The behavior people expect from you based on your position in society.

Stereotypes: A preconceived notion that all members of a group share the same set of characteristics.

Verbal aggression: Causing emotional harm to another person through your language.

References

Abbey, A. (1987). Misperceptions of friendly behavior as sexual interest: A survey of naturally occurring incidents. Psychology of Women Quarterly, 11(2), 173–194.

Abramson, Li, Seligman, M. E., & Teasdale, J. D. (1978). Learned helplessness in humans: Critique and reformulation. Journal of Abnormal Psychology, 87, 49–74.

Aczel, A. D. (2005). Descartes secret notebook: A true tale of mathematics, mysticism, and the quest to understand the universe. New York: Broadway Books.

Adams, R. J. (1987). An evaluation of color preference in early infancy. Infant Behavior & Development, 10(2), 143–150. doi:10.1016/0163-6383(87)90029-4

Ader, R., & Cohen, N. (1977). Behaviorally conditioned immunosuppression. Psychosomatic Medicine, 37, 333–340.

Aguiar, A., & Baillargeon, R. (2003). Perseverative responding in a violation-of-expectation task in 6.5-month-old infants. Cognition, 88(3), 277–316. doi:10.1016/S0010-0277(03)00044-1

Aharon, I., Etcoff, N., Ariely, D., Chabris, C. F, O'Connor, E. & Breiter. H. C. (2001). Beautiful faces have variable reward value: fMRI and behavioral evidence. Neuron, 32, 537–551. et al 2001

Alloway, T., Wilson, G., & Graham, J. (2005). Sniffy the virtual rat: Pro Version 2.0. Belmont, CA: Thomson-Wadsworth.

Allport, G. W. (1937). Personality: A psychological interpretation. New York: Holt.

Allport, G. W. (1966). Traits revisited. American Psychologist, 21, 1–10.

Allport, G. W., & Odbert, H. S. (1936). Trait-names: A psycho-lexical study. Psychological Monographs, 47(1, Whole No. 211).

Allport, G. W., & Vernon, P. E. (1933). Studies in expressive movement. New York: Macmillan.

Alon, U. (2007). An introduction to systems biology: Design principles of biological circuits. New York: Chapman & Hall.

Alwin, D. F. (1990), Historical changes in parental orientations to children. In N. Mandell (Ed.). Sociological studies of child development (Col. 3). Greenwich, CT: JAI Press.

American Psychiatric Association. (2000). Diagnostic and statistical manual of mental disorders: DSM-IV-TR. Washington, DC: Author.

Archer, J. (2004). Sex differences in aggression in real-world settings: A meta-analytic review. Review of General Psychology, 8(4), 291–322.

Aries, E. (1987). Gender and communication. In P. Shaver, & C. Hendrick (Eds.), Sex and gender. (pp. 149–176). Thousand Oaks, CA, US: Sage Publications, Inc.

Aronson, E., & Linder, D. (1965). Gain and loss of esteem as determinants of interpersonal attraction. Journal of Experimental Social Psychology, 1, 156–I 71.

Asch, S. E. (1955). Opinions and social pressure. Scientific American, 193, 31–55.

Asch, S.F. (1946). Forming impressions of personality. Journal of Abnormal and Social Psychology 41, 258–290.

Atkinson, R. (1988). The teenage world: Adolescent self-image in ten countries. New York: Plenum Press.

Bailey, J. M., Gaulin, S., Agyei, Y., & Gladue, B. A. (1994). Effects of gender and sexual orientation on evolutionarily relevant aspects of human mating psychology. Journal of Personality and Social Psychology, 66(6), 1081–1093.

Bailey, J. M., Kirk, K. M., Zhu, G., Dunne, M. P., & Martin, N. G. (2000). Do individual differences in sociosexuality represent genetic or environmentally contingent strategies? evidence from the Australian twin registry. Journal of Personality and Social Psychology, 78(3), 537–545.

Baillargeon, R. (1986). Representing the existence and the location of hidden objects: Object permanence in 6- and 8-month-old infants. Cognition, 23(1), 21–41. doi:10.1016/0010-0277(86)90052-1

Ball, K., Berch, D. B., Helmers, K. F., Jobe, J. B., Leveck, M. D., Marsiske, M., Morris, J. N., Rebok, G. W., Smith, D. M., Tennstedt, S. L., Unverzagt, F. W., & Willis, S. L. (2002). Effects of cognitive training interventions with older adults: A randomized controlled trial. JAMA: Journal of the American Medical Association, 288(18), 2271–2281. doi:10.1001/jama.288.18.2271

Baltes, P. B., Reese, H. W., & Nesselroade, J. R. (1988). Life-span developmental psychology: Introduction to research methods. Hillsdale, NJ, England: Lawrence Erlbaum Associates, Inc.

Bandura A. (1997). Self-efficacy. New York: Freeman.

Bandura A. (1999). Social cognitive theory of personality. In L. A. Pervin & 0. P. John (Eds.), Handbook of personality: Theory and research (2nd ed., pp. 154–196). New York: Guildford Press.

Bandura, A. (1973). Aggression: A social learning analysis. Englewood Cliffs, NJ: Prentice-Hall.

Bandura, A. (1986). Social foundations of thought and action: A social cognitive theory. Englewood Cliffs, NJ: Prentice-Hall.

Bandura, A., & Walters, R. H. (1963). Social learning and personality development. New York: Holt Rinehart, & Winston.

Bandura, A., Ross, D., & Ross, S. (1963). Vicarious reinforcement and imitative learning. Journal of Abnormal and Social Psychology, 67, 601–607.

Barkley, R. A. (1998). Attention-deficit hyperactivity disorder: A handbook for diagnosis and treatment (2nd ed.). New York, NY, US: Guilford Press.

Bartholomew, K. (1990). Avoidance of intimacy: An attachment perspective. Journal of Social and Personal Relationships, 7(2), 147–178. doi:10.1177/0265407590072001

Bartoshuk, L. M. (2000). Comparing sensory experiences across individuals: Recent psychophysical advances illuminate genetic variation in taste perception. Chemical Senses, 25, 447–460.

Bates, J. E. (1989). Applications of temperament concepts. In G. A. Kohnstamm, J. E. Bates & M. K. Rothbart (Eds.), Temperament in childhood. (pp. 322–355). Oxford, England: John Wiley & Sons.

Batson, C. D., & Ahmad, N. (2001). Empathy-induced altruism in a prisoner's dilemma II: What if the target of empathy has defected? European Journal of Social Psychology, 31, 25–36.

Baumeister, R. F. (2005). The cultural animal: Human nature, meaning, and social life. New York, NY, US: Oxford University Press.

Baumeister, R. F., & Tice, D. M. (1990). Anxiety and social exclusion. Journal of Social and Clinical Psychology, 9, 165–195.

Baumeister, R. F., Catanese, K. R., & Vohs, K. D. (2001). Is there a gender difference in strength of sex drive? theoretical views, conceptual distinctions, and a review of relevant evidence. Personality and Social Psychology Review, 5(3), 242–273.

Bem, S. L. (1987). Masculinity and femininity exist only in the mind of the perceiver. In J. M. Reinisch, L. A. Rosenblum, & S. A. Sanders (Eds.). Masculinity/femininity: Basic perspectives. New York: Oxford University Press.

Bem, S. L. (1993). The lenses of gender: Transforming the debate on sexual inequality. New Haven, CT, US: Yale University Press.

Benasich, A. A., & Tallal, P. (1996). Auditory temporal processing thresholds, habituation, and recognition memory over the 1st year. Infant Behavior & Development, 19(3), 339–357. doi:10.1016/S0163-6383(96)90033-8

Benson, P. L. (1992, Spring). Patterns of religious development in adolescence and adulthood. PIRI Newsletter, 2–9.

Benson, P. L., Sharma, A. R., & Roehlkepartain, E. C. (1994). Growing up adopted: A portrait of adolescents and their families. Minneapolis: Search Institute.

Berenbaum, S. A., & Bailey, J. M. (2003). Effects on gender identity of pre-natal androgens and genital appearance. Evidence from girls with congenital adrenal hyperplasia. Journal of Clinical Endocrinology and Metabolism, 88, 1102–1106.

Berenbaum, S. A., & Hines, M. (1992). Early androgens are related to childhood sex-typed toy preferences. Psychological Science, 3(3), 203–206.

Berkowitz, L. (1962). Aggression: A social psychological analysis. New York: McGraw-Hill.

Berkowitz, L. (1989). Frustration-aggression hypothesis: Examination and reformulation. Psychological Bulletin, 106, 59–73.

Bern, D. J., & Allen, A. (1974). On predicting some of the people some of the time: The search for cross-situational consistencies in behavior. Psychological Review, 81, 506–520.

Berndt, T. J. (1992). Friendship and friends' influence in adolescence. Current Directions in Psychological Science, 1(5), 156–159.

Berscheid, E., & Reis, H. T. (1998). Attraction and close relationships. In D. Gilbert, S. T. Fiske, & G. Lindzey (Eds.), Handbook of social psychology (Vol. 2, 4th ed., pp. 193–28 1). Boston: McGraw-Hill.

Berscheid, E., & Walster, E. (1978). Interpersonal attraction. Reading, MA: Addison-Wesley.

Bettencourt, B. A., & Dorr, N. (1997). Collective self-esteem as a mediator of the relationship between allocentrism and subjective well-being. Personality and Social Psychology Bulletin, 23(9), 955–964.

Bettencourt, B. A., & Kernahan, C. (1997). A meta-analysis of aggression in the presence of violent cues: Effects of gender differences and aversive provocation. Aggressive Behavior, 23(6), 447–456.

Blackburne-Stover, G., Belenky, M. F., & Gilligan, C. (1982). Moral development and reconstructive memory: Recalling a decision to terminate an unplanned pregnancy. Developmental Psychology, 18(6), 862–870. doi:10.1037/0012-1649.18.6.862

Blanchard, M., & Main, M. (1979). Avoidance of the attachment figure and social-emotional adjustment in day-care infants. Developmental Psychology, 15(4), 445–446. doi:10.1037/0012-1649.15.4.445

Blanchard, R. J., Blanchard, D. C., Griebel, G., & Nutt, D. (Eds.). (2008). Handbook of anxiety and fear. New York: Elsevier.

Blass, T. (2004). The man who shocked the world: The life and legacy of Stanley Milgram. New York: Basic Books.

Bloom, L. (1974). Talking, understanding, and thinking. Language perspectives: Acquisition, retardation, and intervention. (). Baltimore, MD, US: University Park Press.

Bloom, P. (2000). How children learn the meanings of words. Cambridge, MA, US: The MIT Press.

Bohman, M., & Sigvardsson, S. (1990). Outcome in adoption: Lessons from longitudinal studies. In D. M. Brodzinsky, & M. D. Schechter (Eds.), The psychology of adoption. (pp. 93–106). New York, NY, US: Oxford University Press.

Boker, S. M., & Wenger, M. J. (Eds.). (2007). Data analytic techniques for dynamical systems. Mahwah, NJ: Lawrence Erlbaum Associates.

Bond, M. H. (1988). Finding universal dimensions of individual variation in multicultural studies of values: The Rokeach and Chinese value surveys. Journal of Personality and Social Psychology, 55(6), 1009–1015.

Boneva, B. S., & Frieze, I. H. (2001). Toward a concept of a migrant personality. Journal of Social Issues, 57(3), 477–491.

Bornstein, M. H. (1985). Habituation of attention as a measure of visual information processing in human infants: Summary, systematization, and synthesis. In G. Gottlieb, & N. A. Krasnegor (Eds.), Measurement of audition and vision in the first year of postnatal life: A methodological overview. (pp. 253–300). Westport, CT, US: Ablex Publishing.

Bornstein, M. H., & Benasich, A. A. (1986). Infant habituation: Assessments of individual differences and short-term reliability at five months. Child Development, 57(1), 87–99. doi:10.2307/1130640

Bornstein, M. H., Tal, J., Rahn, C., Galperín, C. Z., Pêcheux, M., Lamour, M., et al. (1992). Functional analysis of the contents of maternal speech to infants of 5 and 13 months in four cultures: Argentina, France, Japan, and the United States. Developmental Psychology, 28(4), 593–603.

Bornstein, M. H., Tamis-LeMonda, C. S., Tal, J., & Ludemann, P. (1992). Maternal responsiveness to infants in three societies: The United States, France, and Japan. Child Development, 63(4), 808–821.

Bosworth, H. B., & Schaie, K. W. (1997). The relationship of social environment, social networks, and health outcomes in the Seattle longitudinal study: Two analytical approaches. The Journals of Gerontology: Series B: Psychological Sciences and Social Sciences, 52B(5), P197–P205.

Bouchard, T. J., & McGue, M. (1990). Genetic and rearing environmental influences on adult personality: An analysis of adopted twins reared apart. Journal of Personality, Special Issue: Biological Foundations of Personality: Evolution, Behavioral Genetics, and Psychophysiology, 58(1), 263–292.

Bouchard, T. J., Jr. (1994). Genes, environment, and personality. Science, 264, 1700–1701.

Bouchard, T. J., Jr. (2004). Genetic influence on human psychological traits: A survey. Current Directions in Psychological Science, 13(4), 148–151.

Bradshaw, J. (1990). Homecoming: Reclaiming and championing your inner child. New York: Bantam Books.

Bregman, A. S. (1990). Auditory scene analysis: The perceptual organization of sound. Cambridge, MA: The MIT Press.

Brehm, S., Kassin, S., & Fein, S. (2005). Social psychology (6th ed.). Boston Houghton Mifflin.

Briscoe, D. (1997, February 16). Women lawmakers still not in charge. Associated Press (in Grand Rapids Press, p. A23).

Brislin, R. W. (1988). Increasing awareness of class, ethnicity, culture, and race by expanding on students' own experiences. In I. S. Cohen (Ed.), The G. stanley hall lecture series, vol. 8. (pp. 137–180). Washington, DC, US: American Psychological Association.

Brodzinsky, David M. (Ed) (1), & Schechter, M. D. (. (Eds.). (1990). The psychology of adoption. New York, NY, US: Oxford University Press.

Brooks, M. (2003). The zombie survival guide: Complete protection from the living dead. New York: Three Rivers Press.

Brown, R. (1973). A first language: The early stages. Oxford, England: Harvard U. Press.

Bruder, C. E. G., et al. (2008). Phenotypically concordant and discordant monozygotic twins display different DNA copy-number-variation profiles. American Journal of Human Genetics, 82, 763–771.

Bryan, J. H., & Test, M. A. (1967). Models and helping: Naturalistic studies in aiding behavior. Journal of Personality and Social Psychology, 6, 400–407.

Buck, L., &Axcl, R. (1991). A novel multigene family may encode odorant receptors: A molecular basis for odor recognition. Cell, 65, 175–187.

Buckley, K. W. (1989). Mechanical man: John Broadus Watson and the beginnings of behaviorism. New York: Guilford Press.

Bureau of Labor Statistics. (2004, September 14). American time-user survey summary. Washington, DC: United States Department of Labor (www.bls.gov).

Burger, J. M., & Cornelius, T. (2003). Raising the price of agreement: Public commitment and the lowball compliance procedure. Journal of Applied Social Psychology, 33, 923–934.

Buss, D. M. (1991). Evolutionary personality psychology. Annual Review of Psychology, 42, 459–491.

Buss, D. M. (1994). The strategies of human mating: People worldwide are attracted to the same qualities in the opposite sex. American Scientist, 82, 238–249.

Buss, D. M. (1995). Evolutionary psychology: A new paradigm for psychological science. Psychological Inquiry, 6(1), 1–30.

Buss, D. M. (1996). Sexual conflict: Evolutionary insights into feminism and the "battle of the sexes.". In D. M. Buss, & N. M. Malamuth (Eds.), Sex, power, conflict: Evolutionary and feminist perspectives. (pp. 296–318). New York, NY, US: Oxford University Press.

Buss, D. M. (2000). Desires in human mating. In D. LeCroy, & P. Moller (Eds.), Evolutionary perspectives on human reproductive behavior. (pp. 39–49). New York, NY, US: New York Academy of Sciences.

Buss, D. M. (2000). Evolutionary psychology. Washington, DC, US: American Psychological Association; New York, NY, US: Oxford University Press.

Buss, D. M. (2000). Natural selection. Washington, DC, US: American Psychological Association; New York, NY, US: Oxford University Press.

Buss, D. M. (2000). The dangerous passion: Why jealousy is as necessary as love and sex. New York, NY, US: Free Press.

Buss, D. M. (2000). The evolution of happiness. American Psychologist, 55(1), 15–23.

Buss, D. M. (2005). The handbook of evolutionary psychology. Hoboken, NJ: Wiley.

Buss, D. M. (2012). Evolutionary psychology: The new science of the mind. New York: Allyn & Bacon.

Buss, W. G. (2000). Measures of intelligence: Legal issues. Washington, DC, US: American Psychological Association; New York, NY, US: Oxford University Press.

Butler, B. Y. (2006). Holy intoxication to drunken dissipation: Alcohol among Quichua speakers in Otavalo, Ecuador. Albuquerque: University of New Mexico Press.

Byrnes, J. P., Miller, D. C., & Schafer, W. D. (1999). Gender differences in risk taking: A meta-analysis. Psychological Bulletin, 125(3), 367–383.

Cahill, L. (2005, May). His brain, her brain. Scientific American, 40–47.

Cameron, J. R., Hansen, R., & Rosen, D. (1989). Preventing behavioral problems in infancy through temperament assessment and parental support programs. In W. B. Carey, & S. C. McDevitt (Eds.), Clinical and educational applications of temperament research. (pp. 155–165). Lisse, Netherlands: Swets & Zeitlinger Publishers.

Caplan, N., Choy, M. H., & Whitmore, J. K. (1992, February). Indochinese refugee families and academic achievement. Scientific American, 36–42.

Carducci, B. J. (1998). The psychology of personality. Pacific Grove, CA: Brooks/Cole.

Carlson, N. R. (2007). Physiology of behavior (9th ed.). New York: Pearson.

Carlson, N. R., Heth, C. D., Miller, H., Donahoe, J. W., Buskist, W., & Martin, G. N. (2007). Psychology: The science of behavior. New York: Pearson.

Carnagey, N. L., Anderson, C. A., & Bushman, B. J. (2007). The effect of video game violence on physiological desensitization to real-life violence. Journal of Experimental Social Psychology, 43, 489–496.

Carpenter, S., & Huffman, K. (2008). Visualizing psychology. Hoboken, NJ: John Wiley & Sons, Inc.

Carter, R. (2010). Mapping the mind. Los Angeles, CA: University of California Press.

Carver, C. S., & Scheier, M. F. (1996). Perspectives on personality. Needham Heights, MA: Simon & Schuster.

Caspi, A. (2000). The child is father of the man: Personality continuities from childhood to adulthood. Journal of Personality and Social Psychology, 78(1), 158–172.

Cattell, R. B. (1973). Personality and mood by questionnaire. San Francisco: Jossey-Bass.

Cheek, J. M., & Melchior, L. A. (1990). Shyness, self-esteem, and self-consciousness. In H. Leitenberg (Ed.), Handbook of social and evaluation anxiety. (pp. 47–82). New York, NY, US: Plenum Press.

Chemelli, R. M., Willie, J. T., Sinton, C. M., Elmquist, J. K., Scammell, T. E., Lee, C., Richardson, J. A., Williams, S. C., Xiong, Y., Kisanuki, Y., Fitch, T. E., Nakazato, M., Hammer, R. E., Saper, C. B., & Yanagisawa, M. (1999). Narcolepsy in orexin knockout mice: Molecular genetics of sleep regulation. Cell, 98, 437–451.

Chess, S., & Thomas, A. (1987). Know your child: An authoritative guide for today's parents. New York: Basic Books.

Choi, I., & Choi, Y. (2002). Culture and self-concept flexibility. Personality and Social Psychology Bulletin, 28(11), 1508–1517.

Chomsky, N. (1957). Syntactic structures. Oxford, England: Mouton.

Chu, D. T., Kim, S. W., Hsu, H. K., Cok, G., Roubec, J., Patil, S., Damyanov, D., West, T., Hall, B., & Altug, S. (2009). Patient attitudes towards chemotherapy and survival: A prospective observational study in advanced non-small cell lung cancer. Lung Cancer, 66, 250–256.

Cialdini, R. B. (2001). Influence: Science and practice (4th ed.). Boston: Allyn & Bacon.

Cialdini, R. B., & Goldstein, N.J. (2004). Social influence: Compliance and conformity. Annual Review of Psychology, 55, 591–621.

Ciccarelli, S. K., & Meyer, G. E. (2006). Psychology. Upper Saddle River, NJ: Pearson.

Clark, R. D. (1990). The impact of AIDS on gender differences in willingness to engage in casual sex. Journal of Applied Social Psychology, 20(9), 771–782.

Clark, R. D., & Hatfield, E. (1989). Gender differences in receptivity to sexual offers. Journal of Psychology & Human Sexuality, 2(1), 39–55.

Colapinto, J. (2000). As nature made him: The boy who was raised as a girl. New York, NY, US: HarperCollins Publishers.

Colarelli, S. M., & Dettmann, J. R. (2003). Intuitive evolutionary perspectives in marketing practices. Psychology & Marketing, 20(9), 837–865.

Colarelli, S. M., Spranger, J. L., & Hechanova, M. R. (2006). Women, power, and sex composition in small groups: An evolutionary perspective. Journal of Organizational Behavior, Special Issue: Darwinian Perspectives on Behavior in Organizations, 27(2), 163–184.

Collins, W. A., Maccoby, E. E., Steinberg, L., Hetherington, E. M., & Bornstein, M. H. (2000). Contemporary research on parenting: The case for nature and nurture. American Psychologist, 55(2), 218–232.

Cossu, G., Ledent, C., Fattore, L, Imperato, A., Bohme, G. A., Parmentier, M., & Fratta, W. (2001). Cannabinoid CB1 receptor knockout mice fail to self-administer morphine but not other drugs of abuse. Behavioural Brain Research, 118, 61–65.

Courage, M. L., & Howe, M. L. (2002). From infant to child: The dynamics of cognitive change in the second year of life. Psychological Bulletin, 128(2), 250–277. doi:10.1037/0033-2909.128.2.250

Cousins, N. (1989). Head first: The biology of hope. New York: Dutton.

Crabtree, S. (2002, January 22). Gender roles reflected in teen tech use. Gallup Tuesday Briefing (www.gallup.com).

Craik, F. I. M. (1994). Memory changes in normal aging. Current Directions in Psychological Science, 3(5), 155–158. doi:10.1111/1467-8721.ep10770653

Craik, F. I. M., Moscovitch, M., & McDowd, J. M. (1994). Contributions of surface and conceptual information to performance on implicit and explicit memory tasks. Journal of Experimental Psychology: Learning, Memory, and Cognition, 20(4), 864–875. doi:10.1037/0278-7393.20.4.864

Crawford, C, Salmon, C. (2004). Evolutionary psychology, public policy and personal decisions. Mahwah, NJ: Lawrence Erlbaum Associates.

Daley, D. C. (2006). Addiction and mood disorders: A guide for clients and families. Oxford: Oxford University Press.

Damasio, A. R., Tranel, D., & Damasio, H. (1990). Face agnosia and the neural substrates of memory. Annual Review of Neuroscience, 13, 89–109.

Darley, J. M., & Batson, C. D. (1973). "From Jerusalem to Jericho": A study of situational and dispositional variables in helping behavior. Journal of Personality and Social Psychology, 27, 100–108.

Darley, J. M., & Latanh, B. (1968). Bystanders intervention in emergencies: Diffusion of responsibility. Journal of Personality and Social Psychology, 8, 377–383.

Dartnall, H. J. A., Bowmaker, J. K., & Mollon, J. D. (1983). Human visual pigments: Microspectrophotometric results from the eyes of seven persons. Proceedings of the Royal Society of London, 220B, 115–130.

Darwin, C. (1859). On the origin of species by means of natural selection. London: Murray.

Davidson R. J. (1993). Cerebral asymmetry and emotion: Conceptual and methodological conundrums. Cognition and Emotion, 7, 115–138.

Davies, P. (1992). The mind of God: The scientific basic for a rational world. New York: Simon & Schuster.

Davies, P. (1999). The fifth miracle: The search for the origin and meaning of life. New York: Simon & Schuster.

Davies, P. (2004, April 14). Into the 21st century. Metaviews (www.metanexus.net).

Davis, J. L., & Rusbult, C. (2001). Attitude alignment in close relationships. Journal of Personality and Social Psychology, 81, 65–84.

Dawkins, R. (1998). Unweaving the rainbow. Boston: Houghton Mifflin.

Dearborn, G. V. N. (1912). Review of biological aspects of human problems. The Journal of Abnormal Psychology, 7, 382–383.

DeCasper, A. J., & Fifer, W. P. (1980). Of human bonding: Newborns prefer their mothers' voices. Science, 208(4448), 1174–1176. doi:10.1126/science.7375928

DeCasper, A. J., & Spence, M. J. (1986). Prenatal maternal speech influences newborns' perception of speech sounds. Infant Behavior & Development, 9(2), 133–150. doi:10.1016/0163-6383(86)90025-1

DeCasper, H. S. (1986). A state-wide survey of teacher use of narrative test report forms for instructional decision-making. ProQuest Information & Learning). Dissertation Abstracts International, 46 (7-A), 1912–1912. (Electronic; Print). (1986-54024-001)

DeGroot, G. J. (2006). Dark side of the moon: The magnificent madness of the American lunar quest. New York: New York University Press.

Descartes, R. (2003). Treatise of man. (T. S. Hall, Trans.) New York: Prometheus Books. (Original work published 1662).

Deutsch, D. (1974). An auditory illusion. Nature, 251, 307–309.

Deutsch, D. (1995). Musical illusions and paradoxes [CD]. La Jolla, CA: Philomel Records.

DeValois, R. L., & DeValois, K. K. (1975). Neural coding of color. In E. C. Carterette & M. P. Friedman (Eds.), Handbook of perception, Vol. 5 (pp. 117–166). New York: Academic Press.

Devane, W. A., Hanus, L., Breuer, A., Pertwee, R. G., Stevenson, I. A., Griffin, G., Gibson, D., Mandelbaum, A., Etinger, A., & Mechoulam, R. (1992). Isolation and structure of a brain constituent that binds to the cannabinoid receptor. Science, 258, 1946–1949.

Dey, E. L., Astin, A. W., & Korn, W. S. (1991). The American freshman: Twenty-five year trends. Los Angeles: Higher Education Research Institute, UCLA.

Dhawan, N., Roseman, I. J., Naidu, R. K., & Rettek, S. I. (1995). Self-concepts across two cultures: India and the United States. Journal of Cross-Cultural Psychology, 26(6), 606–621.

Dhawan, N., Roseman, I. J., Naidu, R. K., & Rettek, S. I. (1995). Self-concepts across two cultures: India and the United States. Journal of Cross-Cultural Psychology, 26(6), 606–621.

Diamond, J. (2001, February). A tale of two reputations: Why we revere Darwin and give Freud a hard time. Natural History, 20–24.

Diamond, M. (1997). Sexual identity and sexual orientation in children with traumatized or ambiguous genitalia. Journal of Sex Research, 34, 199–211.

Diamond, M., & Watson, L. A. (2004). Androgen insensitivity syndrome and Klinefelter's syndrome: Sex and gender considerations. Child and Adolescent Psychiatric Clinics of North America, 13, 623–640.

Diener, E., Diener, M., & Diener, C. (1995). Factors predicting the subjective well-being of nations. Journal of Personality and Social Psychology, 69(5), 851–864.

Diener, E., Diener, M., & Diener, C. (1995). Factors predicting the subjective well-being of nations. Journal of Personality and Social Psychology, 69(5), 851–864.

DiLalla, D. L., Carey, G., Gottesman, I. I., & Bouchard, T. J., Jr. (1996). Heritability of MMPI personality indicators of psychopathology in twins reared apart. Journal of Abnormal Psychology, 105(4), 491–499.

DiLalla, D. L., Carey, G., Gottesman, I. I., & Bouchard, T. J., Jr. (1996). Heritability of MMPI personality indicators of psychopathology in twins reared apart. Journal of Abnormal Psychology, 105(4), 491–499.

Diller, L. H. (2006). The last normal child: Essays on the intersection of kids, culture, and psychiatric drugs. Westport, CT: Praeger.

Dindia, K., & Allen, M. (1992). Sex differences in self-disclosure: A meta-analysis. Psychological Bulletin, 112(1), 106–124.

Dindia, K., & Allen, M. (1992). Sex differences in self-disclosure: A meta-analysis. Psychological Bulletin, 112(1), 106–124.

Dion, K. (2003). Prejudice, racism, and discrimination. In T. Millon & M. Lerner (Eds.), Handbook of psychology: Vol. 5: Personality and social psychology (pp.507–536). Dion, K.K. (1972). Physical attractiveness and evaluations of children's transgressions. Journal of Personality and Social Psychology, 24, 207–213.

Dion, K. K., & Dion, K. L. (1993). Individualistic and collectivistic perspectives on gender and the cultural context of love and intimacy. Journal of Social Issues, 49(3), 53–69.

Dion, K. K., & Dion, K. L. (1993). Individualistic and collectivistic perspectives on gender and the cultural context of love and intimacy. Journal of Social Issues, 49(3), 53–69.

Dion, K. K., & Dion, K. L. (2001). Gender and cultural adaptation in immigrant families. Journal of Social Issues, 57(3), 511–521.

Dion, K. K., & Dion, K. L. (2001). Gender and cultural adaptation in immigrant families. Journal of Social Issues, 57(3), 511–521.

Doetsch, F., & Hen, R. (2005). Young and excitable: The function of new neurons in the adult mammalian brain. Current Opinion in Neuroscience, 15, 121–128.

Dollard, J., Doob, L. W., Miller, N. E.. Mowrer, 0. H.. & Sears, R. R. (1939). Frustration and aggression. New Haven, CT: Yale University Press.

Dowd, M. (1984, March 12). Twenty years after the murder of Kitty Genovese, the question remains: Why? New York Times, pp. B1, B4.

Du Bois, N. F., & Brown, F. L. (1973). Selected relationships between Frostig scores and reading achievement in a first grade population. Perceptual and Motor Skills, 37(2), 515–519.

Eagly, A. H., & Johnson, B. T. (1990). Gender and leadership style: A meta-analysis. Psychological Bulletin, 108(2), 233–256.

Eagly, A. H., & Wood, W. (1999). The origins of sex differences in human behavior: Evolved dispositions versus social roles. American Psychologist, 54(6), 408–423.

Ebbesen, E. B., Kjos, G. L., & Konecni, V. J. (1976). Spatial ecology: Its effect on the choice of friends and enemies. Journal of Experimental Social Psychology, 12, 505–518.

Eddy, N. B., Halbach, H., Isbell, H. & Seevers, M. H. (1965). Drug dependence: Its significance and characteristics. Bulletin of the World Health Organization, 32, 721–733.

Ehrenreich, B. (2001). Nickel and dimed: On not getting by in America. New York: Henry Holt and Company.

Einstein, G. (2007). Sex and the brain. Cambridge, MA: MIT Press.

Eisenberg, N., Cumberland, A., & Spinrad, T. L. (1998). Parental socialization of emotion. Psychological Inquiry, 9(4), 241–273.

Eisenberg, N., Spinrad, T. L., & Cumberland, A. (1998). The socialization of emotion: Reply to commentaries. Psychological Inquiry, 9(4), 317–333.

Elbert, T., Pantev, C., Wienbruch, C., Rockstroh, B., & Taub, E. (1995). Increased cortical representation of the fingers of the left hand in string players. Science, 270, 305–307.

Elkind, D. (1985). Egocentrism redux. Developmental Review, 5(3), 218–226. doi:10.1016/0273-2297(85)90010-3

Ellis, B. J., McFadyen-Ketchum, S., Dodge, K. A., Pettit, G. S., & Bates, J. E. (1999). Quality of early family relationships and individual differences in the timing of pubertal maturation in girls: A longitudinal test of an evolutionary model. Journal of Personality and Social Psychology, 77(2), 387–401. doi:10.1037/0022-3514.77.2.387

Ellyson, S., Kestner, J., Haynes, V. F., Coldren, J. T., Ragozzine, F., Fry, R., & Beckett, P. (2008). General Psychology (3rd ed.). Dubuque, IA: Kendall-Hunt.

Embretson, S. E. (2010). Measuring psychological constructs: Advances in model-based approaches. Washington, DC: American Psychological Association.

Emde, R. N., Plomin, R., Robinson, J., & Corley, R. (1992). Temperament, emotion, and cognition at fourteen months: The MacArthur longitudinal twin study. Child Development, 63(6), 1437–1455.

Engel, G. L. (1977). The need for a new medical model: A challenge for biomedicine. Science, 196, 129–136.

Ephraim, D. (2000). Culturally relevant research and practice with the Rorschach comprehensive system Iberoamerica. In R. H. Dana (Ed.), Handbook of cross-cultural and multicultural personality assessment (pp. 303–327). Mahwah, NJ: Erlbaum.

Epstein, S. (1979). The stability of behavior: I. On predicting most of the people much of the time. Journal of Personality and Social Psychology, 37, 1097–1126.

Epstein, S. (1980). The stability of behavior: II. Implications for psychological research. American Psychologist, 35, 790–806.

Erikson, E. H. (1950). Childhood and society. New York, NY, US: W W Norton & Co.

Erikson, E. H. (1950). Growth and crises of the "healthy personality.". Oxford, England: Josiah Macy, Jr. Foundation.

Ewing, J. A. (1977). A biopsychosocial look at drinking and alcoholism. Journal of the American College Health Association, 25, 204–208.

Eysenck, H. J. (1967). The biological basis of personality. Springfield, IL: Charles C. Thomas (Revised, 1977).

Fabrigar, L. R., MacDonald, T. K., & Wegner, D. T. (2005). The structure of attitudes. In D. Albanacin, B. T. Johnson, & M. P. Zanna (Eds.), Handbook of attitudes (pp. 79–124).

Fantz, R. L. (1961). A method for studying depth perception in infants under six months of age. The Psychological Record, 11, 27–32.

Fantz, R. L. (1961). The origin of form perception. Scientific American, 204(5), 66–72.

Fantz, R. L. (1964). Visual experience in infants: Decreased attention familiar patterns relative to novel ones. Science, 146(Whole No. 3644), 668–670. doi:10.1126/science.146.3644.668

Faraone, S. V., Biederman, J., & Friedman, D. (2000). Validity of DSM-IV subtypes of attention-deficit/hyperactivity disorder: A family study perspective. Journal of the American Academy of Child & Adolescent Psychiatry, 39(3), 300–307. doi:10.1097/00004583-200003000-00011

Faraone, S. V., Biederman, J., Lehman, B. K., & Keenan, K. (1993). Evidence for the independent familial transmission of attention deficit hyperactivity disorder and learning disabilities: Results from a family genetic study. The American Journal of Psychiatry, 150(6), 891–895.

Fegley, D., Kathuria, S., Mercier, R., Li, C., Goutopoulos, A., Makriyannis, A., & Piomelli, D. (2004). Anandamide transport is independent of fatty-acid amide hydrolase activity and is blocked by the hydrolysis-resistant inhibitor. Proceeding of the National Academy of Science, USA, 101, 8756–8761.

Feinfield, K. A., Lee, P. P., Flavell, E. R., Green, F. L., & Flavell, J. H. (1999). Young children's understanding of intention. Cognitive Development, 14(3), 463–486. doi:10.1016/S0885-2014(99)00015-5

Feldman, D. H. (2003). Cognitive development in childhood. In R. M. Lerner, M. A. Easterbrooks & J. Mistry (Eds.), Handbook of psychology: Developmental psychology, vol. 6. (pp. 195–210). Hoboken, NJ, US: John Wiley & Sons Inc.

Feldman, H., Levy, A. R., Hsiung, G. -., Peters, K. R., Donald, A., Black, S. E., Bouchard, R. W., Gauthier, S. G., Guzman, D. A., Hogan, D. B., Kertesz, A., & Rockwood, K. (2003). A Canadian cohort study of cognitive impairment and related dementias (ACCORD): Study methods and baseline results. Neuroepidemiology, 22(5), 265–274. doi:10.1159/000071189

Feldman, R., & Eidelman, A. I. (2003). Direct and indirect effects of breast milk on neurobehavioral and cognitive development of premature infants. Developmental Psychobiology, 43(2), 109–119. doi:10.1002/dev.10126

Felleman, D. J., & Van Essen, D.C. (1991). Distributed hierarchical processing in the primate cerebral cortex. Cerebral Cortex, 1, 1–47.

Feshbach, S. (1984). The catharsis hypothesis, aggressive drive, and the reduction of aggression. Aggressive Behavior; 10, 91–101.

Festinger, L. (1957). A theory of cognitive dissonance. Stanford, CA: Stanford University Press.

Field, T. (2001). Massage therapy facilitates weight gain in preterm infants. Current Directions in Psychological Science, 10(2), 51–54.

Field, T., Hernandez-Reif, M., Feijo, L., & Freedman, J. (2006). Prenatal, perinatal and neonatal stimulation: A survey of neonatal nurseries. Infant Behavior and Development, 29, 24–31.

Fishbein, M., & Ajzen, I. (1974). Attitudes toward objects as predictors of single and multiple behavioral criteria. Psychological Review 81, 59–74.

Fivush, R. (1996). Young children's event recall: Are memories constructed through discourse?. San Diego, CA, US: Academic Press.

Fivush, R. (2004). The silenced self: Constructing self from memories spoken and unspoken. In D. R. Beike, J. M. Lampinen & D. A. Behrend (Eds.), The self and memory. (pp. 75–93). New York, NY, US: Psychology Press.

Fivush, R. (2004). Voice and silence: A feminist model of autobiographical memory. In J. M. Lucariello, J. A. Hudson, R. Fivush & P. J. Bauer (Eds.), The development of the mediated mind: Sociocultural context and cognitive development. (pp. 79–99). Mahwah, NJ, US: Lawrence Erlbaum Associates Publishers.

Fivush, R., & Edwards, V. J. (2004). Remembering and forgetting childhood sexual abuse. Journal of Child Sexual Abuse, 13(2), 1–19. doi:10.1300/J070v13n02_01

Fivush, R., & Nelson, K. (2004). Culture and language in the emergence of autobiographical memory. Psychological Science, 15(9), 573–577. doi:10.1111/j.0956-7976.2004.00722.x

Fivush, R., & Sales, J. M. (2004). Children's memories of emotional events. In D. Reisberg, & P. Hertel (Eds.), Memory and emotion. (pp. 242–271). New York, NY, US: Oxford University Press.

Fivush, R., Bohanek, J., Robertson, R., & Duke, M. (2004). Family narratives and the development of children's emotional well-being. In M. W. Pratt, & B. H. Fiese (Eds.), Family stories and the life course: Across time and generations. (pp. 55–76). Mahwah, NJ, US: Lawrence Erlbaum Associates Publishers.

Fivush, R., Haden, C., & Reese, E. (1996). Remembering, recounting, and reminiscing: The development of autobiographical memory in social context. In D. C. Rubin (Ed.), Remembering our past: Studies in autobiographical memory. (pp. 341–359). New York, NY, US: Cambridge University Press.

Fivush, R., Sales, J. M., Goldberg, A., Bahrick, L., & Parker, J. (2004). Weathering the storm: Children's long-term recall of hurricane Andrew. Memory, 12(1), 104–118. doi:10.1080/09658210244000397

Flannery, S. (2001). In code: A mathematical journey. Chapel Hill, NC: Algonquin Books of Chapel Hill.

Flavell, J. H. (1999). Cognitive development: Children's knowledge about the mind. Annual Review of Psychology, 50, 21–45. doi:10.1146/annurev.psych.50.1.21

Flavell, J. H., & Green, F. L. (1999). Development of intuitions about the controllability of different mental states. Cognitive Development, 14(1), 133–146. doi:10.1016/S0885-2014(99)80021-5

Flavell, J. H., Green, F. L., Flavell, E. R., & Lin, N. T. (1999). Development of children's knowledge about unconsciousness. Child Development, 70(2), 396–412. doi:10.1111/1467-8624.00029

Foster, J. D., Campbell, W. K., & Twenge, J. M. (2003). Individual differences in narcissism: Inflated self-views across the lifespan and around the world. Journal of Research in Personality, 37(6), 469–486.

Franzoi, S. (2003). Social psychology (3rd ed.). New York: McGraw-Hill.

Freud, S. (1920). A general introduction to psychoanalysis. New York: Boni & Liveright.

Funder, D. C., & Ozer, D. J. (1983). Behavior as a function of the situation. Journal of Personality and Social Psychology, 44, 107–112.

Gabbay, F. H. (1992). Behavior-genetic strategies in the study of emotion. Psychological Science, 3(1), 50–55.

Galanter, E. (1962). Contemporary psychophysics. in R. Brown, E. Galanter, E. H. Hess, & G. Mandler (Eds.). New directions in psychology (pp. 87–157). New York: Holt, Rinehart, & Winston.

Galileo Galilei, 3/30/09, Retrieved April 3, 2009, from Wikipedia: http://en.wikipedia.org/wiki/Galileo_Galilei

Gallistel, C. R., & Gibbon, J. (2002). The symbolic foundations of conditioned behavior. Mahwah, NJ: Lawrence Erlbaum Associates.

Ganchrow, J. R., Steiner, J. E., & Daher, M. (1983). Neonatal facial expressions in response to different qualities and intensities of gustatory stimuli. Infant Behavior & Development, 6(4), 473–484. doi:10.1016/S0163-6383(83)90301-6

Gangestad, S. W., & Simpson, J. A. (2000). The evolution of human mating: Trade-offs and strategic pluralism. Behavioral and Brain Sciences, 23(4), 573–644.

Gazzaniga, M. S. (1992). Nature's mind: The biological roots of thinking, emotions, sexuality, language, and intelligence. New York, NY, US: Basic Books.

Geary, D. C. (1998). Male, female: The evolution of human sex differences. Washington, DC, US: American Psychological Association.

Gilligan, C. (. (., Lyons, N. P. (., & Hanmer, T. J. (. (Eds.). (1990). Making connections: The relational worlds of adolescent girls at Emma Willard school. Cambridge, MA, US: Harvard University Press.

Gilligan, C. (1982). New maps of development: New visions of maturity. American Journal of Orthopsychiatry, 52(2), 199–212.

Gilligan, C. (1993). In a different voice: Psychological theory and women's development. Cambridge, MA, US: Harvard University Press.

Gilligan, C. (1993). In a different voice: Psychological theory and women's development. Cambridge, MA, US: Harvard University Press.

Goerke, M., Moller, J., Schulz-Hardt, S.. Napiersky, U., & Frey, D. (2004). "It's not my fault-but only I can change it": Counterfactual and prefactual thoughts of managers. Journal of Applied Psychology, 89, 279–292.

Goldberg, L. R. (1981). Language and individual differences: The search for universals in personality lexicons. In L. Wheeler (Ed.), Review of personality and social psychology (Vol. 2, pp. 14 1–165). Beverly Hills, CA: Sage.

Goldstein, S. (1997). Managing attention and learning disorders in late adolescence and adulthood: A guide for practitioners. Oxford, England: John Wiley & Sons.

Goodale, M. A., & Humphrey, G. K. (1998). The objects of action and perception. Cognition, 67, 181–207.

Gopnik, A., & Schulz, L. (Eds.). (2007). Causal learning: Psychology, philosophy, and computation. New York: Oxford University Press.

Graber, D. R., & Sloane, P. D. (1995). Nursing home survey deficiencies for physical restraint use. Medical Care, 33(10), 1051–1063. doi:10.1097/00005650-199510000-00006

Graber, J. A., & Brooks-Gunn, J. (1995). Models of development: Understanding risk in adolescence. Suicide and Life-Threatening Behavior, 25(Suppl), 18–25.

Graber, J. A., Brooks-Gunn, J., & Warren, M. P. (1995). The antecedents of menarcheal age: Heredity, family environment, and stressful life events. Child Development, 66(2), 346–359. doi:10.2307/1131582

Graber, K. C. (1995). The influence of teacher education programs on the beliefs of student teachers: General pedagogical knowledge, pedagogical content knowledge, and teacher education course work. Journal of Teaching in Physical Education, 14(2), 157–178.

Granrud, C. E. (2006). Size constancy in infants: 4-month-olds' responses to physical versus retinal image size. Journal of Experimental Psychology: Human Perception and Performance, 32, 1398–1404.

Greenough, W. T., & Volkmar, F. R. (1973). Pattern of dendritic branching in occipital cortex of rats reared in complex environments. Experimental Neurology, 40, 491–504.

Greenough, W. T., Black, J. E., & Wallace, C. S. (1987). Experience and brain development. Child Development, 58(3), 539–559.

Gregory, R. L. (1970). The intelligent eye. New York: McGraw-Hill.

Gregory, R. L. (1978). Eye and brain: The psychology of seeing (3rd edition). New York: McGraw-Hill.

Grusec, J. E., Davidov, M., & Lundell, L. (2002). Prosocial and helping behavior. In P. K. Smith & C. H. Hart (Eds.), Blackwell handbook of childhood social development (pp. 457–474). Malden, MA: Blackwell.

Haden, C. A., & Fivush, R. (1996). Contextual variation in maternal conversational styles. Merrill-Palmer Quarterly: Journal of Developmental Psychology, 42(2), 200–227.

Haden, C. A., Reese, E., & Fivush, R. (1996). Mothers' extratextual comments during storybook reading: Stylistic differences over time and across texts. Discourse Processes, 21(2), 135–169.

Hall, C. S. (1954). A primer of Freudian psychology. New York: World.

Hall, C. S., Lindzey, G., & Campbell. J. B. (1998). Theories of personality. New York: Wiley.

Hall, J. A. (1987). On explaining gender differences: The case of nonverbal communication. In P. Shaver, & C. Hendrick (Eds.), Sex and gender. (pp. 177–200). Thousand Oaks, CA, US: Sage Publications, Inc.

Harlow, H. F. (1958). The nature of love. American Psychologist, 13(12), 673–685. doi:10.1037/h0047884

Harris, J. R. (1998). The nurture assumption: Why children turn out the way they do. New York, NY, US: Free Press.

Harris, J. R. (2000). Socialization, personality development, and the child's environments: Comment on Vandell (2000). Developmental Psychology, 36(6), 711–723.

Harris, J. R. (2006). No two alike: Human nature and human individuality. New York, NY, US: W W Norton & Co.

Harris, L., & Jenkin, M. (Eds.). (2007). Computational vision in neural and machine systems. Cambridge: Cambridge University Press.

Hazan, C., & Shaver, P. (1987). Romantic love conceptualized as an attachment process. Journal of Personality and Social Psychology, 52(3), 511–524. doi:10.1037/0022-3514.52.3.511

Hechtman, L., Weiss, G., & Perlman, T. (1984). Hyperactives as young adults: Past and current substance abuse and antisocial behavior. American Journal of Orthopsychiatry, 54(3), 415–425.

Heiberger, M. M., & Vick, J. M. (1992). The academic job search handbook. Philadelphia: University of Pennsylvania Press.

Heider, F. (1958). The psychology of interpersonal relations. New York: Wiley.

Heinicke, C. M., Goorsky, M., Moscov, S., Dudley, K., Gordon, J., Schneider, C., & Guthrie, D. (2000). Relationship-based intervention with at-risk mothers: Factors affecting variations in outcome. Infant Mental Health Journal, 21(3), 133–155. doi:10.1002/1097-0355(200007)21:3<133::AID-IMHJ1>3.0.CO;2-P

Hemmes, N. S., Brown, B. L., Jakubow, J. J., & Cabeza de Vaca, S. (1997). Determinants of response recovery in extinction following response elimination. Learning and Motivation, 28, 542–557.

Herrnstein, R. J., & Murray, C. A. (1994). The bell curve: Intelligence and class structure in American life. New York, NY, US: Free Press.

Higgins, S. T., & Silverman, K. (Eds.). (1999). Motivating behavior change among illicit-drug abusers: Research on contingency management interventions. Washington, D.C.: American Psychological Association.

Hines, M. (2004). Brain gender. New York, NY, US: Oxford University Press.

Hines, M., & Green, R. J. (1991). Human hormonal and neural correlates of sex-typed behaviors. In A. Tasman, & S. M. Goldfinger (Eds.), American psychiatric press review of psychiatry, vol. 10. (pp. 536–555). Washington, DC, US: American Psychiatric Association.

Hock, R. R. (2009). Forty studies that changed psychology: Explorations into the history of psychological research. (6th ed.). Upper Saddle River, NJ: Pearson.

Hodson, D. S., & Skeen, P. (1994). Sexuality and aging: The hammerlock of myths. Journal of Applied Gerontology, 13(3), 219–235. doi:10.1177/073346489401300301

Hogan, R. (1983). A socioanalytic theory of personality. In M. Page & R. Dienstbeir (Eds.), Nebraska Symposium on Motivation, 1982 (pp. 55–89). Lincoln: University of Nebraska Press.

Holden, C. (1980). Identical twins reared apart. Science, 207(4437), 1323–1328.

Howe, M. L., & O'Sullivan, J. T. (1990). The development of strategic memory: Coordinating knowledge, meta-memory, and resources. In D. F. Bjorklund (Ed.), Children's strategies: Contemporary views of cognitive development. (pp. 129–155). Hillsdale, NJ, England: Lawrence Erlbaum Associates, Inc.

Hubel, D. H., & Wiesel, T. N. (1962). Receptive fields, binocular interaction, and functional architecture in the cat's visual cortex. Journal of Physiology, 160, 106–154.

Hudson, J. A., Lucariello, J., Fivush, R., & Bauer, P. J. (2004). Katherine nelson's vision of the mediated mind. In J. M. Lucariello, J. A. Hudson, R. Fivush & P. J. Bauer (Eds.), The development of the mediated mind: Sociocultural context and cognitive development. (pp. 1–11). Mahwah, NJ, US: Lawrence Erlbaum Associates Publishers.

Huesmann, L. R., Moise-Titus, J., Podolski, C., & Eron, L. D. (2003). Longitudinal relations between children's exposure to TV violence and their aggressive and violent behavior in young adulthood: 1977–1992. Developmental Psychology, 39, 201–221.

Hunt, E. (2007). The mathematics of behavior. New York: Cambridge University Press.

Isen, A. M., & Levin, P. F. (1972). Effects of feeling good on helping: Cookies and kindness. Journal of Personality and Social Psychology, 21, 384–388.

Iversen, L. (2003). Cannabis and the brain. Brain, 126, 1252–1270.

Jaffe, J. H. (1985). Drug addiction and drug abuse. In L. S. Goodman & A. Gilman (Eds.). The pharmacological basis of therapeutics (Vol. 7). New York: Macmillan.

Jakubow, J. J. (2011, December 7). It's like reincarnation all over again [Review of the film Uncle Boonmee Who Can Recall His Past Lives]. PsycCRITIQUES—Contemporary Psychology: APA Review of Books, 56 (No. 49), Article 9. Retrieved [12/13/11], from the PsycCRITIQUES database.

Jakubow, J. J. (2010, September 8). Constructing the future constructs [Review of the book Measuring Psychological Constructs: Advances in Model-Based Approaches]. PsycCRITIQUES—Contemporary Psychology: APA Review of Books, 55 (No. 36), Article 1. Retrieved [12/14/10], from the PsycCRITIQUES database.

Jakubow, J. J. (2010, January 20). Communicating more effectively [Review of the book Communimetrics: A Communication Theory of Measurement in Human Service Settings]. PsycCRITIQUES—Contemporary

Psychology: APA Review of Books, 55 (No. 3), Article 7. Retrieved [2/13/10], from the PsycCRITIQUES database.

Jakubow, J. J. (2009, April 1). Everything you always wanted to know about fear but were afraid to ask [Review of the book Handbook of Anxiety and Fear]. PsycCRITIQUES—Contemporary Psychology: APA Review of Books, 54 (No. 13), Article 7. Retrieved [9/2/09], from the PsycCRITIQUES database.

Jakubow, J. J. (2008, August 27). Motoring our behavior [Review of the book A Theory of the Basal Ganglia and Their Disorders]. PsycCRITIQUES—Contemporary Psychology: APA Review of Books, 53 (No. 35), Article 8. Retrieved [9/2/09], from the PsycCRITIQUES database.

Jakubow, J. J. (2008, May 28). Finding out what really matters [Review of the book Causal Learning: Psychology, Philosophy, and Computation]. PsycCRITIQUES—Contemporary Psychology: APA Review of Books, 53 (No. 22), Article 8. Retrieved [9/2/09], from the PsycCRITIQUES database.

Jakubow, J. J. (2008). Quotation: Operant conditioning in popular scientific writing. Journal of the Experimental Analysis of Behavior, 89, 425.

Jakubow, J. J. (2008, January 23). Do behavioral researchers need one diploma in mathematics and another in psychology? [Review of the book Data Analytic Techniques for Dynamical Systems]. PsycCRITIQUES—Contemporary Psychology: APA Review of Books, 53 (No. 4), Article 10. Retrieved [1/27/08], from the PsycCRITIQUES database.

Jakubow, J. J. (2007, December 19). So shall we see the world with new eyes? [Review of the book Computational Vision in Neural and Machine Systems]. PsycCRITIQUES—Contemporary Psychology: APA Review of Books, 52 (No. 51), Article 7. Retrieved [12/31/07], from the PsycCRITIQUES database.

Jakubow, J. J. (2007, August 15). Self-help for the dually diagnosed [Review of the book Addiction and Mood Disorders: A Guide for Clients and Families]. PsycCRITIQUES—Contemporary Psychology: APA Review of Books, 52 (No. 33), Article 4. Retrieved [8/23/07], from the PsycCRITIQUES database.

Jakubow, J. J. (2007, August 8). Education, psychiatry and children: Explaining the social factors behind the next public health threat [Review of the book The Last Normal Child: Essays on the Intersection of Kids, Culture, and Psychiatric Drugs]. PsycCRITIQUES—Contemporary Psychology: APA Review of Books, 52 (No. 32), Article 11. Retrieved [8/8/2007], from the PsycCRITIQUES database.

Jakubow, J. J. (2007). Review of the book Sniffy the Virtual Rat Pro Version 2.0. Journal of the Experimental Analysis of Behavior, 87, 317–323.

Jakubow, J. J. (2007, January 3). Integrating the data, models and theory of psychophysics [Review of the book Relational Psychophysics in Humans and Animals: A Comparative Developmental Approach]. PsycCRITIQUES—Contemporary Psychology: APA Review of Books, 52 (No. 1), Article 17. Retrieved [1/9/2007], from the PsycCRITIQUES database.

Jakubow, J. J. (2006, October 11). Economics, religion and racism: The rise and fall of the Incan drinking ritual [Review of the book Holy intoxication to drunken dissipation: Alcohol among Quichua speakers in Otavalo, Ecuador]. PsycCRITIQUES—Contemporary Psychology: APA Review of Books, 51 (No. 41), Article 8. Retrieved [11/01/2006], from the PsycCRITIQUES database.

Jakubow, J. J., Brown, B. L., & Hemmes, N. S. (2004). The cover-stimulus effect: Role of similarity in durations of the CS and cover cues. Psychological Record, 54, 293–317.

Jakubow, J. J. (2001). Quotation: Hermann Melville on stimulus dimension contrast. Journal of the Experimental Analysis of Behavior, 75, 298.

Jakubow, J. J. (2000). Introduction to canine behavioral pharmacology. In R. DeFranco (Ed.), Companion animal behavior counseling: A manual for applied practitioners. (Available from the American Institute for Animal Science, PO Box 7623, Rego Park, NY 11374–7623)

Jakubow, J. J. (2000). Clinical applications of behavioral pharmacology in canines. In R. DeFranco (Ed.), Companion animal behavior counseling: A manual for applied practitioners. (Available from the American Institute for Animal Science, PO Box 7623, Rego Park, NY 11374–7623)

Jakubow, J., Schlinger, H., & Poling, A. (1989). Pentylenetetrazol-induced seizures in pigeons and the effects of ethosuximide thereon. Pharmacology, Biochemistry and Behavior, 33, 11–15.

Jardine, L. (2003). The curious life of Robert Hooke: The man who measured London. New York: Perennial.

Jensen, A. R. (1969). How much can we boost IQ and scholastic achievement? Harvard Educational Review, 39(1), 1–123.

Johnson, C. B., Stockdale, M. S., & Saal, F. E. (1991). Persistence of men's misperceptions of friendly cues across a variety of interpersonal encounters. Psychology of Women Quarterly, 15(3), 463–475.

Jones, E. E., & Davis, K. E. (1965). A theory of correspondent inferences: From acts to dispositions. In L. Berkowitz (Ed.), Advances in experimental social psychology (Vol. 2, pp. 249–315). New York: Academic Press.

Joseph, J. (2001). Separated twins and the genetics of personality differences: A critique. American Journal of Psychology, 114(1), 1–30.

Juffer, F., & Rosenboom, L. G. (1997). Infant–mother attachment of internationally adopted children in the netherlands. International Journal of Behavioral Development, 20(1), 93–107. doi:10.1080/016502597385469

Kagan, J., & Snidman, N. (2004). The long shadow of temperament. Cambridge, MA, US: Belknap Press/Harvard University Press.

Kagan, J., Arcus, D., Snidman, N., Feng, W. Y., Hendler, J., & Greene, S. (1994). Reactivity in infants: A cross-national comparison. Developmental Psychology, 30(3), 342–345.

Kagan, J., Snidman, N., & Arcus, D. M. (1992). Initial reactions to unfamiliarity. Current Directions in Psychological Science, 1(6), 171–174.

Kalff, A. C., Kroes, M., Vles, J. S. H., Hendriksen, J. G. M., Feron, F. J. M., Steyaert, J., et al. (2001). Neighbourhood level and individual level SES effects on child problem behaviour: A multilevel analysis. Journal of Epidemiology & Community Health, 55(4), 246–250.

Kandel, E. R. (2006). In search of memory: The emergence of a new science of mind. New York: W. W. Norton and Company.

Kantowitz, B. H., Roediger III, H. L., & Elmes, D. G. (1994). Experimental psychology: Understanding psychological research. New York: West Publishing Company

Kaplan (2002). The real Dr. Frankenstein: Christian Gottlieb Kratzenstein? Journal of the Royal Society of Medicine, 95, 577–578.

Karni, A., Meyer, G., Rey-Hipolito, C., Jezzard, P., Adams, M. M., Turner, R., & Ungerleider, L. G. (1998). The acquisition of skilled motor performance: Fast and slow experience-driven changes in primary motor cortex. Proceedings of the National Academy of Sciences, 95, 861–868.

Kashima, Y., Siegal, M., Tanaka, K., & Kashima, E. S. (1992). Do people believe behaviours are consistent with attitudes? towards a cultural psychology of attribution processes. British Journal of Social Psychology, 31(2), 111–124.

Kastenbaum, R., & Costa, P. T. (1977). Psychological perspectives on death. Annual Review of Psychology, 28, 225–249. doi:10.1146/annurev.ps.28.020177.001301

Kather, R., Chesnut, E., & Ellyson, S. L. (2000). Is professional wrestling becoming more violent? Perception versus reality. Proceedings and Abstracts of the 2000 Annual Meeting of the Eastern Psychological Association, Vol. 71, Glassboro, NJ.

Kaufman, L., & Rock, 1. (1962). The moon illusion. Scientific American, 207, 120–132.

Kelley, H. H. (1972). Attribution in social interaction. In E. E. Jones et al. (Eds.), Attribution: Perceiving the causes of behavior (pp. 125–161). Morristown, NJ: General Learning Press.

Kelley, J., & De Graaf, N. D. (1997). National context, parental socialization, and religious belief: Results from 15 nations. American Sociological Review, 62(4), 639–659.

Kenrick, D. T., & Stringfiekl, D. 0. (1980). Personality traits and the eye of the beholder: Crossing some traditional philosophical boundaries in the search for consistency in all the people. Psychological Review, 87, 88–104.

Kenrick, D. T., & Trost, M. R. (1987). A biosocial theory of heterosexual relationships. In K. Kelley (Ed.), Females, males, and sexuality: Theories and research. (pp. 59–100). Albany, NY, US: State University of New York Press.

Keririck, D. T., Nueberg, S., & Cialdini, R. B. (2005). Social psychology: Unraveling the mystery (3rd ed.). Boston: Pearson.

Kermoian, R., & Leiderman, P. H. (1986). Infant attachment to mother and child caretaker in an east african community. International Journal of Behavioral Development, Special Issue: Cross-Cultural Human Development, 9(4), 455–469.

Kessel, R. G., & Kardon, R. H. (1979). Tissues and organs: A text-atlas of scanning electron microscopy. San Francisco, CA: W. H. Freeman.

Kim, H., & Markus, H. R. (1999). Deviance or uniqueness, harmony or conformity? A cultural analysis. Journal of Personality and Social Psychology, 77(4), 785–800.

King, L. A. (2008). The science of psychology: An appreciative view. New York: McGraw-Hill.

Kitayama, S., & Markus, H. R. (2000). The pursuit of happiness and the realization of sympathy: Cultural patterns of self, social relations, and well-being. In E. Diener, & E. M. Suh (Eds.), Culture and subjective well-being. (pp. 113–161). Cambridge, MA, US: The MIT Press.

Koenig, L. B., McGue, M., Krueger, R. F., & Bouchard, T. J., Jr. (2005). Genetic and environmental influences on religiousness: Findings for retrospective and current religiousness ratings. Journal of Personality, 73(2), 471–488.

Kolb, B., & Whishaw, I. Q. (1998). Brain plasticity and behavior. Annual Review of Psychology, 49, 43–64.

Komisaruk, B. R., Beyer-Flores, C., & Whipple, B. (2006). The science of orgasm. Baltimore: The Johns Hopkins University Press.

Korn, S. J. (1984). Continuities and discontinuities in difficult/easy temperament: Infancy to young adulthood. Merrill-Palmer Quarterly: Journal of Developmental Psychology, 30(2), 189–199.

Kosslyn, S. M., & Rosenberg, R. S. (2006). Psychology in context (3rd ed.). New York: Pearson.

Kowalski, R., & Westen, D. (2009). Psychology. Hoboken, NJ: John Wiley & Sons.

Kramer, H. & Sprenger, J. (1487/2007). The malleus maleficarum. (M. Summers, Trans.). New York: Cosimo Classics.

Kranz, G. (2000). Failure is not an option: Mission control from Mercury to Apollo 13 and beyond. New York: Berkley Books.

Kulik, L. (2005). Intrafamiliar congruence in gender role attitudes and ethnic stereotypes: The Israeli case. Journal of Comparative Family Studies, 36, 289–303.

Landrum, R. E., & Davis, S. F. (2010). The psychology major: Career options and strategies for success (4th ed.). Upper Saddle River, NJ: Pearson.

Lapsley, D. K., Milstead, M., Quintana, S. M., Flannery, D., & Buss, R. R. (1986). Adolescent egocentrism and formal operations: Tests of a theoretical assumption. Developmental Psychology, 22(6), 800–807. doi:10.1037/0012-1649.22.6.800

Larsen, R. J., & Diener, E. (1987). Affect intensity as an individual difference characteristic: A review. Journal of Research in Personality, 21(1), 1–39.

Latane, B., & Darley, J. M. (1968). Group inhibition of bystander intervention. Journal of Personality and Social Psychology, 10, 21 5–221.

Lee, C. (1998). Alternatives to cognition: A new look at explaining human social behavior. Mahwah, New Jersey: Lawrence Erlbaum Associates

Lerner, M. J. (1980). The belief in a just world: A fundamental delusion. New York: Plenum.

Leventhal, T., & Brooks-Gunn, J. (2000). The neighborhoods they live in: The effects of neighborhood residence on child and adolescent outcomes. Psychological Bulletin, 126(2), 309–337.

Levine, R. V., & Norenzayan, A. (1999). The pace of life in 31 countries. Journal of Cross-Cultural Psychology, 30(2), 178–205.

Lilienfeld, S. O., Lynn, S. J., Namy, L. L., & Woolf, N. J. (2009). Psychology: From inquiry to understanding. New York: Pearson.

Lilienfeld, S. O., Lynn, S. J., Ruscio, J., & Beyerstein, B. L. (2010). 50 great myths of popular psychology: Shattering widespread misconceptions about human behavior. Malden, MA: Wiley-Blackwell

Lilienfeld, S. 0., Wood, J. M., & Garb, H. N. (2000, November). The scientific status or projective techniques. Psychological Science in the Public Interest, I(2).

Lipsitt, L. P., Kaye, H., & Bosack, T. N. (1966). Enhancement of neonatal sucking through reinforcement. Journal of Experimental Child Psychology, 4(2), 163–168. doi:10.1016/0022-0965(66)90016-6

Loehlin, J. C. (1992). Genes and environment in personality development. Newbury Park, CA: Sage.

Loehlin, J. C., Willerman, L., & Horn, J. M. (1985). Personality resemblances in adoptive families when the children are late-adolescent or adult. Journal of Personality and Social Psychology, 48, 376–392.

Longo, D. A., Lent, R. W., & Brown, S. D. (1992). Social cognitive variables in the prediction of client motivation & attribution. Journal of Counseling Psychology 39, 447–452.

Longuski, J. (2007). The seven secrets of how to think like a rocket scientist. New York: Copernicus Books.

Looy, H. (2001). Sex differences: Evolved, constructed, and designed. Journal of Psychology & Theology, Special Issue: Christianity and Evolutionary Psychology, 29(4), 301–313.

Lorenz, K. (1974). Civilized man's eight deadly sins. New York: Harcourt Brace Jovanovich.

Lucariello, Joan M. (Ed) (1), Hudson, Judith A. (Ed) (2), Fivush, R. (. (., & Bauer, P. J. (. (. (Eds.). (2004). The development of the mediated mind: Sociocultural context and cognitive development. Mahwah, NJ, US: Lawrence Erlbaum Associates Publishers.

Lütkenhaus, P., Grossmann, K. E., & Grossmann, K. (1985). Infant–mother attachment at twelve months and style of interaction with a stranger at the age of three years. Child Development, 56(6), 1538–1542. doi:10.2307/1130472

Lykken, D. T., Bouchard, T. J., Jr., McGue, M., & Tellegen, A. (1993). Heritability of interests: A twin study. Journal of Applied Psychology, 78, 649–661.

Lyons, J. S. (2009). Communimetrics: A communication theory of measurement in humans service settings. New York: Springer.

Lysak, H., Rule, B. G., & Dobbs, A. R. (1989). Conceptions of aggression: Prototype or defining features? Personality and Social Psychology Bulletin, 15, 233–243.

Lytton, H., & Romney, D. M. (1991). Parents' differential socialization of boys and girls: A meta-analysis. Psychological Bulletin, 109(2), 267–296.

Maccoby, E. E. (1990). Gender and relationships: A developmental account. American Psychologist, 45(4), 513–520.

Maccoby, E. E. (1995). Divorce and custody: The rights, needs, and obligations of mothers, fathers, and children. In G. B. Melton (Ed.), The individual, the family, and social good: Personal fulfillment in times of change. (pp. 135–172). Lincoln, NE, US: University of Nebraska Press.

Maccoby, E. E. (1998). The two sexes: Growing up apart, coming together. Cambridge, MA, US: Belknap Press/Harvard University Press.

Macrae, C. N., Stangor, C., & Hewstone, M. (Eds.). (1996). Stereotypes and stereotyping. New York: Guilford Press.

Maddi, S. R. (1972). Personality theories: A comparative analysis. Homewood, IL: The Dorsey Press.

Maestripieri, D. (2003). Similarities in affiliation and aggression between cross-fostered rhesus macaque females and their biological mothers. Developmental Psychobiology, 43(4), 321–327.

Maguire, E. A., Gadian, D. G., Johnsrude, I. S., Good, C. D., Ashburner, J., Frackowiak, R. S, J., & Frith, C. D. (2000). Navigation-related structural change in the hippocampi of taxi drivers. Proceedings of the National Academy of Sciences of the United States, 97, 4398–4403.

Main, M., & Cassidy, J. (1988). Categories of response to reunion with the parent at age 6: Predictable from infant attachment classifications and stable over a 1-month period. Developmental Psychology, 24(3), 415–426. doi:10.1037/0012-1649.24.3.415

Main, M., & Hesse, E. (1990). Parents' unresolved traumatic experiences are related to infant disorganized attachment status: Is frightened and/or frightening parental behavior the linking mechanism? In M. T. Greenberg, D. Cicchetti & E. M. Cummings (Eds.), Attachment in the preschool years: Theory, research, and intervention. (pp. 161–182). Chicago, IL, US: University of Chicago Press.

Main, M., & Solomon, J. (1990). Procedures for identifying infants as disorganized/disoriented during the ainsworth strange situation. In M. T. Greenberg, D. Cicchetti & E. M. Cummings (Eds.), Attachment in the preschool years: Theory, research, and intervention. (pp. 121–160). Chicago, IL, US: University of Chicago Press.

Major, B., Schmidlin, A. M., & Williams, L. (1990). Gender patterns in social touch: The impact of setting and age. Journal of Personality and Social Psychology, 58(4), 634–643.

Mak, M., & de Koning, P. (1995). Clinical research in aggressive patients, pitfalls in study design and measurement of aggression. Progress in Neuro-Psychopharmacology & Biological Psychiatry, 19, 993–1017.

Marcus, G. (2004). The birth of the mind: How a tiny number of genes creates the complexities of human thought. New York, NY, US: Basic Books.

Markus, H. R., & Kitayama, S. (1991). Culture and the self: Implications for cognition, emotion, and motivation. Psychological Review, 98(2), 224–253.

Martin, C. L., & Ruble, D. (2004). Children's search for gender cues: Cognitive perspectives on gender development. Current Directions in Psychological Science, 13(2), 67–70.

Martin, C. L., Ruble, D. N., & Szkrybalo, J. (2002). Cognitive theories of early gender development. Psychological Bulletin, 128(6), 903–933.

Masson, J. M. (1984). The assault on truth. New York: Farrar, Straus, & Giroux.

Matsui, Y. (1981). A structural analysis of helping. Japanese Journal of Psychology, 52, 22–32.

Maunsell, J. H., & Van Essen, D. C. (1983). Functional properties of neurons in middle temporal visual area of the macaque monkey. I. Selectivity for stimulus direction, speed, and orientation. Journal ofNeurophysiology, 49, 1127–1147.

McClelland, D. C. (1987). Human motivation. New York: Cambridge University Press.

McCrae, R. R., Costa, P. T., Jr., Ostendorf, F., Angleitner, A., Hfiebíãková, M., Avia, M. D., et al. (2000). Nature over nurture: Temperament, personality, and life span development. Journal of Personality and Social Psychology, 78(1), 173–186.

McCullough, D. (2005). 1776. New York: Simon and Schuster.

McGue, M., & Bouchard, T. J., Jr. (1998). Genetic and environmental influences on human behavioral differences. Annual Review of Neuroscience, 21, 1–24.

McGue, M., & Lykken, D. T. (1992). Genetic influence on risk of divorce. Psychological Science, 3, 368–373.

McGue, M., & Lykken, D. T. (1992). Genetic influence on risk of divorce. Psychological Science, 3(6), 368–373.

McGuire, W. J., McGuire, C. V., Child, P., & Fujioka, T. (1978). Salience of ethnicity in the spontaneous self-concept as a function of one's ethnic distinctiveness in the social environment. Journal of Personality and Social Psychology, 36(5), 511–520.

Megarry, T. (2001). Society in prehistory: The origins of human culture. New York: New York University Press.

Mehl, M. R., Vazire, S., Ramirez-Esparza, N., Slatcher, R. B., & Pennebaker, J. W. (2007). Are women really more talkative than men? Science, 317, 82.

Melzack, R., & Wall, P. D. (1965). Pain mechanisms: A new theory. Science, 150, 971–979.

Milgram, S. (1974). Obedience to authority. New York: Harper & Row.

Miller, D. T., & Prentice, D. A. (1994). Collective errors and errors about the collective: Special Issue: The self and the collective. Personality and Social Psychology Bulletin, 20, 54 1–550.

Miller, L. C., Putcha-Bhagavatula, A., & Pedersen, W. C. (2002). Men's and women's mating preferences: Distinct evolutionary mechanisms? Current Directions in Psychological Science, 11(3), 88–93.

Miller, R. (2008). A theory of the basal ganglia and their disorders. New York: CRC Press.

Mischel, W. (1968). Personality and assessment. New York: Wiley.

Mischel, W., Shoda, Y., & Smith R. (2004). Introduction to personality toward an integration (7th ed.). New York: Wiley.

Moon, Y. (2003). Don't blame the computer: When self-disclosure moderates the self-serving bias. Journal of Consumer Psychology 13, 125–137.

Morelli, G. A., Rogoff, B., Oppenheim, D., & Goldsmith, D. (1992). Cultural variation in infants' sleeping arrangements: Questions of independence. Developmental Psychology, 28(4), 604–613.

Moskowitz, G. B. (2005). Social cognition: Understanding self and others. New York: Guilford Press.

Myers, D. G. (2000). The American paradox: Spiritual hunger in an age of plenty. New Haven, CT, US: Yale University Press.

Myers, D. G. (2002). Intuition: Its powers and perils. New Haven, CT, US: Yale University Press.

Myers, D. G. (2007). Psychology (8th ed.). New York: Worth.

Myers, D. G. (2008). A friendly letter to skeptics and atheists: Musings on why god is good and faith isn't evil. San Francisco, CA: Jossey-Bass.

Myers, D. G. (2010). Psychology (9th edition). New York: Worth.

Nadeau, K. G. (. (1995). A comprehensive guide to attention deficit disorder in adults: Research, diagnosis, and treatment. Philadelphia, PA, US: Brunner/Mazel.

Nell, V. (2002). Why young men drive dangerously: Implications for injury prevention. Current Directions in Psychological Science, 11(2), 75–79.

Nelson, K. (1993). The psychological and social origins of autobiographical memory. Psychological Science, 4(1), 7–14. doi:10.1111/j.1467-9280.1993.tb00548.x

Nelson, K., & Fivush, R. (2004). The emergence of autobiographical memory: A social cultural developmental theory. Psychological Review, 111(2), 486–511. doi:10.1037/0033-295X.111.2.486

Neubauer, P. B., & Neubauer, A. (1990). Nature's thumbprint: The new genetics of personality. Reading, MA, US: Addison-Wesley/Addison Wesley Longman.

Nolan, P. J. (1993). Fundamentals of college physics. Dubuque, IA: Wm. C. Brown Publishers

Norman, D. K., Murphy, J. M., Gilligan, C., & Vasudev, J. (1981–1982). Sex differences and interpersonal relationships: A cross-sectional sample in the U.S. and India. The International Journal of Aging & Human Development, 14(4), 291–306.

Nyborg, H. (1983). Spatial ability in men and women: Review and new theory. Advances in Behaviour Research and Therapy, 5, 89–140.

Offer, D., Ostrov, E., Howard, K. I., & Atkinson, R. (1988). The teenage world: Adolescents' self-image in ten countries. New York, NY, England: Plenum Medical Book Co/Plenum Press.

Offer, D., Ostrov, E., Howard, K. I., & Atkinson, R. (1988). The teenage world: Adolescents' self-image in ten countries. New York, NY, England: Plenum Medical Book Co/Plenum Press.

Offer, D., Ostrov, E., Howard, K. I., & Atkinson, R. (1988). The teenage world: Adolescents' self-image in ten countries. New York, NY, England: Plenum Medical Book Co/Plenum Press.

Orlean, S. (1998). The orchid thief. New York: Ballantine Books.

Owen, M. T., Easterbrooks, M. A., Chase-Lansdale, L., & Goldberg, W. A. (1984). The relation between maternal employment status and the stability of attachments to mother and to father. Child Development, 55(5), 1894–1901. doi:10.2307/1129936

Oyserman, D., Coon, H. M., & Kemmelmeier, M. (2002). Rethinking individualism and collectivism: Evaluation of theoretical assumptions and meta-analyses. Psychological Bulletin, 128(1), 3–72.

Oyserman, D., Kemmelmeier, M., & Coon, H. M. (2002). Cultural psychology, a new look: Reply to Bond (2002), Fiske (2002), Kitayama (2002), and Miller (2002). Psychological Bulletin, 128(1), 110–117.

Pachter, H. M. (1951/2007). Magic into science: The story of Paracelsus. Sumner Press.

Pedersen, N. L., Plomin, R., McClearn, G. E., & Friberg, L. (1988). Neuroticism, extraversion, and related traits in adult twins reared apart and reared together. Journal of Personality and Social Psychology, 55(6), 950–957.

Pendle, G. (2005). Strange angel: The otherworldly life of rocket scientist John Whiteside Parsons. New York: Harcourt

Peretti, P. 0., & Abplanalp, R. R., Jr. (2004). Chemistry in the college dating process: Structure and function. Social Behavior & Personality, 32, 147–154.

Phelps, J. A., Davis, J. O., & Schartz, K. M. (1997). Nature, nurture, and twin research strategies. Current Directions in Psychological Science, 6(5), 117–121.

Piaget, J. (1952). The origins of intelligence in children. Oxford, England: International Universities Press. doi:10.1037/11494-000

Pierce, S. H., & Lange, G. (2000). Relationships among metamemory, motivation and memory performance in young school-age children. British Journal of Developmental Psychology, 18(Pt 1), 121–135. doi:10.1348/026151000165616

Pinker, S. (2002). The blank slate: The modern denial of human nature. New York, NY, US: Viking.

Pleck, J. H., Sonenstein, F. L., & Ku, L. C. (1993). Masculinity ideology: Its impact on adolescent males' heterosexual relationships. Journal of Social Issues, 49(3), 11–29.

Plomin, R. (1997). Identifying genes for cognitive abilities and disabilities. In R. J. Sternberg, & E. L. Grigorenko (Eds.), Intelligence, heredity, and environment. (pp. 89–104). New York, NY, US: Cambridge University Press.

Plomin, R., & Bergeman, C. S. (1991). The nature of nurture: Genetic influence on "environmental" measures. Behavioral and Brain Sciences, 14(3), 373–427.

Plomin, R., & Crabbe, J. (2000). Dna. Psychological Bulletin. Special Issue: Psychology in the 21st Century, 126(6), 806–828.

Plomin, R., & Daniels, D. (1987). Why are children in the same family so different from one another? Behavioral and Brain Sciences, 10(1), 1–16.

Plomin, R., Corley, R., Caspi, A., Fulker, D. W., & DeFries, J. (1998). Adoption results for self-reported personality: Evidence for nonadditive genetic effects? Journal of Personality and Social Psychology, 75(1), 211–218.

Plomin, R., Fulker, D. W., Corley, R., & DeFries, J. C. (1997). Nature, nurture, and cognitive development from 1 to 16 years: A parent–offspring adoption study. Psychological Science, 8(6), 442–447.

Plomin, R., McClearn, G. E., Pedersen, N. L., Nesselroade, J. R., & Bergeman, C. S. (1988). Genetic influence on childhood family environment perceived retrospectively from the last half of the life span. Developmental Psychology, 24(5), 738–745.

Plomin, R., Reiss, D., Hetherington, E. M., & Howe, G. W. (1994). Nature and nurture: Genetic contributions to measures of the family environment. Developmental Psychology, 30(1), 32–43.

Pollak, S., & Gilligan, C. (1982). Images of violence in thematic apperception test stories. Journal of Personality and Social Psychology, 42(1), 159–167. doi:10.1037/0022-3514.42.1.159

Putnam, R. D. (2000). Bowling alone: The collapse and revival of American community. New York, NY, US: Touchstone Books/Simon & Schuster.

Ramachandran, V. 5. (1992). Blind spots. Scientific American, 266, 85–91.

Ramachandran,V. S., & Hirstein, W. (1998). The perception of phantom limbs: The D. 0. Hebb lecture. Brain, 121, 1603–1630.

Reese, E., Haden, C. A., & Fivush, R. (1996). Mothers, fathers, daughters, sons: Gender differences in autobiographical reminiscing. Research on Language and Social Interaction. Special Issue: Constituting Gender through Talk in Childhood: Conversations in Parent-Child, Peer, and Sibling Relationships, 29(1), 27–56. doi:10.1207/s15327973rlsi2901_3

Reiner, W. G., & Gearhart, J. P. (2004). Discordant sexual identity in some genetic males with cloacal exstrophy assigned to female sex at birth. The New England Journal of Medicine, 350(4), 333–341.

Renfrey, G., Schlinger, H., Jakubow, J., & Poling, A. (1989). Effects of phenytoin and phenobarbital on schedule-controlled responding and seizure activity in the amygdala-kindled rat. Journal of Pharmacology and Experimental Therapeutics, 248, 967–973.

Renner, M. J., & Renner, C. H. (1993). Expert and novice intuitive judgments about animal behavior. Bulletin of the Psychonomic Society, 31(6), 551–552.

Renner, M. J., & Rosenzweig, M. R. (1987). Enriched and impoverished environments: Effects on brain and behavior. New York: Springer-Verlag.

Roberts, T. (1991). Determinants of gender differences in responsiveness to others' evaluations. ProQuest Information & Learning). Dissertation Abstracts International, 51 (8-B), 4092–4092. (Electronic; Print)

Robins, R. W., & Craik, K. H. (1994). A more appropriate test of the kuhnian displacement thesis. American Psychologist, 49(9), 815–816. doi:10.1037/0003-066X.49.9.815

Robinson, A. (2007). The Last Man Who Knew Everything: Thomas Young, the Anonymous Genius Who Proved Newton Wrong and Deciphered the Rosetta Stone, Among Other Surprising Feats. New York: Plume.

Robinson, A. (2007). The last man who knew everything: Thomas Young, the anonymous genius who proved Newton wrong and deciphered the Rosetta Stone, among other surprising feats. New York: Plume

Robinson, J. L., Kagan, J., Reznick, J. S., & Corley, R. (1992). The heritability of inhibited and uninhibited behavior: A twin study. Developmental Psychology, 28(6), 1030–1037.

Rogers, C. R. (1965). Client centered therapy: Its current practice, implication, and theory. Boston: Houghton Mifflin.

Rogoff, B. (1994). Developing understanding of the idea of communities of learners. Mind, Culture, and Activity, 1(4), 209–229.

Rohan, M. J., & Zanna, M. P. (1996). Value transmission in families. In C. Seligman, J. M. Olson & M. P. Zanna (Eds.), The psychology of values: The Ontario symposium, vol. 8. (pp. 253–276). Hillsdale, NJ, England: Lawrence Erlbaum Associates, Inc.

Rohner, R. P. (1986). The warmth dimension: Foundations of parental acceptance-rejection theory. Thousand Oaks, CA, US: Sage Publications, Inc.

Rose, J. S., Chassin, L., Presson, C. C., & Sherman, S. J. (1999). Peer influences on adolescent cigarette smoking: A prospective sibling analysis. Merrill-Palmer Quarterly, Special Issue: Peer Influences in Childhood and Adolescence, 45(1), 62–84.

Rose, R. J., Viken, R. J., Dick, D. M., Bates, J. E., Pulkkinen, L., & Kaprio, J. (2003). It does take a village: Nonfamilial environments and children's behavior. Psychological Science, 14(3), 273–277.

Rosenthal, R., & Fode, K. L. (1963). The effect of experimenter bias on the performance of the albino rat. Behavioral Science, 8, 183–189.

Rosenzweig, M. R. (1984). Experience, memory, and the brain. American Psychologist, 39(4), 365–376.

Rosenzweig, M. R., & Bennett, E. L. (1996). Psychobiology of plasticity: Effects of training and experience on brain and behavior. Behavioural Brain Research, 78, 57–65.

Rothbart, M. K., Ahadi, S. A., & Evans, D. E. (2000). Temperament and personality: Origins and outcomes. Journal of Personality and Social Psychology, 78(1), 122–135.

Rothbaum, F., & Tsang, B. Y. (1998). Lovesongs in the united states and china: On the nature of romantic love. Journal of Cross-Cultural Psychology, 29(2), 306–319.

Rotter, J. B. (1996). Generalized expectancies for internal versus external control of reinforcement. Psychological Monographs, 80, 1–28.

Rovet, J. F. (1993). The psychoeducational characteristics of children with turner syndrome. Journal of Learning Disabilities, 26(5), 333–341.

Rowe, D. C. (1990). As the twig is bent? the myth of child-rearing influences on personality development. Journal of Counseling & Development, 68(6), 606–611.

Rowe, D. C., Vazsonyi, A. T., & Flannery, D. (1995). Ethnic and racial similarity in developmental process: A study of academic achievement. Psychological Science, 6(1), 33–38.

Rowe, D. C., Vazsonyi, A. T., & Flannery, D. J. (1994). No more than skin deep: Ethnic and racial similarity in developmental process. Psychological Review, 101(3), 396–413.

Rubin, Z. (1973). Liking and loving. New York: Holt.

Rushon, J. P.. & Buns, T. A. (2005). Mate choice and friendship in twins. Psychological Science, 16, 555–559.

Rutherford, W. (1886). A new theory of hearing. Journal of Anatomy and Physiology, 21, 166–168.

Sadato, N., Pascualleone, A., Grafman, J., Ibanez, C., Deiber, M. P., Dold, G. & Hallett, M. (1996). Activation of the primary visual cortex by Braille reading in blind subjects. Nature, 380, 526–528.

Salthouse, T. A. (1984). The skill of typing. Scientific American, 250(2), 128–135.

Sampson, E. E. (2000). Reinterpreting individualism and collectivism: Their religious roots and monologic versus dialogic person–other relationship. American Psychologist, 55(12), 1425–1432.

Sapadin, L. A. (1988). Friendship and gender: Perspectives of professional men and women. Journal of Social and Personal Relationships, 5(4), 387–403.

Sarris, V. (2006). Relational psychophysics in humans and animals: A comparative-developmental approach. New York: Psychology Press.

Saudino, K. J., Wertz, A. E., Gagne, J. R., & Chawla, S. (2004). Night and day: Are siblings as different in temperament as parents say they are? Journal of Personality and Social Psychology, 87(5), 698–706.

Schanberg, S. M., & Field, T. M. (1987). Sensory deprivation stress and supplemental stimulation in the rat pup and preterm human neonate. Child Development, 58, 1431–1447.

Schmitt, D. P., & Pilcher, J. J. (2004). Evaluating evidence of psychological adaptation: How do we know one when we see one? Psychological Science, 15(10), 643–649.

Schmitt, H. H. (2006). Return to the moon: Exploration, enterprise, and energy I the human settlement of space. New York: Copernicus Books.

Schwitzgebel, E. (1999). Representation and desire: A philosophical error with consequences for theory-of-mind research. Philosophical Psychology, 12(2), 157–180. doi:10.1080/095150899105855

Scientific American (1998, Winter). Exploring intelligence [Special Issue]. Scientific American, 9(4).

Scott, W. A., Scott, R., & McCabe, M. (1991). Family relationships and children's personality: A cross-cultural, cross-source comparison. British Journal of Social Psychology, 30(1), 1–20.

Segal, N. L. (1999). Entwined lives: Twins and what they tell us about human behavior. New York, NY, US: Dutton/Penguin Books.

Segal, N. L. (2000). Virtual twins: New findings on within-family environmental influences on intelligence. Journal of Educational Psychology, 92(3), 442–448.

Segall, M. H., Dasen, P. R., Berry, J. W., & Poortinga, Y. H. (1990). Human behavior in global perspective: An introduction to cross-cultural psychology. Elmsford, NY, US: Pergamon Press.

Selye, H. (1936). A syndrome produced by diverse nocuous agents. Nature, 138, 32

Sharma, A. R., McGue, M. K., & Benson, P. L. (1998). The psychological adjustment of united states adopted adolescents and their nonadopted siblings. Child Development, 69(3), 791–802.

Sheeber, L. B., & Johnson, J. H. (1992). Child temperament, maternal adjustment, and changes in family life style. American Journal of Orthopsychiatry, 62(2), 178–185. doi:10.1037/h0079329

Sheldon, W. H. (with the collaboration of S. S. Stevens) (1942). The varieties of temperament: A psychology of constitutional differences. New York: Harper.

Shermer, M. (2005). Science friction: Where the known meets the unknown. New York: Henry Holt and Company.

Shopshire, M. S., & Craik, K. H. (1994). The five factor model of personality and the DSM-III—R personality disorders: Correspondence and differentiation. Journal of Personality Disorders, 8(1), 41–52.

Siegler, R. S. (1996). Emerging minds: The process of change in children's thinking. New York, NY, US: Oxford University Press.

Sigelman, C. K., & Rider, E. A. (2006). Life-span human development. Belmont, CA: Thomson-Wadsworth.

Silver, L. B. (2000). Attention-deficit/hyperactivity disorder in adult life. Child and Adolescent Psychiatric Clinics of North America, 9(3), 511–523.

Silverstein, K. (2005). The radioactive boy scout: The frightening true story of a whiz kid and his homemade nuclear reactor. New York: Villard.

Silvia, P. J. (2007). How to write a lot: A practical guide to productive academic writing. Washington, D.C.: American Psychological Association.

Simansky, K. J., Jakubow, J., Sisk, F. C., Vaidya, A. H., & Eberle-Wang, K. (1992). Peripheral serotonin is an incomplete signal for eliciting satiety in sham-feeding rats. Pharmacology, Biochemistry and Behavior, 43, 847–854.

Singelis, T. M., & Sharkey, W. F. (1995). Culture, self-construal, and embarrassability. Journal of Cross-Cultural Psychology, 26(6), 622–644.

Singelis, T. M., Bond, M. H., Sharkey, W. F., & Kriss, S. Y. L. (1999). "Unpackaging culture's influence on self-esteem and embarrassability: The role of self-construals": Erratum. Journal of Cross-Cultural Psychology, 30(5), 657–657.

Singelis, T. M., Bond, M. H., Sharkey, W. F., & Lai, C. S. Y. (1999). Unpackaging culture's influence on self-esteem and embarrassability: The role of self-construals. Journal of Cross-Cultural Psychology, 30(3), 315–341.

Singh, D. (1993). Adaptive significance of female physical attractiveness: Role of waist-to-hip ratio. Journal of Personality and Social Psychology, 65(2), 293–307.

Singh, D., & Young, R. K. (1995). Body weight, waist-to-hip ratio, breasts, and hips: Role in judgments of female attractiveness and desirability for relationships. Ethology & Sociobiology, 16(6), 483–507.

Singh-Manoux, A., Richards, M., & Marmot, M. (2003). Leisure activities and cognitive function in middle age: Evidence from the Whitehall II study. Journal of Epidemiology & Community Health, 57(11), 907–913. doi:10.1136/jech.57.11.907

Siqueland, E. R., & Lipsitt, L. P. (1966). Conditioned head-turning in human new-borns. Journal of Experimental Child Psychology, 3(4), 356–376. doi:10.1016/0022-0965(66)90080-4

Sirevaag, A. M., Black, J. E., Shafron, D., & Greenough, W. T. (1988). Direct evidence that complex experience increases capillary branching and surface area in visual cortex of young rats. Developmental Brain Research, 43, 299–304.

Skinner, B. F. (1938). The behavior of organisms: An experimental analysis. Copley Publishing Group.

Slater, A. (2000). Visual perception in the young infant: Early organization and rapid learning. In D. Muir, & A. Slater (Eds.), Infant development: The essential readings. (pp. 95–116). Malden: Blackwell Publishing.

Slater, A., Morison, V., & Rose, D. (1984). Habituation in the newborn. Infant Behavior & Development, 7(2), 183–200. doi:10.1016/S0163-6383(84)80057-0

Slee, R. M., & Pratt, C. A. (1899). Dr. Berkeley's discovery. New York: The Knickerbocker Press.

Smoreda, Z., & Licoppe, C. (2000). Gender-specific use of the domestic telephone. Social Psychology Quarterly, 63(3), 238–252.

Sokol, D. K., Moore, C. A., Rose, R. J., & Williams, C. J. (1995). Intrapair differences in personality and cognitive ability among young monozygotic twins distinguished by chorion type. Behavior Genetics, 25(5), 457–466.

Solkoff, N., & Matuszak, D. (1975). Tactile stimulation and behavioral development among low-birthweight infants. Child Psychiatry and Human Development, 6, 33–37.

Solkoff, N., Yaffe, S., Weintraub, D., & Blasé, B. (1969). Effects of handling on the subsequent development of premature infants. Developmental Psychology, 4, 765–768.

Spradley, J. P., & Phillips, M. (1972). Culture and stress: A quantitative analysis. American Anthropologist, 74(3), 518–529.

Sternberg, R. J. (1988). Triangulating love. In R. J. Sternberg & M. L. Barnes (Eds.), The psychology of love. New York: Yale University Press.

Stevens, J. C. (1971). Psychophysics. In W. C. Cain & L. E. Marks (Eds.), Stimulus & sensation: Readings in sensory psychology (pp. 5–18). Boston: Little, Brown.

Sulloway, F. J. (1996). Born to rebel: Birth order, family dynamics, and creative lives. New York: Pantheon.

Summers, J. A., & Craik, F. I. M. (1994). The effects of subject-performed tasks on the memory performance of verbal autistic children. Journal of Autism and Developmental Disorders, 24(6), 773–783. doi:10.1007/BF02172285

Tamres, L. K., Janicki, D., & Helgeson, V. S. (2002). Sex differences in coping behavior: A meta-analytic review and an examination of relative coping. Personality and Social Psychology Review, 6(1), 2–30.

Tannenbaum, P. H., & Ziliman, D. (1975). Emotional arousal in the facilitation of aggression through communication. In L. Berkowitz (Ed.), Advances in experimental social psychology (Vol. 8, pp. 149–192). New York: Academic Press.

Taylor, S. E. (1982). Social cognition and health. Personality and Social Psychology Bulletin, 8, 549–562.

Tellegen, A., Lykken, D. T., Bouchard, T. J., Jr., Wilcox, K. J., Segal, N. L., & Rich, 5. (1988). Personality similarity in twins reared apart and together. Journal of Personality and Social Psychology, 54, 1031–1039.

Tesser, A. (1993). The importance of heritability in psychological research: The case of attitudes. Psychological Review, 100, 129–142.

Thomas, A., & Chess, S. (1977). Temperament and development. Oxford, England: Brunner/Mazel.

Thomas, B. (1993). Magic eye. Kansas City, MO: Andrews & McMeel.

Thomson, R., & Murachver, T. (2001). Predicting gender from electronic discourse. British Journal of Social Psychology, 40(2), 193–208.

Tinbergen, N. (1951). The study of instinct. Oxford, UK: Clarendon Press.

Trepanning, 5/8/11, Retrieved May 14, 2011, from Wikipedia: http://en.wikipedia.org/wiki/Trepanning

Triandis, H. C. (1989). The self and social behavior in differing cultural contexts. Psychological Review, 96(3), 506–520.

Triandis, H. C. (1994). Culture and social behavior. New York, NY, England: Mcgraw-Hill Book Company.

Triandis, H. C., Bontempo, R., Villareal, M. J., Asai, M., & Lucca, N. (1988). Individualism and collectivism: Cross-cultural perspectives on self-ingroup relationships. Journal of Personality and Social Psychology, 54(2), 323–338.

Turnbull, C. M. (1961). The forest people. New York: Simon & Schuster.

Turner, A. M., & Greenough, W. T. (1985). Differential rearing effects on rat visual cortex synapses. I. Synaptic and neuronal density and synapses per neuron. Brain Research, 329, 195–203.

Twenge, J. M. (1997). Changes in masculine and feminine traits over time: A meta-analysis. Sex Roles, 36(5-6), 305–325.

Twenge, J. M. (2001). Changes in women's assertiveness in response to status and roles: A cross-temporal meta-analysis, 1931–1993. Journal of Personality and Social Psychology, 81(1), 133–145.

Udry, J. R. (2000). Biological limits of gender construction. American Sociological Review, 65(3), 443–457.

Udry, J. R. (2000). Biological limits of gender construction: Erratum. American Sociological Review, 65(5), 789–789.

Ungerleider, L. G., & Mishkin, M. (1982). Two cortical visual systems. In D. J. Ingle, M. A. Goodale, & R. J. W. Mans_field (Eds.), Analysis of visual behavior (pp. 549–586). Cambridge, MA: The MIT Press.

van Engen, M. L., & Willemsen, T. M. (2004). Sex and leadership styles: A meta-analysis of research published in the 1990s. Psychological Reports, 94(1), 3–18.

Van Leeuwen, M. S. (1978). A cross-cultural examination of psychological differentiation in males and females. International Journal of Psychology, 13(2), 87–122.

Vandell, D. L. (2000). Parents, peer groups, and other socializing influences. Developmental Psychology, 36(6), 699–710.

Vandello, J. A., & Cohen, D. (1999). Patterns of individualism and collectivism across the united states. Journal of Personality and Social Psychology, 77(2), 279–292.

Vartanian, L. R. (2000). Revisiting the imaginary audience and personal fable constructs of adolescent egocentrism: A conceptual review. Adolescence, 35(140), 639–661.

Vygotsky, L. S. (1962). Thought and word. Cambridge, MA, US: MIT Press. doi:10.1037/11193-007

Walker, L. J. (1991). Sex differences in moral reasoning. In W. M. Kurtines, & J. L. Gewirtz (Eds.), Handbook of moral behavior and development, vol. 1: Theory; vol. 2: Research; vol. 3: Application. (pp. 333–364). Hillsdale, NJ, England: Lawrence Erlbaum Associates, Inc.

Wallace, W. (2003). The vibrating nerve impulse in Newton, Willis and Gassendi: First steps in a mechanical theory of communication. Brain and cognition, 51, 66–94.

Warren, R. M. (1970). Perceptual restoration of missing speech sounds. Science, 167, 392–393.

Wartner, U. G., Grossmann, K., Fremmer-Bombik, E., & Suess, G. (1994). Attachment patterns at age six in south Germany: Predictability from infancy and implications for preschool behavior. Child Development, 65(4), 1014–1027. doi:10.2307/1131301

Watson, J. B. (1913). Psychology as the behaviorist views it. Psychological Review, 20, 158–177.

Watson, J. B. (1924/2007). Behaviorism (6th ed.). New Brunswick, CT: Transaction Publishers.

Weale, R. A. (1986). Aging and vision. Vision Research, 26, 1507–15 12.

Weisman, A. (2007). The world without us. New York: St. Martin's Press.

Weisman, A. D. (1972). On dying and denying: A psychiatric study of terminality. Pasadena, CA, US: Behavioral Publications.

Weiss, A., King, J. E., & Figueredo, A. J. (2000). The heritability of personality factors in chimpanzees (pan troglodytes). Behavior Genetics, 30(3), 213–221.

Wender, P. H., Wolf, L. E., & Wasserstein, J. (2001). Adults with ADHD: An overview. In J. Wasserstein, L. E. Wolf & F. F. LeFever (Eds.), 17th annual conference of the new york neuropsychology group, 17, Apr 1996; an earlier version of this article was presented at the aforementioned conference. (pp. 1–16). New York, NY, US: New York Academy of Sciences.

Wertheimer, M. (1912/1961). Experimental studies on the seeing of motion. In T. Shipley (Trans. and Ed.), Classics in psychology (pp. 1032–1038). New York: Philosophical Library.

Wever, E. G., & Bray, C. W. (1930). Action currents in the auditory nerve in response to acoustical stimulation. Proceedings of the National Academy of Science, 16, 344–350.

Whiting, B., & Edwards, C. P. (1988). A cross-cultural analysis of sex differences in the behavior of children aged 3 through 11. Hawthorne, NY, US: Aldine de Gruyter.

Wierzbicki, M. (1993). Psychological adjustment of adoptees: A meta-analysis. Journal of Clinical Child Psychology, 22(4), 447–454.

Williams, J. E., & Best, D. L. (1990). Measuring sex stereotypes: A multination study (rev. ed.). Thousand Oaks, CA, US: Sage Publications, Inc.

Willis, J., & Todorov, A. (2006), First impressions: Making up your mind after a 100-ms exposure to a face. Psychological Science, 17, 592–598.

Wilson, D. H. (2007). Where's my jetpack?: A guide to the amazing science fiction future that never arrived. New York: Bloomsbury.

Wolgin, D. L., & Jakubow, J. J. (2004). Tolerance to amphetamine hypophagia: A real-time depiction of learning to suppress stereotyped movements in the rat. Behavioral Neuroscience, 118, 470–478.

Wolgin, D. L., & Jakubow, J. J. (2003). Tolerance to amphetamine hypophagia: A microstructural analysis of licking behavior in the rat. Behavioral Neuroscience, 117, 95–104.

Wong, M. M., & Csikszentmihalyi, M. (1991). Affiliation motivation and daily experience: Some issues on gender differences. Journal of Personality and Social Psychology, 60(1), 154–164.

Wood, W. (1987). Meta-analytic review of sex differences in group performance. Psychological Bulletin, 102(1), 53–71.

Wood, W., & Eagly, A. H. (2002). A cross-cultural analysis of the behavior of women and men: Implications for the origins of sex differences. Psychological Bulletin, 128(5), 699–727.

Worobey, J., & Blajda, V. M. (1989). Temperament ratings at 2 weeks, 2 months, and 1 year: Differential stability of activity and emotionality. Developmental Psychology, 25(2), 257–263.

Wright, P. H. (1989). Gender differences in adults' same- and cross-gender friendships. In R. G. Adams, & R. Blieszner (Eds.), Older adult friendship: Structure and process. (pp. 197–221). Thousand Oaks, CA, US: Sage Publications, Inc.

Yela. C., & Sangrador, J. L. (2001). Perception of physical attractiveness throughout loving relationships. Current Research in Social Psychology, 6, 57–75.

Zhang, X., Dc la Cruz, 0., Pinto, J. M., Nicolae, D., Firestein, S., & Gilad,Y. (2007, May 17). Characterizing the expression of the human olfactory receptor gene family using a novel DNA microarray. Genome Biology, 8, article R86. Retrieved March 12, 2010, from http://genomebiology.com/2007/8/5/R86.

Zimmer, C. (2004). Soul made flesh: The discovery of the brain—and how it changed the world. New York: Free Press.

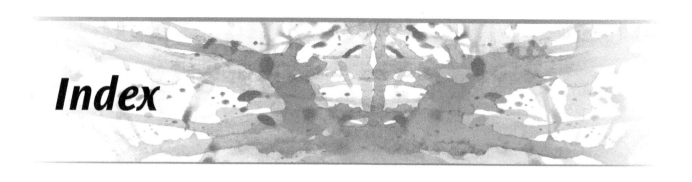

Index